COMMENTARY

on the

LUTHERAN BOOK OF WORSHIP

To Lois

and to our children

Carl
Carolyn
Sarah
Linda

COMMENTARY

on the

LUTHERAN BOOK OF WORSHIP

Lutheran Liturgy in Its Ecumenical Context

PHILIP H. PFATTEICHER

AUGSBURG FORTRESS   Minneapolis

COMMENTARY ON THE LUTHERAN BOOK OF WORSHIP

Library of Congress Cataloging in Publication Data

Pfatteicher, Philip H.
    Commentary on the Lutheran book of worship : Lutheran liturgy in its ecumenical context / Philip H. Pfatteicher.
      p. cm.
    Includes bibliographical references.
    ISBN 0-8006-0392-3 (alk. paper)
    1. Lutheran book of worship — History and criticism. 2. Lutheran Church — North America — Liturgy. I. Title.
    BX8067.A3L7637 1990
    264'.04135 — dc20   90-31528
                                     CIP

Manufactured in the U.S.A.   AF 10-3923

4   5   6   7   8   9   10

CONTENTS

CONTENTS

CONTENTS

CONTENTS

PREFACE

In 1947 Luther Reed, the preeminent liturgical scholar, published his magisterial study of the Common Service, *The Lutheran Liturgy*. He revised the book in 1960 in light of the Common Liturgy in the *Service Book and Hymnal* of 1958. With the publication of the *Lutheran Book of Worship* in 1978 a new study was required. A mere updating and revision of Reed's work was not feasible in view of major developments in systematic theology, history, anthropology, biblical studies, and liturgy. Despite many points of continuity, the new Lutheran service book was built on a significantly altered foundation from that of the Common Service and the Common Liturgy. An entirely new book was necessary.

The explosion of knowledge in the twentieth century has rendered it virtually impossible for one person to do now what Luther Reed did in mid-century. Frank C. Senn and I planned to cooperate on a volume, Senn to do the first half dealing with historical and theological foundations, I to do the second half as a commentary on the *Lutheran Book of Worship* services. Our work soon outgrew the limits of one book and emerged as two complementary yet independent studies: the present volume and Frank Senn's *Christian Worship: Catholic and Evangelical*. The present book is meant to be a companion volume to Dr. Senn's study of the historical and theological foundations which support the liturgical texts examined in these pages.

In writing this commentary, I have taken as the basic liturgical text the *Lutheran Book of Worship* Ministers Edition and throughout this commentary have made reference to page numbers in that book. There are two forms of the Ministers Edition: one in larger format, designed for use as an altar book by presiding and assisting ministers, and one in reduced size, called the Ministers Desk Edition. The forms are identical except in size.

The Ministers Edition is comparable to the Roman Catholic sacramentary and includes all the liturgical texts necessary for conducting the major services of the Lutheran Church. The liturgical portion of the pew edition, on the other hand, is not a complete text; it is a selection from the Ministers Edition of those liturgical texts which the congregation needs for its participation in the services.

The format of this commentary follows that of my *Commentary on the Occasional Services*. For each service in the *Lutheran Book of Worship* there is (1) a list of parallel services in the liturgies of the other principal denominations, together with a list in chronological order of most of the principal North American Lutheran predecessor rites — it is thus a look around at the contemporary liturgical scene and a look back through Lutheran history in order to suggest a view of the whole context in which the service is to be understood; (2) a statement of the purpose of each rite (which may at first seem too obvious to state, but the formulation of such a statement can be most valuable, for what is intended now by a rite — the Holy Communion for example — is not always what was intended by that rite at other times in liturgical history); (3) a description of the principal distinguishing characteristics of each service as it appears in the *Lutheran Book of Worship;* (4) a review of the background of each service, how it developed and was received and used through the centuries until its present form; and (5) a study of the service in detail, giving the sources of the texts, an indication of how the texts have been altered in the borrowing, comparison with what other denominations have provided as an indication of the status of ecumenical understanding, and a commentary on the theological intentions and implications of the texts as specific formulations of our liturgical theology as it is understood at this point in our history.

Reed's *Lutheran Liturgy* was roughly equivalent to Josef A. Jungmann's *The Mass of the Roman Rite,* supplemented with studies of Matins and Vespers and their attendant prayers, the Litany and the Suffrages. Here in the present volume, supplemented by my *Commentary on the Occasional Services,* is for the first time a commentary on the entire body of Lutheran liturgical texts. It is an effort to set those texts in their historical and ecumenical context as documents of the continuing growth and renewal of the church. It must be noted and understood that as wide-ranging as this study is, it is nonetheless still limited. One needs to go beyond the liturgical texts and examine the movements of the various ministers and the congregation, the music of the liturgy, the architectural setting in which the words, movement, and music of the liturgy are done. Beyond that, the church's liturgy is reflected and interpreted in art — in painting and sculpture, music and literature — and such reflections can be instructive to the student of liturgy, indicating how the liturgy has been understood by laypeople. The footnotes and bibliographies are, among other uses, meant to suggest directions in which the student of liturgy may choose to go in search of a fuller picture than that which is possible in this space.

It is a pleasant obligation to acknowledge my debt to Frank C. Senn, who has helped to shape and encourage my work; the worship staff of the Lutheran Church in America and of the Evangelical Lutheran Church in America who carefully read drafts of this manuscript and made detailed suggestions for additions and corrections; my colleagues in the North American Academy of Liturgy who have taught me many things which are included in these pages; the pastors and people of the Church of the Holy Communion in Philadelphia, who developed and maintained a tradition which embodied the stateliness of the Lutheran liturgy; Luther D. Reed, who although long retired when I was a student at the Lutheran Theological Seminary at Philadelphia was still a presence and to me a teacher and friend; Edward C. McCoy, who taught me by vigorous and devout example the liveliness, variety, and dramatic possibilities of the Christian liturgy; George R. Seltzer, who taught me liturgics and from whose store of recondite learning came the subject of my doctoral dissertation; and C. A. Park, whose gracious hospitality allowed me to exercise my ministry in a variety of ways and to participate in the emerging ecumenical consensus of the later twentieth century.

Moreover the whole church is in debt to the authors of the *Church Book* and the Common Service, who gave to the Lutheran Church in North America a liturgy which reflected a consensus of the "pure Lutheran liturgies" of the sixteenth century and by this gift returned the Lutheran Church to the ancient ways of the Church of the West of which Lutheranism has theologically and confessionally always been a part, even when it did not remember it. Thus began the movement of the Lutheran community into the larger ecumenical heritage which was furthered by the *Lutheran Book of Worship*.

PHILIP H. PFATTEICHER

WORKS FREQUENTLY CITED

Apostolic Tradition
Dix, Gregory. *The Apostolic Tradition of St. Hippolytus.* 2d ed. with preface and corrections by Henry Chadwick. London: SPCK, 1968.
Cuming, Geoffrey J. *Hippolytus: A Text for Students.* Bramcote, Notts.: Grove Books, 1976.

Book of Common Prayer
Unless a different edition is cited, reference is to *The Book of Common Prayer.* New York: The Church Hymnal Corporation, 1979.

Book of Concord
The Book of Concord. Translated and edited by Theodore G. Tappert, et al. Philadelphia: Fortress Press, 1959.

Church Book (1868)
Church Book for Use of Evangelical Lutheran Congregations. Philadelphia: Lutheran Book Store, 1868 [1872, 1873, 1882].

Church Book (1891)
Church Book for Use of Evangelical Lutheran Congregations. Philadelphia: General Council Publication Board, 1891 [1892, 1893, 1901, 1903, 1904, 1905, 1906, 1908, 1913, 1915].

Common Service Book
Common Service Book, text edition. Philadelphia: The Board of Publication of the United Lutheran Church in America, 1919. The first edition, with music, 1917; second edition, with music, 1918.

Contemporary Worship [1–10]
Contemporary Worship. A series of resources prepared by the Inter-Lutheran Commission on Worship for Provisional Use. Minneapolis: Augsburg Publishing House; Philadelphia: Board of Publication, Lutheran Church in America; and St. Louis: Concordia Publishing House, 1969–1976.

The Lutheran Hymnal
The Lutheran Hymnal. St. Louis: Concordia Publishing House, 1941.

Luther's Works
Luther's Works, American Edition. 55 volumes. Volumes 1–30: Jaroslav Pelikan, general editor; St. Louis: Concordia Publishing House, 1956–1976. Volumes 31–55: Helmut T. Lehmann, general editor; Philadelphia: Fortress Press, 1957–1986.

Min. Ed., Ministers Edition
Lutheran Book of Worship, Ministers Edition. Minneapolis: Augsburg Publishing House, and Philadelphia: Board of Publication, Lutheran Church in America, 1978.

The Rites
   The Rites of the Catholic Church. New York: Pueblo Publishing Co., 1976, 1983.
The Sacramentary
   The Sacramentary. New York: Catholic Book Publishing Co., 1973, 1985. English translation by the International Consultation on English in the Liturgy.
Service Book and Hymnal
   Service Book and Hymnal. Minneapolis: Augsburg Publishing House, and Philadelphia: Board of Publication, Lutheran Church in America, 1958. Text edition 1967.

The Principal Ancient Sacramentaries (Roman)

Leonine or Verona Sacramentary (manuscript ca. A.D. 600)
   Sacramentum Veronese. Edited by Leo Cunibert Mohlberg. Rome: Herder, 1956.
Gelasian Sacramentary (manuscript of the eighth century):
   Liber Sacramentorum Romanae Aeclesiae Ordinis Anni Circuli. Edited by Leo Cunibert Mohlberg. Rome: Herder, 1968.
Gregorian Sacramentary (manuscript of the late eighth century) with supplement (by Benedict of Aniane?) of the early ninth century: *Le Sacramentaire Gregorien.* Edited by Jean Deshusses. Fribourg: Editions universitaries, 1971.
Gallican Sacramentaries (manuscript of the seventh or eighth centuries):
   Missale Gallicanum vetus. Edited by Leo Cunibert Mohlberg. Rome: Herder, 1958.
   Missale Gothicum. Edited by Leo Cunibert Mohlberg. Rome: Herder, 1961.
   The Bobbio Missal. Edited by Elias Avery Lowe. Vol. 2. London: Harrison and Sons, 1920.

Reformation Church Orders

Richter, Aemilius L., ed. *Die evangelischen Kirchenordnungen des sechzehnten Jahrhunderts: Urkunden und Regesten zur Geschichte des Rechts und der Verfassung der evangelischen Kirche in Deutschland.* Weimar: Landindustriecomptoir, 1846. 2d ed. Leipzig: Günther, 1871.
Sehling, Emil, editor. *Die evangelischen Kirchenordnungen des XVI. Jahrhunderts.* Vols. 1–5; Leipzig: Reisland, 1902–1913. Vol. 6: Tübingen: Mohr, 1955.

1

CONVERGENCE AND COOPERATION

A study of the liturgy used by Lutherans in North America during the transition from the twentieth to the twenty-first century may properly begin not with a Lutheran person or event but with the principal work of a Roman Catholic bishop of Rome. That fact in itself reminds Christians that no longer is any one church or denomination self-sufficient, able to carry on without the support of the rest of Christ's church, and it reminds Lutherans in particular of their origins (reemphasized in recent times) as a confessional movement within the Catholic Church of the West. The meeting of the millennia is a time of remarkable convergence and cooperation.

On January 25, 1959, at the Roman Basilica of Saint Paul outside the Walls, Pope John XXIII announced his intention of convoking a council of the church to open its windows, as he put it, to let in fresh air. The ultimate goal of the council was to be Christian unity. After nearly four years of extensive preparation, the council met in four sessions from October 11, 1962 to December 8, 1965 and was a momentous event not only for the Roman Church but for all of Western Christianity. Before the council opened, invitations were extended to other churches and communities. Jewish and Greek Orthodox groups declined to send observers, but more than forty Lutheran, Anglican, Methodist, Baptist, Congregationalist, Disciples of Christ, Presbyterian, and other groups sent delegate-observers.

"The Ecumenical and Universal Council Held in the Vatican Basilica," known as the Second Vatican Council (the first, which defined papal infallibility, was held in 1869–1870), showed the Church of Rome to be not the monolithic monarchy many thought it to be but rather a living body capable of remarkable change, renewal, and renovation — a model for the rest of Christianity. Moreover, the churches of the Reformation, and Lutherans especially, saw in the working and the documents of the council an acceptance of basic principles of the sixteenth-century Reformation: the primacy of grace, the centrality of Scripture, the understanding of the church as the people of God, the use of the vernacular language. It was as if the Lutheran Reformation had made its point at long last. Indeed, some Lutherans observed that the place in the modern world where the principles of the Reformers were most clearly at work was the Roman Church. This thrilling discovery challenged deep-seated prejudices and stereotypes and evoked an atmosphere of heady optimism.

Convergence of Traditions

The conciliar documents[1] summarized in a concise and provocative way the fruits of decades of scholarship and thus laid the foundation for specific reforms of the church's practice. Significantly, the first completed document of the council was the Constitution on the Sacred Liturgy, *Sacrosanctum Concilium*, completed in two sessions, October 11–December 8, 1962 and September 29–December 4, 1963, passed by a vote of 2147–4, and promulgated by Paul VI on December 4, 1963.

The scholarly research which this document reflected, buttressed by the liturgical movement of the twentieth century, was not peculiar to the Roman Church nor limited to it. Scholars of various traditions and diverse lands and many denominations had been moving in similar directions. With the Second Vatican Council the reform of the Roman Mass began, resulting in what is known as the Missal of Paul VI, published in 1969. In the United States the Episcopal Church through its Standing Liturgical Commission had been conducting a series of studies looking toward the revision of the 1928 *Book of Common Prayer*. These studies were published as a continuing series called *Prayer Book Studies*, which summarized the state of research, explained proposed changes, and offered draft texts for trial and comment. A series of proposed liturgical rites was prepared: *Services for Trial Use* (1971), *Authorized Services* (1973, with an "Expanded Edition" in the same year), the *Draft Proposed Book of Common Prayer* (1976), which with the approval of the church's triennial General Convention became the *Proposed Book of Common Prayer* (1976), and finally the *Book of Common Prayer* (1979). Protestant churches, notably the Presbyterian and United Methodist but others as well, began to take a new interest in aspects of liturgical worship.[2]

---

[1]Collected in *The Documents of Vatican II*, ed. Walter M. Abbott (New York: Guild Press, America Press, 1966).

[2]See, for example,

Charles W. Baird, *Presbyterian Liturgies* (Grand Rapids: Baker Book House, 1960).

John M. Barkley, *Worship of the Reformed Church* (Richmond: John Knox Press, 1967).

John E. Burkhart, *Worship* (Philadelphia: Westminster Press, 1982).

Paul W. Hoon, *The Integrity of Worship: Ecumenical and Pastoral Studies in Liturgical Theology* (Nashville and New York: Abingdon, 1971).

James Hastings Nichols, *Corporate Worship in the Reformed Tradition* (Philadelphia: Westminster Press, 1968).

Hughes Oliphant Old, *The Patristic Roots of Reformed Worship* (Zurich: Theologischer Verlag Zurich, 1975).

Kenneth G. Phifer, *A Protestant Case for Liturgical Renewal* (Philadelphia: Westminster, 1965).

Robert E. Webber, *Worship Old and New* (Grand Rapids: Zondervan Publishing Co., 1982).

James F. White, *Introduction to Christian Worship* (Nashville: Abingdon, 1980).

The Lutheran church in North America could not help being influenced by these developments as well as by the work of its own scholars in Scripture, history, systematic theology, and liturgy; it too shared in the emerging ecumenical consensus of the latter half of the twentieth century.

Gordon Lathrop has identified eight convictions which summarize this consensus. (1) Christian worship involves both words and signs; (2) Sunday is the preeminent Christian feast day; (3) the gathering for worship is the action of a community; (4) regardless of its cultural setting, this gathering follows an ancient shape; (5) in our time, this assembly may best be marked by a kind of simplicity; (6) ritual focus and flow belong to this gathering at its best; (7) the actions of this assembly are intended to proclaim the meaning of Jesus Christ in the midst of the present time; (8) the recovery of the integrity of this assembly matters for the life of the world.[3]

The International Consultation on English Texts

As various English-speaking Christian bodies became increasingly aware of each other the desire was often expressed that common versions of liturgical texts would be desirable as a further evidence of unity and agreement. After several national efforts, the International Consultation on English Texts was convened with Ronald Jasper and Harold Winstone as joint chairmen. In 1969, texts of the Lord's Prayer, Apostles' Creed, Nicene Creed, Gloria in Excelsis, Sanctus and Benedictus, and Gloria Patri were accepted and published together with three texts on which the consultation was still working: Sursam Corda, Agnus Dei, and Te Deum. The booklet which contained these texts was *Prayers We Have in Common* (1970).[4] An enlarged and revised edition appeared in 1972, which added the texts of the Benedictus, Nunc Dimittis, and Magnificat. A second revised edition was published in 1975. The work of this international consultation has been incorporated into the service books of many denominations.

The Consultation on Ecumenical Hymnody

In addition to the desire for common liturgical texts, a desire for a common core of hymns further to unify Christian worship was expressed. A Consultation on Ecumenical Hymnody reviewed the hymnals in use by major Christian denominations in North America to determine which hymns were common to their heritage, which hymns should by common consent be retained and which should be retired; the tune to which each text should be set; the best translation; and, in some cases, which stanzas should be used. A list of 150 hymns and tunes recommended for ecumenical use supplemented by 80 additional hymns and tunes was

---

[3]Gordon Lathrop, "What Are We Hoping For?" *Accent on Worship* 3:4 (Liturgical Conference, 1985), 1.

[4]*Prayers We Have in Common* (Philadelphia: Fortress Press, 1970; enlarged and rev. ed. 1972; 2nd rev. ed. 1975).

adopted September 8, 1971. These hymns are noted by an asterisk in the index of first lines of hymns in the *Lutheran Book of Worship.*

The Consultation on Ecumenical Hymnody list has had less impact than the work of the International Consultation on English Texts. Hymns which had been familiar in common versions were revised differently by various denominations so that an unfortunate but perhaps at this stage inevitable divergence is apparent. Christians seem to find it more difficult to agree on the hymns they sing than on the liturgies they use.

The Inter-Lutheran Commission on Worship

In Lutheran practice, it is usually the hymnal rather than the liturgy which initiates a desire for revision of liturgical books. When the *Common Service Book* was but nineteen years old (1936), the Common Service Book Committee began studies looking toward a revision of the hymnal in that book. The report was submitted to the convention of the United Lutheran Church in America in 1944, and the convention directed the president of the church to invite all Lutheran bodies in the United States and Canada to join in the preparation of a common hymnal.[5] John W. Behnken, the president of the Lutheran Church–Missouri Synod, in part because the Synodical Conference had just published *The Lutheran Hymnal* in 1941, declined the invitation; but eight Lutheran bodies, which through merger were to become two (the American Lutheran Church in 1960 and the Lutheran Church in America in 1962), produced not only a new hymnal but a revised liturgy as well, published together as the *Service Book and Hymnal* (1958).[6] The use of one book encouraged and facilitated the merging of church bodies.

Having declined to participate in the work of the *Service Book and Hymnal*, the Lutheran Church–Missouri Synod in 1953 began steps toward the revision of its book, *The Lutheran Hymnal.* In response to reports of this work to conventions of the Lutheran Church–Missouri Synod, some delegates opposed any unilateral program of liturgical revision and suggested that the work of reform must be done by all the Lutheran bodies in North America.

Meanwhile, following the publication of the *Service Book and Hymnal* (1958), the Commission on Liturgy and Hymnal of the American

---

[5] In a letter of November 5, 1783, Henry Melchior Muhlenberg wrote, "It would be a most delightful and advantageous thing if all the Evangelical Lutheran congregations in North America were united with one another, if they all used the same order of service." Since that time, Lutherans in North America have cherished the dream of "one church, one book."

[6] The original meeting of the Commission on the Hymnal, at the invitation of the President of the United Lutheran Church in America, was held in June 1945 in Pittsburgh. Representatives from the United Lutheran Church in America, the American Lutheran Church, the Augustana Lutheran Church, and the Evangelical Lutheran Church were in attendance. They were later joined by representatives of the United Evangelical Lutheran Church, the American Evangelical Lutheran Church, the Finnish Evangelical Lutheran Church in America (Suomi Synod), and the Lutheran Free Church.

Lutheran Church and the Lutheran Church in America turned to future developments in liturgy and hymns. Henry E. Horn, who chaired the commission, explained that, faced with a deadlock between only two churches — one of which, the American Lutheran Church, voted in a bloc — the commission sought ways whereby the three Lutheran bodies could work together. Conversations between Henry Horn and Walter Buszin, who chaired the Lutheran Church–Missouri Synod commission, explored ways and means for establishing a common commission. The only way this could be accomplished was to have the Missouri Synod commission propose it *de novo* on the floor of their church convention. Then the invitation could be extended to the other two church bodies. The new commission may therefore be understood as an extension of the work of the Commission on Liturgy and Hymnal.[7] The 1965 convention of the Lutheran Church–Missouri Synod adopted a report which declared

that we authorize the President in conjunction with the Vice-Presidents to appoint representatives to pursue a cooperative venture with other Lutheran bodies as soon as possible in working toward, under a single cover:
    a) a common liturgical section in rite, rubric, and music;
    b) a common core of hymn texts and musical settings; and
    c) a variant selection of hymns, if necessary
...that we pledge our joy, willingness, and confidence to the other Lutheran bodies as work in this cooperative project begins....

The American Lutheran Church and the Lutheran Church in America accepted the invitation.

Although the *Service Book and Hymnal* was but seven years old, events in church and society encouraged continued revision of the church's liturgy. The Second Vatican Council reflected the contemporary progress in biblical, historical, and liturgical scholarship not limited to the Roman Church. Taste and styles of music, language, and etiquette were changing in what appeared to be radical ways. Vociferous elements of society with a revolutionary fervor called into question traditional customs and practice. By mid-century a deep alienation was becoming evident in parts of North American society, an alienation from systems of order, authority, and value. By the beginning of the final third of the century this had developed into an emphasis on the subjective experience of the moment, on what was thought to be immediately and obviously relevant. Innovation gained a new respectability. Sexual morality, cultivated manners, and standards of dress for a time reflected a youthful, often indeed an adolescent rejection of the social, political, and moral values of the older generation. Tradition was cast aside; the present moment was what mattered. The popular slogan "do your own thing"[8] captured and expressed the dominant mood. Unplanned occur-

---

[7]Henry Horn in a letter to the editor of *Lutheran Partners* 3:1 (January/February 1987):7.
    [8]Thought by some to have been derived from Ralph Waldo Emerson's essay "Nature."

rences called "happenings" were celebrated, free from history, tradition, and thoughtful preparation. Some perceived what was thought to be the dawning of a new age, the "age of Aquarius," when "peace will guide the planets and love will steer the stars."[9]

This revolution was not without precedent and was similar, for example, to the development of many sects within the fringes of Christianity from the Middle Ages on, which called into question and ultimately rejected the mores of church and society.[10] Nor was the revolution solely an American phenomenon: it was part of a worldwide cultural, social, and political revolution. Colonialism had collapsed. The "third world" had begun to increase in influence, accompanied by demands for justice for minorities and the oppressed. It was a time of declining religious authority, a time of rising secularization. Worship was of course affected by these rapid and widespread changes, and therefore it did not seem too soon to begin work again on the revision of the liturgy.

On February 10–11, 1966 at the invitation of the president of the Lutheran Church–Missouri Synod, Oliver R. Harms, representatives and observers from six American Lutheran church bodies met in Chicago to participate in the Inter-Lutheran Consultation on Worship.[11] The representatives heard papers on tradition and meaning in the worship of the American Lutheran Church, the Lutheran Church in America, and the Synodical Conference; two papers on the *Service Book and Hymnal* — its preparation, and its acceptance and use since 1958; progress reports on the work of the Commission on Worship, Liturgics, and Hymnology of the Synodical Conference; and a definition of the task ahead. At the conclusion of this consultation, resolutions were adopted that this project be approved by the participating churches and implemented by the establishment of an Inter-Lutheran Commission on Worship (ILCW), that working committees be established (such as hymn

---

[9]"Aquarius" by Gerome Ragni and James Rado from the musical *Hair.*

[10]See J. H. Plumb, "The Secular Heretics," *Horizon* 10:2 (Spring 1968):9–12.

[11]The participants were

From the American Lutheran Church:

    Mandus A. Egge, Paul H. Ensrud, Edward A. Hansen, Hans F. Knauer, Theodore S. Liefeld, Alf Romstad, and Herbert Nottbohm, assistant to President Fredrik Schiotz;

From the Lutheran Church in America:

    Conrad J. Bergendoff, Edgar S. Brown, Jr., L. Crosby Deaton, Edward T. Horn III, Ulrich S. Leupold, William R. Seaman;

From the Lutheran Church–Missouri Synod:

    Oliver R. Harms, Paul G. Bunjes, Walter E. Buszin, Herbert E. Kahler, Adalbert R. Kretzmann, Herbert F. Lindemann, Martin L. Seltz, Fred L. Precht (advisory), and David Appelt (advisory);

From the Synod of Evangelical Lutheran Churches:

    Stephen M. Touhy, Jaroslav J. Vajda;

From the Wisconsin Evangelical Lutheran Synod:

    Martin Albrecht, Kurt J. Eggert;

From the Evangelical Lutheran Synod:

    Julian G. Anderson, Stanley Ingebretson, Eivind G. Unseth.

texts, hymn tunes, liturgy, liturgical music), and that the participating churches underwrite the cost of this project.[12]

Formal organization of the Inter-Lutheran Commission on Worship took place in Chicago on November 29–30, 1966. Herbert Lindemann was elected chairman; T. S. Liefeld, vice-chairman; L. Crosby Deaton, secretary; and Herbert Kahler, treasurer. The commission created four working committees: liturgical text, liturgical music, hymn text, hymn music; membership was drawn from the commission and from among other specialists in the participating churches. As the work progressed, these committees appointed smaller groups with still broader representation to draft proposed texts. (A list of members of the Commission is given in Appendix 1, pp. 515–516.)

The committees began their work by gathering a library of basic materials: current revisions by various denominations as well as liturgical rites and hymns prepared by individuals and groups. By 1969 the commission was ready to begin the publication of a series of booklets under the general title *Contemporary Worship*. The preface, printed in each book in the series, set out the commission's understanding of its mandate:

The Inter-Lutheran Commission on Worship, an organization of representatives from the Lutheran churches of North America, was given a mandate to produce common worship materials for the churches. In the face of the growing pluralism of society, the ecumenical movement and new insights into the meaning and uses of liturgy, Christian history and theology, these participating churches voice the need for a common expression of their Christian faith.

Ultimately, the commission expects to produce a new, common liturgy and hymnal for the churches. It is concerned that the richness of the tradition be retained; at the same time it seeks to enhance and enliven that tradition with lively speech and songs for the church of the future.

To that end, the commission is engaged in preparing materials that are provisional in nature, forms intended to supplement those already in use by the participating churches. These materials will include liturgical forms and hymns that are contemporary in text and music and contemporary versions of existing worship forms that are common to the participating churches.

The introduction to the booklets explained with a confidence characteristic of the late '60s and early '70s,

Contemporary Worship is a series of booklets designed to broaden the scope of currently available hymnic and liturgical resources.

Social tensions, new currents in theology and piety, new fears, new hopes — all call for fresh expressions. Each booklet voices petitions and praise which the Holy Spirit urges in the church today.

Ultimately there were ten books in the series:

---

[12] The papers presented at the consultation together with the resolutions adopted were published as *Liturgical Reconnaissance*, ed. Edgar S. Brown, Jr. (Philadelphia: Fortress Press, 1968).

Contemporary Worship 1: Hymns (1969)
Contemporary Worship 2: The Holy Communion (1970)
Contemporary Worship 3: The Marriage Service (1972)
*Contemporary Worship 4: Hymns for Baptism and Holy
    Communion* (1972)
Contemporary Worship 5: Services of the Word (1972)
*Contemporary Worship 6: The Church Year: Calendar and
    Lectionary* (1973)
Contemporary Worship 7: Holy Baptism (1974)
Contemporary Worship 8: Affirmation of the Baptismal Covenant
    (1975)
Contemporary Worship 9: Daily Prayer of the Church (1976)
Contemporary Worship 10: Burial of the Dead (1976).

Beginning in *Contemporary Worship 7: Holy Baptism* (1974) an evaluation form was included in the Contemporary Worship booklets to
encourage responses and by which congregations could report directly
to the Inter-Lutheran Commission on Worship their reactions to the trial
use of the new texts and music. In September 1975 a booklet styled *Contemporary Worship 01: The Great Thanksgiving* was sent to all pastors
of the cooperating churches to solicit reactions to seven quite different
eucharistic prayers: a set of modules from which a great thanksgiving
could be constructed; the third-century prayer of Hippolytus; a revision of the prayer of thanksgiving in the *Service Book and Hymnal;* a
new composition with an invariable preface; a Great Thanksgiving for
Easter, inspired by the Exsultet; a prayer based on the ancient *Birkat-ha-
mazon,* the thanksgiving over the cup at the end of the Jewish meal; an
ecumenical text, published as "A Common Eucharistic Prayer" (1975)
and included in the 1979 *Book of Common Prayer;* and a poetic Great
Thanksgiving composed for the Arauna services in Rotterdam and published in Dutch in the Netherlands in 1968. *Contemporary Worship 01*
was drafted by John W. Arthur, Robert W. Jenson, Gordon Lathrop, Gail
Ramshaw-Schmidt. Its publication completed the series of preparatory
studies.

The service of Eugene L. Brand as project director from 1976 through
the conclusion of the project in 1978 (the publication of the *Lutheran
Book of Worship*) needs to be noted. A systematic theologian, musician,
and ecumenist, possessed of pastoral, linguistic, and artistic sensitivity,
Brand guided the developing manuscript of the book through its final
years of preparation, overseeing the resolution of outstanding problems,
supplying drafts of portions of the book which were as yet incomplete,
and giving the book and its liturgy much of its final shape and sound.

The work of the Inter-Lutheran Commission of Worship was not
an effort by an elitist few but was the result of a clear consensus of
the cooperating churches and their representatives, tested and refined
by theological discussion and by trial use in representative parishes.
Moreover, the passage of a decade gave the churches a longer view of

the work and enabled more informed discussions about what would endure and what was temporary and passing.

In the work of the commission the churches did not ever vote as blocs against each other, and nothing in the resulting work is there as the result of the insistence of one synod. Any disagreements always crossed synodical lines, and no one's opinion or vote was entirely predictable.

The introduction to the *Lutheran Book of Worship*, drafted by Eugene L. Brand, describes succinctly the liturgical goals of the Inter-Lutheran Commission on Worship:

> to restore to Holy Baptism the liturgical rank and dignity implied by Lutheran theology, and to draw out the baptismal motifs in such acts as the confession of sin and the burial of the dead; to continue to move into the larger ecumenical heritage of liturgy while, at the same time, enhancing Lutheran convictions about the Gospel; to involve lay persons as assisting ministers who share the leadership of corporate worship; to bring the language of prayer and praise into conformity with the best current usage; to offer a variety of musical styles. (Min. Ed., p. 12)

None of this was an exclusively Lutheran concern. The work of the Inter-Lutheran Commission on Worship depended to a considerable degree on the work of the Roman Catholic and Episcopal churches. Its task was to do three things at once: (1) be faithful to the Lutheran tradition in continental Europe (as was the Common Service of 1888), in Scandinavia (as was the *Service Book and Hymnal* of 1958) and, more recently, in North America; (2) share in so far as it was possible the work of the Roman Catholic Church which was nearing completion and also the work of the Episcopal Church which was taking place concurrently with the Lutheran revisions; and (3) look beyond the Western liturgical churches to the experience and work of other denominations of Christianity, Orthodox and Protestant. The Methodist *At the Lord's Table* (1981) and the Presbyterian *Service for the Lord's Day* (1984) are indications of the extent of the common tradition that was emerging in most of Western Christianity. The "Lima document" of the World Council of Churches, *Baptism, Eucharist, and Ministry*, Faith and Order Paper no. 111 (Geneva: World Council of Churches, 1982), stands as a powerful and prophetic statement of the emerging ecumenical consensus in three key areas of the church's proclamation of the Gospel.[13]

Understanding any liturgy requires a knowledge of other traditions as well. For as Robert Taft has observed, "Liturgiology, like philology, is a comparative discipline. The liturgiologist who knows only one tradition is like a philologist who knows only one language."[14] In the following chapters, the extent of the borrowing from the work of other churches

---

[13]See *Baptism, Eucharist, and Ministry: A Liturgical Appraisal of the Lima Text*, papers read at the 1985 Congress of Societas Liturgica, ed. Geoffrey Wainwright (Rotterdam: Liturgical Ecumenical Center Trust, 1986). Published as *Studia Liturgica* 16:1–2 (1986).

[14]Robert Taft, *The Liturgy of the Hours in East and West* (Collegeville: Liturgical Press, 1986), 315, also p. xii.

is demonstrated by parallel columns showing the similarity in texts as well as the differences, the latter only infrequently of theological significance and more often merely stylistic or idiosyncratic. It is important, indeed necessary, to show the relationship with other traditions, especially the Roman Catholic and Episcopal churches, in order to document borrowings from other rites, to indicate how other churches have handled similar problems, and to prevent comparison only with previous Lutheran books by those to whom such books remain familiar and who lament the loss of what was beloved in previous books.[15]

As the decade of preparatory work passed, the church, reflecting changes in society, began to lose interest in the avant-garde; and individuals and congregations, having tired of experimental liturgies, began to develop a new appreciation of the traditional forms and some of the more stately language of previous books. One example may suffice at this point. In *Contemporary Worship 6*, the Prayer of the Day for the Ninth Sunday after Pentecost read,

O God, give us bread. Give us bread to nourish our bodies, and in Christ give us the bread of eternal life, that in him we may grow and thrive and serve; through your Son, Jesus Christ our Lord.

The brashness of the opening sentence, initially welcomed by many, did not wear well. The prayer was replaced in the *Lutheran Book of Worship* with the collect from the Leonine sacramentary which in previous books had been appointed for that Sunday:

Pour out upon us, O Lord, the spirit to think and do what is right, that we, who cannot even exist without you, may have the strength to live according to your will; through your Son, Jesus Christ our Lord.

(An echo of the experimental prayer was retained in the alternative Prayer of the Day, appropriate for Year C: "O God, you see how busy we are with many things....")

The revolution of the 1960s and early '70s was flawed because, as Sigurdur Nordal wisely observes in another context, "The preservation of old values is an indispensable counterpart to the creation of new."[16] The church needed by trial and occasional error to come to understand that the new is not always found in opposition to the old but arises from the old as its natural growth and development. Stability and continuity are essential elements of catholic Christianity.

---

[15]See the negative but provocative criticism of the revision of the *Book of Common Prayer* by Margaret A. Doody, " 'How Shall We Sing the Lord's Song upon an Alien Soil?': The New Episcopalian Liturgy," in *The State of the Language*, ed. Leonard Michaels and Christopher Ricks (Berkeley: University of California Press, 1980), 108–124; also Cleanth Brooks, "God, Gallup, and the Episcopalians," *American Scholar* 50 (Summer 1981):313–325; David Crane, "The Price of Benevolence," *Times Literary Supplement* (November 5, 1982), 1227. Dissatisfied Lutherans seem generally less prone to commit their complaints to writing.

[16]Sigurdur Nordal, introduction to *The Prose Edda of Snorri Sturluson*, trans. Jean I. Young (Berkeley: University of California Press, 1964), 13.

Nevertheless, the continuing value of the revolutionary decade was the acknowledgement that there are alternative ways of perceiving reality beyond the familiar historical, philosophical, and theological modes; and this insight opened up vast possibilities for ordering and doing the worship of God. The return to more conservative forms was therefore not necessarily a condemnation of the experiments of the decade. It was healthful for the church to have tried out new ways of prayer and praise, even as it was fortunate not to have bound them within the covers of a permanent book. What emerged finally in the resulting liturgy were not the passing experiments but more lasting concerns.

BIBLIOGRAPHY

Adams Doug. *Meeting House to Camp Meeting: Toward a History of American Free Church Worship from 1620 to 1835.* 2nd ed. Saratoga, CA: Modern Liturgy/Resource Publications and Austin, TX: Sharing Co., 1984 [1981].

Brand, Eugene L. *The Rite Thing.* Minneapolis: Augsburg Publishing House, 1970.

Calinescu, Matei. *Faces of Modernity: Avant-garde, Decadence, Kitsch.* Bloomington: Indiana University Press, 1977.

Coates, Willson and Hayden V. White. *The Ordeal of Liberal Humanism: An Intellectual History of Western Europe.* New York: McGraw-Hill, 1970.

Cooper, Frederick E. *An Explanation of the Common Service with Appendices on Church Hymnody and Liturgical Colors and a Glossary of Liturgical Terms.* 6th ed., rev. and enl. Philadelphia: United Lutheran Publication House, 1941.

Egge, Mandus, ed. *Worship: Good News in Action.* Minneapolis: Augsburg Publishing House, 1973.

Ellmann, Richard, and Charles Feidelson, eds. *The Modern Tradition: Backgrounds of Modern Literature.* Oxford University Press, 1965.

Horn, Edward Traill. "The Lutheran Sources of the Common Service." *Lutheran Quarterly* 21 (1891):239–68.

Horn, Henry E. *Worship in Crisis.* Philadelphia: Fortress Press, 1972.

Jacobs, Henry Eyster. "The Making of the *Church Book.*" *Lutheran Church Review* 31 (1912):597–622.

Koenker, Ernest B. *The Liturgical Renaissance in the Roman Catholic Church.* St. Louis: Concordia Publishing House, 1954.

Lindemann, Herbert F. *The New Mood in Lutheran Worship.* Minneapolis: Augsburg Publishing House, 1971.

Lutheran Forum 3:7 (July-August 1969); 4:6 (June 1970); 5:4 (April 1971); 5:6 (June-July 1971); 5:7 (August-September 1971); 5:8 (October 1971); 7:3 (August 1973).

Mitchell, Leonel L. *Praying Shapes Believing: A Theological Commentary on the Book of Common Prayer.* Minneapolis: Winston-Seabury Press, 1986.

Poggioli, Renato. *The Theory of the Avant-garde.* Translated by Gerald Fitzgerald. Cambridge, MA: Belknap Press of Harvard University Press, 1968.

Principles of Prayer Book Revision. London: SPCK, 1957.

Reed, Luther D. "The Character and Claims of the Church Book." *Lutheran Church Review* 26 (1907): 689–700.

———. "Historical Sketch of the Common Service." *Lutheran Church Review* 36 (1917):501–19.

———. *The Lutheran Liturgy*. Philadelphia: Muhlenberg Press, 1947. Rev. ed. Philadelphia: Fortress Press, 1960.

———. "The Standard Manuscript of the Common Service, and Variata Editions." *Lutheran Church Review* 20 (1901):459–73.

Strodach, Paul Zeller. *A Manual on Worship*. Rev. ed. Philadelphia: Muhlenberg Press, 1946.

Stulken, Marilyn Kay. *Hymnal Companion to the Lutheran Book of Worship*. Philadelphia: Fortress Press, 1981. "Historical Essays," pp. 2–114.

White, James F. "A Protestant Worship Manifesto." *Christian Century* 99:3 (January 27, 1982):82–86.

Zaretsky, Irving I., and Mark P. Leone, eds. *Religious Movements in Contemporary America*. Princeton: University Press, 1975.

2

THE NATURE AND USE OF THE
LUTHERAN BOOK OF WORSHIP

The opening pages of the *Lutheran Book of Worship* contain useful and instructive introductory material which provides a means by which the liturgical rites may be understood.

Title

The Liturgical Text Committee and the Inter-Lutheran Commission on Worship expressed no preferred title for their work, although many indicated their hope that "Lutheran" not be part of the title. With the exception of *The Lutheran Hymnal* of the Missouri Synod, a denominational label had never been added to the primary title of a predecessor book: the *Service Book and Hymnal*, the *Common Service Book*, the *Church Book* (and in other denominations, the *Book of Common Prayer*, the *Worshipbook*, the *Book of Services*). There is, moreover, no such thing as "Lutheran worship"; there is only the worship of the church as used by Lutherans. The introduction to the *Lutheran Book of Worship* declares:

The services of the *Lutheran Book of Worship* embody the tradition of worship which received its characteristic shape during the early centuries of the Church's existence and was reaffirmed during the Reformation era. As such, they are an emblem of continuity with the whole Church and of particular unity with Lutherans throughout the world. (Min. Ed., p. 12)

In the absence of any clear direction from the commission, the publishers selected the title *Lutheran Book of Worship*, which recalls the *Book of Worship* of the General Synod South (1867) and the General Synod (rev. ed. 1870; ninth ed. 1883) as well as the 1964 *Book of Worship* of the United Methodist Church and the *Book of Worship* of the Evangelical and Reformed Church which emerged in 1987 as the *Book of Worship* of the United Church of Christ. Some were relieved that the title at least was not the Book of Lutheran Worship.

It may be argued that the proper title would have been the Common Service Book. This title would parallel the titles of the *Book of Common Prayer*, the *Book of Common Worship* of the Church of South India, the *Book of Common Order* of the Church of Scotland. There is, moreover, no compelling reason to choose a new title for each new liturgical book, as if it were an entirely new work. The range of possibilities in any case is constantly narrowing. The Anglican tradition seems wise in maintaining one title, indicating thereby that the basic worship resource is published in a new and revised edition but that it is nonetheless the continuation of the tradition. The *Lutheran Book of Worship*, more than any of its predecessors, has the right to be the common service book of Lutherans in North America.

The Ministers Edition contains the complete liturgy (supplemented by *Occasional Services*, 1982).[1] The familiar pew edition contains selections from the liturgy which are necessary for congregational participation, so there are no minister's intonations, no proper prefaces, no alternative eucharistic prayers, no psalm prayers. A complete edition of the *Lutheran Book of Worship* would be the Ministers Edition bound with the hymnal (and supplemented by the Accompaniment Edition[2] with keyboard settings for the music of the liturgy).

Publishers

The book was prepared by the representatives of the churches participating in the Inter-Lutheran Commission on Worship: the Lutheran Church in America, the American Lutheran Church, the Evangelical Lutheran Church of Canada, the Lutheran Church — Missouri Synod. The Missouri Synod, at whose invitation the work began, withdrew from the publication of the book just before the book appeared, and so is not one of the publishers. The book was published by Augsburg Publishing House of the American Lutheran Church and by the Board of Publication of the Lutheran Church in America.[3]

The first printing of both the Ministers Edition and the pew edition is dated September 1978. Minor corrections were made in successive printings of the pew edition (second printing October 1978, third printing December 1978, fourth printing April 1979, fifth printing June 1982, sixth printing October 1984. The corrected printing of the Ministers Edition was issued in August 1985. The first printing of the Ministers

---

[1] *Occasional Services: A Companion to Lutheran Book of Worship* (Minneapolis: Augsburg Publishing House and Philadelphia: Board of Publication, Lutheran Church in America, 1982).

[2] *Lutheran Book of Worship Accompaniment Edition: Liturgy* (Minneapolis: Augsburg Publishing House and Philadelphia: Board of Publication, Lutheran Church of America, 1978).

[3] The Lutheran Church–Missouri Synod, apparently uneasy at the prospect of sharing a liturgical book with other Lutherans and aware of the expected goal of Lutheran unity fostered by the use of one book, appointed a "blue ribbon committee" to make a theological evaluation of the *Lutheran Book of Worship*, which it had helped write. (There had been no such response to the preparatory *Contemporary Worship* series.) To no one's surprise, the book was found wanting by the *Report and Recommendations of the Special Hymnal Review Committee* (1978), and the Missouri Synod withdrew at the end of the project and published its own book, *Lutheran Worship* (1982). Bryan D. Spinks in *Worship* (1983), p. 183, found the Report "reminiscent of the Puritan Exceptions against the *Book of Common Prayer* (1660)."

Desk Edition was in September 1978, the second printing in September 1979, the third printing in September 1983.

Copyright

Like its predecessor books, but unlike the *Book of Common Prayer*, the *Lutheran Book of Worship* is copyrighted material. Lutherans in North America have not always respected the creation or ownership of liturgical resources, borrowing and reprinting without acknowledgment of sources.[4] One reason for copyrighting liturgical materials is political. The multiplicity of Lutheran bodies in North America, even after the mergers of the twentieth century, makes those groups which invested in the production of liturgical material wary of its being appropriated by those who did not share in its production. Hymns, both text and music, are, unlike liturgical texts, usually the work of an individual, and more obviously require copyright to protect the interests of those who created the work. (The Episcopal *Hymnal 1982*, unlike the *Book of Common Prayer*, is protected by copyright.)

Notes on the Liturgy

The Notes on the Liturgy (Min. Ed., pp. 13–39) correspond to the General Rubrics of the *Common Service Book* and the *Service Book and Hymnal*. They are, however, cast in a different style and spirit, as the title implies. They are notes rather than directive rubrics, suggestions for the use of the book of worship. In previous books, two levels of use were acknowledged: directive rubrics, expressed by "shall" ("The Minister shall say"); and permissive, expressed by "may" ("A brief silence may be kept before the Introit for the Day").[5] The Notes on the Liturgy, like the General Instruction of the present Roman missal, have an interpretative and instructional function and are not so much directions for use as descriptive comments on possible uses of the services. There are three levels of use in the rubrics of the *Lutheran Book of Worship:* the directive rubrics of previous books have been replaced by indicative statements ("The Psalmody begins with this song of praise"); optional elements supported by tradition are indicated by "should" ("When more than one reading is used at Morning Prayer, the first should always be from the Old Testament"); other optional usage of less importance is indicated by "may" ("Seasonal antiphons for the Gospel Canticle . . . may be used"). The Notes on the Liturgy were drafted by Eugene L. Brand.

The rubrics which appear within the text of the service are printed in red (as the name rubric — from *ruber*, red — implies). They also incorporate headings for the principal parts of the services, indicated by printing certain words in all capital letters: "The PSALMODY begins with this song of praise."

---

[4]See Luther D. Reed, *The Lutheran Liturgy* (Philadelphia: Fortress Press, 1960), 176 n. 9.

[5]*Service Book and Hymnal*, p. 274.

Orthography

In line with modern practice, capitalization has been reduced in the *Lutheran Book of Worship*. The *Service Book and Hymnal*, like the *Book of Common Prayer*, no longer capitalized pronouns which referred to God — a nineteenth-century innovation. The practice was not entirely consistent in any case; "he," "his," and "who" were regularly capitalized but "own" (grammatically an adjective) was not.

"Church" when it refers to the Christian Church is still capitalized as is common in liturgical writing. It is a proper noun, the name of a specific entity, the body of Christ.

The *Lutheran Book of Worship*, unlike the *Book of Common Prayer*, the *Common Service Book*, and the *Service Book and Hymnal*, no longer capitalizes "name" when it refers to the name of God. The unintended effect is to weaken the suggestion made by the capital letter that Name is not to be understood in the usual contemporary sense of a mere appellation or designation. Name is explained by Marion Hatchett as "carrying the idea of God's self-revelation."[6] In biblical use a name is intimately connected with the person who bears it, and thus knowing a name gives one a measure of power. Used in prayer, as "we pray in his name" or "baptizing them in the name of the Father, and of the Son, and of the Holy Spirit," "name" is redolent with the very power of God.

Calendar

The revised calendar of the church year which was introduced in the 1969 Roman Missal removed the pre-Lenten Sundays of Septuagesima, Sexagesima, and Quinquagesima as an unnecessary duplication of the preparatory season of Lent and extended the time after the Epiphany until Ash Wednesday, the beginning of Lent; reduced Passiontide, which had previously begun with Judica (Passion Sunday, the Fifth Sunday in Lent), to one week, Holy Week; and made of the Easter celebration one fifty-day festival lasting through the Day of Pentecost. The Episcopal and Lutheran churches generally accepted the Roman reforms of the calendar.

The celebration of the death and resurrection of Christ, his passage and therefore the passage of his followers from death to life, is the central event of the liturgical calendar. Thus, Sunday is the original Christian feast day[7] and in modern calendars has been restored to its ancient prominence (in the Roman and Episcopal calendars days which correspond to what are called Lesser Festivals in Lutheran practice do not displace the Sunday propers). The Easter Vigil has been recovered as the celebration of the Christian Passover, the principal occasion on which initiation into the Christian community takes place and the people of

---

[6] Marion Hatchett, *Commentary on the American Prayer Book* (New York: Seabury Press, 1980), 188.

[7] *Constitution on the Sacred Liturgy* V. 106, in *Documents of Vatican II*, ed. Walter M. Abbott (New York: Guild Press, America Press, Association Press, 1966), 169.

God reaffirm their solidarity with the risen Lord. Even Christmas has its focus in the passion-Easter event: the Prayer of the Day asks that "his birth as a human child will set us free from the old slavery of our sin." Sunday, therefore, is the first Christian festival and always throughout the year, even in penitential seasons, retains its paschal character.

The Easter Table (of days on which Easter will fall) together with the corresponding Table of Movable Festivals should be restored to the Lutheran service book. The logical place is the calendar section of the Notes on the Liturgy. These two tables were a part of the predecessor books — the *Church Book* (pp. vi–vii giving the date of Easter for the years 1868–1899, 1900–2003), the *Common Service Book* (pp. 492–493 for the years 1918–2005), the *Lutheran Hymnal* (p. 158 for the years 1941–2000), the *Service Book and Hymnal* (pp. 278–279 for the years 1955–2002) — and are essential for liturgical planning as well as research. The Inter-Lutheran Commission on Worship thought the tables were unnecessary since nearly all calendars, secular as well as liturgical, note the date of Easter. The tables given in the *Book of Common Prayer* (pp. 880–885) are convenient and moreover, unlike Lutheran Books, give careful instructions explaining how the date of Easter is determined.

The Week

In the ancient world, weeks were of varying lengths: ten days in ancient Greece, eight days in Rome. The seven-day measurement of time originated in the East, in western Asia, and was little known in Jesus' time except in Jewish colonies. Judaism had a specific name only for the last day of the week, the Sabbath; but when the seven-day week spread during the first three centuries of the common era, the Hellenic areas linked the days of the week with the "seven planets" (including the sun and the moon). The planets, moreover, were in turn dedicated to the principal gods, hence the names of the days of the week in the Romance languages: Sun (Helios), Moon (Selene), Mars (Ares), Mercury (Hermes), Jupiter (Zeus), Venus (Aphrodite), and Saturn (Kronos). In northern Europe, the names of what were considered to be equivalent divinities were used: Mars = Tiu, Mercury = Woden, Jupiter = Thor, Venus = Frigg. Despite opposition by the church, the names came into general currency by the late third century and were retained in nearly all western European languages.

As the planetary week spread, it reinforced the connection, which the church had already noticed, between Christ and the "sun of righteousness" (Mal. 4:2) and the light (John 1:4, 9; 8:12; 9:5, 12:46; Luke 2:32). The church, however, did not adopt the planetary names for the days of the week, connected as they were to other gods, but, following the biblical method, simply numbered the days.

The first day of the week was in the Gospels the day of the Lord's resurrection and the preferred day for his resurrection appearances, the day on which he gave the Holy Spirit to the apostles, and the day on which he sent them forth as his messengers. It was natural, therefore, for the first day of the week to become the principal day for the Christian assembly (Acts 20:7; 1 Cor. 16:2). The day of resurrection (*anastasimos hēmera*) is preserved in the name of the first day of the week in many Slavic languages, including Russian, *woskresenie.* The other days of the week were simply numbered by the church — *feria secunda* (second day), *feria tertia* (third day); the last day of the week, retaining its Jewish title, was called *sabbatum.*

The first day of the week acquired very early a specific designation: it is the Lord's Day.[8] It is so because it is the day of his mighty work, principally his resurrection, but the name may in fact have been inspired by a still older term, the Lord's Supper (1 Cor. 11:20). "We do not know of a Sunday on which the Eucharist was not celebrated."[9] The ancient association of the Lord's Supper and the Lord's Day may be a testimony to the paschal character both of the Supper and of the first day of the week.

The conclusion of the paschal proclamation is not the passion but the resurrection, and so Sunday became known as the Eighth Day.[10] It is the first day of a new and greater creation ("Almighty God, you wonderfully created and yet more wonderfully restored the dignity of human nature," the Prayer of the Day for the First Sunday after Christmas and the prayer after the first lesson in the Easter Vigil declare; see also 2 Cor. 5:17), which will lead to the eternal Sabbath rest of fulfillment.[11] It is the day on which God's work was extended beyond the Sabbath and, with the rising of Christ, broke through the natural boundaries of time into a new dimension. The name Eighth Day, moreover, perhaps has reference also to baptism with which the number eight was often associated (circumcision on the eighth day, the eight survivors of the flood, the four corners of this world combined with the four corners of the next).

From the ninth century certain saints' days took precedence over Sunday, but in the calendar of the Roman Catholic and the Episcopal churches — and to a lesser degree the Lutheran church — the ancient and suggestive primacy of Sunday has been reasserted. This recovery, however, has sharpened the conflict between the liturgical understanding

---

[8]Rev. 1:10; Ignatius, *To the Magnesians* 9:1; *Didache* 14:1; Tertullian, *The Chaplet* or *de Corona* 3:4.

[9]*The Study of Liturgy,* ed. Cheslyn Jones, Geoffrey Wainright, Edward Yarnold (New York: Oxford University Press, 1978), 405.

[10]See John 20:26. Already in post-biblical Judaism the eighth day represented the last age, the time of the new heavens and the new earth. The oldest Christian witness to the name Eighth Day is apparently the Letter of Barnabas 15.9; Origen (PG 12:1624) and Ambrose (PL 15:1735) also make use of the understanding of the Eighth Day as the beginning of the new creation. Justin Martyr (*Dialogues* 41.4) explains the name in relation to circumcision as did Ambrose (PL 14:494). See Augustine *Letter* 55.9, 17.

[11]Adolf Adam, *The Liturgical Year,* trans. Matthew J. O'Connell (New York: Pueblo Publishing Co., 1981), 40. See also the Tantur Report on Worship (1981), B.25–28, in *Worship among Lutherans,* ed. Eugene L. Brand (Geneva: Lutheran World Federation, 1983), 19–20.

of the first day of the week and the prevailing secular understanding of the "weekend" which views Monday as the first day of the (work) week.[12]

A liturgical appreciation of the weekdays developed anciently also. The Jewish fast days were Tuesday and Thursday, but the *Didache*, a very ancient Christian document, instructs Christians to fast on Wednesday and Friday, and Tertullian knew the practice.[13] The mid-third-century Syriac *Didascalia*[14] connects the Wednesday fast with Judas' betrayal of Jesus and the Friday fast with the crucifixion. This twice-weekly fast lasted well into the Middle Ages. Eastern and Gallican traditions, with their penchant for elaboration, observed a fast on Monday as well as on Wednesday and Friday.

In the East, from the fourth century, Saturday was equated with Sunday ("the brother of Sunday"), but in the West it was until the eleventh century a fast day connected with the apostles' mourning over Jesus' death.

Thursday, the day of the ascension as well as the day on which the Holy Communion was instituted, attained prominence in the Middle Ages as a day of rejoicing.

Thus, "the events of holy week played an important role in developing the liturgical character of the weekdays."[15]

Just as Sunday represented a weekly Easter, so the whole week appeared to be a faint copy of Holy Week. The great facts of the story of redemption were to be set before the eyes of the people, not only once a year, but in the course of the weekly cycle as well.[16]

This paschal character of the week's liturgy was obscured during the Middle Ages by the rapid growth of the number of saints' days and the association of particular votive masses with each of the days of the week. Contemporary liturgical reform has restored the richly-freighted paschal emphasis as central to Sunday, the week, and the year.

Lesser Festivals

The church celebrates saints' days as the birthdays of "the martyrs and victors who lead us."[17] But the saints are remembered not for themselves, but for the work of God which is evident in their lives. The saints are not the church's equivalent of the heroes of the world. Rather, in the saints the new creation is perceived and celebrated; the saints' days are

---

[12]See the discussion of the issues in Adam, pp. 49–51; see also *Liturgy* 20:4 (April 1975):105–30 and 20:10 (December 1975):307ff. "Sunday clears away the rust of the whole week," said Joseph Addison and Richard Steele in *The Spectator* no. 112 (Monday, July 9, 1711).

[13]*Didache* 8.1; Tertullian, *de Jejunio* 10.

[14]*Didascalia* V. 14.4ff.

[15]Adam, 52.

[16]Josef A. Jungmann, *Pastoral Liturgy* (New York: Herder and Herder, 1962), 253. Quoted in Adam, 52.

[17]*Syriac Breviary* (5th century) ed. B. Mariani (Rome, 1956), p. 27. Quoted by Paul VI, Apostolic Letter, *The Sacramentary* (New York: Catholic Book Publishing Co., 1985), 62.

celebrations of the transforming grace of God, which lifts and changes and makes new the faltering and the meanness of ordinary human lives.

The celebration of the saints, therefore, is rooted in the creation and renovation of humanity by a gracious and loving and long-suffering God. Saints' days are to be seen in relation to Easter, for they "proclaim and renew the paschal mystery of Christ."[18] The themes of creation and new creation, dying and rising, baptism, and the paschal mystery of Christ's death and resurrection all come together in a particular human focus in each of the saints as in each believer.[19] The difference is only that these themes are more apparent in some than in others.

For over a century the list of festivals and days has been expanding in North American Lutheran service books. The *Church Book* (1868) recognized four "chief festivals": Christmas, or the Nativity of our Lord; the Circumcision of Christ, and New Year's Day; the Epiphany, or the Manifestation of Christ to the Gentiles; and the Festival of the Reformation. (The alternative titles for Christmas and the Epiphany paralleled those of the *Book of Common Prayer*, often a model as Lutherans began to use English in worship.) The intention of this brief list was only to note those important festivals which fell on specific dates; Sundays were assumed as a separate category. Thus Easter and Pentecost were not listed as "chief festivals."

The *Common Service Book* (1918) added to the list not to increase the number of chief festivals but to indicate which days and Sundays took precedence when two days coincided. (North American Lutherans were beginning to ask liturgical questions.) To the four chief festivals noted in the *Church Book*, therefore, were added the Sundays of Advent, the Transfiguration (observed on the last Sunday after the Epiphany), Septuagesima, Sexagesima, Quinquagesima, Ash Wednesday, the Sundays in Lent, the days of Holy Week, the Ascension and the Sunday following, Pentecost and the Day following, the Festival of the Holy Trinity. The *Service Book and Hymnal* (1958) added the Sundays after Easter and All Saints' Day to the list.

The rubric which introduced the list in both the *Common Service Book* and the *Service Book and Hymnal* directed, "The following days shall be observed invariably as appointed in the Calendar."[20] In addition to declaring the precedence of these days, the rubric can be understood as directing congregations to observe these days without omission or variation.

The *Church Book* also listed certain "Minor Festivals observed in some parts of the Lutheran Church." These were the days of St. Andrew, St. Thomas, St. Stephen, St. John, the Conversion of St. Paul, the Presentation of Christ, St. Matthias, the Annunciation, St. Philip and St. James, the Birthday of John the Baptist, St. Peter and St. Paul, the

---

[18]*Constitution on the Sacred Liturgy* V. 104 as quoted in the sacramentary, 62.

[19]Philip H. Pfatteicher, "The Fulfillment of Baptism," *Liturgy* 5:2 (Fall 1985):15–19.

[20]*Common Service Book*, text ed., p. 491; *Service Book and Hymnal*, p. 278.

Visitation, St. James, St. Bartholomew, St. Matthew, St. Michael, St. Simon and St. Jude. St. Mark and St. Luke were not included, perhaps because they were not apostles; All Saints' Day was not listed.

The *Common Service Book* added to this list the days of St. Mark and St. Luke, thus adding the category of Evangelists to those selected, and also listed All Saints' Day. (It also revised the title of June 24 to sound more liturgical — the Nativity of St. John the Baptist — and added "All Angels" to St. Michael's Day).

The Lutheran Hymnal (1941) added Holy Innocents' Day and St. Mary Magdalene. It also added to the title of February 2: the Presentation of Our Lord and the Purification of Mary (following the *Book of Common Prayer*).

The *Service Book and Hymnal* followed *The Lutheran Hymnal* and added Holy Innocents' Day (December 28) to the *Common Service Book* list. It also moved the Transfiguration to the more ancient and universal date, traditional for Roman Catholics and Episcopalians, August 6.

A gradual expansion of propers for the lesser festivals is to be noted, indicating and encouraging increasing frequency of their observance. The *Church Book* provided propers consisting of Introit, Collect, two Old Testament lessons (one from the historical books and one from the poetical books), an Epistle, and a Gospel for the Festival of Harvest, the Festival of the Reformation, a Day of Humiliation and Prayer, and a Day of General or Special Thanksgiving. Propers consisting of Introit, Collect, Epistle, and Gospel were provided for the other days; for evangelists', apostles', and martyrs' days there was one common Introit and three collects. The *Common Service Book* provided for apostles' days a common Introit and Gradual and five collects; for evangelists' days a common Introit, Collect, and Gradual. A proper Introit, Collect, Epistle, Gradual, and Gospel were provided for St. Stephen's Day, the Nativity of St. John the Baptist, St. Michael and All Angels, Reformation Day, All Saints' Day, the Festival of Harvest, a Day of Humiliation and Prayer, and A Day of General or Special Thanksgiving. A proper Introit, Collect, Epistle, and Gospel were provided for the Presentation of Our Lord, the Annunciation, the Visitation. The *Service Book and Hymnal* provided a proper Collect for each of the lesser festivals and a common Introit and Gradual for apostles' days and for evangelists' days.

Commemorations

In addition to the six principal festivals (Easter, Ascension, Pentecost, Trinity Sunday, Christmas, and the Epiphany), Sundays and Days of Special Devotion (Ash Wednesday and the Days of Holy Week), and the Lesser Festivals, the *Lutheran Book of Worship* provides for the commemoration of certain men and women who have been of importance to the Christian tradition.

The limitation of holy days in previous Lutheran books to the festivals of the apostles and the evangelists, certain biblical people (such as Mary Magdalene, the Holy Innocents, Michael, and Stephen), certain biblical events (conversion of St. Paul, presentation of Christ in the temple, the Annunciation, the Visitation, the birth of John the Baptist, the Transfiguration), sometimes an object (the holy cross), and Reformation Day gave the impression — often supported by caricatures of church history — that after the close of the apostolic age there was no history to be celebrated until the gospel broke into the medieval darkness October 31, 1517, in Wittenberg with Luther's posting of his Ninety-five Theses and that since the sixteenth-century Reformation no further events worth celebrating occurred or need occur. The present calendar seeks to give a more balanced picture of the continuity of Christian history and witness.

The principles used in selecting those to be commemorated were these:[21] (1) No century is left without a witness, so that the continuity of the Christian tradition is emphasized. (2) Those selected have distinguished themselves by conspicuous service and witness within the Christian tradition, broadly understood. (3) The men and women chosen are not only ecclesiastics but represent the varied vocations of service. (4) Unless there is a compelling tradition otherwise, the date chosen for commemoration is, in accordance with the usual tradition of Christianity, that of the person's death, the birth into heaven. (5) Even those who have only recently died were understood to be eligible for selection. (6) An attempt has been made at a geographic spread which includes all the various parts of the inhabited world, with an emphasis on those lands in which Lutheranism has been strong. (7) The title "saint" is applied to all New Testament figures whose days are Lesser Festivals with the sole exception of the Virgin Mary to avoid unnecessarily stirring any lingering anti-Catholic sentiment. (It is now apparent that such reticence was unwarranted and that consistency would have been acceptable. It might be argued, however, that not to call her St. Mary, the name of many Lutheran churches in Europe and elsewhere, is to recognize that the God-bearer is not simply one saint among others but the principal person, who in her humility stands above all men and all other women as the human agent of the incarnation.) All those whose days are Commemorations are not given the title "saint" on the Lutheran calendar, for although some, like Francis of Assisi, are universally granted the title, many others are not and to do so would give rise not only to controversy over who has the right to canonize but also to oddities such as "St. George Fox."

The selection of people to be commemorated was made by Charles A. Ferguson and Philip H. Pfatteicher, based in part on the calendars in the Roman sacramentary, the *Book of Common Prayer*, and the Evangelischer Namenkalender in the *Allgemeines Evangelisches Gebetbuch*.[22] Michelangelo was added by vote of the Inter-Lutheran Commission on Worship.

---

[21] See Philip H. Pfatteicher, "The New Lutheran Calendar of Festivals and Commemorations," *Liturgy* 1:2 (1980):9–19.

[22] *Allgemeines Evangelisches Gebetbuch* (Hamburg: Furche-Verlag, 1965), 493–505.

The following table provides an overview of how the present calendar compares with the medieval pattern in use in previous books. The integration of the lesser festivals with the Sundays and major feasts of the church year was a feature of the calendar in the *Common Service Book* (not followed by the *Service Book and Hymnal*) and reflects what some believe may have been the practice of the ancient church.

Table I
THE CALENDAR BEFORE AND AFTER 1969

Church Orders through *Service Book and Hymnal* (and Roman Missal to 1969 and *Book of Common Prayer* to 1979)		*Lutheran Book of Worship* (and Roman sacramentary and *Book of Common Prayer*)
		The Christmas Cycle
The Season of Advent — 4 weeks		Advent Season — 4 weeks
St. Andrew, Apostle	November 30	St. Andrew, Apostle
St. Thomas, Apostle	December 21	St. Thomas, Apostle
		Christmas Season
		The Nativity of Our Lord
	December 24	Christmas Eve
Christmas Day. The Nativity of Our Lord	December 25	Christmas Day
St. Stephen, Martyr	December 26	St. Stephen, Deacon and Martyr
St. John, Apostle, Evangelist	December 27	St. John, Apostle and Evangelist
Holy Innocents (*SBH*)	December 28	Holy Innocents
		1st Sunday after Christmas
Circumcision of Our Lord	January 1	The Name of Jesus
		2nd Sunday after Christmas
The Season of the Epiphany		Epiphany Season
(1 to 6 Sundays)		(4 to 9 Sundays)
The Epiphany of Our Lord	January 6	The Epiphany of Our Lord
		The Baptism of Our Lord
1st to 5th Sundays after the Epiphany		2nd to 8th Sundays after the Epiphany
Transfiguration of Our Lord (*CSB*)		Transfiguration of Our Lord
Septuagesima Sunday		
Sexagesima Sunday		
Quinquagesima Sunday		
	January 18	Confession of St. Peter
Conversion of St. Paul	January 25	Conversion of St. Paul
Presentation of Our Lord	February 2	Presentation of Our Lord
St. Matthias, Apostle	February 24	St. Matthias, Apostle
		The Easter Cycle
The Season of Lent — 40 days		Lenten Season
Ash Wednesday		Ash Wednesday
The Sundays in Lent		
I. Invocabit		1st Sunday in Lent
II. Reminiscere		2nd Sunday in Lent

III. Oculi		3rd Sunday in Lent
IV. Laetare		4th Sunday in Lent
V. Judica. Passion Sunday		5th Sunday in Lent
		Holy Week
VI. Palmarum. Palm Sunday		Sunday of the Passion. Palm Sunday
The Days in Holy Week		
Monday		Monday in Holy Week
Tuesday		Tuesday in Holy Week
Wednesday		Wednesday in Holy Week
Thursday		Maundy Thursday
Good Friday		Good Friday
Saturday, Easter Eve		Saturday in Holy Week
The Easter (or Paschal) Season		Easter Season
		Resurrection of Our Lord
		Vigil of Easter
Easter Day. The Resurrection of Our Lord		Easter Day
		Easter Evening
The Annunciation	March 25	The Annunciation
The Sundays after Easter		
I. Quasi Modo Geniti		2nd Sunday of Easter
II. Misericordia Domini		3rd Sunday of Easter
III. Jubilate		4th Sunday of Easter
IV. Cantate		5th Sunday of Easter
V. Rogate		6th Sunday of Easter
Ascension of Our Lord		Ascension of Our Lord
(VI.) Exaudi		7th Sunday of Easter
St. Mark, Evangelist	April 25	St. Mark, Evangelist
St. Philip & St. James	May 1	St. Philip & St. James
Day of Pentecost. Whitsunday		Pentecost
		Vigil of Pentecost
		Day of Pentecost
		The Time of the Church
The Trinity Season (season after Pentecost) 22–27 Weeks		The Season after Pentecost
Trinity Sunday		The Holy Trinity
		2–27 Sundays after Pentecost
	May 31	The Visitation
	June 11	St. Barnabas
Nativity of St. John the Baptist	June 24	Nativity of St. John the Baptist
St. Peter & St. Paul	June 29	St. Peter & St. Paul
The Visitation	July 2	
	July 22	St. Mary Magdalene
St. James	July 25	St. James
Transfiguration (*SBH*)	August 6	(Transfiguration)
	August 15	Mary, Mother of Our Lord
St. Bartholomew	August 24	St. Bartholomew
	September 14	Holy Cross Day
St. Matthew	September 21	St. Matthew
St. Michael & All Angels	September 29	St. Michael & All Angels
St. Luke	October 18	St. Luke
St. Simon & St. Jude	October 28	St. Simon & St. Jude
Reformation Day	October 31	Reformation Day
All Saints' Day	November 1	All Saints' Day
		Christ the King

Table II
CLASSIFICATION OF OBSERVANCES

Roman sacramentary	*Lutheran Book of Worship*	*Book of Common Prayer*
1. Solemnities	1. Principal Festivals	1. Principal Feasts
	2. Sundays and Days of Special Devotion	2. Sundays
2. Feasts	3. Lesser Festivals	3. Holy Days
		4. Days of Special Devotion
3. Memorials a) obligatory b) optional	4. Commemorations	5. Days of Optional Observance
	5. Occasions	
	6. Weekdays	

BIBLIOGRAPHY

Adam, Adolf. *The Liturgical Year.* New York: Pueblo Publishing Co., 1981.

Bacchiocchi, Samuele. *From Sabbath to Sunday: A Historical Investigation of the Rise of Sunday Observance in Early Christianity.* Rome: Gregorian University, 1977.

Beckwith, Roger T., and Wilfred Scott. *The Christian Sunday: A Biblical and Historical Study.* Grand Rapids: Baker Book House, 1980. Published in London by Morgan and Scott in 1978 as *This Is the Day: The Biblical Doctrine of Sunday in Its Jewish and Early Christian Setting.*

Bynum, Caroline Walker. *Holy Feast and Holy Fast: The Religious Significance of Food to Medieval Women.* Berkeley: University of California Press, 1987.

Cabrol, Fernand. *The Year's Liturgy.* London: Burns, Oates & Washbourne, 1938.

Campbell, Joseph, ed. *Man and Time.* Princeton: University Press, 1983. Bollingen series xxxi:3.

Carrington, Philip. *The Primitive Christian Calendar.* Cambridge: University Press, 1952.

Cowie, Leonard W., and John Gummer. *The Christian Calendar.* Springfield: Merriam, 1974.

Crum, Milton Jr. "Our Approach to the Christian Year: Chronological or Eschatological?" *Worship* 51 (January 1977):24–32.

Denis-Boulet, N. M. *The Christian Calendar.* New York: Hawthorn Books, 1960.

Eliade, Mircea. *Cosmos and History: The Myth of the Eternal Return.* New York: Harper & Row, 1959.

von Franz, Marie-Louise. *Time: Rhythm and Repose.* London: Thames and Hudson, 1978.

Fraser, J. T. *Of Time, Passion, and Knowledge: Reflection on the Strategy of Existence.* New York: George Braziller, 1975.
———. *The Voices of Time.* New York: George Braziller, 1966.
Gale Richard M., ed. *The Philosophy of Time.* Garden City: Doubleday, 1967.
Hall, Edward T. *The Dance of Life: The Other Dimension of Time.* Garden City: Doubleday, 1983.
Halton, Thomas and Thomas K. Carroll. *The Making of the Liturgical Year.* Wilmington, DE: Michael Glazier, 1987.
Horn, Edward T., III. *The Christian Year.* Philadelphia: Muhlenberg Press, 1957.
Lesser Feasts and Fasts together with the Fixed Holy Days, The Proper for the. 4th ed. New York: Church Hymnal Corporation, 1988. See also the preparatory studies, *Prayer Book Studies IX, the Calendar* (1957); *Prayer Book Studies XII, the Collects, Epistles, and Gospels for the Lesser Feasts and Fasts* (1958), together with a *Supplement* (1960); *Lesser Feasts and Fasts* (1963). Rev. ed. (1973), 3rd ed. (1980).
"Liturgical Time." Papers Read at the 1981 Congress of Societas Liturgica. Ed. Wiebe Vos and Geoffrey Wainright. *Studia Liturgica* 14:2, 3, 4 (1982).
Liturgy 1:2 (1980). An issue devoted to the Calendar.
Liturgy 20:10 (December 1975). An issue devoted to Sunday.
Lock, Richard. *Time in Medieval Literature.* New York: Garland, 1984.
McArthur, Alan A. *The Evolution of the Church Year.* New York: Seabury Press, 1955.
Nocent, Adrian. "Liturgical Catechesis of the Christian Year," *Worship* 51 (November 1977):495–505.
———. *The Liturgical Year.* 4 vols. Collegeville: Liturgical Press, 1977.
Park, David. *The Image of Eternity: Roots of Time in the Physical World.* Amherst: University of Massachusetts Press, 1980.
Parsch, Pius. *The Church's Year of Grace.* 5 vols. Collegeville: Liturgical Press, 1953–1964.
Pfatteicher, Philip H. *Festivals and Commemorations: Handbook to the Calendar in the Lutheran Book of Worship.* Minneapolis: Augsburg Publishing House, 1980.
Pieper, Joseph. *In Tune with the World: A Theory of Festivity.* Chicago: Franciscan Herald Press, 1965.
Porter, H. Boone, Jr. *The Day of Light: The Biblical and Liturgical Meaning of Sunday.* Greenwich: Seabury Press, 1960.
———. *Keeping the Church Year.* New York: Seabury, 1977.
Priestly, J. B. *Man and Time.* London: Aldus Books, 1964.
Ricoeur, Paul. *Time and Narrative.* Trans. Kathleen McLaughlin and David Pellauer. 2 vols. Chicago: University of Chicago Press, 1984, 1986.
Rorsdorf, Willy. *Sunday: The History of the Day of Rest and Worship in the Earliest Centuries of the Christian Church.* Trans. A. A. K. Graham. Philadelphia: Westminster Press, 1968.
Searle, Mark, ed. *Sunday Morning: A Time for Worship.* Collegeville: Liturgical Press, 1985.
Stählin, Wilhelm. "Resurrection and Calendar Reform," *Response* 11 (Epiphany and Easter 1971):69–76,
Strodach, Paul Z. *The Church Year.* Philadelphia: United Lutheran Publication House, 1924.

Taft, Robert. "The Liturgical Year: Studies, Prospects, and Reflections." *Worship* 55 (January 1981):2–23.

Talley, Thomas J. *The Origins of the Liturgical Year*. New York: Pueblo Publishing Co., 1986.

The Year of Grace of the Lord. A Scriptural and Liturgical Commentary on the Calendar of the Orthodox Church by a Monk of the Eastern Church. Crestwood, NY: St. Vladimir's Seminary Press, 1980.

Zerubavel, Eviatar. *The Seven Day Circle: The History and Meaning of the Week*. New York: Free Press, 1985.

See also the bibliography for Chapter 6: The Propers.

3

HOLY BAPTISM

Ministers Edition, pp. 308–12, 188–89

Parallel Rites

Roman Catholic
: Rite of Christian Initiation of Adults, *The Rites*, pp. 13–181.
Rites of Baptism for Children, *The Rites*, pp. 183–283.

Episcopal
: Holy Baptism, *Book of Common Prayer*, pp. 297–314

Lutheran
: The Order of Holy Baptism: I. The Baptism of Infants. II. The Baptism of Adults. III. Confirmation. *The Book of Worship* (General Synod 1867), pp. 63–78.

Order for the Baptism of Children. Baptism of Adults. *Liturgy of the Evangelical Lutheran Church* (General Synod 1881), pp. 38–49.

Holy Baptism: I. Order for the Baptism of Infants. II. Order for the Baptism of Adults. *Church Book* (General Council 1891), pp. 345–58.

The Baptism of Infants. The Baptism of Adults. *Forms for Ministerial Acts* (General Synod 1900), pp. 7–33.

Order for the Baptism of Infants. Order for the Baptism of Adults. *A Liturgy for the Use of Evangelical Lutheran Pastors* (Joint Synod of Ohio 1912), pp. 127–34.

Order for the Baptism of Infants. Order for the Baptism of Adults. *Common Service Book*, text ed., pp. 389–98.

Baptism: 1. The Baptism of Infants: First Form; Second Form (without Sponsors). Emergency Baptism. 2. Confirmation of Lay Baptism. 3. The Baptism of Adults. *Liturgy and Agenda* (Lutheran Church–Missouri Synod 1921), pp. 319–29.

The Baptism of Infants (with Sponsors). The Baptism of Infants (without Sponsors). The Baptism of Adults. *The Lutheran Agenda* (Missouri Synod n.d. [194–]), pp. 1–20.

Order for the Baptism of Infants, *Service Book and Hymnal* (1958), pp. 242–44; Order for the Baptism of Adults, *The Occasional Services* (1962), pp. 6–10.

Contemporary Worship 7: Holy Baptism (1974).

Orthodox
: The Office of Holy Baptism, *Service Book* (1975), pp. 276–80.

The Service of Holy Baptism, *An Orthodox Prayer Book* (1977), pp. 55–73.

Methodist   Order for the Administration of Holy Baptism. Children. Adults. *The Book of Worship* (1964, 1965), pp. 7–11.
A Service of Baptism, Confirmation, and Renewal, Supplemental Worship Resources 10 (1980).

Presbyterian The Sacrament of Baptism, *The Worshipbook* (1972), pp. 43–47.

Church of   The Baptism of Persons Able to Answer for Themselves. The
South India   Baptism of Infants. *The Book of Common Worship* (1963), pp. 102–22.

Purpose

Baptism, "the door to life and the kingdom of God,"[1] is the cleansing with water through the power of the living word,[2] by which Christ takes new members into himself and by which they become part of his body, the church. Through the operation of the holy and life-giving Spirit in baptism they are adopted as God's own children, they are built into a living temple, they become a holy nation, they are ordained into a royal priesthood. Sin is washed away, and those made clean in the baptismal waters receive forgiveness, life, and salvation. Baptism is therefore nothing less than a rebirth, a passage from death to life, and is thus a personal appropriation of the paschal mystery.

Characteristics

The New Testament images of baptism and what it accomplishes are abundant and diverse. As summarized in the World Council of Churches' document *Baptism, Eucharist, and Ministry* (1982), baptism is (1) a participation in Christ's death and resurrection, Rom. 6:3–5; Col. 2:12; (2) a washing away of sin, 1 Cor. 6:11; (3) a new birth, John 3:5; (4) an enlightenment by Christ, Eph. 5:14; (5) a reclothing in Christ, Gal. 3:27; (6) a renewal by the Spirit, Titus 3:5; (7) the experience of salvation from the flood, 1 Pet. 3:20–21; (8) an exodus from bondage, 1 Cor. 10:1–2; and (9) a liberation into a new humanity, Gal. 3:27–28, 1 Cor. 12:13.

The service of Holy Baptism is the liturgical formulation and expression of this manifold process by which individuals are incorporated into the body of Christ, the church. Baptism is "the central liturgy of the community"[3] and embraces an ensemble of actions that together constitute initiation into the Christian community. It begins with the call of the Holy Spirit through the gospel, then continues with the response of conversion and faith, the catechumenate, baptismal washing

---

[1] *The Rites,* 4, §3.
[2] Eph. 5:26. See also the Small Catechism, IV.
[3] Marion J. Hatchett, *Commentary on the American Prayer Book* (New York: Seabury Press, 1981), 251

and anointing, and is consummated in eucharistic communion with the Lord and his church.

Because Holy Baptism is intimately bound to the dying and rising of Christ and his people,[4] it is most appropriately celebrated during the Easter Vigil. It joins the experience of Israel passing through the sea to the work of the second Adam passing through crucifixion to resurrection, and it binds the individual to both old and new celebrations of the Passover.

The Roman Catholic liturgy strongly urges the celebration of Holy Baptism at the Easter Vigil:

... Lent achieves its full force as a profound preparation of the elect, and the Easter Vigil is considered the proper time for the sacraments of initiation.[5]

The *Book of Common Prayer* places the liturgy for Holy Baptism immediately following the Great Vigil of Easter (pp. 284–314), thus suggesting the intimate connection between the two. The *Lutheran Book of Worship* (Min. Ed., p. 30), following the *Book of Common Prayer* (p. 312), lists the Vigil of Easter as the first of the occasions appropriate for baptism and suggests rubrically that

after the Easter season, it is appropriate to place the paschal candle near the font. It should be lighted at all baptisms as a reminder of the relationship between Baptism and the death and resurrection of our Lord.

Moreover, the Roman Catholic liturgy,[6] the *Lutheran Book of Worship*, and the *Book of Common Prayer*[7] in structure and in rubrics assume that except under unusual circumstances, baptism will be celebrated within the Holy Communion "as the chief service on a Sunday"[8] "when the Church commemorates the Lord's resurrection,"[9] for "the celebration should be filled with the Easter spirit."[10]

The liturgy of Holy Baptism in the *Lutheran Book of Worship* is designed for infants, children, and adults alike so that the unity of the sacramental action is emphatically clear and that no preference be expressed for a "proper" age for baptism. Earlier Lutheran books provided two separate orders, one for the baptism of infants and one for the baptism of adults. Previous editions of the *Book of Common Prayer* did likewise from 1662 until the 1928 American Prayer Book. Modern rites have, however, moved in the opposite direction, in keeping with the broader tradition of the church. The Eastern Orthodox rite, the *Lutheran Book of Worship*, the *Book of Common Prayer*, and the Presbyterian *Worshipbook* provide only one rite for Holy Baptism. On

---

[4] Tertullian, *On Baptism* 19.
[5] *The Rites*, 22 §8. See also 33, §4; 35, §49; 36, §55; 94, §208.
[6] Ibid., 37, §59; 107, §243.
[7] *Book of Common Prayer*, p. 228.
[8] Ibid.
[9] *The Rites*, 191, §9.
[10] Ibid., 94, §209.

the other hand, however, the Roman Catholic Rite for the Baptism of Children is the first Roman rite of baptism designed especially for children. (The Roman sacramentary also provides masses with eucharistic prayers designed especially for children.) The concerns of all the rites are similar, nonetheless: children who cannot speak for themselves are baptized in the faith of the church; the responsibility of parents and sponsors is affirmed; the role of the congregation in the work of initiation is emphasized; and indiscriminate baptism of infants is discouraged.

Background

In the early church, Christian initiation was received in a series of successive stages, for, Tertullian wrote, Christians "are made, not born."[11] The catechumenate was begun with various symbolic actions, including the candidates being breathed upon to signify the calling by and filling with the Holy Spirit, being signed on their foreheads with a cross denoting their new owner and master, and receiving salt in their mouths for purification.

In the West, where baptism was normally administered at Easter (or, alternatively, Pentecost), Lent was the time when the scrutinies[12] of the catechumens were made, exorcisms done, and the texts of the Creed and the Lord's Prayer given to the catechumens. Then on Easter eve, the litany was sung; the font was blessed; the candidates were again signed with the cross, received the *effeta* (the ritual opening of the ears with saliva), and were anointed with the oil of exorcism. Then came the baptism, including the three-fold renunciation of Satan by the candidates, their three-fold profession of belief in the Father, the Son, and the Holy Spirit, and their three-fold washing in the water. The newly baptized were anointed on the head, vested in white robes, and brought into the church. There the bishop prayed over them, invoking the seven-fold gifts of the Spirit, laid his hand on them, and signed them with chrism on the forehead. In the East, this was the only anointing and included the forehead as well as the heart and sense organs. The newly baptized then took part in the prayers of the church and received Holy Communion.

In the West, from the early sixth century on,[13] infant baptism became the general practice. The preparation was abbreviated and the concern shifted from making Christians to saving children from dying unbaptized. A high infant mortality rate and the widely accepted teaching of Augustine on original sin led to more baptisms by priests and fewer by

---

[11] Tertullian, *Apology* 18. Patristic documents describe baptismal practice in Africa (Tertullian, Cyprian, Augustine), in Rome (Hippolytus, John the Deacon), in Northern Italy (Ambrose), in Spain (Isidore, Hildephonsus), and in the East (Cyril of Jerusalem, John Chrysostom, Theodore of Mopsuestia, Pseudo-Dionysius Areopagiticus).

[12] Originally ritual examinations before the bishop of the candidate's faith, the scrutinies later came to be an assurance that the evil spirit(s) had departed.

[13] John the Deacon, ca. 500; Gelasian sacramentary.

the bishop at Easter and Pentecost. From the tenth century, this custom of a single rite performed on one day, often as soon after birth as possible, became the general rule. It was this rite that the Reformers received, simplified, and, along with the Roman Church, preserved to the twentieth century.[14]

Luther's "Order of Baptism" (*Taufbüchlein*, 1523) followed the rite of the medieval Roman Church with two significant additions. Luther inserted the Gospel reading (Mark 10:13–16) as a (dubious) warrant for infant baptism and replaced the collect after the giving of salt to the candidate with his "flood prayer" (*Sintflutgebet*).[15] Luther's "Order of Baptism Newly Revised" (1526) greatly simplified the ceremonies of exorcism, reduced the number of anointings, and made no provision for the giving of the lighted candle to the newly baptized person or the sponsors. Immensely popular, this revised order influenced the structure of the baptismal rite in the *Common Service Book* (1917) and the *Service Book and Hymnal* (1958).

By the last third of the twentieth century, biblical scholarship, liturgical and historical study,[16] ecumenical understanding, the secularization of previously "Christian" societies, and the expansion of the church into non-Christian areas of the world all combined to require a review and reconstruction of the baptismal rites of the western church. The reforms were fundamental and far-reaching.

The Roman Catholic rite for the baptism of children (1969), for confirmation (1971), and for the initiation of adults (1972) combined early Christian initiation patterns with the insights of pastoral experience in contemporary third world countries and influenced the reforming work of the other churches as well. Also influential on the new Lutheran rite was the work of the Standing Liturgical Commission of the Episcopal Church in *Prayer Book Studies* 18 (1970) and 26 (1973).

The Roman Catholic, Episcopal, and Lutheran churches have gone behind the medieval orders and recovered much more of the ancient and biblical richness of imagery and understanding. The resulting rites of the three churches have achieved consensus on the general shape of the baptismal service.

The liturgy of Holy Baptism was drafted by Hans Boehringer. Herbert Brokering, Sharon Esse, Justin Flak, Benjamin A. Johnson, Leigh D. Jordahl, Richard P. Jungkuntz, Edgar M. Krentz, Gordon W. Lathrop, and Arthur C. Repp served as consultants.

---

[14]For a compendious telling of this history along with commentary on the new rites of baptism, see Frank C. Senn, "The Shape and Content of Christian Initiation: An Exposition of the New Lutheran Liturgy of Holy Baptism," *Dialog* 14 (1975):97–107.

[15]The texts of the "Order for Baptism in the Marburg Agenda" (1497) and Luther's "Order for Baptism" (1523) are presented in parallel columns in J. D. C. Fisher, *Christian Initiation: The Reformation Period* (London: SPCK, 1970), 9ff.

[16]See Aidan Kavanagh, *The Shape of Baptism: The Rite of Christian Initiation* (New York: Pueblo Publishing Co., 1978), 81ff.

THE SERVICE IN DETAIL

Initiation into the Christian church begins with entrance into the cat-echumenate,[17] infant baptism being understood as an exception to the regular pattern. But whether an infant or an adult is baptized, the service of Holy Baptism is but a part of the process of entrance which begins earlier and is not completed until death. The service is nonetheless the central action to which the catechumenate points and from which the Christian life flows.

Propers

It is intended that baptism be celebrated within the context of the worship of the people of God into which the candidates are to be incorporated. Propers for the Holy Communion are therefore provided for optional use when baptism is celebrated on days for which the liturgical color is green.

The prayer (no. 160) which the *Lutheran Book of Worship* gives as the Prayer of the Day for Holy Baptism (Min. Ed., p. 188) was written by Louis Weil for the baptismal rite in the 1979 *Book of Common Prayer* in which it serves as the concluding collect for the prayers for the candidates. The basic thought is drawn from Romans 6:3–4; the phrase "the power of his resurrection" is from Philippians 3:10. In the version in the *Lutheran Book of Worship*, however, the prayer has unfortunately been simplified by the removal of the eschatological note.

The Notes on the Liturgy (Min. Ed., p. 30) permit the use of this prayer after the appointed prayer of the day at times of baptism when the appointed color is other than green. The collect in the *Book of Common Prayer* for use "At Baptism"[18] and the Roman Catholic opening prayers for baptism[19] stress somewhat more clearly the ethical implications of baptism and the moral responsibilities of the baptized.

Book of Common Prayer	*Lutheran Book of Worship*
Grant, O Lord, that all who are baptized into the death of Jesus Christ your Son may live in the power of his resurrection and look for him	Grant to us, Lord, that all who are baptized into the death of Jesus Christ, your Son, may also live with him in the power of his resurrection;

[17] See *Occasional Services* (1982), 13–15, and Philip H. Pfatteicher, *Commentary on the Occasional Services* (Philadelphia: Fortress Press, 1983), 15–29; and William H. Willimon, "Making Christians in a Secular World," *Christian Century* 103:31 (October 22, 1986), 914–17.

[18] Almighty God, by our baptism into the death and resurrection of your Son Jesus Christ, you turn us from the old life of sin: Grant that we, being reborn to new life in him, may live in righteousness and holiness all our days; through Jesus Christ...."

[19] Lord God, in baptism we die with Christ to rise again in him. Strengthen us by your Spirit to walk in the newness of life as your adopted children.
or
Lord God, your word of life gives us a new birth. May we receive it with open hearts, live it with joy, and express it in love.

33

to come again in glory; who	who
lives and reigns	lives and reigns with you and the
now and for ever. (p. 306)	Holy Spirit, now and forever.

Most of the scriptural lessons appointed in the *Lutheran Book of Worship* for Holy Baptism are shared with the Roman Catholic (RC) and Episcopal (*BCP*) rites.

Deut. 30:15–20 (RC)
Jer. 31:31–34 (RC)
Ezek. 36:24–28 (RC, *BCP*)

Psalm   8 (RC)
          23 (RC, *BCP*)
          29
          34:1–9 (RC)
          42:1–2a (RC, *BCP*)
          43:3–4
          84 (*BCP*)
          93
          122

Acts 8:26–38 (RC)
Rom. 5:1–5
Rom. 6:3–5 (RC, *BCP*)
Rom. 8:14–17 (RC, *BCP*)
1 Cor. 12:12–13 (RC, *BCP*)
2 Cor. 5:17–20 (*BCP*)
Eph. 4:1–6
Titus 3:4–8a (RC)
1 Peter 2:4–10 (RC)
Rev. 21:5–7
Matt. 28:16–20 (RC)
Mark 1:9–11 (RC, *BCP*)
Mark 10:13–16 (RC, *BCP*)
John 3:1–8 (RC, *BCP*)
John 4:5–14
John 15:1–11 (RC)

The Verse for Holy Baptism was composed for *Contemporary Worship 7: Holy Baptism* (1974). (1974) It is based on John 3:5 and Colossians 2:12.

The Address

The presiding minister's opening address in the service of baptism, written by Hans Boehringer and the Liturgical Text Committee of the Inter-Lutheran Commission on Worship for the *Lutheran Book of Worship*, refining the address in *Contemporary Worship 7*, is a statement of the nature, effects, and responsibilities of baptism. It replaces an address from predecessor rites, which was adapted from the *Book of*

Common Prayer and which began, "Dearly beloved, forasmuch as all men are conceived and born in sin...."[20] The *Church Book* (1868) declared *how* one knows that: "We learn from the Word of God, and know from our own experience, that all men are conceived and born in sin, and so are under the wrath of God."[21] The clause in the *Lutheran Book of Worship*, "We are born children of a fallen humanity" is an expression of this inheritance of original sin, but less liable to misunderstanding. Being children of a fallen humanity, we are inheritors of death, for "the wages of sin is death" (Rom. 6:23); those who are reborn as children of God are inheritors of eternal life.[22]

But before talking about sin and death, the address speaks of God as gracious, emphasizing the primacy of grace in evangelical theology and in baptism — the prevenient grace of God. The word *liberates* echoes the exodus and recalls the passion and resurrection of Christ and all the struggles against bondage which oppressed people have waged in quest of freedom.[23] Christians are liberated from sin and death by being joined to the death and life of Jesus Christ. Death is the consequence of sin, and both nouns — sin and death — are important: we are at once free from sin and yet continue to sin; we are free from death, and yet we must die. Luther teaches that we are at once justified and sinful, *simul justus et peccator.* "Thus a Christian man is righteous and a sinner at the same time, holy and profane, an enemy of God and a child of God."[24] Baptism begins a process which is not completed until death.[25] The power of sin and death is already broken, but not until death and the last day will the old and last enemy be overcome.

The parallels and paradoxes in the introductory address are noteworthy: our sin and death, Christ's death and resurrection; our birth as children of sin, our rebirth as children of God; our share in fallen humanity, our inheritance of eternal life. The paradoxes remain in tension throughout our life, and a clear understanding of both sides is necessary for a responsible view of the human condition.

Baptism is "by water and the Spirit"[26] (John 3:5), a creation theme recalling Genesis 1 and the Johannine equation of water and spirit. By water and the Spirit creation began; by water and the Spirit the new

---

[20]*Common Service Book*, text ed., p. 389; *Service Book and Hymnal*, p. 242.

[21]*Church Book*, 348. "Born into sin" would have been less liable to misunderstanding than "born in sin."

[22]See Martin Luther, "The Holy and Blessed Sacrament of Baptism," *Luther's Works* 35:30, §3.

[23]See Michael Walzer, *Exodus and Revolution* (New York: Basic Books, 1984).

[24]Martin Luther, "Lectures on Galatians" (1535), *Luther's Works* 26:232. See also Luther, "Lectures on Romans," *Luther's Works* 25:257: "The saints are always sinners in their own sight." See also Luther, "Lectures on Galatians" (1519), *Luther's Works* 27:231.

[25]Martin Luther, "The Holy and Blessed Sacrament of Baptism," *Luther's Works* 35:30–31.

[26]See Alexander Schmemann, *Of Water and the Spirit* (New York: St. Vladimir's Seminary Press, 1974).

creation of Christians is accomplished.[27] Baptism's new birth is an unrepeatable event, but like physical birth it is the beginning of a process of growth and continual liberation. Thus the address concludes with an emphasis on the ethical dimensions of this baptismal growth: living with Christ and his people, we grow in faith, love, and obedience. It is in community that these virtues are learned.

The Presentation and Instruction

In the Lutheran and Episcopal rites the candidates are presented by name to the presiding minister for baptism. The sponsors, who present the candidates, have an obvious liturgical and practical role in getting the candidates to the appropriate place, but their task as spiritual guides and overseers is far more important. Ideally, they will accompany the candidates through the years of incorporation into the Christian community, helping them to persevere in the Christian life.

After the presentation, those candidates able to answer for themselves each affirm their desire for baptism, for coming to be baptized must be a voluntary act if the sacrament is to be efficacious. A candidate must knock on the door of the kingdom like a beggar seeking bread, like a petitioner with a precisely worded request (Matt. 22:12), like "those who know their need of God" (Matt. 5:3 NEB), crying, "I want to be baptized" (Acts 8:36).

If only young children are to be baptized, the minister instructs those who present them concerning their responsibilities: to bring (not send) the children to worship; to teach them the Lord's Prayer, the (Apostles') Creed, and the Ten Commandments;[28] to put the Bible in their hands (not on a table or shelf) and further to provide for their instruction in the faith; to the end that they in union with the church may live their baptismal covenant until the Day of the Lord. The text of this instruction is from the Order for the Baptism of Infants from the *Common Service Book* (text ed., pp. 392–93) and the *Service Book and Hymnal* (p. 243), which was adapted from the address in the *Church Book* (1891). The charge in the *Church Book* and in the *Common Service Book* was given at the end of the rite as an appropriate reminder to the sponsors and parents of their duties to continue the post-baptismal instruction (*mystagogia*) now that the liturgical rite has concluded. In the *Service Book and Hymnal* order, the charge was given immediately prior to the renunciation, as if to give the sponsors one last chance to decline their demanding duties before the action of baptism began.

---

[27]Students of mythology have often noted the sexual overtones of feminine water and masculine spirit and their creative conjunction. See, for example, Alan W. Watts, *Myth and Ritual in Christianity* (Boston: Beacon Press, 1968), 46–47; Mircea Eliade, *Patterns in Comparative Religion*, trans. Rosemary Sheed (Cleveland and New York: World Publishing Co., 1963), chapters 2 and 5.

[28]These are, of course, the first three sections of Luther's Small Catechism, rearranged so as to begin with the easiest and most familiar.

Reading the four texts of this address in chronological order shows a text moving toward a notably satisfying statement of the responsibilities of the present generation of Christians toward the spiritual formation of the next as the living faith is passed on through the centuries.

I now admonish you who have done so charitable a work to *this child* in *its* Baptism, that ye diligently and faithfully teach *it*, or have *it* taught, the Ten Commandments, that thereby *it* may learn to know the will of God; also the Christian Faith, set forth in the Creed, whereby we obtain grace, the forgiveness of sins, and the Holy Ghost; and likewise the Lord's Prayer, that *it* may call upon God, and find help to withstand the devil, and lead a Christian life, till God shall perfect that which He hath now begun in *it*, and bring *it* to life everlasting.

(Church Book, 1891)

I now admonish you who have done so charitable a work to *this child* in *his* Baptism, that ye diligently and faithfully teach *him* the Ten Commandments, the Creed, and the Lord's Prayer; and that, as *he grows* in years, ye place in *his* hands the Holy Scriptures, bring *him* to the Services of God's House; and provide for *his* instruction in the Christian Faith, that, abiding in the covenant of *his* Baptism, and in communion with the Church, *he* may be brought up to lead a godly life until the day of Jesus Christ. Amen.

(Common Service Book, pp. 392–93)

Since in Christian love you present *this Child* for Holy Baptism, I charge you that you diligently and faithfully teach *him* the Ten Commandments, the Creed, and the Lord's Prayer; and that, as *he* grows in years, you place in *his* hands the Holy Scriptures, bring *him* to the services of God's House, and provide for *his* instruction in the Christian Faith; that, abiding in the covenant of *his* Baptism and in communion with the Church, *he* may be brought up to lead a godly life until the day of Jesus Christ. I therefore call upon you to answer in *his* stead: . . . .

(Service Book and Hymnal, p. 243).

In Christian love you have presented *these children* for Holy Baptism. You should, therefore, faithfully bring *them* to the services of God's house, and teach *them* the Lord's Prayer, the Creed, and the Ten Commandments. As *they grow* in years, you should place in *their* hands the Holy Scriptures and provide for *their* instruction in the Christian faith, that, living in the covenant of *their* Baptism and in communion with the Church, *they* may lead *godly lives* until the day of Jesus Christ.

Do you promise to fulfill these obligations?

(Min. Ed., p. 308)

In the *Lutheran Book of Worship* the charge has been made more active: the children are not simply to "abide" in the covenant of their baptism; they are to "live" in it. Here the charge is not an instruction concerning duties but a statement of obligations calling for a promise from the sponsors.

The charge to the sponsors "when older children and adults are baptized also," with its rather vague generalities, is a less successful revision of the inherited statement.

The Prayers

A model text for the Prayers is given with the propers for Holy Baptism (Min. Ed., p. 189). The invitation to the Prayers and the petitions are adapted from the *Book of Common Prayer* for which they were newly composed. (The corresponding Prayer for the Elect in the Roman rite is used in connection with the second scrutiny, celebrated on the Fourth Sunday in Lent. Model intercessions for baptism are also provided.)[29]

Book of Common Prayer	*Lutheran Book of Worship*
Let us now pray for *these persons* who *are* to receive the Sacrament of new birth	Let us pray for *those* who are to receive the Sacrament of Holy Baptism, for *their* sponsors and parents, and for all the baptized everywhere.
[and for those (this person) who *have* renewed *their* commitment to Christ.] Deliver *them*, O Lord, from the way of sin and death.	Deliver *them*, from the way of sin and death. Lord, in your mercy,
Lord, hear our prayer.	*Hear our prayer.*
Open *their hearts* to your grace and truth.	
Fill *them* with your holy and life-giving Spirit.	Fill *them* with the Holy Spirit, so that *they* lack no spiritual gift. [1 Cor. 1:7]
Keep *them* in the faith and communion of your holy Church.	
	Let the examples of *their* sponsors and parents strengthen *them* in faith and life so that together *they* may enter the joy which is prepared for all the faithful. [Matt. 25:21, 23]
Teach *them* to love others in the power of the Spirit.	
Send *them* into the world	
in witness to your love.	Strengthen all who bear the sign of the cross, so that they may always bear witness to the Lord by word and life.

---

[29] *The Rites*, 77–78, 264–67.

Bring *them* to the fullness
of your peace and glory.

We give thanks for all who have
gone before us in the faith [St.
John the Baptist, Mary the mother
of our Lord, apostles and martyrs,
evangelists and teachers, and all
those] who by their lives have
testified to the love of God,
especially ————— .

The final petition in the *Lutheran Book of Worship* form is noteworthy, for it is the one example in the book of how one may follow the rubric in the Prayers of the Eucharist, "The minister gives thanks for the departed. ... " It mentions by name two witnesses (John the Baptist because of his connection with baptism, and the Virgin Mary as the first of the saints and the birth-giver) and four classes of people (apostles and martyrs, evangelists and teachers). The concluding remembrance of the saints is also an allusion to the understanding that in baptism one is united to the communion of saints, the holy men and women of all ages, who in Christ are one and who stand about to support one another (Heb. 12:1–2), an understanding which the Roman rite expresses by its use in the baptismal liturgy of the Litany of the Saints, calling upon many in the cloud of witnesses by name and asking their prayerful support.

The Thanksgiving

In the early church, the water of baptism was to be "living water,"[30] that is, running water, the most honorable of the six Jewish grades of water used for ritual purposes.[31] The *Apostolic Tradition* of Hippolytus (ca. 215) notes, "At cockcrow a prayer is said over the water";[32] the Gelasian sacramentary (nos. 444–48) gives the text of such a prayer using biblical typology involving water.[33] One of the primary purposes of the prayer over the water was to unfold the richness and the depth of the symbol of baptism, and in the present rite the relation between water and baptism is recalled and explicated in the Thanksgiving prayer (no. 245).

The theologians of the early church understood that Jesus' baptism hallowed all water for use in the sacrament of Baptism. Maximus of Turin, for example, declared in a sermon,

---

[30] *Didache* 7. 1–3.

[31] The origins may go back to Lev. 14:5 and Numb. 19:17. See H. L. Strack and P. Billerbeck, *Kommentar zum Neuen Testament aus Talmud und Midrash.* 4 vols. (Munich: Beck, 1922–1928), 108ff. See also the account of Jesus and the woman of Samaria at the well, John 4:1–30, esp. v. 10.

[32] *Apostolic Tradition* 21.

[33] See also the Easter baptismal vigil in the Mozarabic Missale Mixtum and the *Missale Gallicanum vetus* (no. 168).

Someone might ask, "Why would a holy man desire baptism?" Listen to the answer: Christ is baptized, not to be made holy by the water, but to make the water holy, and by his cleansing to purify the waters which he touched. For the consecration of Christ involves a more significant consecration of the water.

For when the Savior is washed all water for our baptism is made clean, purified at its source for the dispensing of baptismal grace to the people of future ages.[34]

The water of baptism, moreover, signifies the continuity between the original and the new creation, "thus revealing the significance of baptism not only for human beings but also for the whole cosmos."[35]

Luther of course knew these traditions, and they appealed to him as a student of Scripture. For him, typology demonstrated the unity of the Bible, showing how the Old Testament "types" foreshadowed Christ and Holy Baptism. The idea that Jesus' baptism sanctified all water demonstrated his understanding that creation is capable of bearing the Creator to the world. The Flood Prayer (*Sintflutgebet*) was thus not Luther's invention but his adaptation of the tradition based on his remarkable insight into the richness of baptism and his understanding of Scripture. His prayer drew upon the biblical accounts of destruction and salvation in Noah's flood and the Red Sea as anticipations or "types" of baptism and also pointed to the baptism of Jesus as the consecration of all water. This prayer had great popularity in the German church orders and was included, although as an optional element, in the baptismal rite in the *Church Book* (1891).

Almighty and Everlasting God, Who of Thy righteous judgment didst destroy the unbelieving world by the waters of the flood, when of Thy great mercy Thou didst save faithful Noah and his family; Who didst drown wicked Pharaoh, with all his army, in the Red Sea, yet didst lead Thy people Israel safely through the midst thereof, prefiguring thereby the washing of Thy Holy Baptism; and Who, by the Baptism of Thy well-beloved Son, Jesus Christ, didst sanctify and appoint Jordan and all waters to a saving flood, and the abundant washing away of sin; We beseech Thee, of Thine infinite mercy, to look graciously upon *this child*, and to bless *it* in spirit with true faith, that, by this salutary flood, whatsoever of the old Adam is inborn and worketh in *it* may be washed away, and that, being delivered out of the number of the unbelieving, *it* may be savingly kept in the holy Ark of the Church, serve Thee in fervency of spirit and joyful hope, and finally, with all believers, be accounted worthy to obtain Thy promise of everlasting life; through Jesus Christ our Lord.[36]

---

[34] Maximus of Turin, *Sermon* 100 On the Holy Epiphany 1.3. The passage is given in the Roman Catholic *Liturgy of the Hours* as the second reading in the Office of Readings for Friday between the Epiphany and the Baptism of Christ.

[35] *Baptism, Eucharist, and Ministry.* Faith and Order Paper no. 111 (Geneva: World Council of Churches, 1982), 7.

[36] *Church Book*, 350. In Luther's 1523 Order of Baptism the *Sintflutgebet* is followed by a wonderfully vigorous exorcism:

Therefore, thou miserable devil, acknowledge thy judgment and give glory to the true and living God, give glory to his Son Jesus Christ and to the Holy Ghost, and depart from this N. his servant; for God and our Lord Jesus Christ has of his goodness called him to his holy grace and blessing, and to the fountain of baptism

Thomas Cranmer included a version of this prayer in the 1549 *Book of Common Prayer*, and it remained in the American Prayer Book until the 1928 revision. The *Church Book* translation of the Flood Prayer is based on that in the Prayer Book.

In the Small Catechism there is a faint echo of the idea that Jesus was baptized in order to baptize water, to consecrate the element for sacramental use. Luther explains, "It is not the water that produces these effects, but the Word of God connected with the water, and our faith which relies on the Word of God connected with the water."[37] The Large Catechism rhapsodizes,

Therefore it is not simply a natural water, but a divine, heavenly, holy, and blessed water — praise it in any other terms you can — all by virtue of the Word, which is a heavenly, holy Word which no one can sufficiently extol, for it contains and conveys all the fullness of God. From the Word it derives its nature as a sacrament, as St. Augustine taught, "*Accedat verbum ad elementum et fit sacramentum.*" This means that when the Word is added to the element...it becomes a sacrament.[38]

Later Lutheran theology tamed this vigorous understanding of the word as the activity of Christ inseparable from Christ himself and implied that the word was simply the biblically based baptismal formula.

In the *Lutheran Book of Worship* the Thanksgiving for baptism, like the comparable Thanksgiving in the *Book of Common Prayer*, is designed to be clearly parallel to the Great Thanksgiving of the Eucharist. It begins with the traditional preface dialogue (a Gallican elaboration of the ancient prayer[39]), but, like the blessing of the palms on the Sunday of the Passion, eliminates the verse "Lift up your hearts" and its response, following the practice described by Hippolytus in the *Apostolic Tradition* that this verse and response was used only in the eucharistic dialogue. The Thanksgiving represents a recovery of a fuller Lutheran practice dating from Luther's Order of Baptism (1523) and is a conflation of Luther's *Sintflutgebet* ("flood prayer"), the Roman Catholic prayer at the blessing of the water,[40] and the thanksgiving over the water, drafted by Leonel Mitchell, in the *Book of Common Prayer*.[41] The extent of the similarities of the three prayers in structure and language in readily apparent when the three are set side by side (see pp. 42–43).

---

so that thou mayest never dare to disturb this sign of the holy cross + which we make on his forehead.... So hearken now, miserable devil, abjured by the name of the eternal God and of our Savior Jesus Christ, and depart trembling and groaning, conquered together with thy hatred.... Come out of and depart from this servant of God, N., for he commands thee, thou miserable one, he who walked upon the sea and stretched forth his hand to sinking Peter (*Luther's Works* 53:97–98).

[37] *Book of Concord* trans. and ed. Theodore G. Tappert et al. (Philadelphia: Muhlenberg Press, 1959), 349.

[38] Ibid., 438. The quotation from St. Augustine is from his Exposition of the Gospel of St. John 80.3 (*Corpus Christianorum: series latina* [Turnhout, Belgium, 1953–] 36:529).

[39] See the *Missale Gallicanum vetus* no. 168.

[40] *The Rites*, 96–98, 175–77.

[41] *Book of Common Prayer*, pp. 306–07.

The Rites of the Catholic Church	Lutheran Book of Worship	Book of Common Prayer
Father,	Holy God, mighty Lord, gracious Father: We give you thanks, for	We thank you, Almighty God,
you give us grace through sacramental signs which tell us of the wonders of your unseen power. In baptism we use your gift of water which you have made a rich symbol of the grace you give us in this sacrament. At the very dawn of creation your Spirit breathed on the waters, making them the wellspring of all holiness.	in the beginning your Spirit moved over the waters and you created heaven and earth. By the gift of water you nourish and sustain us and all living things.	for the gift of water. Over it the Holy Spirit moved in the beginning of creation.
The waters of the great flood you made a sign of the waters of baptism that make an end of sin and a new beginning of goodness. Through the waters of the Red Sea you led Israel	By the waters of the flood you condemned the wicked and saved those whom you had chosen, Noah and his family. You led Israel by the pillar of cloud and fire through the sea, out of	Through it you led the children of Israel
out of slavery to be an image of God's holy people set free from sin by baptism.	slavery into the freedom of the promised land.	out of their bondage in Egypt into the land of promise.
In the waters of the Jordan your Son was baptized by John and anointed with the Spirit.	In the waters of the Jordan your Son was baptized by John and anointed with the Spirit.	In it your Son Jesus received the baptism of John and was anointed by the Holy Spirit as the Messiah, the Christ, to lead us, through his death and resurrection,
Your Son willed that water and blood should	By the baptism of his own death and resurrection your beloved Son has set us free from the bondage to sin and death, and has opened the way to the joy and freedom of everlasting life.	from the bondage of sin into everlasting life.
flow from his side as he hung upon the cross.	He made water a sign of the kingdom and of cleansing and rebirth.	

(continued)

The Rites of the Catholic Church (continued)	Lutheran Book of Worship (continued)	Book of Common Prayer (continued)
		We thank you, Father, for the water of Baptism. In it we are buried with Christ in his death. By it we share in his resurrection. Through it we are reborn by the Holy Spirit. Therefore in joyful obedience to your Son, we bring into this
After his resurrection he told his disciples: "Go out and teach all nations, baptizing them in the name of the Father, and of the Son, and of the Holy Spirit." Father, look now with love upon your Church and unseal for it the fountain of baptism. By the power of the Spirit give to the water of this font the grace of your Son. You created man in your own likeness: cleanse him from sin in a new birth to innocence by water and the Spirit. We ask you, Father, with	In obedience to his command, we make disciples of all nations, baptizing them in the name of the Father, and of the Son, and of the Holy Spirit.	fellowship those who come to him in faith, baptizing them in the Name of the Father, and of the Son, and of the Holy Spirit.
your Son to send the Holy Spirit upon the water of this font. May all who are buried with Christ in the death of baptism rise also with him to newness of life.	Pour out your Holy Spirit, so that *those* who *are* here baptized may be given new life.	Now sanctify this water, we pray you, by the power of your Holy Spirit, that those who here are cleansed from sin and born again may continue for ever in the risen life of Jesus Christ our Savior.
	Wash away the sin of *all those* who *are* cleansed by this water and bring *them* forth as *inheritors* of your glorious kingdom.	
We ask this through Christ our Lord.	To you be given praise and honor and worship through your Son, Jesus Christ our Lord, in the unity of the Holy Spirit,	To him, to you, and to
Amen.	now and forever. *Amen.*	the Holy Spirit, be all honor and glory, now and for ever. *Amen.*
(pp. 96–98)	(Min. Ed., pp. 309–10)	(pp. 306–07)

The purpose of the Thanksgiving is to tie the life of the candidates to the history of salvation, making that history their history, incorporating them into that story so that they may perceive in their lives a continuation of the mighty acts of God. The prayer situates this particular baptism in its larger context: what God has done in the past and what God promises for the future.

The text of the Thanksgiving itself, underscoring its parallel to the Great Thanksgiving of the Eucharist, opens with the same three-fold address to the "holy God, mighty Lord, gracious Father," which will be echoed in reverse order in the baptismal formula "in the name of the Father, and of the Son, and of the Holy Spirit." Three classic biblical accounts of events in which water becomes a type of baptism are brought to remembrance, as they have been since the time of Ambrose:[42] (1) creation, including the continual nourishment and sustenance of all things, following Luther's explanation in the Small Catechism of the first article of the Creed; (2) the flood, a new beginning already seen as a type of baptism in 1 Peter 3:20–21; and (3) the passage through the Red Sea, recalling St. Paul's use of this image in Corinthians 10:1–2. In each of these three stories an enemy is destroyed and a new reality comes into being. Chaos is overcome by light and order; the wicked are drowned,[43] and Noah is saved to renew the race (the allusion to the church as the ark of salvation,[44] explicit in Luther, is now exceedingly indirect); the Egyptian army perishes, and Israel is set free. The creation itself involved three acts of separation: light from darkness, the waters under the firmament from the waters above the firmament, and sea from dry land. Similarly, Luther describes baptism as an act of separation, a new creation (2 Cor. 5:17):

Baptism ... so separates us from all men not baptized that we are thereby known as a people of Christ, our Leader, under whose banner of the holy cross we continually fight against sin.[45]

The description of the passage through the Red Sea no longer gloats over the drowning and destruction of Pharaoh and his armies but emphasizes instead the passage from slavery to freedom, recalling and giving context to the opening address of the rite, "In Holy Baptism our gracious heavenly Father liberates us from sin and death ... " and the eschatological promise of freedom in the Promised Land.

Ambrose sees the Holy Spirit at work in each of the three archetypal stories. The Spirit moves over the water at creation, is represented by the dove Noah sends out which brings peace, and overshadows the fleeing Hebrews like a cloud. The focus of baptism, we are to learn,

---

[42] Ambrose, *De mysteriis* 3.9–13 (assuming with many but not all commentators that Ambrose is the author of this book).

[43] The verb in the prayer in the *Lutheran Book of Worship* is "condemned" as in *Luther's Works* 53:97, on the basis of Heb. 11:7.

[44] Tertullian, *On Baptism* 8.

[45] "The Holy and Blessed Sacrament of Baptism," *Luther's Works* 35:29.

is not the washing with water but the Holy Spirit which distinguishes Christian baptism from other initiatory ablutions.

Ambrose adds to these accounts three further stories: the bitter water at Marah (Exod. 15:22ff.), Naaman the Syrian (2 Kings 5:1ff.), and the paralytic at the pool of Bethsaida (John 5:1–9). The Thanksgiving in the *Lutheran Book of Worship*, however, uses three images from the New Testament instead of the three which Ambrose provides. First, Jesus' baptism in the Jordan and his anointing with the Spirit is cited. (The service of Holy Baptism repeatedly draws on the Fourth Gospel's connection between water and Spirit). Here, the sinless one underwent baptism as an example to his followers, to be revealed as the Child of God, to sanctify the water, to receive the Spirit to consecrate him to his work, and to anticipate his death which will cause the Spirit of forgiveness to be given to the church.[46] In the prayer, Jesus' baptism is perhaps to be understood as a parallel to creation, a new beginning (2 Cor. 5:17) when the Spirit again moves over the water.

Second, Jesus' death and resurrection as the baptism with which he must be baptized (Luke 12:50; see Mark 10:38–39), by which he set us free and opened the way to life (see the Prayer of the Day for Easter, "Almighty God...you opened for us the gate of everlasting life") is a parallel to the story of the crossing of the Red Sea. The language underscores the parallel with the Exodus: the ancient pascha finds its parallel and fulfillment in the Christian pascha.

A less readily apparent image completes this second group of three stories and is parallel to the story of Noah and the great flood: Jesus "made water a sign of the kingdom." He did so when he talked with the Samaritan woman at the well (John 4:7ff.), when he was at the pool of Bethsaida (John 5:2ff.), and when he spoke with reference to the water from the pool of Siloam (John 7:37ff.). Water is also the element through which by baptism one enters the kingdom (John 3:5), and it recalls the river which flows from the throne of God through the holy city (Rev. 22:1). See also Ephesians 5:26 and Hebrews 10:22.

The familiar words of the great commission (Matt. 28:19–20), a passage included in the baptismal rites of the *Common Service Book* and the *Service Book and Hymnal*, are claimed as the warrant for baptism and constitute a fourth element in the New Testament portion of the archetypal stories recalled in the prayer. Therefore seven biblical accounts — creation, the flood, the passage through the Red Sea, Jesus' baptism in the Jordan, Jesus' death and resurrection as his baptism, water as a sign of the kingdom, and the great commission — are brought to mind as the church sets baptism in its scriptural context through this thanksgiving.

The focus of the liturgical action of baptism is not on water or a symbolic spiritual washing but the work of the Holy Spirit of which

---

[46]Oscar Cullmann, *Baptism in the New Testament* (London: SCM, 1950), 9–22.

the washing is an effective symbol (as in Titus 3:5). It is the Spirit who works the regeneration; it is the holy and life-creating Spirit who bestows new life in baptism. Therefore the eighth portion of the Thanksgiving is the prayer for the Holy Spirit, drawing upon the equation of water and spirit in the Fourth Gospel and recalling the conjunction of water and Spirit at the creation as well as the dependence of all life on water, which is itself a gift of God. This section echoes the first paragraph of the prayer. The first sentence makes reference to water as an efficacious sign of the new birth, mentioned in the preceding paragraph of the prayer. The second sentence refers to the washing aspect of baptism, asking a deeper and more spiritual cleansing than mere physical washing. This sentence again sounds the eschatological note heard earlier in references to "the promised land" and "the joy and freedom of everlasting life." In the Roman Catholic rite the celebrant touches the water at the mention of the Spirit, and the water "ripples with life and energy as the Spirit passes over" it[47] (John 5:3-4).

The renewal by the Spirit makes those who are so reborn to be inheritors with Jews (Gal. 3:29; Heb. 11:9) and Gentiles (Eph. 3:6) of the "glorious kingdom" of God and so heirs of eternal life (Titus 3:7; also Heb. 1:14). "All who are led by the Spirit of God are the children of God . . . and if children, then heirs, heirs of God and fellow heirs with Christ" (Rom. 8:14, 17).[48] The entire paragraph from Paul, Romans 8:12-17, is an important background document for understanding the thought of this paragraph of the Thanksgiving. The "glorious kingdom," recalling the splendid antiphon from the burial office *O quam gloriosam,* "O how glorious is that kingdom wherein all the saints do rejoice with Christ,"[49] is not precisely a biblical phrase, although it draws upon such passages as 1 Thessalonians 2:12; Ephesians 5:27; Hebrews 2:10; 1 Peter 1:21 and 5:10.

The doxology of the Thanksgiving is similar to that of the Great Thanksgiving in the Eucharist, ascribing three-fold praise, honor, and worship according to the ancient formula of the Gloria Patri: to the Father, through the Son, in the Holy Spirit.[50] The Holy Spirit, moreover, as in the doxology of the Great Thanksgiving and elsewhere (for example, the Prayer of the Church, Min. Ed., p. 117), serves as "a certain ineffable communion of the Father and the Son" and is understood as the guarantee of unity within the godhead.[51]

---

[47] Mark Searle, *Christening: The Making of Christians* (Collegeville: Liturgical Press, 1980), 76.

[48] See also Gal. 4:7; Heb. 6:17; 9:15; Col. 1:12.

[49] *Service Book and Hymnal,* p. 263.

[50] *Prayers We Have in Common,* 2nd rev. ed. (Philadelphia: Fortress Press, 1975), 19.

[51] Augustine, *On the Trinity* 5.11.12; 6.5.7; *Creed of Leo III;* Ephesians 4:3. See Jaroslav Pelikan, *The Christian Tradition,* vol. 2: *The Spirit of Eastern Christendom (600–1700)* (Chicago and London: University of Chicago Press, 1974), 196–197. See also David L. Miller, *Three Faces of God: Traces of the Trinity in Literature and Life* (Philadelphia: Fortress Press, 1986), 95.

The Renunciation, Profession, and Washing

All is now prepared for the central action, the mystical washing in the waters of baptism, the radical redirection and renovation of the lives of the candidates. It is a vivid portrayal of the gospel, which is a call to repentance and conversion, a summons to put away the old and to put on the new (Eph. 4:22–24; cf. Acts 3:19).

The presiding minister's invitation to the renunciation of Satan and the profession of faith serves a dramatic function, setting the stage and informing the candidates and the congregation of the profound significance of what is about to be done.[52] The invitation asks three actions. (1) "Profess your faith in Christ Jesus" is perhaps best understood here not to refer to the recitation of the creed but to the general desire to be joined to the body of Christ expressed by presenting oneself for baptism. Then (2) the candidates are to "reject sin," that is, Satan (the phrase is troublesome, but the commission believed that sin was less liable to misunderstanding than Satan is for modern people); and (3) "confess the faith of the Church" by professing the Creed. It is in this faith that the ministers of Christ's church baptize.

The renunciation is very ancient, mentioned by Hippolytus[53] and Tertullian.[54] In the tradition known to both men, the renunciation took place after the candidate entered the water immediately prior to the baptismal washing which took place as the Creed was professed. Through the centuries since, the renunciation has remained in close association with the profession of faith and the baptismal washing.

In Luther's two baptismal orders the renunciation was three-fold, as it had been since ancient times, corresponding to the three articles of the profession of faith. The Notes on the Liturgy in the *Lutheran Book of Worship* (Min. Ed., p. 31, n. 10) permit the continuation of this pattern. The renunciation was reduced to one question in later church orders and in the *Church Book* (p. 351) and the *Common Service Book* (text ed., p. 396); it was made optional in the *Service Book and Hymnal* (p. 243). The language of the renunciation, at least since the time of Hippolytus, was "the devil and all his works and all his ways."[55]

Satan is a problematic figure and concept for most moderns, and the rites of the Roman Catholic and Episcopal and Lutheran churches are all clearly struggling to make the figure meaningful in the modern world. The Roman Catholic rite offers a choice of two kinds of language: "Do you reject Satan and all his works and all his empty promises?" or "Do you reject sin so as to live in the freedom of God's children...do you reject the glamor of evil and refuse to be mastered by sin...do you reject

---

[52]The language of the invitation is drawn from the Roman Catholic order for the baptism of children of catechetical age: "N. and N., before you are baptized, reject Satan and profess your faith in the presence of Christ's Church" (*The Rites*, 145).

[53]*Apostolic Tradition* 21.

[54]Tertullian, *De spectaculis* 4; *De corona militis* 3; *De anima* 35.

[55]See Luther's rites, *Luther's Works* 53:99, 108.

Satan, father of sin and prince of darkness?"[56] The *Book of Common Prayer* asks

Do you renounce Satan and all the spiritual forces of wickedness that rebel against God?

Do you renounce the evil powers of this world which corrupt and destroy the creatures of God?

Do you renounce all sinful desires that draw you from the love of God[57]

If the existence of Satan is not altogether rejected — Satan's most effective tactic as Baudelaire observes in *Short Prose Poems*[58] — his figure has become trivialized in recent decades. Yet the reality to which Satan language points is alive and active, real and objective evil, a force driving humanity to evil often beyond our imagining.[59] Auschwitz and Hiroshima are but two modern examples, racism is another.

By the act of renunciation, this evil mastery is rejected, and ancient rites made the rejection dramatic indeed.[60] In the *Apostolic Tradition* the renunciation is said facing west, the place of the setting sun, to show the waning of Satan's power. Still today in the Eastern rites, the candidate sometimes spits toward the west as a further sign of detestation.[61] In the *Apostolic Tradition* of Hippolytus and through the medieval rites, after the renunciation of Satan, the candidates were anointed with the cleansing, healing, and protective oil of exorcism with the command, "Let every evil depart from you!"

The candidate then turned toward the east, the place of the rising sun (Son)[62] and made an act of adherence, replacing the rejected master with another Lord and master. The Apostles' Creed has its origin in such statements of faith as candidates were baptized,[63] and so has its primary use remained. The creed here and elsewhere in the liturgy is

---

[56]*Rites*, 98–99. Further adaptation by conferences of bishops is permitted.

[57]*Book of Common Prayer*, p. 302. To these questions are added additional questions summarizing what it means to be a Christian.

[58]Noted also by Denis de Rougemont, *The Devil's Share: An Essay on the Diabolic in Modern Society*, trans. Haakon Chevalier (New York: Meridian Books, 1956), 17ff., and by C. S. Lewis, *The Screwtape Letters* (London: Collins, 1942).

[59]Jeffrey Burton Russell, *The Devil: Perceptions of Evil from Antiquity to Primitive Christianity* (Ithaca: Cornell University Press, 1977); also his *Satan: The Early Christian Tradition* (Ithaca: Cornell University Press, 1981); *Lucifer: The Devil in the Middle Ages* (Ithaca: Cornell University Press, 1984); and *Mephistopheles: The Devil in the Modern World* (Ithaca: Cornell University Press, 1987). See also Neil Forsyth, *The Old Enemy: Satan and the Combat Myth* (Princeton: University Press, 1987), and Walter Wink, *Naming the Powers: The Language of Power in the New Testament*, vol. 1 of *The Powers* (Philadelphia: Fortress Press, 1984); and *Unmasking the Powers: The Invisible Forces That Determine Human Existence*, vol. 2 of *The Powers* (Philadelphia: Fortress Press, 1986).

[60]See Cyril of Jerusalem, *Mystagogical Catecheses*, 1.2, 9.

[61]*Service Book*, trans. Isabel Florence Hapgood, rev. ed. (Englewood, NJ: Antiochian Orthodox Christian Archdiocese of New York and All North America, 1975), 274.

[62]Note the baptismal connection with the Exsultet of the Easter Vigil (Min. Ed., p. 145): "that morning star which never sets...which...rising again from the grave, faithfully sheds light on all the human race."

[63]See J. N. D. Kelly, *Early Christian Creeds*, 3rd ed. (London: Longmans, 1972); O. Sidney Barr, *From the Apostles' Faith to the Apostles' Creed* (New York: Oxford University

to be understood not so much as a list of doctrines which are to be believed but as a summary of history — past, present, and future — by which God has made himself known to his creation.[64]

Luther's 1523 baptismal order followed the profession of faith with the anointing on the breast and back with "the oil of salvation." (In ancient rites there was a pre-baptismal anointing on the back and breast with the oil of exorcism, and, after baptism, the *Apostolic Tradition* describes an anointing on the crown of the head by the presbyter with the oil of thanksgiving, that is, oil over which the thanksgiving has been said,[65] as a celebration of joy. See Psalm 45:7.) Luther deleted this anointing in his 1526 rite, and Lutheran orders have not reinstituted the practice. The present Roman Catholic rite prescribes the anointing with the oil of catechumens, "the oil of salvation," on the breast or both hands "or even on other parts of the body,"[66] but a rubric notes that the episcopal conference may choose to omit this anointing. The *Book of Common Prayer* allows for the bishop to consecrate chrism at this point in the rite for use in the sealing after the baptism.

The mode of baptism has varied through the centuries, but immersion in some form is clearly the preferred method because of the clarity of the symbol of washing and of drowning and rising.[67] In the early church, immersion probably meant that the candidate stood in the water while water was poured over his or her head. In many ancient representations John the Baptist is shown standing with Jesus in the water of the Jordan and touching Jesus' head with his hand. The *Didache*[68] directs, "... baptize in running water.... If you do not have running water, baptize in some other. If you cannot in cold, then in warm. If you have neither, then pour water on the head three times 'In the name of the Father, Son, and Holy Spirit.'" This direction can be read as suggesting total immersion but permitting pouring if immersion was not feasible, but more likely in view of the iconographical evidence from the early church the three-fold pouring was done whether or not the candidate was able to stand in water. The *Apostolic Tradition* is not entirely clear as to the precise practice but seems to imply an immersion. The candidate goes down into the water with a deacon; the baptizer lays his hand on the candidate and asks, "Do you believe in God, the Father almighty?" The candidate answers, "I believe." The rubric then directs, "Let him baptize him a first time, keeping his hand on the person's head," the baptizer apparently in effect pushing the candidate under the water. The washing is done a second and a third time. The baptizer's hand remains on the candidate's head after each of the washings

---

Press, 1964); Wolfhart Pannenberg, *The Apostles' Creed* (Philadelphia: Westminster Press, 1973).

[64] Searle, 84.

[65] Ambrose, *De mysteriis* 6.29.

[66] *The Rites*, 99.

[67] See the splendid exposition by Cyril of Jerusalem, *Mystagogical Catecheses* 2.4–5.

[68] *Didache* 7.1–3.

to show the continuity of the three-fold action. In Syria, Theodore of Mopsuestia testifies to the practice of the candidate bowing down under the water of baptism (poured over the head), giving affirmation to the bishop's words of the baptismal formula.[69]

Immersion at least of infants in the water continued until Reformation times,[70] when there were three methods of baptizing: immersion of the child in the font;[71] *superfusio*, holding the naked child over the font and pouring water over the child; and *infusio*, dipping only the head of the child in the font.[72] Luther himself was strongly in favor of immersion. "It would be proper, according to the meaning of the word *Taufe*, that the infant, or whoever is to be baptized, should be put in and sunk completely into the water and then drawn out again."[73] Both of Luther's baptismal orders direct the minister to "take the child, dip it in the font, and say...."[74] The oldest baptismal order for the Münster diocese (ca. 1400–1414) prescribes triple immersion. Bucer and Zwingli preferred pouring.

Matthew 28:19 gives the formula "in the name of the Father, and of the Son, and of the Holy Spirit," reflected in the *Didache* (7.1), but according to Acts (2:38; 8:16; 10:48; 19:5) and Paul (1 Cor. 1:13; 6:11; Gal. 3:27; Rom. 6:3) baptism was simply "in the name of Jesus." Whether this was an actual baptismal formula is not clear. By the beginning of the third century the confession of faith was the baptismal formula, as in the *Apostolic Tradition;* it was given as questions to which the candidate gave answer. (In Acts 8:37 the Ethiopian eunuch's declaration of belief immediately preceded his baptism.) The use of the three formulaic questions that the candidate answered remained in the Roman rite as the baptismal formula until the eighth century as is evidenced by the Gelasian sacramentary (no. 449). Some time after the third century a formula based on Matthew 28:19 was developed. The first time such a declarative formula accompanied the three-fold immersion seems to have been in the East in a fifth-century Syrian adaptation of the *Apostolic Tradition*, the *Canons of Hippolytus*. The minister immersing the candidate said, "I baptize you in the name of the Father, and of the Son, and of the Holy Spirit." In the West, the formula is found in the Gallican sacramentaries: the eight-century *Missale Gothicum* (no. 260), the *Missale Gallicanum vetus* (no. 174), and the Bobbio missal (no. 248).[75] It was introduced into the Roman rite in the eighth century and is found in the Hadrian recension of the Gregorian sacramentary (no. 982) at the end of the eighth century. The "I" who speaks

---

[69] Theodore of Mopsuestia, *Baptismal Homily* 3.18.

[70] See Thomas Aquinas, *Summa Theologica* III.66.7.

[71] A sixteenth-century woodcut showing this practice was reproduced in *Contemporary Worship 7: Holy Baptism*, 3.

[72] Paul Zeller Strodach, *The Works of Martin Luther*. The Philadelphia Edition. (Philadelphia: Muhlenberg Press, 1932), 6:203. Reproduced in *Luther's Works* 53:100, n. 2.

[73] "The Holy and Blessed Sacrament of Baptism," *Luther's Works* 35:29.

[74] Ibid., 100, 109.

[75] Hatchett, 277–78.

the formula, it should be understood, is ultimately Christ, who acts through the church's sacraments.

As an alternative to the universal practice of the West, the *Lutheran Book of Worship* provides an even more ancient wording of the baptismal formula used in the Antiochene church of the fourth century[76] (it may be even older) and found to this day in the rites of the Eastern churches. This formula emphasizes the action of the triune God and the minister's function as a principal witness of what God is doing. The formula used at the distribution of Holy Communion in the Eastern churches is similar: "The servant of God, *N.*, partaketh of the precious and holy Body and Blood of our Lord...."[77]

The Laying On of Hands

In the gospel accounts of Jesus' baptism, the dove descended upon him as Jesus emerged from the waters of the Jordan. Thus, the action of confirmation follows immediately after the baptismal washing. The New Testament provides no clear pattern of the relationship of the Spirit to the baptismal washing.[78] Conversion, the Spirit, and the bath are distinguishable but are never totally separated. The various descriptions in Acts may or may not be a picture of the developing practice of the early church. Some distinguish the prophetic Spirit of the primitive enthusiastic community (Luke) from the life-giving Spirit described by Paul and John and find this a ground for understanding baptism and confirmation as separate sacraments.[79] Others argue that the New Testament offers no basis for a distinction between baptism and confirmation.[80] Tertullian in *De baptismo* (ca. 200) separates the washing from the imposition of hands and says that "in the water we are made clean...and made ready for the Holy Spirit" which is attributed to the laying on of hands. The *Apostolic Tradition* (ca. 215) describes in addition to both the pre-baptismal anointing with the oil of exorcism and the post-baptismal anointing with the oil of thanksgiving a series of actions by the bishop: prayer with the bishop's hands extended over the newly-baptized, an anointing (an imposition of the hand performed with oil), and a signing (sealing) on the forehead with the cross. Thus washed, dressed, and prepared, the candidates were ready for their first communion. Although the order and manner in which these elements were combined subsequently varied, this Roman pattern was through the centuries imposed on the Western church. The post-baptismal anointing by the presbyter

---

[76]Theodore of Mopsuestia, *Baptismal Homily* 3.15; John Chrysostom, *Baptismal Instruction* 2.26.

[77]*Service Book*, 119.

[78]See Reginald Fuller, "Christian Initiation in the New Testament" in *Made, Not Born* (Notre Dame, IN: University Press, 1976), 14.

[79]Thomas Marsh, "A Study of Confirmation," *Irish Theological Quarterly* 39 (1972), 161.

[80]Raymond Brown, "We Profess One Baptism for the Forgiveness of Sins," *Worship* 40 (1966), 265.

was understood to have its completion in the bishop's anointing of the candidate's forehead.[81]

In the Roman rite the bishop's actions were associated with the gift of the Spirit, but in other rites of the Latin West this may not have been the case. In Gaul and Spain a simple post-baptismal anointing of the forehead with oil consecrated by the bishop was performed by the presbyter who had done the baptism. In the early Syrian church no such post-baptismal action intervened between the washing and the Holy Communion, water perhaps being understood as the primary sign by which the Spirit was imparted. By the time of the *Apostolic Constitutions* (ca. 375) and the Catecheses of Cyril of Jerusalem a post-baptismal anointing is known, probably imported from the Western churches.

By about the fifth century, anointing with chrism and an accompanying prayer after baptism had become nearly universal. The bishop's prayer in the *Apostolic Tradition* has been expanded by the time of the early sixth-century Gelasian sacramentary and later Western books, and listed the seven-fold gifts of the Holy Spirit, taken from Isaiah 11:2 in the Vulgate translation.[82]

Apostolic Tradition	Gelasian sacramentary
O Lord God	Almighty God, Father of our Lord Jesus Christ,
who didst count these worthy of deserving the forgiveness of sins by the laver of regeneration make them worthy to be filled with thy Holy Spirit. and send them thy grace, that they may serve thee according to thy will;	who hast made thy servants to be regenerated of water and the Holy Spirit, and hast given them remission of all their sins, do thou, Lord, pour upon them thy Holy Spirit, the Paraclete, and give them the spirit of wisdom and understanding, the spirit of counsel and might, the spirit of knowledge and godliness, and fill them with the spirit of fear of God,
to thee is the glory, to the Father and to the Son with the Holy Ghost in the holy Church, both now and forever.... [83]	in the name of our Lord Jesus Christ, with whom thou livest and reignest ever God with the Holy Spirit, throughout all ages... [84]

In the baptismal order of the *Lutheran Book of Worship*, therefore, following a practice as ancient as the *Apostolic Tradition*, after the baptismal washing, the minister(s), those who are being baptized, and their

---

[81] E. C. Whitaker, ed., *Documents of the Baptismal Liturgy*, 2nd ed. (London: SPCK, 1970), 229–230.

[82] "It is instructive to read the first part of the eleventh chapter of Isaiah and to see the glorious and imperial context of the 'spirit of wisdom and understanding, the spirit of counsel....'" H. Boone Porter, "Holy Baptism: Its Paschal and Ecumenical Setting," *Response* 13:1 (Easter 1973), 10.

[83] *Apostolic Tradition* 22: Whitaker, 6.

[84] Gelasian sacramentary 44; Whitaker, 178.

sponsors move to a place before the altar to pray for the Holy Spirit. (For brief scriptural verses and songs from ancient liturgies which may be appropriate for use during this little procession, see *The Rites*, 177–180, 271–273.) The prayer for the Spirit (no. 246) is a revision of the prayer from the sixth-century Gelasian sacramentary, which derives from the early third-century *Apostolic Tradition* of Hippolytus. The enumeration of the seven gifts of the Spirit had perhaps been made in Rome in the fourth century. Pope Siricus wrote to Bishop Himerius of Tarragona in 385 that converts were to be received "by the invocation of the seven-fold Spirit and by the imposition of the bishop's hand." And Ambrose wrote, "Remember that you received the seal of the Spirit; the Spirit of wisdom and understanding, the Spirit of counsel and strength, the Spirit of knowledge and godliness, and the Spirit of holy fear."[85]

The Roman Catholic, Episcopal, and Lutheran books have revised the prayer in similar ways.

The Rites of the Catholic Church	*Lutheran Book of Worship*	*Book of Common Prayer*
All-powerful God, Father of our Lord Jesus Christ, by water and the Holy Spirit you freed your sons (and daughters) from sin and gave them new life. Send your Holy Spirit upon them to be their Helper and Guide. Give them the spirit of wisdom and understanding, the spirit of right judgment and courage, the spirit of knowledge and reverence. Fill them with the spirit of wonder and awe in your presence. (pp. 103–04)	God, the Father of our Lord Jesus Christ, we give you thanks for freeing your sons and daughters from the power of sin and for raising them up to a new life through this holy sacrament. Pour your Holy Spirit upon ____name____: the spirit of wisdom and understanding, the spirit of counsel and might, the spirit of knowledge and the fear of the Lord, the spirit of joy in your presence. (Min. Ed., p. 311)	Heavenly Father, we thank you that by water and the Holy Spirit you have bestowed upon *these* your *servants* the forgiveness of sin, and have raised *them* to the new life of grace. Sustain *them*, O Lord, in your Holy Spirit. Give *them* an inquiring and discerning heart, the courage to will and to persevere, a spirit to know and to love you, and the gift of joy and wonder in all your works. (p. 308)

The Lutheran rite, like the Roman Catholic rite, directs the minister to lay both hands on each of the baptized while the prayer is said. The Episcopal form of the prayer softens the emphasis on the invocation of the Spirit in order to preserve the separate character of confirmation. The earlier Lutheran baptismal rites gave an abbreviated form of the prayer in the form of a blessing of the newly baptized, with only the most subtle allusion to the gifts of the Spirit:

Almighty God, the Father of our Lord Jesus Christ, Who hath begotten thee again of water and the Holy Ghost, and hath forgiven thee all thy sin, strengthen thee with his grace unto life everlasting.[86]

---

[85] Ambrose, *On the Sacraments* 7.42.

[86] *Church Book* (1891), p. 352; *Common Service Book* (1919), text ed., p. 392; *Service Book and Hymnal* (1958), p. 244.

The fuller traditional form of the prayer was given in the service of Confirmation:

Almighty and Everlasting God, Who hast vouchsafed to regenerate these Thy servants by water and the Spirit, and hast forgiven them all their sins: Strengthen them, we beseech Thee, with the Holy Ghost, the Comforter; and daily increase in them Thy manifold gifts of grace: the spirit of wisdom and understanding; the spirit of counsel and might; the spirit of knowledge and of the fear of the Lord, now and forever; through Jesus Christ, Thy Son, our Lord.[87]

The baptismal sealing follows. The concept of seal (Greek, *sphragis*) has a long history and a bewildering variety of meanings in antiquity, Old Testament and Judaic use, and New Testament and early Christian literature. In Christianity "seal" was used to describe the sign of the cross,[88] baptism as a whole,[89] confirmation,[90] the washing with water.[91] In the New Testament "sealing" and "anointing" are used to describe the communication of the Holy Spirit to God's people, guaranteeing God's protection in this life and guaranteeing a share in the life to come. By such anointing the baptized are made one with the Lord Jesus, whose title "Christ" means the anointed of God. The gift of the Spirit is intended to unite the baptized with Christ and to make them like him, for the Spirit is the Spirit of Christ, released by his death and resurrection.

In the *Lutheran Book of Worship*, the seal is understood to be the "seal of the Spirit" mentioned by Theodore of Mopsuestia.[92] This seal, following St. Paul (2 Cor. 1:21–22), is the mark of ownership signifying that those who are thus indelibly sealed/branded/tatooed belong to the Lord as his inalienable property, his own possession. The *Lutheran Book of Worship* baptismal rite joins two separate actions of the practice described in the *Apostolic Tradition* — anointing with oil and marking the forehead with the cross — and makes of them one dual action. The anointing of those who are being baptized is connected with the anointing of priests in the Old Testament and with the anointing of Christ, the Messiah.[93] Kings were also anointed (Isa. 9:1–6) as were prophets (Ps. 110:4; Rev. 1:5–6). To be anointed in baptism, then, is to be joined to Christ and to share in his prophetic, priestly, and royal ministry. Oil in the ancient world had a cleansing function, like water; it was also used for healing, for cooking, and for lighting. But the oil of baptism is

---

[87] *Common Service Book*, text ed., p. 400; *Service Book and Hymnal*, p. 246.

[88] Maronite Liturgy, see Donald Attwater, *Eastern Catholic Worship* (New York: Devin-Adair Co., 1945), 157. "Christ hath . . . signed the Church and her children by the power of the cross."

[89] Syrian Liturgy, see Attwater, p. 138, "You are redeemed by the Lord's victorious cross, sealed with the seal of holy baptism. . . . "

[90] Gregory Dix, *The Theology of Confirmation in Relation to Baptism* (London: Dacre, 1946); L. S. Thornton, *Confirmation: Its Place in the Baptismal Mystery* (London: Dacre, 1954).

[91] Shepherd of Hermas, *Similitudes* 9.16.

[92] Theodore of Mopsuestia, *Baptismal Homily* 2.28.

[93] Tertullian, *On Baptism* 7.

not merely olive oil, as rich a symbol as that was for the early church and as is the oil of exorcism and the oil of catechumens. The oil of baptism is chrism, perfumed oil, heavily scented, the heady after-bath lotion of the new bride. The chrism, perfumed oil, has been used in the Western church since the sixth century and, according to the early church, has romantic and marital overtones (Song of Sol. 1:3; 3:6; 2 Cor. 2:15).[94] This chrism is a cosmetic, called in the East *myron* or "myrrh," changed like the elements of the Holy Communion, John Chrysostom says, to become God's grace.[95] Anciently, the anointing was done with an abundance of oil, as in Psalm 133:2–3.

The sealing is done on the forehead, and, in its vestigial form in modern rites chary of pouring oil liberally, it is made in the sign of the cross. Marking animals and slaves with a sign of ownership is very ancient and widespread. Basil claims that the marking with the cross had been handed down by the apostles themselves,[96] and indeed the sign on the forehead may derive from the mark of the Hebrew letter *taw*, the last letter of the Hebrew alphabet and therefore the sign of God himself, inscribed on the forehead of those who underwent Jewish baptism, a sign recalling God's mark made that people might be spared and survive.[97] (See Gen. 4:15; Ezek. 9:3ff.; Rev. 7:3; 14:1.) Until late in the Middle Ages the sign of the cross was made in private devotion on the forehead, retracing the mark made in baptism. Tertullian wrote,

At every forward step and movement, at every going in and out, when we bathe, when we sit at table, when we light the lamps, on couch, on seat, in all the ordinary actions of daily life, we trace upon the forehead the sign.[98]

The sign urges likeness to Christ, growing into the image of God (Gen. 1:26–27; Eph. 1:3). It is an indelible reminder that those baptized have been "bought with a price"[99] and made forever a part of Christ, the anointed one, with an eternal share in his priesthood and kingship, having been anointed like him and into him and bearing forever his mark on their brow.[100] Thus the sign of the cross on the forehead becomes an impulse to witness, impelling the baptized to make visible by their actions what is invisible on their foreheads. (See the third stanza of hymn 377, "Lift High the Cross.")

The text which in the *Lutheran Book of Worship* accompanies the sealing declares boldly and succinctly (1) baptism as adoption into the

---

[94] Searle, 36.

[95] John Chrysostom, *Mystagogical Catecheses* 3.3; Searle, 97.

[96] Basil, *On the Holy Spirit* 27.

[97] Hatchett, 280.

[98] Tertullian, *De Corona* 3; see also Cyril of Jerusalem, *Mystagogical Catecheses* 4.14; 13.36.

[99] 1 Cor. 7:23; John Chrysostom, *Sermons on St. Matthew* 54.7. See Arthur Carl Piepkorn, "As You Get Out of Bed — As You Go to Bed," *Response* 5:1 (Pentecost 1963), 35–40.

[100] See 2 Cor. 1:21–22 and Victor Paul Furnish, *II Corinthians*, Anchor Bible vol. 32A (Garden City, NY: Doubleday, 1984), 137–38, 149–50. See also Gen. 4:15; Ezek. 9:4–6; Eph. 1:13; Rev. 9:4.

family of God (the newly baptized is now in a new way a "child of God"); (2) the significance of the prayer for the Holy Spirit and the marking with the cross (in oil) — "you have been sealed by the Holy Spirit"; and (3) the effect and duration of the signation in baptism — "marked with the cross of Christ forever." It is a permanent, indelible, eternally durable sign. More than that, the words point to the completion of baptism, which Luther explains:

> The lifting up out of the baptismal water is quickly done, but the thing it signifies — the spiritual birth and the increase of grace and righteousness — even though it begins in baptism, lasts until death, indeed, until the Last Day. Only then will that be finished which the lifting up out of baptism signifies.[101]

The Lutheran formula derives from the Roman Catholic rite, which uses a fifth-century Byzantine form,[102] and from the *Book of Common Prayer*. (See Eph. 1:13.)

The Rites of the Catholic Church	*Lutheran Book of Worship*	*Book of Common Prayer*
N., be sealed with the Gift of Holy Spirit. (p. 104)	___name___ , child of God, you have been sealed by the Holy Spirit and marked with the cross of Christ forever. (Min. Ed., p. 311)	N., you are sealed by the Holy Spirit in Baptism and marked as Christ's own for ever. (p. 308)

The Notes on the Liturgy in the *Lutheran Book of Worship* observe, "Other uses of the sign of the cross — at the beginning of the Brief Order for Confession and Forgiveness or at a benediction — become acknowledgements and affirmations of Baptism" (Min. Ed., p. 31, #14). The consoling strength of baptism is its eternal permanence.

The Clothing

In the ancient church, when candidates went down into the baptismal water naked (to be reborn), the action immediately following their emergence from the water was their being clothed in a white garment, which was soon seen as more than a utilitarian action. Following Galatians 3:27 (which is sung in the Eastern churches to welcome the newly-baptized), the clothing was a richly significant dramatization of what baptism had done to the person. The garment was understood to show that the baptized had put on Christ the risen Lord,[103] as St. Paul had

---

[101] "The Holy Blessed Sacrament of Baptism," *Luther's Works* 35:31.

[102] See Gerard Austin, *Anointing with the Spirit* (New York: Pueblo Publishing Co., 1985), 45–46.

[103] Cyril of Jerusalem, *Mystagogical Catecheses* 3.1; John Chrysostom, *Catecheses* series Stavronikita 2.17; Ambrose, *De mysteriis* 36.

commanded, "Put on the Lord Jesus Christ" (Rom 13:12–14; Col. 3:9–10; Eph. 4:24). The new robe signified the new person. The robe was a bridal garment,[104] bright with the radiance of the *eschaton*.[105] It was a symbol of purity of life,[106] and a symbol of the forgiveness of sins. Cyril of Jerusalem quotes Psalm 32:1, "Blessed is he whose transgression is forgiven, whose sin is covered." Again and again the radiance of the robe is mentioned; it is a sign of the fulfillment of the kingdom. John Chrysostom quotes Matthew 13:43 in this regard, "Then the righteous will shine like the sun in the kingdom of their Father." The brightness of the garments is connected with the robes of God (Dan. 7:9), the transfiguration of Christ (Matt. 17:2; Mark 9:3; Luke 9:29) and thus a glimpse of the transfigured glory of the baptized,[107] and the elders in heaven (Rev. 4:4; 7:9–13). The robes are also related to the veil with which the priests of the Old Testament covered their heads, indicating yet again the priestly character of the baptized. Peter Lombard wrote that by repentance "the old garment is put away again and the new garment, which was lost, is resumed."[108] The medieval morality play *Everyman* (11.638ff.) speaks of the garment of sorrow and contrition, recalling either the baptismal garment or the garment of penance.

Luther understood the richness of the symbolism of the baptismal garment, which makes use of a familiar and necessary daily action as a powerful and personal symbol. At the conclusion of the explanation of baptism in the Large Catechism he wrote,

Therefore let everybody regard his Baptism as the daily garment which he is to wear all the time. Every day he should be found in faith and amid its fruits, every day he should be suppressing the old man and growing up in the new.[109]

In his treatise on "The Holy and Blessed Sacrament of Baptism" he wrote of the Last Day,

Only then will that be finished which the lifting up out of baptism signifies. Then we shall arise from death, from sins, and from all evil, pure in body and soul, and then we shall live eternally. Then shall we be truly lifted up out of baptism and be completely born, and we shall put on the true baptismal garment of immortal life in heaven.[110]

In his 1523 baptismal order and in his 1523 tract "How One Shall Properly and Intelligibly Baptize a Person into the Christian Faith"[111] Luther retained the custom of giving a white robe (*Hauben*, hood) immediately

---

[104]Ambrose, *De mysteriis* 7.35ff; John Chrysostom, *Catecheses* series Papadopoulos-Kerameus 3.6–7.

[105]Theodore of Mopsuestia, *Baptismal Homily* 3.26.

[106]Cyril of Jerusalem, *Mystagogical Catecheses* 4.3, 8; John Chrysostom, *Catecheses* series Stavronikita 5.18; Ambrose, *De mysteriis* 41.

[107]Theodore of Mopsuestia, *Baptismal Homily* 3.26.

[108]Peter Lombard, *Sentences* Book IV, Dist. xiv, chap. 1.

[109]*Book of Concord*, 446.

[110]*Luther's Works* 35:31.

[111]*Works of Martin Luther*, Philadelphia Ed., 6:210–11.

after the baptismal anointing. In his revised rite of 1526 the *Wester-hembd*, or christening robe, is put on the child following the baptismal washing. (There is no anointing in this rite.) Various Lutheran congregations retained or have restored the giving of the white robe "calling attention to a significant biblical image of Baptism, Galatians 3:37" (Min. Ed., p. 31, n. 15) which was noted by many of the early Christian fathers. The text suggested for a representative of the congregation to say, "Put on this robe, for in Baptism you have been clothed in the righteousness of Christ, who calls you to his great feast" (Min. Ed., p. 31, n. 15), was written for *Contemporary Worship 7: Holy Baptism* (1974), and recalls other biblical images such as Matthew 22:11–12. (The medieval text used by Luther in his 1523 order to accompany the giving of the robe remains in the second sentence of the present Roman Catholic rite: "N. and N., you have become a new creation and have clothed yourselves in Christ. Take this white garment and bring it unstained to the judgment seat of our Lord Jesus Christ so that you may have everlasting life."[112])

The use of the baptismal garment gives particular point to the use of funeral pall when the baptized reach the end of this life and the completion of what was begun in Holy Baptism.

Luther's baptismal order of 1523 also retained the long-standing practice of giving a lighted candle to the baptized.[113] The practice perhaps dates from Pseudo Ambrosius[114] and may be an amplification of the imagery of radiance associated with the garments and its nuptial suggestions. (See Hebrews 6:4, 10:32.) The giving of the candle is not mentioned in Luther's tract of 1523 nor in his order of 1526; he evidently found the robe a more significant symbol than the candle. The *Lutheran Book of Worship*, however, so as not to burden the rite with two unfamiliar actions, relegated the giving of the robe to the Notes on the Liturgy, which appear only in the Ministers Edition; the text of the service mentions only the giving of the candle. The use of baptismal candles was already common in many congregations and easier to introduce in others. Moreover, modern congregations might more readily associate the baptismal candle with the paschal candle, reflecting the ancient association of baptism and the Easter Vigil and indicating a personal appropriation of the Easter mystery. In addition, twentieth-century people apparently love to play with fire — witness the popularity of candlelight services in congregations and candlelight vigils in secular society. The commission also had the example of the *Book of Common Prayer*, which makes no mention of the garment but which in a rubric permits a candle "which may be lighted from the Paschal

---

[112]*The Rites*, 102.

[113]The accompanying text was, "Receive this burning torch and preserve thy baptism blameless, so that when the Lord cometh to the wedding thou mayest go to meet him to enter with the saints into the heavenly mansion and receive eternal life." The present Roman rite retains this medieval text.

[114]Pseudo Ambrosius, *De lapsu virginis* 5.

Candle" to be given "to each of the newly baptized or to a godparent" (p. 313).

The text that Luther retained in his 1523 order accompanying the candle presentation recalls Jesus' parable of the ten maidens (Matt. 25:1–13). This verse, in teaching the responsibility to be prepared for the sudden arrival of the bridegroom, is both ethical and eschatological in emphasis. Its counterpart in the *Lutheran Book of Worship* (Matt. 5:16, in a translation adapted from the Authorized Version) loses both the connection with the bridal imagery of the garment and the eschatological promise but has the virtue of pointing those who have been baptized beyond themselves to a life of service to others.

Prayer for Parents of Small Children

The prayer for parents when small children are baptized (no. 247), written for the *Lutheran Book of Worship*, has drawn a few phrases from the Roman Catholic Rite of Baptism for Children at the conclusion of which "the celebrant first blesses the mothers, who hold the children in their arms, then the fathers, and lastly the entire assembly."[115] The "gift" which the parents have been given is three-fold: their own life, their child's life, and the new life of the baptized.

Welcome

Finally, the newly baptized are welcomed not only into the congregation but into the whole Christian community, specifically into the priesthood of God's people. Baptism, as has been suggested at several points in the rite, is the ordination of the laity, the incorporation into Christ the high priest, giving those who are thus made part of his body a share in the holy nation and the royal priesthood.

The statement by the representative of the congregation — by design and intent a layperson — gives a clear definition of that often misunderstood and misused phrase "the priesthood of all believers." (See 1 Peter 2:5, 9.) There are two responsibilities of this priesthood: to pray, offering the sacrifice of prayer, praise, and thanksgiving; and to serve others, mediating Christ to one's neighbor. Despite popular notions to the contrary, in Lutheran theology this universal priesthood does not confer the privilege to every member of the church to preside at celebrations of the Eucharist, to exercise a ministry of Word and Sacrament. The ordained and the laity have equally important and necessary ministries, but they are separate ministries nonetheless. The ordained ministry does not derive from the general priesthood of all the baptized.

The welcome by the congregation, written for *Contemporary Worship 7: Holy Baptism* using phrases and ideas borrowed from the *Book of Common Prayer* (p. 308), emphasizes the equality of all the baptized (it is baptism which makes one a member of the church, not confirmation or some other rite or the attainment of a certain age), their unity as

---

[115] *The Rites*, 211, §70.

"children of the same heavenly Father" (this phrase will recall to many the hymn beloved throughout Scandinavia, "Children of the Heavenly Father"), and their responsibilities for service in the kingdom of God of which they are now a part.

The baptized have been welcomed into the community with the exchange of the peace at least since the second century as evidenced by the *Apology* of Justin Martyr.[116] Peace is an ancient greeting, which continues in the Middle East as *shalom* and *salaam*. It was the greeting of the risen Christ (John 20:19, 21). Moreover, the prophets associated peace with the last days of messianic fulfillment (Isa. 9:7; Ezek. 34:25; 37:26), and in Christianity the word retains its eschatological thrust. Thus, to conclude, dramatize, and effect the welcome of the newly-baptized into the Christian community, the peace is exchange.[117]

The welcome, made real with the sharing of the peace, should be understood as an introduction to the *mystagogia*, the post-baptismal instruction, which continues long after the rite is ended.

Historically, the first privilege of the baptized was to join in the prayers of the church.[118] In the *Lutheran Book of Worship* order this privilege has already been exercised after the Presentation and before the Thanksgiving. In the usual parish practice of the present, however, those who have not been baptized are free to join the prayers of the church as they choose, for the church's worship is a public event, no longer a closely-guarded secret for the initiated. The second ancient privilege of the baptized, however, retains its power and its mystery: to share in the eucharistic communion of the church. In the baptismal rites of the Roman Catholic, Episcopal, and Lutheran churches the baptismal initiation therefore continues. As in the *Apostolic Tradition*, in which the order was baptism-sealing-eucharist, the incorporation continues with the celebration of the Eucharist in which those who have been baptized are expected to share.[119]

The "communion of saints" confessed in the baptismal creed is ambiguous in both Latin and Greek, perhaps deliberately so. *Communio sanctorum* can mean, taking *sanctorum* as masculine, the "communion of holy people" into which the neophyte has now been incorporated, or, taking *sanctorum* as neuter, "communion of holy things," that is, the Holy Communion.[120] "Holy things for holy people"[121] is the priest's in-

---

[116]Justin, *Apology* I.65. (The peace is exchanged after the prayers). See also the *Apostolic Tradition* 21.

[117]In the Roman rite, after the confirmation sealing, the celebrant speaks to each one confirmed, "Peace be with you," and the newly-confirmed reply, "And also with you." (*The Rites*, 104.) The physical exchange of the peace is done in the eucharistic rite, prior to the distribution, its usual place in the Roman liturgy. See Kavanagh, 140–41.

[118]Justin, *Apology* I.65; Tertullian, *On Baptism* 20.

[119]See Kavanagh, 175.

[120]See Jaroslav Pelikan, *The Christian Tradition*, vol. 3: *The Growth of Medieval Theology (600–1300)* (Chicago: University Press, 1978), 174ff.

[121]Literally "Holy things for the holy." In the present *Book of Common Prayer* the invitation is "The gifts of God for the people of God."

vitation to communicants in the Byzantine liturgy, derived from Eastern liturgies of the fourth century and the *Apostolic Constitutions.* To this invitation the people reply, "One is holy, only one is Lord, Jesus Christ in the glory of God the Father," downplaying their own holiness as if to instruct the priest concerning the locus of all holiness.

Ordo Romanus XI, reflecting the practice of the sixth century, says that after baptism and confirmation "all the infants receive communion." The communion was received under both kinds (bread and wine), but after the tenth century the practice was to offer the infants only wine. With the withdrawal of the cup from the laity around 1200 "infants were left with no communion at all."[122] The Fourth Lateran Council (1215) decreed that communion was not necessary until one reached the age of discretion, and the Council of Trent declared that baptized infants had no need of communion because they were not capable of losing the grace of their baptism and anathematized those who claimed that infants needed communion before the age of discretion. The formulation "brought about the final dismemberment of the three sacraments of initiation: baptism, confirmation, and eucharist."[123]

For the baptismal Eucharist the *Lutheran Book of Worship* appoints a proper preface for Holy Baptism, which was adapted from the preface written for the 1979 *Book of Common Prayer.*

Book of Common Prayer	**Lutheran Book of Worship**
Because in Jesus Christ our Lord you have received us as your sons and daughters, made us citizens of your kingdom, and given us the Holy Spirit to guide us into all truth. (p. 381)	...through Christ our Lord. In him you have received us as your children, made us citizens of your kingdom, and given us your Holy Spirit to guide us into all truth. (Min. Ed., p. 189)

The scriptural allusions include Ephesians 2:19 and John 16:13.

The early church at Rome, recalling Old Testament parallels, gave the newly-baptized a drink of milk and honey before the chalice of Holy Communion as a sign of their inheritance of the promised land. In baptism they had already crossed the river and entered upon the joys of their true and permanent homeland. (See hymns 337, 347, 348.)

The post-communion prayer (#161, Min. Ed., p. 189), written for *Contemporary Worship 7: Holy Baptism,* is an unusual form, not following the traditional pattern but being instead a simple ascription of praise. The eschatological overtones of the prayer, which looks at the present experience of baptism and communion and which also looks toward the consummation and the messianic banquet, are to be noted. The scriptural allusions include Isaiah 25:6–9; 49:12; Matthew 8:11; 22:1–10; 26:29; Luke 14:16–24; and Revelation 19:9, 17.

---

[122]Austin, p. 19.
[123]Ibid.

The process of initiation is not yet completed when the Eucharist has concluded. The period of post-baptismal teaching (*mystagogia*) follows, during which the newly-baptized (the neophytes) are to be assisted by their sponsors and the general community of believers into full and joyful participation in the life of the community. In the Roman rite[124] the liturgical observance of this period includes a special place for the neophytes and their sponsors for Sunday masses and mention of them in the sermon and the intercessions. At the end of the Easter season some form of celebration is held. Moreover, on the anniversary of their baptism the neophytes should "gather together again to give thanks to God, to share their spiritual experiences with one another, and to gain new strength."[125] *Occasional Services* (1982) includes a form for the Anniversary of a Baptism designed for use in the home. The yearly liturgical remembrance of baptism is made at the Easter Vigil.

In the Large Catechism Luther wrote of the daily use of baptism, observing that every day each of the baptized

should be found in faith... suppressing the old man and growing up in the new. If we wish to be Christians, we must practice the work that makes us Christians.[126]

Baptism is the beginning of a spiritual journey,[127] a lifelong struggle of continuing renewal. Thus the life of conversion continues: "When our Lord and Master Jesus Christ said, 'Repent' [Matt. 4:17], he willed the entire life of believers to be one of repentance."[128] The great commission given in Matthew 28 is to "make disciples," obedient followers of Christ, who seek constantly to learn the will of God for them and then seek to do it in their lives, learning obedience (Rom 16:26), that entire trust and complete submission which are to characterize the disciples of Jesus Christ. This life of constant renewal is kept alive in the weekly celebration of Holy Communion as the Christian community gathers week by week to renew its identity, and it is kept alive by daily repentance and renewal.

The post-baptismal instruction includes, among other things, drawing implications for the Christian life from the privilege of being able to pray the Our Father with new understanding. The newly-baptized are now no longer strangers but citizens of the city of God (an image used in many rites' prayers of thanksgiving over the water), who accept its constitution, rule, and order.[129] The new life which now is theirs is replete with privilege and with consequent responsibility. The rest

---

[124] See *The Rites*, 105–106.
[125] Ibid., 105. They are thus to form what in current jargon is called a support group.
[126] *Book of Concord*, 446.
[127] *Decree on the Missionary Activity of the Church* of the Second Vatican Council, 13.
[128] The first of Luther's *Ninety-five Theses*. (*Luther's Works* 31:25).
[129] Karl Barth, *Prayer*, 2nd ed., ed. Don E. Saliers from the trans. of Sara F. Terrien (Philadelphia: Westminster Press, 1985), 12, 37.

of their life will unfold the implications of the mystery of Holy Baptism until it is completed in death when the fullness of the new life will be theirs.

The Small Catechism remains a most useful guide to meditation on these responsibilities and privileges. This little book should be supplemented with spiritual reading in the ancient classics of devotion and a regular course of prayer in the morning and in the evening of each day. Moreover, all the baptized should each year make devotional use of Lent leading to the renewal of their baptismal vows in the Easter Vigil.

Table I
DEVELOPMENT OF THE RITE

Magdeburg Agenda 1497	Luther 1523	Luther 1526	Common Service Book (1919) and Service Book and Hymnal (1958)		Lutheran Book of Worship
			INFANTS	ADULTS	
			In the Name...		
			Address	Address	Address
					Questions to candidates
					Charge to candidates
			Prayer	Prayer	(The Prayers)
At Entrance of the church					
Exsufflation	Exsufflation — exorcism of the eyes	Exorcism			
Signing with cross	Signing with cross	Signing with cross			
Prayer	Prayer	Prayers			
Giving of salt	Giving of salt — exorcism of the mouth				
Prayer	Sintflutgebet	Sintflutgebet			
Exorcism	Exorcism	Exorcism			

(continued)

Table I (continued)
DEVELOPMENT OF THE RITE

Magdeburg Agenda 1497	Luther 1523	Luther 1526	Common Service Book (1919) and Service Book and Hymnal (1958)		Lutheran Book of Worship
At Entrance of the Baptistry					
Apostles' Creed					
	Salutation				
	Mark 10:13–16	Mark 10:13–16	Mark 10:13–16; Matt. 28:18–20	Matt. 28:18–20	
Our Father	Our Father	Our Father ...evil.	Our Father ...ever.	Our Father ...ever.	
Ephpheta = exorcism of ears and nostrils	Exorcism of ears and nostrils				
	Into the church	*To the Font*			
					Thanksgiving
Renunciation	Renunciation & Profession	Renunciation & Profession	(Renunciation &) Profession	Renunciation & Profession	Renunciation & Profession
Anointing on breast	Anointing on breast				
In the Baptistry					
Profession					
Baptism	Baptism	Baptism	Baptism	Baptism	Baptism
					Prayer for Holy Spirit
Anointing on head	Anointing on head				Sealing with sign of cross
			Laying hand on head & prayer	Laying hand on head & prayer	
Peace	Peace		Peace	Peace	
Presentation of white robe	Presentation of white robe	Presentation of christening robe & blessing			(Presentation of robe)
		Peace			
Presentation of candle	Presentation of candle				(Presentation of candle)
			Prayer for Holy Spirit	Prayer for Holy Spirit	
					(Prayer for parents)
				Welcome	Welcome
			Admonition to sponsors	Admonition to congregation	
					Peace
Dismissal			Blessing	Blessing	

Table II
COMPARISON OF RITES

The Rites of the Catholic Church		Lutheran Book of Worship	Book of Common Prayer
ADULTS	CHILDREN		
Reception	Reception		
	Naming child		
	(Psalm)		(Hymn, psalm, anthem)
			Verses
		Prayer of the Day	Collect of the Day
Lessons	Lessons	Lessons	Lessons
Sermon		Sermon	Sermon
		Hymn of the Day	
Prayer			
Address		Address	
		Presentation	Presentation
		Question to candidates	
		Charge to candidates (& sponsors)	Examination of candidates (& sponsors)
			Renunciation
			Profession of Faith
(Litany of the saints)	Litany	(The Prayers)	Prayers for candidates
	Exorcism & anointing		
(Thanksgiving)	Thanksgiving	The Thanksgiving	Thanksgiving (Consecration of chrism)
Renunciation	Renunciation	Renunciation	
(Anointing with oil of catechumens)			
Profession of faith	Profession of faith	Profession of faith	
The Baptism	The Baptism	The Baptism	The Baptism
		(Psalm or hymn)	
		Prayer for Holy Spirit	Prayer with mention of Spirit
(Anointing after Baptism)	Anointing with chrism	Sealing	Sealing
		Sign of cross	Sign of cross

(continued)

Table II (continued)
COMPARISON OF RITES

The Rites of the Catholic Church		Lutheran Book of Worship	Book of Common Prayer
ADULTS	CHILDREN		
Clothing with white garment	Clothing with white garment	(Clothing with white garment)	
Presentation of candle	Presentation of candle	(Presentation of candle)	
		(Prayer for parents)	
		Welcome into priesthood	Welcome into household of God
Celebration of Confirmation			
Address Prayer for Spirit			
Laying on of hands			
Sealing with oil & sign of cross			
Peace		Peace	Peace
	Song		
	Address		
	Lord's Prayer		
	Blessing		

AFFIRMATION OF BAPTISM
Ministers Edition, pp. 324-27, 35-36

Parallel Rites

Roman Catholic	Rite of Confirmation, *The Rites*, pp. 285-334.

Episcopal	Confirmation with Forms for Reception and for the Reaffirmation of Baptismal Vows, *Book of Common Prayer*, pp. 412-19.

Lutheran	The Order of Confirmation, *The Book of Worship* (General Synod 1867), pp. 72-78.

Order for Confirmation of Persons Baptized in Infancy, Order for Receiving Members from Other Congregations, *The Liturgy of the Evangelical Lutheran Church* (General Synod 1881), pp. 50-54, 55.

Confirmation, *Church Book* (General Council 1891), pp. 358-364.

Confirmation, Reception of Members from Other Churches, *Forms for Ministerial Acts* (General Synod 1900), pp. 34-43.

Order for Confirmation, *A Liturgy for the Use of Evangelical Lutheran Pastors* (Joint Synod of Ohio 1912), pp. 134-36.

Order for Confirmation, *Common Service Book*, text ed., pp. 399-402.

Confirmation, the Reception of Converts, The Reception of Voting Members, Announcement of Excommunication and of Restoration, *Liturgy and Agenda* (Lutheran Church–Missouri Synod 1921), pp. 330-39.

Office for the Public Reception of Fellow-Members of the Household of Faith; Office for the Restoration of One Who Has Lapsed, To Membership in the Church, "Additional Orders and Offices" in *The Occasional Services* (United Lutheran Church in America 1930), pp. 179-82.

The Rite of Confirmation, The Reception of Converts, *The Lutheran Agenda* (Lutheran Church–Missouri Synod n.d. [194-]), pp. 21-31.

Order for Confirmation, *Service Book and Hymnal* (American Lutheran Church and the Lutheran Church in America 1958), pp. 245-47.

Admission to Membership (By Transfer, Restoration or Renewal), "Additional Orders and Offices," *The Occasional Services* (American Lutheran Church and the Lutheran Church in America 1962), pp. 189-90.

Contemporary Worship 8: Affirmation of the Baptismal Covenant (1975).

Orthodox	The Office of Holy Chrismation, The Office for Receiving into

the Orthodox Faith Such Persons As Have Not Previously Been Orthodox, *Service Book*, pp. 281–85, 454–67.
The Service of Holy Baptism, *An Orthodox Prayer Book*, pp. 55–73.

Methodist	The Order for Confirmation and Reception into the Church, *The Book of Worship* (1964, 1965), pp. 12–14.
Presbyterian	The Commissioning of Baptized Members, the Order for Their Confirmation, and the Reception of Members from Other Churches, *The Worshipbook* (1972), pp. 48–52.
Church of South India	An Order of Service for the Reception of Baptized Persons Into the Full Fellowship of the Church, Commonly Called Confirmation, *Book of Common Worship* (1963), pp. 123–30.

Purpose

Affirmation of Baptism is one rite designed to serve three occasions: confirmation (understood as the completion of a period of instruction in the Christian faith as confessed in the teachings of the Lutheran Church); reception of Christians from other denominations into membership in the Lutheran Church through reception into a local congregation; and restoration of the lapsed to active participation in the life of the church. Moreover, the use of the Affirmation of Baptism by the whole congregation (beginning at section 12) may be appropriate on the festival of the Baptism of Our Lord to join the baptism of Christ with the baptism into him of each individual believer and on the Day of Pentecost to celebrate the life-giving role of the Holy Spirit in Holy Baptism and in the lives of the baptized. (See the *Book of Common Prayer*, p. 312, for a parallel practice.) The principal renewal of baptismal vows is made annually at the Easter Vigil.

Characteristics

Each of the three uses of this rite find a common point of reference in the affirmation of God's gift of baptism. Instruction in the teachings of the Lutheran church precedes each of the three uses, and in each a public profession of the baptismal faith is appropriate.

In each of the three uses, the candidates are understood by virtue of their baptism already to be members of the church, and this rite adds nothing to that enduring foundation and well-spring of the Christian life. Holy Baptism is necessary; this service is not.

In the Roman Catholic Rite of Confirmation, it is the bishop in his role as teacher and guardian of the faith who confirms the candidates' profession of faith.[130] The idea that it is the confirmands who confirm their baptismal vows dates only from the time after the Reformation

---

[130]"The bishop confirms their profession of faith by proclaiming the faith of the Church: This is our faith. This is the faith of the Church. We are proud to profess it in Christ Jesus our Lord" (*The Rites*, 310).

as the Lutheran churches were searching for reasons to preserve and explain the rite of confirmation. In the *Lutheran Book of Worship* the prayer at the laying on of hands reveals a new interpretation: it is God the Father who confirms the faith of the confirmands.

Background

The baptismal theology of the major churches of Christianity is returning to a more faithful adherence to what is already clear in the ancient tradition, which has always been preserved in the Eastern church: the unity of the initiatory sequence of water baptism, sealing in and by the Holy Spirit, and the Holy Communion.

Confirmation by a bishop emerged as the unity of Christian initiation dissolved.[131] The old Roman practice, recorded in the *Apostolic Tradition* and the Gelasian sacramentary, of signation with the laying on of hands and a second anointing with chrism after the washing in water and anointing with the "oil of thanksgiving," was accepted reluctantly by the other churches of the West under pressure from the Carolingian government. The strongly resisted signation and anointing were performed after communion or a week after the baptism at the Easter Vigil, on the eighth day of Easter. Since in much of Europe there were but few baptisms, this second anointing was delayed even longer until the bishop's visit.

From the third century the bishop of Rome insisted that the baptized receive the seal of the Spirit from the bishop,[132] and the practice spread with the Roman liturgy in the eighth and ninth centuries. As early as the fourth century the unity of the rite of initiation was divided and the "confirmation" was explained apart from baptism.[133] The 38th canon of the Synod of Elvira (306) allowed that in case of necessity a sick person may be baptized by a layperson, but if the one who was sick recovered that person was to be taken to the bishop for the laying on of hands. Leo the Great (440–461) used "confirmation" in connection with the admission of heretics to the Christian community. Those baptized by heretics need only confirmation with the invocation of the Spirit through the imposition of hands which supplies the power lacking in baptism at the hands of a heretic.

In much of Christianity "confirmation" was used to describe the Holy Communion. The chalice "completes" the eating of the bread, or the bread and cup "confirm" the participants. But in fifth-century Gaul, Faustus, bishop of Reiz, delivered a sermon on Pentecost which stands as the first doctrinal explanation of a separate action of "confirmation," episcopal hand-laying, other than in cases of rebaptism or the

---

[131]Kavanagh, 68. In the East, the association of the bishop with the anointing is maintained by his consecration of the oil used by the priest for the anointing.

[132]Eusebius (*Church History* 4.43.15–16) tells of Pope Cornelius's insistence that Novatian, after baptism while sick, come before the bishop for the laying on of hands.

[133]*De rebaptismate* 1.4. See Frank Quinn, "Confirmation Reconsidered: Rite and Meaning," *Worship* 59 (1985), 360.

admission of heretics. "In baptism we are washed, after baptism we are strengthened," he declared. For him, baptism is received passively, but confirmation stresses human effort and struggle. By the early ninth century the separation of baptism and confirmation had become the normal practice, and the new separate action of confirmation was explained as giving an increase of baptismal grace.[134] Faustus's sermon reemerged and gained enormous influence when it was included in the mid-ninth century *False Decretals* and attributed to a (fictitious) Pope Melchiades.

The earliest texts suggest that the bishop only stretched out his right hand over all the newly-baptized, but from the twelfth century at Rome the imposition of the bishop's hand was given to each confirmand individually rather than collectively, and this action gave added emphasis to the separate significance of the confirmation. In the East, the imposition of hands is hardly known; it is the anointing that is significant.

About 1150, Peter Lombard enumerated the seven sacramental actions which by then had become traditional, among which was the action now known as confirmation.[135] The list was accepted by Thomas Aquinas and was formally affirmed at the councils of Florence (1439 in the *Decretum pro Armenis*) and Trent (1545–1563). "Confirmation" was not used as the title of the Roman rite until 1520 in conjunction with signation; and, after the Council of Trent defined confirmation as one of the seven sacraments, "confirmation" became the exclusive title of the rite in the Roman Pontifical of Clement VIII (1596).

Confirmation as a separate practice had gone in search of a supporting theology[136] and was explained as the anointing, or the imposition of the bishop's hand, or both. Increasingly, it came to be explained that as baptism gave the Spirit for rebirth and salvation, so confirmation gave the Spirit to arm and strengthen the Christian for service in the world. It was therefore normally delayed until the child had need of such assistance, which at the Council of Trent was defined as seven to twelve years of age. But until the end of the Middle Ages infant confirmation was not unknown in the West.

The separation of confirmation from baptism and its enumeration as one of the seven sacraments was attacked by the Reformers. Wycliffe called confirmation "frivolous"; Luther dismissed it as "that deceitful mumbo-jumbo of the episcopal idols."[137] In a more temperate moment he explained, "We seek sacraments that have been divinely instituted, and among them we see no reason for numbering confirmation.... It is sufficient to regard confirmation as a certain churchly rite or sacramental ceremony...."[138] In view of its history as well as Luther's comments it

---

[134]Nathan Mitchell, "Dissolution of the Rite of Christian Initiation" in *Made, Not Born*, 55–56.

[135]Peter Lombard, *Sentences* Book 4, dist. 1, no. 2.

[136]Austin, 23–31.

[137]"The Persons Related by Consanguinity and Affinity Who Are Forbidden to Marry according to the Scriptures," Leviticus 18, *Luther's Works* 45:8.

[138]"The Babylonian Captivity of the Church," *Luther's Works* 36:92.

is not surprising that the understanding of confirmation in the Lutheran churches has been varied and inconsistent.[139] In the sixteenth century there was in some places an emphasis on instruction: continuing, life-long catechesis. In other areas, especially those under the influence of Martin Bucer, the emphasis was on church discipline, and confirmation became the occasion for a child willingly to submit to the authority of the church and so be admitted to Holy Communion. A third understanding of confirmation was sacramental and stressed the addition of gifts and privileges to those bestowed in baptism — an increase in the Holy Spirit and fuller church membership. A fourth understanding was set forth by Philip Melanchthon in his *Loci communes* of 1543: examination in the catechism, public confession of faith, and an intercessory consecration of confirmands by laying-on of hands. This understanding is found in the Wittenberg church order (1545) and had Luther's approval. Admission to the Holy Communion was not part of this understanding and could occur before confirmation. (An assembly of theologians at Celle in 1548 on the matter related admission to communion not to confirmation but to Jesus' invitation, "Let the children come to me. . . .") Martin Chemnitz developed the most complete confirmation order that has survived from the sixteenth century. It included remembrance of baptism, personal confession of faith, examination in the catechism, admonition to remain faithful and to remain true to the baptismal covenant, prayer of intercession with the laying-on of hands.

In the seventeenth century, under Pietistic influence, confirmation was often understood as a subjective acceptance of Christ as Lord, a conversion experience. In the next century, influenced by rationalism, confirmation became a kind of graduation from the church's rigorous educational program and appeared to many to be superior to baptism. In the nineteenth century, children were examined publicly and admitted as a group to the Holy Communion.

In 1968, a joint study of the theology and practice of confirmation, representing the American Lutheran Church, the Lutheran Church in America, and the Lutheran Church–Missouri Synod, issued its report to the churches. It defined confirmation as "a pastoral and educational ministry of the church that is designed to help baptized children identify with the life and mission of the adult Christian community and that is celebrated in a public rite." Confirmation in this definition thus is not the rite but a ministry.[140] Nevertheless, there was widespread desire to have a rite which celebrated the completion of this ministry. Such a rite was drafted by Hans C. Boehringer (chair), C. Richard Evenson, Frank W. Klos, Jr., and Frank C. Senn, and published as *Contemporary*

---

[139]See Arthur C. Repp, *Confirmation in the Lutheran Church* (St. Louis: Concordia Publishing House, 1964); Frank W. Klos, *Confirmation and First Communion* (Minneapolis, Philadelphia, St. Louis: Augsburg Publishing House, Board of Publication of the Lutheran Church in America, Concordia Publishing House, 1968).

[140]For a detailed history of these various understandings of Confirmation see Repp.

Worship 8: Affirmation of the Baptismal Covenant, the precursor of the "Affirmation of Baptism" in the *Lutheran Book of Worship*.[141]

THE SERVICE IN DETAIL

Addressing the candidates for confirmation, reception, and restoration as "friends" may be understood as an allusion to Jesus' use of that intimate term for his disciples (John 15:13–15).

The address to the confirmands uses the description of the purpose of confirmation given in the *Service Book and Hymnal* rite (p. 245), "You now desire to make public profession of your faith." (An indication of the varying understandings of confirmation that have obtained in just one stream of Lutheran liturgies may be found by comparing the definitions given in the addresses in the rite of confirmation in the *Church Book*, the *Common Service Book*, and the *Service Book and Hymnal*. Nearly all other rites have shown a remarkable consistency in language and understanding; confirmation, however, has not.) The concluding phrase in the *Service Book and Hymnal* address, "and to be confirmed," is changed, however, to make the action not one of receiving something but rather of doing something: "assume greater responsibility in the life of our Christian community and its mission in the world."

The address to those being received into membership acknowledges that they are already members of the one, holy, catholic, and apostolic church and are simply moving from one fellowship or local assembly to another.

The address to those being restored to membership makes it clear that baptism lasts forever and those who have strayed can return to the household of God (Eph. 2:8) and claim again their inheritance which is eternal (1 Pet. 1:4; Heb. 9:15). For in Holy Baptism they "have been sealed by the Holy Spirit and marked with the cross of Christ forever." (Min. Ed., p. 311).

The address by the presiding minister to all who have been presented stresses the sufficiency of baptism by which one is made a member of the church (affirmation adds nothing to baptism); the community setting of their instruction (noteworthy is the movement beyond the individual to God's purpose for "all creation," including the natural world); and the call to service and witness to the gospel. Some of these themes echo phrases in the long instruction by the bishop in the Roman Catholic Rite of Confirmation.[142]

The invitation ("...I ask you to profess your faith..."), the renunciation of "all the forces of evil, the devil, and all his empty promises"; and the profession of faith are the same as those in Holy Baptism (Min. Ed., p. 310), recalling and reaffirming what was vowed then.

---

[141] On the rationale of *Contemporary Worship 8: Affirmation of the Baptismal Covenant* see Frank C. Senn, "An End for Confirmation?" *Currents in Theology and Mission* 3 (1976), 45–52.

[142] *The Rites*, 306–07.

The Prayers (no. 238, Min. Ed., p. 326) recall in part the prayers at Holy Baptism (p. 189) and are drawn from the prayers for the candidates for Holy Baptism in the *Book of Common Prayer* (pp. 305–306), for which they were newly composed. The prayers provide an outline of the essential elements of the Christian life and focus on the work of the Holy Spirit in those who have been gathered in Holy Baptism. The Spirit enlightens the baptized, opening their hearts; preserves them in communion with the church; leads them out to witness to the world; and at last gathers them into the fullness of the kingdom of peace and glory. These petitions reflect the description of the work of the Holy Spirit which Luther gives in the explanation of the third article of the Creed in the Small Catechism. In part because the prayer is for "all the baptized everywhere," which includes the company of saints of all times and all places, the faithful departed are not otherwise mentioned by explicit reference or by name as they are in the Prayers at Holy Baptism.

The examination of the candidates is a revision of the questions which in the *Book of Common Prayer* follow the Apostles' Creed in the Baptismal Covenant, and the examination is an expansion of the two further questions asked of the candidates in the Common Service.

Common Service Book	*Book of Common Prayer*	*Lutheran Book of Worship*
Do you promise to abide in this Faith?	Will you continue in the apostles' teaching and fellowship, in the breaking of bread, and in the prayers?	Do you intend to continue in the covenant God made with you in Holy Baptism to live among God's faithful people, to hear his Word and share in his supper,
Yes, by the help of God	*I will, with God's help.*	
Dost thou promise, as a member of the Evangelical Lutheran Church, to remain faithful to its teachings and to be diligent in the use of the Means of Grace?	Will you persevere in resisting evil, and whenever you fall into sin, repent and return to the Lord? *I will, with God's help.*	
	Will you proclaim by word and example the Good News of God in Christ?	to proclaim the good news of God in Christ through word and deed,
Yes, by the help of God. (text ed., p. 400)	Christ? *I will, with God's help.* Will you seek and serve Christ in all persons,	
		to serve all people, following the example of our Lord Jesus,
	loving your neighbor as yourself? *I will, with God's help.* Will you strive for justice and peace among	and to strive for justice and peace

all people, and respect	in all the earth?
the dignity of every	
human being?	
I will, with God's help.	*I do, and I ask God*
(pp. 417, 304–05)	*to help and guide me.*
	(Min. Ed., p. 326)

The Inter-Lutheran Commission on Worship avoided the language of the *Book of Common Prayer,* "Will you . . ." not requiring the candidates to declare a future course of events which they cannot know for sure — one cannot be certain what one will do in the future — and asks instead only a declaration of intent.

Those making affirmation kneel for prayer, and silence is kept so that prayer may be made for them by the congregation. Such silence before a spoken prayer allows for the involvement of the congregation, which offers in silence its petitions and intercessions, and is a regular feature of the present Roman rite before all major prayers. After the silence, the presiding minister gathers the intentions of the congregation in an ancient prayer (no. 274), a version of the prayer in the *Apostolic Tradition* and the Gelasian sacramentary (see above, p. 52, which was preserved in the *Common Service Book* and the *Service Book and Hymnal* in their orders for confirmation[143] and placed before the laying on of hands. The ancient prayer is used also in the Roman Rite of Confirmation at the laying on of hands by the bishop;[144] It is preceded by an invitation to pray for the Holy Spirit and by silent prayer. Another version of the same prayer is used by the *Lutheran Book of Worship* in the Service of Holy Baptism at the sealing by the Holy Spirit (#246, Min. Ed., p. 311). The prayer in Affirmation of Baptism is closer to the Roman Catholic version and to the original in the Gelasian sacramentary.

The Rites of the Catholic Church	*Lutheran Book of Worship*
All-powerful God, Father of our Lord Jesus Christ, by water and the Holy Spirit you freed your sons and daughters from sin and gave them new life. Send your Holy Spirit upon them to be their Helper and Guide. Give them the spirit of wisdom and understanding, the spirit of right judgment and courage, the spirit of knowledge and reverence. Fill them	Gracious Lord, through water and the Spirit you have made these *men and woman* your own. You forgave them all their sins and brought them to newness of life. Continue to strengthen them with the Holy Spirit, and daily increase in them your gifts of grace: the spirit of wisdom and understanding, the spirit of counsel and might, the spirit of knowledge and the fear of the Lord,

---

[143] *Common Service Book,* text ed., p. 400; *Service Book and Hymnal,* p. 246.
[144] *The Rites,* 309.

with the spirit of wonder	the spirit of joy
and awe in your presence.	in your presence;
We ask this through Christ	through Jesus Christ, your Son,
our Lord.	our Lord.
(p. 309)	(Min. Ed., p. 327)

The prayer in the *Lutheran Book of Worship* asks God to "continue to strengthen them with the Holy Spirit" as an acknowledgement that the Spirit has been at work since baptism and indeed before baptism.

Following the prayer for the Holy Spirit, the confirmands receive the laying-on of hands. The formula which accompanies the action (no. 275) is a revision of the form in use since the *Church Book* (1891) taken from German church orders, which was based on 2 Peter 3:18; 1 Peter 2:20; Philippians 3:10; and Titus 2:13. In prior books the formula was directed to the candidate, but in the *Lutheran Book of Worship*, as in the *Book of Common Prayer*, it is in the form of a prayer.

Book of Common Prayer	*Church Book, Common Service Book, Service Book & Hymnal*	*Lutheran Book of Worship*
	The Father in Heaven,	Father in heaven,
Strengthen, O Lord,	for Jesus' sake, renew	for Jesus' sake,
your servant *N.* with	and increase in thee	stir up in __name__
your Holy Spirit;	the gift of the Holy	the gift of your Holy
	Ghost, to thy	Spirit;
	strengthening in	confirm *his/her*
	faith, to thy growth	faith, guide *his/her*
	in grace, to thy	life,
empower *him* for		empower *him/her* in
your service; and		*his/her* serving,
		give *him/her*
sustain *him* all the	patience in suffering,	patience in suffering,
days of *his* life.[145]	and to the blessed hope	and bring *him/her*
(p. 148)	of everlasting life.	to everlasting life.
		(Min. Ed., p. 327)

The verb in the *Lutheran Book of Worship* form of the prayer, "confirm" rather than "strengthen" as in the previous books, is of course a clearer allusion to confirmation and to what happens in the rite: God confirms our faith.

In the Lutheran and Episcopal rites the peace is exchanged to conclude the rite. The Roman Catholic rite concludes with the anointing with oil ("N., be sealed with the Gift of the Holy Spirit") and the exchange between the bishop and the newly confirmed — "Peace be with you" with the response "And also with you" — but the passing of the

---

[145] *Or:* Defend, O Lord, your servant *N.* with your heavenly grace, that *he* may continue yours forever, and daily increase in your Holy Spirit more and more until *he* comes to your everlasting kingdom." (p. 418).

peace does not occur until immediately prior to the reception of Holy Communion, its regular place in the Roman mass.

COMPARISON OF RITES

The Rites of the Catholic Church	Common Service Book	Lutheran Book of Worship	Book of Common Prayer
Confirmation	Confirmation	Affirmation	Confirmation
Liturgy of the Word through the Gospel	Liturgy of the Word through the General Prayer	Liturgy of the Word through the Gospel	Liturgy of the Word through the Gospel
Presentation			
Homily		Sermon	Sermon
		Hymn of Day	
		Presentation	Presentation
	Address	Address	
Renunciation	Renunciation	Renunciation	Renunciation
Profession of faith	Profession of faith	Profession of faith	Profession of faith
		Prayers	Prayers
	Promises	The Affirmation	
	Prayer for Holy Spirit	Prayer for Holy Spirit	
Laying-on of hands and prayer for Holy Spirit	Laying-on of hands and confirmation prayer	Laying-on of hands and confirmation prayer	Laying-on of hands and confirmation prayer
			Reception
			Reaffirmation
	Welcome		
	Admonition to congregation		
	Prayer		
	Our Father		
Anointing with chrism			
Peace		Peace	Peace
	Blessing		

CORPORATE CONFESSION AND FORGIVENESS
Ministers Edition, pp. 318–21, 33–34, 191

Parallel Rites

Roman Catholic	Rite for Reconciliation of Several Penitents with General Confession and Absolution, *The Rites*, pp. 376–79.
	Rite for Reconciliation of Several Penitents with Individual Confession and Absolution, *The Rites*, pp. 365–75.
Episcopal	A Penitential Order, *Book of Common Prayer*, pp. 319–21, 351–53.
Lutheran	The Order of Confession Preparatory to the Celebration of the Lord's Supper. *The Book of Worship* (General Synod 1867), pp. 79–82.
	Order for Confession and Absolution, Preparatory to the Celebration of the Lord's Supper, *Liturgy of the Evangelical Lutheran Church* (General Synod 1881), pp. 56–62.
	Confession and Absolution, Preparatory to the Holy Communion, *Forms for Ministerial Acts* (General Synod 1900), pp. 44–52.
	Public Confession and Absolution, *A Liturgy for the Use of Evangelical Lutheran Pastors* (Joint Synod of Ohio 1912), pp. 139–41.
	Order for Public Confession and Absolution, *Church Book* (General Council 1891), pp. 367–73.
	Order for Public Confession Preparatory to the Holy Communion, *Common Service Book* (United Lutheran Church in America 1919), text ed., pp. 403–08.
	The Order of the Confessional Service, *The Lutheran Hymnal* (Missouri Synod 1941), pp. 46–49.
	The Order for Public Confession, *Service Book and Hymnal* (American Lutheran Church and Lutheran Church in America 1958), pp. 249–52.
Methodist	An Order of Worship for Such as Would Enter into or Renew Their Covenant with God, *The Book of Worship* (1964, 1965), pp. 382–88.
Presbyterian	Order for a Service of Preparation for the Sacrament of the Lord's Supper or Holy Communion, *Book of Common Order* (Church of Scotland 1952), pp. 105–10.
Church of South India	The Covenant Service, *Book of Common Worship* (1963), pp. 130–38.

Purpose

This rite has been prepared to serve a variety of purposes: confession and absolution of individuals within the context of corporate worship as a regular discipline to deepen and enrich the spiritual life; the reconciliation of those individuals or families or factions who are estranged from one another; the acknowledgment of a share in corporate wrongs or the corporate guilt of industries, governments, groups.

Characteristics

The rite has its source in baptism, which establishes the Christian community and to which one returns by repentance and renewal. Because of its intimate connection with the gospel and with baptism, Confession and Absolution has been understood by Lutherans to be a sacrament.[146]

The rite is a flexible form designed to stand by itself as a separate service, either in preparation for Holy Communion or other occasions when a general confession of sin and complicity in wrongdoing and evil may be pastorally useful.

Background

The immediate ancestor of this service is the Order for Public Confession which was included in the *Church Book*, the *Common Service Book*, and the *Service Book and Hymnal*. That was a service in preparation for the reception of the Holy Communion. The Eucharist was then celebrated infrequently, sometimes only quarterly, and an extended public preparation a few times a year was customary and useful. The rubric in the *Common Service Book* explained that the order "should be appointed for the afternoon or evening of the Friday or Saturday preceding the Holy Communion, when all who purpose to commune should be present."[147] The service, the rubrics allowed, could also be used with slight alternation immediately preceding the service of Holy Communion, and it was so used as the custom of a preparatory service on a day preceding the celebration began to disappear. In the *Service Book and Hymnal*, which provided a separate "Brief Order for Public Confession When the Confession Occurs Immediately before the Service of the Day" (pp. 247–48), the Order for Public Confession was "for a specially appointed preparatory service" and was provided "for use when a Service of Preparation for Holy Communion is held on a day before the administration of the Sacrament" (p. 249).

General absolutions were a recognized liturgical form from the ninth through the fourteenth centuries and were usually given in the context of another liturgy, especially the Holy Communion. They focused on the Word of God in Scripture and sermon, an examination of conscience, a general confession, and an absolution given collectively to those who desired it.[148] In eighteenth-century Lutheranism public con-

---

[146]See Martin Luther, "The Babylonian Captivity of the Church," *Luther's Works* 36:81ff.; the Large Catechism, *Book of Concord*, 445; Apology of the Augsburg Confession XII.41, XIII.4 in the *Book of Concord*, 187, 211.

[147]*Common Service Book*, text ed., p. 403. For further discussion of this service see Chapter 14: "Conducting the Service Preparatory to the Holy Communion" in G. H. Gerberding, *The Lutheran Pastor* (Philadelphia: Lutheran Publication Society, 1902), 329–36.

[148]James Dallen, *The Reconciling Community: The Rite of Penance* (New York: Pueblo Publishing Co., 1986), 125–26.

fession developed as a replacement for private confession, which had been the universal practice inherited from the medieval church.[149] The new service was in effect a return to ancient practice. (In the 1950s and '60s the Roman Catholic Church began a recovery of general confession and absolution, for that church "the first new form of penance in a millennium."[150])

In the early church, the pronunciation of absolution was a public event as the Greek liturgical name for the rite, *exomologesis* (a confession of faith, the praise of God, and an appeal for the community's prayerful support[151]) implies. Sinners were reconciled in the presence of the congregation after they had done public penance.[152] Although Clement of Rome (d. 96),[153] Ignatius of Antioch (ca. 110),[154] Polycarp (156),[155] and the author of Second Clement (ca. 150)[156] reveal a relatively generous spirit, by the third century a system of public penance had developed, which was regarded as a second baptism.[157] Jerome called penitence "a second plank after shipwreck"[158] (the first plank was baptism). Penitence was oriented to the restoration of the wholeness of the church (the imposition of the priest's hands signifying a renewal of the Spirit), and a restoration of baptism and baptismal spirit. Jerome's description was quoted by Peter Lombard and by Luther.[159] Like baptism, the course of penitence could be undertaken only once in a lifetime. In this system, the penitent made a confession acknowledging sin to a bishop or his representative, a priest-penitentiary, asked for discipline and punishment, was enrolled in the order of penitents (note the parallels with baptism and the catechumenate), wore a special robe of goatskin (sackcloth) to show separation from the sheep of Christ's flock, was covered with ashes, worshiped separately from the congregation in the west end of the nave between the catechumens and the faithful, was excluded from the liturgy at the prayer of the faithful and deprived of Holy Communion, and was committed to a rigorous course of prayer, fasting, and almsgiving. The length of this course of penitence was determined by the gravity of the sin. When the penitence was completed, the penitent was liturgically reconciled to the congregation on Maundy

---

[149]For an account of the situation in Leipzig see Günther Stiller, *Johann Sebastian Bach and Liturgical Life in Leipzig*, trans. Herbert J. A. Bouman, Daniel F. Poellot, Hilton C. Oswald; ed. Robin A. Leaver (St. Louis: Concordia Publishing House, 1984).

[150]Dallen, 230, 247, n. 62.

[151]See Dallen, 20, 32–33, 39–40.

[152]See *Didache* 4.14.

[153]*First Clement* 57.

[154]Ignatius, *To the Philadelphians* 3.

[155]Polycarp, *To the Philippians* 6.

[156]*Second Clement* 18.

[157]See Tertullian, *On Penitence.*

[158]Jerome, *Letter* 130.9. See also *Letter* 122.4. The image of extending a plank to the shipwrecked, a favorite with Jerome, was derived from Seneca and Cicero.

[159]Peter Lombard, *Sentences* Book IV, dist. xiv, chap. 1. Martin Luther, "The Babylonian Captivity of the Church," *Luther's Works* 36:58.

Thursday. Following the reconciliation, the penitent was often committed to life-long continence and was not permitted to serve in the armed forces or to engage in public trade.

In Asia Minor, penitent sinners came to the grade of penitents by a series of steps. They were first mourners, who remained outside the church, asking the prayers of those who entered; then they were hearers, who participated in the Liturgy of the Word; then fallers or penitents, who received the imposition of hands and the prayers of the community; and finally standers (the usual grade for those who did not deserve public penance), who remained during Holy Communion but who could not receive the sacrament.

The severity of such systems was appropriate for those of a monastic devotion, and because of the rigors penitence was nearly always postponed until one was near death.

Through the influence of Celtic and Anglo-Saxon missionaries in the sixth century a new system of penitence was developed and administered through the more flexible approach of Penitential Books (which had a significant role in developing secular law). Penance remained public, long, and arduous. Confession was in private and absolution was withheld until the completion of the course of penitence. By the eleventh century, however, the absolution had been moved back to follow confession and precede penance. Such a system still entailed severe disruption of one's life, and a system of commutation developed involving the performance of certain religious acts (such as praying the entire Psalter in a posture of physical discomfort) and the payment of money. Abuses of this system led to the practice of selling and buying indulgences, which at last ignited the Reformation.

Sacramental theory developed during the scholastic period. The Schoolmen distinguished between *culpa* (guilt) and *poena* (punishment) and between *poena damnationis* (damnation) and *poena temporalis* (temporal punishment). The guilt and the eternal punishment were removed by confession and absolution; the temporal punishment was removed by doing penance. This was understood to involve three acts: contrition, confession, and satisfaction. The Fourth Lateran Council (1215) required every Christian to make such confession of sin at least once a year.

The relationship between baptism and penance had never been entirely lost. Jerome and Peter Lombard, as noted above (p. 79), maintained the connection. Luther had a great regard for confession and absolution because of his profound understanding of baptism.[160] He made the connection clear by devoting a special section in the Small

---

[160]Martin Luther, "The Sacrament of Penance," *Luther's Works* 35:9–22; "The Babylonian Captivity of the Church," *Luther's Works* 36:58–64, 81–91; "Confession Concerning Christ's Supper" (1528), *Luther's Works* 37:368, 370; "A Discussion on How Confession Should Be Made" (1520), *Luther's Works* 39:27–47; "The Keys" (1530), *Luther's Works* 40:325–77. See also the Large Catechism, Fourth Part: Baptism; Augsburg Confession XII.

Catechism to Confession and Absolution and placing it between Baptism and the Sacrament of the Altar. Confession is the daily use of baptism and was intended by Luther especially for those who were about to receive Holy Communion. Thus the medieval discipline of private confession was maintained in the Lutheran churches, and after languishing largely unused for some centuries was recovered by the nineteenth-century confessional and liturgical revival.

The penitential rites were drafted for the *Lutheran Book of Worship* by Walter R. Bouman, John R. Cochran, and Paul K. Peterson, who chaired the subcommittee.

THE SERVICE IN DETAIL

The service begins with the invocation (and the sign of the cross) as a reminder of the baptismal covenant to which this service marks a return, for baptism, as Gustav Aulén says, "is an expression of the open arms of the Father."[161] And indeed, a biblical image that lies behind this service is the parable of the prodigal son (Luke 15:11–32). All the participants say the words (and make the sign), for all are bound together by their common baptism. Anciently, the sign was more important than the accompanying words and was in use long before the words were attached to it.[162] The liturgy in the German Lutheran tradition gave the invocation a prominence not found elsewhere and saw in it an affirmation of faith, an expression of the awareness of God's presence, an invocation of the triune God in whose name the congregation assembles.

The prayer for purity (no. 236), reminiscent of Psalm 51 which follows, is a late Gregorian collect found in the eleventh-century Leofric missal and the Sarum missal as the Prayer of the Day for a mass of the Holy Spirit. In the Sarum missal it was also used as a prayer to be prayed by the priest after *Veni creator spiritus* as part of the preparation for mass. The collect was retained in the *Book of Common Prayer* as part of the initial rite of the Holy Communion. A much-beloved prayer, it was borrowed by the *Church Book* and included among its "special collects"[163] and by the *Common Service Book* for the Order for Public Confession and also as number 33 of its Collects and Prayers. From those books it made its way into the *Service Book and Hymnal* Order for Public Confession and the abbreviated Brief Order for Public Confession When the Confession Occurs Immediately Before the Service of the Day (p. 247) and as number 66 of its Collects and Prayers.

The alternative prayer (no. 271) is adapted from an alternative opening prayer in the Roman Catholic rite for the Reconciliation of Several Penitents.

---

[161] Gustav Aulén, *The Faith of the Christian Church*, trans. Eric H. Wahlstrom and G. Everett Arden (Philadelphia: Muhlenberg Press, 1948), 380.

[162] See Luther D. Reed, *The Lutheran Liturgy*, rev. ed. (Philadelphia: Fortress Press, 1959), 253–54.

[163] *Church Book* (1868), 109, no. 66.

The Rites of the Catholic Church	*Lutheran Book of Worship*
Father of mercies and God of all consolation, you do not wish the sinner to die but to be converted and live. Come to the aid of your people, that they may turn from their sins and live for you alone. May we be attentive	Father of mercies and God of all consolation,
	come to the aid of your people, turning us from our sin to live for you alone. Give us the power of your Holy Spirit, that we may
to your Word, confess our sins, receive your forgiveness, and be always grateful for your loving kindness. Help us to live the truth in love and grow into the fullness of Christ, your Son, who lives and reigns for ever and ever.	attend to your Word, confess our sins, receive your forgiveness,
	and grow into the fullness of your Son Jesus Christ, our Lord and our Redeemer.
(p. 386)	(Min. Ed., p. 318)

The opening address of the prayer quotes 2 Corinthians 1:3 (see also Ezek. 33:11; 18:20–32). The Lutheran version of the prayer stresses the work of the Holy Spirit in the congregation's attending to the word, confessing sin, receiving forgiveness, and growing into the fullness of Christ.

Psalm 51 has been in the Lutheran order for public confession since the *Church Book* (1891) and is also familiar from the use of some its verses as the Offertory in the Holy Communion. It is, however, no longer the required psalm. Other psalms and (Old Testament, Epistle, and Gospel) lessons are cited on page 191 of the Ministers Edition. A reading from the Gospels is normally included, the rubric (p. 319, #6) observes; it would be most unusual for a Christian congregation to gather to confess its sins and not want to hear the good news from the gospel. The proclamation of the Word of God helps to focus the service not on the sinner's actions but on the reconciling work and power of God in Christ.[164]

The prayer of confession is a revision of the confession in the Order of the Confessional Service before the Holy Communion in *The Lutheran Hymnal* (pp. 16, 47), which is a version of the confession at the beginning of the Common Service (1888).

Common Service Book	*The Lutheran Hymnal*	*Lutheran Book of Worship*
Almighty God, our Maker and Redeemer, we poor sinners	O almighty God merciful Father, I, a poor, miserable	Almighty God, merciful Father, I, a troubled and

---

[164] Dallen, 256.

confess unto Thee,
that we are by
nature sinful and
unclean, and that
we have sinned
against Thee by
thought, word, and
deed. Wherefore we
flee for refuge to
Thine infinite
mercy, seeking and
imploring Thy grace,
for the sake of our
Lord Jesus Christ.

O most merciful God,
Who hast given Thine
Only-begotten Son to
die for us, have mercy
upon us, and for His
sake grant us
remission of all
our sins:

and by Thy Holy Spirit
increase in us true
knowledge of Thee,
and of Thy will, and
true obedience to Thy
Word, to the end that by
Thy grace we may come to
everlasting life;
through Jesus Christ our Lord.
Amen.

(text ed., pp. 7–8)

sinner, confess unto
Thee all my sins and
iniquities
with which I have
ever offended Thee
and justly deserved
Thy temporal and
eternal punishment.
But I am heartily
sorry for them and
sincerely repent of
them, and I pray Thee
of Thy boundless
mercy and for the
sake of the holy,
innocent, bitter
sufferings and death
of Thy beloved Son,

Jesus Christ, to be
gracious and merciful
to me, a poor, sinful
being.

(p. 47)

penitent sinner, confess
to you all my sins and
iniquities
with which I have
offended you
and for which I justly
deserve your
punishment.
But I am
sorry for them, and
repent of them,
and pray for
your boundless mercy.
For the
sake of the

suffering and death
of your Son,

Jesus Christ, be
gracious and merciful
to me, a poor sinful
being;
forgive my sins, give
me your Holy Spirit
for the amendment
of my sinful life,

and bring me to
life everlasting.

Amen.
(Min. Ed., p. 319)

The texts are derived primarily from Melanchthon's order for Mecklenburg (1552), as later adopted in Wittenberg (1559); behind this may lie the work of John Riebling (1534).[165]

Anciently the absolution was (de)precatory, a prayer that God would forgive. That form is still used in the East, and in the Roman rite it is used in the liturgy as at the beginning of mass.[166] Like the modern Roman Catholic formula, the absolution in the Lutheran order begins with God's mercy in Christ and declares that humanity's reconciliation is a participation in the Easter passage from darkness to light by the power of the Spirit. The first sentence of the absolution is adapted from the opening of the declaration of grace at the beginning of the Common Service.

---

[165] Reed, 258.
[166] "May Almighty God have mercy on us,
forgive us our sins,
and bring us to everlasting life."

Common Service	Lutheran Book of Worship
Almighty God, our Heavenly Father, hath had mercy upon us, and hath given His only Son to die for us, and for His sake forgiveth us all our sins.[167]	Almighty God in his mercy has given his Son to die for us and, for his sake, forgives us all our sins.

The sentence is derived, like the paragraphs above, chiefly from Melanchthon's order for Mecklenburg. The second sentence, incorporating the proclamatory language of 1 Peter 2:9, expands on the work of the Holy Spirit in God's people to cleanse, enlighten, and empower for witness. The third sentence, the actual absolution, is from the Order for Public Confession from the Common Service.

Common Service	Lutheran Book of Worship
As a minister of the Church of Christ, and by His authority, I therefore declare unto you who do truly repent and believe in Him, the entire forgiveness of all your sins: In the Name of the Father, and of the Son, and of the Holy Ghost.[168]	As a called and ordained minister of the Church of Christ and by his authority, I therefore declare to you the entire forgiveness of all your sins, in the name of the Father, and of the + Son, and of the Holy Spirit.

The interpolated phrase, "called and ordained," is from *The Lutheran Hymnal* (p. 48) and describes the foundation of the pastor's authority to exercise the power of the keys and announce the forgiveness of sin.

Although the general absolution grants "the entire forgiveness of all your sins," those convinced of their sin and guilt may desire a more individual and personal confirmation of the absolution. Absolution of an entire congregation is the usual and familiar practice among Lutherans, as in the Brief Order for Confession and Forgiveness which many use at every service without variation. A general absolution may therefore be by itself too familiar a form to be fully effective for those whose complicity in sin is particularly apparent and burdensome. Individuals may need to hear these words spoken directly to them and perhaps even more importantly may need to see the absolution being granted individually to those with whom they may have been at variance. The

---

[167] *Church Book*, p. 4; *Common Service Book*, text ed., p. 8; *Service Book and Hymnal*, p. 1.

[168] *Church Book*, p. 372; *Common Service Book*, text ed., p. 407; *Service Book and Hymnal*, pp. 248, 252.

individual absolution is a personal application of what has been granted to the assembly in the general absolution.

The laying on of hands was the most ancient form of absolution, signifying a return and renewal of the Holy Spirit to the penitent and a reconciliation to the community. Later, words praising God's compassion and asking for mercy were added to the gesture. Gregory the Great observed that reconciliation of heretics was accomplished through the laying on of the hand,[169] while in the East it was done through anointing with chrism. Leo the Great (440–461) used "confirmation," meaning the imposition of the bishop's hand, in connection with the reconciliation of heretics.

Originally absolution (*absolutio*) was a concluding blessing for any liturgy. From the ninth-century Carolingian reformation onward, absolution began to take on the meaning of pardon and remission indicating that the period of penance had been completed. References to the power of the keys became increasingly frequent, and the absolution became either a deprecatory prayer of supplication addressing God and asking forgiveness for the sinner or an optative prayer addressed to the penitent, speaking of God in the third person and expressing the desire for the penitent's forgiveness. From the tenth and eleventh centuries an indicative form of absolution with the priest in a judicial role came into use, usually in conjunction with one or both of the other form, and was in common use by the end of the twelfth century. With the use of this formula the laying on of hands disappeared and the judicial formula replaced the gesture.[170]

The words at the individual absolution, "In obedience to the command of our Lord Jesus Christ, I forgive you all your sins," are an example of the indicative form of absolution, and they ground the pastor's declaration of forgiveness in the authority and command of Christ given in John 20:22–23; Matthew 16:19; 18:18. The words accompany the primary action, the minister laying both hands on each person's head.

The forgiveness of sins having been bestowed, the spirit of the service turns to praise, gratitude, and peace, the characteristic attitude of the ancient *exomologesis*. The hymn, which, the rubrics direct, is to be a hymn of praise, is an expression of joyful thanksgiving for the freedom of forgiveness, a confession of faith in the God who reconciles the world to himself. The salutation and response which introduce the prayers underscore the sense of unity and mutual concern which have been restored by the confession and absolution. The first prayer after the hymn (no. 272) takes its first phrase, "you reconciled the world to yourself," from the absolution in the Roman Catholic Rite for the Reconciliation of Individual Penitents;[171] the reference is to 2 Corinthians

---

[169] Gregory the Great, *Letter* 11.52.
[170] Dallen, 141–42.
[171] *The Rites*, 362–63, 378.

5:19. The concluding prayer (no. 255), the collect for peace which was used in the Common Service to conclude Vespers and also the Order for Public Confession,[172] is the prayer of the day in a mass for peace in the Gelasian sacramentary (no. 1472), the Gregorian sacramentary (no. 1343), and the Sarum missal. It was used at Vespers in the Sarum breviary. From there it passed into Evening Prayer in the *Book of Common Prayer* and thence into Vespers in the Lutheran Common Service.

The blessing is identical with that at the conclusion of the Holy Communion and is derived from various medieval versions of the Roman missal. The dismissal is from the Roman Catholic Rite for the Reconciliation of Individual Penitents.

The Rites of the Catholic Church	*Lutheran Book of Worship*
The Lord has freed you from your sins. Go in peace. (p. 363)	The Lord has made you free. Go in peace. *Thanks be to God.* (Min. Ed., p. 321)

COMPARISON OF RITES

The Rites of the Catholic Church	*Common Service Book*	*Lutheran Book of Worship*	*Book of Common Prayer*
	Verses		Verse & response
Song			
Greeting		In the name...	
		Hymn	
Prayer		Prayer	
	Psalm 51	Psalm 51	
Lesson(s)	Lesson(s)	Lesson(s)	
			(Exhortation)
Homily	Sermon	Sermon	(Sermon)
	Exhortation		
	Prayer for purity		
Examination of conscience	Examination of conscience		
			(Sentences)
Confession	Confession	Confession	Confession
Our Father			
Absolution	Absolution	Absolution	Absolution
	Our Father		
Song or hymn		Hymn of praise	
Prayer of thanksgiving		Prayer of thanksgiving	

[172] *Church Book*, p. 33, 373; *Common Service Book*, text ed., pp. 35–36, 408; *Service Book and Hymnal*, pp. 148, 252.

Prayer for peace	Prayer for peace	Prayers
	Our Father	
Blessing	Blessing	Blessing	Blessing
Dismissal		Dismissal	

INDIVIDUAL CONFESSION AND FORGIVENESS
Ministers Edition, pp. 322–23

Parallel Rites

Roman Catholic	Rite of Reconciliation of Individual Penitents, *The Rites*, pp. 337–64.
Episcopal	The Reconciliation of a Penitent, *Book of Common Prayer*, pp. 446–52.
Lutheran	Order for Private Confession and Absolution, *Church Book* (1891), pp. 364–67.
	Order for Confession and Absolution (Private), *A Liturgy for the Use of Evangelical Lutheran Pastors* (Joint Synod of Ohio 1912), pp. 137–38.
	Order for Private Confession and Absolution, *Common Service Book* (United Lutheran Church in America 1919), text ed., p. 409.
	Order for Private Confession and Absolution, *Occasional Services* (American Lutheran Church and the Lutheran Church in America 1962), pp. 31–32.
Orthodox	The Rite of Confession, *Service Book*, pp. 286–90.
	The Sacrament of Holy Confession, *An Orthodox Prayer Book*, pp. 135–39.

Purpose

Individual Confession and Forgiveness is intended for use as a personal application of the gospel through the forgiveness of sins. It is a traditional use of what the Lutheran Confessions, drawing on a long tradition in Christianity, call "the power (or office) of the keys," based on Matthew 16:19; 18:18; John 20:22–23, to disclose "a sure and firm consolation for the conscience."[173]

Characteristics

The form for Individual Confession and Forgiveness in the *Lutheran Book of Worship* is a simple one, based primarily on the model which Luther suggested in the Small Catechism, part 5, "Confession and Absolution. How Plain People are to be Taught to Confess."[174]

---

[173] Apology of the Augsburg Confession X in the *Book of Concord*, 180.
[174] *Book of Concord*, 350–51. See also Luther's sermon of March 16, 1522 at Wittenberg on Confession, *Luther's Works* 51:97–100.

In Lutheran use, the form for Individual Confession and Forgiveness is basically a prayer of confession, which may or may not include an enumeration of particular sins, and absolution. Luther explained in the Small Catechism,

Confession consists of two parts. One is that we confess our sins. The other is that we receive absolution or forgiveness from the confessor as from God himself, by no means doubting but firmly believing that our sins are thereby forgiven before God in heaven.[175]

The Lutheran Confessions, reacting to medieval abuses, insist that "we should confess only those sins of which we have knowledge and which trouble us." One should not "search for and invent other sins, for this would turn confession into torture."[176] So a rubric in the *Church Book* warns:

The enumeration of sins in Private Confession is entirely free; and the Minister should not curiously inquire into special forms of transgression, or otherwise burden penitents by questions about what is not voluntarily confessed: for the ministry of divine Absolution is not appointed to investigate secret sins, neither is such investigation necessary to their forgiveness. But penitents should be encouraged to confess the sins which specially burden their souls, that proper direction and consolation may be given them.[177]

Luther intended Confession and Absolution especially for those who were about to receive Communion,[178] and the Lutheran churches have maintained that connection. The initial rubric in the *Church Book* regarding Private Confession relates confession first to the reception of Holy Communion and then secondly to spiritual growth.

It is of great importance that the Minister should have personal knowledge of those whom he admits to the Lord's Supper, and to this end should inquire into the spiritual condition especially of the young and inexperienced, that he may instruct and encourage them as need may be. Christian people also, for their growth in knowledge and grace, should use their privilege to confer personally with those appointed to watch over their souls, in order to have the instructions and consolations of the Word of God ministered to them individually.[179]

The second rubric reflects customary Lutheran insistence that Private Confession is traditional and acceptable in evangelical use on the one hand but on the other that it is not to be required.

Private Confession and Absolution is a service which has been used by the Church for such personal ministrations. It is not to be regarded as necessary, nor to be exacted of any one; but it is provided and recommended for such as are particularly distressed and burdened in conscience on account of sin.[180]

---

[175] *Book of Concord*, 349–50.
[176] Ibid., 350.
[177] *Church Book*, p. 365.
[178] *Book of Concord*, 349, n. 5.
[179] *Church Book*, pp. 364–65.
[180] Ibid., p. 365.

Confession is to be genuine, and it is to be free.

Absolution is to be given only to such persons as are truly penitent, and sincerely determined to amend their ways; for without genuine repentance there is no forgiveness.

The person making Confession may use his or her own words, or the words here given, or any other suitable words.[181]

The form in the *Common Service Book* (1919), from which is derived the one in *Occasional Services* (1962), is simple and straightforward: a confession, the absolution, and a blessing. *Occasional Services* (1962) permits the pastor to lay a hand on the head of the penitent as the absolution is said and includes the sign of the cross in the absolution. The form in both books is introduced with this rubric:

Private Confession and Absolution has been used by the Church from ancient times, and persons who are burdened in conscience on account of sin may always seek the personal ministration of the Pastor before the Holy Communion or at any other time.[182]

Background

In the early church, as outlined above, p. 79, absolution was pronounced in the presence of the congregation after the penitent had made a private confession and done public penance. From about the eighth century *ex-omologesis* meant individual confession of sins to a priest and a private hearing of the absolution. The form of the absolution was declaratory, a pronouncement that God forgives those who repent, or it was (de)precatory, a prayer that God may forgive the penitent. The precatory form remains the liturgical form in the Roman rite and is used also in the East, even with individuals.[183] In the West in the thirteenth century, when confession had become almost totally a private act, the indicative form, "I absolve you," was adopted for use with individuals, and the pronouncement of this form was reserved to priests.

In the seventeenth and eighteenth centuries the idea that going to Holy Communion was to be preceded by confession and absolution had gained complete supremacy among Lutherans.[184] In Leipzig throughout the eighteenth century only the form of private confession was used, and for this purpose opportunity was given before the celebrations of Holy Communion as well as on the previous day.[185]

---

[181] Ibid.

[182] *Common Service Book*, text ed., p. 409.

[183] For example, the *Service Book*, p. 290, where it is joined with an indicative form: "May our Lord and God Jesus Christ, through the grace and bounties of his love towards mankind, forgive thee, my child, N., all thy transgressions. And I, his unworthy Priest, through the power given unto me by him, do forgive and absolve thee from all thy sins, in the Name of the Father, and of the Son, and of the Holy Spirit. Amen."

[184] Stiller, 140.

[185] Stiller, 44–45, 257–58.

The Roman Catholic Church numbers Penance among the seven sacraments.[186] In addition to the Rite for Reconciliation of Individual Penitents, which continues the long tradition of individual private confession and absolution, two other rites are provided which emphasize the relation of the sacrament to the community and place confession and absolution in the context of a celebration of the word of God: Rite for Reconciliation of Several Penitents with Individual Confession and Absolution, and the Rite for Reconciliation of Several Penitents with General Confession and Absolution.[187]

The *Book of Common Prayer* gives two forms for what is called the "Reconciliation of a Penitent." The first form is derived from general medieval practice and is like forms used in recent revisions in various Anglican provinces; the second is a fuller rite, closer to recent Roman Catholic reforms and the Byzantine form for confession. It is "particularly appropriate when a person has turned or returned to the Christian Faith, or at other possible 'crisis' points in a person's life."[188]

The penitential rites were drafted for the *Lutheran Book of Worship* by Walter R. Bouman, John R. Cochran, and Paul K. Peterson, who chaired the subcommittee.

Preparation for the Service

The introduction to the Roman Catholic rite of penance observes wisely:

In order to fulfill his ministry properly and faithfully the confessor should understand the disorders of soul and apply the appropriate remedies to them. He should fulfill his office of judge wisely and should acquire the knowledge and prudence necessary for this task by serious study, guided by the teaching authority of the Church and especially by fervent prayer to God. Discernment of spirits is a deep knowledge of God's action in the hearts of men; it is a gift of the Spirit as well as the fruit of charity.[189]

The personal pronouns of the passage are not inclusive enough for Lutherans, but the thought is worth pondering. A confessor must be a person of prayer and study as well as a person of sympathy.

The more immediate preparation for Confession and Forgiveness also requires prayer. Again, the Roman Catholic introduction observes,

Priest and penitent should first prepare themselves by prayer to celebrate the sacrament. The priest should call upon the Holy Spirit so that he may receive enlightenment and charity. The penitent should compare his life with the example and commandments of Christ and then pray to God for the forgiveness of his sins.[190]

---

[186]See *The Rites*, 344–47.
[187]*The Rites*, 365–75, 376–79.
[188]Hatchett, 453.
[189]*The Rites*, 348. A footnote to the section refers the reader to Phil. 1:9–10.
[190]*The Rites*, 350.

Lutherans will also recall Luther's advice in the Small Catechism, "Reflect on your condition in the light of the Ten Commandments."[191]

Physical preparations need also to be made to ensure privacy for the confession. The pastor may want to draw the curtain around the hospital bed as an indication that others should not intrude. In a home the pastor should sit next to the penitent. Kneeling should be encouraged if the person is able to do so, but many infirm people will not find this possible.

THE SERVICE IN DETAIL

Individual Confession and Forgiveness begins with the pastor greeting the penitent. The purpose of the greeting is to relax the penitent and to set the proper tone for what follows. The Roman Catholic rite suggests several verses of scripture as possible greetings:

> Ezekiel 33:11
>
> Luke 5:32
>
> 1 John 2:1–2
>
> May God, who has enlightened every heart,
> help you to know your sins
> and trust in his mercy.
>
> May the grace of the Holy Spirit
> fill your heart with light,
> that you may confess your sins with loving trust
> and come to know that God is merciful.
>
> May the Lord be in your heart
> and help you to confess your sins with true sorrow.

Psalm 51 is used in the Byzantine confession, and phrases from it were used in the Confession in the *Church Book*.

The pastor's invitation to the penitent,

You have come to make confession before God. In Christ you are free to confess before me, a pastor in his Church, the sins of which you are aware and the sins which trouble you.

is to clarify what is about to happen, especially for those to whom confession and absolution is unfamiliar.

The comfort and consolation which confession and absolution confers is drawn from the Scripture. In the Roman Catholic rite scriptural verses are used before the confession to proclaim God's mercy and to call people to conversion: Isaiah 53:4–6; Ezekiel 11:19–20; Matthew 6:14–15; Mark 1:14–15; Luke 6:31–38; Luke 15:1–7; John 10:19–32; Romans 5:8–9; Ephesians 5:1–2; Colossians 1:12–14; Colossians 3:8–10, 12–17; and 1 John 1:6–7, 9 are suggested. In the *Book of Common Prayer* the "comfortable words" from the confession in the Eucharist

---

[191] *Book of Concord*, 350.

are used also in the Reconciliation of a Penitent: Matthew 11:28, John 3:16, 1 Timothy 1:15, and 1 John 2:1–2. In the *Lutheran Book of Worship* the confession is surrounded by Scripture, beginning with verses from Psalm 51 and following the confession with passages from Scripture as comfort and consolation and concluding the act of confession with verses from Psalm 51, the psalm of repentance. The readings from Scripture help counter the subjective piety that came to prevail in the late medieval, and therefore also Lutheran, understanding of confession and forgiveness. "It shifts the focus from the sinner's deeds to the reconciling power of God in Christ."[192]

The penitent is invited to make confession. The wording of the invitation emphasizes that the confession is made to God in the presence of the pastor and that the pastor's personality and character are irrelevant to what is to take place, for the pastor functions here as a representative of the church and not in an individual capacity as friend or as adversary.

The confession acknowledges first, before God, that the penitent is "guilty of many sins," many of which are not known even to the penitent. Then, before the pastor, the penitent makes confession to those sins of which the penitent is aware and which are troubling. The intent of the invitation and of the suggested form of confession is to avoid excessive enumeration of every sin the penitent might be able to recall (or indeed imagine or invent). It is those sins which trouble the penitent which are to be confessed in Individual Confession and Forgiveness.

Following the confession, counsel, and psalm verses, the absolution is pronounced. The pastor stands in order conveniently to lay hands on the penitent's head and declares God's forgiveness. (The Roman Catholic form calls for the priest only to extend the hands, or at least the right hand, over the penitent's head as the absolution is pronounced. In the *Book of Common Prayer*, Form 1 makes no mention of a gesture; Form 2 allows either a hand on the head or over the head of the penitent.)

The absolution used in the form for Individual Confession and Forgiveness given in the *Lutheran Book of Worship* combines the ancient declaratory form with the indicative form adopted in the thirteenth century by the Roman rite for use with individuals. The first sentence, which declares God's merciful nature, recalls Psalm 67:1 in the Authorized Version. The second sentence is the indicative form of absolution, adapted from the form in the Order of the Holy Communion in *The Lutheran Hymnal* (p. 16), clearly grounding in ordination the pastor's authority to forgive. The "command" of Christ to forgive sins derives from such scriptural passages as Matthew 16:19 and John 20:22–23. Although there is no explicit command in Scripture to forgive sins in this way, Luther understood the power of the keys to be such a command. The keys "are an office, a power or command given by God through Christ to all of Christendom for the retaining and remitting of the sins

---

[192]Dallen, 256.

of men."[193] Thus, in the form suggested in the Small Catechism, Luther has the confessor say, "According to the command of our Lord Jesus Christ, I forgive you your sins...."[194]

In some ways the absolution from Corporate Confession and Forgiveness is a superior prayer, declaring God's initiative in sending Christ and recalling indirectly the Easter passage from darkness to light by the power of the Spirit. A deficiency of the prayer and the corresponding Roman formula is that there is no mention of reconciliation with the church.[195]

A time of silence is appropriate as the penitent savors the words of absolution. Gratitude for forgiveness may then be spoken with the words of Psalm 103:8–13. The Roman rite concludes more simply, "Give thanks to the Lord, for he is good. His mercy endures forever" (Ps. 136:1).

The dismissal,

> Blessed are those whose sins have been forgiven,
> whose evil deeds have been forgotten.
> Rejoice in the Lord, and go in peace

is from the Roman rite.[196] The first sentence is from Psalm 32:1, which Cyril of Jerusalem used in relation to the baptismal garment: "whose sins have been covered." The concluding words of the dismissal were added by Luther to the absolution recalling such passages as Mark 5:34; Luke 7:50; 8:48. "Peace" may be seen in relation to the exchange of the peace with which the newly-baptized were welcomed into the Christian community. The reconciliation of the sinner with God and with the church has been restored.

---

[193]Martin Luther, "The Keys," *Luther's Works* 40:366.
[194]*Book of Concord*, 351.
[195]Dallen, 335.
[196]*The Rites*, 364.

Table I
DEVELOPMENT OF THE RITE
INDIVIDUAL CONFESSION AND FORGIVENESS

Church Book 1892	Common Service Book 1919	Occasional Services 1962	Lutheran Book of Worship 1978
			Greeting
			Psalm 51:16–18, 1–2
			Invitation
Confession	Confession	Confession	Confession
			Consolation from Scripture
			Psalm 51:1, 11–13
Absolution	Absolution	Absolution	Absolution
			Psalm 103:8–13
"The Peace of the Lord be with thee."	Blessing	Blessing	Dismissal
			(The Peace)

Table II
COMPARISON OF RITES
INDIVIDUAL CONFESSION AND FORGIVENESS

The Rites of the Catholic Church	Book of Common Prayer		Lutheran Book of Worship
	FORM 1	FORM 2	
Reception of the Penitent			Greeting
		Psalm 51:1–3	Psalm 51:16–18, 1–2
(Scripture)		Scripture	
			Invitation to Confession
Confession	Confession	Confession	Confession
	(Consolation, direction, and comfort)	(Consolation, direction, and comfort)	
			Psalm 51:1, 11–13
Prayer of the Penitent			
Expression of Sorrow		Expression of sorrow	
		Questions to the penitent	
Absolution	Absolution	Absolution	Absolution
Praise of God		Praise	Psalm 103:8–13
Dismissal	Dismissal	Dismissal	Dismissal

BRIEF ORDER FOR CONFESSION AND FORGIVENESS
Ministers Edition, pp. 195, 233, 269

Parallel Rites

Roman Catholic — Penitential Rite, *Sacramentary*, pp. 357–65.

Episcopal — A Penitential Order, *Book of Common Prayer*, pp. 319–21, 351–53.

Lutheran — The Confession of Sins, *Church Book* (1868), pp. 3–5.
The Confession of Sins, *Common Service Book* (1919), text ed., pp. 7–8.
The Confession of Sins, *Service Book and Hymnal* (1958), pp. 1, 15–16, 41–42.
A Brief Order for Public Confession When the Confession Occurs Immediately Before the Service of the Day, *Service Book and Hymnal* (1958), pp. 247–48.

Presbyterian — The Law of God and Summary of the Law, Confession of Sin and Declaration of Pardon, *Worshipbook* (1972), pp. 17, 26–27.

Purpose

The Brief Order is a rite of confession and absolution for use immediately prior to the Holy Communion at those times when such a penitential preparation is desired. It is not intended to be used alone as a separate service.

Characteristics

The Brief Order is similar to the confessional rites which previous Lutheran liturgies have provided for use at the beginning of the Holy Communion. Like the Brief Order provided by the *Service Book and Hymnal*, the one in the *Lutheran Book of Worship* is a shortened form of the longer and separate for Corporate Confession and Forgiveness (Public Confession).

Background

The *Confiteor* ("I confess"), a late element in the liturgy, developed from the prayers originally said by the priest in the sacristy while vesting as part of his private preparation for mass. Early liturgies had no such penitential portion, but increasingly emphasis was laid on (private) confession and absolution in preparation for receiving the sacrament. After the seventh century, under Frankish influence, the once silent prayers of the priest were spoken aloud, the priest "lying prostrate on the ground" before the altar.[197] The congregation did not participate. By the begin-

---

[197]Josef A. Jungmann, *The Mass of the Roman Rite*, rev. Charles K. Riepe (New York: Benziger, 1959), 203; Dallen, 126, 138, n. 71.

ning of the eleventh century there was a general confession, *Confiteor* ("I confess"), which came from the monastic offices of Prime and Compline, followed by the *Misereatur* of those whose intercession had been requested. ("Almighty God have mercy on you, pardon your sins, and bring you to everlasting life.") After mutual use of *Confiteor* and *Misereatur*, the priest then gave the *Indulgentiam* ("The almighty and merciful Lord grant us pardon, absolution, and remission of our sins") — a favorite form of absolution used in private confession ca. 1000. The purpose of this confession at the beginning of mass was make the priest worthy of offering the eucharistic sacrifice.

From the office of the communion of the sick a second confession entered the mass. After the communion of the celebrant, the *Confiteor*, *Misereatur*, and *Indulgentiam* were said again, this time to prepare the people for their communion. The text of the Roman *Confiteor* was adopted in 1314 by the Synod of Ravenna and became part of the Missal of Pius V (1570).

Luther attacked these ritual preparations designed to make people worthy of communion as part of his general assault on the mass as sacrifice. His orders had no such confession and absolution. In his Formula Missae he wrote, "...private confession before communion...neither is necessary nor should be demanded.... For the best preparation is — as I have said — a soul troubled by sins, death, and temptation and hungering and thirsting for healing and strength,"[198] and in the Small Catechism, "...he is truly worthy and well prepared who believes these words: 'for you' and 'for the forgiveness of sins.'"[199] In fact, the Holy Communion is the primary sacrament of reconciliation.[200] The Eucharist expresses and celebrates the continual conversion begun at baptism and carried on daily in the lives of Christians.

The Reformers, however, were shaped by the medieval emphasis on penitential preparation for reception of Holy Communion and generally included some kind of preparation in their church orders. By the seventeenth and eighteenth centuries the idea that communion was to be preceded by confession and absolution had gained complete supremacy. Friedrich Kalb cites three different uses of preparation for communion: (1) the private preparation of the clergy; (2) the public preparation of the congregation at the beginning of the liturgy; (3) an acknowledgement of guilt after the sermon as a general confession and absolution, an admonition to true faith, or as petition and intercession.[201].

An experimental form of confession is found in the Nuremberg missal (1525). The *Confiteor* was retained as the private prayer of the pastor in Brandenburg-Nuremberg (1533), Schleswig-Holstein (1542),

---

[198] *Luther's Works* 53:34.

[199] *Book of Concord*, 352.

[200] Dallen, 257.

[201] Friedrich Kalb, *Grundriss der Liturgik* (Munich: Claudius Verlag, 1955), 100; Jungmann, 480

Pfalz-Neuburg (1543), Hildesheim (1544), and Pomerania (1563). Congregational forms are found in Sweden (1531), Hamburg (1537), and the Reformation of Cologne (1543).[202] In eighteenth-century Leipzig at every celebration of the Holy Communion, in addition to the usual provisions for private confession, there was at the beginning of the announcement section a general public confession in the church. For those with a reputation of being advanced (*geförderte*) Christians this was deemed sufficient.[203]

Contemporary Worship 2: The Holy Communion (1970), in an effort to make the service clearly begin with the opening Entrance Hymn and because of the psychological insight that one cannot admit one's guilt until one is assured of acceptance, moved the confession to a position between the liturgy of the word and the liturgy of the meal. This was a recovery of a practice which had obtained in some Lutheran areas after the Reformation, continuing the practice of certain medieval orders, and which also was the location of confession in the *Book of Common Prayer*. The resulting liturgy of 1970 was awkward, attempting to squeeze too much into the sandwich between two principal parts of the service, the Sermon and the Offering: Hymn of the Day, Creed, Act of Reconciliation, the Peace, and Intercessions. Moreover, Lutherans had been too well trained by the North American tradition and its commentators to take to innovation at this point. As one washes one's hands before coming to the dinner table, the explanation went, so one washes one's soul by confession before coming to the altar of God. The logic of the order seemed too compelling to be altered, and confession at the outset continued to be expected.

The *Church Book*, the *Common Service Book*, and the *Service Book and Hymnal* at the beginning of the Service gave a corporate confession spoken by the minister on behalf of the congregation; a prayer for mercy, forgiveness, and the Holy Spirit said by the congregation and the minister together; a declaration of grace said by the minister (a Reformation use found also in Morning and Evening Prayer in the *Book of Common Prayer*). The *Service Book and Hymnal* provided as an alternative a precatory absolution, "...God grant unto you...pardon and remission...." To provide an individual form of confession, the Order for Public Confession was often substituted when the Holy Communion was being celebrated. *The Lutheran Hymnal* gave an individual confession, "I...confess unto thee all my sins..." with an explicit sacramental absolution, "...I forgive you all your sins."

The *Church Book* and the *Common Service Book* began the Service with the confession of sins and declaration of grace. The *Service Book and Hymnal* began an effort to divide the confessional portion from the rest of the service by a rubric, "A brief silence may be kept before

---

[202]Reed, 258. See Edward T. Horn, *Outlines of Liturgics*, 2nd rev. ed. (Philadelphia: Lutheran Publication Society, ca. 1912), 110.
[203]Stiller, 140.

the Introit for the Day" and, following the rubric, by a rule across the page. The *Lutheran Book of Worship* carried this further and clearly divided the Brief Order for Confession and Forgiveness from the Holy Communion as a separate action. It is printed on a separate page of its own, the symbol and title "Holy Communion" follow the Brief Order, the first rubric of the Holy Communion says that the Brief Order "may be used before this service," and the opening hymn, the Entrance Hymn, is sung following the Brief Order. Moreover, the Notes on the Liturgy not only permit but encourage at least the occasional omission of the Brief Order.

The Brief Order for Confession and Forgiveness may be used before the Holy Communion begins. While it is neither theologically nor liturgically necessary that a congregational act of confession and forgiveness precede the Holy Communion, pastoral discernment may indicate the need for such a practice most of the time. (Min. Ed., p. 26)

This was not an innovation. *Contemporary Worship 2: The Holy Communion* (1970) noted concerning the act of reconciliation, "Occasionally this portion of the service may be omitted,"[204] and the *Common Service Book* and the *Service Book and Hymnal*, while not explicitly saying that the confession may be omitted, directed in the general rubrics, "When The Service begins with the Introit, the Minister shall go immediately to the altar."[205]

In the Roman Catholic and Episcopal orders the penitential rite is integrated into the Eucharist. In the Roman mass the Kyrie can be used as a penitential text;[206] in the *Book of Common Prayer*, the confession is placed between the liturgy of the word and the liturgy of the meal. In the Roman liturgy this is an innovation; in the Prayer Book it is the continuation of the Anglican tradition.

The penitential rites were drafted for the *Lutheran Book of Worship* by Walter R. Bouman, John R. Cochran, and Paul K. Peterson, who chaired the subcommittee.

THE SERVICE IN DETAIL

The rite begins with the invocation (and the sign of the cross) as a reminder of the baptismal covenant to which this rite marks a return. The words and the cross together are a sign of endurance and victory in suffering (Rom. 8:31–39), a sign confessing that one's faith, justification, righteousness, and salvation are all gifts of God and not of one's own doing (Gal. 6:14).

The prayer for purity (no. 236) is a late Gregorian collect found in the eleventh-century Leofric missal and in the Sarum missal as the Prayer

---

[204] *Contemporary Worship 2: The Holy Communion*, 8.

[205] *Common Service Book*, text ed., p. 485; *Service Book and Hymnal*, p. 274.

[206] "A common penitential rite in the eucharistic liturgy is absolutely an innovation of the Missal of Paul VI." John F. Baldovin, "Kyrie Eleison and the Entrance Rite of the Roman Eucharist," *Worship* 60 (1986), 335. See also pp. 345–347.

of the Day for a mass of the Holy Spirit; in the Sarum rite it was also used as a prayer by the priest as part of his preparation for mass. It passed into the *Book of Common Prayer*, where it continues to be used at the beginning of the Eucharist (pp. 323, 355), and from there it was taken into the *Church Book* and the Common Service for the Order for Public Confession.

The two sentences that follow the prayer are from 1 John 1:8–9, slightly altered from the Revised Standard Version and the translation in the *Book of Common Prayer*, in which they are the second of three "sentences" provided for optional use in the Penitential Order "for use at the beginning of the Liturgy, or as a separate service." (pp. 319–20, 351–52. The other two sentences are Matthew 12:29–31 and Hebrews 4:14–16.)

Kneeling for the confession was prescribed in the Church Order of Austria (1571).[207] It was permitted by the General Rubrics of the *Common Service Book* (text ed., p. 485) and by a rubric printed in the text of the Service in the *Service Book and Hymnal* (p. 1).

The prayer of confession is a revision of the confession in the Eucharist in the Episcopal Church, and draws upon both the form published in *Services for Trial Use* (1971) and *Authorized Services* (1973), and upon the revised form published in the 1979 *Book of Common Prayer*. Those prayers are based on a form proposed by a British ecumenical organization, the Joint Liturgical Group.[208] That form was in turn a revision of a prayer written by John Hunter in *Devotional Services for Public Worship*[209] and used in John Doberstein's *Minister's Prayer Book*[210] (see p. 100).

The opening of the Lutheran version of the prayer is significant: "...we are in bondage to sin and cannot free ourselves." This clause may seem to contradict the bold declaration of the address in the baptismal service, "In Holy Baptism our gracious heavenly Father liberates us from sin and death...." It is, however, not a contradiction but a useful paradox expressing our condition as forgiven sinners. The clause "we are in bondage to sin" is an attempt to express the doctrine of original sin. By this phrase the congregation expresses and confesses its solidarity with Adam and with the whole human race. The *Church Book* and the Common Service expressed this idea with the phrase "we are by nature sinful and unclean,"[211] language misleading at least. The Epitome of the Formula of Concord, for example, says,

We believe, teach, and confess that there is a distinction between man's nature and original sin, not only in the beginning when God created man pure and holy and without sin, but also as we now have our nature after the Fall. Even after

---

[207]Reed, 259.

[208]*The Daily Office* (London: SPCK, 1968). The text of that prayer is in Hatchett, 343.

[209]John Hunter, *Devotional Services for Public Worship* (London: Dent, 1901), 52.

[210]John Doberstein, *Minister's Prayer Book* (Philadelphia: Muhlenberg Press, 1959), 18–19, no. 35.

[211]*Church Book*, p. 2; *Common Service Book*, text ed., pp. 7–8; *Service Book and Hymnal*, pp. 1, 16, 42.

Hunter, Devotional Services	Services for Trial Use	Book of Common Prayer	Lutheran Book of Worship
Almighty and most merciful God, we acknowledge and confess that	Most merciful God, we confess that	Most merciful God, we confess that	Most merciful God, we confess that we are in bondage to sin and cannot free ourselves.
we have sinned against thee in thought, word and deed;	we have sinned against you in thought, word and deed:	we have sinned against you in thought, word, and deed, by what we have done and by what we have left undone.	We have sinned against you in thought, word, and deed, by what we have done and by what we have left undone.
that we have not loved thee with all our heart and soul, with all our mind and strength; and that we have not loved our neighbor as ourselves. We beseech	we have not loved you with our whole heart; we have not loved our neighbors as ourselves. We pray	We have not loved you with our whole heart; we have not loved our neighbors as ourselves. We are truly sorry and we humbly repent. For the sake of your Son Jesus Christ, have mercy on us and forgive us;	We have not loved you with our whole heart; we have not loved our neighbors as ourselves. For the sake of your Son, Jesus Christ, have mercy on us. Forgive us,
thee, O God, to be forgiving to what we have been, to help us to amend what we are, and of thy mercy to direct what we shall be, so that the love of goodness may ever be first in our hearts, that we may always walk in thy commandments and ordinances blameless, and follow unto our life's end in the footsteps of Jesus Christ our Lord.	you of your mercy forgive what we have been, amend what we are, direct what we shall be; that we may delight in your will, and walk in your ways, through Jesus Christ our Lord. (p. 63)	that we may delight in your will and walk in your ways, to the glory of your Name. (p. 353)	renew us, and lead us, so that we may delight in your will and walk in your ways, to the glory of your holy name. (Min. Ed., p. 195)

100

the Fall our nature is and remains a creature of God. The distinction between our nature and original sin is as great as the difference between God's work and the devil's work.[212]

Jesus declares, "Everyone who commits sin is a slave to sin" (John 8:34). St. Paul, in his agonized confession, describes what it means to be in bondage to sin and be unable to free himself:

I am carnal, sold under sin. . . . I do not do what I want, but I do the very thing I hate. . . . I can will what is right, but I cannot do it. For I do not do the good I want, but the evil I do not want is what I do. Now if I do what I do not want, it is no longer I that do it, but is which dwells within me. (Rom. 7:14–20)

He has previously said (6:22), "You have been set free from sin," yet he still experiences the effects of sin in himself. It is the now/not yet of biblical eschatology: here yet still anticipated, inaugurated but not yet consummated. The future has broken into the present, hope has entered our history. The outcome is assured, so we may have confidence; but the warfare continues until the last day. Luther's term for this now/not yet (which be borrowed from Augustine) was *simul justus et peccator:* we are at the same time justified and sinful.[213] Sin persists in the life of the redeemed, and sanctification remains a lifelong struggle of daily dying and daily rising.

Indeed, it is the "justified" person, the one who has been incorporated into the divine fellowship, who understands with increasing clarity that he is still a sinner.[214]

The liberation which baptism makes available is real and effective, but it does not remove the necessity of death, nor does it remove our hereditary sin of being turned away from God and turned inward toward ourselves.[215] Moreover, not to be overlooked in the reference to bondage are the experiences of Israel in Egypt and in exile. Like ancient Israel, the church is entirely dependent upon God's act of deliverance; unaided escape is not possible. The latter half of the phrase, "we . . . cannot free ourselves," recalls the exhortation to communicants from the *Common Service Book,* "we . . . find in us nothing but sin and death from which we can in no wise set ourselves free."[216] We are dependent entirely upon God's mercy.

The confession acknowledges complicity in all manner of evil — active sins of commission, "what we have done" in thought, word, and deed; and the passive sins of omission, "what we have left undone" in thought, word, and deed. The confession acknowledges having broken

---

[212] Epitome I.1, *Book of Concord,* 466.
[213] See, for example, Luther's Lectures on Galatians (1535), *Luther's Works* 26:232; and his lectures on Galatians (1519), *Luther's Works* 27:231.
[214] Aulén, 168; see also Luther, "The Bondage of the Will," *Luther's Works* 33:130.
[215] Smalkald Articles III.1 in the *Book of Concord,* 510. See Walter R. Bouman, "Bondage?" *The Lutheran Standard* (January 8, 1980), 8–10.
[216] *Common Service Book,* text ed., p. 405.

both of the commandments — to love God with all one's being and to love one's neighbor as oneself (Matt. 22:34–40; Mark 12:28–31; Luke 10:25–28; Micah 6:8) — by which Jesus answered the lawyer's question, "Which is the great commandment in the law?" The prayer asks a three-fold renovation by which God will forgive what is past, renew the being of each one who prays, and lead those so renewed in a life of faithfulness and service. The renovation which is prayed for is such a complete dying and being reborn that obedience to God's will may no longer be an onerous duty but a delight (Ps. 1:2). Behind the prayer lies the thought of Luther's explanation of the Ten Commandments in the Small Catechism: we should so fear and love God that keeping the commandments comes naturally. Commandments two through ten then become examples of how one lives who fears, loves, and trusts in God above all things.

Two forms of absolution are provided in the Brief Order to accommodate the desires of the varied constituencies of the Lutheran Church in North America, some desiring a strong priestly indicative statement of absolution, following the medieval tradition which Lutheranism inherited, and others seeking a less judicial form which proclaimed God's forgiving nature, as in the earliest known forms of absolution. The two forms also preserve two valid Lutheran traditions: the priestly absolution form of *The Lutheran Hymnal* and the declarative statement of the *Service Book and Hymnal* and its predecessor books.

The first form, "I declare to you the entire forgiveness of all your sins," is perhaps a bit too full and powerful for regular use every week without vitiating its strength, and perhaps ought to be reserved for penitential days and those times when a particular sin weighs heavily on the community and the need for release is evident. This first form of absolution is from Corporate Confession and Forgiveness with the second sentence (1 Peter 2:9) deleted. The formula derives from the declaration of grace at the beginning of the Common Service and the absolution in the Order for Public Confession in the Common Service[217] with the interpolation of "called and ordained" taken from *The Lutheran Hymnal*.

The second form of absolution, the declaration of grace, is no less powerful and forceful — "God forgives you all your sins" — but emphasizes the continuing struggle to make the life of Christ evident in

---

[217]Order for Public Confession in the *Common Service Book*, text ed., p. 407: "Almighty God, our Heavenly Father, hath had mercy upon us, and for the sake of the sufferings, death, and resurrection of His dear Son, Jesus Christ, our Lord, forgiveth us all our sins. As a Minister of the Church of Christ, and by His authority, I therefore declare unto you who do truly repent and believe in Him, the entire forgiveness of all your sins: In the Name of the Father, and of the Son, and of the Holy Ghost." The text was retained in the *Service Book and Hymnal*, p. 252.

The Declaration of Grace at the beginning of the Service began, "Almighty God, our Heavenly Father, hath had mercy upon us, and hath given His Only Son to die for us, and for His sake forgiveth us all our sins. To them that believe on His Name, He giveth power to become the sons of God, and bestoweth upon them His Holy Spirit." (*Church Book*; *Common Service Book*; *Service Book and Hymnal*.)

the lives of those who believe in him. It is a more active statement, urging renewed commitment and growth in grace. This second form is a revision of the declaration of grace, based on John 1:12 (see also Rom. 8:16, 21; Gal. 3:26; Eph. 1:19; 3:20), which was used at the beginning of the service in the *Church Book* and the Common Service,[218] rendered in the second person, for the speaker — the presiding minister — is an ordained representative of the church.

Common Service	*Lutheran Book of Worship*
Almighty God, our Heavenly Father, hath had mercy upon us, and hath given his only Son to die for us, and for His sake forgiveth us all our sins. To them that believe on His Name, He giveth power to become the sons of God, and bestoweth upon them His Holy Spirit. He that believeth and is baptized shall be saved. Grant this, O Lord, unto us all.	In the mercy of almighty God, Jesus Christ was given to die for you, and for his sake God forgives you all your sins. To those who believe in Jesus Christ he gives the power to become the children of God and bestows on them the Holy Spirit.

The text derives from Melanchthon's order for Mecklenburg (1552) as later adopted in Wittenberg (1559).[219]

The absolution formula is to be said by an ordained minister only, but to require that is not clericalistic. Of course laypeople can announce and declare God's forgiveness to one another, but not in the context of services of the church. One of the pastor's jobs is to represent the church in speaking the absolution in connection with "the third sacrament,"[220] and "the called and ordained" phrase reminds both pastor and congregation that the pastor's authority to do so derives from Christ through the church. It is not spoken as a boast ("I'm ordained, and you're not") but as a reminder of the pastor's subservient role.

---

[218] *Church Book*, pp. 2–3; *Common Service Book*, text ed., p. 8; *Service Book and Hymnal*, p. 1.

[219] Reed, 258.

[220] Apology of the Augsburg Confession XI, *Book of Concord*, 180ff.

Table I
DEVELOPMENT OF THE RITE

Common Service	Service Book and Hymnal	Lutheran Book of Worship
	Brief Order	
Invocation	Invocation	Invocation
Invitation		
Versicles	Collect for purity (Psalm 51)	Prayer for purity
		1 John 1:8–9
Confession	Confession	Confession
Declaration of grace	Absolution	Absolution or Declaration of grace

Table II
COMPARISON OF RITES

Roman Catholic*	Lutheran Book of Worship	Book of Common Prayer
		Penitential Order
Entrance Song		
Invocation	Invocation	Verse & response
Greeting		
		(Decalogue)
	Prayer for purity	
		Matt. 22:37–40
	1 John 1:8–9	1 John 1:8–9
		Heb. 4:14, 16
Invitation		
Confession	Confession	Confession
Absolution	Absolution	Absolution
	Entrance Hymn	
	Apostolic Greeting	
Kyrie & Gloria	Kyrie/Hymn of Praise	Gloria/Kyrie/Trisagion

---

*In the Roman rite the invocation and the absolution are the only fixed texts of the penitential rite; all the rest may be adapted by the priest.

BIBLIOGRAPHY

Baptism and Christian Initiation

Aland, Kurt. *Did the Early Church Baptize Infants?* Translated by G. R. Beasley-Murray. Philadelphia: Westminster Press, 1963.

Baptism, Eucharist, and Ministry. Faith and Order Paper no. 111. Geneva: World Council of Churches, 1982.

Baptism in the New Testament: A Symposium. Translated by D. Askew. London: Geoffrey Chapman, 1964.

Barth, Karl. *The Teaching of the Church Regarding Baptism.* Translated by E. A. Payne. London: SCM, 1948.

Beasley-Murray, G. R. *Baptism in the New Testament.* New York: Macmillan, 1962.

Bedard, Walter M. *The Symbolism of the Baptismal Font in Early Christian Thought.* Washington, D.C.: Catholic University Press, 1951.

Brand, Eugene L. *Baptism: A Pastoral Perspective.* Minneapolis: Augsburg Publishing House, 1975.

———. "Baptism and Communion of Infants: A Lutheran View." *Worship* 50 (1976):29–42.

———, and S. Anita Stauffer. *By Water and the Spirit.* Philadelphia: Parish Life Press, 1979.

Brock, S. "Studies in the Early History of the Syrian Orthodox Baptismal Liturgy." *Journal of Theological Studies* new series XXIII (April 1972):16–64.

Brown, Raymond E. "We Profess One Baptism for the Forgiveness of Sins." *Worship* 40 (1966):260–71.

Cullmann, Oscar. *Baptism in the New Testament.* Translated by J. K. S. Reid. London: SCM, 1950.

Davies, J. G. *The Architectural Setting of Baptism.* London: Barrie and Rockliff, 1962.

Davis, Charles. *Sacraments of Initiation: Baptism and Confirmation.* New York: Sheed and Ward, 1964.

Eliade, Mircea. *Birth and Rebirth: Rites and Symbols of Initiation.* Translated by Willard R. Trask. New York: Harper & Bros., 1958. Published as *Rites and Symbols of Initiation.* New York: Harper & Row, 1965.

———. *Myths, Dreams, and Mysteries.* New York: Harper & Row, 1960.

Ellebracht, Mary Pierre. *The Easter Passage: The RCIA Experience.* Minneapolis: Winston, 1983. [RCIA = (Roman Catholic) Rite of Christian Initiation of Adults]

Fahey, Michael. *Catholic Perspectives on Baptism, Eucharist, and Ministry.* Lanham, MD: University Press of America, 1986.

Fisher, J. C. D. *Christian Initiation: Baptism in the Medieval West.* London: SPCK, 1965.

———. *Christian Initiation: The Reformation Period.* London: SPCK, 1970.

Gros, Geoffrey, ed. "The Search for Visible Unity: Baptism, Eucharist, and Ministry." *Journal of Ecumenical Studies* 21:1 (1984) New York: Pilgrim Press, 1984.

Holeton, David R. *Infant Communion — Then and Now.* Grove Liturgical Study no. 27. Bramcote, Notts.: Grove Books, 1981.

Jagger, Peter J. *Christian Initiation: 1552–1969*. London: SPCK, 1970.

Jeremias, Joachim. *Infant Baptism in the First Four Centuries*. Translated by D. Cairns. Philadelphia: Westminster Press, 1962.

Jones, Cheslyn, Geoffrey Wainwright, and Edward Yarnold, eds. *The Study of Liturgy*. New York: Oxford University Press, 1978. "Initiation," pp. 79–146.

Kartsonis, Anna D. *Anastasis: The Making of an Image*. Princeton: University Press, 1986.

Kavanagh, Aidan. *The Shape of Baptism: The Rite of Christian Initiation*. New York: Pueblo Publishing Co., 1978.

Kelly, J. N. D. *Early Christian Creeds*. London: Longmans, Green, 1950.

Kretschmar, Georg. "Recent Research on Christian Initiation." *Studia Liturgica* 12 (1977):87–103.

Lampe, G. W. H. *The Seal of the Spirit: A Study in the Doctrine of Baptism and Confirmation in the New Testament and the Fathers*. Rev. ed. London: SPCK, 1967.

Limouris, Gennadios, and Nomikos Michael Vaporis, eds. "Orthodox Perspectives on Baptism, Eucharist, and Ministry. *Orthodox Theological Review* 30:2 (Summer 1985), Brookline, MA: Holy Cross Orthodox Press, 1985.

Liturgy. Journal of the Liturgical Conference. 18:7 (August/September 1973); 19:10 (December 1974); 22:1 (January 1977).

Luther, Martin. "The Holy and Blessed Sacrament of Baptism, 1519. Translated by Charles M. Jacobs. *Luther's Works* 35:23. Philadelphia: Muhlenberg Press, 1960.

"Luther, Baptism, and Christian Formation." *The Bulletin* of the Lutheran Theological Seminary at Gettysburg 59:1 (February 1979).

Made, Not Born: New Perspectives on Christian Initiation and the Catechumenate. Edited by the Murphy Center for Liturgical Research. Notre Dame, IN: University Press, 1976.

Marsh, Thomas. *Gift of Community: Baptism and Confirmation*. Wilmington, DE: Michael Glazier, 1984.

Marthaler, Berard L. *The Creed*. Mystic, CT: Twenty-Third Publications, 1986.

Mitchell, Leonel L. "Ambrosian Baptismal Rites." *Studia Liturgica* 1 (December 1962):241–53. See also vol. 4 (Winter 1965).

———. *Baptismal Anointing*. London: SPCK, 1966.

———. "Mozarabic Baptismal Rites." *Studia Liturgica* (Autumn 1964):78–106.

Porter, H. Boone. "Holy Baptism: Its Paschal and Ecumenical Setting," *Response* 13 (Easter 1973):5–11.

Riley, Hugh. *Christian Initiation: A Comparative Study of the Interpretation of the Baptismal Liturgy in the Mystagogical Writings of Cyril of Jerusalem, John Chrysostom, Theodore of Mopsuestia, and Ambrose of Milan*. Washington, D.C.: Catholic University of America Press, 1974.

Schlink, Edmund. *The Doctrine of Baptism*. St. Louis: Concordia Publishing House, 1972.

Schmemann, Alexander. *Of Water and the Spirit*. New York: St. Vladimir's Seminary Press, 1974.

Schnackenburg, Rudolf. *Baptism in the Thought of St. Paul: A Study in Pauline Theology*. Translated by G. R. Beasley-Murray. New York: Herder, 1964.

Searle, Mark. *Christening: The Making of Christians*. Collegeville: Liturgical Press, 1980.

————, ed. *Baptism and Confirmation.* Vol. 2 of Alternative Futures for Worship. Collegeville: Liturgical Press, 1987.

Sedgwick, Timothy F. *Sacramental Ethics: Paschal Identity and the Christian Life.* Philadelphia: Fortress Press, 1987.

Stauffer, S. Anita. "Holy Baptism in the *Lutheran Book of Worship.*" *Currents in Theology and Mission* 13 (December 1986):339–45.

Stevick, Daniel B. "Types of Baptismal Spirituality." *Worship* 47 (January 1973):11–26.

Studia Liturgica 10:1 (1974) and 12:2/3 (1977). Issues on Christian Initiation.

Thurian, Max. *Churches Respond to B.E.M.: Official Responses to the Baptism, Eucharist, and Ministry Text.* Faith and Order Paper no. 129. Geneva: World Council of Churches, 1986.

————, and Geoffrey Wainwright, eds. *Baptism and Eucharist: Ecumenical Convergence in Celebration.* Geneva: World Council of Churches; Grand Rapids: Eerdmans, 1983.

Wainwright, Geoffrey. *Christian Initiation.* Richmond: John Knox, 1969.

————. *The Baptismal Liturgy: An Introduction to Baptism in the Western Church.* London: Faith Press, 1965.

Whitaker, E. C., ed. *Documents of the Baptismal Liturgy.* 2nd ed. London: SPCK, 1970.

Winkler, Gabrielle. "The Original Meaning and Implications of the Prebaptismal Anointing," *Worship* 52 (January 1978):24–45.

Vischer, Lukas. *Ye Are Baptized: A Study of Baptism and Confirmation Liturgies as the Initiation to the Ministry of the Laity.* Geneva: Department on the Laity, World Council of Churches, 1964.

Yarnold, Edward. *The Awe-inspiring Rites of Initiation: Baptismal Homilies of the Fourth Century.* Slough: St. Paul Publications, 1972.

Confirmation

Austin, Gerard. *Anointing with the Spirit: The Rite of Confirmation. The Use of Oil and Chrism.* New York: Pueblo Publishing Co., 1986.

————. "What Has Happened to Confirmation?" *Worship* 50 (1976):420–426.

Dix, Gregory. *The Theology of Confirmation in Relation to Baptism.* London: Dacre, 1946.

Fischer, J. D. C. *Confirmation Then and Now.* Alcuin Club Collections 60. London: Alcuin Club/SPCK, 1978.

Hatchett, Marion J. "'The Rite of Confirmation' in the Book of Common Prayer and in Authorized Services 1973." *Anglican Theological Review* 56 (1974):292–310.

Holmes, Urban T., III. *Confirmation: The Celebration of Maturity in Christ.* New York: Seabury Press, 1975.

Kavanagh, Aidan. "Confirmation: A Suggestion from Structure." *Worship* 58 (1984):386–95.

————. *Confirmation: Its Origins and Reform.* New York: Pueblo Publishing Co., 1988.

Kett, Joseph F. *Rites of Passage: Adolescence in America, 1790 to the Present.* New York: Basic Books, 1977.

Marsh, Thomas. "A Study of Confirmation." *Irish Theological Quarterly* 39 (1972):149–63.

Powers, Joseph M. "Confirmation: the Problem of Meaning." *Worship* 46 (1972):22–29.

Quinn, Frank. "Confirmation Reconsidered: Rite and Meaning." *Worship* 59 (1985):354–70.

Report of the Joint Commission on the Theology and Practice of Confirmation. Minneapolis: Augsburg Publishing House; St. Louis: Concordia Publishing House; Philadelphia: Board of Publication of the Lutheran Church in America, 1970.

Repp, Arthur C. *Confirmation in the Lutheran Church.* St. Louis: Concordia Publishing House, 1964.

Shepherd, Massey H., Jr. "Confirmation: the Early Church." *Worship* 46 (1972): 15–21.

Stevick, Daniel B. "Confirmation Today: Reflections on the Rite Proposed for the Episcopal Church." *Worship* 44 (1970):541–60.

Thornton, L. S. *Confirmation: Its Place in the Baptismal Mystery.* London: Dacre, 1954.

Winkler, Gabrielle. "Confirmation or Chrismation?: A Study in Comparative Liturgy." *Worship* 58 (1984):2–17.

Confession and Forgiveness

Bieler, Ludwig, ed. *The Irish Penitentials.* Dublin: Irish Institute for Advanced Studies, 1963.

Bouman, Walter R. "Bondage?" *The Lutheran Standard* (January 9, 1980):8–10.

———. "Confession and Absolution in the Eucharistic Liturgy." *Lutheran Quarterly* 26 (1974):204–20.

Braswell, Mary Flowers. *The Medieval Sinner: Characterization and Confession in the Literature of the English Middle Ages.* Cranbury, NJ: Fairleigh Dickinson University Press, 1983.

Crichton, J. D. *The Ministry of Reconciliation.* London: Geoffrey Chapman, 1974.

Dallen, James. "The Imposition of Hands in Penance: A Study in Liturgical History." *Worship* 51 (1977):224–47.

———. *The Reconciling Community: The Rite of Penance.* New York: Pueblo Publishing Co., 1986.

Fink, Peter E. *Reconciliation.* Vol. 4 of Alternative Futures for Worship. Collegeville: Liturgical Press, 1987.

Gallen, John. "A Pastoral-Liturgical View of Penance Today." *Worship* 45 (1971):132–50.

Gunstone, J. T. A. *The Liturgy of Penance.* London: Faith Press, 1966.

Hater, Robert J. "Sin and Reconciliation: Changing Attitudes in the Catholic Church." *Worship* 59 (1985):18–31.

Hellwig, Monika. *Sign of Reconciliation and Conversion.* Wilmington, DE: Michael Glazier, 1982.

McNeill, John T. A. *A History of the Cure of Souls.* New York: Harper and Row, 1965.

McNeill, John T., and Helena M. Garner. *Medieval Handbooks of Penance.* New York: Columbia University Press, 1938. Reprint, New York: Octagon Books, 1965.

Oakley, Thomas P. *English Penitential Discipline and Anglo-Saxon Law in Their Joint Influence.* New York: Columbia University Press, 1923. Reprint, New York: AMS Press, 1969.

Palmer, Paul F. *Sacraments and Forgiveness.* Westminster, MD: Newman Press, 1959.

Payer, Pierre J. *Sex and the Penitentials. The Development of a Sexual Code 550–1150.* Toronto: University Press, 1985.

Poschmann, Bernhard. *Penance and the Anointing of the Sick.* New York: Herder and Herder, 1964.

Rahner, Karl. *Allow Yourself to be Forgiven: Penance Today.* Denville, NJ: Dimension Books, 1978.

Senn, Frank C. "Structures of Penance and the Ministry of Reconciliation." *Lutheran Quarterly* 35 (1973):270–283.

Studia Liturgica 18:1 (1988). An issue devoted to penance in contemporary scholarship and practice.

Telfer, W. *The Forgiveness of Sins.* London: SCM, 1959.

Thurian, Max. *Confession.* London: SCM, 1958.

Watkins, Oscar D. *A History of Penance.* 2 vols. New York: Longmans, Green, 1920. Reprint, 1960.

4

HOLY COMMUNION

Ministers Edition, pp. 25–29, 196–307

Parallel Rites

Roman Catholic	*The Roman Missal revised by the decree of the Second Vatican Council.* Promulgated by Paul VI April 3, 1969, published 1970; 2nd ed. 1975. *The Sacramentary.* English translation (ICEL) 1973, 1985.
Episcopal	The Holy Eucharist. *Book of Common Prayer* (1979), pp. 315–409.
Lutheran	The Order of Morning Service. The Holy Communion. *Church Book* (1868), pp. 3–23.
	The Common Service (1888).
	The Service. *Common Service Book* (1917, 2nd rev. ed. 1918), text ed. (1919), pp. 7–25.
	The Order of the Holy Communion. *The Lutheran Hymnal* (1941), pp. 15–31.
	The Service. *Service Book and Hymnal* (1958), pp. 1–70. Text ed. (1967), pp. 1–20.
	Contemporary Worship 2: The Holy Communion (1970).
Orthodox	The Divine Liturgy of St. John Chrysostom, The Divine Liturgy of St. Basil the Great, *Service Book*, pp. 67–126.
Methodist	The Sacrament of the Lord's Supper (1972).
Presbyterian	Service for the Lord's Day, *Worshipbook* (1972), pp. 21–42.
Consultation on Church Union	An Order of Worship for the Proclamation of the Word of God and the Celebration of the Lord's Supper (1968).
Church of South India	An Order for the Lord's Supper or the Holy Eucharist, *Book of Common Worship* (1963), pp. 21–41.

Purpose

In response to Jesus' command when he lay at supper on the night in which he was betrayed — "Do this for my remembrance" — the Christian community since its beginning has regularly gathered to hear the Word of God and to take bread and wine; to recall and give thanks for the Lord's sacrifice of himself for all the world; to receive his gift of himself, his body and blood for forgiveness, life, and salvation; to be joined in intimate communion with him and with one another, those in this world and those in the next, in joyful anticipation of the fulfillment of the kingdom of God.

Characteristics

The Holy Communion in North American Lutheran use has been moving from an infrequent addition to "the Morning Service" (in many early liturgies and agendas it was an "occasional service"[1]) to its rightful position as the central celebration of the Christian community.

Typologically, as Holy Baptism is connected with the passage through the sea from slavery to freedom and death to life, the Holy Communion is connected with the marvelous bread from heaven by which God's people were fed during their time in the wilderness.

The Holy Communion is characterized by a spirit of joyful celebration involving action and movement and is the work of the entire assembly in union with other parts of the Christian community, in which the past is made alive as a contemporary experience and the future is enjoyed proleptically. Through receiving it, a pilgrim people are sustained "until he comes again."

To emphasize the corporate nature of the eucharistic celebration, the chief minister is designated the presiding minister.[2] The presence also of assisting ministers is assumed.

Music is expected in the Lutheran use of the church's liturgy. Although a spoken liturgy is permitted ("Any portion of any service which is set to music may be spoken rather than sung," Min. Ed., p. 13), the Holy Communion is not printed in the *Lutheran Book of Worship* without a musical setting as it was in the *Service Book and Hymnal* (pp. 1ff.) and the text editions of the *Common Service Book* and the *Service Book and Hymnal*.

In the twelfth century, Richard of St. Victor in his *Of the Four Degrees of Passionate Charity* identified four periods of growth in prayer: (1) purgation, (2) illumination, (3) union with God, and (4) service to

---

[1] For example, in the *Book of Worship* of the General Synod South (1867) the Holy Communion is included not with the services for morning and evening but in Section II, The Order of Ministerial Acts. In the 1881 *Liturgy* of the General Synod it is included in Part Second after baptism, confirmation, reception of members, confession and absolution, and sentences for the collection of alms and offerings. It occupies the same place in *Forms for Ministerial Acts* (1900) of the General Synod.

[2] The title has roots as ancient as Justin Martyr's *First Apology*, which uses presidential terminology in describing the leader of the eucharistic celebration (65.3).

one's neighbor in need. These four stages may be seen as having parallels in the movement of the Holy Communion, its preparation, celebration, and effect: (1) confession and absolution, (2) the liturgy of the Word, (3) the liturgy of the Eucharist, (4) ministry in the world. When one is united to God, one lives the life of God, which, as Jesus demonstrated, is a life given to and for humanity. The assembly, having gathered, then disperses into the world to do the reconciling work of God which the church has experienced in Word and sacrament.

THE SERVICE IN DETAIL

There are four musical settings of the Holy Communion in the *Lutheran Book of Worship*. The first setting is a new composition by Richard W. Hillert (1923–). The second setting is by Ronald A. Nelson (1927–), in part a revision of his hymnic setting of the Holy Communion in *Contemporary Worship 2*. The third setting is a revision of the second setting of the Service in the *Service Book and Hymnal*, which was based on the ancient chant setting of the Swedish Mass Book of 1942. The revision includes settings by Gerhard M. Cartford (1923–) of the new texts "Worthy is Christ," "Return to the Lord," "Let the vineyards be fruitful," "What shall I render to the Lord," "Through him, with him, in him," and "Thank the Lord and sing his praise"; it was originally published in *Contemporary Worship 2* as the third setting of that service. The fourth setting (called the "Chorale Service of Holy Communion") is in the tradition of Luther's German Mass in which the ordinary of the mass (Kyrie, Gloria in Excelsis, Creed, Sanctus, Agnus Dei) plus the Gradual and the Post-Communion Canticle are replaced with hymns and metrical paraphrases.

The Entrance Rite

ENTRANCE HYMN. The liturgy may be understood to begin with a kind of procession of individuals from their homes to gather in the assembly of the congregation at the church.[3] At Constantinople, ministers and people went to church together in a grand public processional event, and all entered the church at the same time. (Witness the great number of doors in early Byzantine churches such as Hagia Sophia.)

In the West, when the congregation has gathered, the Holy Communion opens with the entrance of the ministers during the singing of the entrance hymn or psalm. This opening action of entrance and singing corresponds to the Introit in previous Lutheran and Roman Catholic books; there is no comparable element in the Eastern churches' liturgy.

Until the fourth or fifth century the Holy Communion began with the readings from Scripture, but after the legalization of Christianity and the erection of large church buildings, the church could invest its worship

---

[3] Alexander Schmemann, *For the Life of the World: Sacraments and Orthodoxy* (Crestwood, NY: St. Vladimir's Seminary Press, 1973), 27.

with special dignity.[4] The ministers could enter in a formal procession, bearing the Book of the Gospels, often preceded by candles and incense, like civic officers. At the latest, it was Pope Celestine I (422–432) who introduced the antiphonal singing of a psalm by a double choir as the ministers came from the sacristy to the altar.[5] A single verse was selected to highlight a theme of the psalm and was sung by the congregation as an antiphon before and after the psalm and, on festivals, after each verse or group of verses of the psalm. Only as much of the psalm as was needed for the entrance was used. Beginning in the fifth century, the Gloria Patri was added to the psalm to bring it to a conclusion and to signal the first reading. Late in the Middle Ages in the low (spoken) mass the processional psalm was abbreviated to its initial verse, preceded by the antiphon and followed by the Gloria Patri and antiphon. This remnant was known as the Introit. Lutheran use preserved the introits from the medieval church. In older Lutheran and Roman Catholic books the Sundays in Lent and after Easter took their names from the first words of the Introit in Latin.

Luther in his *Formula Missae*, while approving the Introits for Sundays and festivals of Christ, expressed his preference for whole psalms.[6] Only one or two German church orders followed his suggestion (Schwäbisch Hall [1526]); the great majority retained the historic Gregorian series whenever there were choirs to sing the Latin texts. Many of the church orders simply refer to the Introits, leaving the texts and music to be supplied from the old choir books (the *Graduale*) or the later evangelical cantionales. The full series with Latin texts and music is given in Johann Spangenberg, *Kirchengesänge lateinisch und deutsch* (1545); Lucas Lossius, *Psalmodia sacra* (1553); Franz Eler, *Cantica sacra* (1588), and the Nuremberg *Officium sacrum* (1664). Some of the church orders attempt to come to terms with the difficulties in introducing a vernacular service. Brandenburg-Nuremberg (1533) directed the pastor to read the Introit when there were no choir boys; Hoya (1573) permits the pastor to sing it. Osnabrück (1652) seems to have been the first church order to omit the Introit.[7] Difficulties in translating the Latin texts into German led many orders to devise a single Introit for each season. The *Church Book* (1868) returned the series of historic Introits to English Lutheran use.

The 1549 *Book of Common Prayer* followed Luther's suggestion and appointed short psalms or a portion of Psalm 119 as the Introit for each

---

[4]See Ralph A. Kiefer, "Our Cluttered Vestibule: The Unreformed Entrance Rite," *Worship* 48 (May 1974):270–77.

[5]*Liber pontificalis*. See *The Study of Liturgy*, ed. Cheslyn Jones, Geoffrey Wainwright, and Edward Yarnold (New York: Oxford University Press, 1978), 182.

[6]*Luther's Works* 53:22. In the twentieth century, Luther Reed said the same of the Introit: "A historic reconstruction of its full body and earliest use would help to a better understanding of its function and value in our services today." *Lutheran Liturgy*, rev. ed. (Philadelphia: Fortress Press, 1960), 262.

[7]Reed, 265.

Sunday and festival, but the revision of 1552 and all subsequent Prayer Books omitted the Introit entirely.

In the *Deutsche Messe* (1526) Luther moved toward a more congregational form of song: "To begin the service we sing a hymn or a German Psalm in the First Tone...."[8] In towns and villages when there were no adequate choirs, vernacular hymns of the season were regularly substituted for the Introit.

The *Lutheran Book of Worship* returns to Luther's suggestion and directs the singing of the entrance hymn or psalm. The Notes on the Liturgy (Min. Ed., p. 27, #4) permit the substitution of "a classic introit or an entire psalm" for the entrance hymn.

"Late in the nineteenth century a practice without precedent was accepted in many Anglican churches — the choir entered with the clergy in procession during the entrance song."[9] The practice spread to Lutheran congregations and throughout the Protestant churches. The Notes on the Liturgy attempt to discourage the practice as a regular weekly custom.

The Roman rite of 1969 begins with an entrance hymn or, if there is no singing, with the entrance antiphon, a relic of the old Introit (which was itself a relic of an entire psalm). The entrance antiphon serves the useful function of announcing the theme of the day (at least for those Sundays which may be said to have a central theme). Then, at the insistence of Paul VI, follows the formula "In the name of the Father, and of the Son, and of the Holy Spirit."

APOSTOLIC GREETING. The initial liturgical text of the Holy Communion is the Apostolic Greeting, from 2 Corinthians 13:14. (The translation "*our* Lord Jesus Christ" is from the Roman rite.) It was printed as a prayer and doxology, not a benediction,[10] at the conclusion of the Litany in the 1559 *Book of Common Prayer* and was added to Morning and Evening Prayer in 1662. From there it was taken into Lutheran use to conclude Matins and Vespers in the 1891 *Church Book*.

Older liturgical use, however, testified in the *Apostolic Constitutions* (8.2.5), had transformed the verse into a greeting: In the liturgy of St. John Chrysostom it is used at the beginning of the preface dialogue in the Great Thanksgiving. In the Roman sacramentary of 1969 it follows the entrance song as one of three options with which the celebrant greets the people.[11] In the *Lutheran Book of Worship* the verse is to be understood not as a blessing but as a trinitarian doxology and prayerful greeting. The sign of the cross is therefore inappropriate in connection with this use.

---

[8] *Luther's Works* 53:69.

[9] Marion J. Hatchett, *Commentary on the American Prayer Book* (New York: Seabury Press, 1980), 317.

[10] Massey H. Shepherd, Jr., *The Oxford American Prayer Book Commentary* (New York: Oxford University Press, 1950), 20.

[11] The others are "The grace and peace of God our Father and the Lord Jesus Christ be with you" and the familiar "The Lord be with you." The response to each is "And also with you."

The fullest and most elaborate of all Pauline closings, this three-fold doxology summarizes the Christian experience out of which the later formal doctrine of the Trinity developed. The grace of Christ leads to the love of the Father, which yields participation in the Spirit and produces communion between God and his people.[12] It is thus a summary of the principal gifts of the three persons of the Holy Trinity[13] which will be unfolded as the liturgy progresses. Like an overture to an opera, this verse of apostolic greeting introduces the themes which will be developed as the work proceeds and by this statement prepares the assembly for what follows, alerting them to the significant themes.

KYRIE. Until the end of the fourth century the Eucharist began with a silent entrance and a simple greeting followed by the readings.[14] As the entrance procession was elaborated to suit public celebrations of the liturgy in large public buildings (no longer private, even secret, meetings in private houses), litanies and canticles, often from the daily office, were sung, followed by a prayer. The action points of the liturgy are most subject to ritual expansion, as may be seen in the ceremonies of gathering and presenting the offering in many Protestant traditions.

Kyrie eleison was a widespread secular and religious shout throughout the ancient world. It was a cry of Persian and Egyptian sunworshipers and an acclamation used at the approach of an emperor.[15] It was a shout of praise resembling the Hebrew *hosanna* ("save now"), a cry for favor and help rather than a petition for forgiveness. The pagan uses persisted; in the fifth century a preacher in Alexandria found it necessary to denounce the custom still observed by some Christians of bowing to the rising sun and crying *Kyrie eleison*. The pervasive popular use of this cry of acclamation and petition made it nearly inevitable that it would be drawn into the Christian liturgy, for the phrase can be found in Scripture.[16] It has been explained as

the most comprehensive and most expressive of all prayers.... To beg God's mercy is to ask for the coming of His kingdom, that kingdom which Christ promised to give to those who seek it, assuring them that all other things will be added (Matthew 6:33). Because of this, it is a perfect example of a universal petition.[17]

---

[12] *The New Oxford Annotated Bible with the Apocrypha*, expanded ed., Revised Standard Version (New York: Oxford University Press, 1977), 1409.

[13] Hatchett, 132. On the foundational character of grace see Franz Josef van Beeck, *Grounded in Love: Sacramental Theology in an Ecumenical Perspective* (Lanham, MD: University Press of America, 1981).

[14] Augustine, *City of God* 22.8.22; John Chrysostom, *Sermon on Matthew* 12.6.

[15] Franz Dölger, *Sol Salutis, Gebet und Gesang im christlichen Alterum*, Liturgiewissenschaftliche Quellen und Forschungen 4/5 (Münster in Westf., 1925), 77–82; Reed, 268; Hatchett, 319.

[16] Ps. 25:16; 26:11; 41:4; 51:1; 123:3; Matt. 9:27; 15:22; Mark 10:47; Luke 17:13; 18:38; Tob. 8:10; Jth. 7:20.

[17] *The Liturgy of St. John Chrysostom* with commentary by Basil Shereghy (Collegeville: Liturgical Press, 1961), 14–15.

At first a cry of acclamation, the Kyrie revealed in its Christian context a rich depth of meaning.

In the fourth century in the East the Kyrie became the people's response to the petitions of a litany led by a deacon.[18] Egeria reports hearing it as the people's response to the petitions at the close of Vespers.[19] It later appeared in the Greek Clementine Liturgy and the liturgies of St. James (Jerusalem), St. Mark (Alexandria), and St. John Chrysostom (Constantinople). In these instances, it was used, at the beginning of the liturgy and after the Gospel, in the form of an *ektene*, a deacon's litany in which the people repeated *Kyrie eleison* a number of times in a row at the conclusion of the last petition, and associated in Constantinople originally with outdoor processions. These litanies spread to the West in the fifth century. During the pontificate of Gelasius I (492–96), who was responsible for several changes in the Roman liturgy, such a litany was introduced, the so-called *deprecatio Gelasii*, at the beginning of the mass before the readings.[20] Both the petitions and the responses (*Domine, exaudi et miserere*) were in Latin. In the Ambrosian liturgy still there is a litany between the Introit and the Collect, with the responses in Latin.

The first appearance of *Kyrie eleison* in the West seems to have been in the first half of the fifth century in the Ambrosian rite in the *Litania divinae pacis*, where it was repeated three times at the end of the litany. The repeated *Kyrie eleison* seems to have been treated as a separable element which sometimes was used alone. The sixth-century *Rule* of St. Benedict (9 and 17) makes reference to a litany at Lauds and Vespers, and a three-fold Kyrie was used before the Lord's Prayer at the other hours. During the time of Gregory I (590–604), the use of the litany in the mass was eliminated on certain days and was replaced by an independent chant repeated nine times as nine precatory acclamations.[21] The three middle acclamations were changed to *Christe eleison*, giving the nine-fold text a Trinitarian appearance, although in fact the whole prayer is addressed to Christ the Lord. By the eighth century this use of acclamations had become the practice at all masses (*Ordo Romanus IV*). The litany had disappeared, and the acclamations, freed from their original context, took on penitential overtones as a plea for forgiveness. They remain so in the Missal of Paul VI (1969).

By the ninth and tenth centuries elaborate musical settings led to the development of "farsed" or troped Kyries, which were filled out with

---

[18] *Apostolic Constitutions* 8.6.

[19] *Egeria's Travels* 24.5, 6.

[20] The text of this litany is given in Josef Jungmann, *The Mass of the Roman Rite*, rev. Charles K. Riepe (New York: Benziger, 1959), 224–36. See John F. Baldovin, "Kyrie Eleison and the Entrance Rite of the Roman Eucharist," *Worship* 60 (July 1986):334–47.

[21] For the origin of this phrase see W. Jardine Grisbrooke, "Kyrie," *The New Westminster Dictionary of Liturgy and Worship*, ed. J. G. Davies (Philadelphia: Westminster Press, 1986), and *Prayers We Have in Common*, 2nd rev. ed. (Philadelphia: Fortress Press, 1975), 10.

additional words or paraphrased.[22] A body of sacred pre-Reformation German folk hymns called *Leisen* concluded each stanza with *Kyrie eleison*, often contracted to *Kyrieleis*. In these Hymns this was not so much a petition for forgiveness as a prayer for strength or even an exultant cry to a conqueror, equivalent to the Hebrew shout *Hosanna*. The *Leisen* were sung on pilgrimages, in processions, and occasionally during the mass; later in the Middle Ages certain of them were sung by the congregation in the vernacular in alternation with the choir singing in Latin. "Kyrie, Gott Vater in Ewigkeit" (*Lutheran Book of Worship* hymn 168) is an example of a trope turned into a hymn. The earliest of the *Leisen* may be the twelfth century (or earlier) "Christ Is Arisen" (hymn 136); other *Leisen* are "All Praise to You, Eternal Lord" (hymn 48) and "To God the Holy Spirit Let Us Pray" (hymn 317).

The Kyrie was the first of the five texts (Kyrie, Gloria in Excelsis, Creed, Sanctus, and Agnus Dei) comprising the countless musical masses of later centuries.

Luther's *Formula Missae* accepted the Kyrie Eleison "in the form in which it has been used until now"[23]; the German mass reduced it to a three-fold form, but retaining the Greek. So it has remained in German liturgies. (See, for example, the *Kirchenbuch*, 1877.) The more elaborate nine-fold musical settings of the Kyrie continued in many places, especially on festivals (Wittenberg [1533]).[24] Later German church orders alternated Greek and German texts (as, for example, in the *Kirchenbuch*, 1877). The minister intoned "Kyrie eleison," and the congregation responded, "Herr, erbarm Dich unser." Some orders required the Kyrie to be sung in Greek, Latin, and German (Prussia [1525]; Riga [1531]; Brandenburg [1540]; Pomerania [1563]). Occasionally, the Kyrie, no longer understood as an acclamation, was combined with the confession (Naumburg [1537]; Sweden [1541]; *Liturgie und Agenda* [New York, 1857]).

The Kyrie was originally an acclamation, and then it became a response in a litany. The *Service Book and Hymnal* (1958) suggested both historic uses by preserving the six-fold Kyrie of the Common Service (although as an alternate use) —

> Lord, have mercy upon us. *Lord, have mercy upon us.*
> Christ, have mercy upon us. *Christ have mercy upon us.*
> Lord, have mercy upon us. *Lord, have mercy upon us.*

— and by restoring a brief litany of petition and intercession as the first prayer of the service. A litany form of the general intercessions had been

---

[22]The earliest evidence for such a practice is found in Amalarius of Metz (ca. 780–850), *De ecclesiasticis officiis* 3.6. Willi Apel, in *Gregorian Chant* (Bloomington: University of Indiana Press, 1958), 431, cites Ekkehard IV of St. Gall (ca. 980–1060) who attributed the trope *Kyrie fons bonitatis* to a monk of the monastery, Tuotilo (d. 913).

[23]*Luther's Works* 53:23.

[24]Reed, 271.

provided in the 1948 liturgy for the Rhineland and Westphalia and elsewhere, and the *Common Service Book* had permitted a congregational response "We beseech Thee to hear us, good Lord" after each paragraph of the General Prayer of intercession. The source of the five petitions in the newly-devised Kyrie was the Litany of Peace or the Great Litany at the beginning of the enarxis of the Byzantine Liturgy. This Eastern *synapte*[25] has twelve petitions; the *Service Book and Hymnal* used the first four and the one prior to the concluding commemoration of the saint. The introduction of this litany proved popular and durable in Lutheran use and was retained in the *Lutheran Book of Worship*. (It had not been included in the 1972 *Contemporary Worship 2: The Holy Communion* but was returned by popular demand.) The option of a three-(or six- or nine-)fold Kyrie in the medieval manner was not continued, for, outside of the Missouri Synod, congregations had generally abandoned its use in favor of the litany.

The grace of the Apostolic Greeting leads to the Kyrie's prayer for peace. In his epistles, St. Paul frequently joins the two and wishes grace and peace for those to whom he writes (Rom. 1:7; 1 Cor. 1:3; et al.). When grace, understood as the undeserved favor of God, is felt in one's inmost being, the result is peace of spirit and conscience (Col. 3:15) and a secure enjoyment of the love of God (Rom. 5:1, 8:6), which will be perfected in heaven beyond the reach of all enemies. A favorite prayer in the liturgy has been the collect for peace at the conclusion of Vespers, which gives voice to similar sentiments. The root meaning of the Hebrew *shalom* is wholeness and well-being, the proper condition for humanity, the ideal state of life in all its manifold relationships. It is in this sense and in this spirit that the Kyrie litany in the entrance rite prays for peace.

The Byzantine Great Litany	Service Book and Hymnal	Lutheran Book of Worship
In peace let us pray to the Lord. *Lord, have mercy.*	In peace let us pray to the Lord *Lord, have mercy.*	In peace let us pray to the Lord. *Lord, have mercy.*
For the peace that is from above, and for the salvation of our souls, let us pray to the Lord. *Lord, have mercy.*	For the peace that is from above, and for the salvation of our souls, let us pray to the Lord. *Lord, have mercy.*	For the peace from above, and for our salvation, let us pray to the Lord. *Lord, have mercy.*
For the peace of the	For the peace of the	For the peace of the

[25]In the Byzantine rite the *synapte* ("linked together" or "series") form is a series of biddings by the deacon to the congregation to which the congregation responds *Kyrie eleison;* the series is concluded with a prayer by the priest. In the *ektene* or "insistent" litany the deacon's bids are direct petitions to God, not bids to pray, intercessory verbs are multiplied at the end of each prayer, and the people repeat *Kyrie eleison* a number of times at the end of the last petition.

whole world; for the
welfare of God's
holy Churches, and
for the union of all,
let us pray to the Lord.
Lord, have mercy.

For this holy Temple,
and for those who
with faith, devoutness,
and in the fear
of God have entered
therein,
let us pray
to the Lord.
Lord, have mercy.

for our Most Holy
Synod; for our
Bishop, N.; for the
honorable Presbytery,
the Diaconate in
Christ; for all the
clergy and the laity,
let us pray to the Lord.
Lord, have mercy.

[petitions for those
in civil authority]

That he will aid them
and subdue under
their feet every
foe and adversary,
let us pray to the Lord.
Lord, have mercy.
For this city, for
this holy Temple,
and for every city
and land, and for
those who with faith
dwell therein, let
us pray to the Lord.
Lord, have mercy.

For healthful seasons;
for abundance of the
fruits of the earth,
and for peaceful times
let us pray to the Lord.
Lord, have mercy.

for those who travel

whole world, for the
well-being of the
churches of God, and
for the unity of all,
let us pray to the Lord.
Lord, have mercy.

For this holy house,
and for them that
in faith, piety
and fear
of God offer here
their worship and
praise, let us pray
to the Lord.
Lord, have mercy.

whole world, for the
well-being of the
Church of God, and
for the unity of all,
let us pray to the Lord.
Lord, have mercy.

For this holy house,
and for all who

    offer here
their worship and
praise, let us pray
to the Lord.
Lord, have mercy.

by sea or by land; for
the sick and the
suffering; for those
who are in captivity,
and for their salvation,
let us pray to the Lord.
Lord, have mercy.

That he will deliver us
from all tribulation,
wrath, and necessity,
let us pray to the Lord.
Lord, have mercy.

Succor us, save us,	Help, save,	Help, save,
have mercy upon us,	pity, and	comfort, and
and keep us, O God,	defend us, O God,	defend us,
by thy grace.	by thy grace.	gracious Lord.
Lord, have mercy.	*Amen.*	*Amen.*
(*Service Book*, pp. 80–81)	(p. 2)	(pp. 57–58)

The first petition of the Kyrie reminds the worshiper that peace is a requirement for genuine worship.[26]

Surrounded, protected, and comforted by this peace, the next three petitions then locate the peace which is asked. First it comes as a gift from God, who is the source of peace (Judg. 6:24; John 14:27; Phil. 4:7), and it involves our salvation.[27] Peace, the removal of estrangement, and the creation of a new relationship (which is really the restoration of the original divinely-intended relationship of paradise) is the essence of the Gospel; it is almost synonymous with eternal life. Salvation in the Old Testament has the root meaning of entering into a spacious place, free from confinement and restriction to grow without hindrance. It came to have the meaning of victory in battle (1 Sam. 14:45), the victor being the people's savior whom God had raised up (Judg. 2:18, 6:14; Exod. 14:30; 1 Sam. 10:19). Those in need of salvation are the oppressed or threatened, and their salvation consists of deliverance from danger and tyranny, their rescue from imminent peril (1 Sam. 4:3, 7:8, 9:16). The last of the servant songs (Isa. 53) suggests that the saving work is carried out through suffering. Moreover, to save someone is to give that person one's own prevailing strength (Job 26:2) and the power to maintain that necessary strength. It is therefore preeminently the work of God (Ps. 3:8, 47:9, 62:11; 1 Sam. 14:39; 1 Chron. 16:35). In the synoptic gospels the purpose of Jesus' ministry is to seek those who are lost (Luke 19:10) and to save his people from their sins (Matt. 1:21). The gospel can be summarized

---

[26]Acts 10:36; Rom. 5:1; 8:6; 15:33; Eph. 6:15; Phil. 4:7, 9; Col. 1:20; 1 Thess. 5:23.

[27]Isa. 26:12; 49:22–26; 53:5; 54:11–17; 57:19; 60:12–17; Jer. 33:8–14; Zech. 8:16–19; Ps. 29:11; 72:7; 85:8; 119:165; Lev. 26:6; 1 Kings 2:33.

and comprehended as the saving power of God at work in the world (Rom. 1:16).[28]

The third petition acknowledges that peace is needed on earth in a three-fold way — in the whole world (Matt. 5:9), in the church (Mark 9:50; Eph. 4:3), and in the uniting of all the people of the earth — for peace is the restoration of harmony to the whole creation (Col. 1:19–22, 3:15; Heb. 12:14; Rom. 12:18–19; Matt. 5:38–48; Luke 6:27–36).

The fourth petition asks for peace among those in the present congregation (Rom. 4:19; 1 Cor. 14:33; 2 Cor. 13:11; 1 Thess. 5:13; Mark 9:50; Heb. 12:14; 2 Tim. 2:22).

The final petition summarizes the gifts which this peace brings: help, salvation, comfort, and defense against all enemies (Phil. 4:7). Peace is the way along which God's people are to walk (Luke 1:79; Rom. 14:19; 2 Tim. 2:22), the message of the gospel (Eph. 2:17; Phil 6:15), God's gift to humanity (Luke 2:14; 12:51; John 14:27), the name of the Messiah (Isa. 9:6; Eph. 2:14), and the sign of the messianic kingdom (Luke 19:38).

The Notes on the Liturgy (Min. Ed., p. 27, #6) permit the occasional substitution of "Kyrie! God, Father in Heav'n Above" (hymn 168) or "Your Heart, O God, Is Grieved, We Know" (hymn 96) for the Kyrie, thus preserving the medieval practice of farsing the Kyrie.

The Kyrie is an optional element in the Holy Communion in the *Lutheran Book of Worship*. It is not intended that it be used invariably at every service throughout the year. The entrance rite had become cluttered by accretions through the Middle Ages, and it has been the intention of each of the Western liturgical churches (Roman, Episcopal, Lutheran) to simplify the entrance. (See the Notes on the Liturgy, Min. Ed., p. 27, #6.)

HYMN OF PRAISE. In the liturgies of St. Basil and St. John Chrysostom, the entrance is separated from the Trisagion by variable hymns. The Gallican church, influenced by the East, included a canticle after the entrance at all masses.[29] As the Kyrie was imported to the Holy Communion in part from the daily office, so the Hymn of Praise was brought in from the same source.

GLORIA IN EXCELSIS. The Gloria in Excelsis is called the greater doxology or the greater Gloria (in distinction from the lesser doxology, the Gloria Patri) and is called the angelic hymn (*hymnus angelicus, laus angelorum, laus* or *hymnus angeli cum carmine*).[30] The hymn is alluded to in the treatise *De virginitate*, attributed to Athanasius. There are three principal versions of the early text: (1) the Syrian, from Nestorian liturgies; (2) the Greek from the *Apostolic Constitutions* 7.47 (ca. 380); and

---

[28] F. J. Taylor has suggested that the phrase "God saves" or "God is salvation" could "almost be likened to a primitive creed." ("Save, Salvation," *Theological Word Book of the Bible*, ed. Alan Richardson [New York: Macmillan, 1958].)

[29] Hatchett, 321.

[30] See Luther in his *Formula Missae* (*Luther's Works* 53:23). Luther Reed (*Lutheran Liturgy*, 273) reports, without citation, Luther's remark that the Gloria "did not grow, nor was it made on earth, but it came down from heaven."

(3) the Greek from the Byzantine liturgy, which is closest to the Western text. It is found with the title "Morning Hymn" among the canticles at the end of the Psalter in the Codex Alexandrinus (fifth century). The Latin text dates from the Antiphonary of Bangor (ca. 690) and is a literal translation of the Greek text in the Codex Alexandrinus. The hymn was used at Morning Prayer and also at Vespers. The first complete version of the text in use until 1969 is found in the ninth-century Psalter of Abbot Wolfcoz of St. Gall.

The text of the Gloria in Excelsis used in the *Lutheran Book of Worship* (and the Roman sacramentary, the *Book of Common Prayer*, and elsewhere) is in the translation by the International Consultation on English Texts, which has transposed certain lines and phrases to enhance their clarity and omits others to avoid unnecessary redundancy. It was reasoned that "since it is not a dogmatic text, such as the creeds, a modern vernacular version may adapt its pattern to hymn structures that are more readily understood in English, without any basic modification of its substance and spirit."[31]

Like the evening hymn Phos Hilaron ("Joyous light of glory"), the "morning hymn" Gloria in Excelsis is an example of the *psalmi idiotici* (private psalms), popular non-rhythmic hymns in imitation of the biblical psalms and canticles.

The Gloria in Excelsis has been used at Morning Prayer since the fourth century — it still remains in the Byzantine *Orthros* — and was most popular. Indeed, its great popularity enabled it to withstand the ban of the fourth Council of Toledo (633) on church hymns created "by merely human endeavor" and contributed therefore to the explanation that it was not a human composition but the song of the angels. The Rule of Caesarius of Arles (d. 542) appointed it for Matins until the spread of the Roman liturgy. According to the *Liber Pontificalis*, it was first used at a mass at Christmas midnight by Pope Telesophorus (d. 136). Pope Symmachus (498–514) introduced the custom of including the Gloria in Excelsis on festivals of martyrs at masses celebrated by the pope or bishops (because the bishop is a shepherd of the church or is a messenger, angel, to the church). In the Gregorian sacramentary the Gloria in Excelsis was placed after the Kyrie on Sundays (except in Advent and Lent) and on certain feast days. In the seventh century priests were permitted to intone the Gloria but only at the Easter Vigil mass. The ninth-century Ordo of St. Amand permitted a priest to sing the Gloria at the Easter Vigil and on the day of his ordination. By the end of the eleventh century the Gloria had become customary at masses celebrated by priests on Sundays and feasts except in Advent, pre-Lent, and Lent and was thus a mark of a more festive mass.

The Gloria in Excelsis was occasionally used as a hymn of thanksgiving like the Te Deum.[32]

---

[31] *Prayers We Have in Common*, 2nd rev. ed.,, 2nd rev. ed. 11–13.

[32] Gregory of Tours, *De gloria martyrum* 1.63.

The Gloria was originally a song of the congregation and not a choir piece, but it inspired many notable musical compositions, and from the tenth to the sixteenth centuries farsed forms of the Gloria as well as the Kyrie were developed. These tropes were discarded by the Reformers although hymn paraphrases were used in many places, and the tropes were banned by the Council of Trent and the Missal of Pius V (1570).

Although in the *Formula Missae* Luther included the Gloria in Excelsis in its usual place, he allowed the bishop-pastor to omit it as often as he chose and made no mention of it in the German Mass. Olavus Petri included the Gloria in Excelsis in his Swedish Mass of 1531. Many German church orders substituted vernacular versifications, especially those by Luther, "All Ehr und Preis soll Gottes sein," and Decius, "Allein Gott in der Höhe sei Ehr."

The Gloria begins with an antiphon (Luke 2:14; cf. Ps. 118:26; Luke 19:38), an acclamation of the glory of God and the coming of his deliverance to his people.

> Glory to God in the highest
> and peace to his people on earth.

The biblical text is of uncertain interpretation.[33]

The hymn itself follows. The first stanza is addressed to the Father under three groups of titles — Lord God, heavenly King, almighty God and Father — and three expressions of praise. This is set out as two pairs of parallel lines which climax in "glory," echoing the first word of the antiphon.

> Lord God, heavenly King,
> almighty God and Father,
>   we worship you, we give you thanks,
>   we praise you for your glory.

The second stanza, addressed to Christ as the only Son of the Father, is built around the Agnus Dei (John 1:29). Two lines of titles correspond to two lines of petition.

> Lord Jesus Christ, only son of the Father,
>   Lord God, Lamb of God,
> you take away the sin of the world:
>   have mercy on us;
> you are seated at the right hand of the Father:
>   receive our prayer.

The third stanza continues to acclaim Christ, and the lines have a trinitarian shape. The three titles given to Christ — Holy One, Lord, Most High — are those which also belong to the Father, and the final three lines are a concluding trinitarian doxology.

---

[33]See *Prayers We Have in Common*, 11–12; Joseph A. Fitzmyer, *The Gospel According to St. Luke I–IX* (Garden City, NY: Doubleday, 1981), 395–97, 410–12.

> For you alone are the Holy One,
> you alone are the Lord,
> you alone are the Most High,
>> Jesus Christ,
>> with the Holy Spirit,
>> in the glory of God the Father.

This third stanza may be related to the Eastern acclamation made just before communion when the priest says to the people, "Holy things for the holy" and the people respond, "One is holy, one Lord Jesus Christ."[34] The verse, moreover, recalls the primitive confession of faith (Phil. 2:11; Acts 2:36; 1 Cor. 8:6).

The Notes on the Liturgy (Min. Ed., p. 27, #7) give clear preference to the greater Gloria as the Hymn of Praise and observe that the Gloria in Excelsis, "the traditional Hymn of Praise, is appropriate on Sundays and all festivals, especially from Christmas Day through the Epiphany season." The Notes permit the occasional substitution of "All Glory Be to God on High" (hymn 166), Nikolaus Decius's metrical paraphrase of the Gloria (Min. Ed., p. 27, #7).

WORTHY IS CHRIST. In Western use the Gloria in Excelsis was a canticle employed like the Te Deum, a festive song occasionally added to the Eucharist. In rites other than that of Rome (Ambrosian, Mozarabic, Celtic) other options for the Hymn of Praise besides the Gloria in Excelsis were provided. In Gaul in the sixth century the Benedictus was sung after the Kyrie at mass. The *Lutheran Book of Worship* also has provided an alternative hymn of praise, especially appropriate for the Sundays of Easter, Christ the King, and All Saints' Day. The use of this hymn in praise of the feast on those occasions when there is no eucharistic feast and the service is confined to the ante-communion is incongruous and should be avoided. The hymn, written by John Arthur for *Contemporary Worship 2: The Holy Communion* (1970), is a kind of "prose" — a rhythmic composition in elevated language — based on much the same material as the canticle *Dignus est Agnus* (Rev. 5:12, 13; 15:3–4; 19:5, 6), which was included in the *Common Service Book* and *The Lutheran Hymnal*.[35]

"Worthy is Christ" consists of an antiphon-refrain drawn from Revelation 19:7, 9, and a series of verses. The arrangement varies from setting to setting of the service. "Worthy is Christ" is from Revelation 5:9; "Power, riches..." is from Revelation 5:12–13; "Sing with all the people of God" is adapted from Revelation 15:2–4; 19:5–6; "For the Lamb who was slain" is adapted from Revelation 11:17.

The antiphon-refrain, "This is the feast of victory for our God," is, like many traditional antiphons in the church's liturgy, not an exact bib-

---

[34]Note that in this interesting exchange it is the priest who ascribes holiness to the laity, and it is the laity who correct the priest and ascribe holiness to Christ alone.

[35]*Common Service Book*, text ed., p. 363; *The Lutheran Hymnal*, p. 122. The canticle was not preserved in the *Service Book and Hymnal*.

lical quotation but rather a gathering and a restatement of the many biblical references and allusions to banquets and feasting as signs of the gladness and intimacy of God's kingdom. It draws upon the picture of the messianic banquet in Isaiah 25:6, which celebrates the destruction of death and which proclaims therefore God's victory and triumph (see also Rev. 5:5; 22:6, 17; Isa. 55:1). The New Testament image for the gladness of the kingdom is often the wedding feast (as in Matt. 22:1ff.; Rev. 19:9) but is sometimes simply a "feast" as in Matthew 8:11. Nonetheless, the image looks back to the Passover meal which celebrates Israel's deliverance from slavery, to the Easter victory both in its past and present (and future) dimensions, and to the messianic banquet of the future, when the kingdom comes in all its fullness.

In the antiphon, "this" refers to the eucharistic celebration, which itself points to the Passover, Easter, and the messianic banquet — past, present, future. By this celebration we share now in a remembrance of the past as well as a "foretaste of the feast to come."

The celebration is described as "the feast of victory for our God," that is to say, a feast of God's victory: it is victory for God that we celebrate and proclaim, the victory over death won by Christ. It is the feast of victory of our God, but it is also a feast *for* God, that is to say, in honor and celebration of his triumph.

The figure of the slain and triumphant Lamb of God is the point of unity in the two hymns of praise, "Glory to God in the highest" and "Worthy of Christ."

"During Advent, Lent and Holy Week, a hymn of praise is not appropriate because of the preparatory and penitential nature of these times," the Notes on the Liturgy advise (Min. Ed., p. 27, #7). Both the Kyrie and the Hymn of Praise should be omitted in services on weekdays, and the presiding minister should proceed directly from the Apostolic Greeting to the Prayer of the Day.

PRAYER OF THE DAY. In the daily office from which they both come, the Kyrie and the Gloria in Excelsis were each concluded with a prayer.

Anciently, before the development of the entrance rite, the readings which began the Eucharist were sometimes preceded by a salutation which called the assembly to order and attention. The ancient forms varied, drawn from several biblical passages, principally Ruth 2:4 and also Luke 1:28; Judges 6:12; 2 Chronicles 15:2; 2 Thessalonians 3:16. The original Latin of the salutation, *Dominus vobiscum*, lacks a verb, but English requires one. The traditional translation takes the phrase to be optative, a wish, "The Lord be with you"; but some, remembering Matthew 18:20 and 28:20, prefer the indicative, "The Lord is with you."[36] The people's response parallels that of the reapers to Boaz, "The Lord bless you." In the Vulgate, 2 Timothy 4:22 is rendered *Dominus cum*

---

[36]W. C. van Unnik, "Dominus Vobiscum: The Background of a Liturgical Formula," *New Testament Essays — Studies in Memory of Thomas Walter Manson 1893–1958*, ed. A. J. B. Higgins (Manchester: Manchester University Press, 1959), 270–305.

spiritu tuo ("The Lord be with your spirit" in the RSV; cf. Philem. 25; Gal. 6:18; Phil. 4:23). The meaning of *et cum spiritu tuo* has been debated, some finding great significance in the older rendering "and with thy spirit." (Chrysostom took it to refer to the Holy Spirit bestowed upon the priest at ordination.) Modern liturgies, however, take the phrase to be a Semitism in which "spirit" is the person, simply "you."[37] The purpose is to establish a climate of mutuality (Matt. 18:20); Loehe says, "The bonds of love and unity between pastor and people are tied anew."[38] Moreover, Josef Jungmann observes that "thus in the greeting and its response we have the same double note that reappears at the end of the oration; the *Dominus vobiscum* seems to anticipate the *per Christum* of the close of the oration, and the *Et cum spiritu tuo* is a forerunner of the people's agreement expressed in the Amen."[39]

In the Roman liturgy the salutation and response were inserted before each new action of the liturgy to renew the attention of the people: before the Collect of the day, before the Gospel, before the Offertory, before the Great Thanksgiving, before the post-communion prayer, before the blessing. In the Missal of Paul VI the number of uses has been reduced. The salutation and response may be used as the greeting after the entrance song, and is used before the reading of the Gospel, at the beginning of the Great Thanksgiving, and before the blessing.

In the *Lutheran Book of Worship* the salutation and response may be used before the Prayer of the Day (it is an optional element); it is omitted if the Kyrie or Hymn of Praise is omitted so as to avoid duplicating the Apostolic Greeting, and it is used at the beginning of the Great Thanksgiving. Its third use in the Common Service, before the Benediction, has been eliminated.

The summons "Let us pray" (*Oremus*) indicates the corporate character of the prayer which follows, which, although voiced by the presiding minister, is the prayer of the assembly.

In addition to the traditional *Oremus*, the Roman sacramentary provides an optional expansion of the invitation to pray which relates the prayer to the theme of that particular day or occasion. If the alternative opening prayer is used, the invitation may be expanded further.[40]

The *Lutheran Book of Worship* assumes, although it does not explicitly direct, that a period of silence will be kept between "Let us pray" and the reading or intoning of the Prayer of the Day. The Notes on the Liturgy explain, "A brief silence between the invitation to pray and the prayer itself gives people time to collect their thoughts" (Min. Ed., p. 27, #8). The Roman sacramentary directs that, following the invitation to prayer, "Priest and people pray silently for a while. Then the priest extends his hands and sings or says the opening prayer...."[41] The

---

[37] Jungmann, 224.
[38] Quoted in Reed, 278.
[39] Jungmann, 244.
[40] *The Sacramentary* (New York: Catholic Book Publishing Co., 1974), 2ff.
[41] Ibid., 368.

silence between "Let us pray" and the prayer is a recovery of what was apparently ancient practice. The name *collect* (*collecta*) derives from the Gallican liturgy[42] and probably describes the function of the prayer in the Roman liturgy called simply *oratio* (prayer), which collected and summed up the people's intercessions.[43] Because the Prayer of the Day functions thus to gather the people's prayers into one pointed petition, it is a presidential prayer, offered by the presiding minister on behalf of all. In the Western church it is traditionally the responsibility of the presiding minister to voice all the principal prayers of the liturgy, giving continuity to the service and clarity to the articulation of the prayer.

The Collect was originally a free composition, and improvisation continued until the sixth century.[44] The Egyptian sacramentary of Bishop Serapion mentions the "first prayer of the Lord's Day," a prayer related to the lessons which follow. In later liturgies the Collect functions both as a conclusion to the elaborated entrance rite (as a kind of "station collect" following the entrance procession or a psalm prayer following the Hymn of Praise) and also as a prayer introducing the lessons which follow.

According to the oldest traditions of the church, all prayers are addressed "to the Father through the Son in the Holy Spirit."[45] Most collects in the church's treasury, therefore, are addressed to the Father; a few (none earlier than the Gregorian sacramentary) are addressed to Christ; a very few (chiefly Mozarabic) are addressed to the Holy Spirit.

The collect, peculiar to Western liturgies, is, with the eucharistic prayer and the litany, one of the three basic forms of Western liturgical prayer. In the Roman rite, the prayer of the day (called the opening prayer), the prayer over the gifts, and the post-communion prayer are indistinguishable in form. The collect is a "prayer that puts point to thought."[46] It is a literary form in which terse yet elegant thoughts are arranged in definite patterns of rhythmic prose,[47] a form which "is as rigid in structure as a sonnet or haiku."[48] The simplest form of the collect has three parts: an address or invocation, a petition, and a conclusion. The complete collect has five parts: (1) the address to God, the invocation; (2) the antecedent reason, a relative or participial clause referring to some attribute or saving act of God which forms the basis for the petition; (3) the petition; (4) the desired result or benefit from the granting of the petition; and (5) the doxological conclusion.

---

[42] Canon 30 of the Synod of Agde (A.D. 506).

[43] Bernard Capelle, "Collecta," *Reallexikon für Antike und Christentum* i (1957) cols. 243–45; "Collecta," *Revue Bénédictine* XLII (1930):197–204; reprinted in *Travaux Liturgiques* II (1962):192–203; derived from Walafrid Strabo (ca. 808–49).

[44] Augustine, *On the Catechising of the Uninstructed* 9.13; *The Study of Liturgy*, 184.

[45] Council of Hippo (393).

[46] Ezra Pound, *Shih Ching* (Cambridge, MA: Harvard University Press, 1954), 218.

[47] See Jungmann, 250, on the rhythm of the *cursus* which influenced the cadence of the collects.

[48] Hatchett, 164, from Leonel L. Mitchell, "The Collects in the Proposed Book of Common Prayer," *Worship* 52 (March 1978):138.

The second or the fourth part is sometimes absent, and occasionally both are omitted.[49]

The collects of the Roman rite came into use during the time of Celestine (422–32) or Leo (440–61) and are the literary gems of the Latin liturgy, having a place in the daily office as well as the mass. On special days the collect was related to the readings or the theme of the occasion; at other times the collect was more general. This was a time of repeated barbarian threats to Rome, and so the collects often pray for protection and peace.

The old Roman rule was that there should be only one collect at mass, but about the eleventh century it became customary, especially in Gallican rites, to use more than one collect before the lessons. In the thirteenth century the number of collects was prescribed according to the rank of the feast. For days of highest rank only one collect was appointed; the simplest day could have five or seven collects. The multiplication of such commemorations, as the additional collects were called, was abolished in the Roman rite by the Second Vatican Council. Luther restricted the number of collects to one[50] and in the German Mass seems to suggest that one fixed collect always be used.[51]

The Lutheran reformers translated and adapted many of the historic collects which had been in unbroken use for a thousand years and which were recognized to be an important part of the liturgical treasure of the church. Luther himself translated many collects.[52] Other important collections are found in the catechism of Andreas Althamer (1528); and the church orders of Prussia (1525), which gave sixty-seven translations of Roman collects; Brandenburg-Nuremberg (1533), which gave twenty-seven collects, eleven of which were new translations; Duke Henry of Saxony (1539–55); Spangenberg (1545), which gave eighty-seven in Latin and thirty-five in German; Mecklenburg (1552), edited by Melanchthon; Pomerania (1568), which gave sixty-three collects; and Austria (1571), which gave nearly two hundred.[53] Veit Dietrich, friend of Luther and Melanchthon and pastor of St. Sebaldus Church in Nuremberg (1543), and Johan Mathesius, the first biographer of Luther and leader in Bohemia (1563), composed collects of somewhat fuller form and related to the Epistles and Gospels. The Dietrich series, although "limited in content and stereotyped in form,"[54] attracted great popularity and was used in Germany and Sweden as "text collects" in the pulpit before or after the sermon; in the Danish church it supplanted the historic series. The more extensive and

---

[49] Hatchett, 164; Shepherd, 70; John Wallace Suter, Jr., *The Books of English Collects* (New York and London: Harper and Bros., 1940), xxviii–li; Eric Milner-White and G. W. Briggs, eds., *Daily Prayer* (Harmondsworth: Penguin, 1959), 200.
[50] *Formula Missae* (*Luther's Works* 53:23).
[51] *Deutsche Messe* (*Luther's Works* 53:72).
[52] *Luther's Works* 53:127–46.
[53] Reed, 284–85.
[54] Ibid., 285.

varied Mathesius series was incorporated in the Austrian church order of 1571.

In Lutheran use the collects were generally intoned by the minister in simple inflections. Swedish immigrants continued the practice in North America, but the Germans from the Palatinate, by that time unaccustomed to the practice, considered the practice "papistical."[55] The *Lutheran Book of Worship* in the Notes on the Liturgy (Min. Ed., p. 18) provides "a simple method for intoning the prayers."

Translation of the classic collect language and form has become increasingly difficult to accomplish in a satisfying way.

The classical Latin sentence, with its subordination (hypotaxis) of clauses, its massive but controlled length, its delayed verb, its sense not completed till the last word had been written, its skillful intricacy and artful, rhythmical devices, was a challenge to renaissance virtuosity, and it was speedily imitated so far as (and sometimes beyond what) the mechanics of the English sentence would permit.[56]

In particular the prayers or collects "are Latin periodic sentences of astonishing virtuosity." Cranmer's problem — "triumphantly solved — was to create an English prose for oral delivery which would match the Latin in dignity, rhythm, and resonance."[57] As the English language changes, Cranmer's solutions are no longer entirely satisfying. The 1979 *Book of Common Prayer* chose a conservative rendering of the elevated language of previous Prayer Books and provided two forms of the collects, "traditional" and "contemporary."[58] The *Lutheran Book of Worship* opted for a somewhat bolder approach, reducing relative clauses, shortening sentences, and simplifying the language.[59] Moreover, in a departure from tradition, the *Lutheran Book of Worship* gives several alternative prayers for Sundays and other days. In the *Church Book*, the *Common Service Book*, and the *Service Book and Hymnal* there were no alternative collects for Sundays but only for Ascension Day (to preserve an ancient antiphon) and Reformation Day, and a series of "other collects" for Advent, Good Friday, and Easter. Faced with a new three-year lectionary which gave little thematic coherence to many Sundays, and testing various styles of prayer for modern use, *Contemporary Worship 6: The Church Year: Calendar and Lectionary* (1973) provided alternative Prayers of the Day for Epiphany 7, Ash

[55] Henry Melchior Muhlenberg, *The Journals of Henry Melchior Muhlenberg*, trans. Theodore G. Tappert and John W. Doberstein, vol. 1 (Philadelphia: Evangelical Lutheran Ministerium of Pennsylvania and Muhlenberg Press, 1942), 193 [April 28, 1748].

[56] Ian A. Gordon, *The Movement of English Prose* (Bloomington and London: Indiana University Press, 1966), 77.

[57] Ibid., 81–83.

[58] Mitchell, 138–45.

[59] Charles A. Ferguson, "The Collect as a Form of Discourse," in *Language in Religious Practice*, ed. W. J. Samarin (Rowley, MA: Newbury House, 1976). See also John Arthur, *Prayers, Psalms, and Days' Songs* (Chicago: Lutheran Council in the USA, Department of Campus Ministry, 1970).

Wednesday, Lent 1, Monday, Tuesday, Wednesday, Thursday, and Friday in Holy Week, Easter 4, Pentecost, Pentecost 20, Pentecost 24, the Annunciation, and Reformation Day. It also noted when alternative prayers would be appropriate for each of the years of the lectionary cycle for various days, and provided "additional prayers" for Advent, Christmas-Epiphany, Lent, Easter, and after Pentecost. To accommodate a widespread desire to preserve many of the traditional collects and to preserve the more successful new compositions, the *Lutheran Book of Worship* deleted the "additional prayers" and provided alternative Prayers of the Day for Advent 3, Epiphany 7, the Transfiguration (the Last Sunday after the Epiphany), Lent 1, Lent 2, Maundy Thursday, Good Friday, Easter Day, Easter 4, Easter 7, Pentecost, Trinity Sunday, Pentecost 8, Pentecost 9, Pentecost 11, Renewers of Society, Pastors and Bishops, Dedication and Anniversary, and the Stewardship of Creation. The Lutheran book, however, did not take into account the reordering of the collects which the Roman rite had initiated and which the *Book of Common Prayer* followed.

The Roman sacramentary, in addition to a relatively conservative rendering of the Latin collect, provides an "alternative prayer" for Sundays and certain other festivals, "suggested by the Latin text and in harmony with its theme" but generally more concrete and expansive than the "succinct and abstract character of the original Latin." The addition of such texts was prompted by the practice of other Roman liturgical books of offering alternatives and by the 1969 instruction on translation, which observed,

Texts translated from another language are clearly not sufficient for the celebration of a fully renewed liturgy. The creation of new texts will be necessary. But translation of texts transmitted through the tradition of the Church is the best school and discipline for the creation of new texts so "that any new forms adopted should in some way grow organically from the forms already in existence" (no. 143).[60]

The English translation of the Roman missal is undergoing revision and is scheduled for completion in 1991. The revision (and, one might add, notable improvement) of the translation of the opening prayers (formerly called the collects) is especially to be noted.

The original conclusion to the collects seems to have been simply "through Jesus Christ our Lord" (*per Christum dominum nostrum*). The conclusion of the collects in earlier Roman and Lutheran use was always the most rigidly constrained part: "through thy Son, Jesus Christ our Lord, who liveth and reigneth with thee and the Holy Ghost, one God, world without end,"[61] added in fifth-century Spain in reaction to the Arians. There were prescribed variants if the Son or the Holy Spirit is

---

[60]Foreword, *The Sacramentary*, 12.

[61]The Latin phrase translated by the odd "world without end" is literally "through all ages of ages" (*per omnia saecula saeculorum*). "World" in a now obsolete use could mean "age," a long period of time in earthly or human existence or history, and "world without

addressed or mentioned in the prayer, and a shortened form for when the collect is used as a second prayer of "commemoration."[62] In medieval Roman missals the termination was never given in full; only a cue phrase is indicated, *per dominum* (through our Lord) or *qui vivis* (who lives). Beginning in the 1662 *Book of Common Prayer* more of the traditional ending was printed, followed by Amen, and the terminations varied. It has been noted that "this seems to have been part of the general plan of leaving nothing to chance, tradition or caprice; but the variations do not seem to rest on any principle, and the frequent curtailment of the familiar, sonorous and profoundly theological conclusion seems little better than a wanton maiming of an artistic form."[63]

Luther in his own translations and adaptations of collects used a great variety of endings, but Lutheran usage soon stabilized again. The *Lutheran Book of Worship* has introduced a limited variety in the conclusion by printing a simple conclusion — some form of "through Jesus Christ our Lord" — at the end of the Prayers of the Day for the "ordinary" time after the Epiphany and after Pentecost, and the full termination for the other Sundays and festivals. The Notes on the Liturgy, however, permit more freedom. "Either simple or full terminations may be used for any Prayer of the Day as circumstances suggest" (Min. Ed., p. 18). The prayers were drafted by John W. Arthur, Leslie S. Brandt, Richard Du Brau, Charles A. Ferguson, who chaired the committee, Adalbert R. Kretzmann, Jack E. Lindquist, Paul K. Peterson, and Edward D. Roe.

The Liturgy of the Word of God

THE LECTIONARY. The Bible is the church's principal liturgical book. Reading Scripture in the Christian assembly is, therefore, entirely natural and appropriate, for the texts have to do with the assembly of God's people and the worship of God, and the texts often have their origin in the assemblies of the Christian community. Even the biblical canon is rooted there, for the canon is the list of books authorized to be read in public worship.

The public reading of Scripture was a Jewish custom which the Christians continued in their services (Luke 4:16–21; Acts 13:27). To the reading of the Hebrew Scriptures, the Christians added readings from Christian writings; "the books of the New Testament were in fact largely selected from Christian writings which had come into general use in the church's worship"[64] (1 Thess. 5:27; Col. 4:16).

---

end" can be dated from ca. 1225 (*Ancren Riule* 182). See "world without end" in the *Oxford English Dictionary*.

[62] General Rubrics in the *Common Service Book*, text ed., p. 484; abbreviated in the *Service Book and Hymnal*, p. 274.

[63] *Liturgy and Worship*, ed. W. K. Lowther Clarke and Charles Harris (London: SPCK, 1932), 378.

[64] Hatchett, 324.

In the first century, in Justin's time, "the memoirs of the apostles or the writings of the prophets are read as long as time permits."[65] For centuries there seems to have been considerable latitude in the selection of the readings, which were interspersed with psalms. In fourth-century Antioch there were, as in the synagogue, two lessons from the Law and the Prophets, one from the Epistles or Acts, and one from the Gospels,[66] but the use of three lessons (one from the Old Testament and two from the New Testament) seems more common and was standardized in the Armenian, Mozarabic, Milanese, and Gallican liturgies. Already in the fourth century, however, the number of lessons was being reduced to two, and at Constantinople in the fifth and at Rome in the sixth century the readings were increasingly reduced to two: two New Testament readings on Sundays and on weekdays one Old Testament lesson and the Gospel. Since the seventh century the Eastern Church has had but two readings, both from the New Testament.

The lessons at Easter seem to have been the first to become fixed; Acts was read in both East and West. During the fourth century the lessons for Christmas, Epiphany, and Ascension Day became fixed. Sundays began to have appointed lessons in Antioch in Chrysostom's time. The time after Pentecost was the last to acquire fixed readings.

In the middle of the fifth century, Venerius, bishop of Marseilles, devised a lectionary for the feast days of the year. The first complete lectionaries date from the seventh century. The oldest extant Roman lectionary is the Würtzburg lectionary (late sixth to early seventh century); the *Comes* (= companion, which gave the texts of the lessons)[67] of Murbach, containing both Epistles and Gospels, is probably from the end of the eighth century. Alcuin (?735–804) standardized the mass lectionary from existing local provisions, using the Roman series for the Gospels and the Gallican for the Epistles. The combinations were therefore largely fortuitous, although traces of older cycles remained, as in the Epistles for the Sundays after Pentecost. Alcuin's series was not quite complete for the last Sundays after the Epiphany and after Pentecost.

The lectionary was at first a separate book, but with the appearance of the missal in the tenth century, all materials necessary for the celebration of mass were incorporated into one volume. Diocesan missals varied in Western Europe until the Roman Missal of 1570 prescribed a single order and lectionary for the entire Roman Church. (In the 1969 Missal of Paul VI the biblical readings were omitted and again issued as a separate lectionary.)

---

[65] Justin Martyr, *First Apology* 67.

[66] *Apostolic Constitutions* 8.5.11; Liturgy of St. James.

[67] A *comes* (*liber comitis* or *liber comicus*) is a book containing passages to be read at mass as Epistles and/or Gospels. It was originally a list of opening words (*incipit*) of readings to serve as a reference. The beginning (*incipit*) and the ending (*explicit*) was noted in the margin of the church Bible, and a capitulary or table of incipits and explicits was made for reference. The name *liber comicus* later came to be applied to books with the complete text of the readings.

The German church orders, with few exceptions, retained the historic lessons, and Luther, Melanchthon, Bugenhagen, and others published *postils* (homilies) on these lessons. Continuing pre-Reformation usage, the lessons were regularly intoned by the minister in sixteenth-century Lutheran services, particularly in Mark Brandenburg (1540), Herzogin Elizabeth (1542), Pomerania (1563), and Hoya (1581).

Through the centuries, certain areas of the Lutheran church developed alternative series of readings for use as preaching texts. The private lectionary of Gottfried Thomasius (d. 1875) in Bavaria and the lectionaries of the Eisenach Conference of 1852 and the Church of Hannover were included in the *Common Service Book*.[68] The *Church Book* included a "Table of Scriptural Lessons for the Sundays and Festivals of the Church-Year,"[69] which gave four lessons for each Sunday and festival: from the Gospels, from the Epistles, from the historical books of the Old Testament, and from the poetical books of the Old Testament. The *Common Service Book* like the *Church Book* before it gave precedence to the historic series of Epistles and Gospels, however, and the primary value of the alternative series was to provide additional sermon texts and to provide lessons for Matins and Vespers.

A two-year cycle of lessons, designed to give a larger portion of Scripture for liturgical reading and preaching, was devised in Germany in 1896. The *Hymnal* of the Augustana Lutheran Church provided a three-year cycle of lessons, and *The Lutheran Hymnary* of the Evangelical Lutheran Church provided a two-year cycle. These were preserved in the 1967 text edition of the *Service Book and Hymnal* (pp. 651–55) and in its Altar Book (pp. 378–85) "for the convenience of those congregations which have desired their inclusion," although a note at the head of the supplementary tables declares that they are "in no sense a part of the Common Liturgy adopted by the Churches." *The Lutheran Hymnal* (1941) also provided an alternative series of Epistles and Gospels and an optional series of Old Testament readings.

The Second Vatican Council of the Roman Catholic Church (1962–65) in its Constitution on the Sacred Liturgy directed that in the liturgical rites "there is to be more reading from holy Scripture, and it is to be more varied and suitable," and that in the Eucharist in particular, "the treasures of the Bible are to be opened up more lavishly, so that richer fare may be provided for the faithful at the table of God's Word. In this way a more representative portion of the holy Scriptures will be read to the people over a set cycle of years."[70] In the revised lectionary which resulted from these directives, *Ordo lectionum missae* (1969 and 1980), three lessons rather than the two, Epistle and Gospel, were appointed

---

[68] *Common Service Book*, text ed., pp. 499–506; these lectionaries were also included in the *Service Book and Hymnal* Altar Book, pp. 371–77 and the text edition, pp. 644–50; they were not in the pew edition.

[69] *Church Book*, pp. x–xi.

[70] *The Documents of Vatican II*, ed. Walter M. Abbott (New York: Guild Press, America Press, Association Press, 1966), 149, 155 §51.

for each Sunday, and the lectionary was composed of three yearly cycles rather than the one which had been common to the liturgical churches since very early in the Christian era. This three-year cycle attracted wide attention and, with alterations, was introduced in the Episcopal Church beginning with *The Church Year: Prayer Book Studies 19* (1970), in another form in the Presbyterian *Worshipbook* (1970), and in the Lutheran churches in North America in *Contemporary Worship 6: The Church Year: Calendar and Lectionary* (1973). The Lutheran version of the three-year lectionary was prepared by Samuel Boda, Victor R. Gold, John V. Halvorson, Herbert F. Lindemann, Norman E. Nagel, Louis G. Nuechterlein, John H. P. Reumann who chaired the committee, Stanley D. Schneider, the secretary of the committee, and Walter T. Weind; Wilhelm T. Linss was a consultant.[71] The Presbyterian revision was subsequently adopted by the United Church of Christ and the Christian Church (Disciples of Christ) and, in another form, by the United Methodist Church and the Consultation on Church Union.

European Lutherans have rather consistently chosen to revise the older one-year lectionary rather than adopt the three-year cycle, and therefore the first lectionary prepared by the Inter-Lutheran Commission on Worship was a revision of the one-year historic series (1971).[72] Its use, however, has been minimal.

In 1978 the Consultation on Common Texts undertook a revision of the various forms of the three-year lectionary in an effort to achieve greater consensus and to meet the criticisms, especially regarding the absence of the great Old Testament historical narratives. The result of their work, the *Common Lectionary* (1982),[73] moreover follows the Roman Catholic and Episcopal and United Methodist practice of adjusting the propers by eliminating extra propers at the beginning of the time after Pentecost rather than the Lutheran and Presbyterian method of removing the extra appointments from the end of the year before the festival of Christ the King. Cutting at the beginning rather than the end preserves the eschatological emphasis of the propers which occur at the end of the year, which had been a significant Lutheran emphasis.[74]

---

[71] For an account of this work by a participant see John H. P. Reumann, "A New Lectionary for Lutherans," *Lutheran Forum* 7:3 (August 1973), 6–8. See also his "A History of Lectionaries: From the Synagogue at Nazareth to Post Vatican II," *Interpretation* 31 (1977), 116–30.

[72] Given in the Ministers Ed., 192–94. It does not appear in the pew edition.

[73] Published as *Common Lectionary: The Lectionary Proposed by the Consultation on Common Texts* (New York: Church Hymnal Corporation, 1983). For accounts of the work see Horace T. Allen, Jr., "The Promise of the Common Lectionary," *Accent on Worship* 3:2 (1985):4, 8; Hans Boehringer, "The Other New Lectionary," *Lutheran Forum* 18 (Reformation 1984):27–28; Lewis A. Briner, "A Look at New Proposals for the Lectionary," *LCA Partners* 5 (October 1983):26–28; Aelred Tegels, "Chronicle: Common Lectionary," *Worship* 58 (November 1984):536–39.

[74] See *Common Service Book*, text ed., p. 507; *Service Book and Hymnal*, p. 105: "The propers for the following three Sundays may be used on the last three Sundays after Trinity."

The Old Testament readings in the 1969 Roman Catholic lectionary were chosen in accordance with the typological principle to harmonize with the Gospel readings. Such an approach presents problems. The exegesis on which such correlation is based may be dubious, the results of this approach involve a comparative neglect of the Wisdom literature, and a lectionary based on the typological principle "is not conducive to a proper appreciation of the Hebrew Scriptures as such," suggesting that the Hebrew Bible has no intrinsic religious value of its own.[75]

In the Consultation's lectionary, Year A, the year of Matthew, presents the patriarchal and Mosaic sagas read in sequence: twenty Sundays of pentateuchal material beginning with the call of Abraham and ending with the death of Moses, plus three Sundays from Ruth and three of prophetic eschatological material. In Year B, the year of Mark, there are fourteen Sundays of Davidic narrative from his anointing to his death, together with fourteen Sundays of Wisdom literature. In Year C, the year of Luke, the Elijah-Elisha account is read over ten Sundays, beginning with Solomon's dedication of the Temple and concluding with Elisha's death, followed by fifteen Sundays of readings from major and minor prophets. There is a general correlations with the Gospels, although not on a week-to-week basis. To read the Pentateuch in connection with Matthew is in accordance with the interest of that evangelist; so is the correlation of David with Mark and the prophets with Luke.

The story of the successive translations of the Bible into English has often been told.[76] In the *Book of Common Prayer* the officially-approved

---

[75]See Tegels, 536–39.

[76]F. F. Bruce, *History of the Bible in English*, 3rd ed. (New York: Oxford University Press, 1978); Douglas Bush, *English Literature in the Early Seventeenth Century 1600–1660*, 2nd rev. ed., Oxford History of English Literature, vol. 5 (Oxford: Clarendon Press, 1962):65–73; Charles C. Butterworth, *The Literary Lineage of the King James Bible 1340–1611* (Philadelphia: University of Pennsylvania Press, 1941); *Duke Divinity School Review* 44:2 (Spring 1979), eight essays on the nature and quality of modern English translations; Frederick C. Grant, *Translating the Bible* (Greenwich, CT: Seabury Press, 1961); S. L. Greenslade, ed., *The West from the Reformation to the Present Day*, vol. 3 of the Cambridge History of the Bible (Cambridge: University Press, 1963); Gerald Hammond, *The Making of the English Bible* (Manchester: Carcanet Press, 1982); *Interpreter's Dictionary of the Bible*, ed. George A. Buttrick (Nashville: Abingdon Press, 1962, supplement 1976), articles on "Versions, English"; Ronald A. Knox, *On Englishing the Bible* (London: Burns & Oates, 1949); Sakae Kubo and Walter Specht, *So Many Versions? Twentieth Century English Versions of the Bible*, rev. and enl. ed. (Grand Rapids: Zondervan, 1983); C. S. Lewis, *English Literature in the Sixteenth Century, Excluding Drama*, Oxford History of English Literature, vol. 3 (Oxford: Clarendon Press, 1954), esp. pp. 204–215; C. S. Lewis, "The Literary Impact of the Authorized Version," *They Asked for a Paper: Papers and Addresses* (London: Geoffrey Bles, 1962), published separately by Fortress Press, 1963; (cf. Lane Cooper, *Certain Rhythms in the English Bible* (Ithaca: Cornell University Press, 1952); T. R. Henn, *The Bible as Literature* (New York: Oxford University Press, 1970); Geddes Macgregor, *A Literary History of the Bible: From the Middle Ages to the Present Day* (Nashville: Abingdon Press, 1968); Eugene Nida and Charles Taber, *The Theory and Practice of Translation* (Leiden: Brill, 1969); A. C. Partridge, *English Biblical Translation* (London: Andre Deutsch, 1973); A. W. Pollard, *Records of the English Bible* (Oxford: Clarendon Press, 1911); John H. P. Reumann, *Four Centuries of the English Bible* (Philadelphia: Muhlenberg, 1961); Allen Wikgren, "The English Bible," *The Interpreter's Bible*, vol. 1 (Nashville: Abingdon Press, 1952).

135

Great Bible (1539, 2nd ed. 1540 with a preface by Thomas Cranmer) was established as the standard translation. By the time Lutherans began to worship in English in the early nineteenth century, the stately and deliberately archaic Authorized Version of 1611, "appointed to be read in churches" (that is, parishes of the Church of England) had become the accepted English translation for all non-Roman denominations of the West. It was therefore only natural to use its translation in Lutheran service books. In the latter part of the nineteenth century and the early decades of the twentieth century new translations began to appear, chiefly to supplement, clarify, and occasionally to correct the King James Version.[77] By the middle of the twentieth century other translations, principally the Revised Standard Version (NT 1946, OT 1952), a conservative revision of the Authorized Version, had begun to challenge the supremacy of the King James Bible. With difficulty the committee which prepared the *Service Book and Hymnal* drove back attempts at adopting the Revised Standard Version as the basic translation. The language of the liturgy remained Tudor English; biblical quotations in Introits, Graduals, and elsewhere remained in the King James translation, but as a compromise the texts of the Epistles and Gospels were not included in the pew edition of the book (as they had been in the *Common Service Book*). Instead, two separate lectionaries were prepared: one in the King James Version and the other in the Revised Standard Version. The text edition of the *Service Book and Hymnal* (1967) gave the Lessons in the Authorized Version. T. R. Henn, a professor of English at Cambridge University had written, "The Authorized Version of 1611... alone of all the versions is the product of one of the great ages, and the first stable age, of English literature [and]... will remain with Bacon, the Voyages, the sermons of Donne and Jeremy Taylor, the prose poems of Traherne, among the literary monuments of the time."[78] The preparers of the *Service Book and Hymnal*, like those who prepared the *Common Service Book* before them, were conscious of maintaining not only a particular liturgical tradition but a particular literary tradition as well. That concern was, however, being undermined by changing language, culture, and taste and was soon to be rendered largely impossible to implement. At the end of the twentieth century there was no one Bible translation which commanded authoritative preeminence; there was no standard version.[79]

A yet more vexing question with regard to the lectionary has to do with what has generally been called inclusive language. Do modern users

---

[77] English Revised Version (NT 1881, OT 1885); American Revised Version (1901); Ferrar Fenton, *Holy Bible in Modern English* (1895); R. F. Weymouth, *The New Testament in Modern Speech* (1903); A. S. Way, *Twentieth Century New Testament* (1904); James Moffatt, *The Bible: A New Translation* (1926, rev. 1935); Edgar J. Goodspeed, et al., *The Complete Bible: An American Translation* (1933); Ronald A. Knox, NT (1947), OT (1958); J. B. Phillips, *The New Testament in Modern English* (1958).

[78] T. R. Henn, *The Bible as Literature* (New York: Oxford University Press, 1970), 10–11.

[79] See John H. J. Westlake "The Liturgical Use of Modern Translations of the Bible," *Studia Liturgica* 8:2 (1971/1):98–118.

of the Bible have the freedom to alter the reflections of the patriarchal context of ancient Israel and the New Testament world to accommodate current sensitivities? Respect for the historical context of God's great acts seem to preclude such an approach, however attractive it may seem to some. How one is to name and refer to God in contemporary public English is a more difficult question when it is applied to the translation of Scripture. At this point the foundations of appropriate answers are just being laid, and satisfactory solutions lie still in the future.[80]

In the Byzantine liturgy, "Wisdom. Let us attend" is said before the reading of a scriptural pericope to remind the assembly that special attention and perception is required, for God himself is to speak at that very moment.[81]

The custom of announcing individual lessons dates from the twelfth century. The 1549 *Book of Common Prayer* introduced the citation of the chapter which was to be read. Verse divisions were introduced in the Geneva Bible (1557, 1560), and the 1662 Prayer Book required the citation of the verse as well as the chapter. North American Lutheran service books in English borrowed the practice. The *Lutheran Book of Worship* does not provide for the citation of the verse, only the chapter from which a lesson is taken, for verse numbers are of no significance to those who listen to the reading of a lesson. (The *Book of Common Prayer* makes the citation of chapter and verse optional.)

THE FIRST LESSON. The First Lesson, except during Easter, is from the Old Testament. This lesson is read not in isolation, by itself alone, but in the context of Christian worship. The First Lesson usually correlates in one way or another, direct or indirect, with the Gospel for the day, and so the ancient scriptures are opened to speak ultimately of Jesus Christ — his death, his risen presence, and the death and resurrection of his people. (See Luke 4:16–21; 24:25–35, 44–49.)

RESPONSORIAL PSALM. The use of a psalm after the Old Testament lesson is the oldest regular use of psalmody in the liturgy. The practice is mentioned by Athanasius (ca. 293–373) and prescribed by the *Apostolic Constitutions* (ca. 380). "It is in the very nature of things that the grace-laden message which God proclaims to men would awaken an echo of song."[82]

In early Christian times the psalm was sung in the responsorial manner, which flourished until the fourth century. A solo voice sang the psalm; the people answered by repeating after each section the unchanging *responsum* or refrain. This refrain seems to have been a verse, often the first verse, of the psalm being sung. The refrains were highly hon-

---

[80]See Gordon Lathrop and Gail Ramshaw, eds., *Lectionary for the Christian People: Cycle A* (New York: Pueblo Publishing Co., 1986); Cycles B and C published by Paulist Press and Fortress Press. Also see Gail Ramshaw-Schmidt, "Lutherans and an Inclusive Language Lectionary," *LCA Partners* (May/June 1985):25–30.

[81]Emilianos Timiadis, *The Nicene Creed: Our Common Faith* (Philadelphia: Fortress Press, 1983), 31.

[82]Jungmann, 275.

ored; Augustine and Chrysostom again and again speak of them as a starting point for a deeper study of the psalms.[83] As the refrains were elaborated poetically and musically, the psalm itself began to be pruned away and the people participated less and less in the singing. The psalm became a choir piece, and when the First Lesson was dropped from the liturgy, because of their beauty the psalm refrains were not sacrificed with it but were joined with the Alleluia to form what was known as the Gradual, sung between the Epistle and Gospel.

One of the most important features of the liturgical reforms of the twentieth-century liturgies, rooted in the Reformation of the sixteenth century, is the restoration of psalm singing to the congregation. The Roman sacramentary and the *Lutheran Book of Worship* appoint a psalm for use after the first lesson. There is no provision for the psalm to be replaced by a hymn. (The *Book of Common Prayer* allows a psalm, hymn, or anthem.)

The other principal psalm use in the Western liturgy was the Introit, Offertory, and Communion, introduced in the fifth century, which were examples of antiphonal psalmody: the verses of the psalm sung alternately by two groups of singers. A characteristic feature of antiphonal psalmody was the use of the Gloria Patri as a doxology at the end of the psalm. The origins go back to the beginning of antiphonal psalmody at Antioch, and the purpose was to give a Christian conclusion to the psalm. The three antiphonal psalms in the liturgy were sung to accompany processions (of the ministers as they entered, of the people as they presented their gifts, of communicants as they came to the altar) and were sung as long as necessary to cover the action. If the action, which was the principal thing, was completed before the psalm was finished, the Gloria Patri was interposed to bring the singing to a close.

The responsorial gradual psalms between the lessons were more integral to the liturgy and were regarded as a kind of added Old Testament lesson. The gradual psalms, which did not cover an action, were never cut and never had the Gloria Patri associated with them.[84] It is thus undesirable, remembering the origin and use of the responsorial psalmody, to add the Gloria Patri to the psalm between the lessons in the present liturgy. The proper psalms, based on the Roman Catholic appointments, were chosen by Ralph W. Doermann, Herbert F. Lindemann, who chaired the committee, and Charles D. Trexler, Jr. Further information on the Psalter is found in chapter 6, Daily Prayer (below, pp. 381–385).

THE SECOND LESSON. St. Paul intended his letters to be read in the assembly (1 Cor. 16:22–24; Col. 4:16), and the Second Lesson is from one of the New Testament epistles (or Hebrews) or the Acts of the Apostles.

---

[83] Ibid., 275–76.

[84] Massey H. Shepherd, Jr., *The Psalms in Christian Worship: A Practical Guide* (Collegeville: Liturgical Press, 1976), 36–47; Hatchett, 328. Music for the antiphons is provided in Roger Petrich, *Psalm Antiphons for the Church Year* (Philadelphia: Fortress Press, 1979).

The Second Lesson generally provides the "horizon of the church," the plane from which the axis of the First Lesson and the Gospel is to be understood, by suggesting the present religious and social context in which the ancient Scriptures are read.[85] The Second Lesson often is the most suggestive of concerns for prayer to those preparing the intercessions.

After the First Lesson and after the Second Lesson the reader may say, "Here ends the reading" (inverting the natural order, "The reading ends here" or "Here the reading ends") on the basis of the older formula "Here endeth the lesson," introduced in the Scottish Prayer Book of 1637 and the 1662 *Book of Common Prayer*.[86] In the Roman Catholic mass the reader says, "This is the Word of the Lord"; in the *Book of Common Prayer* "the Reader may say, 'The Word of the Lord,'" (borrowed from the Taizé Office). In both the Roman Catholic and Episcopal rites the response is "Thanks be to God," which dates from the medieval period as an acknowledgement of having heard what was said.[87] The present function is to involve the congregations in a brief expression of thanks for what has just been proclaimed. The Lutheran rite is alone in not providing a congregational response.

THE VERSE. The Psalm serves not simply as an interlude between the first two lessons, but as a bridge between the two readings, an echo of the first and a transition to the second, binding the two readings together as a unit. The Verse before the Gospel looks entirely ahead to the third reading and forms a unit with it, welcoming the Gospel, except in Lent, with the song of heaven, "Alleluia." As early as the third-century *Martyrdom of Matthew*, alleluias were sung to welcome the Gospel. "For the Alleluia is the perpetual voice of the church, just as the memorial of His passion and victory is perpetual."[88] Hallelujah (= "[let us] praise the Lord"), a word restricted in the Old Testament to Psalms 104–150, was originally a religious cry, probably used to encourage congregational participation in the liturgical recitation of the psalms, and later became a stereotyped cry of joy. In Christian use, usually employed in its Greek form Alleluia (in the Ambrosian rite and in the *Common Service Book* the Hebrew form "Hallelujah" is used), the word took on profound overtones as a sign of the eternal praise of heaven, for "it is in praising God that we shall rejoice forever in the life

---

[85] William Skudlarek, *The Word in Worship* (Nashville: Abingdon Press, 1982).

[86] "Here ends the reading" is no longer a current English form. Beginning a sentence with a demonstrative word like "here" or "then" followed by the verb was once a common Old English structure, often encountered in the *Anglo-Saxon Chronicle* (ninth–twelfth centuries). The order survived in elevated contexts after it disappeared from ordinary speech; examples are the "here lies" of epitaphs, the "here beginneth" and the "here endeth" of the Prayer Book. Thence it passed into Lutheran use, as, for example, "Then shall be sung or said the Gloria in Excelsis" (*Service Book and Hymnal*, p. 3). See Ian Gordon, 28.

[87] Jungmann, 274; Hatchett, 327.

[88] Martin Luther, *Formula Missae* (*Luther's Works* 53:24). *Alleluia vox perpetua est ecclesiae, sicut perpetua est memoria passionis et victoriae Christi.*

139

to come," wrote Augustine.[89] "Alleluia" points to what Christians do not yet possess entirely and urges those who sing it to a wholehearted life of praise doing what is pleasing to God.

When in the Middle Ages the Old Testament lesson disappeared from the liturgy, the psalm verses sung between the first and second lessons were united with the Alleluia sung before the Gospel to form one choir piece, called the Gradual[90] (apparently from *gradus*, the step of the altar from which the chant was sung). Luther retained the Gradual in his *Formula Missae*, but in his German Mass he suggested a vernacular hymn between the Epistle and Gospel. The *Church Book* of 1868 restored the Introits to North American Lutheran use; the Graduals were not restored until the *Common Service Book* (1917).

Anciently, a psalm was sung using "alleluia" as its antiphon-refrain. By the Middle Ages only a remnant remained: an alleluia was sung by a single voice and the choir repeated it, the verse which replaced the whole psalm was sung by a solo voice, and the choir repeated the alleluia. The practice continues in the present Roman rite. From the Second Sunday of Easter to Pentecost a double alleluia replaced the Gradual and alleluia, and a second verse followed with a final alleluia.

The *Lutheran Book of Worship* has replaced the Graduals with the (Alleluia) Verses. (The present Roman rite permits the older texts of the Graduals to be sung in place of the responsorial psalm.) The Lutheran book provides a full series of proper Verses, drawn from the Roman liturgy. The Verse consists of a scriptural verse, usually from the New Testament (for it comes between two New Testament readings), with a single alleluia before and after. During Easter, from Easter Evening through the seventh week of Easter, the Verse consists of two scriptural verses; the first is always Romans 6:9; tying the season together as one fifty-day festival. Alleluia is sung before, in the middle of, and after the double verse. The Verse for Easter Day has alleluia only before the first and after the second scriptural verse because the sequence hymn (137), which elaborates the Easter song of praise, may follow.

During Lent the scriptural verse is sung simply, without the refrain-antiphon alleluia. The omission of alleluia (peculiar to the Western Church; the Eastern church always uses it) goes back at least to the fifth century. St. Augustine wrote, "We sing alleluia indeed on certain days, but every day we think it. For if in this word is signified the praise of God, though not in the mouth of the flesh, yet surely in the mouth of the heart."[91]

As a concession to those congregations without a choir able or willing to sing the proper Verse, the Verse for the Sixth Sunday after the Epiphany (John 6:68) is appointed for general use and the Verse proper for Ash Wednesday (Joel 2:13) is appointed for use throughout Lent.

---

[89] Augustine, *Discourse* on Psalm 148:1–2. See also his *Discourse* on Psalm 111:1. See Revelation 19:1–8.

[90] The name is found in Rhabanus Maurus (784 or 786–856).

[91] Augustine, *Discourse* on Psalm 107:1.

But the Notes on the Liturgy (Min. Ed., p. 27, #14) strongly encourage the singing of the proper Verse by a choir or a single voice rather than the singing of an invariable Verse by the congregation.

During the last half of the ninth century, the lengthy continuations of the final vowel (the *jubilus*) of the Alleluia developed into metrical hymns called sequences, of which more than five thousand are known and which form an important part of medieval literature.[92] Notker Balbulus, a monk of St. Gall (d. 912), provided texts which gave one note to a syllable. The rhythmic, elevated texts were called *sequentia cum prosa*, or, in English, "sequences" or "proses." After the beginning of the eleventh century rhymed sequences began to appear. The most famous writer of these was Adam of St. Victor (d. ca. 1192). The *Lutheran Book of Worship* like the Roman sacramentary, appoints two sequences — one for Easter day and one for the Day of Pentecost (see below, pp. 290, 299) — thus beginning and ending the Fifty Days with sequence hymns.

THE HOLY GOSPEL. The reading of the Gospel has always occupied the last place, the place of honor, as the climax of the readings. From the fourth century it was read not by a lector but by a deacon (first among the assisting ministers) or a priest; in Jerusalem the bishop read the Gospel every Sunday.[93] Many rich and great ceremonies clustered about this reading, all designed to emphasize its outstanding importance and to crown it with every honor.

The books in which the Gospels were written, called sometimes the *Textus* and later the *Evangelium*, were ornamented with gold and precious stones, carried in formal procession to the place of reading, held by specific servers, read by specific ministers. Certain lights were lit at this time; incense was burnt; all uncovered their heads — bishops removed their mitres, kings their crowns — staves and weapons were laid down; all was quietness, order, attention; all stood slightly bowing in posture of deepest reverence, for these are the words of the Lord Jesus or the narrative of his life and work.[94]

Standing for the reading of the Gospel can be traced to the *Apostolic Constitutions* (ca. 380). The movement of the reader of the Gospel to the place from which it was to be read became a procession led by two servers carrying torches. The richly-decorated book of the Gospels was often carried into the church during the entrance and placed on the reading desk or on the altar. Both the book and reading from it symbolized the presence of Christ among his people, comparable to his

---

[92]See Charles W. Jones, *Medieval Literature in Translation* (New York: Longmans, 1950); F. A. March, *Latin Hymns* (New York: Harper, 1883); William A. Merrill, *Latin Hymns* (Boston: Sanborn, 1904); Ruth Ellis Messenger, *The Medieval Latin Hymn* (Washington, D.C.: Capital Press, 1953) with an extensive bibliography; Helen Waddell, *Medieval Latin Lyrics* (Baltimore: Penguin, 1952); James J. Wilhelm, *Medieval Song* (New York: Dutton, 1971).

[93]Jungmann, 284.

[94]Paul Z. Strodach, *A Manual on Worship*, rev. ed. (Philadelphia: Muhlenberg Press, 1946), 222.

presence in the Eucharist. Thus Luther's insistence on the proclamation of Christ in preaching is comparable to his insistence on the real presence in the sacrament; both are continuations of catholic tradition. "For the preaching of the Gospel is nothing else than Christ coming to us, or we being brought to him."[95] St. Augustine told his congregation,

So let us therefore listen to the Gospel just as if the Lord himself were present. And do not let us say: "How fortunate were those who were able to see him!" For many of those who saw him also killed him, while many of us who have not seen him have yet believed in him. The precious truth that came from the mouth of the Lord was written down for us and kept for us and read aloud for us, and will be read by our children too, until the end of the world. The Lord is above, but the Lord, the truth, is here. The Lord's body in which he rose from the dead can be only in one place; but his truth is everywhere.[96]

Christ comes to his people in Scripture and in sacrament, and they stand (or kneel) to receive him. The Holy Gospel is heard as the voice of the living Lord in the midst of his people, who is soon to break bread with them and enter them in a yet more personal and intimate way in the Supper.

The Gospel is announced; the form varies in each of the rites:

Roman Catholic	**Lutheran**	**Episcopal**
The Lord be with you. *And also with you.* A reading from the holy Gospel according to N.	The Holy Gospel according to St. _____, the _____ chapter.	The Holy Gospel of our Lord Jesus Christ according to _____.

The congregation acknowledges the real presence of the Lord in the proclamation of the Gospel by acclamations before and after:

Roman Catholic	**Lutheran**	**Episcopal**
Glory to you, Lord.	Glory to you, O Lord.	Glory to you, Lord Christ.
This is the gospel of the Lord	The Gospel of the Lord.	The Gospel of the Lord.
Praise to you, Lord Jesus Christ.	Praise to you, O Christ.	Praise to you, Lord Christ.

The acclamations before and after the Gospel entered the liturgy quite early, from northern Europe. The form of the first was fixed at an early

---

[95] Martin Luther, "A Brief Instruction on What to Look for and Expect in the Gospels" (1521), *Luther's Works* 35:121.

[96] Augustine, *Sermon on St. John's Gospel* 30.1.

date; the exact form of the second varied somewhat. In the ninth century the practice of signing one's forehead with a cross at the announcement is found, and about the eleventh century the signing of forehead, mouth, and breast, which is still in use.[97]

The traditional Latin introductory formula for the Gospel pericope is *in illo tempore*, "at that time."[98] Mircea Eliade has found deep significance in these apparently simple words. The phrase for him becomes a technical phrase which makes reference to a primordial event which occurred in the archetypal time, the mythological period which gives justification and purpose to all succeeding ages. For "only that which was effected *in illo tempore* is real, meaningful, exemplary, and of inexhaustible creativity."[99]

SERMON. From earliest times, the sermon, an element inherited from Judaism, was a constituent part of the liturgy.[100] Its usual and logical place, also inherited from Judaism, is in close proximity to the readings, for the sermon serves as an exposition of the Scriptures which have just been read. Luther, in his *Formula Missae*, took a different approach:

We do not think that it matters whether the sermon in the vernacular comes after the Creed or before the introit of the mass; although it might be argued that since the Gospel is the voice crying in the wilderness and calling unbelievers to faith, it seems particularly fitting to preach before mass. For properly speaking, the mass consists in using the Gospel and communing at the table of the Lord.[101]

In his German Mass the sermon follows the Creed, which follows the Gospel.

In the *Lutheran Book of Worship*, as in the Roman sacramentary and the *Book of Common Prayer*, the sermon directly follows the Gospel. The sermon need not be on the Gospel for the day, of course, but it is always to be related to the gospel of what God has done for his people in Jesus Christ. Whatever the content of the sermon, worthy or unworthy, the location of the sermon immediately following the Gospel can help remind the congregation as it should remind the preacher of what the content of the message should be.

For Luther, as for the church which bears his name, hearing the word is not simply listening to a sermon but is an encounter with the risen

---

[97]Jungmann, 287–88; Hatchett, 331.

[98]The formula was used in the lectionary which accompanied the *Service Book and Hymnal, Epistles and Gospels together with Lessons from the Old Testament from the Service Book and Hymnal of the Lutheran Church in America: Authorized Version of 1611 A.D.* (Minneapolis: Augsburg Publishing House et al., 1959), p. 12 (Holy Innocents), 65 (Rogate), 67 (Exaudi), 68, 69, 71, 74, 78, 86, 97, 98, 99, 100.

[99]Mircea Eliade, *Australian Religions: An Introduction* (Ithaca: Cornell University Press, 1973), 40. See also his *Cosmos and History: The Myth of the Eternal Return* (New York: Harper and Row, 1959), 24ff. et passim; *Myth and Reality* (New York and Evanston: Harper and Row, 1963). See also Northrop Frye, *The Great Code: The Bible and Literature* (New York and London: Harcourt Brace Jovanovich, 1982), 84.

[100]Luke 4:16ff.; Acts 13:15; Justin Martyr, *First Apology* 67.

[101]*Luther's Works* 53:25.

and reigning Lord, who comes to liberate his people. The sermon cannot be understood apart from an understanding of the creative energy of language, for language can be charged with power, creating the conditions for an encounter with the Lord of life. The creative word works still, creating the presence of God, showing God in relation to creation, and bringing human life into relationship with God and the world. It is therefore the preacher's task to bring the energies of language to bear upon the ancient story to recreate and enliven and charge with power the inexhaustible wonder of the living Christ coming again, desiring of us some fresh avowal of our love, some new deep experience of what it means in Paul's matchless phrase to be "in Christ."

Preaching is not the act of the preacher alone, and the congregation is not an audience listening to a lecturer, a performer, or an entertainer. The sermon arises from a dialogue between the people of God and the Word of God, between the laity and the preacher, between the people of the world and the people of God. It is a conversation in which both preacher and congregation engage. The Bible delivers its message to its hearers, the preacher delivers a message to the congregation, and the congregation delivers the message to the world, translating the words into action. Thus the gospel engages the world, and the world engages the gospel.

Moreover, the sermon participates in the unity of the liturgical action of which it is a part. The sermon is set in the larger context as part of one great action of praise and proclamation. The liturgy is to be understood as a total sign involving the preacher and other ministers, readings and proclamation, a meal, and service in the world. Thus the sermon is the testimony of a representative of the church in whose life and manner and words is heard the living voice of the Gospel, the purpose of which is to assist in the creation of a total experience of encounter with the Most High who is paradoxically most near.

In Roman Catholic, often in Episcopal, and sometimes in Lutheran use the custom has developed to begin the sermon "In the name of the Father, and of the Son and of the Holy Spirit," thus placing all that follows under the power and guidance of the Holy Trinity. The preacher by this formula declares that the sermon is not a collection of private thoughts or personal notions but is what the triune God wants and helps to be said and heard. The sermon often closes with the same invocation of the Trinity. In Episcopal use, an ascription of praise to the Holy Trinity is sometimes employed instead.[102]

In Lutheran use, an additional custom has developed. It is the use of the Pauline formula of greeting, "Grace to you and peace, from God our Father and from the Lord Jesus Christ" (2 Cor. 1:2). Since the Holy Communion now begins with the Apostolic Greeting, the use of

---

[102] A popular form is "And now to God the Father, God the Son, and God the Holy Ghost be ascribed, as is most justly due, all honor, power, might, majesty, and dominion henceforth and forevermore."

such a formula again at the beginning of the sermon seems redundant, even misleading, suggesting that the service is beginning again. It is nonetheless an expression of the Lutheran conviction that the sermon is to be a proclamation of the gospel, setting the tone for what is to follow, indicating to the preacher the theme of what is to be said and to the congregation what is to be heard. If the sermon is otherwise unworthy, the greeting at least provides the congregation with a summary of the gospel which should have been preached.

No formula has been prescribed in Lutheran, Roman, or Episcopal service books, and none should be understood as necessary or as always desirable.

In the medieval period, Prone, a vernacular office, was often attached to the sermon. The form was at the discretion of the preacher and ordinarily consisted of the bidding of prayers, expositions of the Lord's Prayer and Creed, notices of ensuing feasts and fasts, and the banns of marriage and ordination. The name apparently derives from the French *prône*, originally a grille which marked off the chancel or the place where the notices were read.

HYMN OF THE DAY. The Hymn of the Day as practically an additional proper is a distinctive Lutheran contribution to the church's liturgy. Many sixteenth-century church orders established a yearly cycle of hymns for each Sunday of the year, but by the eighteenth century these as well as the gradual hymn suggested by Luther in his German Mass had fallen into disuse. After several nineteenth-century efforts, a yearly cycle of hymns was reestablished in the German *Evangelisches Gesangbuch* of 1950 and elsewhere in Europe.

The Hymn of the Day is, among other things, a doxological action, a sacrifice of praise as Wolfhart Pannenberg understands the term: a surrender to God of our reading from the ancient holy books and the words of the sermon, opening them to be filled by him and given ultimate meaning.[103]

The varied and elaborate musical treatment of this hymn — sung in unison or in polyphonic settings, antiphonally or in alternation with the choir, in conjunction with organ chorale settings, or accompanied by other instruments — indicate the high regard in which this hymn was held and suggest manifold ways of unfolding its text.

The index of Hymns for the Church Year (Min. Ed., pp. 470–72) incorporates a contemporary adaptation of the traditional Lutheran *de tempore* series. This index might perhaps more usefully and appropriately be included with the propers for the church year (pp. 121–70) of which it is in fact a part.

THE CREED. The principal creedal declaration in the liturgy is the eucharistic prayer. Before the beginning of the fourth century all creeds and summaries of faith were local statements. There was no one origi-

---

[103]Wolfhart Pannenberg, "Analogie und Doxologie," in W. Jöst and W. Pannenberg, eds., *Analogie und Denkstrukturen* (Göttingen: Vandenhoeck & Ruprecht, 1963), 96–115.

nal stock, but their roots were embedded in the action of baptism and the instruction of catechumens. The creed which came to be associated with the Eucharist began in the East, modelled on Matthew 28:19. The Council of Nicaea (325) amplified the creed in response to the Arians; it was further expanded at Constantinople (381) to combat Apollinarianism, and was adopted at Chalcedon in 451.[104] The Creed entered the eucharistic liturgy in the East during the christological controversies of the fifth century. It was introduced in 473 by a Monophysite bishop, Peter the Fuller (d. 488), to show his "orthodoxy" to his Orthodox adversaries.[105] In 511 the Monophysite Patriarch of Constantinople introduced the Nicene Creed into the liturgy in his diocese. It was said, never sung, by the congregation after the Great Entrance with the bread and wine. By the end of the sixth century the practice had spread to the West. The Third Council of Toledo (589) inserted the *filioque* ("and the Son") clause, which was not part of the text adopted at the ecumenical council at Chalcedon,[106] and introduced the Creed before the Lord's Prayer as a preparation for communion. It became the custom for the congregation to sing the Creed as was done with all the principal congregational parts of the mass. In the ninth century Charlemagne moved the Creed to a position immediately following the Gospel, and under the influence of the empire its use spread throughout the West. Rome adopted the liturgical use of the Creed in 1014 and regarded the Creed as a festal element which could be omitted on weekdays. In the tenth century Germany followed Celtic use and put the Creed after the Gospel and sermon and prior to the intercessions; many church orders (Liegnitz [1534], Brandenburg [1540], Reformation of Cologne [1543]) continued this location.[107]

The Greek text of the original conciliar form of the Creed begins "We believe," and so the present translation by the International Consultation on English Texts restores the plural. After the vocal participation of the people in the mass has ceased, the custom of the priest beginning the Creed, "I believe" spread and became established in the Western liturgy.[108] The use of the singular pronoun has led to the explanation that in the Creed one professes one's own faith. While there is an element of personal involvement in the profession to be sure, what in fact one does in professing the Creed is to bind oneself to the faith of the church, and so "we believe" is altogether appropriate.

---

[104] For a fuller discussion of the development of the Creed, see J. N. D. Kelly, *Early Christian Creeds*, 3rd ed. (London: Longmans, 1972).

[105] Timiadis, 26; Shepherd, 71.

[106] See Jaroslav Pelikan, *The Christian Tradition: The Spirit of Eastern Christendom (600–1700)*, vol. 2 (Chicago and London: University of Chicago Press, 1974), 183–98; see also *Spirit of God, Spirit of Christ: Ecumenical Reflections on the Filioque Controversy*. Faith and Order Paper 103, ed. Lukas Vischer (Geneva: World Council of Churches, 1981).

[107] Reed, 302.

[108] *Prayers We Have in Common* (p. 7) allows that "the use of the singular is, of course, an established legitimate variation."

In the opening sentence of the Creed God is called "*the* Almighty"; the definite article was added in the translation to bring out the significance of the Greek *pantocrator*, a noun not an adjective (see Rev. 1:8; 4:8). God is described as the maker "of all that is, seen and unseen," which refers to "heaven and earth" and to such things as angels but also may be understood to include further creative processes as part of the divine plan.[109]

Jesus Christ is "begotten" of the Father, describing his unique relationship with the Father as distinct from the mere process of birth. He is "eternally begotten," an explicitly anti-Arian description, directed at the denial of the Son's eternity. The Son who is not made but begotten shares the same kind of being as the Father and is "one in being (*homoousios*) with the Father." The Son, "through whom all things were made," is the Father's agent in creation (Heb. 1:2).

The translation by the International Consultation on English Texts has "For us men and for our salvation he came down from heaven," the Consultation explaining that " 'men' is here generic. Alternatives were sought to avoid the exclusive use of one gender, but the suggested variants tended to weaken the main statement." Nevertheless, the *Lutheran Book of Worship*, like the *Book of Common Prayer*, deleted "men" from the translation.

The Son "became incarnate from the Virgin Mary and was made man." This refers not only to the actual birth but to the entire process beginning with conception through which the Son of God took human flesh. He "suffered death," the Greek *pathonta* being made to bear the notions of both suffering and death," in accordance with the [Old Testament] Scriptures" (1 Cor. 15:4). The risen and ascended Lord "is seated at the right hand of the Father," emphasizing the permanence of Christ's position of honor.

The Holy Spirit is both Lord of life and the giver of life, and "proceeds from the Father." The International Consultation on English Texts translation puts "and the Son" (*filioque*), a Western addition to the Creed, in square brackets "indicating that some churches may include the words and other churches may not. It was not considered within the province of this Consultation to make recommendations as to its excision or retention."

The Latin text of the creed has "I believe one holy, catholic, and apostolic church," but the Greek has "We believe *in* one, holy, catholic, and apostolic church," expressing belief in the church as well as in God and in Christ "though some Western Fathers argue from the Latin text that belief in the church is a different order from belief in God." The line is printed as part of the third article, in subordination to "We believe in the Holy Spirit...."

---

[109]This and the comments on the translation of the Nicene and Apostles' Creeds which follow are from *Prayers We Have in Common*, 2nd rev. ed. (1975), and are given here because that useful book is not always easy to come by.

In common vernacular use in Germany before the Reformation, the church was described in the creed as *eine heilige christiliche Kirche;* German Roman Catholics after the Reformation continued to use the phrase rather than "one, holy, catholic, and apostolic church." Luther followed this custom in the Small Catechism, and the church orders continued the use of the word "Christian" rather than "catholic" and established a phraseology peculiar to the German Lutheran church.[110] The Scandinavian and French Lutheran churches used "catholic." The *Service Book and Hymnal* (1958) continued the translation "Christian" but in a footnote allowed "catholic" (curiously not capitalized to indicate that it did not mean Roman Catholic: "I believe one Holy, catholic, and Apostolic Church") and noted that it was "the original and generally accepted text."[111] In France, Germany, and Italy it was customary for the people to sing the Creed to a simple plainsong chant; the practice survived the Reformation in many Lutheran orders. Such congregational singing of the Creed is another indication that, as George Lindbeck has observed, the Nicene Creed "has acquired liturgical and expressive functions that are in some respects more important than its doctrinal use for large parts of Christendom. The act of reciting it is for millions a mighty symbol of the church's unity in space and time."[112]

A few church orders — Nuremberg, church orders (1525), Strasbourg, (1525), Sweden (1531), Austria (1571) — permitted the use of the Apostles' Creed for Sundays and the Nicene Creed for festivals. The *Lutheran Book of Worship*, in an effort not to lose congregational familiarity with the Apostles' (baptismal) Creed and following long Lutheran custom, appoints the Nicene Creed for all festival and penitential times and the Apostles" Creed for Sundays for which the color is green ("ordinary time") after the Epiphany and after Pentecost regardless of whether the Holy Communion is celebrated or abbreviated to ante-communion. The *Book of Common Prayer* permits the use of the baptismal (Apostles') Creed at the Burial of the Dead.[113]

The Latin text of the Apostles' Creed on which the translation is based is from the eighth century but is related to texts of earlier origin.[114] In its single unilateral departure from consistent use of the translations of the International Consultation on English Texts, the *Lutheran Book of Worship* gives the older translation "he descended into hell" because some Lutherans found this to be a confessional issue: since the Formula of Concord, Epitome IX and Solid Declaration IX used the expression "descent into hell," it was insisted that the old language be retained.[115]

---

[110]Reed, 303.

[111]*Service Book and Hymnal*, pp. 4–5.

[112]George Lindbeck, *The Nature of Doctrine: Religion and Theology in a Postliberal Age* (Philadelphia: Westminster Press, 1984), 95.

[113]*Book of Common Prayer*, 480, 496, where it is introduced, "In the assurance of eternal life given at Baptism, let us proclaim our faith and say...."

[114]See Kelly, chaps. 12–13. On this creed see Wolfhart Pannenberg, *The Apostles' Creed*, trans. Margaret Kohl (Philadelphia: Westminster Press, 1973).

[115]"We let matters rest on the simple statement of our Christian Creed, to which

The Latin phrase *descendit ad infernam* (literally "he descended to the lower [world]") has been variously understood: an underscoring of the assertion of Jesus' death; the beginning of Christ's victory, setting free the souls of the dead (1 Pet. 3:19); Christ's going to do battle with Satan and thus guaranteeing the deliverance of the saints. The International Consultation on English Texts provided a text, "he descended to the dead," which, it was thought, was open to all three interpretations.[116] This rendering is included in the *Lutheran Book of Worship* in a footnote whenever the Apostles' Creed appears.

Although "he rose again" may be questioned on biblical and theological grounds ("he was raised" would be more accurate) the phrase is an accurate translation of the Latin *resurrexit*. "The *again* is simply an English colloquialism which is appropriate to the spatial metaphor." "Ascended" is retained also for the sake of the metaphor, because of the biblical picture of which it is a part, and because the feast of the Ascension has a prominent place on the church's calendar.

"Catholic" with its emphasis on wholeness is a richer word than such substitutes as "universal" and has been the common translation of the vast majority of English-speaking churches. The description of the church as "Christian" rather than "catholic" was a common vernacular practice in Germany before and after the Reformation and was given currency in the Lutheran movement by Luther's use of it in the Small Catechism.

Many have seen the church and the communion of saints in apposition, following Luther, who wrote in the Large Catechism, "The creed calls the holy church a 'communion of saints.' Both expressions have the same meaning."[117] Thus, the two phrases were separated by a comma in the older translation of the Apostles' Creed and the two-phrase unit separated from the rest of the elements in the third article by semicolons. The "communion of saints," however, is ambiguous in the Latin. It can mean the communion of holy people or the communion in holy things. (See above, p. 60.) Helpful comments on particular words and phrases of the present translation of each creed are given in *Prayers We Have in Common*, second revised edition (Philadelphia: Fortress, 1975).[118]

In the *Lutheran Book of Worship* certain texts which are to be read — the Nicene and Apostles' Creeds, the eucharistic prayers, the Lord's Prayer, benedictions — are printed in sense lines to facilitate reading. This practice is followed in Roman Catholic and Episcopal books as well.

Dr. Luther directs us . . . 'I believe in the Lord Christ, God's Son, who died, was buried, and descended into hell.'" *Book of Concord*, 610. See also the Epitome of the Formula of Concord, article IX, p. 492.

[116] *Prayers We Have in Common*, 4–5.

[117] *Book of Concord*, 416.

[118] For a discussion of the contemporary problems of conception and translation see S. Mark Hein, "Gender and Creed: Confessing a Common Faith," *Christian Century* 102 (April 17, 1985):379–81.

THE PRAYERS. The prayers of intercession followed the readings as early as the second century.[119] In the East by the end of the fourth century these prayers had taken the form of a litany with biddings by the deacon. In the fifth century at Rome the prayers were also in bidding form, followed by silence and a collect by the presiding minister — a form preserved in the Bidding Prayer of the Good Friday liturgy. In the late fifth century at Rome the *deprecatio Gelasii*, a litany, began the service. Eventually, in part because intercessions were attached to the eucharistic prayer beginning in the fourth century, the prayers disappeared, and the Roman liturgy was left without a prayer of intercession.[120]

The loss was significant for in the prayers of intercession the "priesthood of believers" is seen in its proper exercise: the unselfish concern for the church and for all the world and everyone in it in their several callings and necessities, in harmony with the Apostle's admonition, "I urge that supplications, prayers, intercessions, and thanksgivings be made for all, for kings and all who are in high positions, that we may lead a quiet and peaceable life, godly and respectful in every way" (1 Tim. 2:1–2).[121] Anciently, the first act of the newly baptized was to join in the prayers of the faithful.[122]

Following Luther's *Deutsche Messe* (1526) in which he suggested an expanded paraphrase of the Lord's Prayer following the sermon,[123] drawing on the vernacular pulpit office called Prone, the Lutheran church orders developed the general prayer of the church (*Allgemeine Kirchengebet*). Such a general prayer and its location following the sermon is suggested in the Wittenberg Reformation (1545). The nineteenth-century American Lutheran liturgists beginning with the *Church Book* gathered material from Hesse Cassel (1657), Austria (1571), Baden (1556), Pfalz Zweibrücken (1557), and Strasbourg (1598) and formed the General Prayer. It was expanded in the *Common Service Book* (1919) and replaced with a new and superior text in the *Service Book and Hymnal* (1958), which survives in the *Lutheran Book of Worship* (Min. Ed., pp. 116–17).

Despite an abundance of general prayers of the church from the Lutheran church orders,[124] to encourage relevance to immediate needs and

---

[119] Justin Martyr, *First Apology* 65.

[120] See W. Jardine Grisbrooke, "Intercession at the Eucharist," *Studia Liturgica* 4:3 (Autumn 1965):129–55; 5:1 (Spring 1966):20–44; 5:2 (Summer 1966):87–103.

[121] See C. F. Miller, "Intercessory Prayer: History, Method, Subjects, and Theology," *Studia Liturgica* 3:1 (Summer 1964):20–29.

[122] Justin Martyr, *First Apology* 65; *Apostolic Tradition* 22.5.

[123] *Luther's Works* 53:78–80.

[124] See Mecklenburg (1540), Pomerania (1542), Brunswick-Lüneburg (1564), Austria (1571), Baden (1556), Calenberg (1569), the Reformation of Cologne (1543), Mark Brandenburg (1540), Rhein-Pfalz (1543), Saxony (1906), Bavaria (1879), the liturgy of Henry Melchior Muhlenberg (1748, 1786), and especially the *Common Service Book* (text ed., pp. 253–57), *Collects and Prayers* (Philadelphia: Board of Publication of the United Lutheran Church in America, 1935), 177–216; *Service Book and Hymnal*, pp. 238–41.

particularity in reference to the contemporary situation of the assembly the *Lutheran Book of Worship* (expect for Holy Baptism) provides no models prayers as does the *Book of Common Prayer* (pp. 383–95). Instead, the range of concerns for which prayers are to be offered is listed ("Prayers are included for the whole Church, the nations, those in need, the parish, special concerns"), and two forms are given which are to shape the intercessions written by those who prepare the service.[125] The introduction, "Let us pray for the whole people of God in Christ Jesus and for all people according to their needs" recalls the Byzantine *Book of Needs*[126] and the double concern of the prayers: the church and the world. The formula "Lord, in your mercy, *hear our prayer*" is from the Roman and Episcopal form; "Let us pray to the Lord. *Lord have mercy*" recalls the Kyrie as well as the litany in Evening Prayer, taken from the Byzantine liturgy. The conclusion to the prayers, "Into your hands, O Lord, we commend all for whom we pray," recalls Jesus' prayer on the cross (Luke 23:46), echoed in the responsory in Compline; the final clause, "trusting in your mercy; through Jesus Christ our Lord" recalls such passages as 2 Corinthians 3:4 and Psalm 52:8.

The Liturgy of the Eucharistic Meal

THE PEACE. The Peace, comparable in spirit and intention to the Apostolic Greeting, begins the second half of the Holy Communion, the liturgy of the eucharistic meal. Anciently it was a greeting of the communicants after the dismissal of the catechumens.[127] The holy kiss of peace, a symbol of family love, is referred to in the New Testament (Rom. 16:16; 1 Cor. 16:20; 2 Cor. 13:12; 1 Thess. 5:26; 1 Pet. 5:14), and there are constant references to it in succeeding centuries.

In the Armenian liturgy the deacon says, "Greet one another with a holy kiss" (Rom. 16:16) and the people bow to one another saying, "Christ is in the midst of us." Justin Martyr says that at the conclusion of the prayers, concluding the synaxis and forming a bridge to the offering of the bread and wine, "we greet one another with a kiss." This location, still the place of the peace in Eastern liturgies and in the Ambrosian rite, recalls Christ's admonition "If you are offering your gift at the altar, and there remember that your brother has something against you, leave your gift there before the altar and go; first be reconciled to your brother, and then come and offer your gift" (Matt. 5:23–24).

In the fourth century, St. Augustine reports that in the African church the kiss was exchanged after the Lord's Prayer and before communion. In the next century the Roman rite followed the African church and moved the Peace to just prior to the distribution of the sacrament as

---

[125]See Walter C. Huffman, *The Prayer of the Faithful: Understanding and Creatively Using the Prayer of the Church* (Minneapolis: Augsburg Publishing House, 1986).

[126]*Book of Needs of the Holy Orthodox Church* (New York: AMS Press, 1969 [1894]).

[127]Justin Martyr, *First Apology* 65. For a brief history of the Peace and a review of the literature see Robert F. Taft, *The Great Entrance* (Rome: Pont. Institutum Studiorum Orientalium, 1975), 375–78.

a dramatic illustration of the petition in the Lord's Prayer which immediately precedes it, "as we forgive those who sin against us," and as an expression of the peace-bestowing presence of the risen Christ (John 20:19–23). This has remained its location in the Roman rite. It was therefore the location of the peace in the Common Service and is an alternate location of the peace in the *Lutheran Book of Worship.* ("The Peace is shared at this time or after the Lord's Prayer, prior to the distribution" — Min. Ed., pp. 205, 242, 278.) The actual kiss of peace in late medieval times was a formal exchange, beginning with the celebrant receiving the peace of the Lord symbolically from the Lord himself by kissing the altar, the paten,[128] the consecrated bread, or a pax-board (*osculatorium*) — a board bearing the image of the crucifixion or of a saint. The peace would then be received by the ministers in descending order of rank. If a pax-board was used, it would be passed among the communicants. Eventually the kiss of peace was limited to a formal exchange between the celebrant and deacon on certain occasions.

The accompanying words, "The peace of the Lord be with you always," were much appreciated by Luther, who in the *Formula Missae* (1523) says that the greeting is "a public absolution of the sins of the communicants, the true voice of the gospel announcing remission of sins, and therefore the one and most worthy preparation for the Lord's Table, if faith holds to these words as coming from the mouth of Christ himself. On this account I would like to have it pronounced facing the people, as the bishops are accustomed to do...."[129] (Luther then unaccountably omitted the sentence from his *Deutsche Messe* [1526].) Yngve Brilioth commented that Luther's interpretation "was a violent importation of his favorite idea into a phrase which was originally intended to convey a different meaning; but is it not another sign that the phrase 'forgiveness of sins' had for him a deeper meaning than the words normally bear?"[130]

The response "and also with you" ("and with thy spirit" in the older language), the usual response to a liturgical salutation, is given in the Roman Catholic, Episcopal, and Lutheran rites. Until the *Service Book and Hymnal* (1958), however, the Common Service had the congregation say "Amen," influenced by Luther's understanding of the verse as an announcement of the gospel of the forgiveness of sins. Most worshipers in recent centuries, however, seemed to understand the one-word reply as a simple liturgical thank-you, and thus it seemed unsatisfactory.

The action of sharing the peace was revived in the *Book of Common Worship* of the Church of South India (1963) as an optional element following the prayers and before the offering.[131]

---

[128] A cross is still often marked on the rim of patens so that the presiding minister does not kiss a plate but the sign of the Lord whose peace the kiss conveys.

[129] *Luther's Works* 53:28.

[130] Yngve Brilioth, *Eucharistic Faith and Practice: Evangelical and Catholic*, trans. A. G. Hebert (London: SPCK, 1930), 117.

[131] The Directions explain the practice: "When the Peace is given, the giver places his

OFFERING. The most ancient accounts of the liturgy lay no stress on the presentation and preparation of the gifts. In Justin's account bread and wine and water are simply brought in. In the second century, in opposition to those who repudiated the material universe, the presentation of the gifts of bread and wine was invested with symbolic meaning and liturgical action. Tertullian and Hippolytus describe the people making individually their offerings of bread and wine and other gifts for the poor and needy and presenting them separately at the altar. A mosaic on the floor of a large Christian church in Aquileia shows that the gifts were often elaborate: grapes, wine, birds, fruit, wool, oil, honey, olives, cheese, silver, and gold. The *Apostolic Tradition* provides prayers for the "first fruits of the field." Grapes, apples, figs, olives, pears, pomegranates, peaches, cherries, and almonds are to be blessed; lotus, onions, garlic, pumpkins, and cucumbers are not. Roses and lilies are acceptable gifts, but other flowers are not.

After the fourth century, when reception of communion became infrequent, many offerings were no longer received at the Eucharist. In the Eastern churches a procession of the gifts of Great Entrance bread and wine, the Great Entrance, arose and spread to many churches of the West apart from Rome.

In the fourth century the gifts had so proliferated that they had to be restricted to bread and wine, but the impulse proved difficult to repress. By the ninth and tenth centuries efforts were made at least to distinguish between the offering of bread and wine and the presentation of other gifts at other times (before mass or before the Gospel).

As the entrance of the ministers at the beginning of the Eucharist was covered by the entrance psalm, so the offertory procession was accompanied by the antiphonal singing of a psalm.[132] By the eighth century this offertory psalm had been reduced to one or two verses. After the offering had been presented, the celebrant said a prayer over the gifts. Ceremonies multiplied, and "as a result the Mass books of the later Middle Ages contain at the oblation a veritable jungle of new prayers and texts."[133] It is small wonder therefore, that Luther fumed,

that utter abomination follows which forces all that precedes in the mass into its service and is, therefore, called the offertory. From here on almost everything smacks and savors of sacrifice. And the words of life and salvation [the words of

---

right palm against the right palm of the receiver, and each closes his left hand over the other's right hand. The Peace is given before the offertory (see Matthew 5:23, 24) as a sign of fellowship, and the offertory sentences [Ps. 133:1; 1 Cor. 10:17; Ps. 2:6] recall St. Augustine's teaching that the sacrifice we offer is our unity in Christ. The presbyter gives the Peace to those ministering with him, and these in turn give it to the congregation. It may be passed through the congregation either along the rows, or from those in front to those behind. Each person as he gives the Peace may say in a low voice, 'The peace of God,' or 'The Peace of God be with you.'" (*Book of Common Worship*, p. xiii.)

[132] Augustine, *Retractations* II.11.

[133] Jungmann, 335.

Institution] are embedded in the midst of it all....Let us, therefore, repudiate everything that smacks of sacrifice.... [134]

The Lutheran church orders, therefore, came generally to provide for the singing of psalm verses while the gifts were received and no more. The Common Service appointed Psalm 51:10–12; the *Common Service Book* (1919) provided Psalm 51:17–19 as an alternative and permitted "any other suitable Offertory." The *Service Book and Hymnal* (1958) added Psalm 116:12–14, 19 as another option. The *Lutheran Book of Worship* is the first North American Lutheran service book to provide a full course of proper offertories for every Sunday and festival of the year. [135] The present Roman Catholic sacramentary makes provision only for an "offertory song" without specifying the text. The texts of the optional offertory songs are available in the *Graduale Romanum* (Chicago: G.I.A. Publications, 1974) and the *Graduale Simplex*, editio typica altera (Vatican City State: Libreria Editrice Vaticana, 1975). The Lutheran texts are based on a preliminary draft of the optional series drafted for the Roman rite. The *Book of Common Prayer* makes no provision for such an offertory verse. Nine offertory sentences and one bidding of offerings and oblations are given under the rubric, "One of the following, or some other appropriate sentence of Scripture, may be used." In all three rites, the offertory verse, song, or sentence is optional.

As an alternative to the proper offertories, the *Lutheran Book of Worship* provides two texts set to music within the liturgy. The first, "Let the vineyards be fruitful, Lord," is a text by John Arthur, written for *Contemporary Worship 2: The Holy Communion* (1970). The biblical allusions include Isaiah 5:1; Hosea 10:1; Ezekiel 19:10; Psalm 23:5; Revelation 14:15; John 6:48. The second offertory text is Psalm 116:12, 17, 13–14, 19, a text traditionally associated with the Holy Communion. It is part of the Hallel (Psalms 113–118), recited at all the principal Jewish festivals, and is supposed by some to be the "hymn" which Jesus and the apostles sang before his arrest on Maundy Thursday evening. The translation by the Inter-Lutheran Commission on Worship is a modernization of the Authorized Version used in the *Service Book and Hymnal* (p. 6), which introduced this text to North American Lutheran use.

When the gathered offerings are brought to the altar, the rubrics (Min. Ed., p. 28, #5) direct that the assisting minister who receives the alms basin elevate it slightly to suggest the self-offering of the assembly. The two offertory prayers explicate this gesture.

From the fifth century, before the medieval elaborations, the old Roman rite provided simply a prayer over the gifts (called the "secret" because it was said inaudibly) when the offerings had been presented

---

[134] *Formula Missae* (*Luther's Works* 53:25–26).

[135] This is not to say that the proper offertories were unknown or not available before 1978. See, for example, Albert Olai Christiansen and Harold Edward Schuneman, *Proper of the Service* (New York: H. W. Gray, 1947), 46–55. The rubrics of the *Common Service Book* (p. 13) and the *Service Book and Hymnal* (p. 5) permitted such use: "One of the Offertories here following, or any other suitable Offertory, may be used."

at the altar. The *Lutheran Book of Worship*, increasing the contact of the Lutheran use with the broader Christian tradition,[136] and suggesting a reinterpretation of the concept of sacrifice as the self-offering of the church (Rom. 12:1–2), has introduced a simple offertory prayer, the purpose of which is to acknowledge our use of God's gifts of creation which have blessed and enriched human life.[137] God's gifts to us, grain and grapes, are returned to him as human labor has transformed them into bread and wine for use in the Holy Supper.[138] God's gifts of grain and grapes have been harvested, baked or pressed, packaged or bottled, delivered, stored, displayed, purchased, and presented in a world of economic inflation and depression, marketing analyses, price negotiations, collective bargaining, injustice and greed, sacrifice and concern. The elements are rich with suggestive meanings and connections with life in a complex modern world, and they will not allow the congregation which celebrates the Holy Communion to leave the world behind when they enter into the holy place. The bread, a necessity of life, suggests the wonderful aroma of the bakery and food of which some have too little and others, far too much. The wine, an enrichment of life, suggests the drink which makes glad human hearts and warms and cheers the spirit and also which is the cause of drunkenness, violence, and degradation. Moderation and excess, nourishment and deprivation, enrichment and intoxication are all gathered in the bread and wine which are offered to God for blessing and redemption, justice and purification and renewal.

Both offertory prayers were written for the *Lutheran Book of Worship*. The first (no. 239), a revision of a prayer drafted for *Contemporary Worship 2: The Holy Communion* (1970), stresses our imitation of God's prior self-giving love. The second (no. 240), written by Eugene L. Brand, is similar to Jewish prayers of thanksgiving. It emphasizes the offering of the lives of those who offer the gifts, following the admonition of the Apostle, "Present your bodies as a living sacrifice" (Rom. 12:1), and also touches on responsible stewardship of creation — the life of all the natural world and not human life only.[139]

The assisting minister prepares the table and leads the prayer. The association of deacons with the preparation of the altar is traceable from the second-century *Apology* of Justin Martyr. The Inter-Lutheran Commission on Worship, however, contrary to the traditional practice of having the presiding minister voice all the principal prayers of the liturgy, gave this prayer to the assisting minister and the congregation so

---

[136]This was an acknowledged goal of the Inter-Lutheran Commission on Worship, as expressed in the Introduction to the Lutheran Book of Worship: "... to continue to move into the larger ecumenical heritage of liturgy...." (Min. Ed., p. 12.)

[137]Shepherd, 71–73. See also Ralph A. Kiefer, "Preparation of the Altar and Gifts or Offertory?" *Worship* 48 (December 1974):595–600; W. Jardine Grisbrooke, "Oblation at the Eucharist," *Studia Liturgica* 3:4 (1964):227–39; 4:1 (Spring 1965):37–55.

[138]See John A. T. Robinson, *Liturgy Coming to Life* (Philadelphia: Westminster Press, 1964), 61–63, 90.

[139]See H. Paul Santmire, *The Travail of Nature: The Ambiguous Ecological Promise of Christian Theology* (Philadelphia: Fortress Press, 1985).

that the presiding minister need not approach the altar until the beginning of the preface. It might be observed that the people have already raised their voices in the offertory song, which, although optional, is only very rarely omitted in Lutheran practice.

THE GREAT THANKSGIVING. The Great Thanksgiving (*eucharistia me-gale*, an early title) begins with the opening dialogue, the Preface, and concludes with the great Amen at the conclusion of the prayer of thanksgiving (or with the Words of Institution in the two other forms which the *Lutheran Book of Worship* provides). In the East the great prayer was often called the Anaphora (from the Greek *anapherō*, I carry up, I offer in sacrifice), a name still preferred by many liturgists. In the West it was sometimes called "the action"; the phrase in ancient sacramentaries, *incipit canon actionis* (the order of the action begins), gave rise to the use of "canon" to refer to the Great Thanksgiving. It was also called simply "the prayer," in Latin *oratio* or *prex* or *praedicatio* or *prefatio*.

The Great Thanksgiving derives from Jewish table blessings (thanksgivings) such as Jesus said at the Last Supper.[140] The religious character of the Jewish meal found expression in the prayers (*berakoth*, singular *berakah*) which accompanied it. There was a short *berakah* over the bread, a blessing, at the beginning of a meal, and after the meal there was another *berakah* over the cup, a thanksgiving (1 Cor. 10:16). This second prayer, the more important prayer which could never be omitted, was the *Birkat ha-mazon*, the thanksgiving after the meal. The full text of the *Birkat ha-mazon* dates only from the ninth century C.E., but doubtless it has more ancient roots. It is in three parts: a benediction, blessing God for the food which he gives to Israel; a thanksgiving for the land; and a supplication for Jerusalem. There is a close relation between the *Birkat ha-mazon* and the prayers of *Didache* 10, noted by Kohler in the *Jewish Encyclopedia* (1925), although the *Didache* reverses the order of the first two parts of the Jewish prayer (thanksgiving, benediction, supplication) and although there is in the *Didache* no concluding benediction or *chatimah*. The reorganization appears to be deliberate so as to emphasize thanksgiving for redemption over the blessing of God

---

[140]There has developed a considerable series of studies of the literary structure of the eucharistic prayer as a genre of liturgical prayer, initiated by Jean-Paul Audet, "Literary Forms and Contents of a Normal *Eucharistia* in the First Century," *Studia Evangelica*, Texte und Unterschungen 73 (1959):643–62; Robert J. Ledogar, "The Eucharistic Prayer and the Gifts over Which It Is Spoken," *Worship* 41 (1967):578–96; Robert J. Ledogar, *Acknowledgement: Praise Verbs in the Early Greek Anaphoras*, doctoral dissertation (Rome, 1968); Louis Ligier, "The Origins of the Eucharistic Prayer: From the Last Supper to the Eucharist," *Studia Liturgica* 9 (1973):176–85; Thomas J. Talley, "From *Berakah* to *Eucharistia*: A Reopening Question," *Worship* 50 (1976):115–37; Thomas J. Talley, "The Eucharistic Prayer of the Ancient Church according to Recent Research: Results and Reflections," *Studia Liturgica* 11 (1976):138–58; *Studia Liturgica* 11:3/4 (1976) is devoted to eucharistic prayer; Thomas J. Talley, "The Eucharistic Prayer: Directions for Development," *Worship* 51 (1977):316–25; Thomas J. Talley, "The Literary Structure of the Eucharistic Prayer," *Worship* 58 (1984):404–20; Enrico Mazza, *The Eucharistic Prayers of the Roman Rite* (New York: Pueblo Publishing Co., 1986), 12–22.

for his gifts of creation. To the basic pattern of praise, thanksgiving, and supplication additions were made on the model of the festal embolisms in the *Birkat ha-mazon*, inserted in the manner of a scriptural citation. But the Jewish *berakah* which became a central form of prayer was in its biblical origins not a prayer addressed to God at all but a praise of God stated in the third person, like the creedal forms in Christian liturgies (see Luke 1:68; Eph. 1:3; 1 Pet. 1:3).[141] The *berakah* itself derives from *todah* (from a root meaning "to confess" faith or "to confess" sin), which comprises two coordinated parts: an account of the works of God (an anamnesis) and a petition that the prayers of Israel may be heard (an epiclesis). The basic structure is bipartite, account and invocation, and it appears that the real source of the Christian Great Thanksgiving is not the *berakoth* but the *todah*.[142] *Todah*, a prayer form, is in Greek *eucharistein*. The result is a reduction of the tripartite formula to a bipartite form — praise followed by supplication — which is visible also in the anaphoras of Addai and Mari and of Hippolytus.[143]

This basic pattern of the great prayer was soon enriched with the addition of three elements: (1) the Preface, the purpose of which was to join the congregation's praise with that of heaven, and which led into the second additional piece (2) the Sanctus, the song of heaven; and (3) intercessions, inserted before the concluding doxology.

The prayers of Israel are not formulas to be repeated verbatim; they are rather outlines to guide those who pray. Similarly, for the first centuries of the church's life the text of the Great Thanksgiving was not fixed, and the presiding minister elaborated on the basic pattern according to ability and the occasion. The *Apostolic Tradition* of Hippolytus (ca. 215) gives the text of the Great Thanksgiving which seems to have been derived from the *Birkat ha-mazon* through the *Didache* and which turns the thanksgiving into a telling of the history of salvation.[144] The basic structure is bipartite: account and invocation. The structure may be further divided into (1) introductory dialogue, (2) thanksgiving, (3) institution narrative, (4) anamnesis, (5) epiclesis or invocation, (6) concluding doxology. All the Great Thanksgivings of the known eucharistic rites contain these parts in this order. The one exception is the mid-fourth-century anaphora of Serapion, which conflates the institution narrative and the anamnesis. The East Syrian Anaphora of the Holy Apostles Addai and Mari has no institution narrative, but it is often thought once to have contained one. The structure of the eucharistic prayer, a genre of liturgical prayer, is thus a nearly universal order throughout the church in East and West: (1) dialogue, (2) Preface, (3) Sanctus, (4) post-sanctus, (5) institution narrative,

---

[141]Thomas J. Talley, "The Literary Structure of the Eucharistic Prayer," *Worship* 58 (1984):406.
[142]Mazza, 15–17.
[143]Frank C. Senn, "Toward a Different Anaphoral Structure," *Worship* 58 (1984):349.
[144]See Mazza, 19–21.

(6) anamnesis, (7) epiclesis, (8) intercessions, (9) concluding doxology, (10) the amen.[145]

Dialogue. In the opening dialogue the presiding minister asks and the congregation grants authority to proclaim the Great Thanksgiving in the name of all.

Since earliest times all the liturgies of East and West have begun the Great Thanksgiving with an introductory dialogue. In the Bible and in the liturgy, the dialogue is the crucial relationship in the light of which all other relationships and actions are judged.[146] Dialogue brings the limitations of human contingency, powerlessness, and finitude into combination with the Lord God, the Eternal One of unlimited power,[147] by whom humans break through their limitations. Human wholeness cannot exist apart from relationships to others; Martin Buber observed, "All real living is meeting."[148] In the Eucharist, the dialogue is two-fold. It is a dialogue between human beings (the presiding minister and the congregation) and also between humanity and God.

The translation of the introductory dialogue is by the International Consultation on English Texts.[149]

The first pair of verses is usually a salutation, in Roman and Egyptian liturgies "The Lord be with you" (Ruth 2:4), in Syrian and Byzantine liturgies some form of the Apostolic Greeting, "The grace of our Lord Jesus Christ ... " (2 Cor. 13:14). The response is always "And also with you." Large problems make the translation of these verses difficult.[150] Some (e.g., Van Unnik) believe that "the Lord" in the first line *Dominus vobiscum* refers to the Holy Spirit; others (e.g., Jungmann) believe it refers to Christ. Moreover, the Latin phrase has no verb, but English requires one. Some suggest that the verb should be the indicative *is;* the majority, however, on the basis of 1 Corinthians 16:23, 2 Corinthians 13:13, and the Latin phrase later in the mass *Pax domini sit semper vobiscum* (The peace of the Lord be with you always) believe that the verb should be the subjunctive *be.*

The congregation's response, *et cum spiritu tuo,* is also unclear. Some (e.g., John Chrysostom) find deep significance in "spirit" as a reference to the indwelling Holy Spirit; most understand it as a Semitism meaning simply the person, "you."

The second pair of verses, "Lift up your hearts. We lift them to the Lord" (*Sursam corda. Habemus ad dominum.*),[151] although their pre-

---

[145]W. Jardine Grisbrooke, "Anaphora," *The New Westminster Dictionary of Liturgy and Worship.*

[146]Leonard L. Thompson, *Introducing Biblical Literature: A More Fantastic Country* (Englewood Cliffs, NJ: Prentice-Hall, 1978), 12–13.

[147]See Northrop Frye, *Anatomy of Criticism* (Princeton: University Press, 1971), 120.

[148]Martin Buber, *I and Thou* (New York: Scribners, 1970), 17, 11, 6, 8. See Maurice S. Friedman, *Martin Buber: The Life of Dialogue,* 3rd ed. rev. (Chicago: University Press, 1976).

[149]See *Prayers We Have in Common,* 2nd rev. ed., p. 14.

[150]See above, p. 125 sin connection with the salutation before the Prayer of the Day.

[151]The 2nd rev. ed. of *Prayers We Have in Common* (1975) was not available when the

cise origin is unknown, are a most ancient Christian tradition, being found in the *Apostolic Tradition* (ca. 215). Cyprian (ca. 252) comments on them, saying that every worldly thought is to be suppressed and the mind turned solely to the Lord.[152] St. Augustine refers to this verse again and again,[153] finding in it the Pauline injunction to "seek the things which are above" (Col. 3:1-2; John 11:41; see also Lam. 3:41; Ps. 86:4). Origen observes that one must "lift up the soul before lifting the eyes, and, before standing to pray, lift up the spirit from the things of earth and direct it to the Lord of all."[154] The original intent of these verses, however, seems to have been practical: they were a command to the people to stand, to assume the priestly posture of prayer.[155]

The third pair of verses, "Let us give thanks to the Lord our God. It is right to give him thanks and praise" (*Gratias agamus domino deo nostro. Dignum et justum est.*) is an introduction to the prayer of thanks in Jewish prayer. Following the Jewish tradition, the Christian liturgies blessed God by praising and thanking him for his works. The first line therefore appropriately begins "Let us give thanks," and the second concludes with the word "praise," giving emphasis to the central thought of these verses.[156] "Let us give thanks" was a request by the presiding minister to be allowed to offer thanks in the name of all present. Their consent was given in the response, *Dignum et justum est* (It is fitting, it is right") as the people endorsed the request in language not uncommon throughout the ancient world.[157]

The Preface. Following the opening dialogue the Great Thanksgiving continues with thanksgiving to God "through Jesus Christ our Lord." (In the form of the prayer in the *Apostolic Tradition* — the earliest extant text of the Great Thanksgiving — there is no preface. The prayer moves from dialogue to the thanksgiving without interruption.)

The Preface is always addressed to the first person of the Holy Trinity, God the Father, and praises him for what he has done or praises him through Jesus Christ. In the West, the part of the praise before the Sanctus acquired a character of its own as a seasonal variable, of-

---

English translation of the Roman sacramentary was prepared (1970), and so the English translation of the Roman mass follows the earlier version of the texts prepared by the International Consultation on English Texts, "We lift them up to the Lord" (1970, 1971), as did the preparatory drafts of the Lutheran and Episcopal books.

[152]Cyprian, *On Prayer* 31; Jungmann, 369. The Liturgy of St. John Chrysostom has the congregation sing, "Let us, who mystically represent the cherubim, now lay aside all earthly care...."

[153]E.g., Augustine, *Sermon* 227; see W. Rötzer, *Des hl. Augustinus Schriften als liturgiegeschichtliche Quelle* (Munich, 1930), 118f.

[154]Origen, *Prayer* 31.2; *Exhortation to Martyrdom* 3.

[155]Hatchett, 361.

[156]*Prayers We Have in Common*, 14. It has been suggested by Edward Yarnold (*Study of Liturgy*, 190 note 6) that a form of the dialogue may have already existed when St. Paul wrote 2 Thess. 1:3.

[157]Jungmann, 369; Hatchett, 361; Grisbrooke, "Anaphora" in *the New Westminster Dictionary of Liturgy and Worship*.

ten called the Proper Preface. This preface had its focus on one aspect of salvation history appropriate to the season of the church year being celebrated. The early prefaces,[158] and the Eastern prefaces still, were lengthy and elaborate, a fixed text reviewing the history of salvation. In the West, the characteristic terse style prevailed. The most ancient collection of Roman mass texts, the Leonine sacramentary, has a proper preface for each mass — 267 are provided, and the sacramentary is incomplete. This number was drastically reduced in the Gregorian sacramentary to some ten prefaces. From time to time others were introduced and suppressed.[159] The reforms of the liturgy in the twentieth century have provided an increased number of prefaces. These are given and commented on in chapter 5 in connection with the propers for seasons and days.

The purpose of the Preface is to give reasons for rendering thanksgiving at the particular occasion and to join the praise of the church on earth with that of the church in heaven (Heb. 12:22ff.). Modern revisions of the eucharistic prayer follow both Eastern and Western traditions, providing anaphoras which use a variable preface as in the Western tradition and providing at least one anaphora with an invariable preface as in the Eastern tradition. In the *Lutheran Book of Worship*, Eucharistic Prayer IV, the prayer of Hippolytus, does not use a variable preface (or the Sanctus).

In Lutheran and Episcopal use, the Preface concludes with a fixed formula:

Lutheran Book of Worship	*Book of Common Prayer*
And so, with the Church on earth and the host of heaven, we praise your name and join their unending hymn:	Therefore we praise you, joining our voices with Angels and Archangels and with all the company of heaven, who for ever sing this hymn to proclaim the glory of your Name: (Eucharistic Prayer A [p. 362] and B [p. 367])

(The loss of the older series of strong verbs — "laud...magnify... evermore praising...and saying" — in exchange for two weaker ones, "praise" and "join," has been seen by some as a flattening of the language of praise.[160]) The Roman Catholic, Methodist, and Presbyterian prefaces exhibit a variety of conclusions. In either case, the purpose of the conclusion is to unite the praise of the Preface with the Sanctus of the whole company of heaven.

---

[158] *Apostolic Constitutions* 8, 12.

[159] Jungmann, 373.

[160] Margaret A. Doody, in *The State of the Language*, ed. Leonard Michaels and Christopher Ricks (Berkeley: University of California Press, 1980), 116.

160

Sanctus. The Sanctus, with which the Preface continues, is the hymn of praise in the liturgy of the table, corresponding to the Hymn of Praise in the liturgy of the word.

The Sanctus was absent from the *Apostolic Tradition* of Hippolytus and from the fourth-century Syrian document *The Testament of Our Lord Jesus Christ*, closely dependent on the *Apostolic Tradition*, but by the fourth century it is found in all the liturgies of East and West. It is perhaps referred to by Clement of Rome in his first letter[161] and by Origen.[162]

The Sanctus, the first and fullest acclamation of the Great Thanksgiving, with which the congregation joins the voice of the presiding minister as together they join the choirs of heaven, derives from Isaiah's breathtakingly majestic vision of the transcendent otherness of the All-Holy in confounding contrast to the mortality and impurity of humanity (Isa. 6:3; see Dan. 7:10; Rev. 4:8). The prophet sees the exalted and utterly unapproachable Thrice-Holy enthroned as sovereign, surrounded with seraph attendants who hide their faces from the divine glory. The swirling incense becomes the robes of the Holy One whose glory fills the earth, whose holiness radiates upon the world. Isaiah was terrified by what he saw. A sinful man had penetrated the heavenly court and gazed upon the face of God.[163]

At an early stage in liturgical use, to increase the picture of God's grandeur, the church added "heaven" to the second line and, instead of making a statement, addressed the phrase to God in praise: "Heaven and earth are full of your glory." Lord God of Sabaoth is an ancient title for God the divine warrior rooted in holy war (Ps. 89:6–8; cf. James 5:4, Rom. 9:29). It is a troublesome concept for the modern world, and Sabaoth is better understood as describing all the forces which operate at God's command throughout the whole of creation.[164]

"Hosanna" (= save, I/we pray) is used in Psalm 118:25, a psalm which came to be associated with messianic expectation, and in the New Testament Jesus was hailed as Messiah by use of the word.[165]

In all the anaphoras but the Alexandrian, the *Benedictus qui venit* (Mark 11:9–10; cf. Matt. 21:9; John 12:13; Luke 19:38) was attached to the Sanctus. In the Anglican Reformation there was opposition to this addition, for it seemed to suggest an understanding of the real presence which was unacceptable to many Protestants, and so the Benedictus was not part of the Sanctus in Anglican rites until the 1979 Prayer Book. In

---

[161] 1 Clement 34:6–7.

[162] Origen, *Sermon on Isaiah* 1.2.

[163] See Gerald Moultrie's hymn based on the Liturgy of St. James, "Let All Mortal Flesh Keep Silence" (hymn 198).

[164] See *Prayers We Have in Common*, 15.

[165] See Donald McIlhagga, "Hosanna, Supplication and Acclamation," *Studia Liturgica* 5 (Autumn 1966):129–50.

the *Apostolic Constitutions* and the Byzantine rites, *Benedictus qui venit* is used as the people's response to the invitation to communion, "Holy things for the holy people."

The translation of the Sanctus and the Benedictus is by the International Consultation on English Texts. The melody for the Sanctus in setting two of the *Lutheran Book of Worship* (Min. Ed., p. 257) derives from eleventh-century plainsong adapted by J. S. Bach (Steinau, 1726) and revised by Regina H. Fryxell for the *Service Book and Hymnal* (1958).

Bowing low during the Sanctus is very ancient;[166] it clearly accords well with Isaiah's vision of God. The use of the sign of the cross at the *Benedictus qui venit*, the practice of some Lutherans, is mentioned as early as the eleventh century;[167] the practice is not continued in the Missal of Paul VI (1969).

In his *Formula Missae* (1523) Luther placed the Sanctus after the words of institution, and the church orders of Brandenburg-Nuremberg (1533), Sweden (1531), and Riga (1530) did likewise.[168] The first reference to the use of the Sanctus in the West is in Peter Chrysologus, who gave it a christological interpretation.[169] The Sanctus supported Luther's emphasis on the real presence of Christ in the consecration of the bread and wine.[170] His German Mass (1526) provided a hymn paraphrase of the Sanctus ("Isaiah in a Vision Did of Old," hymn 528) for use between the consecration and distribution of the bread and the consecration and distribution of the cup, and he said that this "German Sanctus or the hymn, 'Let God be blest,' or the hymn of John Hus, 'Jesus Christ, Our God and Savior' could be sung. Then shall the cup be blessed and administered, while the remainder of these hymns are sung...."[171]

Post-Sanctus. The post-Sanctus begins with words which recall and echo the words of the Sanctus, continuing its praise. Frequently the post-Sanctus marks a transition from the proclamation of the works of God reported in the Old Testament to those reported in the New Testament, a continuity noted in 1 Peter 2:5; Malachi 1:11, and *Didache* 14.3 This section links the verbal thanksgiving of the Sanctus to the ritual thanksgiving of the institution narrative and the actions with the bread and cup.

In liturgical history the post-Sanctus takes one of two forms. It may be a continuation of the thanksgiving, as it was in most of the historic liturgies, or, as in the Alexandrine and Roman rites, it may be a prayer

---

[166] Jungmann, 384.
[167] Ibid.
[168] Reed, 332.
[169] Peter Chrysologus, *Sermon* 170.
[170] Senn, "Toward a Different Anaphoral Structure," 358; see Reed, 332, who refers to Adrian Fortescue, *The Mass: A Study of the Roman Liturgy* (New York: Longmans, 1937), 323.
[171] *Luther's Works* 53:81–82.

often called the preliminary epiclesis, asking that the gifts of bread and wine may be filled with God's blessing.

Institution Narrative. The narrative of the institution of the Supper, the *verba testamenti*, turns from the opening section of praise of the Father to a second section, praise of the Son. The prayer, nonetheless, is still directed to the Father.

In the West, from the early Middle Ages the recitation of the *verba institutionis* (words of institution) was held as itself constituting the consecration. This view was made precise by Thomas Aquinas, who focused on the words "This is my body" and "This cup is the new covenant in my blood" without reference to their context within the institution narrative, itself a part of the Great Thanksgiving which is addressed to the Father. (Thomas further taught that the consecration thus effected by the words was instantaneous, for the bread and wine cannot gradually become the substance of the body and blood of Christ: either they are that substance or they are not.[172] Thus, in view of the development of the liturgy in East and West, a "disproportionately privileged place was thus given to the account of the institution."[173] In the view of the early church, however, it was the whole prayer, representing the church's version of the prayer which Jesus offered at the table of the Last Supper, the text of which we do not possess, which effected the consecration of the elements.

The view that the recitation of the *verba* effected the consecration corresponded well with Luther's understanding of the power of the living Word and the centrality of the proclamation of the Gospel. Luther therefore followed in the medieval tradition when he made his most radical liturgical reform and removed the entire prayer of thanksgiving except for the words of institution (called in the *Formula Missae* the *verba benedictionis*, words of blessing), which alone remain of the canon and which alone are understood to consecrate.[174]

The institution narrative is a liturgical text and is therefore not a reading of a Bible passage but a pastiche of the four New Testament accounts of the institution of the supper (Matt. 26:26–28; Mark 14:22–25; Luke 22:17–20; 1 Cor. 11:23–26). In his use of the Verba, Luther omitted several medieval embellishments and added the scriptural (and Mozarabic) phrase "which is given for you." There is no common version of the Verba in general ecumenical use (see table p. 164). The translation "he gave it for all to drink" is an effort to render the older "Drink, ye all, of it" in clear contemporary English. Moreover, it better represents the joint witness of Paul, Mark, and Matthew. "The new covenant in my blood" is a way of saying that the covenant was sealed by the blood of Christ, the sacrificial Lamb. "Shed for you and for all people" is literally "for many" or "for the many," which in biblical use

---

[172]Thomas Aquinas, *Summa Theologicae* III:75, 7c.

[173]For the argument see Mazza, 250–66.

[174]See Frank C. Senn, "Martin Luther's Revision of the Eucharistic Canon in the Formula Missae of 1523," *Concordia Theological Monthly* 44 (March 1973):101–18.

Roman Sacramentary	Lutheran Book of Worship	Book of Common Prayer
	In the night in which he was betrayed	On the night he was handed over to suffering and death,
	our Lord Jesus took bread, and gave thanks; broke it, and gave it to his disciples, saying: Take	our Lord Jesus Christ took bread; and when he had given thanks to you, he broke it, and gave it to his disciples, and said, "Take,
Take this, all of you, and eat it: this is my body which will be given up for you.	and eat; this is my body	eat: This is my Body, which is given for you. Do this for the remembrance of me." After supper he took the cup
	given for you. Do this for the remembrance of me. Again, after supper, he took the cup,	
Take this, all of you, and		
		of wine; and when he had given thanks, he gave it to them, and said, "Drink this, all of you:
drink from it:	gave thanks, and gave it for all to drink, saying:	
This is the cup of my blood, the blood of the new and everlasting covenant. It will	This cup is the new	This is my Blood of the new
	covenant in my blood, shed for you and for all people for the forgiveness of sin. Do this for the remembrance of me.	Covenant,
be shed for you and for all men so that sins may be forgiven. Do this in memory of me.		which is shed for you and for many for the forgiveness of sins. Whenever you drink it, do this for the remembrance of me."

can mean all (see Isa. 53:12; Rom. 5:18–19, where the two words "all" and "many" seem interchangeable; Mark 10:45, 1 Tim. 2:5–6, Rom. 8:32, and 1 Cor. 15:22). "The forgiveness of sin" is one metaphor for the gift of Holy Communion in which forgiveness means life and salvation. "Do this for the remembrance of me" is a most difficult phrase to render adequately. The Greek suggests that it is properly, "Do this for my remembrance" or "for my memorial,"[175] so the stress falls on the memorial action. But such language is apt to be mistaken by modern hearers, who associate "memorial" with cemeteries ("memorial parks") and with honoring the dead and to whom "my remembrance" may suggest a keepsake left by a departed loved one. The *Lutheran Book of Worship* and the *Book of Common Prayer* both therefore continue their older and more familiar rendering, "Do this for the remembrance of me," which, although awkward, stresses that the object of remembering is Christ. Thus, when the institution narrative is used alone as a proclamation of the gospel, the last word, "me," is Christ, the living Lord.

The Roman rite has attempted to make the bread-word and the cup-word parallel. The Lutheran and Episcopal rites have chosen not to do so, but they repeat "Do this for the remembrance of me" after the bread-word and after the cup-word as in St. Paul, tying the two parts together as one unified action.

Eucharistic Prayers I and II in the *Lutheran Book of Worship*, following St. Paul in 1 Corinthians 11:23–26, add to the Verba the verse "For as often as we eat of this bread and drink from this cup, we proclaim the Lord's death until he comes." ("*Of* this bread" was suggested by the rendering of this verse in the exhortation in the Order for Public Confession of the *Common Service Book; "from* this cup" is the translation of Goodspeed and Today's English Version.) The verse was included in the liturgies of St. Basil, St. Mark, St. James, the Anaphora of the Twelve Apostles, the Gallican rite, and the Mozarabic rite.

In the eucharistic prayer, after the words of institution, as in many Eastern liturgies, the congregation responds with an acclamation. Most of the anaphoras of the Eastern church included numerous acclamations, often as a response to the command of Christ, "Do this for the remembrance of me." The congregational response says in effect, "We do indeed remember." The use of such a response was recovered in the twentieth century by the Communion rite in the *Book of Common Worship* of the Church of South India (1963). The acclamation in Eucharistic Prayers I and II in the *Lutheran Book of Worship*, like Eucharistic Prayer A in the *Book of Common Prayer*, is borrowed from the first of four options in the English translation of the Roman mass. (The first two options are variations of the same Latin original: "Mortem

---

[175]Fritz Chenderlin, *"Do This as My Memorial": The Semantic and Conceptual Background and Value of Anamnesis in 1 Corinthians 11:24–25* (Rome: Biblical Institute Press, 1982).

tuam annuntiamus, Domine, et tuam resurrectionem confitemur, donec venias," literally, "We proclaim your death, Lord, and we confess your resurrection, until you come.") These acclamations are newly composed on the model of the Syrian Liturgy of St. James ("Your death, Lord, we proclaim and your resurrection we confess") and Egyptian liturgies ("We proclaim your death, we confess your resurrection, and we pray . . .").[176] The acclamation succinctly recalls the three-fold aspect of the paschal mystery which is at the heart of the Christian faith: death, life, parousia. As in *maranatha* (Rev. 22:20) and the Church of South India liturgy, the acclamation is addressed to Christ according to the usual pattern of congregational acclamations in the liturgy — "Lord, have mercy," "Glory to you, O Lord," "Praise to you, O Christ," "Lamb of God."

Anamnesis. The institution narrative gives the authority for proceeding to the next section of the Great Thanksgiving, the anamnesis. ("Do this for my *anamnēsin*," Luke 22:19; 1 Cor. 11:24, 25.) The word *anamnesis* is most difficult to render into English. Memorial, commemoration, remembrance all suggest something past and absent. But biblically and liturgically when one remembers, the past, brought into the here and now, is made present. What was past becomes a living contemporary experience.[177] The whole Eucharist is *anamnesis*, for in the Eucharist we recall before the Father the saving deeds of the Son, and in fulfillment of his promise Christ makes himself present to the congregation in all his redeeming activity.[178] The anamnesis is the statement that the church, in obedience to the Lord's command, offers the bread and cup to remember and proclaim the death-resurrection of Christ in all its accomplished fullness. Often the ascension and the second coming were added to the specific events recalled. "With this bread and cup we remember . . . ," Eucharistic Prayers I and II proclaim. The present memorial action depends on, derives from, and points to the self-offering of Christ, the dying, rising, and reigning Lord. In certain ancient liturgies of the Byzantine rite and the Roman canon the offering of the bread and cup includes the offering of the whole created order. In the ancient liturgies the bread and cup are "offered" to recall the self-offering of Christ; the bread and cup and all that they represent are lifted to God through the thanksgiving of those who remember and give thanks. Thus the idea

---

[176]*Prayers of the Eucharist: Early and Reformed*, trans. and ed. R. C. D. Jasper and G. J. Cuming (New York: Oxford University Press, 1980), 63, 45. See Bernard Botte, "Mysterium Fidei," *Bible et Vie Chrétienne* 80 (1968):29–34; James Dallen, "The Congregation's Share in the Eucharistic Prayer," *Worship* 52 (1978):329–41.

[177]See Mircea Eliade, "Mythologies of Memory and Forgetting," chapter 7 of *Myth and Reality* (New York and Evanston: Harper and Row, 1963). Northrop Frye notes "Plato's view of knowledge as *anamnesis* or recollection, the *re*-cognizing of the new as something identifiable with the old." (*The Great Code*, 81.)

[178]*Anamnesis* is "the re-calling before God of the one sacrifice of Christ in all its accomplished fullness so that it is here and now operative by its effects in the souls of the redeemed." Gregory Dix, *The Shape of the Liturgy* (Westminster: Dacre, 1945), 243. "The anamnesis is the moment in which the Mass defines itself," and the purpose of the anamnesis memorial is to evoke and express a response of gratitude and also to secure God's continued blessing (Mazza, 75).

that the Eucharist is a spiritual sacrifice enters the classic *anamneses*. (See Mal. 1:11 and Justin, *Dialogue* 41.)

Epiclesis. An epiclesis (= invocation) follows, a universal component of the Great Thanksgiving at this point. The liturgy is always celebrated in the power of the Holy Spirit (Rom. 8:27), who prompts the prayers of the community, in whom the proclamation of the lessons is always done (Luke 4:18), who makes the crucified and risen Christ present in the Supper in fulfillment of the promise inherent in the words of institution. The whole Eucharist has an epicletic character because it all depends on the work of the Holy Spirit. In the liturgy the presence of the risen and reigning Lord — Christ filled with the Spirit — is actualized.

Specifically at this point in the prayer the epiclesis asks God's response to the church's obedience to the command of Christ to "Do this in *anamnesis* of me."

Two forms of the epiclesis are usually identified: (a) consecratory, the invocation of the Spirit on the offering (*Apostolic Constitutions* 8) so that the elements might "be made" or be "shown to be" the body and blood of Christ; and (b) sanctificatory, the invocation of the Spirit on the assembly, asking for the fruits of communion with the Lord, as in the *Apostolic Tradition*. In the early understanding the Spirit was invoked to apply the Eucharist to the lives of those who share it, and thus it appropriately appears after the Verba.[179] Later understandings suggest that the epiclesis was consecratory; indeed in the Eastern Church some have claimed that the consecration is effected solely by the epiclesis of the Spirit. In response to such views the Council of Florence (1439–45) declared that the words of institution were the consecrating form, not the invocation of the Spirit. In the Alexandrine and Roman rites there is a preliminary epiclesis before the Verba to prepare the elements for consecration.

The eucharistic prayer of Serapion gave an epiclesis of the Word rather than the Spirit.

Although the trinitarian shape of the eucharistic prayer is evident — to the Father through the Son in the Holy Spirit — the prayer is nonetheless entirely directed to the Father. Thus, the epiclesis is not precisely an invocation of the Spirit, a prayer addressing the Spirit directly to come. It is addressed rather to the Father asking for the gift of the Spirit promised by the risen Christ to guide the church into all truth in order to continue his redeeming work.

Intercessions. The intercessions follow. The epiclesis is a prayer for the congregation which is present, in its fullest form asking the Father to send the Spirit to transform the bread and wine to sanctify the faithful. The intercessions are prayers for the church throughout the world. The *Apostolic Tradition*, the oldest text of a eucharistic prayer that the church

---

[179]Lukas Vischer, "Epiklesis: Sign of Unity and Renewal," *Studia Liturgica* 6 (1969): 30–39.

possesses, contained no intercessions, but the epiclesis in that prayer asking unity and the fruits of communion is a basis for the intercessions within the anaphora which are a feature of the Antiochene-Byzantine and the Roman traditions. The *Didache*, a still older document than the *Apostolic Tradition*, gives the text of this prayer in connection with the bread of the Eucharist:

As this bread was scattered over the hills and then was brought together and made one, so let your church be brought together from the ends of the earth into your kingdom

and after the meal this prayer:

Remember, Lord, your church; save it from all evil and make it perfect by your love. Make it holy and gather it together from the four winds into your kingdom which you have prepared for it.[180]

The intercessions extend the anamnesis to include those who benefit from the history of salvation which the anamnesis recalls.

Before the congregation partakes of the heavenly food, one last act is necessary: intercession.[181] As the writer to the Hebrews (7:25) notes, Christ lives to make intercession; therefore we must make his intercessory work our own as we prepare to partake of Christ who gave himself for the life of the world. The world and its concerns, apparently put aside or risen above in the preface dialogue ("Lift up your hearts"), returns here in all of its reality, need, and urgency. The Eucharist is not an escape from the world but a participation in Christ and therefore a participation in the world which he redeemed and for which he intercedes. An intercessory portion is found in all but the Spanish and Gallican rites where it occurs between the offering and the anaphora.[182]

Doxology. The doxology concludes the thanksgiving. The great prayer, addressed to the Father, evolved in a trinitarian direction, praising the Father for all he has done in creation and redemption; describing the saving work of Christ the Son, especially his death and resurrection; invoking the gift of the Holy Spirit to sanctify the offering (both the gifts and the people who offer and receive them). This trinitarian structure is summed up on the concluding doxology which gathers the themes of the anaphora in a proclamation of the divine Name. The prayer to the Father rises through Christ, in Christ, with Christ, as the Eucharist like life itself derives all value and meaning from its Christ-centeredness. The honor and glory rise to the Father "in the unity of the Holy Spirit" because the only acceptable worship is in Spirit and

---

[180] *Didache* 9, 10.

[181] Alexander Schmemann, *The World as Sacrament* (London: Darton, Longman & Todd, 1966), 53. Published originally as *Sacraments and Orthodoxy* (New York: Herder and Herder, 1965).

[182] See W. Jardine Grisbrooke, "Intercession at the Eucharist," *Studia Liturgica* 4 (1965):129–55; 5 (1966):20–44, 87–103.

truth and because the unity of God the Holy Trinity enters God's people through the working of that Spirit. Moreover, according to the grand vision of the Old Testament (Mal. 1:11; Joel 3:5), the doxology has an eschatological dimension, longing for that day when all creation will ascribe honor and glory to God who at last is all in all (1 Cor. 15:28).

The elevation of the bread and cup which accompanies the doxology makes it clear that this is the culmination of the entire prayer, a triumphal proclamation of the divine Name (Numb. 6:24–27).[183] The prayer thus ends as it began, with praise and thanksgiving to the Holy Trinity.

Amen. The Great Amen is attested to as early as Justin Martyr: when the eucharistic prayer is finished, "all the people present assent saying, 'Amen.'"[184] Jerome (d. ca. 420) declared that this Amen thundered in the churches of Rome and made pagan temples tremble.[185] The people's Amen to the Great Thanksgiving is of equal importance to their response in the preface dialogue, assenting to and participating in the words and actions of the presiding minister on their behalf.

To emphasize its importance, the Amen is sung by the congregation together with the doxology as a grand and joyful conclusion to the Great Thanksgiving, affirming all that has been proclaimed in the central prayer of the whole liturgy.

Recension of the Canon. To the Lutheran reformers the text of the canon with which they were familiar was the most offensive part of the mass. To them it reeked with sacrificial language, turning the sacrament on its head and making God's gift to us into a gift we presumed to offer to God. The canon was therefore subject to radical surgery as the reformers attempted to cut away what were thought to be accretions in order to reveal the central evangelical core.

The vast majority of Lutheran church orders followed Luther's *Formula Missae* (1523) and *Deutsche Messe* (1526) in providing the Verba alone, preserving with still more pronounced emphasis the medieval isolation of a moment of consecration by separating the words of Christ from their surrounding context of prayer. The resulting form continued in North America in the Common Service of 1888, the *Common Service Book* (1917), and *The Lutheran Hymnal* (1941); it was an option in the *Service Book and Hymnal* (1958) and remains an option in the *Lutheran Book of Worship.* Such a practice focuses all attention on the narrative of the action and words of Christ and expressed the view of consecration expounded in the Formula of Concord:

For the truthful and almighty words of Jesus Christ which he spoke in the first institution were not only efficacious in the first Supper but they still retain their

---

[183]Mazza, 87, 189–90.
[184]Justin Martyr, *First Apology* 65.
[185]Jerome, *Letter to the Galatians* 2.

validity and efficacious power in all places where the Supper is observed according to Christ's institution and where his words are used, and the body and blood of Christ are truly present, distributed, and received by the virtue and potency of the same words which Christ spoke in the first Supper. For wherever we observe his institution and speak his words over the bread and cup and distribute the blessed bread and cup, Christ himself is still active through the spoken words by virtue of the first institution, which he wants to be repeated.[186]

This tradition that the words of Christ constitute the act of consecration can be traced from Ambrose of Milan (339–97).[187] But Lutherans, sensing the barrenness of the bare and naked Verba, have never been entirely comfortable with such a singular element in their liturgy. Prior Kaspar Kantz of Nördlingen in the first German liturgy (1522) substituted for the canon a paraphrase of one of the prayers of the Roman canon to introduce the words of institution and a series of private prayers in German for the presiding minister before and after the reception of communion. Oecolampadius in 1523 prepared a series of prayers for the congregation which included a prayer of self-offering. Other church orders — Nuremberg (1525), Strasbourg (1525), Nördlingen (1538), Waldeck (1556), Austria (1571), Hesse (1574) — provided a prayer of humble access for the communicants. The first attempt at a German canon was made by Anton Firm and others in Strasbourg in 1523. The church order (1524) attempted an evangelical recasting in the vernacular of some of the prayers of the medieval Roman canon. After the Sanctus the order continues,

All-kind Father, merciful and eternal God, grant that this bread and wine may become and be for us the true body and the innocent blood of your beloved Son, our Lord Jesus Christ, who on the day before his passion, took bread.... [188]

The Verba and the Lord's Prayer follow, then the Agnus Dei and a prayer to Christ imploring salvation

through this your holy body and precious blood. Grant that we may accomplish your will at all times and that we may never be separated from you in eternity.

The church order of Pfalz-Neuburg (1543); the German *Agende* (1855) of the Ministerium of Pennsylvania, the New York Synod, and the Ohio Synod; and the *Agende* of the Lutheran Church of Bavaria (1879) provided a prayer of thanksgiving followed by an epiclesis and the Verba and then a prayer of praise to Christ, which introduces the Our Father. The liturgy of the Joint Synod of Ohio (1904) gave an English version of these prayers (except for the epiclesis) but moved the Lord's Prayer to a position before the Verba to bring the order in line with the form in the *Church Book* and the Common Service.

---

[186] Solid Declaration VII §75–76 (*Book of Concord*, 583).
[187] Ambrose, *On the Mysteries* 54; *On the Sacraments* 4.14–15; see Mazza, 260–61.
[188] Reed, 343.

Agende 1855	Joint Synod of Ohio
Preface with Proper Preface	Preface with Proper Preface
Sanctus	Sanctus
Exhortation	(Exhortation)
Alternate Prayer:	*During the Consecration the Minister shall turn toward the Altar.*

Herr Jesus Christus, Du einiger warer Sohn des lebendigen Gottes (ewiger Hoherpriester),* der Du deinen Leib für uns alle in den bittern Tod hast dargegeben, und dein Blut zur Vergebung unserer Sünden hast vergossen; dazu denselben Leib und dasselbige dein Blut (in dem heiligen Sakrament) allen deinen Jüngern zu essen und zu trinken deines Todes dabei zu gedenken befohlen hast: wir bringen vor deine göttliche Majestät diese deine Gaben, Brod und Wein, und bitten, Du wollest diesselben (nach deinem Wort) durch deine göttliche Gnade, Güte und Kraft heiligen, segnen und schaffen, dass dieses Brod dein Leib und dieser Wein dein Blut sei, und allen denen, die (mit bussfertigen Herzen) davon essen und trinken, zum ewigen Leben es lassen gedeihen: der Du mit Gott dem Vater in einigkeit (= Gemeinschaft) des Heiligen Geistes lebest und regierest immer und ewiglich.

Glory to to Thee, O Lord Jesus Christ, Thou almighty and everlasting Son of the Father, that by the sacrifice of Thyself upon the cross, offered up once for all, Thou didst perfect them that are sanctified, and ordain, as a memorial and seal thereof, Thy Holy Supper, in which Thou givest us Thy body to eat, and Thy blood to drink, that being in Thee, even as Thou art in us, we may have eternal life, and be raised up at the last day. Most merciful and exalted Redeemer, we humbly confess that we are not worthy of the least of all the mercies, and of all the truth, which Thou hast shown to us, and that, by reason of our sins, we are too impure and weak worthily to receive Thy saving gifts, Sanctify us, therefore, we beseech Thee, in our bodies and souls by Thy Holy Spirit, and thus fit and prepare us to come to Thy Supper, to the glory of Thy grace, and to our own eternal good. And in whatsoever, through weakness, we do fail and come short, in true repentance and sorrow on account of our sins, in living faith and trust in Thy merits, and in an earnest purpose to amend our sinful lives, do Thou graciously supply and grant,

---

*Words added in 1855 to Pfalz-Neuburg (1543) upon which the prayer is based are enclosed within parentheses.

171

Amen.
O Heiliger Geist, heilige uns
und reinige mir Herz und Lippen,
dass ich würdlich im Namen des
Herrn und in Kraft seines Wörtes
das heilige Testament verwalte!
*The Minister turns to the Altar
and says*
Words of Institution
Lob und Ehre und Preis sei Dir,
O Christe! Das gesegnete Brod
ist deines heiligen Leibes und
der gesegnete Kelch deines
heiligen Blutes Gemeinschaft.
O Du unser Mittler zur Rechten
des Vaters, Du wollest uns
theilhaftig machen deines
heiligen Leibes und Blutes, dass
wir gereinigt von Sünden uns
vereinen mit allen Gliedern
deiner Gemeinde im Himmel und
auf Erden. Herr Jesu, Du hast
uns erkauft, Dir leben wir, Dir
sterben wir, Dein sind wir in
Ewigkeit. In deinem Namen beten
wir für uns and für die ganze
Christenheit zum Vater:
Vater unser...
Pax and Communion

out of the fullness of the merits
of Thy bitter sufferings and
death; to the end that we, who
even in this present world desire
to enjoy Thee, our only comfort
and Saviour, in the Holy Sacrament,
may at last see Thee face to face
in Thy heavenly kingdom, and
dwell with Thee, and with all
Thy saints, for ever and ever.
Amen.
Our Father...

Words of Institution
Praise and honor, and glory,
be unto Thee, O Christ! The
bread which we bless is the
communion of Thy holy body, and
the cup which we bless is the
communion of Thy holy blood. O
Thou everlasting Son of the
Father, sanctify us by Thy Holy
Spirit, and make us worthy
partakers of Thy sacred body and
blood, that we may be cleansed
from sin and made one with all
the members of Thy Church in
heaven and on earth. Lord Jesus!
Thou hast bought us: to Thee will
we live, to Thee will we die, and
Thine will we be forever. Amen.

Agnus Dei and Communion

The *Church Book* (1868), which like its successor the Common Service (1888) had the Lord's Prayer follow the Sanctus and exhortation and precede the Verba, treated the Our Father as a prayer of consecration, directing "Then the minister, turning to the altar, and extending his hands over the Bread and Wine, shall say: Let us pray. Our Father...."

In Lutheran use the Lord's Prayer is the all-purpose prayer, used here to consecrate, used commonly to conclude meetings. The use of the Lord's Prayer as the prayer of consecration may be rooted in a letter of Gregory the Great to Bishop John of Syracuse in which Gregory said that in the apostolic period the Lord's Prayer (*oratio dominum*) had provided the only words used in celebrating the Eucharist. Thus, when the rest of the canon was stripped from the Verba by the Lutheran reformers the Lord's Prayer remained, whether before or after the Verba, as the sole prayer associated with the consecration, which was understood to be effected by the proclamation of the institution narrative.[189] The rubric in the *Church Book*, moreover, gives the Our Father an epicletic character, corresponding to the preliminary epiclesis of the Roman rite before the institution narrative, asking for the sanctification of the bread and wine that they may become for the congregation the body and blood of Christ.

In the *Church Book* order, moreover, the exhortation which precedes the Our Father preserves the themes of the eucharistic prayer in the form of admonition rather than prayer and thanksgiving:

Dearly Beloved! Forasmuch as we purpose to come to the Holy Supper of our Lord Jesus Christ, in which He giveth us His Body to eat and His Blood to drink, in order to strengthen and confirm our faith, it becometh us diligently to examine ourselves, as St. Paul exhorteth us. For this Holy Sacrament hath been instituted for the special comfort and strengthening of those who humbly confess their sins, and who hunger and thirst after righteousness.

Our own conscience accuseth us that we are by nature sinners, and have grievously offended the Lord our God; but our Lord Jesus Christ hath had mercy upon us, and by His death and passion hath wrought perfect redemption for us. And to the end that we should the more confidently believe this, and be strengthened by our faith in a cheerful obedience to His holy will, He hath given us His Body to eat and his Blood to drink.

Therefore whoso eateth of this bread, and drinketh of this cup, firmly believing the words of Christ, dwelleth in Christ, and Christ in him, and hath eternal life.

We should also do this in remembrance of Him, showing his death, that He was delivered for our offences, and raised again for our justification, and rendering unto Him most hearty thanks for the same, take up our cross and follow Him, and according to His commandment, love one another even as He hath loved us. For we are all one bread and one body, even as we are all partakers of this one bread, and drink of this one cup.[190]

When this exhortation was removed by the Common Service and placed in the Order for Public Confession in the *Common Service Book*, the resulting eucharistic rite of Preface and Sanctus, Lord's Prayer, Verba, and the Pax was rendered remarkably bare, indeed empty.

---

[189] Mazza (250–52) suggests that the "Lord's Prayer" included the Our Father which came down verbatim and also the Lord's thanksgiving at the Last Supper which was unrecorded. On the discussion of the place of the Our Father before or after the Verba in the Common Service see Luther Reed, *The Lutheran Liturgy*, 1st ed. (Philadelphia: Muhlenberg Press, 1947), 188–89.

[190] This exhortation was revised in the Common Service and the 1891 edition of the *Church Book*.

The Inter-Lutheran Commission on Worship, therefore, remembering these various historical precedents, gave a second option besides the Verba alone: a brief prayer of thanksgiving followed by the Verba. The prayer, which is a thanksgiving and an epiclesis, is translated from the 1942 *Missale för Svenska Kyrkan*. In the *Lutheran Book of Worship*, as in the Swedish mass, it is followed by the Verba and the Lord's Prayer. (The Church of Sweden has since replaced that form with a more traditional eucharistic prayer which includes the Verba within it. The *Lutheran Book of Worship* thus preserves here a now archaic use.) The intention of the option of this prayer followed by the Verba was to satisfy those who objected, they said, not to a prayer of thanksgiving but to the inclusion of the Verba within such a thanksgiving.[191] Such a prayer followed by (the Lord's Prayer and) the Verba is found in the order of the Presbyterian *Worshipbook* (1972) and the *Book of Common Order* of the Church of Scotland.

A third option is provided by the *Lutheran Book of Worship*, reflecting the movement of the Lutheran tradition into the wider ecumenical heritage,[192] which has been slowly developing since the sixteenth century: a eucharistic prayer which contains the words of institution.

In the twentieth century, Paul Zeller Strodach prepared a full eucharistic prayer consisting of extracts from the liturgies of St. James, St. John Chrysostom, St. Basil, Gaul, and the 1549 *Book of Common Prayer*.[193] The prayer was included in the liturgy of the Federation of Lutheran Churches in India (1936). Luther D. Reed in the first edition of his *The Lutheran Liturgy* (1947) proposed a text of a eucharistic prayer "in the spirit of the early liturgies and in agreement with Lutheran teaching."[194] The reports of the Lutheran World Federation's Commission on Liturgy (Hannover 1952 and Minneapolis 1957) approved of a eucharistic prayer. The *Agende für evangelisch-lutherische Kirche und Gemeinden* prepared by the Lutheran Liturgical Conference of Germany (1955) provided a eucharistic prayer which included the Verba within it. The *Service Book and Hymnal* (1958) included a prayer of thanksgiving

---

[191] *Contemporary Worship 2: The Holy Communion* (1970) had only a eucharistic prayer, and no objections were raised throughout the trial use of this booklet. The committee was therefore surprised, as the publication of the *Lutheran Book of Worship* drew near, by objections to the inclusion of the Verba within a eucharistic prayer, for, some said, the Verba are a proclamation of the Gospel. The arguments were not new; they had been raised prior to the publication of the *Service Book and Hymnal* in 1958. Since the issue could not be resolved, the commission suggested that two options be included in the book: a eucharistic prayer and a thanksgiving followed by the Verba. This did not satisfy some, who, desiring to preserve the then current practice, insisted on the option of the use of the Verba alone without a prayer. The commission reluctantly conceded.

[192] Note the eucharistic prayers provided by the Presbyterian Church, *The Service For the Lord's Day* (Philadelphia: Westminster Press, 1984) and by the United Methodist Church, *At the Lord's Table*. Supplemental Worship Resources 9 (Nashville: Abingdon Press, 1981).

[193] The text is given in his *Manual on Worship*, rev. ed. (Philadelphia: Muhlenberg Press, 1946), 253–54. See Addendum I below, pp. 199–200.

[194] Reed, *The Lutheran Liturgy*, 1st ed., 336–37. See Addendum II below.

(a eucharistic prayer) based on the prayers compiled by Strodach and Reed from ancient sources and which followed the triune order of the creed, beginning with the praise of the Father, continuing with praise of the work of the Son, and invocation of the sanctification of the Holy Spirit, and concluding with praise of the Holy Trinity.[195] This praise-worthy prayer appeared in a Spanish translation in *El Culto Cristiano* (1958) and then in an English translation of that version in *Worship Supplement* (1969).[196] The eucharistic prayer of the *Service Book and Hymnal* is preserved in the *Lutheran Book of Worship* as Eucharistic Prayer III.

Contemporary Worship 2: The Holy Communion (1970) employed a eucharistic prayer and made no provision for a prayer followed by the Verba or for the use of the Verba alone, and throughout the period of its trial use the order elicited no objections.

The *Lutheran Book of Worship* provides four eucharistic prayers. Eucharistic Prayers I and II and set in parallel columns in the Ministers Edition so that the presiding minister may, if desired, move from one column to the other, weaving a prayer appropriate to the occasion. (See Min. Ed., p. 29, #31.) Prayer I is a revision of the prayer composed for *Contemporary Worship 2;* Prayer II, a festive elaboration of Prayer I, was drafted for *The Great Thanksgiving: Contemporary Worship 01* (1975) and revised by Frank C. Senn for the *Lutheran Book of Worship.* Prayers I and II are both noteworthy for the full review of the mighty works of God under the Old Covenant. The Praise of the Father, which begins with the preface dialogue, resumes in the prayer and spans the history of salvation from creation to consummation, and, as is usual in eucharistic prayers, is christological throughout.

Eucharistic Prayer I follows this development and draws on these sources:

1. *Praise of the Father*

Holy God, mighty Lord, gracious Father:	The three-fold titles of God, each joined with an adjective, derive from the Liturgy of St. James and from Prayer III and echo the three-fold "holy" of the Sanctus.
Endless is your mercy and eternal your reign.	
You have filled all creation	a. *for creation*
with light and life;	Gen. 1:1ff.; John 1:1–5 Roman Catholic Prayers III and IV

---

[195] The prayer was referred to with approval in Louis Bouyer's assessment of the Lutheran liturgy in his *Eucharist: Theology and Spirituality of the Eucharistic Prayer* (Notre Dame, IN: University Press, 1968), 441.

[196] *Worship Supplement authorized by the Commission on Worship of the Lutheran Church–Missouri Synod and the Synod of Evangelical Lutheran Churches* (St. Louis: Concordia Publishing House, 1969), p. 45. The variations from the form in the *Service Book and Hymnal* occur in the next to last paragraph of the prayer, the anamnesis-epiclesis. The references to the Holy Spirit have been excised and the statement of the real presence strengthened.

heaven and earth
are full of your glory

Isa. 6:3, an echo of the Sanctus

Through Abraham you promised
to bless all nations

b. *for salvation history*

Gen. 12:2; Roman Prayer IV

Naming Abraham without mention of Sarah, troubling to some, is admittedly patriarchal, but the church has no authority to change the canonical record: the biblical promise came to Abraham. More important than adding Sarah here is a recognition of the New Testament analogue, Mary, the woman to whom and in whom the promise was fulfilled.

You rescued Israel,
your chosen people.
Through the prophets
you renewed your promise;

Exod. 12:51–15:21

St. Basil; Roman Prayer IV;
Episcopal Eucharistic Prayers B, C, D

c. *for Christ*

and, at this end of all the ages,

Acts 2:17; Heb. 9:26; *Apostolic Tradition*

"This" modifies the entire phrase "end of all the ages" and not simply "end" as if to say "this end" as opposed to some other end. The church is living in the last days, which began with the advent of Christ.

you sent your son,
who in words and deeds
proclaimed your kingdom
and was obedient to your will,
even to giving his life.

Roman Prayer IV

see Roman Prayer IV

In the night

in which he was betrayed . . .

2. *Narrative of the Institution*

The Verba are a recital of a particular event which justifies the present act of praise. The liturgical narrative is not a reading of part of the Bible; it is our telling the story now.

. . . for the remembrance of me.

For as often as we eat
of this bread
and drink from this cup,

1 Cor. 11:26; Liturgy of St. Basil, St. Mark, St. James, Anaphora of the Twelve Apostles, Gallican rite, Mozarabic rite.

we proclaim the Lord's death
until he comes.
Christ has died.
Christ is risen.
Christ will come again.

In the Sacrament "the sum of the whole gospel is contained," said Luther (*LW* 36:183)

In the twentieth century a three-fold acclamation by the people was introduced in the *Book of Common Worship* of the Church of South India (1963): "Amen. Thy death, O lord, we commemorate, thy resurrection we confess, and thy second coming we await. Glory be to thee, O Christ." (p. 16)

The people's acclamation is common to the four Roman prayers and Eucharistic Prayer A in the *Book of Common Prayer*.

3. *The Remembrance (Anamnesis) of the Son*

Therefore, gracious Father,
with this bread and cup
we remember the life

We recall Jesus' life, death, and resurrection to memory before God and the fellowship. Since the institution narrative has brought the bread

our Lord offered for us.

And, believing the witness
of his resurrection,
we await his coming in power
to share with us
the great and promised feast.

Amen. Come, Lord Jesus.

Send now, we pray,
your Holy Spirit,

the spirit of our Lord

and of his resurrection,
that we who receive
the Lord's body and blood

may live to the praise
of your glory
and receive our inheritance
with all your saints in light.

Amen. Come, Holy Spirit.

Join our prayers
with those of your servants
of every time and every place,

and cup to the center of attention, this calling to memory is done both with words and with the presence of the bread and cup.

From that moment when the Son of God emptied himself and became a human being (see Phil. 2), everything that he did was an offering of himself. His entire life as the Savior is the sacrifice he offered, and the church remembers the events of that life.

That the human act of thanksgiving using the bread and cup does not save humanity is acknowledged as the remembrance turns into anticipation of that fulfillment of Christ's work which lies beyond all human working. Moreover, to be at table with Jesus is already to be in the eschatological kingdom.

Rev. 22:20.

This acclamation voices the eschatological emphasis which runs throughout the Eucharist and implores the presence of him without whom all human work is insufficient.

4. *The Epiclesis of the Holy Spirit*

The prayer is for the sending of the Spirit to the meal, so that it and all God's acts and promises may come to fulfillment.

The lower-case "spirit" is deliberately ambiguous: it is the Pauline understanding of the Holy Spirit as the Spirit of Christ; it is also the spirit of Christ in the sense of his mind, essential quality, characteristic attitude.

Those who receive the body of Christ are the body of Christ, made so by the Holy Spirit and given power to do his work in the world, which for his people as for him means living and suffering for others.

Eph. 1:12
Liturgy of St. Basil;
El Culto Cristiano;
Roman Catholic Eucharistic Prayer III

The congregation's prayer for the Spirit derives from the Pentecost antiphon "Come, Holy Spirit, fill the hearts of the faithful and kindle in them the fire of your love." It balances the "Come, Lord Jesus" above.

Roman Eucharistic Prayers II and III have, following the (second) invocation of the Holy Spirit, petitions for the unity of the church in communion with the saints. The Liturgy of St. John Chrysostom does likewise.

Here is a faint expression of the intercessions which have a part in nearly all the historic anaphoras, expanding the assembly's consciousness of the wider fellowship of all hu-

177

manity and the whole church, militant and triumphant.

and unite them
with the ceaseless petitions

In Holy Communion individuals are united with Christ and with Christians throughout the world and with all those who have received the holy food through the centuries since Pentecost. With them they share the hope of the victorious coming of the Lord.

of our great high priest
until he comes
as victorious Lord of all.

5. *Concluding doxology*

Through him, with him, in him,
in the unity of the holy Spirit,

From the Roman canon.

In Western Trinitarian theology, the Holy-Spirit is the bond between the Father and the Son, the guarantee of unity within the godhead. (See Augustine, *On the Trinity* 5.11.12; 6.5.7; Creed of Leo III; Eph. 4:3)

all honor and glory
is yours, Almighty Father,
now and forever. Amen.

Only the *Lutheran Book of Worship* assigns the concluding doxology to the people, again to emphasize the corporate character of the eucharistic assembly over which the president presides. The doxology is sung to a melody which recalls the Sanctus, emphasizing the unity of the Great Thanksgiving, which began with singing the dialogue, Preface, and Sanctus.

In the Roman and Episcopal rites the doxology is said or sung by the celebrant, and the people respond with the Great Amen.

The beginning of Eucharistic Prayer II is borrowed from the beginning of Eucharistic Prayer II in the Roman rite, "Lord, you are holy indeed, the fountain of all holiness." The Father is praised for three mysteries of creation: light from darkness, life from death, speech from silence. Each is a Johannine theme, set forth in the prologue to the Fourth Gospel (John 1:1–18). God the Father is praised for our lives, the world in which we live, the new world to come, and the love that will at the consummation triumph as God is all in all. The love that paradoxically will rule is seen most clearly in Christ, love himself who will be judge and pantocrator.

The review of salvation history is more detailed in this prayer than in the corresponding section of Prayer I, as befits a festive elaboration of praise.

The institution narrative, the quotation from 1 Corinthians 11:26, and the people's acclamation are identical with those in Prayer I for the convenience of both the presiding minister and the congregation.

The anamnesis of the life and work of Christ is more detailed than in the corresponding section of Prayer I and is written for use especially during the fifty days of Easter.

The invocation of the Spirit is for the purpose of uniting all who share in the Holy Supper (the phrase "the fellowship of the Holy Spirit" recalls the apostolic greeting with which the Eucharist begins) and who, made one, may enter upon the inheritance of the saints in light.

The concluding paragraph and doxology are identical with the conclusion of Prayer I.

Eucharistic Prayer III is the Prayer of Thanksgiving from the *Service Book and Hymnal* (1958), which was based on the work of Strodach and Reed. The prayer has been revised into contemporary language. Its sources are these:[197]

You are indeed holy, almighty and most merciful God; you are most holy, and great is the majesty of your glory.	Liturgy of St. James, Jerusalem Liturgy of St. John Chrysostom
You so loved the world that you gave your only son, that whoever believes in him may not perish but have eternal life.	John 3:16; Liturgy of St. John Chrysostom
Having come into the world, he fulfilled for us your holy will and accomplished our salvation. In the night in which he was betrayed....	Liturgy of St. John Chrysostom John 19:28; St. John Chrysostom
Remembering, therefore, his salutary command, his life-giving Passion and death, his glorious resurrection and ascension, and his promise to come again, we give thanks to you, Lord God Almighty,	Liturgy of St. James, Jerusalem, amplified by the Scottish Presbyterian *Book of Common Order* (1940)
not as we ought, but as we are able;	*Apostolic Constitutions*
and we implore you mercifully to accept our praise and thanksgiving,	1549 *Book of Common Prayer*
and, with your Word and Holy Spirit,	Liturgy of St. John Chrysostom
to bless us, your servants, and these your own gifts of bread and wine;	1549 *Book of Common Prayer*
that we and all who share in the body and blood of your Son may be filled	

---

[197]Reed, 357.

with heavenly peace and joy	Roman canon as translated in *Worship Supplement* (1969)
and, receiving the forgiveness of sin, may be sanctified in soul and body,	Liturgy of St. James, Jerusalem
and have our portion	Paul Zeller Strodach
with all your saints. All honor and glory are yours, O God, Father, Son, and Holy Spirit,	
in your holy Church	*Apostolic Tradition*
now and forever.	

Noteworthy in this prayer is the inclusion of a prayer for the Holy Spirit (epiclesis), a part of all the classic Byzantine eucharistic prayers. The Eastern tradition from the *Catecheses* of Cyril of Jerusalem (ca. 348) holds, in distinction from the Western tradition which relies on the Verba, that the invocation of the Spirit constitutes the act of consecration.

Eucharistic Prayer IV is a translation of the most ancient prayer of thanksgiving which the church possesses, the eucharistic prayer in chapter 4 of the *Apostolic Tradition* of Hippolytus (ca. 215).[198] Because of its antiquity and its fidelity to the Gospel it is of immense ecumenical significance.[199] In its original context the prayer immediately follows the opening dialogue without Preface or Sanctus. This remains the way it is intended to be used in the *Lutheran Book of Worship:* "Note that when this prayer is used it should follow immediately the third sentence of the preface dialog, 'Let us give thanks to the Lord our God. . . .' The preface itself and the *Sanctus* are omitted. Prayer IV is recommended for use especially on weekdays or whenever a simple service is desired" (Min. Ed., p. 29, #31).

The spareness of this prayer may reflect a time when the Sanctus was not yet in common use[200] or perhaps reflects a deliberate deletion for some theological reason such as a reaction against the use of Jewish elements in Christian worship.[201] The prayer is Johannine in its ascription of the work of creation to the Word. For this prayer, there clearly was never a time when the Son was not. Inseparable from God, it is he through whom all things were made and in whom the Father

---

[198]The document known as the *Apostolic Tradition* was first published as the "Egyptian Church Order" in 1891 by H. Achelis from a Coptic manuscript. Edouard Schwartz (1910) and Richard H. Connolly (1916) first identified it as the lost work of Hippolytus, the title of which was inscribed on the chair of his third-century statue, discovered in 1551.

[199]*The Great Thanksgiving: Contemporary Worship 01* (New York: Inter-Lutheran Commission on Worship, 1975), 8.

[200]Hans Lietzmann, *Mass and Lord's Supper*, trans. Dorothea H. G. Reeve (Leiden: Brill, 1953), 134–35.

[201]Brilioth, 236.

delights. The dominant theme of this carefully-crafted prayer, however, is Christ's work of redemption, his passion and atonement, described in the mythological language of the conquering hero (cf. the Advent hymn of St. Ambrose, translated as "Savior of the Nations, Come," hymn 28). For all of its emphasis on the work of the vigorous and heroic Son, the prayer nonetheless reveals a three-fold shape, corresponding to the three persons of the Holy Trinity.

The form of the Verba in this prayer varies somewhat from the form in the other options in the *Lutheran Book of Worship* in order to preserve Hippolytus's text. The Verba are used in this prayer not as a consecratory formula but as a sign of the climax of salvation history.

Out of concern for Lutheran sensitivity about eucharistic sacrifice, the straightforward Latin *offerimus tibi panem et calicem* (we offer to you this bread and cup) is ambiguously rendered "we lift this bread and cup before you." The Holy Spirit is invoked explicitly first on the elements so that all who partake of the holy gifts may be made one, and then is invoked on all communicants.

This prayer had been introduced into Lutheran use in *Worship Supplement* (1969).[202] An English translation was prepared by the (Roman Catholic) International Consultation on English in the Liturgy in January 1983, based on existing English translations and Dom Bernard Botte's *La Tradition Apostolique de Saint Hippolyte*. The translation of the prayer in the *Lutheran Book of Worship* is by Gordon Lathrop.

The prayer given in the *Apostolic Tradition* is probably not to be understood as a fixed liturgical form but rather as a model, a sample prayer of thanksgiving, incorporating favorite ideas of Hippolytus.[203] It has been adapted in the Roman sacramentary as the Second Eucharistic Prayer[204] and in the *Book of Common Prayer* as Eucharistic Prayer B.[205]

Under the auspices of the Episcopal Church an unofficial committee was formed in 1974 to consider the possibility of a common text for the Great Thanksgiving with the hope that it might become one of several prayers authorized for use in the various churches. The result of that endeavor was a text which is drawn from early versions of the Anaphora of St. Basil and from Eucharistic Prayer IV in the Roman sacramentary because of its widespread use, its ancient roots, its broad scope, and its wide appeal in Eastern and Western Christianity. The prayer has an invariable preface and concludes with optional intercessions, like Eastern and Western prayers since the fourth century. The prayer appears as Eucharistic Prayer D in the *Book of Common Prayer* (pp. 372–75); *The Service for the Lord's Day* (Great Thanksgiving E),

---

[202] *Worship Supplement*, pp. 46–47.
[203] Jungmann, 20. See Maxwell E. Johnson, "Eucharistic Prayer IV: An Alternate Proposal," *Lutheran Forum* 19 (Reformation 1985):25–28.
[204] For a discussion of the text see Mazza, 88–122.
[205] For a discussion of the text see Hatchett, 375.

a Presbyterian resource;[206] and *At the Lord's Table* (no. 6), a United Methodist publication.[207] It was not included in the *Lutheran Book of Worship* only because of its length and the desire not to overwhelm users of the book with too many eucharistic prayers when such prayers have not yet become familiar to many and are not even accepted by all Lutherans.

The Manual Acts. Two "manual acts" are directed by the rubrics, as they have been since the *Church Book* (1868). At the Words of Institution which refer to the bread, the minister takes and holds the bread or the paten with the bread on it (in the Common Service the minister took the paten; in the *Service Book and Hymnal* the minister took the bread) and replaces it on the corporal after the first "Do this for the remembrance of me." At the words which refer to the cup, the minister takes and holds the cup, replacing it on the corporal after the second "Do this for the remembrance of me."

When a eucharistic prayer is used, a third action is suggested. "It is appropriate to lift the bread and cup together at the words 'all honor and glory are yours....' Note the rationale for such a gesture in Luther's German Mass" (Min. Ed., p. 29, #30). There Luther said,

We do not want to abolish the elevation, but retain it because it goes well with the German Sanctus [which Luther's order placed after the consecration and administration of the bread and before the consecration and administration of the cup] and signifies that Christ has commanded us to remember him. For just as the sacrament is bodily elevated, and yet Christ's body and blood are not seen in it, so he is also remembered and elevated by the word of the sermon and is confessed and adored in the reception of the sacrament. In each case he is apprehended only by faith; for we cannot see how Christ gives his body and blood for us and even now daily shows and offers it before God to obtain grace for us.[208]

In Luther's understanding, the elevation is a wonderfully rich and suggestive gesture.

Luther rejected the sign of the cross in connection with the consecration, and no sixteenth-century church order except Münzer (Alstädt, 1523) expressly indicates its use over the bread and wine. Johann Gerhard reintroduced it, and Coburg (1626) gives it; modern German and Swedish liturgies universally include it.[209]

The Roman sacramentary of 1969 has only one sign of the cross during the Great Thanksgiving and it is associated not with the Verba but with the invocation of the Holy Spirit. The use of the sign of the cross at the Verba is unwise, for it enforces a magical interpretation of the

---

[206] *The Service for the Lord's Day*, Supplemental Liturgical Resource 1 (Philadelphia: Westminster Press, 1984).

[207] *At the Lord's Table*, Supplemental Worship Resources 9 (Nashville: Abingdon Press, 1981).

[208] Martin Luther, "German Mass" (*Luther's Works* 53:82).

[209] Reed, 361.

words of institution, suggesting that it is their repetition which effects the consecration. Modern liturgical theology understands the consecration more broadly and takes the Great Thanksgiving to be all of one piece. The consecration thus takes place within the whole eucharistic action.

Consecration of Additional Elements. The repetition of the words of institution to set apart additional elements (*Nachkonsekration*) is not required.[210] The *Common Service Book* rubrics directed, "If the consecrated *Bread* or *Wine* be spent before all have communed, the Minister shall set apart more, saying aloud so much of the *Words of Institution* as pertaineth to the Element to be consecrated."[211] Many Lutherans find such a consecration unnecessary. The practice was not mentioned in the *Service Book and Hymnal* nor is it mentioned in the *Lutheran Book of Worship*. Luther Reed explained, "If the Verba are said as a declaration there is no sense in repeating them. If they be taken as a prayer, the repetition would be superfluous, just as no house father would think of repeating the grace every time a new dish was brought to the table.[212] On the other hand, the Formula of Concord, Solid Declaration connects the consecration with the recitation-proclamation of the Verba.[213] Peter Brunner defends the *Nachkonsekration* as the most visible and audible means by which supplemental elements are placed in the service of the Memorial commanded by Christ and connected with his words, which are the constitutional basis of the Sacrament.[214] It is sometimes argued that the relevant words ought to be repeated if for no other reason than to assure communicants that what they receive is the sacramental body and blood of Christ and not simply ordinary bread and wine.

Anglican practice since the Scottish Prayer Book of 1637 and the *Book of Common Prayer* since 1662 have required repetition of the appropriate words of institution; the 1979 Prayer Book continues the practice.[215] Some Anglicans insist that one element should never be consecrated by itself and that in any supplemental consecration both elements must always be set apart.

In Roman Catholic practice there is no reconsecration because no further supplies of bread and wine are used beyond those consecrated during the canon of the mass. There is usually additional supply available from previous masses, or the priest breaks the host into parts as tiny as necessary. If the supply nonetheless runs out, the distribution of communion ceases.

---

[210]This is the view of the *Statement on Communion Practices* adopted by the American Lutheran Church and the Lutheran Church in America in 1978 (II.C.2).

[211]*Common Service Book* (text ed.), p. 486.

[212]Reed, 361.

[213]Formula of Concord, Solid Declaration VII §79–84, 121 (*Book of Concord*, 584, 590).

[214]Peter Brunner, *Worship in the Name of Jesus*, trans. M. H. Bertram (St. Louis: Concordia Publishing House, 1968), 181. Marion Hatchett incorrectly observes that "supplementary consecration of additional bread and wine is a uniquely Anglican tradition" (Hatchett, 420, 388).

[215]*Book of Common Prayer*, 408.

With the doxology and the great Amen, the Great Thanksgiving is concluded. The communion follows, beginning with the preparation by prayer and the breaking of the bread.

The Lord's Prayer. Gregory the Great (590–604) placed the Our Father immediately after the Amen of the eucharistic prayer, where it functioned as a conclusion to the prayer and an extended Amen.[216] The Our Father is a wonderfully appropriate communion prayer. From the time of Tertullian and Cyprian, "daily bread" has been associated with the Eucharist. The prayer is offered in obedience to the command of Christ, as Luther explains in the Small Catechism, even as the Eucharist is celebrated in obedience to the command "Do this." The prayer is rooted in the intercession of Christ, gathering the themes of the eucharistic prayer and expressing solidarity with all who have prayed, all who pray, all who do not yet pray, indeed with all humanity, for to pray the Our Father and to pray with the church is to address God through Christ on behalf of all humanity. The prayer invites the assembly which prays it to participate in the rule and reign of God's life and kingdom, here and now and in the life to come, not only by speaking the words which Jesus gives and commands but by receiving him and living his life of service. The ultimate goal of the prayer is eschatological, yearning for the consummation of the kingdom.[217]

The introduction to the prayer, "Our Father in heaven," as well as the petitions of the prayer indicate the heavenly reference of the spiritual life, even the service of neighbors. The prayer encourages the Christian community that offers it to keep its life and work in perspective, maintaining the proper frame of reference for all that it believes and does. The prayer is closely related to Matthew 6:33, "Set your mind on God's kingdom and justice before everything else." The Our Father is therefore a fitting response to the Great Thanksgiving, which began with the *sursam corda*, "Left up your hearts." The Amen to the Lord's Prayer corresponds to the congregation's reply in the preface dialogue, "It is right to give him thanks and praise." The Great Thanksgiving ends as it began, with conviction and confidence: Yes, it must be so.

Throughout the *Lutheran Book of Worship* and in the *Book of Common Prayer* also, the Our Father is always given in two versions: the 1789 form and the translation prepared by the International Consultation on English texts. The Inter-Lutheran Commission on Worship knew that many people would be reluctant to learn a new translation of the familiar and beloved prayer.

There has been no single invariable translation in common use throughout the English-speaking world, and even the two versions in the Bible (Matt. 9:6–13 and Luke 11:2–4) do not agree. The Presbyterian form of the prayer uses "debts" rather than "trespasses"; the

---

[216]Hatchett, 378.

[217]See Karl Barth, *Prayer*, 2nd ed., trans.. Sara F. Terrien, ed. Don E. Saliers (Philadelphia: Westminster Press, 1985). See also Arthur Carl Piepkorn, "Our Father," *Response* 5 (Easter 1964):183–87.

Methodist version concludes "for ever" rather than "for ever and ever." The doxology was added early; its first known appearance is in the *Didache* (8.2). The use of the doxology is common in Byzantine liturgies but not in the Roman rite. "For ever and ever" is a Semitism carried over into early Christian use (Gal. 1:5; Heb. 13:21; Rev. 1:6).[218] The prayer was translated into English quite early and learned by the common people.[219] No attempt was made at creating a standardized version until the sixteenth century when English translations of the Bible became common. The version in the *King's Book* of 1543 supplanted the several English translations then in use, and, with only one petition changed ("let us not be led into temptation"), maintained its supremacy even after the appearance of the Authorized Version in 1611. The form which Lutherans in North America came to learn was borrowed from the 1789 American *Book of Common Prayer*, which is a slight revision of the version in the English Prayer Book, "Our Father, *which* art in heaven... *in* earth as it is in heaven... *them that* trespass against us...."

In the Roman rite, the Lord's Prayer is introduced, "Let us pray with confidence to the Father in the words our Savior gave us." This is a clearer translation of the intent of the older formula, "Taught by his saving precepts, and informed by his divine instruction, we are bold to say" (*Praeceptis salutaribus moniti, et divina institutione formati, audemus dicere*), in which "bold to say" connoted not so much presumption as assurance and confidence.[220] In the *Book of Common Prayer* the Lord's Prayer is introduced, "And now, as our Savior Christ has taught us, we are bold to say" (a rendering of the invitation in previous Roman missals) or "As our Savior Christ has taught us, we now pray." Luther in his *Formula Missae* introduced the prayer with the Roman formula familiar to him and his readers, and his explanation in the Small Catechism of the introduction to the Lord's Prayer echoes the Roman formula:

---

[218]See Willy Rordorf, "The Lord's Prayer in the Light of Its Liturgical Use," *Studia Liturgica* 14:1 (1980/1):1–20. See also Richard J. Dillon, "On the Christian Observance of Prayer (Matthew 5:5–13)," *Worship* 59 (1985):413–26; also Dikran Hadidian, "The Lord's Prayer and the Sacraments of Baptism and the Lord's Supper in the Early Church," *Studia Liturgica* 15:3/4 (1982/1983):132–44; also Joachim Jeremias, *Das Vater-unser im Lichte der neuern Forschung*, 3rd ed. (Stuttgart, 1965); also Ernst Lohemyer, *"Our Father": An Introduction to the Lord's Prayer*, trans. John Bowden (New York: Harper and Row, 1966).

[219]Albert S. Cook, "The Evolution of the Lord's Prayer in English," *American Journal of Philology* 12 (1891):59–66; Herbert Thurston, "The Our Father in English" in *Familiar Prayers, Their Origin and History*, ed. Paul Grosjean (London: Burns & Oates, 1953); John H. Fisher and Diane D. Bornstein, *In Forme of Speche is Chaunge* (Lanham, MD: University Press of America, 1984), 52–55: texts of the Lord's Prayer in Latin, Anglo-Saxon Koine (before 1000), Late West Saxon (after 1150), Northumbrian (ca. eighth century), Mercian (ca. ninth century), the Wycliffite Bible (ca. 1395), and the King James Bible (1611); Charles A. Ferguson, "Some Forms of Religious Discourse," *International Yearbook of the Sociology of Religion* 8 (1973):224–35.

[220]Shepherd, 81–82.

Here God would encourage us to believe that he is truly our Father and we are truly his children in order that we may approach him boldly and confidently in prayer, even as beloved children approach their dear Father.[221]

Later Lutheran liturgies have generally not used an introduction. The Common Service introduced the prayer with a simple "Let us pray," for the prayer followed the Sanctus.

In the Roman rite from the time of Gregory the Great, the Lord's Prayer was said by the priest alone, although from the eighth century the congregation answered by saying the concluding phrase "but deliver us from evil." Following the most ancient manuscripts of the New Testament, the doxology was not attached to the prayer (as it is not in the German text of Luther's Small Catechism). The Lord's Prayer was chanted by the minister in nearly all the sixteenth-century church orders. In the Common Service, therefore, the minister prayed the Our Father alone; the *Service Book and Hymnal* followed those German church orders (Mark Brandenburg, Herzogin Elizabeth, Pomerania, Hoya, Saxony) which assign the liturgical doxology and the Amen to the congregation. Music was provided for the Lord's Prayer in the third setting (plainsong) of the Service, which was published separately (1958). *The Lutheran Hymnal* followed a similar scheme. In the *Lutheran Book of Worship*, music is provided in the third setting of the Holy Communion. In the present Roman sacramentary, because the prayer is a communion prayer, the assembly says the Our Father together with the priest. This is in accord with Eastern and Gallican use. The *Lutheran Book of Worship* follows the same custom.

Breaking of the Bread. The most ancient name for the Holy Communion seems to have been the Breaking of the Bread, following Lucan terminology (Luke 24:35; Acts 2:42, 46). The *Lutheran Book of Worship* has reintroduced the fraction to Lutheran use in its original, utilitarian function: the bread is broken for distribution.[222] Christianity saw in the unity of the one loaf a sign of gathering into unity,[223] but the breaking of the bread, called the fraction, came to be invested with symbolic significance also. It suggested the sacrificial breaking of the body of Christ.

In the Middle Ages, when the people did not often commune, the celebrant broke his host so that he could reserve a portion of the bread for the communion of the sick. In some places a portion of the bread from a mass celebrated by a bishop was sent to parishes of the diocese to add to the chalice as a sign of the unity of the church under the bishop. In other places, a piece of bread was reserved to be placed in the chalice at a later mass as a sign of continuity. As these customs died out, the practice of commingling a piece of the bread in the chalice at each mass arose and was given allegorical interpretations.

---

[221] *Book of Concord*, 346.
[222] Augustine, *Letter* 149.16: the bread is broken small for distribution.
[223] 1 Cor. 10:17; *Didache* 9.4.

The Notes on the Liturgy permit the presiding minister to say at the breaking of the bread, "When we eat this bread, we share the body of Christ." Then, in a parallel but largely non-utilitarian action, the presiding minister may lift the cup and say, "When we drink this cup we share the blood of Christ." The congregation may then respond, "Reveal yourself to us, O Lord, in the breaking of the bread, as once you revealed yourself to your disciples" (Min. Ed., p. 29, #34). These optional elements are continued from *Contemporary Worship 2: The Holy Communion*, which had introduced them. The congregation's prayer derives from the *Book of Common Worship* of the Church of South India,

Be present, be present, O Jesus, thou good High Priest, as thou wast in the midst of thy disciples, and make thyself known to us in the breaking of the bread, who livest and reignest with the Father and the Holy Spirit, one God, world without end.[224]

The perhaps early ninth-century Stowe missal accompanied the fraction with Luke 24:35.

When the bread is broken, the breaking is to be done at this point in preparation for the distribution. Breaking the bread at the words in the institution narrative "he broke it" was required in the 1662 *Book of Common Prayer* and has been adopted by some Lutheran pastors, but such a practice confuses the progress of the eucharistic action. The eucharistic prayer (or the prayer and Verba or the Verba alone) is our imitation of Jesus' thanksgiving at the Last Supper (he "gave thanks"). The breaking is the preparation for the distribution: he "broke it, and gave it to his disciples." To introduce the fraction into the Verba would require for consistency the separation of the Verba from their surrounding context of prayer and an expansion and enactment of each clause of the narrative: "Our Lord Jesus took bread" (take the bread in hand), "gave thanks" (say a prayer of thanksgiving), "broke it" (break the bread), "and gave it to his disciples" (distribute the bread to the congregation); then the taking, thanksgiving, and distribution of the cup. (Note Luther's German Mass.)

Communion. In the early church the Sacrament was received standing, and in the Eastern churches this is still the practice. After the twelfth century, kneeling became general throughout the West, especially on fast days.

The words which accompanied the distribution in the early church were simply "The body of Christ," "The blood of Christ," to each of which the communicant responded "Amen," giving assent to the minister's creedal affirmation. Special stress was placed on the response. The simple declaration was expanded in various ways in various places: "the body of Christ received unto life," "the holy body of our Lord and God and Savior Jesus Christ" (liturgy of St. Mark), "the body of Christ for the forgiveness of sins and unto eternal life" (Byzantine), "This is

---

[224]*Book of Common Worship*, p. 14, in which it is the offertory prayer.

in truth the body and blood of Emmanuel, our Lord" (Coptic). Luther in his *Formula Missae* followed the formulas of his time, "The body (blood) of our Lord preserve your soul unto everlasting life."

The Lutheran rites in North America have undergone a simplification at this point. The *Church Book* had

Take, eat, this is the Body of our Lord Jesus Christ, which was given for you; may it strengthen and preserve you in the true faith unto everlasting life.

Take and drink, this is the Blood of our Lord Jesus Christ, which was shed for you and for many for the remission of sins; may it strengthen and preserve you in the true faith unto everlasting life.

The Common Service provided,

Take and eat, this is the Body of Christ, given for thee.

Take and drink, this is the Blood of the New Testament, shed for thy sins.

The *Service Book and Hymnal* simplified the formula further:

The body of Christ, given for thee.

The blood of Christ, shed for thee.

The *Lutheran Book of Worship* has retained the simple formula. Both the *Service Book and Hymnal* and the *Lutheran Book of Worship* rubrically encourage the communicant to say "Amen" after each element has been received.[225]

During the distribution, psalms and hymns may be sung, an ancient custom, at least as early as the fourth century, found in Celtic (especially a seventh-century hymn best known in the translation "Draw nigh and take the body of the Lord"), Mozarabic, and other Gallican rites centuries before the Reformation. Psalm 34, with verse 8 as the antiphon, and Psalm 145, with verse 16 as the antiphon, seem to have been the most popular.[226]

One of the hymns sung during the distribution may be the Agnus Dei, a hymn originally part of the Gloria in Excelsis and introduced as an independent song, according to the *Liber pontificalis*, by Pope Sergius I around A.D. 700.[227] It was, at that time, used as a devotion during the fraction; the one-line hymn — *Agnus Dei, qui tollis peccata mundi, miserere nobis* ("Lamb of God, who takest away the sins of the world, have mercy on us") — was repeated as long as the breaking of the bread lasted. The fraction was gradually abandoned after the ninth or tenth

---

[225]On the issue of the health hazards of the chalice see Frank C. Senn, "The Cup of Salvation: Take and Drink," *Lutheran Forum* 20 (Reformation 1986):19–28. Individual glasses were introduced into North American Lutheran churches during the influenza epidemics early in the twentieth century. In England they were introduced into nonconformist worship in the Horningsham Old Meeting House in Wiltshire in 1816; see Ralph Whitlock, "The Suspect Chalice," *Manchester Guardian Weekly* (April 12, 1987):20.

[226]Hatchett, 387.

[227]Jungmann, 485.

century, and the Agnus Dei, freed from its association with the breaking of the bread, assumed its three-fold form with the last words changed to *dona nobis pacem* ("grant us peace"). The new form appeared in other associations besides the fraction — with the Pax ("The peace of the Lord be with you always") or as a song during communion.

The canticle refers to Christ but more specifically to Christ present in the Eucharist as a sacrificial offering.[228] It is "a greeting of him who has been made present under the form of bread,"[229] and is comparable to the hymns of the book of Revelation. The Agnus Dei joins the Old Testament sacrifice of the paschal lamb with the triumphant lamb at the consummation of the universe (Isa. 53:7; John 1:29; Rev. 5:6ff.; 1 Pet. 1:18–19). In the Fourth Gospel, Jesus, the sacrificial offering, dies at the hour when the passover lambs are being slain (see 1 John 1:7).

Nearly all the Lutheran church orders included the Agnus Dei. Luther had written, "Particularly the Agnus Dei, above all songs, serves well for the sacrament, for it clearly sings about and praises Christ for having borne our sins and in beautiful, brief words powerfully and sweetly teaches the remembrance of Christ."[230] Some of the church order — Erfurt (1525) and Bayreuth (1755) — place it between the Verba and the Lord's Prayer. Others — Brunswick (1528), Hamburg (1529), Wittenberg (1533), and Oldenburg (1573) — give it after the distribution of communion and before the final collect. It was frequently used as a hymn sung during the distribution as in the Roman rite in which the celebrant received communion while the Agnus Dei was being sung.

During the later Middle Ages, various tropes on the Agnus Dei appeared, which serve as an indication of the ideas which were associated with the hymn.[231] Luther added "Christ" at the beginning of each of the three lines of the hymn, a unique Lutheran interpolation, found nowhere else.[232] Its first appearance was in the Brunswick order (1528). In the Reformation liturgies of England and Germany, *pacem* at the conclusion of the hymn was rendered "your peace" (see John 14:27).

The International Consultation on English Texts gave two translations of the Agnus Dei. The first, given as Canticle 1 in the *Lutheran Book of Worship*, was adapted by the Consultation in the hope that it would reveal more clearly and immediately the richness of meaning in the phrase "lamb of God." The name Jesus is prefixed to "lamb of God," the name Jesus rather than the title Lamb of God is repeated, and instead of simply repeating "you take away the sins of the world" three times, the phrase is explained as "lamb of God," "bearer of our sins," and "redeemer of the world."[233] The alternative version, prepared

---

[228] Ibid., 486.

[229] Ibid.

[230] Martin Luther, "Admonition Concerning the Sacrament of the Body and Blood of Our Lord" (1530), *Luther's Works* 38:123.

[231] Jungmann, 489; Reed, 370; *Prayers We Have in Common*, 17.

[232] Reed, 370.

[233] *Prayers We Have in Common*, 17.

by the International Commission on English in the Liturgy (the Roman Catholic commission), is given in the text of the Holy Communion in the *Lutheran Book of Worship*. It was proposed for liturgies in which the Agnus Dei is used to accompany a sometimes lengthy breaking of bread; the invocation "Lamb of God, you take away the sins of the world: have mercy on us" may be repeated as many times as necessary.[234]

The *Church Book* rite dismissed the communicants with the Pax, "The peace of the Lord be with you always." The Common Service abbreviated the distribution formulas of the *Church Book* and, having moved the Pax to the conclusion of the Verba, made the deleted phrases into a blessing of the communicants:

The Body of our Lord Jesus Christ and His precious Blood strengthen and preserve you in true faith unto everlasting life.

The language is traceable to the eighth century.[235] The *Lutheran Book of Worship* has simplified the blessing slightly, permitted variation and adaptation ("these or similar words"), and made the whole blessing optional because it no longer functions as a dismissal of each "table" of communicants and because the Benediction follows soon afterward.

The Post-Communion. Before the fourth century the Holy Communion apparently ended with the communion of the people. By the fourth century a dismissal can be documented in some places, and soon it was preceded by a prayer either of thanksgiving for the good effect of the Sacrament in the lives of the communicants[236] or for those who were being sent into the world.[237] The ministers then left the church and carried the Sacrament to those who were absent. The simple conclusion gave way to added ceremonies such as the ablutions and private prayers by the presiding minister.

The post-communion canticle of the Lutheran service corresponds to the *communio* or communion antiphon of the Roman rite, a fragment of a psalm sung to cover the action of the distribution to the people. Such a practice is attested in the fourth-century *Apostolic Constitutions* (8.13, 16). In the Middle Ages the song shrunk to an antiphon read or sung after the distribution was completed and followed immediately by the post-communion prayer; in 1958 its original use as a song during the communion of the people was restored by Pius XII.

The Nunc Dimittis is part of the priest's final devotions in the Liturgy of St. John Chrysostom, and in the Mozarabic rite also it is sung at the close of the liturgy. Luther's orders do not mention the Nunc Dimittis, but the Swedish liturgy (1531) gives it, as do some of the earliest German orders — Nuremberg (1525) and Strasbourg (1525). The Common Service (1888) was based on the consensus of the sixteenth-century church orders, and since most of them followed the Roman

---

[234]Ibid., 18.

[235]Jungmann, 514.

[236]Serapion, *The Euchologion* (A.D. 350).

[237]*Apostolic Constitutions* (ca. 380) 8.2.15.

structure and did not include the canticle, it could not, under a strict application of the rule which determined the preparation of the Common Service, become part of that order. But in response to a general desire for it and on the basis of good although limited precedent the Nunc Dimittis was inserted as a permissive use.[238] The emphasis on peace in the Nunc Dimittis recalls and echoes the prayer of the Kyrie at the beginning of the service. The congregation assembles and disperses with a prayer for the peace of God which passes understanding.

As an alternative to the Nunc Dimittis, the *Lutheran Book of Worship* provides another canticle, a liturgical prose by John Arthur, "Thank the Lord and Sing His Praise." The song marks the transition from encounter with Christ in the sacrament to joyful service in the world. The melody to which "Thank the Lord" is set in setting two of the liturgy is from an African folk tune adapted by Ronald Nelson for setting two of *Contemporary Worship 2: The Holy Communion* (1970). Because of the concluding Alleluias, this canticle is inappropriate for use during Lent.

In the *Lutheran Book of Worship*, the post-communion canticle is no longer optional as it was in the Common Service and in the *Service Book and Hymnal*.

A post-communion prayer follows. The first (no. 241) is from Luther's German Mass and is found in nearly every Lutheran liturgy. The thought of the prayer is not original with Luther, although the expression of it is.[239] The translation has developed through the editions of the *Church Book*, the Common Service, the *Service Book and Hymnal, Worship Supplement, Contemporary Worship 2*, and the *Lutheran Book of Worship*. Luther's prayer from the *Deutsche Messe* was

Wir danken dir, allmächtiger Herr Gott, dass du uns durch diese heilsame Gabe hast erquicket, und bitten deine Barmherzigkeit, dass du uns solches gedeihen lassest zu starkem Glauben gegen dich und zu brünstiger Liebe unter uns allen, um Jesu Christi unsers Herrn willen.

The version in the 1868 *Church Book* was influenced by the opening of the post-communion thanksgiving in the *Book of Common Prayer:*

Almighty God, our Heavenly Father, we most heartily thank Thee that Thou hast again vouchsafed to feed us with the most precious Body and Blood of Thy dear Son, our Saviour Jesus Christ; and we humbly beseech Thee, graciously to strengthen us, through this Holy Sacrament, in faith toward Thee, in charity toward one another, and in the blessed hope of everlasting life; through Jesus Christ, Thy dear Son our Lord, who liveth and reigneth with Thee, in the unity of the Holy Spirit, world without end. (pp. 22–23)

The version in the 1891 *Church Book* was simpler and closer to Luther:

We thank Thee, Lord God Almighty, that Thou hast vouchsafed to refresh us with this Thy salutary gift; and we beseech Thee, of Thy mercy, to strengthen

---

[238] Reed, 379–80.
[239] *Luther's Works* 53:84; Reed, 381–82; Paul Zeller Strodach in the Philadelphia Edition of the *Works of Martin Luther*, vol. 6 (Philadelphia: Muhlenberg Press, 1932):329–32.

us through the same, in faith toward Thee, and in fervent love toward one another; through Jesus Christ, Thy dear Son, our Lord, Who liveth and reigneth with Thee and the Holy Ghost, ever one God, world without end. (p. 21).

In the *Common Service Book* (1917) the translation was

We give thanks to Thee, Almighty God, that Thou hast refreshed us with this Thy salutary gift; and we beseech Thee, of Thy mercy, to strengthen us through the same in faith toward Thee, and in fervent love toward one another; through Jesus Christ, Thy dear Son, our Lord, Who liveth and reigneth with Thee and the Holy Ghost, ever one God, world without end. (pp. 27, 64)

In the *Service Book and Hymnal* (1958) the translation was the same except that one word was inserted — "strengthen us through the same *gift*" — and, as throughout the book, "ever" was deleted from the doxology. In *Worship Supplement* (1969), published by the Commission on Worship of the Lutheran Church–Missouri Synod, the translation was

We give thanks to you, almighty God, that you have refreshed us through this salutary gift; and we pray you that of your mercy you would strengthen us through the same in faith toward you and in fervent love toward one another; through Jesus Christ, our Lord, who lives and reigns with you and the Holy Spirit, one God, forever and ever. (p. 47)

In *Contemporary Worship 2: The Holy Communion* it became

We thank you, almighty God, for the healing power of the gift of life, and we pray that it may strengthen our faith in you and our love for each other; through Jesus Christ, our Lord. (p. 21)

The version in the *Lutheran Book of Worship* returned to the previous phrasing of the concluding clause.

The second collect (no. 242), "Pour out upon us," is a free translation of the post-communion collect in the Roman sacramentary for the Easter Vigil and Easter Day. It was introduced to Lutheran use in the *Service Book and Hymnal* (1958). The original collect is from the Leonine sacramentary (no. 1049):

Spiritum nobis domine tuae caritatis infunde ut quos uno caelesti pane satiasti una facias pietate concordes.

The prayer makes allusion to the bread of heaven given during the exodus and given in Christ, joining old covenant and new in the paschal mystery.

The third collect (no. 243), "Almighty God, you gave your Son," was introduced to Lutheran use in the *Service Book and Hymnal*. It is the collect for the Second Sunday after Easter in the 1928 *Book of Common Prayer* and appointed for Proper 15 in the 1979 Prayer Book. It was written for the 1549 Prayer Book and draws upon the Epistle then appointed for the Second Sunday after Easter, 1 Peter 2:19–15. Massey Shepherd comments, "The Collect summarizes as does no other formulary in the Prayer Book the meaning of God's gift of His Son for our redemption."[240]

Like the rubrics of the *Service Book and Hymnal,* the Notes on the Liturgy in the *Lutheran Book of Worship* (Min. Ed., p. 29, #40) permit the use of the Maundy Thursday prayer (no. 38), "Lord God in a wonderful Sacrament," as a post-communion prayer. It was composed by Thomas Aquinas in 1264 for the then-new feast of Corpus Christi, the Thursday after Trinity Sunday. It was appointed as an alternative to Luther's post-communion collect in several church orders, such as Duke Henry of Saxony (1539), Spangenberg (1545), and Austria (1571).

A fourth post-communion collect was provided in the *Service Book and Hymnal,* "Almighty God, who givest the true Bread which cometh down from heaven." It is included in the *Lutheran Book of Worship* among the Petitions, Intercessions, and Thanksgivings for After Communion (no. 209).

It is the intention in the *Lutheran Book of Worship* that the Holy Communion end with dispatch, and that none of the common additions prolong the conclusion — elaborately sung Amens, extinguishing candles, organ music, silent prayer. Once the blessing has been given (and the dismissal said), the people are to disperse into the world. If the dismissal is said, it must in fact be a dismissal after which those dismissed leave. Therefore, the rite provides for silent prayer and meditation by the congregation before the benediction rather than after it.[241]

The silence is a time for meditation upon the great gift of the Son of God in the Sacrament. It is a recognition that despite all the sounds of the liturgy, hymns, and sermon, the truth of God is "veiled in silence,"[242] that "God's truth often is silent, mysterious, invisible," and that this truth can be known only through and within the church.[243] The silent meditation is a time to listen to that truth and to adore, for "love's favorite language is silence."[244] Ignatius of Antioch said that "the one who possesses in truth the word of Jesus can hear even his silence."[245] Those who have eaten the holy meal and have partaken of the divine mysteries are now bidden to listen to that silence.

Benediction. Before the fourth century there is no evidence of a blessing at the end of the liturgy, although blessings may have been used

---

[240]Shepherd, 170–71.

[241]*Common Service Book* (text ed.), p. 484; "*Silent prayer* should be offered after all Services." *Service Book and Hymnal,* p. 274: "Worshippers should offer Silent Prayer upon entering and before leaving the Church."

[242]Basil, *De spiritu sancto* 27.

[243]Timiadis, 22, 54–55.

[244]Joseph McSorley, *A Primer on Prayer* (New York: Paulist Press, 1969 [1934]), 61.

[245]Ignatius, *Letter to the Ephesians* 15.2. See also Matt. 11:15; Gustav Aulén, *Dag Hammarskjöld's White Book: The Meaning of Markings* (Philadelphia: Fortress Press, 1969), 60, 70: "...the last word about God is *mystery.*" Also Simone Weil, *On Science, Necessity, and the Love of God,* essays collected, translated, and edited by Richard Rees (New York: Oxford University Press, 1968), 197: "The speech of created beings is with sounds. The word of God is silence. God's secret word of love can be nothing else but silence."

which were not recorded in the liturgical texts. Many Eastern liturgies have a prayer with the laying on of hands by the presiding minister if the group was small and with the extending of the hands over the group if the congregation was larger. In the oldest Roman sacramentary, the Leonine, there is a prayer after the post-communion prayer, called a *super populum* (over the people), for every mass. It was a prayer by the presiding minister for God's blessing on the people. The Gregorian sacramentary restricted the *super populum* to the weekdays of Lent; the 1969 Roman sacramentary provides a solemn blessing or a prayer over the people for Sundays and most days of the year.[246] The Episcopal Church has made similar provisions in the *Book of Occasional Services*.[247] The Gallican sacramentaries have a blessing, reserved to the bishop, prior to communion; whether the blessing is upon the communicants or upon those who are about to leave is not clear. The Aaronic blessing (Numb. 6:24–26) was used in this rite on certain occasions.

The eighty-century Ordo Romanus Primus describes a blessing given by the bishop as he leaves the church, but no forms are provided. Late in the Middle Ages the bishop before leaving the church gave this blessing from the altar. Priests in France and Germany during the eleventh century took up this blessing at the end of the mass, and thus it passed through Luther to the German church orders.

Very few of the medieval missals provide a text for this blessing. Luther in his *Formula Missae* says, "The customary benediction may be given; or else the one from Numbers 6[:24–27], which the Lord himself appointed:

The Lord bless us and keep us. The Lord make his face shine upon us and be gracious to us. The Lord lift up his countenance upon us and give us peace.

Or the one from Psalm 67[:6–7]:

God, even our own God shall bless us. God shall bless us; and all the ends of the earth shall fear him.

I believe Christ said something like this when, ascending into heaven, he blessed his disciples [Luke 24:50–51]."[248] The German Mass gives only the Aaronic benediction.

The Reformation church orders generally followed this tradition, explaining the choice as "the only benediction commanded by God" (see Numb. 6:22).[249] Brandenburg-Nuremberg, church orders (1553), Mecklenburg (1540), Württemberg (1553), Worms (1560), and other church orders give the Roman mass form — "May almighty God bless you, the Father, the Son, and the Holy Spirit"[250] — in conjunction with the

---

[246]See Thomas A. Krosnicki, "New Blessings in the Missal of Paul VI," *Worship* 45 (1971):199–205.

[247]*The Book of Occasional Services*, 2nd ed. (New York: Church Hymnal Corporation, 1988), 20–27: "Seasonal Blessings."

[248]*Luther's Works* 53:30.

[249]Reed, 385.

[250]The form appears, among other places, at the Synod of Albi (1230).

Aaronic benediction. The Swedish liturgy, Muhlenberg's liturgy for the Ministerium of Pennsylvania (1748), and the *Service Book and Hymnal* attached to the Aaronic benediction "In the name of the Father, and of the Son, and of the Holy Ghost."

In middle and north Germany the benediction was intoned by the minister, and the church orders and cantionales provide many musical settings for it. The minister usually lifted both hands over the people as the blessing was given in imitation of Moses and Aaron and Jesus before the ascension blessing his disciples "with uplifted hands" (Luke 24:50). The sign of the cross frequently accompanied the concluding words, recalling Colossians 1:20, "making peace by the blood of his cross."

The first benediction in the *Lutheran Book of Worship* is an adaptation of the blessing in the Roman sacramentary used with the prayer over the people.

Roman sacramentary	Lutheran Book of Worship	Book of Common Prayer
May almighty God bless you, the Father, and the Son, + and the Holy Spirit.		
or, *with the prayer* *over people*		
And may the blessing of almighty God, the Father, and the Son, + and the Holy Spirit, come upon you, and remain with you for ever.	Almighty God, Father, + Son, and Holy Spirit, bless you now and forever.	The blessing of God Almighty, the Father, the Son, and the Holy Spirit, be upon you and remain with you for ever. (p. 339)

The *Lutheran Book of Worship*, continuing a long tradition rooted in the temple cult and synagogues of Judaism and adopted by Luther, gives the Aaronic benediction as an alternative blessing.[251] The translation of this benediction — a most difficult Hebrew text — was made for the *Lutheran Book of Worship* by the Inter-Lutheran Commission on Worship. (See below, p. 454.)

Dismissal. The *Apostolic Constitutions* and other early Eastern liturgies give the first evidence of a dismissal. The deacon announces simply, "Depart in peace." (The Ulm church order of 1747 used "Depart in peace" at the conclusion of the liturgy.) A typical response in the early rites was "In the name of Christ." The formula is still in use in Milan.

---

[251] The Aaronic benediction is given once in the *Book of Common Prayer* (p. 114) in the three-fold form typical of its use in the Middle Ages.

The Roman rite at least from the eighth century (it may be much older)[252] had *Ite, missa est*. The meaning is disputed; it may have meant "Go, it is over," or "The assembly is concluded; you are dismissed." The response to the announcement was *Deo gratias*, "Thanks be to God," a response used after announcements and after readings as an acknowledgement that the message has been heard; it also of course conveys an expression of gratitude.

The Gallican rites may have used *Benedicamus domino*, "Let us bless the Lord." It was taken into the Roman rite and eventually the rule was developed that *Ite, missa est* was used whenever the Gloria in Excelsis was used (i.e., festive masses); *Benedicamus domino* was used on other days, especially when other prayers or rites were added to the mass.

Modern liturgies have restored the dismissal to its original function after the Blessing. The Roman sacramentary provides three options for the deacon (or priest):

> Go in the peace of Christ
> *or* The mass is ended, go in peace.
> *or* Go in peace to love and serve the Lord.

The *Book of Common Prayer* provides four options for the deacon or celebrant:

> Let us go forth in the name of Christ.
> *or* Go in peace to love and serve the Lord.
> *or* Let us forth into the world, rejoicing in the power of the Spirit.
> *or* Let us bless the Lord.

The *Lutheran Book of Worship* has one dismissal for the assisting minister, a more terse and abrupt form of the one dismissal common to the Roman and Episcopal rites, "Go in peace. Serve the Lord" (Rom. 12:11b). The response in all cases in all the rites is "Thanks be to God." (During Easter the Roman sacramentary adds two alleluias to "The mass is ended, go in peace" and to the response as well. The *Book of Common Prayer* permits two alleluias to be added during Easter to any of the dismissals and responses.)

Whether or not the dismissal is said, the idea of service in the world is essential. In the twelfth century, Richard of St. Victor added to the three traditional periods of growth in prayer — purgation, illumination, and union with God — a fourth, service to one's neighbor in need.[253] For when one is united to God, one lives the life of God, which, as Jesus demonstrated, is a life given to and for humanity. What Richard said about prayer is, as Luther noted, especially true of the church's consummate prayer, the Holy Communion: "When you have partaken of this sacrament, therefore, or desire to partake of it, you must in turn

---

[252] See Jungmann, 535–36.
[253] See Kristopher L. Willumsen, "Christian Initiation, Apprenticeship in Prayer," *Liturgy* 5 (Summer 1985):18.

share the misfortunes of the fellowship...all the unjust suffering of the innocent, with which the world is everywhere filled to overflowing. You must fight, work, pray, and — if you cannot do more — have heartfelt sympathy."[254] On a similar note, the reformer wrote, "I will therefore give myself as a Christ to my neighbor, just as Christ offered himself to me....We conclude, therefore, that a Christian lives not in himself, but in Christ and in his neighbor."[255] So strengthened by the Holy Communion, the congregation departs to live its baptism.

In the *Lutheran Book of Worship* there is no longer a provision for a hymn after the benediction. Earlier rites never encouraged such a use; the permission was included not in the text of the service, but only in the General Rubrics: "A hymn may be sung after the benediction at any service."[256]

Treatment of Remaining Elements. There is little agreement among Lutherans about what to do with any eucharistic bread or wine which may remain after the celebration.[257] The *Common Service Book* gave specific instructions:

When *The Service* has been completed, a Deacon or other Officer shall remove the Sacramental Vessels from the Altar to the Sacristy, and dispose of that part of the *Bread* and *Wine* which remaineth as follows: He shall carefully remove the Bread from the Paten and Ciborium to a fit receptacle, there to be kept against the next Communion. He shall carry the Chalice to a proper and convenient place without the Church and pour the *Wine* upon the ground.[258]

Nothing was said about what to do with wine remaining in the flagons or cruets. (It was usually returned to the bottle from which it came.) These directions were not preserved in the *Service Book and Hymnal* because there was no longer consensus on how the sacramental elements were to be treated.

If the doctrine of the real presence is still believed, one might expect that elements remaining after the distribution (with careful planning there ought not be large quantities) should be reverently consumed at the altar or in the sacristy, except for what may be reserved for the communion of the sick.

---

[254] Martin Luther, "The Blessed Sacrament of the Holy and True Body of Christ and the Brotherhoods" (1519), *Luther's Works* 35:54.

[255] Martin Luther, "Freedom of a Christian" (1520), *Luther's Works* 31:367, 371.

[256] *Common Service Book* (text ed.), p. 484; *Service Book and Hymnal*, p. 274.

[257] In the early church what was left after communion was taken to the sacristy and kept for at least a day, according to the law in Lev. 7:16, and then either consumed or burned (Lev. 7:17). See "Disposal of Eucharistic Remains," *The New Westminster Dictionary of Liturgy and Worship.* Also see William Lockton, *The Treatment of the Remains of the Eucharist after Holy Communion and the Time of the Ablutions* (Cambridge: University Press, 1920).

[258] *Common Service Book* (text ed.), p. 486.

WHEN THERE IS NO COMMUNION

Recognizing that the movement to restore the ancient association of the Lord's Supper with every Lord's Day would take time to achieve, the Inter-Lutheran Commission on Worship reluctantly and only after considerable debate decided on pastoral grounds that the *Lutheran Book of Worship* should provide for concluding the service "when there is no communion." (In the *Common Service Book* and in the *Service Book and Hymnal* the chief service was called The Service; in the *Lutheran Book of Worship* it is called the Holy Communion, yielding, when the service is limited to ante-communion, the curiosity "The Holy Communion without Holy Communion.") In previous books the order of sermon, offering, general prayer was easily terminated with the Lord's Prayer and benediction. The order in the *Lutheran Book of Worship* is more clearly directed to the celebration of Holy Communion — creed, prayers, peace, offering, offertory — and yields a less satisfying form if it is prematurely terminated. A revised order is therefore provided for "when there is no communion": offering, offertory, prayers, Lord's Prayer, benediction. This was the order in previous books.

The offertory is the one from the Common Service, Psalm 51:10–12, "Create in me a clean heart, O God." The translation is that used in previous books, the Authorized Version, with the second person pronouns modernized and "unto" simplified as "to."

The prayer (no. 244) "O Lord our God, you have commanded the light to shine out of darkness" is a condensation and adaptation of one of the prayers said at Matins and before the holy door in the services of the Orthodox churches.[259] Reed comments, "Its origin is shrouded in the dim light of the early Christian centuries."[260] It was introduced to Lutheran use in the *Service Book and Hymnal* (1958) as the first of the additional General Prayers (p. 258) in a translation borrowed from *A Chain of Prayer across the Ages*[261] and, because of its excellence, was preserved in the *Lutheran Book of Worship* in this manner. The form of prayer used in Holy Communion is provided as an alternative.

The Aaronic benediction is used to conclude the service because of its familiarity to Lutherans for generations.

---

[259] *Service Book of the Holy Orthodox–Catholic Apostolic Church*, trans. Isabel Florence Hapgood, 5th ed. (Englewood, NJ: Antiochian Orthodox Christian Archdiocese of New York and All North America, 1975), 21.

[260] Reed, 661.

[261] *A Chain of Prayer across the Ages*, comp. Selina Fitzherbert Fox, 5th ed. (New York: E. P. Dutton & Co., 1928), 74.

ADDENDUM I

Eucharistic Prayer drafted by Paul Zeller Strodach before 1936
and published in his *Manual on Worship*, rev. ed.
(Philadelphia: Muhlenberg Press, 1946), pp. 253–54.

The Minister standing before the altar shall say:

It is fitting and due to praise Thee, to hymn Thee, to bless Thee, to worship
Thee, to give thanks to Thee,
Therefore, we also, with this Blessed Host, cry aloud and say:

Holy art Thou, O God, Thou and Thine Only-Begotten Son and Thy Holy Spirit.
Holy art Thou, and great is the Majesty of Thy Glory, O Father and Lover of
men, Who didst so love the world as to give Thine Only-Begotten Son, that
whosoever believeth in Him might not perish, but have everlasting life;
Who having come into the world, and having fulfilled for us Thy Holy Will, and
being obedient unto the end,

(THE INSTITUTION)

In the night in which He was betrayed took bread,* and when He had given
thanks, He brake it and gave it to His disciples, saying: Take, eat; this is My
Body,[†] which is given for you; this do in remembrance of Me.

After the same manner also, when He had supped, He took the Cup,[‡] and when
He had given thanks, He gave it to them, saying: Drink ye all of it; this Cup is
the New Testament in My Blood[§] which is shed for you and for many, for the
remission of sins; this do, as oft as ye drink it, in remembrance of Me.

(THE ANAMNESIS)

Therefore remembering His salutary precept, and all that He endured for us: His
Passion and Death, His Resurrection and Ascension, His Session on the Right
Hand, and His Glorious Coming Again, we give thanks to Thee, O Lord God
Almighty, not as we ought, but as we are able; and we offer to Thee, according
to his Institution, these Thy Gifts of Bread and Wine, giving thanks to Thee
through Him, that Thou has deemed us worthy to stand before Thee, celebrating
and making the Memorial which Thy Son hath willed us to make.

(THE EPIKLESIS)

And we beseech Thee: send down Thy Holy Spirit upon us and upon these
Gifts here before Thee, that according to the Word of Thy dear Son they may
be sanctified and blessed, and so used by us, that this Bread may be the Body of
Christ and this Wine His precious Blood, that all who eat and drink thereof in
true faith and with contrite hearts may be sanctified in soul and body, that we
may be one body and one spirit, and may have our portion with all Thy Saints
who have been well-pleasing unto Thee; through the Same, Christ Our Lord;

Here he shall take the Paten with the Bread in his hand.
[†]*At the words,* This is My Body, *he may elevate the Paten with the Bread.*
[‡]*Here he shall take the Cup with the Wine in his Hand.*
[§]*At the words,* In My Blood, *he may elevate the Cup with the Wine.*

(THE LORD'S PRAYER–PRAYER OF HUMBLE ACCESS)

Who has taught us to pray and through Whom we make bold to say:

Our Father, Who art in heaven; Hallowed be Thy Name; Thy Kingdom come; Thy Will be done on earth, as it is in heaven; Give us this day our daily bread; and forgive us our trespasses, as we forgive those who trespass against us; And lead us not into temptation; But deliver us from evil.

(THE EMBOLISM)

Deliver us, O Lord, from all evil, the past, the present, and that which may come; grant us gracious peace in our days: that in all things Thy Holy Name may be hallowed, praised, and blessed, for to Thee is due all glory, worship, adoration, O Father, Son, and Holy Ghost, One God, now and evermore. *Amen.*

ADDENDUM II

Eucharistic Prayer Proposed by Luther Reed,
The Lutheran Liturgy, first ed.
(Philadelphia: Muhlenberg Press, 1947), pp. 336–37

Holy art Thou, O God, Who art from everlasting, the Master and the Lover of men, Who didst so love the world as to give Thine Only-begotten Son, that whosoever believeth in Him might not perish but have everlasting life;

Who, although He was eternal God, yet deigned to become man, and, having fulfilled for us Thy holy will and accomplished all things for our salvation;* in the night in which He was betrayed, took bread; and when He had given thanks, He brake it and gave it to His disciples, saying, Take, eat; this is My Body, which is given for you. This do in remembrance of Me.

After the same manner also, He took the cup, when He had supped, and when He had given thanks, He gave it to them, saying, Drink ye all of it; this cup is the New Testament in My Blood, which is shed for you, and for many, for the remission of sins; this do, as oft as ye drink it, in remembrance of Me.

Remembering, therefore, His holy Incarnation, His perfect Life on earth, His life-giving Passion, His glorious Resurrection and Ascension, His continual Intercession and Rule at Thy right hand, His gift of the Holy Spirit and the promise of His coming again, we give Thee thanks, not as we ought but as we are able; and we make here before Thee the Memorial which Thy dear Son hath willed us to make. And we humbly pray Thee graciously to accept this the sacrifice of our thanksgiving and praise, and to bless and sanctify with Thy Word and Holy Spirit these Thine own gifts of bread and wine, so that in very truth the bread which we break may be the communion of the Body of Christ and the cup of blessing which we bless may be the communion of the Blood of Christ.

And we beseech Thee to send Thy Holy Spirit, the Lord and Giver of Life into our hearts, so that we and all who partake of these gifts consecrated by

---

*Or, instead of the phrase "and accomplished all things for our salvation," insert the following magnificent passage from Hippolytus: "stretched out His hands for suffering, that He might free from suffering those who believed in Thee"; and in the night, etc....

Thy grace and power, may be filled with all heavenly benediction and grace, may receive the remission of our sins, be sanctified in soul and body, be united in one body and one spirit, and finally have our portion and lot with all Thy saints who have been well-pleasing unto Thee, unto Whom be glory now and evermore; through the same Jesus Christ, Thy Son, our Lord, Who taught us when we pray to say:

Our Father, Who art in heaven...

BIBLIOGRAPHY

von Allmen, Jean-Jacques, et al. *Roles in the Liturgical Assembly.* Translated by Matthew J. O'Connell. New York: Pueblo Publishing Co., 1981.

Aulén, Gustav. *Eucharist and Sacrifice.* Translated by Eric H. Wahlstrom. Philadelphia: Muhlenberg Press, 1958.

Baumstark, Anton. *Comparative Liturgy.* London: Mowbray, 1958.

Bouley, Allan. *From Freedom to Formula: The Evolution of the Eucharistic Prayer from Oral Improvisation to Written Texts.* Studies in Christian Antiquity 21. Washington, DC: Catholic University Press, 1981.

Bouyer, Louis. *Eucharist: Theology and Spirituality of the Eucharistic Prayer.* Translated by Charles Underhill Quinn. Notre Dame, IN: University Press, 1968.

Brilioth, Yngve. *Eucharistic Faith and Practice: Evangelical and Catholic.* Translated by A. G. Herbert. London: SPCK, 1930.

Buxton, Richard. *Eucharist and Institution Narrative.* Alcuin Club collections no. 57. Great Wakering, England: Mayhew-McCrimmon, Ltd., 1976.

Cabie, Robert. *The Eucharist.* Translated by M. J. O'Connell. Volume 2 of *The Church at Prayer,* ed. Aime G. Martimort. Collegeville: Liturgical Press, 1986.

Cochrane, Arthur. *Eating and Drinking with Jesus.* Philadelphia: Westminster Press, 1974.

Cullmann, Oscar. and F. J. Leenhardt. *Essays on the Lord's Supper.* Ecumenical Studies in Worship no. 1. Translated by J. G. Davies. Richmond, VA: John Knox Press, 1958.

Dallen, James. "The Congregation's Share in the Eucharistic Prayer," *Worship* 54 (1978):329–41.

Daly, Robert J. *The Origins of the Christian Doctrine of Sacrifice.* Philadelphia: Fortress Press, 1978.

Dix, Gregory. *The Shape of the Liturgy.* With additional notes by Paul V. Marshall. New York: Seabury Press, 1982.

Elert, Werner. *Eucharist and Christian Fellowship in the First Four Centuries.* St. Louis: Concordia Publishing House, 1966.

Eucharist and Ministry. Lutherans and Catholics in Dialogue IV. Edited by Paul C. Empie and T. Austin Murphy. Minneapolis: Augsburg Publishing House, 1979.

The Eucharist as Sacrifice. Lutherans and Catholics in Dialogue III. New York: USA National Committee of the Lutheran World Federation, 1967.

Feeley-Harnik, Gillian. *The Lord's Table.* Philadelphia: University of Pennsylvania Press, 1981.

Hanggi, A., and Irmgard Pahl. *Prex Eucharistica*. Freiburg: University Press, 1968.

Herrlin, Olov. *Divine Service: Liturgy in Perspective*. Philadelphia: Fortress Press, 1966.

Jasper, Ronald C. D., and Geoffrey J. Cuming, eds. *Prayers of the Eucharist: Early and Reformed*. 2nd ed. New York: Oxford University Press, 1980.

Jeremias, Joachim. *The Eucharistic Words of Jesus*. Philadelphia: Fortress, 1966.

———. *The Lord's Prayer*. Facet Book Biblical Series 8. Philadelphia: Fortress Press, 1964.

Jones, Cheslyn, Geoffrey Wainwright, and Edward Yarnold, eds. *The Study of Liturgy*. New York: Oxford University Press, 1978. Part I, chapters 1–14; Part III.

Jungmann, Joseph A. *The Eucharistic Prayer*. Translated by Robert L. Batley. Chicago: Fides, 1956.

———. *The Liturgy of the Word*. Translated by H. E. Winstone. Collegeville: Liturgical Press, 1966.

———. *The Mass of the Roman Rite*. Revised by Charles K. Riepe. New York: Benziger, 1959.

———. *The Place of Christ in Liturgical Prayer*. London: Geoffrey Chapman, 1965.

Kavanagh, Aidan. *On Liturgical Theology*. New York: Pueblo Publishing Co., 1984.

Klauser, Theodor. *A Short History of the Western Liturgy*. New York: Oxford University Press, 1968.

Lee, Bernard J., ed. *The Eucharist*. Vol. III in Alternative Futures for Worship. Collegeville: Liturgical Press, 1987.

Lietzmann, Hans. *Mass and the Lord's Supper: A Study in the History of the Liturgy*. Leiden: Brill, 1953.

Marxsen, Willi. *The Lord's Supper as a Christological Problem*. Translated by Lorenz Neiting. Philadelphia: Fortress Press, 1970.

Mazza, Enrico. *The Eucharistic Prayers of the Roman Rite*. Translated by Matthew J. O'Connell. New York: Pueblo Publishing Co., 1986.

McKenna, John H. *Eucharist and Holy Spirit: The Eucharistic Epiklesis in Twentieth Century Theology (1900–1966)*. Great Wakering, England: Mayhew-McCrimmon, 1975.

Mitchell, Nathan. *Cult and Controversy: The Worship of the Eucharist Outside of Mass*. New York: Pueblo Publishing Co., 1982.

Reumann, John H. P. *The Supper of the Lord: The New Testament, Ecumenical Dialogues, and Faith and Order on "Eucharist."* Philadelphia: Fortress Press, 1985.

Rordorf, Willy, et al. *The Eucharist of the Early Christians*. New York: Pueblo Publishing Co., 1978.

Schmemann, Alexander. *For the Life of the World*. Crestwood, NY: St. Vladimir's Seminary Press, 1973.

Schnitker, T. A., and W. A. Slaby, ed. *Concordantia Verbalia Missalis Romani*. Münster: Aschendorff, 1983.

Schweitzer, Eduard. *The Lord's Supper According to the New Testament*. Translated by Joseph M. Davis. Philadelphia: Fortress Press, 1971.

Senn, Frank C., ed. *New Eucharistic Prayers: An Ecumenical Study of their Development and Structure.* Ramsey, NJ: Paulist Press, 1987.

Smolarski, Dennis C. *Eucharistia: A Study of the Eucharistic Prayer.* New York and Ramsey, NJ: Paulist Press, 1982.

Srawley, J. H. *The Early History of the Liturgy.* 2nd ed. Cambridge: University Press, 1947.

Stevenson, Kenneth. *Eucharist and Offering.* New York: Pueblo Publishing Co., 1986.

Taft, Robert J. *The Great Entrance: A History of the Transfer of Gifts and Other Preanaphoral Rites of the Liturgy of St. John Chrysostom.* Orientalia Christiana Analecta. Rome: Pontifical Oriental Institute, 1975.

Thompson, Bard, ed. *Liturgies of the Western Church.* Cleveland: World, 1962.

Thurian, Max. *The Eucharistic Memorial.* Translated by J. G. Davies. 2 vols. Richmond, VA: John Knox Press, 1961.

————, and Geoffrey Wainwright. *Baptism and Eucharist: Ecumenical Convergence in Celebration.* Grand Rapids: Eerdmans, 1983.

Wainwright, Geoffrey. *Eucharist and Eschatology.* London: Epworth, 1971.

The Collects

Althaus, Paul. *Zur Einführung in die Quellengeschichte der kirchlichen Kollekten in der lutherischen Agenden des 16. Jahrhunderts.* Leipzig: Edelmann, 1919.

Dietz, Otto. *Die Evangelien-Kollekten des Veit Dietrich.* Leipzig: Wallmann, 1930. English translation by Sigfrid Estborn, *A Church Year in Prayers — The Gospel Collects of Veit Dietrich.* Guntur: Board of Publication of the Federation of Evangelical Lutheran Churches in India, 1937.

Goulburn, E. L. *The Collects of the Day.* 2 vols. London: Longmans Green & Co., 1880.

Kulp, Hans-Ludwig. "Das Gemeindegebet in christlichen Gottesdienst" in *Leiturgia: Handbuch des evangelischen Gottesdienstes.* Vol. 2: Gestalt und Formen des evangelischen Gottesdienstes 1. Der Haupt-gottesdienst. Ed. Karl F. Muller and Walter Blankenburg. Kassel: Johannes Stander-Verlag, 1955. Pp. 355–419.

Strodach, Paul Zeller. *The Collect for the Day.* Philadelphia: United Lutheran Publication House, 1939.

————. "The Collect: A Study," *Lutheran Church Review* 44 (1925):34–42.

————. "The Collects in the Church Book," *Lutheran Church Review* 35 (1916):401–25; 36 (1917): 105–36.

————. "The Collects in the Common Service Book," *Lutheran Church Review* 40 (1921):57–74, 242–66.

Suter, John Wallace, Jr. *The Book of English Collects.* New York: Harper and Bros., 1940.

Weil, Louis. *Gathered to Pray: Understanding Liturgical Prayer.* Cambridge, MA: Cowley Publications, 1986.

Lectionary

Borsch, F. H. *Introducing the Lessons of the Church Year: A Guide for Lay Readers and Congregations.* New York: Seabury Press, 1978.

Brown, Schuyler. "The Good News for Today: Reflections on the Sunday Lectionary," *Worship* 49:4 (April 1975) through 50:3 (May 1976).

Danielou, Jean. *The Bible and the Liturgy.* Notre Dame, IN: University Press, 1956.

Fontaine, G. "The Ordo Lectionum Missae," *Notitiae* 5 (1969):256–82.

Hagen, Kenneth, Daniel Harrington, Grant Osborne, and Joseph A. Burgress. *The Bible in the Churches: How Different Churches Interpret the Scriptures.* Ramsey, NJ: Paulist Press, 1985.

Maertens, Thierry, and Jean Frisque. *Guide for the Christian Assembly.* 9 vols. Notre Dame, IN: Fides Press, 1971–74.

Sloyan, Gerard S. "The Bible as the Book of the Church," *Worship* 60 (1986): 9–21.

Psalter

Lamb, John A. *The Psalms in Christian Worship.* London: Faith Press, 1962.

Leaver, Robin A., ed. *Ways of Singing the Psalms.* London: Collins Liturgical Publications, 1984.

Shepherd, Massey H., Jr. *The Psalms in Christian Worship.* Collegeville: Liturgical Press and Minneapolis: Augsburg Publishing House, 1976. Contains a useful annotated bibliography.

Sermon

Biertz, Karl-Heinrich. "Patterns of Proclamation," *Studia Liturgica* 15:1 (1982/1983):18–33.

Brilioth, Yngve. *Landmarks in the History of Preaching.* London: SPCK, 1950.

Burghardt, Walter J. *Preaching: The Art and the Craft.* Mahwah, NJ: Paulist Press, 1987.

Buttrick, David G. *Homiletic: Moves and Structures.* Philadelphia: Fortress Press, 1987.

Esbjornson, Robert. "Preaching as Worship," *Worship* 48 (1974):164–70.

Fuller, Reginald H. *Preaching the Lectionary: The Word of God for the Church Today.* 2nd ed. Collegeville: Liturgical Press, 1984.

———. "Preparing the Homily," *Worship* 48 (1974):442–57.

———. *The Use of the Bible in Preaching.* Philadelphia: Fortress Press, 1981.

Henderson, J. Frank. "The Minister of Liturgical Preaching," *Worship* 56 (1982): 214–30.

Killinger, John. *Fundamentals of Preaching.* Philadelphia: Fortress Press, 1985.

Lischer, Richard, ed. *Theories of Preaching: Selected Readings in the Homiletic Tradition.* Durham, NC: Labyrinth Press, 1988.

Liturgy 19:5 (May 1974). An issue devoted to preaching.

Owst, G. R. *Literature and Pulpit in Medieval England: A Neglected Chapter in the History of English Letters and of the English People.* 2nd ed. Oxford: Clarendon Press, 1961.

———. *Preaching in Medieval England: An Introduction to Sermon Manuscripts of the Period ca. 1350–1450.* Cambridge: University Press, 1926.

Peerlinck, Francis. "Rudolf Bultmann: Preaching and the Liturgy," *Worship* 47 (1973):450–62.

Ritschl, Dietrich. *A Theology of Proclamation.* Richmond, VA: John Knox Press, 1960.

Schmidt, Edward W. "Another Look at Christian Preaching," *Worship* 55 (1981):427–36.

Sleeth, Ronald E. *God's Word and Our Words: Basic Homiletics.* Richmond, VA: John Knox Press, 1986.
Skudlarek, William. *The Word in Worship.* Nashville: Abingdon Press, 1982.
Smyth, Charles. *The Art of Preaching and Practical Survey of Preaching in the Church of England 747–1939.* London: SPCK, 1953.

Hymns

Allen, Cecil J. *Hymns and the Christian Faith.* London: Pickering and Inglis, 1966.
Bailey, Albert E. *The Gospel in Hymns: Background and Interpretations.* New York: Scribners, 1950.
Benson, Louis F. *The English Hymn.* Richmond, VA: John Knox Press, 1962 [1915].
———. *The Hymnody of the Christian Church.* Richmond, VA: John Knox Press, 1956 [1927].
Clark, Keith C. *A Selective Bibliography for the Study of Hymns.* Papers of the Hymn Society of America XXXIII. Springfield, OH: Hymn Society of America, 1980.
Concordance to Hymn Texts — Lutheran Book of Worship, compiled by Robbin R. Hough in consultation with Gordon A. Thorpe. Minneapolis: Augsburg Publishing House, 1985.
Dearmer, Percy. *Songs of Praise Discussed.* London: Oxford University Press, 1933.
Diehl, Katharine Smith. *Hymns and Tunes: An Index.* New York: Scarecrow Press, 1966.
Ensrud, Paul, et al. *The Development of Lutheran Hymnody in America.* Minneapolis: Augsburg Publishing House, 1967.
Eskew, Harry, and Hugh McElrath. *Sing with Understanding: An Introduction to Christian Hymnody.* Nashville: Broadman Press, 1980.
Foote, Henry Wilder. *Three Centuries of American Hymnody.* Hamdon, CT: Shoe String Press, 1961 [1940].
Frost, Maurice. *Historical Companion to Hymns Ancient and Modern.* London: William Clowes & Sons, 1962.
Gillman, Frederick, Jr. *The Evolution of the English Hymn: An Historical Survey of the Origins and Development of the Hymns of the Christian Church.* London: George Allen and Unwin, 1927.
Halter, Carl, and Carl Schalk, ed. *A Handbook of Church Music.* St. Louis: Concordia Publishing House, 1978.
The Hymnal 1940 Companion. 3rd rev. ed. New York: Church Pension Fund, 1956.
Julian, John. *Dictionary of Hymnology.* 2 vols. New York: Dover Publications, 1957 [1907].
Leaver, Robin A. *Catherine Winkworth: The Influence of Her Translations on English Hymnody.* St. Louis: Concordia Publishing House, 1978.
———. *The Liturgy and Music: A Study of the Use of the Hymn in Two Liturgical Traditions.* Grove Liturgical Studies no. 6. Bramcoate, Notts.: Grove Books, 1976.
Lovelace, Austin C. *The Anatomy of Hymnody.* New York: Abingdon Press, 1965.

Lovell, John, Jr. *Black Song: The Forge and the Flame: The Story of How the Afro-American Spiritual Was Hammered Out.* New York: Macmillan, 1972.

Lowther Clarke, W. K. *A Hundred Years of Hymns Ancient and Modern.* London: William Clowes & Sons, 1960.

McCutchan, Robert Guy. *Hymn Tune Names: Their Sources and Significance.* Nashville: Abingdon Press, 1957.

Messenger, Ruth Ellis. *Christian Hymns of the First Three Centuries.* Papers of the Hymn Society of America IX. New York: Hymn Society of America, 1942.

————. *The Medieval Latin Hymn.* Washington, DC: Capital Press, 1953.

————, and Helen E. Pfatteicher. *A Short Bibliography for the Study of Hymns.* Papers of the Hymn Society of America XXV. New York: Hymn Society of America, 1964.

Northcott, Cecil. *Hymns in Christian Worship: The Use of Hymns in the Life of the Church.* Richmond, VA: John Knox Press, 1965.

Patrick, Millar. *The Story of Christian Song.* Rev. ed. Richmond, VA: John Knox Press, 1962.

Polack, William G. *The Handbook to the Lutheran Hymnal.* St. Louis: Concordia Publishing House, 1942.

Raby, F. J. E. *A History of Christian Latin Poetry from the Beginnings to the Close of the Middle Ages.* Oxford: University Press, 1927.

Reynolds, William Jensen, and Milburn Price. *Joyful Sound: Christian Hymnody.* 2nd ed. New York: Holt, Rinehart, and Winston, 1963.

Riedel, Johannes. *The Lutheran Chorale: Its Basic Traditions.* Minneapolis: Augsburg Publishing House, 1967.

————. *Soul Music, Black and White: The Influence of Black Music on the Church.* Minneapolis: Augsburg Publishing House, 1975.

Routley, Eric. *Hymns and Human Life.* Rev. ed. Grand Rapids: Eerdmans, 1959.

————. *The Music of Christian Hymnody: A Study of the Development of the Hymn Tune Since the Reformation with Special Reference to English Protestantism.* London: Independent Press, 1957.

————. *A Panorama of Christian Hymnody.* Collegeville: Liturgical Press, 1979.

Ryden, Ernest E. *The Story of Christian Hymnody.* Rock Island, IL: Augustana Press, 1959.

Seaman, William R. *Companion to the Hymnal of the Service Book and Hymnal.* Minneapolis: Augsburg Publishing House, 1976.

Stulken, Marilyn K. *Hymnal Companion to the Lutheran Book of Worship.* Philadelphia: Fortress Press, 1981.

Tamke, Susan S. *Make A Joyful Noise Unto the Lord: Hymns as a Reflection of Victorian Social Attitudes.* Athens, OH: Ohio University Press, 1978.

Thurman, Howard. *Deep River: An Interpretation of Negro Spirituals.* Rev. and enl. ed. New York: Harper and Bros., 1955.

Wellesz, Egon. *A History of Byzantine Music and Hymnography.* 2nd ed., rev. and enl. Oxford: Clarendon Press, 1961.

5

THE PROPERS

ADVENT

By the eighth century,[1] Advent, the origins of which are apparently to be found some three or four centuries earlier in Gaul, had become an integral part of the Christmas cycle and was understood to be the beginning of the church year. The season has two parts. From the first Sunday through December 16 there is an eschatological emphasis, and the days from December 17 to Christmas Eve look toward Jesus' birth.[2] The Nativity is thus properly understood as the guarantee of the second advent: as Christ came once in humility, so he will come again in glory.

The First Sunday in Advent

The propers for the First Sunday in Advent focus on the second coming of Christ and on the church's vigilant waiting for his appearing. The traditional Gospel for this Sunday, Matthew 21:1–9, remains a key to understanding the relationship between Advent and Christmas, the second coming and the birth in Bethlehem. The long-expected first coming is the promise and guarantee of the second. The Gospel of the triumphal entry is rightfully preserved, if only as an alternative as in the *Lutheran Book of Worship*, as the Gospel for this Sunday and is to be understood not chronologically (and therefore out of sequence) but symbolically and eschatologically: "Behold, your king comes to you."

The Prayer of the Day in the *Lutheran Book of Worship* (no. 1) is an adaptation of prayer no. 778 in the Gregorian sacramentary, appointed for "the first Lord's Day of the month of December." In the single word "come" the prayer, which is addressed directly to Christ, voices the longing appeal of the church for the advent of its Lord.[3] Moreover, the opening petition, "stir up" (*excita*) ties together the prayers of the

---

[1] Massey H. Shepherd, Jr., *The Oxford American Prayer Book Commentary* (New York: Oxford University Press, 1950), 50. Fernand Cabrol, *The Year's Liturgy* (London: Burns Oates & Washbourne, 1938) 1:19, says "since the seventh century at least"; Francis X. Weiser, *Handbook of Christian Feasts and Customs* (New York: Harcourt, Brace, World, 1958), 62, says the tenth century.

[2] See the Roman Catholic *General Norms for the Liturgical Year and the Calendar* title II. v. 39–42.

[3] Luther D. Reed, *The Lutheran Liturgy*, rev. ed. (Philadelphia: Fortress Press, 1960), 466.

First, Second, and Fourth Sundays in Advent. The translation derives from that made originally for the *Church Book* (1868) and preserved in the *Common Service Book* and in the *Service Book and Hymnal.*

The style of the prayers in the *Lutheran Book of Worship* is clear in the adaptation of this prayer: straightforward, even to the point of bluntness; without gratuitous but gracious interjections ("we beseech thee"); avoiding repetition even when part of rhetorical balance. The concluding formula is a standard formula, as it is in the Roman rite; the *Book of Common Prayer* admits variation.

The Roman sacramentary of 1969 (the Missal of Paul VI) appoints this prayer for the Friday after the First Sunday in Advent and has for this Sunday appointed a prayer from the Gelasian sacramentary (no. 1139) "that we may take Christ's coming seriously." The Anglican reformers prepared a new collect for this Sunday, and it is retained in the 1979 Prayer Book.

The medieval Roman rite had no preface for Advent (indicating the relatively recent introduction of the season into the conservative Roman tradition), and therefore the earlier European and American Lutheran service books had none. Except for *The Lutheran Hymnal* (1941), the *Service Book and Hymnal* (1958) was the first North American Lutheran book to provide a proper preface for Advent. The preface was written by a committee of Paul Z. Strodach, George R. Seltzer, and Edward T. Horn III for the *Common Service Book* revision committee and was incorporated into the *Service Book and Hymnal.* It was based on various scripture passages (Isa. 40:1; 43:1–21; Rev. 21:5) and on the preface for Advent which appeared in the 1929 Scottish Prayer Book and the 1940 *Book of Common Order* of the Church of Scotland. (See also the *Book of Common Worship* of the Church of South India.) The preface for Advent in the *Lutheran Book of Worship* is that of the *Service Book and Hymnal* rendered into modern English. The Roman sacramentary of 1969 provides two prefaces for Advent, corresponding to the two parts of the season;[4] the preface for use from the First Sunday in Advent through December 16 is drawn from two prefaces for the month of May in the Leonine sacramentary (nos. 184 and 179), and a preface for use from December 17 through December 24 is drawn from a Christmas preface in the Leonine sacramentary (no. 1241). The preface for Advent in the 1979 *Book of Common Prayer* was composed for the trial Liturgy of the Lord's Supper (1967).[5]

An appointed color sequence is found for the first time at the beginning of the twelfth century;[6] usage varied, and a general rule for the

---

[4]For the various sources see Antoine Dumas, "Les sources du noveau Missel Romain," *Notitiae* (1971), 37–42, 75–76, 94–95, 134–36, 276–79, 409–10. See also Raymond Avery, "A Preview of the New Prefaces," *Worship* 42 (December 1968):587–98.

[5]Marion Hatchett, *Commentary on the American Prayer Book* (New York: Seabury Press, 1980), 399.

[6]It is found in the use of the Augustinian Canons at Jerusalem and suggested black for Christmas and festivals of the Virgin Mary, blue for Epiphany and the Ascension. The

entire Roman Church was not formally defined in rubrics until 1570 in the Missal of Pius V, and even then a certain latitude was permitted. The nineteenth-century Oxford Movement promoted the Roman color sequence in the Anglican Church. The drafters of the *Common Service Book* and the *Service Book and Hymnal* knew the tradition out of which they came and so specified "violet" as the proper color for Advent and Lent, translating *violaceus* of the Roman rubrics. The name, in Latin and in English, was intended to describe a blue-purple.[7] The editors of the *Lutheran Book of Worship*, bowing to prevailing popular practice, used "purple" to describe the color rather than "violet," but the book encourages the use of blue, listing it first. Blue was used for Advent in the diocese of Bath and Wells in England and in the Mozarabic rite in Spain.[8]

The Second Sunday in Advent

The focus of this Sunday and the next is the herald of the Advent, John the Baptizer. The Gospels for the Second Sunday in Advent proclaim John's call to prepare the way for the coming of Christ, as reported in each of the three synoptic Gospels and presented successively in the three-year cycle of lessons.

The Prayer of the Day in the *Lutheran Book of Worship* (no. 2) is based on prayer no. 1125 in the Gelasian sacramentary, no. 39 in the *Missale Gallicanum vetus*, and no. 781 in the Gregorian sacramentary, originally appointed for an Advent mass. It is the most widely used of all the Advent collects. Although it begins like the prayer for the First Sunday in Advent and continues the "stir up" theme, the prayer is addressed to God the Father. The translation derives from the *Church Book* (1868), but the *Lutheran Book of Worship* expands the expression of the desired result, anticipating the central metaphor of darkness and light from the traditional prayer for the Third Sunday in Advent, drawn from the waning light in December in the northern hemisphere. Moreover, it is to be noted that here and elsewhere in the *Lutheran Book of Worship*, instead of "only-begotten" (thought to be unnecessarily obscure to modern congregations), Christ is described as the "only Son" of God (see the RSV of John 1:18; 3:16, 18; also hymn 375). It is intended to mean the same as "only-begotten"; no theological differ-

---

color sequence is mentioned in a treatise by Innocent III (1198–1216), *De sacro altaris mysterio* 1.65, which seems to be the use of the church at Rome: white for feasts, red for martyrs, black for penitential seasons, green for other times.

[7] "The 'violet' for Advent does not of course mean the unpleasant colour (so remote from the colour of the violet flower) at present provided by the shops. There is no such restriction as to tints, and a rather dark blue, or even a bright blue, or purple is equally suitable for Advent." Percy Dearmer, *The Parson's Handbook*, 12th ed. (London: Oxford University Press, 1932), 113.

[8] For further information see John W. Legg, *Notes on the History of the Liturgical Colours* (London: J. S. Leslie, 1882); Gilbert Cope, "Liturgical Colours," *Studia Liturgica* 7:4 (1970):40–49; and "Colours, Liturgical," *The New Westminster Dictionary of Liturgy and Worship*, ed. J. G. Davies (Philadelphia: Westminster Press, 1986).

ence or departure was intended. The *Book of Common Prayer* retains "only-begotten" in several collects.

The Sacramentary has moved this collect to Thursday of the second week of Advent and appoints a prayer from the Gelasian sacramentary (no. 1153) for the Sunday mass.

The 1979 Prayer Book has a new composition based on the collect for the Third Sunday in Advent in the *Book of Common Worship* of the Church of South India. The prayers in all three rites place the responsibility not only on the ministers of God's message but on all the people to be prepared for Christ's return.

The Third Sunday in Advent

Again this Sunday, the Gospels present the person and ministry of John the Baptist. This Sunday "is characterized by anticipatory joy and expectation"[9] which are to be expressed in a life lived according to the spirit of Christ.

The first Prayer of the Day provided in the *Lutheran Book of Worship* (no. 3) is an adaptation of the collect for the Third Sunday in Advent that had been used in the *Book of Common Prayer* from 1662 until the revision of 1979.

Book of Common Prayer (1928) Second Sunday in Advent	*Lutheran Book of Worship* Third Sunday in Advent
O Lord Jesus Christ, who at thy first coming didst send thy messenger to prepare thy way before thee; Grant that the ministers and stewards of thy mysteries may likewise so prepare and make ready thy way, by turning the hearts of the disobedient to the wisdom of the just, that at thy second coming to judge the world we may be found an acceptable people in thy sight, who livest and reignest with the Father and the Holy Spirit ever, one God, world without end.	Almighty God, you once called John the Baptist to give witness to the coming of your Son and to prepare his way. Grant us, your people, the wisdom to see your purpose today and the openness to hear your will, that we may witness to Christ's coming and so prepare his way; through Jesus Christ our Lord, who lives and reigns with you and the Holy Spirit, one God, now and forever.

The ministry of all the people of God is likened to that of John the Baptist, bearing witness to the coming of Christ. The prayer asks wisdom to see and openness to hear in order to witness to his past, present, and future coming and to prepare the way for his present and future advent.

The alternative Prayer of the Day in the *Lutheran Book of Worship* (no. 4) is a translation of prayer no. 1137 in the Gelasian sacramentary, appointed for the second Sunday before Christmas, and no. 787 in the Gregorian sacramentary, appointed for the third Sunday in December.

---

[9] Adolf Adam, *The Liturgical Year* (New York: Pueblo, 1981), 136.

The collect is addressed to Christ and is the one exception to the "stir up" opening of the prayers for the other three Sundays of the season, even as the third Sunday has always had its own character, a lessening of the rigor and discipline of the season, sometimes indicated by the use of rose vestments. The emphasis on light in this prayer may have been related to the popular observance of St. Lucy's Day (December 13) and the winter solstice.[10] The English translation was first made for the *Church Book* (1868) and continued in the *Common Service Book* and the *Service Book and Hymnal*. The present Roman sacramentary appoints this prayer for the Monday of the third week in Advent, and for the Third Sunday in Advent uses prayer no. 1356 from the Leonine sacramentary.

The collect in the *Book of Common Prayer* for the Third Sunday in Advent is a translation of the prayer which the *Lutheran Book of Worship* appoints for the Fourth Sunday.

The Fourth Sunday in Advent

The propers for the Fourth Sunday in Advent look toward the celebration of the birth of Christ and tell of the expectancy of the Virgin Mary. It is a celebration of the richness of the Annunciation: to Joseph (Year A), to Mary (Year B), to Elizabeth (Year C). Anciently, this Sunday was called *Praeparatio*, the Preparation. Later, it was often called "Rorate" from the antiphon of the Introit, "Drop down, ye heavens, from above: and let the skies pour down righteousness" (Isa. 45:8), preserved in the Entrance Antiphon of the present Roman rite. The verse captures the mounting expectancy and insistent earnestness which almost approaches impatience as the church waits for its Lord.

The Prayer of the Day in the *Lutheran Book of Worship* (no. 5) is a translation of prayer no. 1121 in the Gelasian sacramentary in which it is appointed for an Advent mass. Notably similar to the collect appointed for the First Sunday in Advent, the prayer is addressed to Christ; in the Gregorian sacramentary (no. 805) it is changed to a prayer addressed to the Father. The opening address is based on Psalm 80:2, and the prayer joins the themes of the first advent and the second: in the first Christ came in humility to save; in the second he will come in power to aid and relieve.[11] The translation in the *Lutheran Book of Worship* derives from that made for the *Church Book* (1868) and continued in the *Common Service Book* and the *Service Book and Hymnal*. The Roman sacramentary of 1969 appoints this collect for Thursday of the first week in Advent and appoints for this Sunday the prayer used in the Lutheran and Episcopal books on the feast of the Annunciation (March 25).

The *Book of Common Prayer* appoints a revised version of an Advent prayer from the Gelasian sacramentary (no. 1127).

---

[10]See John Donne's poem "A Nocturnall upon S. Lucies Day, Being the shortest day."
[11]Shepherd, 94–95; Hatchett, 167.

The "other collects for the season of Advent" provided in the *Church Book*, the *Common Service Book*, and the *Service Book and Hymnal* are all worth preserving. The second of these given in the *Church Book*,

O God, Who dost gladden us with the yearly anticipation of our Redemption: Grant that we who now joyfully receive Thine Only-Begotten Son as our Redeemer, may also behold him without fear when He cometh as our Judge; Who liveth and reigneth with Thee and the Holy Ghost, ever one God, world without end,

derives from the Gelasian sacramentary (no. 1156). In the Gregorian sacramentary (no. 33) it is appointed for the Vigil of Christmas. It makes an excellent transition from Advent to Christmas and is especially appropriate for a service on December 24.

THE NATIVITY OF OUR LORD: CHRISTMAS DAY

The observance of Christmas originated in the West, probably in Rome, in the early fourth century, and by 336 Christmas was considered in Rome to be the beginning of the church year.[12] Three masses came to be associated with the celebration and are first mentioned by Gregory the Great (d. 604). There was a celebration at midnight in St. Mary Major; another at dawn in St. Anastasia's Church; the public service was "during the day" in the Church of St. Peter.

The First Service of Christmas: at Midnight

The prayer common to the *Lutheran Book of Worship* (no. 6), *The Sacramentary*, and the *Book of Common Prayer* is taken from the Gelasian sacramentary (no. 5, for the Vigil) and the Gregorian sacramentary (no. 36, for the midnight mass at St. Mary Major). The Lutheran version derives from the translation given in the *Church Book* and continued in the *Common Service Book* and in the *Service Book and Hymnal*.

The Service During the Day

The second Prayer of the Day for Christmas in the *Lutheran Book of Worship* (no. 7) is a free translation of the collect for Christmas in the Gelasian sacramentary (no. 6) and the Gregorian sacramentary (no. 49). The adaptation has its roots in the translation made for the *Church Book* ("Collect for Christmas Day") and continued in the *Common Service Book* and in the *Service Book and Hymnal* ("For the Later Service"):

Grant, we beseech Thee, Almighty God, that the new birth of Thine Only-Begotten Son in the flesh may set us free who are held in the old bondage under the yoke of sin; through the same, Thy Son, Jesus Christ our Lord, Who liveth and reigneth with Thee and the Holy Ghost, ever one God, world without end.

---

[12] A. A. McArthur, "Christmas," *Dictionary of Liturgy and Worship*, ed. J. D. Davies (New York: Macmillan, 1972); R. F. Buxton, "Christmas," *The New Westminster Dictionary of Liturgy and Worship*.

Noteworthy is the clear contrast between Christ's new birth and our old bondage, which is somewhat obscured in the adaptation in the *Lutheran Book of Worship*.

The opening prayer in the Roman rite for the Christmas mass during the day is the same as that appointed in the *Lutheran Book of Worship* for the First Sunday after Christmas and in the *Book of Common Prayer* for the Second Sunday after Christmas.

The collect in the *Book of Common Prayer* comparable to the prayer in the *Lutheran Book of Worship* was composed for the 1549 Prayer Book for use "At the Second Communion."

The Roman sacramentary provides for the second service of Christmas the collect for the mass at dawn from the Gregorian sacramentary (no. 42).

In its listing of the propers for Christmas, the *Lutheran Book of Worship* gives prominence to those for the midnight service, recounting the historical event, and for the service during the day, presenting especially through the Gospel its theological significance. A rubric following the propers acknowledges the traditional use, but like the Roman and Episcopal use encourages flexibility and pastoral sensitivity.

The proper preface for Christmas in the *Lutheran Book of Worship* is from the Gregorian sacramentary (no. 38, for the midnight mass at St. Mary Major, and no. 51, for the mass during the day at St. Peter's) and its supplement (no. 1537, for the Presentation of Our Lord). The translation derives from that made for the *Church Book* (1868).

The *Book of Common Prayer* appoints a Preface of the Incarnation for use on the twelve days of Christmas and on the festival of St. Mary the Virgin (August 15). It is a revision of a preface composed for the 1549 Prayer Book.

The Roman Missal of Paul VI appoints three prefaces (from the Gregorian sacramentary, no. 51; from sermon 22.2 by Leo the Great; from the Leonine sacramentary, no. 1260) for Christmas and its octave and weekdays of the season. Each is appropriate to one of the three masses of Christmas, although any one may be used at any time during the season.

Nearly everywhere, white is the proper color associated with feasts of Christ.

Since ancient times, certain saints, called the "companions of Christ" (*comites Christi*),[13] have been commemorated following Christmas Day. They are mentioned by Gregory of Nyssa (d. ca. 385) in his sermon in praise of Basil[14] and are found in all the sacramentaries. The Gelasian sacramentary, for example, calls Christmas Day *In natale domini* (the birthday of the Lord), December 26 *In natale Sancti Stephani martyris*, December 27 *In natale Sancti Johannis euangelistae*, and December 28

---

[13]William Durandus, *Rationale divinorum officiorum* 7.42.1.
[14]*Oratio funebris in laudem fratris Basilii*, PG 46:798.

In natale innocentium. Thus the birthdays of Christ and of his companions are joined together.[15]

St. Stephen, Deacon and Martyr. December 26

The feast day of St. Stephen dates from the fourth century in the East and from the fifth century in the West. The prayers for this day in the Lutheran, Roman, and Episcopal rites are free translations of collect no. 62 in the Gregorian sacramentary. The Lutheran version (no. 111) derives from the Collect for the Day in the *Service Book and Hymnal,* which was borrowed from the 1928 *Book of Common Prayer.*

St. John, Apostle and Evangelist. December 27

The day of St. John dates from the fourth century in the East. The Prayer of the Day in the *Lutheran Book of Worship* (no. 112) as in the Roman and Episcopal books, is one of the few prayers in the Lutheran rite from the earliest Roman sacramentary, the Leonine (no. 1283); it was originally said *super populum* (over the people as a blessing). In an unusual procedure, it was somewhat shortened in the Gregorian sacramentary (no. 67). The collect is notable for its use of the metaphors of light, truth, and life, which are characteristic of the writings attributed to St. John.[16] The version in the first American *Book of Common Prayer* (1789) was brought into Lutheran use by the *Common Service Book* (1917) and was continued in the *Service Book and Hymnal* (1958).

The Holy Innocents, Martyrs. December 28

This feast may have originated in Bethlehem in the fourth century. By the end of the fifth century it seems to have been celebrated in Rome and elsewhere in the East. Under Gallican influence the festival acquired a sorrowful character; thus the three saints' days following Christmas each had its own character and color (Stephen red, John white, Innocents violet) portraying the richness of the implications and cost of the Incarnation. The Prayer of the Day in the *Lutheran Book of Worship* (no. 113) is borrowed from the 1979 *Book of Common Prayer;* it was composed for that book by Charles Mortimer Guilbert. The prayer in *The Sacramentary* originates in the Gelasian sacramentary (no. 42) and the Gregorian (no. 75).

The Lutheran and Episcopal prayer suggests that the theme of the day is broad, inclusive of all innocent victims of violence.[17]

---

[15] Medieval commentators spoke of the three-fold martyrdom which the three days presented: Stephen, a martyr in will and deed; John, a martyr in will although not in deed; the Innocents, martyrs in deed although not in will. To reinforce the interrelatedness of the days of these companions of the Christ-child, in the medieval church the order of collects at Vespers on St. John's Day was St. John (the collect of the feast), Holy Innocents' Day (the eve of that feast), Christmas Day (to mark the continuation of the twelve days of celebration), St. Stephen's Day (for in some calendars these three saints' days had octaves).

[16] Shepherd, 101.

[17] See the list of representative examples in Philip H. Pfatteicher, *Festivals and Commemorations* (Minneapolis: Augsburg Publishing House, 1980), 470–71.

The First Sunday after Christmas

The propers for a mass for this Sunday are first found in the eighth century. In present Lutheran use, since December 26, 27, and 28 each have their own propers, the propers for this Sunday are used only on December 29, 30, or 31. In Roman use, this Sunday within the octave of Christmas is the Feast of the Holy Family, established in 1893, suppressed in 1911, and reintroduced in 1920.

The Prayer of the Day in the *Lutheran Book of Worship* (no. 8) is from the Leonine sacramentary (no. 1239), where it is appointed for the first Christmas mass. The petition echoes a sentence attributed to Leo the Great, "The Son of God became the Son of Man so that the sons of man might become the sons of God."[18] Behind that lies the famous sentence of Athanasius, "He was humanized so that we might be deified."[19] The Gelasian sacramentary includes this prayer among the Christmas prayers for Matins and Vespers (no. 27); the Gregorian sacramentary includes it among "other prayers for the birthday of the Lord" (no. 59). The collect was appointed for the Second Sunday after Christmas in the English proposed Prayer Book of 1928 and was introduced into the American Prayer Book in 1979. The *Lutheran Book of Worship* borrowed it from there but moved it to the First Sunday after Christmas, closer to its original use on Christmas Day.

The Name of Jesus. January 1

Because of what the church perceived as the excesses of the pagan celebration of the new year, the Second Council of Tours (567) prescribed penitential devotions for the first three days of January; the Fourth Council of Toledo (633) ordered a strict fast. In Rome, January 1 became the Anniversary (*Natale*) of the Mother of God, said to be the oldest feast of Mary in the Roman liturgy.[20] The present Roman calendar has restored this celebration. By the time of the Gelasian and Gregorian sacramentaries, the observance had yielded to a celebration of the octave (eighth) day of Christmas. The circumcision became the primary emphasis of the day in Spain and especially in Gaul but was not established in Rome until the thirteenth or the fourteenth century. Since the fifteenth century there has been a particular interest in the holy name of Jesus. In 1721, Innocent XIII assigned the feast of the Name of Jesus to the Second Sunday after the Epiphany; in 1913 it was moved to the Sunday between the first and sixth of January or to January 2 if no Sunday occurred. The present Roman calendar has incorporated the celebration into the Solemnity of Mary the Mother of God on January 1. Recognizing that of the events recorded as taking place on the eighth day after the birth of Christ, the circumcision is of

---

[18]Hatchett, 170.

[19]*On the Incarnation* 54.

[20]Adrian Nocent, *The Liturgical Year*, vol. 1, *Advent, Christmas, Epiphany*, trans. Matthew J. O'Connell (Collegeville: Liturgical Press, 1977), 229, 246; Pius Parsch, *The Church's Year of Grace* 1 (Collegeville: Liturgical Press, 1962):246.

less specifically Christian significance than the bestowal of the name of the Savior, the *Book of Common Prayer* calls the day "The Holy Name" and the *Lutheran Book of Worship* calls it "The Name of Jesus."

The Prayer of the Day in the *Lutheran Book of Worship* (no. 114) is borrowed, with slight condensation, from the collect in the *Book of Common Prayer*, which in turn is a revised version of a prayer from a *Cambridge Bede Book* (1936).[21] The prayer replaces the prayer for the Circumcision which the Lutheran rite had borrowed and revised from the 1549 Prayer Book, which was an adaptation of an episcopal benediction for the Octave of Christmas, found in the supplement to the Gregorian sacramentary (no. 1743) and included in various medieval liturgical books.

The Second Sunday after Christmas

The Prayer of the Day in the *Lutheran Book of Worship* (no. 9) is an adaptation of the collect for the Second Sunday after Christmas Day in the 1928 *Book of Common Prayer*, introduced on this Sunday by the Irish Prayer Book of 1926. The collect is from the Gregorian sacramentary (no. 42) in which it is a second collect for the mass at dawn on Christmas Day. The translation in the 1928 Prayer Book derives from that made by Atwell M. Y. Bayley in *A Century of Collects* (1913).[22] The prayer in the 1969 Roman sacramentary is from the Gregorian sacramentary (no. 94).

EPIPHANY

Before Christmas came into existence in the fourth century, there was in the East an ancient festival, the Feast of the Epiphany,[23] reported from the third century on. The date may have been chosen because April 6, the Quartodecimian pascha, was also taken to be the date of the conception of Jesus, whose birth, nine months later, would have occurred on January 6.[24] In the second half of the fourth century, Christmas was introduced into the East, and the Epiphany was introduced into the West

---

[21] Hatchett, 169.

[22] Shepherd, 105–06; Hatchett, 169.

[23] In the Greek and Roman world, *epiphaneia* or *adventus* was an official state visit by a king or an emperor to a city of his realm, especially on an occasion when he would show himself publicly to the people. The term was also (perhaps originally) used for the manifestation or intervention of a god. *Epiphaneia* is used of Christ in the New Testament in John 2:11, 2 Tim. 1:10, Titus 2:11 and 3:14. James Joyce in *Stephen Hero* defines "epiphany" as a "sudden spiritual manifestation" when the "soul" or "whatness" of an object "leaps to us from the vestment of appearance." From Joyce's use the term has come to be employed in literary criticism to describe a moment of revelation, insight, or clarification.

[24] See Thomas Talley, *Origins of the Liturgical Year* (New York: Pueblo Publishing Co., 1986), 120–21, 129–34; Louis Duchesne, *Christian Worship: Its Origin and Evolution* (London: SPCK, 1910), 264.

perhaps by way of Spain[25] or Africa[26] and came to be associated with the manifestation of Christ to the Gentiles.[27]

The Epiphany. January 6

The prayer of the Day which is common to the *Lutheran Book of Worship* (no. 10), *The Sacramentary*, and the *Book of Common Prayer* is from the Gregorian sacramentary (no. 87). The antithesis on which the original Latin collect turns (2 Cor. 5:7) has been brought out more clearly in the revisions which the Episcopal and Lutheran books have made in their previous versions.

The preface for Epiphany in the Lutheran and Episcopal books derives from the Gelasian sacramentary (no. 59); in the Gregorian sacramentary it becomes the preface for the Epiphany (no. 89) and in its supplement (no. 1526) the preface for the First Sunday after the Epiphany. The preface in the Roman rite combines the Gelasian preface with no. 1247 from the Leonine sacramentary.

The proper color for the Epiphany (through the Sunday following) is white, as in the Roman use, the early list of Innocent III, the English use of Sarum and the diocese of Wells. (Red was used at Litchfield.)

The Baptism of Our Lord. The First Sunday after the Epiphany

The teachers of the church in its formative years laid great stress on Jesus' baptism, seeing it as a revelation of Jesus' divine sonship (Matt. 3:17), the anointing and appointment of Jesus to his messianic office at the beginning of his public ministry, a declaration of Jesus' solidarity with the sinful human race in undergoing baptism by John, and a baptism of the water to give the element power to cleanse from sin.

The Roman sacramentary provides two alternative collects for this Sunday based on traditional ideas associated with the baptism of Christ and on the collect which had been appointed for the octave of the Epiphany in the previous Roman missal and which in the Gelasian sacramentary (no. 62) and the Gregorian sacramentary (no. 93) was appointed for the Epiphany. The Episcopal collect is based on these two Roman Catholic prayers and was drafted by Charles M. Guilbert. The Prayer of the Day in the *Lutheran Book of Worship* (no. 11) is a revision of the collect in the Episcopal book, altered to avoid any implication that the baptismal covenant is something that mortals can make and safeguarding the biblical understanding of God's unilateral covenant with his people.

The Roman sacramentary provides a proper preface for the Baptism of the Lord. The *Lutheran Book of Worship* recognizes the time after the Epiphany as a continuation of the Epiphany theme of the manifestation

---

[25] Bernard Botte, *Les Origines de la Noël et de l'Epiphanie* (Louvain: Abbaye de Mont César, 1932), 57.
[26] J. LeClercq, "Aux origines du cycle de Noël," *Ephemerides liturgicae* 60 (1946):25.
[27] Homilies of St. Leo on the *Theophania*.

of Christ by appointing the proper preface for the Epiphany throughout the season. The *Book of Common Prayer* takes a middle course, appointing the preface of the Epiphany or the preface of the Lord's Day.

The festival of the Baptism of Our Lord brings the Christmas cycle to a close. The green season, which the Roman calendar calls "ordinary time," begins the next day (Monday). The Roman sacramentary assigns to the six weekdays following the Baptism of Our Lord the collect from the Gregorian sacramentary (nos. 86 and 1096) previously assigned to the First Sunday after the Epiphany in previous Lutheran, Roman, and Episcopal books.

The Second Sunday after the Epiphany

In the Roman sacramentary, the opening prayer for this Sunday (the Second Sunday in Ordinary Time) is the collect from the Gregorian sacramentary (no. 922) which had been appointed for this Sunday in previous Roman, Lutheran, and Anglican books. In the *Lutheran Book of Worship* it has been moved to the Eighth Sunday after the Epiphany and in the *Book of Common Prayer* to the Fourth Sunday after the Epiphany. The prayer is a distant echo of Christmas with its supplication for peace.

The Lutheran and Episcopal prayers for this Sunday are more explicitly related to the themes of Epiphany: glory and light, healing and joy. The Prayer of the Day in the *Lutheran Book of Worship* (no. 12) is a new composition written for *Contemporary Worship 6*, where it was appointed for the Fifth Sunday after the Epiphany. The Episcopal collect is based on the collect for the Twentieth Sunday after Pentecost in the *Book of Common Worship* of the Church of South India.

To separate the festive Sundays from the green or "ordinary" Sundays the *Lutheran Book of Worship* prints the prayers of the day for the time after the Epiphany and after Pentecost with the simple termination "through Jesus Christ our Lord," although flexibility is allowed.[28] The *Book of Common Prayer* is not so consistent and varies the termination to suit the prayer, although in the 1979 Prayer Book some form of the full termination is always used.

The Third Sunday after the Epiphany

The Prayer of the Day in the *Lutheran Book of Worship* (no. 13) is a new composition written for *Contemporary Worship 6* (1973) and based primarily on the Gospel for Year C, Jesus' appropriation of the messianic description by Isaiah reported in the First Lesson for the day; but it also reflects the call of Peter and Andrew and of James and John (Year A and Year B), inviting them to share in Jesus' ministry. By extension, all those who follow Jesus are to share in his messianic office.

The collect in the *Book of Common Prayer* was written by Massey H.

---

[28]"Either full or simple terminations may be used for any Prayer of the Day as circumstances suggest." Min. Ed., p. 18.

Shepherd, Jr., and recalls phrases from the Gospels for each of the three years of the lectionary cycle.[29]

The prayer in the Roman sacramentary (the Third Sunday in Ordinary Time) is the collect previously appointed for the Sunday within the Octave of Christmas, in Lutheran and Episcopal use the First Sunday after Christmas. It is from the Gregorian sacramentary (no. 1093).

The Fourth Sunday after the Epiphany

The opening prayer for the Fourth Sunday in Ordinary Time in *The Sacramentary* is from the Leonine sacramentary (no. 432). The *Lutheran Book of Worship* (no. 14) continues the appointment of the collect which had been assigned to this Sunday in medieval missals and in previous Lutheran books. It is from the Gregorian sacramentary (no. 193) in which it is appointed for Ember Saturday in Lent. The English translation in the 1549 Prayer Book was considerably altered in the revision of the Prayer Book in 1662 and in this form entered Lutheran use through the *Church Book* and its successors. The opening of the prayer echoes the Gospel formerly appointed for this Sunday in the Roman and Lutheran books, Matthew 8:23–27 — Jesus stilling the tempest and calming the disciples' fear. The collect has been a favorite among Lutherans; it appears in Luther's German Litany (1529)[30] and in many Lutheran church orders.

The Episcopal collect for this Sunday is the one which the *Lutheran Book of Worship* appoints for the Eighth Sunday after the Epiphany.

The Fifth Sunday after the Epiphany

The *Lutheran Book of Worship* prescribes a Prayer of the Day (no. 15) first written for *Contemporary Worship 6*, where it was appointed for the First Sunday after Christmas. The primary scriptural inspiration for the prayer is 1 John 1:1–3.

The collect in the *Book of Common Prayer* is a new composition written by Massey H. Shepherd, Jr. The Roman Catholic opening prayer for this Fifth Sunday in Ordinary Time is the collect previously appointed for this Sunday in Roman, Lutheran, and Anglican use. It is from the Gregorian sacramentary (no. 1108).

The Sixth Sunday after Epiphany

The Prayer of the Day in the Lutheran book (no. 16) is the collect previously assigned to the First Sunday after the Epiphany. It is from the Gregorian sacramentary (no. 86) for one of the Sundays after Christmas; in the supplement to the sacramentary (no. 1096) it is appointed for the First Sunday after the Epiphany. The Latin original has been

---

[29] Hatchett, 171.
[30] *Luther's Works* 53:169.

praised for its excellence;[31] its teaching concerning prayer is worth pondering.[32]

For this Sunday the *Book of Common Prayer* appoints the Gelasian collect (no. 566) used by the *Lutheran Book of Worship* on the Third Sunday after Pentecost.

The opening prayer in the present Roman rite is from the Gelasian sacramentary (no. 587), in which it is appointed for the Sunday after the Ascension.

The Seventh Sunday after the Epiphany

The first Prayer of the Day in the *Lutheran Book of Worship* (no. 17) is a free translation of the collect *super populum* (over the people) from the Gregorian sacramentary (no. 228) for Saturday after the Second Sunday in Lent. It had previously been appointed for the Fifth Sunday after the Epiphany in Roman, Lutheran, and Anglican use. "The thought behind the Collect is that of a household (*familia*) dependent upon its head for sustenance and protection."[33]

The alternative Prayer of the Day (no. 18) was composed for the *Lutheran Book of Worship* and is based on the Gospel for Year A and Year C. It also echoes the thought of the Prayer of the Day (no. 111) for St. Stephen's Day, December 26. The collect for this Sunday in the *Book of Common Prayer* presents a similar thought. It was previously appointed for Quinquagesima, the Sunday before Ash Wednesday, and was composed for the 1549 Prayer Book.

The Roman Catholic opening prayer for this Sunday is from the Roman missal of 1952 (no. 875).

The Eighth Sunday after the Epiphany

The Lutheran Prayer of the Day (no. 19) is from the Gregorian sacramentary, where it is found among the daily prayers (no. 922) and in the supplement (no. 1099). In previous Roman, Lutheran, and Anglican use it had been appointed for the Second Sunday after the Epiphany. In the *Book of Common Prayer* it is now appointed for the Fourth Sunday after the Epiphany. The Prayer Book accurately translates the Latin, "and in our time grant us your peace"; in the free translation of the *Lutheran Book of Worship* the idea is muted.

The Roman sacramentary appoints the collect previously assigned to the Fourth Sunday after Pentecost (the Fifth Sunday after Pentecost in Lutheran use), from the Leonine sacramentary (no. 633). The Prayer

---

[31] Reed, 481: "The original of the Collect is of such excellence that Dr. Horn was moved to say, 'Such a collect makes one wish that we always said our prayers in Latin.'"

[32] Shepherd, 108–09: "The Collect contains a general teaching on the meaning of prayer. Not all our prayers are according to God's will, so that not all of them are answered with a 'yes.' One of the purposes of prayer is to determine what God's will is, that is, to learn what we 'ought to do' — and then we should seek His strength to accomplish it. Also, it is possible that we may know what God's will is, but have no will to perform it. (Cf. James iv.17; John xiii.17; Luke xii.47.)"

[33] Shepherd, 115.

Book appoints the collect by William Bright given in the *Lutheran Book of Worship* as no. 204 (Min. Ed., p. 111).

The Transfiguration of Our Lord. The Last Sunday after the Epiphany

A feast of the Transfiguration appears as early as the fifth century in East Syria. In the West it is found for the first time in the tenth century in Franco-Roman churches. In 1457 Calixtus III added it to the calendar of the entire Western church "in grateful commemoration of the victory which John of Capistrano and John Hunyadi had won over the Turks at Belgrade in the previous year."[34]

The celebration of the Last Sunday after the Epiphany as the Transfiguration is a Lutheran contribution begun by the sixteenth-century reformers Johannes Bugenhagen and Veit Dietrich. Their sermons on this day, which used the Transfiguration as a text, revealed their knowledge of the structure of the Gospels in relation to the chronology of the church year. The baptism and the transfiguration are both epiphanies of Jesus as he is and as he will be and are therefore like the first manifestation of Jesus in Matthew's account, to the Magi.[35]

The Episcopal Church observes the Last Sunday after the Epiphany in effect as the Transfiguration, for the Gospels each year recount the story, but the title is reserved for August 6, the traditional date. In the *Lutheran Book of Worship*, the Notes on the Liturgy (Min. Ed., p. 14) permit the observance of the Transfiguration on August 6 in addition to the Last Sunday after the Epiphany.

Observing the Transfiguration at the end of the Epiphany season is a happy contribution. It remembers an epiphany which brings the Old Testament law and prophets into Jesus' time, provides a glimpse of Jesus in all his divine splendor, and offers a preview of his glory to come before descending into the shadowed valley of Lent and Holy Week.

The first Prayer of the Day in the *Lutheran Book of Worship* (no. 20) is a revision of the collect for the Feast of the Transfiguration (August 6) in the *Book of Common Prayer*. The collect was written by William Reed Huntington and was introduced in the 1892 American Prayer Book. A Lutheran revision of that collect was included in *Contemporary Worship 6*. The biblical allusion to the beauty of the King (Isa. 33:17, Ps. 27:4) has been obscured by the change to "glory" in the *Lutheran Book of Worship*.

The alternative Prayer of the Day (no. 21) is a translation of the Latin collect of perhaps the fifteenth century, which may have been composed by Calixtus III himself when he extended the celebration of the Transfiguration to the whole Western church in 1457. Its unusual length and complex structure, with double antecedent clauses and

[34] Adam, 180–81.
[35] See J. C. Fenton, *Saint Matthew* (Baltimore: Penguin Books, 1963), 275; G. B. Caird, *Saint Luke* (Baltimore: Penguin Books, 1963), 131–32; D. E. Nineham, *Saint Mark* (Baltimore: Penguin Books, 1963), 234.

parallel construction throughout, are evidence that it is not an early Latin composition.[36] The Lutheran translation derives from that made originally for the *Church Book* (1868). The present Roman sacramentary appoints this collect as the opening prayer for the Transfiguration (August 6).

The collect in the *Book of Common Prayer* for the Last Sunday after the Epiphany is from the 1928 revision of the English Prayer Book. It effectively marks the transition from the celebration of the manifestations of Christ's glory to the contemplation of his call to discipleship and his passion.

The Lutheran and Episcopal books both appoint the preface of the Epiphany as the proper preface for the Transfiguration; the Roman sacramentary provides a preface specifically for the feast.

The prescribed color is white, suggested by the color of Jesus' garments. Thus the green time after the Epiphany is, like the green time after Pentecost, framed by a white festival at the beginning and end of the season. Moreover, the two earlier festivals are echoed by the two later ones: the baptism of Jesus which presents the voice of the Father, the presence of the Son, and the descent of the Spirit, corresponds to the festival of the Holy Trinity at the beginning of time after Pentecost; the Transfiguration, which gives a glimpse of "the King in all his beauty" has its fulfillment in the feast of Christ the King, the last Sunday of the church year.

At the beginning of the fourth century Basil in his Rule reports that Alleluia was discontinued during Lent and was resumed at Easter.[37] The hymn *Alleluia dulce carmen*, an application of Psalm 137 to the situation of the Christian church facing the Lenten exile, is first found in manuscripts of the eleventh century.[38] Particularly in Gaul, the suspension of Alleluia came to be surrounded with ceremony. "We part from Alleluia as from a beloved friend," William Durandus wrote in 1296.[39]

In many parts of the world, Carnival has been a popular celebration as Lent draws near. A socially useful time of release before the onset of the Lenten discipline,[40] it is more than a period of feasting and revelry. It is also a celebration of the common fate of the members of the human race. Its laughter is an act of acceptance, protesting the fact of universal mortality and laughing in acceptance of the democ-

---

[36] Reed, 486.

[37] Cabrol, 1:102.

[38] It is found, for example, in the eleventh-century Anglo-Saxon *Leofric Collector*. The hymn in John Mason Neale's translation was included in the *Service Book and Hymnal* as no. 58. The second stanza draws on Tobit 13:22 and Gal. 4:21ff.

[39] See *The Hymnal 1940 Companion*, 3rd rev. ed. (New York: Church Pension Fund, 1951), 41.

[40] See Johann Wolfgang von Goethe, *Italian Journey (1786–1788)*, trans. W. H. Auden and Elizabeth Mayer (New York: Pantheon, 1962), 445–69; also W. H. Auden, "Forgotten Laughter, Forgotten Prayer," *New York Times*, February 2, 1971. Curiously, Auden here gives the date of Goethe's visit to Rome incorrectly as 1776.

racy of death.[41] Thus, Carnival is an appropriate transition to Ash Wednesday.

LENT

The origin of Lent is to be found first in the preparation for the Christian Passover, the *Pascha*, a nocturnal festival of Saturday-Sunday, which commemorated in a unitive way the passion and resurrection of Christ.[42] This paschal preparation had by the early third century expanded to become Holy Week, the Great Week.[43] The week of fasting then came to be extended to six weeks, the Forty Days (*Quadragesima*) of preparation of candidates for baptism at Easter. Canon 52 of the Council of Laodicaea (363) made Lent a closed time (*tempora clausa*) during which marriages were not performed. The practice has been maintained in both East and West since then.

In the fifth century, Good Friday and Holy Saturday were separated from the Easter event (the Triduum) and were included in the preparatory fast, thus making six weeks of six days each, thirty-six days.[44] In the sixth century, before the time of Gregory the Great, the four weekdays before the First Sunday in Lent were added to the season, bringing the number to exactly forty days (excluding Sundays, which are always feast days). By the seventh century, in the Gelasian sacramentary, the Wednesday before the First Sunday in Lent is called "the beginning of the fast" (*caput jejunii*). As the centuries passed, the strict discipline was relaxed, and after the Reformation, fasting became in Lutheran churches a personal matter not regulated by service books, although the Good Friday fast was nearly always strictly kept.

Ash Wednesday

The observance of Lent and Easter is characterized by the primacy of community, for baptism incorporates those who are washed in its life-giving water into the community of the faithful people of God. Anciently, Ash Wednesday was not a time for confession but for excommunication, excluding sinners, for a time, from the community in this world so that they might return from their erring ways and not be excluded forever in the next world. Later privatized notions led to the emphasis on the confession of one's sins.

---

[41] See C. L. Barber, *Shakespeare's Festive Comedy* (Princeton: University Press, 1959), chap. 1, "Introduction: The Saturnalian Pattern," especially the section "Through Release to Clarification."

[42] "Unitive" is A. A. McArthur's description of the single celebration of the passion-resurrection event. See Thomas J. Talley, "The Origin and Shape of Lent," *Liturgy* 4 (Winter 1983):9–13.

[43] Dionysus of Alexandria, *Letter to Basilides* (*PG* 10:1273); Adam, p. 91.

[44] This was explained as the offering of a tithe of the 365 days of the year. See Gregory I, *Homily 16 on the Gospels* 5 (*PL* 76:1137); John Cassian, *Collationes* 21, 25–27 (*CSEL* 13/2:600–613).

The name Ash Wednesday (*dies cinerum*) derives from the custom which seems to have originated in Gaul in the sixth century of sprinkling ashes on the heads of penitents. In the tenth and eleventh centuries the custom was adopted voluntarily by all the faithful as a sign of penitence and a reminder of their mortality.

In the *Lutheran Book of Worship* the liturgy of penitence, with the optional use of the symbol of the ashes,[45] takes place before the Holy Communion as an adaptation and deepening of the order of confession and forgiveness, which Lutherans have generally come to expect as prelude to the celebration of the Holy Communion. In the Roman Catholic and Episcopal liturgies the Ash Wednesday liturgy takes place within the celebration of Eucharist, after the Gospel and sermon.[46] The comparative structure of the three rites may be seen in this outline:

Roman Catholic	Lutheran	Episcopal
after the homily	after the entrance	after the sermon
	Psalm 51	
	Exhortation	Exhortation
	Litany of Penitence	
Prayer of blessing		(Prayer and
Imposition of ashes	(Imposition of ashes)	Imposition of ashes)
(Antiphons and Ps. 51)		Psalm 51:1–18
	Conclusion of Litany	Litany of Penitence
	Address to congregation	Address to congregation
Intercessions and	Prayer of the Day	The Peace and
Offertory		Offertory

Psalm 51, the best known and most used of the seven penitential psalms, has long been associated with Ash Wednesday. Since it is used in the Lutheran rite not as a responsorial psalm between lessons but rather in its entirety as a kind of antiphonal entrance hymn sung after the solemn entrance of the ministers in silence, it is concluded with the Gloria Patri.

The exhortation is a new composition drafted for the *Lutheran Book of Worship* by Brian Helge and Paul Marshall. Its opening address, "Brothers and sisters," is an acknowledgement of the equal station of minister and people, a democracy underscored by the significance of the ashes into which all must one day return. The first two sentences of the exhortation recall Genesis 1–3, the creation and the fall, God's good

---

[45] On the various meanings of ashes, see Philip H. Pfatteicher and Carlos R. Messerli, *Manual on the Liturgy* (Minneapolis: Augsburg Publishing House, 1979), 307ff.

[46] *Contemporary Worship 6: The Church Year: Calendar and Lectionary* (1973), which quietly returned the imposition of ashes to the Lutheran liturgy by means of two rubrics, suggested that the imposition take place following the sermon.
    In the historic Ash Wednesday liturgy, ashes are applied to the forehead of each person who comes forward, while the minister says, "Remember, O man, that you are dust, and to dust you shall return." Imposition of ashes may take place following the sermon and should be preceded by an invitation to Lenten discipline. (p. 67)

will for his creation and human corruption of that intention. By the rebellion described in Genesis 3, the man and the woman set themselves against God, against each other, and against the natural world. Driven from the garden of paradise, their original equality broken, the man ruling over the woman, the earth would yield its fruit to the man only after hard labor, childbearing would no longer be entirely pleasurable, hostility between the woman and the serpent emerged. None of this was according to the will of God, who had viewed the freshness of the whole creation and had pronounced it "very good."

But with sin came the knowledge of God not only as Creator and Master but as a loving parent, grieved by the children's destructive rebellion, whose good desires for the whole creation remain unchanged. The phrases in the concluding sentence of the first paragraph anticipate the opening of the Prayer of the Day (from Wisdom of Solomon 11:24, 25, 27) and such passages as Amos 5:4, Ezekiel 33:11, Isaiah 55:3, and Micah 7:18–20.

The second paragraph of the exhortation begins with an echo of a favorite Lucan phrase, "the Lord Jesus,"[47] and describes the Lenten discipline by the "evangelical counsels" of the medieval period — fasting, prayer, and good works — to which is prefixed "repentance," recalling Luther's recovery of the New Testament primacy of repentance in the sense of *metanoia*, turning around, changing the direction of one's life. At the outset of his career Luther wrote,

1. When our Lord and Master Jesus Christ said, "Repent" [Matt. 4:17], he willed the entire life of believers to be one of repentance....
3. Yet it does not mean solely inner repentance; such inner repentance is worthless unless it produces various outward mortifications of the flesh.[48]

The concept of spiritual warfare is rooted in St. Paul's description of the armor which protects combatants in the battle against "principalities, powers, and world rulers of this present darkness, and the spiritual hosts of wickedness in the heavenly places" (Eph. 6:10–17;[49] see also Phil. 2:25; 2 Tim. 2:3–4; Philem. 2). Behind these New Testament images is the Old Testament picture of the Lord God of Sabaoth, the Lord of Hosts, the leader of the angelic armies and the God of battles. Moreover, Job 7:1 uses the image of "hardship" in the sense of onerous compulsory military service.[50] (See also Job 14:14; Isa. 40:2.) The idea of spiritual warfare was prominent in the early church and through the Middle Ages. Lorenzo Scupoli's *Combattimento spirituale* (1589) is a classic spiritual writing of the Counter-Reformation period and was received, adapted,

---

[47]See Acts 1:21; 7:58; 8:16; 11:20; 16:31; 19:17; 20:35; Luke 24:3 (textual footnote in the RSV). See also 1 Cor. 11:23; 2 Cor. 1:14; 1 Thess. 2:15; 4:1–2; 2 Thess. 1:17; Heb. 13:20; 2 Pet. 1:2.

[48]Ninety-five Theses, *Luther's Works* 31:25.

[49]See Markus Barth, *Ephesians* 4–6, Anchor Bible, vol. 34A (Garden City, NY: Doubleday, 1974), 759–803.

[50]Marvin H. Pope, *Job*, Anchor Bible, vol. 15 (Garden City, NY: Doubleday, 1965), 57.

and revised according to the ancient traditions of the Eastern church as well.[51] Spiritual warfare is a vigorous, active, and compelling metaphor for the work of Lent.

The exhortation in the *Book of Common Prayer*, which was taken from the Canadian Prayer Book, is an historical review of the purposes of Lent. There is no comparable exhortation in the Roman rite.

The litany of penitence in the *Lutheran Book of Worship* is borrowed from the *Book of Common Prayer* with only minor changes in punctuation. The litany was drafted for the Prayer Book by Massey H. Shepherd, Jr. It opens with a version of the confession used in the *Lutheran Book of Worship* at Compline (Min. Ed., p. 72) and the prayer in the Brief Order for Confession and Forgiveness (Min. Ed., pp. 195, 233, 116–17), and the prayers in the services of Morning and Evening Prayer in the *Book of Common Prayer*. In the *Lutheran Book of Worship* the litany is interrupted for the imposition of ashes; if ashes are not distributed, the litany continues as in the Prayer Book to its conclusion. The Lutheran book breaks the prayer at a logical point, the verse which is taken from Psalm 85:4, "Restore us, good Lord, and let your anger depart from us" and the congregation's reply (from Ps. 69:17), which brings that part of the litany to a temporary conclusion.

Medieval rites employed a series of prayers of blessing over the ashes. The present Roman rite has a simple invitation calling ashes "the mark of our repentance" (not mortality) and a prayer of blessing upon the ashes or a prayer of blessing upon the penitents. Because the blessing of ashes seems to be a late medieval development (eleventh century),[52] because both Lutherans and Anglicans often express a dislike of blessing things rather than people[53] (an idea derived from Martin Bucer's evaluation of the 1549 Prayer Book, particularly the epiclesis), and because "the use of unblessed ashes would be a more potent sign of mortality and penitence than were there some sense of holiness attached,"[54] the *Lutheran Book of Worship* and the *Book of Common Prayer* make no provision for the blessing of the ashes. The Prayer Book does, however, provide a prayer for the proper use of the ashes, that they "may be to us a sign of our mortality and penitence."

The rule that the ashes are to be obtained by burning the palm branches left over from the previous year occurs for the first time in the twelfth century.[55]

The sentence used at the imposition of the ashes, from Genesis 3:19, is that used in the medieval rites. The Latin, *Memento, homo, quia*

---

[51] *Unseen Warfare, being the Spiritual Combat and Path to Paradise of Lorenzo Scupoli as edited by Nicodemus of the Holy Mountain and revised by Theophan the Recluse* (London: Faber and Faber, 1963).

[52] Adam, 98.

[53] See Shepherd, 124; Edward T. Horn III, *The Christian Year* (Philadelphia: Muhlenberg Press, 1960), 106.

[54] Hatchett, 221.

[55] Adam, 98.

pulvis es, et in pulverum reverteris, includes the general name *homo* ("human" in the sense of "mortal") as an additional reference to the fragility of the life of each one who receives the ashen mark. The English versions in the *Lutheran Book of Worship* and in the *Book of Common Prayer* omit the word, which is not present in the Genesis text; the Roman rite preserves it: "Remember, man, that you are dust." The Roman liturgy, however, gives preference to another verse of Scripture, "Turn away from sin and be faithful to the Gospel" (Mark 1:15), which looks to the whole season of repentance and renewal. The traditional verse from Genesis 3:19 is given as an alternative.

During the imposition of ashes the Roman rite provides for the singing of antiphons, a responsory, "or other appropriate songs."[56] It also provides for the imposition of ashes outside of mass.

Following the imposition of ashes the *Book of Common Prayer* uses Psalm 51, the last two verses being omitted to give a better climax (an innovation of the 1928 Prayer Book), without the Gloria Patri. Then the Litany of Penitence is said by the celebrant and people.

After the Litany, or, in the *Lutheran Book of Worship*, after the last two verses of the litany following the imposition of ashes, the minister stands and addresses the people. The Episcopal form, which the *Lutheran Book of Worship* has borrowed and abbreviated, is from the 1552 Prayer Book and incorporates phrases from a liturgy based on Calvin's work, the *Forma ac ratio,* and perhaps from Bucer; the phrase from Ezekiel 33:11 was used in the Sarum rite for the blessing of ashes as well as in the opening prayer of masses provided in the Gelasian sacramentary (no. 1377) and the Gregorian sacramentary (no. 1007) for use in time of great mortality.[57]

The Lutheran book has simplified the address by the deletion of the reference to the authority of ministers to pronounce forgiveness (never an issue among Lutherans) and moves from the statement of God's gracious disposition toward his rebellious people to a prayer for repentance and the Holy Spirit, that actively dedicated to doing God's will we may at last enter into the joy of the Lord. The Liturgy of Ash Wednesday "marks the beginning of a season of penitence. The Maundy Thursday absolution is the structural response to the Ash Wednesday confession, marking off Lent as a penitential time" (Min. Ed., p. 22). In the *Lutheran Book of Worship,* therefore, there is no absolution in the Ash Wednesday service and reference to it has been deleted from the address because all Lent is to be a time of repentance and renewal. The absolution is to be understood as being postponed until Maundy Thursday when the absolution given then before the Holy Communion begins brings to a close the preparatory season of Lent before the celebration of the Triduum (Maundy Thursday, Good Friday, Holy Saturday) begins.

---

[56] *The Sacramentary*, 76.
[57] Hatchett, 222.

The silence which the Lutheran book directs after the minister's address to the congregation is to give the people time to contemplate how their sanctification may be made real in their own individual lives as well as to provide a break between the introductory penitential rite and the beginning of the Holy Communion.

The Prayer of the Day in the *Lutheran Book of Worship* (no. 22) is a slightly revised version of the collect written by Thomas Cranmer for the 1549 *Book of Common Prayer*. The opening clause is based on the Introit appointed for Ash Wednesday in the Roman missal of the time (Wisd. of Sol. 11:24, 25, 27) and on the first collect at the blessing of the ashes ("Almighty, everlasting God, spare those who are penitent . . . "). The petition is inspired by Psalm 51, which had long been associated with this day.[58] The collect was introduced to Lutheran use in the *Church Book* (1868).

A rubric in the Prayer Book from 1662 to the revision of 1928 directed that this collect was to be said daily throughout Lent;[59] the 1928 American Prayer Book qualified the practice by adding "until Palm Sunday." The Ministers Edition of the *Lutheran Book of Worship* (p. 129) permits the practice on weekdays during Lent, but in the 1979 Prayer Book the rubric has been deleted.

The opening prayer in the Roman sacramentary is derived from the collect that in the earlier rite for the blessing of ashes followed the imposition. It is from the Gelasian sacramentary (no. 654); in the Gregorian sacramentary (no. 153) it is appointed for the Wednesday after Quinquagesima.

One set of lessons serves all three years of the lectionary cycle. The First Lesson in the Lutheran lectionary is that of the earliest Roman epistolary and the Sarum rite; the Gospel has been associated with Ash Wednesday since the earliest extant Roman lectionaries.

When the Ash Wednesday liturgy is used, to prevent duplication the *Lutheran Book of Worship* (Min. Ed., p. 22) directs that Psalm 103:8–14 replace Psalm 51 following the First Lesson, since Psalm 51 is used at the beginning of the Ash Wednesday liturgy.

The Roman rite, following the Gregorian sacramentary, provides a proper preface for each Sunday in Lent (those for the first two Sundays are new compositions, those for the next three Sundays are from the supplement to the Gregorian sacramentary, nos. 1556, 1571, 1573) and also provides prefaces for weekday masses during Lent. These prefaces are statements of the renewed understanding of the character of Lent, which is never to be understood except in relation to Easter and never to be practiced except in relation to others. These prefaces are worthy of careful study and meditation.

The proper preface for Lent in the *Lutheran Book of Worship* is an

---

[58] Hatchett, 173.

[59] "A custom analogous to the use of memorials after the collect of the day late in the medieval period." Hatchett, 173.

adaptation of the second of two prefaces for Lent provided by the *Book of Common Prayer*. (Before the 1979 book the American Prayer Book did not have a preface for Lent; the Lutheran rite used the passiontide preface of the cross.) The Episcopal preface is a paraphrase by Howard E. Galley of the first preface for Lent in the Roman sacramentary, a new composition written for the Roman missal of 1969. In the Lutheran version of the preface the Christian faith and the Christian life are brought together, for believing and living are the two sides of the Christian's vocation. Moreover, the phrase "the children of God" is an allusion to the baptismal covenant which commits Christians to faithful living and living the faith.

The First Sunday in Lent

Lent is a participation in the labors of Christ, going with him into the cycle of darkness.[60] The Sunday lessons present not defeats but a series of victories, beginning with the temptation. The association of this Sunday with the temptation of Christ is universal in the Western church. The Gospel is one of the oldest assigned lessons, dating back to the time of Leo the Great in the fifth century,[61] and antedates the extension of the days of Lent to the previous Wednesday. As the Gospel for the beginning of Lent it sets before the church the example of Christ withdrawing into the wilderness and relates his forty-day fast to the *quadragesima* of Lent. The First Sunday of Lent, therefore, tells not only of struggle, fasting, temptation, and testing, but also of Christ's victory over hostile powers and anticipates his glorification ("angels came and ministered to him"). "It is an overture to the paschal mystery of Easter."[62] Anciently, the First Sunday in Lent was the time for the enrollment of candidates for baptism.[63]

The two Prayers of the Day in the *Lutheran Book of Worship* (no. 24, 25) are new compositions. They first appeared in *Contemporary Worship 6: The Church Year, Calendar, and Lectionary* (1973).

The collect in the *Book of Common Prayer* is also new to the book. It is a revision of an original collect in the appendix of William Bright's *Ancient Collects*.[64]

---

[60]The lunar associations are to be noted, especially in view of the lunar basis of the dating of the Passover and therefore also of Easter. The symbolic journey with Christ to his cross and tomb, the Stations of the Cross, has been used in several Lutheran congregations during Lent, but it has never appeared in an official service book. See the Way of the Cross in the Episcopal *Book of Occasional Services*, 54–71.

[61]Horn, 107–08; Shepherd, 126–27.

[62]Adam, 100.

[63]See Philip H. Pfatteicher, *Commentary on the Occasional Services* (Philadelphia: Fortress Press, 1983), 21ff.; Adrian Nocent, *The Liturgical Year*, vol. 2: Lent and Holy Week, trans. Matthew J. O'Connell (Collegeville: Liturgical Press, 1977), 63–66.

[64]William Bright, *Ancient Collects and Other Prayers Selected for Devotional Use from Various Rituals* (Oxford and London: J. H. and James Parker, 1862), 237–38. Marion Hatchett comments (p. 174) that the prayer "is particularly fitting as we enter this season of penitence in preparation for baptism or for renewal of baptismal vows."

The opening prayer in the Roman sacramentary derives from the Gelasian (no. 104) and the Gregorian sacramentary (no. 166). It makes reference not to the temptation, for that is done in the proper preface for this Sunday, but to the spirit of the entire season of Lent as a preparation for the celebration of the *pascha*.

The Second Sunday in Lent

In the Roman calendar the focus of this Sunday is the Transfiguration, which derives from the Gospel for the ordination mass that was the culmination of the Lenten Ember Days and was celebrated during the night between Saturday and Sunday.[65] The opening prayer is from the Mozarabic sacramentary (no. 385).

The first Prayer of the Day in the *Lutheran Book of Worship* (no. 26) is a revision of the collect for this Sunday in the *Book of Common Prayer*. It is derived from one of the solemn collects for Good Friday in the *Missale Gallicanum vetus* (no. 107), the Gelasian sacramentary (no. 413), and the Gregorian sacramentary (no. 351). In the Good Friday liturgy it is a prayer for the return of heretics and schismatics to the Catholic faith; in its new context of the Second Sunday in Lent it is a prayer for the return of those who have abandoned the practice of the Christian faith.[66] The opening of the Lutheran version, "it is your glory always to have mercy," echoes the prayer of humble access from the *Book of Common Prayer*, "thou art the same Lord whose property is always to have mercy" (p. 337) and the prayer in the Penitential Office in the 1928 Prayer Book (p. 63), "whose nature and property is ever to have mercy and to forgive." The phrase "erred and strayed from your ways" in taken from the familiar confession of sin, which appears in Morning Prayer I and Evening Prayer I in the *Book of Common Prayer:* "we have erred and strayed from thy ways like lost sheep, we have followed too much the devices and desires of our own hearts..." (pp. 41, 62).

The alternative Prayer of the Day in the Lutheran book (no. 27) is a new composition. It is for optional use in Year A, when the Gospel in the Lutheran lectionary is the account of Jesus and the woman of Samaria. The prayer first appeared in *Contemporary Worship 6* among the "Additional Prayers" for Lent and Holy Week. In that context, the reference was not to the woman of Samaria but to the "woman who was a sinner" who anointed Jesus' feet (Luke 7:36–50).

Psalm 115:18 in Year B of the Lutheran lectionary presents problems because of its use of Hallelujah, which traditionally is not used during Lent.

The Third Sunday in Lent

Beginning this Sunday the Roman lectionary for Year A makes use of three stories from the Gospel which the church has long associated with

---

[65] See Nocent, 2:64, 77–92.
[66] Hatchett, 174.

baptism: the woman of Samaria at the well, the man born blind, and the raising of Lazarus from the dead. Anciently, on the Third Sunday in Lent the scrutinies of baptismal candidates began. These were exorcisms to prepare the candidates for the reception of the Holy Spirit in baptism.[67]

The Prayer of the Day in the *Lutheran Book of Worship* (no. 28) is a new composition, which was written for *Contemporary Worship 6*.

The collect in the *Book of Common Prayer* is from the Gregorian sacramentary (no. 202), appointed for the Second Sunday in Lent and printed among the "Daily Prayers" (no. 876). The prayer had been used in previous Lutheran books on the Second Sunday in Lent in a translation which was made for the *Church Book* (1868). It is a loss no longer to have this prayer in the Lutheran liturgy.

The Roman sacramentary appoints a prayer from the Gelasian sacramentary (no. 249).

The Fourth Sunday in Lent

This mid-Lent Sunday has been characterized by a note of joy. Before the reform of the lectionary which began in 1969 the Gospel was John 6:1–15, and thus the day came to be known as Refreshment Sunday or *Brotsonntag* ("Bread Sunday"). The rose vestments worn on this day in some places are first mentioned in the sixteenth century.

The Prayer of the Day in the Lutheran rite (no. 29) was written for the *Lutheran Book of Worship*, based loosely on the Gregorian collect appointed for this Sunday (no. 256). The translation in previous Lutheran books was borrowed from the Prayer Book.

The collect in the *Book of Common Prayer* is a revision of a collect written by Frederick Brodie Macnutt.[68] The prayer in the Roman sacramentary derives from the Gelasian sacramentary (no. 178) and a sermon by Leo the Great (2.4).

The Fifth Sunday in Lent

The Fifth Sunday in Lent anticipates the liberating message of the *pascha*. The central picture is the raising of Lazarus (Year A) in anticipation of the victory of Christ, the resurrection and the life, which is shared by all the baptized.[69]

Before the reorganization of the calendar introduced by the Roman Catholic Church in 1969, this Sunday began Passiontide, a two-week period of intensified contemplations of the sufferings of Christ. It was characterized by a distinct liturgical color, often red, the veiling of all crosses and statues, derived perhaps from the *Hungertuch* ("hunger cloth") hung in the chancel in front of the altar during Lent, a custom

---

[67]See Pfatteicher, *Commentary on the Occasional Services*, 23–25; Nocent, 2:102–07, 63–66.

[68]*The Prayer Manual* (London: Mowbray, 1952), no. 488.

[69]See Nocent, 2:117–20; Adam, 104–05.

which appears from the eleventh century.[70] The name "Passion Sunday," a secondary title found in some north European missals, was introduced to North American Lutherans in the *Common Service Book* (1917).

The Prayer of the Day in the *Lutheran Book of Worship* (no. 30) is a new composition, drafted for *Contemporary Worship 6*. It is a departure from the traditional collect form; no previous collect of the day made a confession of sin.[71]

The *Book of Common Prayer* appoints a collect from the Gelasian sacramentary (no. 551) and the Gregorian supplement (no. 1120) in which it had been appointed for the third Sunday after the octave of Easter. The collect is found in the *Lutheran Book of Worship* on its traditional day, now accounted the Fifth Sunday of Easter.

The Roman sacramentary appoints a collect from the Mozarabic sacramentary (no. 706).

HOLY WEEK

Holy Week, culminating in the Great Sabbath, is a recapitulation of the week of creation which concluded with the Sabbath rest. The Sunday of the Resurrection, Easter Day, becomes the eighth day of the new creation.

Called the "Great Week" in the Slavic languages following an ancient custom,[72] and *Karwoche* (week of mourning) in German, Holy Week is older than Lent and is one of the sources from which Lent was to develop. The week is itself an early extension of the preparation for the *pascha*, a time not of mourning but of preparation for the celebration of Christ's victory. Red was the liturgical color in a great many places.

An important part of the liturgy of Holy Week is the reading of the passion accounts in the four Gospels. The medieval practice was to read St. Matthew's Passion on Palm Sunday, St. Mark's Passion on Tuesday, St. Luke's Passion on Wednesday, and St. John's Passion on Good Friday. A conflation of the four accounts into one History of the Passion developed,[73] and in many Lutheran churches these harmonizations displaced the traditional medieval practice. For a long time Lutheran service books contained a History of the Passion (the most popular was by Bugenhagen), divided into seven parts for use on each

---

[70]Adam, 106; Weiser, 176–77.

[71]A more traditional form would be

Almighty God, our Redeemer, renew us by your Holy Spirit so that we may follow your commands and proclaim in the world your reign of love; through your Son. . . .

[72]Egeria refers to Great Week "as they call it here" in Jerusalem (*Egeria's Travels* 30.1).

[73]For example, the Mozarabic (Spanish) rite has a cento of the four passion accounts which was read on Good Friday (Horn, 113–14). Tatian's popular mid-second-century *Diatessaron* was a conflation of the four Gospels into a single narrative. On the separate passion accounts see Raymond E. Brown, *A Crucified Christ in Holy Week: Essays on the Four Gospel Passion Narratives* (Collegeville: Liturgical Press, 1985); Michael Ramsey, *The Narratives of the Passion* (London: A. R. Mowbray and Co., 1962).

of the days of Holy Week. As biblical scholarship came to appreciate the distinct emphases and point of view of each of the four Gospels such harmonizations declined in popularity.

The Sunday of the Passion. Palm Sunday

The most distinctive feature of the Sunday of the Passion, the procession with palms, originated in the church in Jerusalem during the fourth century.[74] The oldest Greek and Latin liturgical texts understand the branches as symbols of hope, life, and victory,[75] The hero's welcome accorded Jesus was seen as anticipating his impending victory over death. The earliest blessing of palms is found in the sixth-century *Liber Ordinum* of the (Spanish) Mozarabic rite and is attested to in the mid-eighth-century Gallican Bobbio Missal. Since palm and olive branches were not available in northern Europe, the use of any green or blossoming branches became common: beech and boxwood in England, in Germany pussy willows with their catkins.[76] At the end of the eighth century the number of witnesses to a procession with palms increases. Bishop Theodolph of Orleans (ca. 750–821), while imprisoned at Angiers on a charge of conspiring against King Louis the Pious, composed *Gloria, laus, et honor* ("All Glory, Laud, and Honor," hymn 108) for the procession. It is "a charming and devotional little poem explaining the meaning of all this ceremonial."[77] The blessing of the palms came to be

---

[74] *Egeria's Travels* 30.1–31.4; Shepherd, 134; Adam, 107; Hatchett, 223.

[75] 1 Maccabees 13:51; also the martyrs' palms of victory in Rev. 7:9 (Adam, 107). See, for example, Caravaggio's paintings of St. Catherine of Alexandria and of the Martyrdom of St. Matthew.

[76] On the honor anciently accorded to trees and branches see Gerardus Van der Leeuw, *Religion in Essence and Manifestation*, trans. J. E. Turner, vol. 2 (New York: Harper & Row, 1963), 394–95; Tacitus, *Germania* 39 ("In this wood, the cradle of the race, the sovereign divinity resides"); James G. Frazer, *The Golden Bough*, abridged ed. (New York: Macmillan, 1963), chap. 9, "The Worship of Trees"; chap. 10, "Relics of Tree Worship in Modern Europe," pp. 126–38, 139–56; see also p. 86. See also Bishop Evind Berggrav's moving description of his "homecoming to the woods" in *Land of Suspense* (Minneapolis: Augsburg Publishing House, 1943), 83–84. In Germany and Scandinavia a guardian tree beside a dwelling place or a temple was honored, and the tradition was remarkably persistent. One finds ancient trees by English church doors still, as for example, the two great yews which dominate the entrance to the church of SS. Peter and Paul at Cudham. (See T. J. White, "Country Diary," *Manchester Guardian Weekly*, April 3, 1971; see also Percy Dearmer, "Notes on the Church-yard Garden," *Parson's Handbook*, 41–42.) The custom of "topping out" the frame of a building by nailing an evergreen tree to its highest point survives occasionally in North America, even in that most sophisticated place, New York City. The custom doubtless has its roots in honoring the guardian tree.

[77] Cabrol, 1:169. John Mason Neale, whose translation is still used in English-speaking churches, notes concerning the hymn he translated, "Another verse was usually sung, till the seventeenth century, at the pious quaintness of which we can scarcely avoid a smile:

Be thou, O Lord, the Rider,
And we the little ass,
That to God's Holy City
Together we may pass."

(Quoted in *The Hymnal 1940 Companion*, 47.) See also Richard Crashaw's epigrams "Upon the Asse that bore our Savior," "The Master is carried on an ass," and "On the Ass the bearer of Christ."

so elaborate that it resembled the structure of the mass,[78] and it may be largely for this reason that the Lutheran and Anglican reformers did not retain the blessing. In Lutheran Germany, however, the procession was retained in some places, for example Brandenburg (1540), and many Lutheran orders retained the distribution of palms.

In 1955, the Roman Catholic Church greatly revised its Holy Week rites to make them more accessible to the people and to encourage congregational participation. The rites were simplified, and ancient understandings and practices were restored. The reform of the rites encouraged non-Roman churches to give renewed attention to them. In the Episcopal Church *The Book of Offices* (1960) provided a form for the blessing of palms and a procession for Palm Sunday.[79] The 1979 *Book of Common Prayer* included a full rite for the liturgy of the palms. In the Lutheran Church, *Occasional Services* (1962) included among the "Additional Orders and Offices,"[80] on the last page, three prayers of blessing (of palms, of a fishing boat, of a wedding ring).[81] *Contemporary Worship 6* (1973) introduced the blessing of palms and the procession to general North American Lutheran use. Despite the absence of liturgical provision in Lutheran books, Palm Sunday processions and the distribution of palms (often after the service as a kind of memento of attendance) had long since caught the popular fancy and had become

---

[78]There was an antiphon (Matt. 21:9) comparable to the Introit, sung by the choir; a collect by the celebrant; the Old Testament lesson (Exod. 15:27–16:7) read by the subdeacon; a responsory (Jer. 11:47–50 or Matt. 26:39–41) sung as a Gradual; the processional Gospel (Matt. 21:1–9); the blessing of the palms with a collect comparable to the prayer over the gifts, the eucharistic preface dialogue and preface (taken from the preface for All Saints), the Sanctus with the Benedictus qui venit, five more collects of blessing, the blessing with incense and holy water and another collect; the distribution of the palms to the congregation while anthems were sung; a final collect was said before the procession. The blessing thus amounted to a dry mass (*missa sicca*) in which the blessing of the palms replaced the consecration of the bread and wine. (Cabrol, 1:167).

[79]One source of the rite is found in *Holy Week Offices*, ed. Massey H. Shepherd, Jr., for the Associated Parishes, Inc., published under the auspices of the Department of Christian Education of the Protestant Episcopal Church (Greenwich, CT: Seabury Press, 1958), 106.

[80]These orders and offices were "prepared by the Commission on the Liturgy and Hymnal at the request of Churches and pastors" and supplemented the Occasional Services which had been approved by the cooperating churches and were part of the Common Liturgy. The "Forms of Blessing" were given on page 215. The title page for these additional orders (p. 157) lists "Prayers and Blessings for Special Occasions."

[81]The uneasiness of the church at that time with such forms is plain in the rubric which preceded the three prayers of blessing (of palms, of a fishing boat, of a wedding ring):

In the use of the following forms of blessing, it must be clear that all of God's creation is good, and that these forms are intended to set apart certain things for specific use, and that the principal blessing is upon those that use them for the specific purpose.

The prayer provided for the blessing of palms is

O God, who for our salvation didst send into this world thy Son, Jesus Christ our Lord, before whom, as he entered Jerusalem, a multitude of people spread palm branches in his path: Let thy blessing rest upon these palms and those who bear them, that we may ever prepare before him the way of faith, and go forth in the sure confidence of his victory over sin and death; through the same Jesus Christ our Lord.

It is an admirable condensation of the extended prayers of the 1570 Roman rite.

rooted in congregational practice. The new rite was therefore readily accepted.[82] The rites of the three churches were further revised in the Roman sacramentary of 1969, the *Lutheran Book of Worship* of 1978, and the *Book of Common Prayer* of 1979. The liturgy that resulted from these reforms and restorations is similar in the three rites.

Roman Catholic	Lutheran	Episcopal
Matt. 21:9	Matt. 21:9b	Luke 19:38
Address		
Prayer of blessing	Prayer	Prayer
Processional gospel	Processional gospel	Processional gospel
(Homily)		
	Preface and Blessing	Preface and Blessing (Matt. 21:9)
"Let us go forth..."	"Let us go forth..."	"Let us go forth..."
Procession with antiphons or hymn	Procession with "All Glory, Laud, and Honor"	Procession with "All Glory, Laud, and Honor"; Ps. 118:19–29 Station with collect
Responsory at entrance of church	Matt. 21:9c at altar	

The Roman and Episcopal books permit the adaptation of this liturgy for use at services other than the principal celebration.

The Roman rite requires the use of red vestments on Passion Sunday, indicating the prominence of two themes in this rite: the theme of the kingship of Christ, whose hour of glorification has come and who is soon to reign from the tree of the cross,[83] and the theme of the church's joy in his mighty work.

In the Roman rite the priest's address to the people invites them to participate in "the celebration of our Lord's paschal mystery." Similar ideas are expressed in the prayer which follows the opening verse in the Lutheran (no. 32) and Episcopal rites. The prayer is based on a collect used as a post-communion for Monday in Holy Week in the Roman

---

[82]The 1973 rite began with the Apostolic Greeting ("The grace of our Lord Jesus Christ...") and the verse "Blessed is the King who comes in the name of the Lord. *Glory to God in the highest*"; a prayer of blessing derived from the prayer in *Occasional Services* (1962):

O God, we praise you as we remember how your Son, before his passion, entered Jerusalem and was welcomed as king by those who shouted "Hosanna," and spread their clothing and branches of palm in his path. Accept our words of praise, bless these branches and bless us who carry them, in the Name of the King who came to save, Jesus Christ, your Son, our Lord.

The processional Gospel for the year was then read; the procession followed during which "All Glory, Laud, and Honor" was sung, and the verse from Matt. 21:9 concluded the procession (*Contemporary Worship 6*, 74).

[83]See hymn 124/125, "The Royal Banners Forward Go," stanza 3. The reference is to a nonexistent psalm verse referred to by Tertullian (*Against Marcion* 3) and others; Justin Martyr (*Against Trypho*) accused the Jews of erasing it from the Hebrew text.

missal and as a prayer over the people for Monday in Holy Week in the Sarum missal and the Gregorian sacramentary (no. 318) and used in the Gelasian sacramentary (no. 74) as the second collect for Sexagesima. The 1928 American Prayer Book appointed the collect for Wednesday of Holy Week. The *Lutheran Book of Worship* has borrowed and slightly revised the translation from the Prayer Book.

The processional Gospel for the appropriate year of the lectionary cycle is read. The citations are the same in the three rites except that the Prayer Book extends the reading from St. Mark to verse 11a and the Roman rite provides John 12:12–16 (the only account to mention palm branches) as an alternative to the reading from St. Mark.

The 1969 Roman sacramentary no longer includes the preface and thanksgiving characteristic of the earlier rite of blessing the palms, substituting instead alternative prayers for the blessing of the branches or the blessing of the people. The form of blessing in the *Lutheran Book of Worship* (no. 33) is a slight revision of the form in the *Book of Common Prayer*, which is based in part on the alternative Roman prayer blessing the people and on the form in the *Book of Offices*.

Although all three rites suggest the use during the procession of the ninth-century hymn "All Glory, Laud, and Honor," the Lutheran book is the only one to require its use. The Prayer Book suggests also, following precedent at least as old as Egeria's time (fourth century), Psalm 118. The Roman rite provides traditional antiphons for use with Psalms 24 and 47 and a responsory; all three, like "All Glory, Laud, and Honor," make use of the theme of the children of Jerusalem welcoming Christ the King. The reference to the children has been in the liturgy since the time of Egeria, who refers to "the Gospel about the children"; it derives from Matthew 21:15–16 (see 11:25).

The *Book of Common Prayer* provides for an optional pause in the procession — a station — "at a suitable place" and the praying of a collect; the collect for Monday in Holy Week is suggested. The *Lutheran Book of Worship* provides for a pause at the conclusion of the procession before the altar and the singing of the verse from Matthew 21:9, which echoes the verse at the beginning of the Liturgy of the Palms.

The procession concluded, each of the three rites begins the Holy Communion with the opening Prayer (collect) of the Day. The Eucharist on the Sunday of the Passion, like the service on the other Sundays of Lent, is given its character by the Gospel, which is the solemn reading of the passion narrative from the synoptic Gospel of the particular year of the lectionary cycle.

The opening Prayer of the Day in each of the three rites is a translation of a collect in the Gelasian sacramentary (no. 329) and the Gregorian sacramentary (no. 312), "a noble and beautiful prayer which perfectly summarizes the divine plan of redemption,"[84] inspired by the

---

[84]Reed, 498.

Second Lesson for the day, Philippians 2:5–11, appointed in the earliest Roman lectionary. The Lutheran version of the prayer (no. 31) softens the note of humility. Cranmer in the 1549 Prayer Book expanded the invocation by adding "of thy tender love for mankind."

The Common Service (1888) and the *Church Book* of 1891 appointed St. Luke's Passion (Luke 22:1–23:42) as the Gospel for Wednesday in Holy Week and St. John's Passion (John 18:1–19:42) as the Gospel for Good Friday. The *Service Book and Hymnal* (1958) restored the Passion of St. Matthew (Matt. 26:1–27:66) as the alternative Gospel for the Sixth Sunday in Lent and St. Mark's Passion (Mark 14:1–15:46) as the alternative Gospel for Tuesday in Holy Week. The present lectionaries of the Roman Catholic, Lutheran, and Episcopal churches rotate the synoptic passion accounts through the three years of the lectionary cycle on the Sunday of the Passion to give each account equal prominence. St. John's Passion is established as the Gospel for Good Friday.

As the proper preface for the Sunday of the Passion the *Lutheran Book of Worship* appoints the Preface of the Cross from the Gregorian sacramentary (no. 1837), which previous Lutheran books had appointed for the entire season of Lent. (Lutherans had been accustomed to making the whole of Lent a season of the passion.) The Roman sacramentary appoints the Preface of the Cross only for masses of the Holy Cross, notably the Festival of the Triumph of the Cross (September 14), and provides a new preface for Passion Sunday drawn from a sermon (59.7) of Leo the Great. The *Book of Common Prayer* provides a preface for Holy Week based on the 1929 revision of the Prayer Book of the Church of Scotland.

The Roman sacramentary appoints red as the proper color for Holy Week. The *Lutheran Book of Worship* appoints "scarlet" (by which a deep blood-red is meant, what some would call crimson, to distinguish it from the bright red of Pentecost) or the continuation of the Lenten purple.

Monday in Holy Week

Egeria described the worship in fourth-century Jerusalem on Monday in Holy Week.[85] At Rome until the fifth century there apparently were no services on Monday or Tuesday; Leo the Great's homily on the passion began on Sunday and was continued on Wednesday, which was with Friday one of the two ancient fast days. From the time of the *Church Book* (1868) the Lutheran Church in North America has made provision for the liturgical observance of the days of Holy Week.

The opening prayer in the Roman rite is from the Gregorian sacramentary (no. 315) and was appointed for this day in previous missals and earlier Lutheran books. The Lutheran translation was made for the *Church Book*.

---

[85] *Egeria's Travels* 32.

The Prayer of the Day in the *Lutheran Book of Worship* (no. 34) is an adaptation of the collect in the *Book of Common Prayer*, which was written by William Reed Huntington, published in his *Materia Ritualis* (1882), and proposed for inclusion in the 1892 revision of the Prayer Book. The 1928 American book appointed it for Monday in Holy Week; in the 1979 book it is also appointed as a collect for Fridays in Morning Prayer and as a station collect for the Palm Sunday procession. The words "went not up to joy... before he was crucified" are drawn from the Consultation of Hermann of Cologne.[86]

The appointed Gospel, John 12:1–11, was in the early church read on the preceding Saturday, thus exactly "six days before the Passover" as the reading declares.

The Roman sacramentary appoints a preface from the supplement to the Gregorian sacramentary (no. 1584).

Tuesday in Holy Week

Egeria describes the ceremonies on this day in fourth-century Jerusalem;[87] its observance in Rome began in the fifth century. Mark's Gospel was thought to be but an abbreviation of Matthew and was therefore not highly regarded liturgically,[88] but in later lectionaries Mark's passion was assigned to Tuesday in Holy Week.

The opening prayer in the Roman sacramentary is from the Gregorian sacramentary (no. 319) and was appointed for this day in previous Roman and Lutheran books. The translation in the *Church Book* was revised in the *Common Service Book*.[89]

The Prayer of the Day in the *Lutheran Book of Worship* (no. 35) is a new composition, written for *Contemporary Worship 6*. It is a departure from the general rule that prayers in the liturgy are addressed to the Father through the Son in the Holy Spirit, and is an oddity in that it lacks a termination of any sort.

The collect in the Prayer Book is a revision of a collect provided in the proposed English book of 1928 for Holy Cross Day and recalls the Introit appointed for Tuesday in Holy Week in previous Lutheran and Roman Catholic books.

The Roman sacramentary appoints a preface from the supplement to the Gregorian sacramentary (no. 1585).

Wednesday in Holy Week

The Gospel for this day, like the Gospel for Tuesday, deals with betrayal, this time from the perspective of its treachery and the resulting curse upon the betrayer.[90] Thus the tradition which gave the nickname

---

[86] Hatchett, 176.

[87] *Egeria's Travels* 33.

[88] Hatchett, 228; Horn, 118.

[89] Reed (p. 500) observes, "The Collect is Gregorian and in the terse Latin of the original has more strength and meaning than the colorless English translation indicates."

[90] Nocent, 2:203.

"Spy Wednesday" to this day because of Judas' betrayal of Jesus is preserved.

The Roman Catholic opening prayer is from the Gregorian sacramentary (no. 324), a version of which was provided in the *Common Service Book* (p. 95) and in the *Service Book and Hymnal* (p. 88) as the second of two "Other Collects for Good Friday."

In the *Lutheran Book of Worship* the Prayer of the Day (no. 36) is a new composition written for *Contemporary Worship 6* in which it was the alternative prayer for Monday, Tuesday, and Wednesday of Holy Week. It is based on the collects for those three days in the *Book of Common Prayer*. The collect for the day in previous Lutheran books was from the Gregorian sacramentary.

The Episcopal collect was proposed for the 1892 revision of the Prayer Book and included in the 1928 book for Tuesday in Holy Week. Its author is unknown.

The Roman sacramentary appoints the preface from the previous missal.

Maundy Thursday

Originally this day was one of preparation for the celebration of the paschal event. Penitents who had been excluded from the community at the beginning of Lent were returned to the community and, from the seventh century on, the oils needed for the Easter baptisms were consecrated. Thursday was apparently the first weekday of Holy Week to have a Eucharist. The oldest name of the day (fourth century) seems to have been the Thursday of the Lord's Supper (*in coena domini*). The name Maundy Thursday comes through Old French *mande* from the Latin *mandatum novum*, the new commandment of John 13:34. The celebration of the evening mass of the Lord's Supper came to be understood as the beginning of the passion, and at least the evening of Maundy Thursday was drawn into the original Triduum of Friday-Saturday-Sunday.

THE TRIDUUM

The concentrated fullness of the Easter event of Christ's death and resurrection, which originally was celebrated in the great Vigil of Easter, in the fourth century was divided into its component parts and developed into what Augustine called "the most holy triduum of the crucified, buried, and risen Lord."[91] These three days were understood to be the culmination of the entire liturgical year.

Maundy Thursday evening

In the *Lutheran Book of Worship* the Maundy Thursday liturgy is understood not so much as the observance of the anniversary of the institution

---

[91] Augustine, *Letter* 55.24. (*CSEL* 34/2:195).

of the Holy Communion but rather as a celebration of the intimacy of the Christian community, its mutual forgiveness, absolution, and peace. It returns to the theme of the primacy of the community which was announced in the Ash Wednesday liturgy. Anciently, those who were excommunicated then were reconciled now, and all the community shares in a common mortality and a common hope of life.

A Christian celebration of the Seder, the Jewish Passover meal, is questionable, for the relation of the Lord's Supper to the Passover meal is uncertain. Jewish-Christian relations cannot be advanced when significant differences between Jewish and Christian celebrations of the Passover are obscured.[92]

The Maundy Thursday liturgy in the *Lutheran Book of Worship* was drafted by Brian Helge and Paul Marshall. It begins with a rite of reconciliation, reminiscent of the ancient reconciliation of penitents on this day in preparation for the celebration of the *pascha*. The sermon, which may be preceded by a hymn, begins the liturgy. This unusual arrangement gives the preacher an opportunity to explain the meaning of the day and the actions that are about to take place so that they may flow uninterruptedly and dramatically from this evening through Good Friday and into Easter. Moreover, this reconciliation rite marks the transition from Lent to the Triduum and corresponds to the extended confession on Ash Wednesday with which Lent began.

The instruction describes (1) the struggle against all that prevents humanity from loving God and one another, the struggle to which baptism commits those who are washed in its waters, the spiritual warfare spoken of in the exhortation on Ash Wednesday; (2) God's gift of forgiveness, echoing Luther's simple and eloquent words in the Small Catechism;[93] (3) the responsibility of responding to God's gift by serving others in imitation of the self-sacrificing love of Christ; and (4) the Holy Communion as the intimate participation in God's love.

After the confession of sin and the absolution, the peace is exchanged as an enactment of the Apostolic Greeting which usually begins the Holy Communion. At the Maundy Thursday liturgy, more than most, actions speak louder than words: the greeting is done personally and individually with movement and gesture and physical contact, acting out what is usually just spoken.

In the Roman rite, in the evening mass of the Lord's Supper the Gloria in Excelsis, not otherwise used during Lent, is sung during which "the church bells are rung and then remain silent until the Easter vigil."[94] The silence of the bells during this time is an ancient custom going back at least to the Carolingian period, the second Frankish dynasty, founded

---

[92] For a careful discussion of the issues see Frank C. Senn, "The Lord's Supper, Not the Passover Seder," *Worship* 60 (July 1986):362–68.

[93] Martin Luther, Small Catechism part V, Confession and Absolution in answer to the question, "What is confession?" *Book of Concord*, 349–50.

[94] *The Sacramentary*, 135.

in 751.[95] It was also customary to suspend the use of the organ during the Triduum (although the missal did not mention the practice). The silence of the bells and the organ, these instruments of festive sound, constituted a "fast of the ears" corresponding to the "fast of the eyes" from the veiled crosses, statues, and pictures (and from the altar itself obscured by the *Hungertuch*)[96] and the fast of the mouth from certain food during the entire penitential season.

Although — confusingly — the *Lutheran Book of Worship* provides three sets of lessons for Maundy Thursday, its Maundy Thursday liturgy, to underscore its understanding of the day as centering in the new commandment, gives preference to one set of lessons for all three years: Jeremiah 31:31–34 (from Year C), 1 Corinthians 11:17–32 (from Year A), and John 13:1–17, 34 (from Year A). The Roman lectionary and the *Book of Common Prayer* also have one set of lessons for all three years. The proposed revision by the Consultation on Common Texts, while providing separate lessons for each of the three years, notes that those who desire the emphasis on foot-washing would use the readings for Year A in each year.

The opening prayer in the Roman sacramentary is a new composition. The first Prayer of the Day in the *Lutheran Book of Worship* (no. 37) is a new composition that first appeared in *Contemporary Worship 6* (1973). It makes clear that the focus of the day in the Lutheran rite, as it was anciently, is primarily on the new commandment of love. The final phrase of the petition echoes the First Lesson (Year C), Jeremiah 31:33. The alternative prayer in the Lutheran rite (no. 38) is the collect written by Thomas Aquinas in 1264 for the then-new feast of Corpus Christi. Although the reformers rejected the feast, they appropriated the collect for use on Maundy Thursday[97] or, in a number of instances, as an alternative to Luther's post-communion collect.[98] The address, as the termination makes clear, is to God the Son. The collect in the *Book of Common Prayer* was written for the 1928 American Prayer Book.

In the Roman, Lutheran, and Episcopal rites the optional washing of the feet follows the Gospel. Foot-washing has its origins in a simple act of charity, mentioned in the Gospels. It became part of the baptismal liturgy in the fourth century, except in Rome. As the Roman liturgy spread, the washing of feet slowly disappeared. It began to return again

---

[95]Amalarius of Metz (died ca. 850) understands the silence to be a sign of a humility that imitates Jesus' humiliation; he suggests that wooden clappers are better suited to the expression of such humility (*Liber officialis* I.12.33 and IV.21.7–8 in J. M. Hanssens, ed., *Amalarii episcopi opera liturgica omnia* 2 [Rome, 1948], 79, 470). Others suggest that wooden clappers are a survival of ancient practice before the use of bells was known in the church. See Adam, 65.

[96]Adam, 66.

[97]It was used in the *Church Book*, the *Common Service Book*, and the *Service Book and Hymnal*.

[98]The church orders of Duke Henry of Saxony (1539), Spangenberg (1545), Austria (1571).

in monasteries; the Seventeenth Council of Toledo (694) required the action to be performed on Holy Thursday in all churches in Spain and Gaul. The rite is attested in Rome since the twelfth century.[99] In Milan in the time of Ambrose the foot-washing took place on Holy Saturday.[100] Toward the end of the nineteenth and the early twentieth century, various Protestant groups recovered the practice. They understood that the "Ordinance of Humility" was commanded by Christ and ranked it with Baptism and Holy Communion.

In the Roman and Episcopal rites, which follow the standard order in which the sermon immediately follows the Gospel, foot-washing is preceded by the sermon. This gives the preacher the opportunity to explain or comment on the action which will follow. In the Lutheran rite the sermon has been preached at the beginning of the service, before the confession. Thus, the washing of feet, when it is practiced, immediately follows the Gospel as an enacted sermon, a dramatic action showing the meaning of the Gospel's call to love and service. Its function as an enactment of what has just been heard thus corresponds to the function of the peace at the conclusion of the service of confession and forgiveness on this night.

In each rite foot-washing is optional. The simplicity of the ceremony in all three rites is noteworthy. The Roman sacramentary directs,

Depending on pastoral circumstances, the washing of the feet follows the homily.

The men who have been chosen are led by the ministers to chairs prepared in a suitable place. Then the priest (removing his chasuble if necessary) goes to each man. With the help of the ministers, he pours water over each one's feet and dries them.[101]

(Male representatives are required for they are understood symbolically to signify the apostles.) The *Lutheran Book of Worship* rubric reads,

The Washing of Feet may follow. The minister lays his [*sic*] vestments aside, puts on an apron or towel, and washes the feet of a representative group of the congregation (Min. Ed., p. 138).[102]

The *Book of Common Prayer* says simply,

When observed, the ceremony of the washing of feet appropriately follows the Gospel and homily (p. 274).

Each rite suggests singing during the action. The Roman sacramentary provides six antiphons (verses from John 13 and 1 Cor. 13:13). The Prayer Book arranges John 13:12, 15; 14:27a; 13:34, 35 so that the verses may be read by the congregation. The *Lutheran Book of Worship*

---

[99] Adam, 67.

[100] Ambrose, *On the Sacraments* 3:4, 5, 7.

[101] *The Sacramentary*, 136. In the Missal of 1570 the rite took place after mass after the stripping of the altar.

[102] This rubric is the one place in the *Lutheran Book of Worship* in which the masculine pronoun only is used for the minister. It is a slip that went unnoticed throughout the editorial process.

directs that "Where Charity and Love Prevail" (hymn 126) be sung; other hymns may be sung also. Hymn 126 is a translation of a Latin antiphon of the Carolingian era or earlier based on 1 John and associated with the washing of the feet. The Roman sacramentary now appoints this song for the procession of the faithful with their gifts for the poor, which follows the prayers of intercession.[103]

In each of the three rites the Creed is omitted (the Roman sacramentary alone explicitly says so)[104] and following the washing of the feet the service continues with the prayers of intercession. The Roman rite provides a proper preface for the mass of the Lord's Supper; the Lutheran book uses the Preface of the Passion as on the other days of Holy Week; the Prayer Book uses the Preface of Holy Week.

In the Roman and Lutheran rites the Eucharist is understood to conclude with the post-communion prayer; the usual blessing is omitted. The Roman sacramentary says explicitly, "Mass concludes with this prayer."

In the Roman and Episcopal rites provision is made for the consecration of the sacrament which will be reserved for administration on Good Friday. The practice arose after Good Friday became the one day on which the mass was not celebrated, perhaps in the eleventh century.

The Roman and Lutheran rites direct that the altar be stripped. The Roman sacramentary says simply,

Then the altar is stripped and, if possible, the crosses are removed from the church. It is desirable to cover any crosses which remain in the church.[105]

The Lutheran rubric is slightly more detailed to describe the action to those unfamiliar with it.

The Stripping of the Altar follows: Linens, paraments, ornaments, and candles are removed. As this is done Psalm 22 is sung or said, the congregation kneeling (Min. Ed., p. 138).

The action has its origins in a utilitarian act: the removal of the altar cloths after the celebration of the Eucharist. This action also facilitated the washing of the altars in preparation for the Easter Holy Communion.[106]

At the end of the Maundy Thursday liturgy there is no benediction or dismissal. The three-day, three-part liturgy of the Triduum has begun; it continues with the liturgy of Good Friday.

Good Friday

The Friday of Preparation (*feria sexta in Parasceve,* derived from the Greek *paraskeve,* from the Jewish preparation for the Sabbath, as in

[103] *The Sacramentary,* 137–38.
[104] Ibid., 137: "The profession of faith is not said in this mass."
[105] Ibid., 139.
[106] Adrian Nocent, *The Liturgical Year,* vol. 3, The Paschal Triduum, the Easter Season, trans. Matthew J. O'Connell (Collegeville: Liturgical Press, 1977), 63–64.

Matt. 27:62, Mark 15:42, Luke 13:54, John 19:31, 42) is known in the Roman missal as the Friday of the Passion and Death of the Lord (*feria VI passione domini* in the Gelasian sacramentary). The day is called Good Friday in English and Dutch, apparently from "God's Friday." It is called *Karfreitag* in German, the Friday of mourning. In Norway it is Long Friday, Great Friday in the Slavic languages, and Holy Friday in the Latin nations.

The earliest witness to a feast on Friday as well as Saturday before Easter is from the second century, in the apocryphal *Gospel according to the Hebrews* and in Irenaeus, Bishop of Lyons (ca. 130–ca. 202). In the third century the *Pascha* was dividing into two parts: the Pasch of Crucifixion and the Pasch of Resurrection. Friday eventually was detached altogether from the *Pascha* and became a commemoration of the death of Jesus. The development of Holy Week in Jerusalem in the late fourth century transformed the Friday of the Paschal fast into what is now known as Good Friday. The Good Friday fast became the principal fast in the calendar, and even after the Reformation in Germany many Lutherans who observed no other fast scrupulously kept Good Friday with strict fasting.

The liturgy for Good Friday in the *Lutheran Book of Worship* was drafted by Brian Helge and Paul Marshall. The understanding of the Good Friday liturgy set forth in the Lutheran book and in the Roman sacramentary is similar. The Lutheran rubrics observe that "the note of austerity does not preclude the note of triumph, however, as the final hymns indicate. The congregation gathers to *celebrate* our Lord's sacrifice on the cross" (Min. Ed., p. 23). The Roman sacramentary calls the Good Friday liturgy the "Celebration of the Lord's Passion."[107] The Lutheran book observes that "the logic of the continuing celebration which began on Maundy Thursday suggests that it is not appropriate to celebrate the Holy Communion." The Roman sacramentary says, "According to the Church's ancient tradition, the sacraments are not celebrated today or tomorrow."

The Sacramentary	*Lutheran Book of Worship*
The celebration of the Lord's passion takes place in the afternoon, about three o'clock,	It is most appropriate to hold this service in the afternoon near 3:00, the traditional hour of Jesus' death.
unless pastoral reasons suggest a later hour.	Local circumstances, however may indicate another hour.
The altar should be completely bare, without cloths, candles, or cross.	The altar, having been stripped of its ornaments and linens, is not used in this service. The rite centers, rather, at one or more reading desks. If paraments are
The priest and deacon, wearing	

[107] *The Sacramentary*, 410.

| red Mass vestments, go to the altar. | used, they should be scarlet or black. |
| | Ministers are vested only in albs or surplices with cassocks. It is Inappropriate to wear additional vestments. |

The Lutheran rubrics (Min. Ed., p. 139) preserve the "fast of the ears" by limiting the use of the organ or other musical instruments to supporting the singing.

The Roman, Lutheran, and Episcopal books all direct the ministers to enter in silence. The Roman and Episcopal books direct kneeling for silent prayer; the Roman sacramentary suggests that the ministers make "a reverence and prostrate themselves." The liturgy begins with the prayer, in the Roman and Lutheran books without the salutation or "Let us pray."

The Roman prayers are notable for the simplicity of the termination ("We ask this through Christ our Lord"; "who lives and reigns for ever and ever"). In the Good Friday rite elaborations are stripped away. The first prayer in the Roman rite is from the Gelasian sacramentary (no. 334). The alternative prayer is adapted from a collect in the Gelasian (no. 398) and the Gregorian sacramentary (no. 324), an alternative collect for Wednesday in Holy Week; the prayer was given in the *Church Book*, the *Common Service Book*, and the *Service Book and Hymnal* as another collect for Good Friday:

Almighty and everlasting God, Who has willed that Thy Son should bear for us the pain of the Cross, that Thou mightest remove from us the power of the adversary: Help us so to remember and give thanks for our Lord's Passion that we may obtain remission of sin and redemption from everlasting death; through the same, our Lord Jesus Christ.[108]

The prayer in the *Lutheran Book of Worship* (no. 39) and in the *Book of Common Prayer*, which had been used in the predecessor books of both communions, is from the Gregorian sacramentary (no. 327), where it is used as a prayer over the people at the end of mass on Wednesday of Holy Week. (This use explains the reference to betrayal). The Sarum missal appoints it also as the post-communion prayer on Good Friday; the Gallican *Missale Gothicum* appoints it for the noon office (Sext) on Good Friday and Holy Saturday; the *Missale Gallicanum vetus* included it among the office prayers for Maundy Thursday, Good

---

[108] The three earlier Lutheran books (*Church Book*, *Common Service Book*, *Service Book and Hymnal*) also gave another prayer for Good Friday, translated from the Saxon Agenda of 1540:

Merciful and everlasting God, who hast not spared thine only Son, but delivered him up for us all, that he might bear our sins upon the Cross: Grant that our hearts may be so fixed with steadfast faith in him that we may not fear the power of any adversaries; through the same, thy Son, Jesus Christ our Lord.

Friday, and Holy Saturday (no. 113)[109] as did the Roman Breviary. The prayer alludes to John 11:52 and is the only instance in the *Lutheran Book of Worship* of the full termination concluding other than "now and forever."

In the Good Friday propers but not in the Good Friday liturgy the *Lutheran Book of Worship* provides an alternative Prayer of the Day (no. 40). The prayer, written for *Contemporary Worship 6*, derives from the Gregorian sacramentary (no. 324) given above. It is addressed to the second person of the Holy Trinity and makes reference to 1 Peter 2:24.

The Roman sacramentary appoints a new composition and as an alternative a collect from the Gelasian sacramentary (no. 398).

In the lessons also there is an unfortunate and confusing discrepancy between the propers, which like the Roman and Episcopal rites give preference to Isaiah 52–53 and provide a psalm and a Second Lesson, and the Good Friday liturgy, which, influenced by the 1570 Roman missal, gives preference to Hosea 6 and makes no provision for a psalm or a Second Lesson.

Between the Lesson and the Gospel, the *Lutheran Book of Worship* directs that the classic hymn "O Sacred Head Now Wounded" (or another appropriate hymn) be sung. The indicated hymn derives from a long poem of seven sections attributed to Bernard of Clairvaux (1091–1153), *Salve mundi salutare*, each section of which is addressed to a member of Jesus' body as it hung on the cross: feet, knees, hands, side, breast, heart, and head. The hymn to the crucified Savior was written during the "golden age of Latin hymnody" (the twelfth century, which produced Latin poetry of singular lyric beauty) and is "the most gripping of all Good Friday hymns."[110] It did not achieve unusual fame, however, until five centuries later when it was translated into German by the greatest of all Lutheran hymnists, Paul Gerhardt (1607–1676). The seventh section, addressed to Jesus' head (*O Haupt voll Blut und Wunden*), was included with seventeen other hymns by Gerhardt in the third (1656) edition of Johann Crüger's *Praxis pietatis melica*. Gerhardt's version was in turn translated by a Presbyterian, James W. Alexander, moving Philip Schaff to write in *Christ in Song,*

The classical hymn has shown as imperishable vitality in passing from the Latin into the German, and from the German into English, and proclaiming in three tongues, and in the name of three Confessions — the Catholic, Lutheran, and Reformed — with equal effect, the dying love of our Saviour and our boundless indebtedness to him.[111]

The "remarkable minor melody" to which the hymn is sung was adapted by Hans Leo Hassler in 1601 from a German folk song. The chorale

---

[109] Hatchett, 177.

[110] Ernest Edwin Ryden, *The Story of Christian Hymnody* (Rock Island, IL: Augustana Press, 1961), 39.

[111] *The Hymnal 1940 Companion*, 57; Ryden, 40.

tune was such a favorite of Johann Sebastian Bach that he set it five times in his St. Matthew Passion (1729) alone.

The use of St. John's Passion as the Gospel for Good Friday was traditional by the time of Egeria's visit to Jerusalem in the late fourth century. The old Armenian lectionary gives further testimony to its use. It has been universal since that time.[112] It was restored to Lutheran use by the Common Service (1888) and the 1891 *Church Book*. (The 1868 *Church Book*, reflecting contemporary German practice, had appointed "The Passion History" as the Gospel for Good Friday.) St. John's Passion, through which the glory of the victorious King radiates, is most appropriate for this solemn day which commemorates the destruction of death by death. The usual acclamations before and after the Gospel ("Glory to you, O Lord"; "Praise to you, O Christ") are omitted as a sign of the solemnity of the day.[113] The Roman sacramentary also forbids the use of candles and incense at the reading of the Passion.[114]

Following the reading of the Passion, the *Lutheran Book of Worship* appoints "Lamb of God, Pure and Sinless" (or another appropriate hymn). This metrical rendering by Nicolaus Decius (1490–1541) of the Agnus Dei is appropriate after St. John's Passion, which emphasizes the sacrificial death of the Lamb of God. The melody is Decius's adaptation of a thirteenth-century (or earlier) plainsong Agnus Dei and was used by Bach in his *St. Matthew Passion*. The text and the tune were in Roman Catholic use by 1631.[115]

Through the centuries the simplicity and conservatism of the Good Friday liturgy preserved in its solemn prayers the prayer of the faithful which had disappeared from the Roman mass after the time of Gelasius (492–496). Indeed, the solemn intercessions of Good Friday formed the pattern of the basic structure of the prayers of intercession which are again part of every mass in the Roman sacramentary. The Good Friday intercessions date from the time of Leo the Great in the fifth century. References to the officers of the church, the Roman Empire, the catechumenate, the turbulence of society all reflect conditions in Rome in the fifth century. The earliest extant form of the collects is in the Gelasian sacramentary (nos. 400–17), the Gregorian sacramentary (nos. 338–55), and the *Missale Gallicanum vetus* (nos. 94–111). The biddings may be more ancient than the collects.

After each bid by the presiding minister, the Gelasian and later sacramentaries have the deacon invite kneeling for silent prayer and then standing for each collect: *Flectamur genua...Leuate*, "Let us bend the knee...Arise."

---

[112]See Raymond E. Brown, "The Passion according to John: Chapters 18 and 19," *Worship* 49 (March 1973):126–34; and his *A Crucified Christ in Holy Week*.

[113]Min. Ed., p. 23. The *Book of Common Prayer* (p. 277) directs, "The customary responses before and after the Gospel are omitted."

[114]*The Sacramentary*, 141, 126.

[115]Marilyn Kay Stulken, *Hymnal Companion to the Lutheran Book of Worship* (Philadelphia: Fortress Press, 1981), 210.

Many Lutheran church orders, especially in south and southwestern Germany (Schwäbisch Hall, 1543; Pfalz Neuburg, 1543; Baden, 1556; Württemberg, 1582; Ulm, 1656) retained these traditional bids and intercessions for Good Friday, which came to be known in Lutheran books as the Bidding Prayer. It is found in the *Church Book*, the *Common Service Book*, and the *Service Book and Hymnal*[116] with other General Prayers. The Bidding Prayer in the *Lutheran Book of Worship* is thus a continuation of the prayer that had been preserved in many of the Lutheran church orders in Europe and North America.

Schwäbisch Hall, 1543	*Church Book, Common Service Book, Service Book and Hymnal*	*Lutheran Book of Worship*
for the Christian Church	for the holy Church of God	for the Church
	for the chief pastor of the Church[117]	
	for pastors and people	for the pastors and people of God
	for catechumens[118]	for those preparing for Baptism
		for the unity of Christians
		for the Jewish people
		for those who do not believe in Christ
		for those who do not believe in God
for all in authority	for all in authority	for all in public office
for all in special need	for all in special need	for all in special need
	for all without the Church[119]	
for peace	for peace	
for our enemies	for our enemies	
for pregnant women		
for the fruits of the earth	for the fruits of the earth	
Our Father	Our Father	Our Father

---

[116] *Church Book* (1868), p. 124; *Common Service Book* (text ed.), p. 249 prefaced by the rubric, "By ancient usage this Prayer was specifically appointed for Good Friday"; *Service Book and Hymnal*, p. 236, prefaced by the same rubric.

[117] *Service Book and Hymnal* only. The reference was intended to be to the President of the national church, but the description is that of the Roman pontiff.

[118] Not in the *Church Book*.

[119] *Service Book and Hymnal* only. In addition to this collect, the *Service Book and Hymnal* lists three optional collects: for the heathen, for the Jews, for Islam. The *Common Service Book*, instead of this section, lists three optional collects; for unity, for the heathen, for the Jews.

248

The prayer for one's enemies was an especially appropriate addition, particularly on Good Friday when Jesus prayed for those who crucified him.

The General Intercessions in the Roman sacramentary and the Bidding Prayer in the *Lutheran Book of Worship* (nos. 42–50) are nearly identical in order and language, drawn primarily from the Gelasian sacramentary. The Solemn Collects in the *Book of Common Prayer* are comparable.

Roman Catholic General Intercessions	Lutheran Bidding Prayer	Episcopal Solemn Collects
		Invitation
1. for the Church	for the Church (no. 42)	1. for the Church: its unity,
2. for the pope		clergy,
3. for the clergy and laity of the Church	for the pastors and people of God (no. 43)	people,
4. for those preparing for baptism	for those preparing for baptism (no. 44)	those about to be baptized
5. for the unity of Christians	for the unity of Christians (no. 45)	
6. for the Jewish people	for the Jewish people (no. 46)	
7. for those who do not believe in Christ	for those who do not believe in Christ (no. 47)	
8. for those who do not believe in God	for those who do not believe in God (no. 48)	
9. for all in public office	for all in public office (no. 49)	2. for nations, governments, and peoples
10. for those in special need	for those in special need (no. 50)	3. for the suffering
		4. for those who have not received the Gospel
		5. for the grace of a holy life

Noteworthy in the twentieth-century revision of these ancient prayers is a changed attitude toward the Jews and toward those outside the church. The change is to be understood as more than an increased tolerance necessitated by a pluralistic society. It represents a changed theology. The older triumphalist confidence in the exclusive truth of Christian doctrine is gone, and in its place is a new appreciation of the honesty and validity of the positions of many who are outside the church and an acknowledgement of the role of the church in turning many away. Here is evidence of Christianity adapting itself to a new understanding of its minority role in the modern world, done not with a sense of loss but with a clear sense of gain.

The addition of the Lord's Prayer to the Bidding Prayer is an innovation of the sixteenth-century German church orders and came to be the usual Lutheran conclusion to the General Prayer in the anticommunion. The bid to pray the Our Father is also from the church orders, particularly Schwäbisch Hall (1543):

Lassent vns auch sonst bitten für alles so vnser Herr gebeeten sein wil sprechent, Vater vnser....

Finally, let us pray for all those things for which our Lord would have us ask. Our Father....

The Bidding Prayer concludes the first part of the Good Friday liturgy, the liturgy of the word.

The second part of the Good Friday liturgy consists of the devotions before the cross and the adoration of the crucified. The Lutheran and Episcopal rites include the option of bringing a wooden cross into the church and setting it up in front of the altar. The *Lutheran Book of Worship* provides for the cross to be set up before the service begins or to be carried in procession through the church; the *Book of Common Prayer* provides only the option of bringing the cross into the church following the solemn collects.

The Roman sacramentary requires the use of the cross but offers two forms of its veneration. "Pastoral demands will determine which of the two forms is more effective and should be chosen" (p. 156). In the first form of showing the cross, the veiled cross is carried to the altar and is successively unveiled by the priest — first the upper part, then the right arm of the cross, finally the entire cross; the priest saying each time, "This is the wood of the cross, on which was hung the Savior of the world"; the people respond, "Come, let us worship." In the second form of showing the cross, the priest or deacon goes to the door of the church and takes the uncovered cross and carries it in procession through the church, pausing three times (anticipating the procession with the Paschal Candle at the Easter Vigil) to sing, "This is the wood of the cross."

In the Roman rite, the clergy and people come to the cross in a procession to venerate it by means of a genuflection or a kiss. The Lutheran book directs the congregation to kneel and keep silence "for meditation on the mystery of the crucified Savior, the mystery of redemption." The *Book of Common Prayer* says simply, "Appropriate devotions may follow...."

The verses at the procession with the cross (in the Roman rite, "This is the wood of the cross on which was hung the salvation of the world. *Come, let us worship*"; in the Lutheran rite, "Behold, the life-giving cross on which was hung the salvation of the whole world. *Oh, come, let us worship him*") appear in the eighth and ninth centuries in connection with the veneration of the cross.

The Roman rite provides three songs for use during the veneration of the cross. The first is the first verse of Psalm 67 with an antiphon of Byzantine origin, known to Amalarius,[120] sung before and after it.

> We worship you, Lord,
> we venerate your cross,
> we praise your resurrection.
> Through your cross you brought joy to the whole world.
>
> May God be gracious to us and bless us;
> and let his face shed its light upon us.
>
> We worship you, Lord. . . .

The *Book of Common Prayer* has a more literal translation of the antiphon and adds two more verses of the psalm and prints the resulting anthem in such a way that it may be read responsively by a leader and congregation.

> We glory in your cross, O Lord,
> *and praise and glorify your holy resurrection;*
> *for by virtue of your cross*
> *joy has come to the whole world.*
> May God be merciful to us and bless us,
> show us the light of his countenance, and come to us.
> *Let your ways be known upon earth,*
> *your saving health among all nations.*
> Let the peoples praise you, O God;
> let all the peoples praise you.
> *We glory in your cross, O Lord,*
> *and praise and glorify your holy resurrection;*
> *for by virtue of your cross*
> *joy has come to the whole world.*

The second song which the Roman sacramentary appoints for use during the veneration of the cross is the series of verses called *Improperia* (complaints) or Reproaches of Christ against his people. The original is in Latin with a refrain in Greek, perhaps showing a Byzantine origin; it reached Rome by way of Gaul. The reproach as a rhetorical device is very ancient, employed by parents from antiquity to the present. The language of the Reproaches is traceable to Micah 6:3ff. and to 2 Esdras 1:12ff.[121] There are traces of components of the Reproaches in the seventh century; in the York Breviary there is a responsory for the Fourth Sunday in Lent in which "populus meus" ("O my people") consists of a recital of benefits conferred upon God's people without mention of the pains of the passion. (Passiontide did not begin until the following Sunday). The developed form of the hymn is in two parts. The first three verses are found in documents of the late ninth and early tenth

---

[120]*Liber Officialis* 1.14; Nocent, 3:71.
[121]*The Old Testament Pseudopigrapha*, ed. James H.Charlesworth, vol. 1 (Garden City, NY: Doubleday, 1983):525–26.

centuries, the *Antiphonale Sylvanectense* [of Senlis] ca. 880[122] and the *Pontificale Romano-Germanicum* (ca. 950).[123] The first part of the hymn in the translation of *The Sacramentary* is:

> My people, what have I done to you?
> How have I offended you? Answer me!
> I led you out of Egypt, from slavery to freedom,
> but you led your Savior to the cross.
> My people, what have I done to you?
> How have I offended you? Answer me!
> > Holy is God!
> > Holy and strong!
> > Holy immortal One,
> > have mercy on us!
> For forty years I led you safely through the desert.
> I fed you with manna from heaven
> and brought you to a land of plenty;
> but you led your Savior to the cross.
> > Holy is God!
> > Holy and strong!
> > Holy immortal One,
> > have mercy on us!
> What more could I have done for you?
> I planted you as my fairest vine,
> but you yielded only bitterness:
> when I was thirsty you gave me vinegar to drink,
> and you pierced your Savior with a lance.
> > Holy is God!
> > Holy and strong!
> > Holy immortal One,
> > have mercy on us!

The second part of the hymn is not found until the eleventh century. It consists of nine verses, each beginning with *Ego* ("I").

> For your sake I scourged your captors and their firstborn sons,
> but you brought your scourges down on me.
> > My people, what have I done to you?
> > How have I offended you? Answer me!
> I led you from slavery to freedom
> and drowned your captors in the sea,
> but you handed me over to your high priests.
> > My people, what have I done to you?
> > How have I offended you? Answer me!
> I opened the sea before you,
> but you opened my side with a spear.

---

[122]*Antiphonale missarum sextuplex*, ed. R. Hesbert (Brussels, 1935).

[123]M. Hittorp, *De catholicae ecclesiae divinis officiis* (Cologne, 1568). See H. A. P. Schmidt, *Hebdomada sancta* ii, part 2 (Rome, 1957), 794ff.

My people, what have I done to you?
How have I offended you? Answer me!
I led you on your way in a pillar of cloud,
but you led me to Pilate's court.
My people, what have I done to you?
How have I offended you? Answer me!
I bore you up with manna in the desert,
but you struck me down and scourged me.
My people, what have I done to you?
How have I offended you? Answer me!
I gave you saving water from the rock,
but you gave me gall and vinegar to drink.
My people, what have I done to you?
How have I offended you? Answer me!
For you I struck down the kings of Canaan,
but you struck my head with a reed.
My people, what have I done to you?
How have I offended you? Answer me!
I gave you a royal scepter,
but you gave me a crown of thorns.
My people, what have I done to you?
How have I offended you? Answer me!
I raised you to the height of majesty,
but you have raised me high on a cross.
My people, what have I done to you?
How have I offended you? Answer me!

This powerful and moving hymn in which the church hears the disappointed voice of Christ as an anguished parent (see 2 Esdras 1:28–29) achieved immense popularity even beyond its liturgical use.[124]

Because of the extraordinary emotional impact of this hymn, the Reproaches were included in the Good Friday liturgy in the *Draft Proposed Book of Common Prayer* (1976) and in review material circulated by the Inter-Lutheran Commission on Worship. But because the Reproaches were perceived by some as anti-Jewish,[125] they were removed

---

[124]See the lyrics by Friar William Herebert (d. 1333), "My folk, what habbe I do thee," and from the *Commonplace Book of John of Grimestone* (1372), "My folk, now answer me." Given in *Religious Lyrics of the XIVth Century*, ed. Carleton Brown, 2nd rev. ed. by G. V. Smithers (Oxford: Clarendon Press, 1965), no. 15 and no. 72; given also in *Middle English Lyrics*, ed. Maxwell S. Luria and Richard L. Hoffman (New York: W. W. Norton and Co., 1974). See also John Stevens, "Medieval Lyrics and Music" in *Medieval Literature: Chaucer and the Alliterative Tradition*, ed. Boris Ford (New York: Penguin Books, 1982), 262–64. Rosemary Woolf, *The English Religious Lyric in the Middle Ages* (Oxford: Clarendon Press, 1968), 37, 40–42, 188, 213, 217. See also Rosemond Tuve's study of George Herbert's poem "The Sacrifice" with reference to the Reproaches in her *A Reading of George Herbert* (Chicago: University Press, 1952), 19–99.

[125]John T. Townsend, " 'The Reproaches' in Christian Liturgies," *Face to Face: An Interreligious Bulletin* II (Summer/Fall 1976):8–11; Thomas A. Indinopulos, "Old Forms of Anti-Judaism in the New Book of Common Prayer," *Christian Century* 93 (August 4–11, 1976):680–84; Eric Werner, "Melito of Sardis, The First Poet of Deicide," *Hebrew Union College Annual* 37 (1966):191–210. See Melito of Sardis (A.D. 120–185), "Homily on

from the *Book of Common Prayer* and, despite some additional verses composed by Charles A. Ferguson to make clear that the Reproaches were directed not against Israel but against Christianity, they were not included in the *Lutheran Book of Worship*. In their place, to conclude the meditation on the mystery of the crucified Savior, the Lutheran book appoints the hymn, "Ah, Holy Jesus, How Hast Thou Offended." This hymn by Johann Heermann, "a precious classic in the hymnals of many denominations,"[126] first appeared in Heermann's *Devoti Musica Cordis* (1630). It is a paraphrase of a passage from chapter seven of the fifteenth-century *Meditationis* attributed erroneously to St. Augustine[127] and which derives from the twelfth-century *Orationes* attributed to St. Anselm of Canterbury. The passage used by Heermann was one drawn by Anselm from the writings of Jean de Fécamp (d. 1078).[128] Heermann's hymn, "Ah, Holy Jesus," therefore, is another expression of that devotional tradition which gave rise to the Reproaches. In the hymn the "I" who speaks is the individual, in the Reproaches the "I" is God; the hymn is personal, the Reproaches are communal; but the effect is the same — "I crucified thee." The Reproaches and Heermann's hymn both provide the wilderness experience of rebellion and denial of God's gifts and promises as the church becomes Israel wandering in the desert and the mob denouncing Jesus and demanding his execution. It is an essential element in the Christian celebration of the Passover.

The third song which the Roman sacramentary suggests during the veneration of the cross is the sixth-century hymn by Venantius Fortunatus, *Pange, lingua, gloriosi proelium certaminis*. The *Book of Common Prayer* appoints the same hymn, "Sing, My Tongue, the Glorious Battle," or "some other hymn extolling the glory of the cross." The *Lutheran Book of Worship* requires the use of "Sing, My Tongue, the Glorious Battle" and/or "The Royal Banners Forward Go."

"Sing, My Tongue, the Glorious Battle" by Fortunatus was perhaps connected with the procession of the relics of the cross to Queen Rhadegunda's new monastery at Poitiers on November 19, 569. The hymn was not generally used in the Middle Ages except in the Mozarabic liturgy. It was either divided into two groups of five stanzas each for use at Matins and Lauds or else the last three stanzas were used alone on the feast of the Finding of the Holy Cross (May 3). The hymn was used by Thomas Aquinas as a model for his hymn in praise of the blessed sacrament, *Pange, lingua, gloriosi corporis* ("Of the Glorious Body Telling"). The second stanza of Fortunatus's hymn, not translated in the *Lutheran Book of Worship* version, alludes to several medieval legends which traced the

---

the Passion," *Journal of Theological Studies* 52:6 (1943) and *Harvard Theological Review* (1943), 316–19.

[126] *Hymnal 1940 Companion*, 54.

[127] Given in the *Hymnal 1940 Companion*, 53.

[128] Stephen A. Hulbut, *The Picture of the Heavenly Jerusalem in the Writings of Johannes of Fecamp* (Washington: St. Alban's Press, 1943). Dom Andre Wilmart, "La Tradition des prières de Saint Anselm," *Revue Bénédictine* XXXVI (1924):52–71.

wood of the cross back through Jewish history to the Garden of Eden. The traditions vary greatly. In some, Adam brought wood from the tree of life or the tree of the knowledge of good and evil when he was expelled from Eden and used it as his staff throughout his life. Others say that Adam, dying, had his son Seth return to the Garden to beg from the sentinel angel balsam to relieve the agony of death. Seth received three seeds of the tree of life, which he put in Adam's mouth at his burial. Three trees — cedar, cypress, and pine — grew and merged into a single trunk. The wood became the rod of Moses; it became a beam in Solomon's temple; it made its way to Joseph's carpenter shop where Judas acquired it and eventually turned it over to the Roman executioners. Other accounts have the wood discarded by Solomon's builders because it proved unworkable and buried it where the pool of Bethesda was later dug, giving the pool miraculous qualities. When Jesus was condemned to die, the wood rose to the surface of the pool and was taken by the Roman soldiers for Jesus' cross.[129]

"The Royal Banners Forward Go" (*Vexilla regis prodeunt*) is thought also to have been written by Venantius Fortunatus for the procession on November 19, 569 when the relics of the cross which Queen Rhadegunda had obtained from Emperor Justinian II were brought from Tours to her new monastery of St. Croix at Poitiers. Gregory of Tours describes the splendid procession:

Eufronius, Bishop of Tours, came with his clergy with much singing and gleaming of tapers and fragrance of incense, and in the absence of the bishop of the city brought the holy relics to the monastery.[130]

Fortunatus's eight-stanza text is found in an eighth-century manuscript from St. Petersburg. In the eleventh century two additional anonymous stanzas are found. The hymn was used at Vespers from the first Sunday of the Passion through Wednesday of Holy Week. The banners (*vexilla*) of the king were the old Roman cavalry standards which, after Constantine, were surmounted by the cross instead of the Roman eagle. The reference in the third stanza is to Psalm 96:10; "reign in triumph from a tree" (*regnabit a ligno deus*) is an addition to the Hebrew in some Old Latin and Septuagint manuscripts. Tertullian refers to the verse,[131] and Justin Martyr in *Against Trypho* 73 accuses the Jews of having erased it from the Hebrew. John Mason Neale[132] calls this hymn "one of the grandest in the treasury of the Latin Church"; it has a place in Randolph's *Seven Great Hymns of the Medieval Church.*

The Good Friday liturgy in the *Lutheran Book of Worship* concludes with a verse and response that were used as an antiphon in medieval rites

---

[129] See A. S. Rappoport, *Medieval Legends of Christ* (New York: Scribners, 1935), chap. 2; Sabine Baring-Gould, *Curious Myths of the Middle Ages* (London, Oxford, and Cambridge: Rivingtons, 1869).

[130] Migne, *PL* 71:518.

[131] Tertullian, *Against Marcion* 3.

[132] *Medieval Hymns and Sequences*, trans. John Mason Neale (London, 1851).

after the devotions before the cross. The antiphon is used in Anthem 2 in the *Book of Common Prayer* as an antiphon to 2 Timothy 2:11b–12a and in the Roman sacramentary in another form as the antiphon to Psalm 67 at the veneration of the cross.

In the Roman sacramentary the Good Friday liturgy concludes with the distribution of the Holy Communion. The *Book of Common Prayer* provides for the optional "administration of Holy Communion from the reserved sacrament." A final prayer concludes the service; no blessing or dismissal is added.

Roman sacramentary	Book of Common Prayer
	(A Confession of Sin
The Lord's Prayer	The Lord's Prayer
The Communion Prayer	The Communion)
Prayer over the People	Prayer

The Mass of the Pre-Sanctified may be said to go back to the second century. On weekdays, when no mass was celebrated, the people communed from the reserved sacrament which they took home with them from the Sunday Eucharist. The earliest evidence for this custom having been transferred to the church is from the seventh century in Constantinople.[133]

The Roman sacramentary notes, "Evening Prayer is not said by those who participate in this afternoon liturgical service" (p. 167).

As on Maundy Thursday, at the conclusion of the Good Friday liturgy there is no benediction or dismissal. The three-day, three-part liturgy of the Triduum, begun on Thursday, continues with the Easter Vigil on Holy Saturday.

Holy Saturday

Saturday in Holy Week, called anciently "The Great Sabbath," had no liturgy of its own. It was a day of meditation, reflection, and fasting in preparation for the celebration of Easter.

After infant baptism had become common and baptisms were no longer administered at the Easter Vigil, the Vigil began to be moved to earlier in the day on Holy Saturday. In the Missal of Pius V (1570), the vigil began early Saturday morning.

The Reformers discarded the Easter Vigil, which made little sense early in the morning of the day before Easter, and restructured the day. The 1549 Prayer Book appointed a proper Epistle (1 Pet. 3:17–22) and Gospel (Matt. 27:57–66) commemorating Jesus' burial and descent to the dead; the Palm Sunday collect was used throughout Holy Week. The

---

[133] *The Study of Liturgy*, ed. Cheslyn Jones, Geoffrey Wainwright, Edward Yarnold (New York: Oxford University Press, 1978), 409; see Nocent, 3:72–75.

1662 revision of the Prayer Book provided a collect based on a collect from the Scottish Prayer Book of 1637, paraphrasing Romans 6:3ff. and preserving the ancient association of Holy Saturday with baptism.[134]

The *Church Book* and the *Common Service Book* provided only the Gelasian collect (no. 454) — also found in the Gregorian sacramentary (no. 377), the Bobbio missal (no. 258), and the Sarum missal — for Easter Eve, with its subtle allusion to the new fire and baptism. The translation was made for the *Church Book* (1868).

O God, Who didst enlighten this most holy night with the glory of the Lord's Resurrection: Preserve in all Thy people the spirit of adoption which Thou hast given, so that renewed in body and soul they may perform unto Thee a pure service; through Thy Son, Jesus Christ our Lord, who liveth and reigneth with Thee and the Holy Ghost, ever one God, world without end.

It is the proper collect for the Easter Vigil and is so appointed in the Roman sacramentary and in the *Book of Common Prayer.* Curiously, while the collect was introduced into the Prayer Book in the 1979 revision, it disappeared from the Lutheran book as the Easter Vigil was introduced.

The *Lutheran Book of Worship* provides propers only for Morning and Evening Prayer on Holy Saturday; no Prayer of the Day is provided (an unfortunate oversight); there are no eucharistic propers. The absence of provision for services other than daily prayer is not only because few congregations will have services other than the Easter Vigil on this day; the absence of liturgical provision is historic and symbolic, for this is the supreme day of rest and anticipation.

The Roman rite likewise provides only for the liturgy of the hours. *The Sacramentary* has only these two paragraphs for Holy Saturday:

On Holy Saturday the Church waits at the Lord's tomb, meditating on his suffering and death. The altar is left bare, and the sacrifice of the Mass is not celebrated. Only after the solemn vigil during the night, held in anticipation of the resurrection, does the Easter celebration begin, with a spirit of joy that overflows into the following period of fifty days.

On this day holy communion may be given only as viaticum (p. 167).

The *Book of Common Prayer* likewise directs, "There is no celebration of the Eucharist on this day." A new collect and lessons are provided for a liturgy of the word.

The Vigil of Easter

The people of Israel observed the night of the Passover each year by a vigil of prayer and praise according to the ancient commandment:

And at the end of four hundred and thirty years, on that very day, all the hosts of the Lord went out from the land of Egypt. It was a night of watching by the Lord, to bring them out of the land of Egypt; so this same night is a night of

---

[134]The *Service Book and Hymnal* imitated the Prayer Book and appointed, in addition to the collect, three lessons for Holy Saturday (Exod. 13:17–22; 1 Pet. 3:17–22; Matt. 27:57–66) and created an Introit and Gradual for the day.

watching kept to the Lord by all the people of Israel throughout their generations (Exod. 12:41–42; see also Luke 12:35–38).

This prayerful watch kept the past alive in remembrance of the origin of the nation and in affirmation of the responsibilities of that nation as God's chosen people. The vigil nourished memory, and it nourished hope as well, looking to the future and to another yet more decisive intervention by God.

The infant church found in the Passover, which commemorates the killing of the first-born, the deliverance from slavery, and the entrance into the land of promise, a preparation for and an anticipation of the saving events which it had experienced in the death and resurrection of Christ. It was natural therefore that the paschal vigil would develop in Christianity.

The great Vigil of Easter is a repetition of actions and gestures initiated long ages before, a conscious replaying of paradigmatic actions from that time behind time encountered in the depths of Christian consciousness. In the celebration of this Vigil are found powerfully expressed the characteristics of ritual action noted by anthropologists and historians of religion. Space is transcended: the act of remembering takes place at a grave, but the grave is anywhere the event is recalled. The church building and with it the congregation moves from darkness to light, and in the font the baptized move from death to resurrection, boldly challenging the threatening powers of darkness and death. Time is transcended: "this is the night" the Exsultet sings again and again, for the Passover and the Resurrection and the church's celebration of Easter all merge and become contemporary events. The Vigil is a participation in the Event it proclaims, and the original deed lives again. What happened once *in illo tempore* (at that time) is repeated again and again *hic et nunc* (here and now) as an experienced reality. It is a re-creation of what happened in the archetypal event, newly activated in the here and now of each celebration. The fullness of the Christian faith is found in the Vigil; more than that, the fullness of Judaism as well, for this is the Christian Passover. And behind that lies the general experience of humankind in the wonder of new birth in the springtime, a death and resurrection. The movement from Lent through Easter parallels the four stages of the new year celebration in many primal cultures: the *mortification* of Lent, the *purgation* of Holy Week, the *invigoration* of the Resurrection, and the *jubilation* of the Fifty Days of Easter.[135] Finally, in its deepest sense, this Passover celebration is not the festival of an individual, a hero, but of a people; the heroic and victorious deeds of Christ were accomplished not

---

[135]See Mircea Eliade, *The Sacred and the Profane: The Nature of Religion* (New York: Harcourt, Brace & World, 1959), 79–80, 104–05; the four-fold pattern is given in Theodor H. Gaster, *Thepis: Ritual, Myth and Drama in the Ancient Near East* (New York: Harper & Row, 1966), 26ff.

for himself but for the people of God, ultimately the whole human race.[136]

The paschal vigil, "the mother of all vigils,"[137] was first of all a preparation for baptism. The *Apostolic Tradition* of Hippolytus (ca. 215) describes the ceremony, which was doubtless developed in the previous century, perhaps even in New Testament times. Candidates for Baptism and others with them fasted Friday and Saturday; Saturday night was spent in a vigil of prayer and instruction. At cockcrow the baptismal water was blessed, and the chrism ("the oil of thanksgiving") blessed and exorcised. The candidates renounced Satan, his servants, and all his works; they were then anointed with the oil of exorcism and baptized, giving assent to a profession of faith, were anointed with chrism and received the laying on of hands by the bishop. The newly-baptized then shared in the Holy Communion.

Later, the sacramentaries show how the Vigil had been elaborated to begin with a *lucernarium* (the blessing of the new fire and the singing of the Easter Proclamation); a series of four to twelve lessons followed, interspersed with psalms, canticles, and prayers. A prayer of thanksgiving was said over the water before the baptisms took place. In Gallican rites a cleric washed the feet of the newly-baptized. In the Roman rites, anointing, common to all liturgies from the fifth century on, was followed by a second anointing, done by the bishop. The newly-baptized were clothed in white garments, and the Eucharist would be celebrated in which the lessons and prayers abounded in baptismal references, relating the celebration of the death and resurrection of Christ to the dying and rising of the baptized in the baptismal water.

As the custom of baptizing infants within a short time after birth became common, the Easter Vigil was no longer the principal time for baptisms and the night of fasting and preparation for baptism was no longer necessary. As late as the fourth century, the Vigil seems to have continued all night, and no further liturgy was celebrated on Easter Day.[138] Toward the end of the sixth century the Vigil was ending before midnight and Easter Day had its own mass; by the middle of the eighth century, the Vigil could begin when the first star appeared; the ninth-century Einsiedeln *Ordo* gives the hour of *none* (around 3 P.M.) as the time for the beginning of the Vigil mass, the preparatory vigil beginning therefore about noon. In the fourteenth century, fasting regulations were relaxed, and the mid-afternoon office of *None* was allowed to be read in the morning and the feast day mass immediately to follow it: the preparatory parts of the Vigil thus began in the early morning. The 1570 missal of Pius V made this odd and anomalous pattern obligatory. The number of lessons was shortened to four (the creation, the exodus, Isa. 4, Deut. 31:22–30). After the Eucharist, an abbreviated

---

[136] Joseph Campbell, *The Masks of God: Occidental Mythology* (New York: Viking Press, 1970), 138.
[137] Augustine, *Sermon* 219, *PL* 38:1088.
[138] Adam, 96.

form of Vespers was sung before the post-communion prayer. The Vigil moreover had become so clericalized that only a small number of laity attended.

The Easter candle was lit and carried to the altar, to the accompaniment of the threefold *Lumen Christi* [light of Christ], at an hour when bright sunshine was already filling the church; the solemn Easter alleluia was sung and the Easter message was proclaimed in the liturgy of the word and the preface, but the people leaving the church knew that the fast did not end until noon![139]

Such practice was far removed from the ancient vigil with its contrasts of darkness and light, night and dawn, fasting and feasting, grief and gladness, dying and rising, death and life, Satan and Christ, the old age and the new age.

Interest in the celebration of the Easter Vigil at a more appropriate and symbolically effective hour revived in the twentieth century as scholars explored the history and meaning of the rites of Holy Week and Easter, enriched by broader studies of the significance of ritual and symbols. A revised order for Holy Saturday was undertaken in 1950 at the request of the Roman Catholic bishops of Germany, France, and Austria, and in a decree of February 9, 1951, the Congregation of Rites as an experiment allowed the Vigil to be celebrated the night before Easter. The reform was used, studied, revised, and extended to the whole liturgy of Holy Week. The new order for Holy Week was introduced November 16, 1955. Anglican groups adopted the Roman revisions and issued their translations of the rites.[140] The Commission on Worship of the Lutheran Church in America, aware of these revisions, in 1968 issued *Holy Week and Easter: Liturgical Orders Supplementing the Service Book and Hymnal.*[141] Holy Week rites, drafted by Brian Helge and Paul Marshall, were included in the Ministers Edition of the *Lutheran Book of Worship.* Revised Holy Week rites were also included in the *Book of Common Prayer* of 1979.

In keeping the Easter Vigil the church celebrates the entire paschal mystery, the passage of Christ through suffering and death to resurrection and new life. The Vigil of Easter consists of four parts: (1) the Service of Light, (2) the Liturgy of the Word, (3) the Celebration of Baptism, and (4) the Celebration of the Holy Communion.

1. THE SERVICE OF LIGHT. The Vigil begins in utter darkness, the desolation of Holy Saturday with Christ lying in the tomb and the lives and hopes of his followers shattered. But suffering, as Elie Wiesel teaches,

---

[139] Ibid., 76.

[140] For Example, *The Order for Holy Week: The Revised Rites for Palm Sunday, Maundy Thursday, Good Friday, Holy Saturday* (London: The Church Union Church Literature Association, 1957); *Holy Week Offices*, ed. Massey H. Shepherd, Jr. (Greenwich, CT: Seabury Press, 1958).

[141] Philadelphia: Fortress Press, 1968; an edition in Modern Speech was published in 1969.

contains the secret of creation.[142] So the Vigil begins with a return to the moment before creation, prior to the separation of God and humanity. It is a return to a time behind time containing all possibilities, pregnant with potentiality, before any commitment to particular forms was begun.

The Service of Light has its origin in the Jewish custom of blessing the lamp at the beginning of the Sabbath on Friday evening. The ancient church continued the practice, transforming it into a thanksgiving to Christ the light of the world.[143] The Christian *lucernarium* was held every Saturday as the day of resurrection began with a service in Christian homes at the lighting of the lamps. Eventually this service fell into disuse except for its continuation in the Easter Vigil where its function is a reenactment of the creation.

The *lucernarium* as it developed in the Easter Vigil consists of three parts: (a) the blessing of the new fire, (b) the procession with the paschal candle, and (c) the chanting of the proclamation of Easter, the Exsultet.

a. The Blessing of the New Fire. The old Roman liturgy had no blessing of fire. In the eighth century no lights (candles) were permitted in the church on Good Friday, but a lamp was kept burning in a place other than the church and was brought into the church for the readings on Holy Saturday to provide illumination for the readers.

The lighting of the new fire began in Celtic lands or in Germany, most likely as a continuation of pre-Christian customs.[144] The practice of striking the new fire from flint is first recorded in the seventh century in Spain. The association between the stone of the flint and Christ the cornerstone developed in the Middle Ages.

The present Roman sacramentary has simplified the rite. After "a large fire is prepared in a suitable place outside the church," the priest, "in these or similar words," addresses the congregation; the *Book of Common Prayer* begins its Great Vigil of Easter with another translation of that model address:

Roman Catholic	**Episcopal**
Dear friends in Christ,	Dear friends in Christ:
on this most holy night,	On this most holy night,
when our Lord Jesus Christ	in which our Lord Jesus
passed from death to life,	passed over from death to life,
the Church invites her children	the Church invites her members,
throughout the world	dispersed throughout the world,
to come together in vigil and prayer.	to gather in vigil and prayer.
This is the passover of the Lord:	For this is the Passover of the Lord,
if we honor the memory of his	

---

[142] Elie Wiesel, *The Gates of the Forest*, trans. Frances Frenaye (New York: Schocken, 1982), 201; see also pp. 189, 202, 213–14.

[143] *Apostolic Tradition* 26.18.

[144] See Mircea Eliade, *Patterns in Comparative Religion* (Cleveland and New York: World, 1963), 398–99; Frazer, 705–53.

death and resurrection
by hearing his word and
celebrating his mysteries,
then we may be confident that
we shall share his victory over death
and live with him for ever in God.

in which, by hearing his Word and
celebrating his Sacraments,

we share in his victory over death.

The fire is blessed with a prayer, which in the Roman Catholic and Episcopal rites is a simplification of the first of three prayers for blessing the new fire in the Missal of 1570 and its predecessors.

Roman Catholic	**Episcopal**

Father,
we share the light of your glory
through your Son, the light of the world.
Make this new fire + holy,
  and inflame us with new hope.
Purify our minds by this Easter celebration
and bring us one day to the feast of eternal
  light.
We ask this through Christ our Lord.

O God, through your Son you
have bestowed upon your
people the brightness of your
light: Sanctify this new fire, and
grant that in this Paschal feast
we may so burn with heavenly
desires, that with pure minds
we may attain to the festival of
everlasting light; through Jesus
Christ our Lord.

The use of the paschal candle goes back at least to the sixth century. Ennodius, bishop of Pavia 513–521, has left two forms for the blessing of the candle.[145]

The Roman rite provides two optional rites "to stress the dignity and significance of the Easter candle." After the blessing of the new fire, the candle is brought to the celebrant, who cuts a cross in the wax with a stylus (in the earliest documents relating to the Easter *lucernarium* — Toledo and Milan — the candle was anointed with chrism in the form of a cross), traces the Greek letter alpha above the cross and omega below, the numerals of the current year between the arms of the cross (this custom first appears in Spain and then in Italy and France), saying,

1. Christ yesterday and today   *tracing the vertical arm*
2. the beginning and the end   *tracing the horizontal arm*
3. Alpha   *alpha, above the cross*
4. and omega;   *omega, below the cross*
5. all time belongs to him   *first numeral, in upper left corner of the cross*
6. and all the ages   *second numeral, in upper right corner*
7. to him be glory and power   *third numeral, in lower left corner*
8. through every age for ever.   *last numeral, in lower right corner*
   Amen.

The priest may then insert five grains of incense in the candle (a later medieval custom) in the form of a cross, saying:

---

[145] Migne, *PL* 63:257, 261.

1. By his holy	*in upper vertical part*
2. and glorious wounds	*at crossing of beams*
3. may Christ our Lord	*in lower vertical part*
4. guard us	*in left arm*
5. and keep us. Amen.	*in right arm*

The *Lutheran Book of Worship* makes a similar provision (Min. Ed., pp. 143, 24), except that the grains of incense, following the medieval practice, are inserted in the candle during the Easter Proclamation.

The paschal candle is then lighted from the new fire. In the Roman and Lutheran rites the minister says,

May the light of Christ, rising in glory, dispel the darkness of our hearts and minds.

The reference is to the paschal candle, which for the Fifty Days represents "the light of Christ."

The Roman sacramentary since 1970 permits adaptation of the ceremonies to suit local circumstances.

The purpose of the preparatory ceremonies is to treat the candle ritually as if it were Christ himself. It is marked with his cross and symbol, Alpha and Omega; it is set with five grains of incense marking the five wounds of Christ's body. The candle participates in the reality to which it points; from the Vigil of Easter through Pentecost the candle *is*, as will be proclaimed in the procession, "the light of Christ."

b. The Procession. The general idea of symbolizing the resurrection with lighted lamps seems to have come from Jerusalem,[146] and in the Eastern churches still today the resurrection is celebrated by the congregation holding lighted candles.

In many medieval rites, because the paschal candle had grown to enormous size (at Sarum it was thirty-six feet high), the deacon carried a lighted taper and lit the great candle during the Exsultet. In the revised and restored Easter Vigil, the deacon or assisting minister carries the paschal candle itself, the symbol of the risen Christ, into the darkened church, leading the procession. (The Roman and Lutheran rites note that if incense is used, the thurifer goes before the deacon.) Three times (at the church door, in the church, before the altar) the deacon pauses, lifts the candle high,[147] and sings,[148] "The light of Christ" (*The Sacramentary* translates the Latin *Lumen Christi* as "Christ our light"), and the congregation answers, "Thanks be to God." Other candles are lighted from the paschal candle during the procession. William O'Shea comments, "This is something infinitely more than a pretty candlelight ceremony. It is a vivid dramatization of the resurrection."[149] Ritually,

---

[146] William J. O'Shea, *The Meaning of Holy Week*, 2nd rev. ed. (Collegeville: Liturgical Press, 1965), 104.
[147] Rubrics in the Roman sacramentary and in the *Lutheran Book of Worship.*
[148] "or says," *Book of Common Prayer.*
[149] O'Shea, 107.

the candle *is* the light of Christ, echoing and fulfilling the first action of the creation and the pillar of fire of the exodus in the mighty rising of Christ, including the descent to the dead and leading them into the land of light and life. The procession is the triumph of the risen Christ.[150]

In the Roman and Episcopal rites, the congregation's candles are lighted from the paschal candle during the procession (in the Roman rite, specifically after the second "Christ our light"). In the Lutheran rite, the congregation's candles are lighted during the singing of the Exsultet.

c. The Exsultet. As the service of light in Evening Prayer concludes with a thanksgiving for light, so the Service of Light, the *lucernarium*, which began the Easter Vigil, concludes with a song of praise of the light newly kindled and spread through the church to give light to the entire community during the nocturnal vigil until the morning star (sun/Son) finally arises.

The text of the Easter Proclamation (or *Praeconium*), called the Exsultet from its first word in Latin (*Exsultet jam angelica turba caelorum*), is very ancient, drawing upon the thought of Ambrose and Augustine and making use of still older texts, among which is the oldest known hymn of praise to the night of Easter, dating from the first half of the fourth century and found in the Easter sermons of Asterius the Sophist and in turn dependent upon the Jewish liturgy of the Passover.[151]

A famous letter (by Jerome?) written in 384 refuses the favor requested by Praesidius to help in the composition of a *laus cerei* (praise of the candle), another name for the Exsultet. St. Augustine in the *City of God* quotes from the first three hexameters of a *laus cerei* which he had composed years before.[152]

Until the sixth century there was considerable freedom left to the presiding minister at the eucharistic celebration to make up appropriate texts; the deacon, likewise, was free to compose an appropriate text for the Easter Proclamation. The present form of the Exsultet probably arose in the world of the Gallican liturgy at the beginning of the seventh century,[153] although the tradition that is was composed by St. Ambrose may not be entirely without foundation.[154]

Nine texts of Easter Proclamations in praise of the candle have survived in their entirety:

1 the Exsultet in use in the Roman rite and followed by the *Book of Common Prayer* and the *Lutheran Book of Worship*, which may be the oldest of the proclamations, found for the first time in the seventh-century *Missale Gothicum* (no. 225), the *Missale Gallicanum vetus* (nos. 132–34), the Bobbio missal (no. 227), and also included in the Gregorian supplement (nos. 1021–22);

---

[150]Ibid., 108.

[151]Adam, 79. "Exsultet," *Orate Fratres* 21 (March 1947):193–205.

[152]Augustine, *City of God* 15.22

[153]Adam, 80.

[154]Nocent, 3:112; "Exsultet," *New Catholic Encyclopedia*.

2 the formula in the "old" Gelasian sacramentary, beginning *Deus mundi conditor* ("God, Creator of the world"), nos. 426–29;

3 the Ambrosian text, still sung in Milan;

4, 5 the two *benedictiones cerei* (blessings of the candle of Ennodius, bishop of Pavia (d. 521);

6 a text of the Visigothic period preserved in the Escorial;

7 the *Vetus Italiana*, or Beneventan, text;

8, 9 the *Benedictio lucernae* and *Benedictio cerei* in the Visigothic Hispanic (Mozarabic) ordinal, the *Liber ordinum*.

By the ninth century the Roman-Gallican form had completely displaced all others.

The Sacramentary directs that "the deacon or, if there is no deacon, the priest sings the Easter proclamation at the lectern or pulpit. All stand and hold lighted candles. If necessary, the Easter proclamation may be sung by one who is not a deacon. In this case the bracketed words 'My dearest friends' up to the end of the introduction are omitted, as is the greeting The Lord be with you."[155]

The Roman, Lutheran, and Episcopal rites all provide a long and a short form of the Exsultet. The sections which may be omitted are marked with brackets in the texts below.

To emphasize the dignity of the Easter Proclamation, the Roman rite has the deacon, as at mass before reading the Gospel, ask the blessing of the priest, who says,

The Lord be in your heart and on your lips, that you may worthily proclaim his Easter praise.
In the name of the Father, and of the Son, + and of the Holy Spirit. *Amen.*[156]

The Exsultet is a noble and rich proclamation and prayer, an extraordinary composition, "one of the rarest treasures of the Roman liturgy,"[157] and the chant to which it is traditionally sung is one of the finest in the Latin liturgy. (It has been adapted by Mark P. Bangert in *Music for the Vigil of Easter* as settings two and three.)

The theme is the victory of Christ the King, and the church's offering of the candle is an act of thanksgiving for all the blessings which the night of Passover-Easter has brought to all creation. The pattern of the Great Thanksgiving from preface through anamnesis to the concluding intercessions is evident.

The Exsultet is in two sections. The first part, a prologue, is a universal invitation to paschal joy,[158] an elaborate invitatory, which moves in ever-decreasing circles, calling first upon heaven and its citizens, then

---

[155] *The Sacramentary*, 174.
[156] Ibid.
[157] O'Shea, 110, but see the comment of Nocent, 3:112–13.
[158] Jean Galliard, *Holy Week and Easter*, trans. William Busch, 3rd rev. ed. (Collegeville: Liturgical Press, 1964), 121.

the earth, the church, and the congregation to rejoice in the victory of Christ, asking as did the bard in ancient epic poetry that the one who sings may be able to do justice to the noble theme.

Roman Catholic	Lutheran	Episcopal
Rejoice, heavenly powers! Sing, choirs of angels! Exult, all creation around God's throne!	Rejoice now, all heavenly choirs of angels, and celebrate the divine mysteries with exultation; and, for the victory of so great a King,	Rejoice now, heavenly hosts and choirs of angels,
Jesus, Christ, our King, is risen! Sound the trumpet of salvation.	sound the trumpet of salvation.	and let your trumpets shout Salvation for the victory of our mighty King.
Rejoice, O earth, in shining splendor, radiant in the brightness of your King! Christ has conquered! Glory fills you!	Exult, also, O earth, enlightened with such radiance; and, made brilliant by the splendor of the eternal King,	Rejoice and sing now, all the round earth, bright with a glorious splendor,
Darkness vanishes for ever!	know that the ancient darkness has been banished from all the world.	for darkness has been vanquished by our eternal King.
Rejoice, O Mother Church! Exult in glory! The risen Savior shines upon you! Let this	Be glad also, O mother Church, clothed with the brightness of such a light, and let this	Rejoice and be glad now, Mother Church,
place resound with joy, echoing the mighty song of all God's people!	house resound with the triumphant voices of the peoples.	and let your holy courts, in radiant light, resound with the praises of your people.
[My dearest friends, standing with me in this holy light, join me in asking God	[Wherefore, dearly beloved, who stand in the clarity of this bright and holy light, join with me, I ask you, in praising the	[All you who stand near this marvelous and holy flame, pray with me to

for mercy, that he may give his unworthy minister the grace to sing his Easter praises.]

lovingkindness of almighty God;

God the Almighty for the grace to sing the worthy praise of this great light;

through our Lord, Jesus Christ, your Son, who lives and rules with you in the unity of the Holy Spirit, one God, now and forever. *Amen.*]

through Jesus Christ his Son our Lord, who lives and reigns with him in the unity of the Holy Spirit, one God, for ever and ever. *Amen.*]

The second part of the Exsultet, the actual praise of the candle (*laus cerei*) and proclamation of Easter (a paschal "preface" in the original liturgical sense of the word, a solemn proclamation of praise) begins with the traditional dialogue establishing a sense of mutuality and interdependence.

The Lord be with you.
And also with you.
Lift up your hearts.
We lift them up to the Lord.
Let us give thanks to the Lord our God.
It is right to give him thanks and praise.

The Lord be with you.
And also with you.

Let us give thanks to the Lord our God.
It is right to give him thanks and praise.

The Lord be with you.
And also with you.

Let us give thanks to the Lord our God.
It is right to give him thanks and praise.

The Lutheran and Episcopal forms of the dialogue follow the rule of the *Apostolic Tradition* and reserve the second of the three exchanges for the Eucharist.

The great hymn is a thanksgiving for the history of salvation: the ransom of fallen Adam, the prefiguring of redemption in the Passover lamb, the Red Sea, the pillar of fire; the triumphant victory of Christ. The theme of light connects creation and redemption, as in Paul: "For it is the God who said, 'Let light shine out of darkness,' who has shone in our hearts to give the light of the knowledge of the glory of God in the face of Christ" (2 Cor. 4:6). Christ's victory parallels and fulfills the Passover: *that* night is set beside *this* night, type and antitype, preparation and fulfillment. In a lyrical meditation on the second chapter of Philippians, the deacon rapturously praises the wonder of the *kenosis* of the Son of God, who emptied himself of his divine glory in order to ransom his people.

It is truly right

It is indeed right and salutary

It is truly right and good, always and

267

		everywhere, with our whole
that with full hearts and minds and voices we should praise the unseen God, the all-powerful Father, and his only Son, our Lord Jesus Christ.	that we should with full devotion of heart and mind and voice praise the invisible God, the Father Almighty, and his only Son, our Lord, Jesus Christ;	heart and mind and voice, to praise you, the invisible, almighty, and eternal God, and your only-begotten Son, Jesus Christ our Lord;
For Christ has ransomed us with his blood, and paid for us the price of Adam's sin to our eternal Father!	who paid for us the debt of Adam to the eternal Father, and who by his precious blood redeemed us from the bondage to the ancient sin.	for he is the true Paschal Lamb, who at the feast of the Passover paid for us the debt of Adam's sin and by his blood delivered your faithful people.

The present liturgical moment, this night, is praised in raptured joy.

This is our passover feast, when Christ, the true Lamb, is slain, whose blood consecrates the homes of all believers.	For this indeed is the Paschal Feast in which the true Lamb is slain, by whose blood the doorposts of the faithful are made holy.	
This is the night when first you saved our fathers: you freed	This is the night in which, in ancient times, you delivered our forebears,	This is the night, when you brought our fathers,
the people of Israel from their slavery and led them dry-shod through the sea.	the children of Israel, from the land of Egypt; and led them, dry-shod, through the Red Sea.	the children of Israel, out of bondage in Egypt, and led them through the Red Sea on dry land.
[This is the night when the pillar of fire destroyed the darkness of sin!] This is the night when Christians everywhere, washed clean of sin	[This, indeed, is the night in which the darkness of sin has been purged away by the rising brightness.] This is the night in which all who believe in Christ are rescued from evil	This is the night, when all who believe in Christ are delivered from

and freed from all defilement, are restored to grace and grow together in holiness.	and the gloom of sin, are renewed in grace, and are restored to holiness.	the gloom of sin, and are restored to grace and holiness of life.
This is the night when Jesus Christ broke the chains of death and rose triumphant from the grave.	This is the night in which, breaking the chains of death, Christ arises from hell in triumph.	This is the night, when Christ broke the bonds of death and hell, and rose victorious from the grave.
[What good would life have been to us, had Christ not come as our Redeemer?]	[For it would have profited us nothing to be born had we not also been redeemed.	
Father, how wonderful your care for us! How boundless your merciful love !	[Oh, how wonderful the condescension of your lovingkindness! Oh, how inestimable the goodness of your love,	[How wonderful and beyond our knowing, O God, is your mercy and loving-kindness to us;
To ransom a slave you gave away your Son.	that to redeem a slave you delivered up your Son!	that to redeem a slave, you gave a Son.

The fullness of the emotion of this soaring hymn gives rise to language that strains the bounds of logic and the usual liturgical restraint. The expansive paradox of the *felix culpa*, the happy fault, has found its way into the fourth stanza of Frederick W. Faber's hymn "There's a Wideness in God's Mercy" (no. 290) as well as John Milton's *Paradise Lost* (Book xii, ll. 473–78). (See Rom. 5:20.)[159]

O happy fault, O necessary sin of Adam, which gained for us	[O necessary sin of Adam that is wiped away by the death of Christ! [O happy fault that was worthy to have
so great a Redeemer!	so great a Redeemer!]
[Most blessed of all nights, chosen by God to see Christ	O night truly blessed which alone was worthy to know the time and the hour wherein Christ
rising from the dead!	rose again from hell!

[159]See Arthur O. Lovejoy, "Milton and the Paradox of the Fortunate Fall," chap. 14 of his *Essays in the History of Ideas* (Baltimore: Johns Hopkins Press, 1948).

[Of this night
scripture says:
"The night will be as
clear as day:
it will become my
light, my joy."]

[This is the night of
which it is written:
"and the night is as
clear as the day"; and,
"then shall my night
be turned into day."]

The reference is to Psalm 139:12. This night of Christ's rising returns humanity to the perfection of paradise, restoring what was lost through the fall and establishing the messianic kingdom.

The power of this holy
night dispels all evil

washes guilt away,
restores lost innocence,
brings mourners
joy;
[it casts out hatred,
brings us peace, and
humbles earthly
pride.]

Night truly blessed
when heaven is wedded
to earth and
man is reconciled with
God!

[The holiness of this
night puts to flight
the deeds of wicked-
ness; washes away sin;
restores innocence to
the fallen, and joy
to those who mourn;
casts out hate;
bring peace; and
humbles earthly
pride.]

[How holy is this
night, when wickedness
is put to flight, and
sin is washed away.
It restores innocence
to the fallen, and joy
to those who mourn.
It casts out pride
and hatred, and brings
peace and concord.

[How blessed is this
night, when earth and
heaven are joined and
man is reconciled to
God.]

The *Lutheran Book of Worship* follows the earlier medieval practice of fixing grains of incense in the candle during the singing of the Exsultet. (In the present Roman rite it is part of the preparation of the candle.) The use of the grains of incense arose apparently through a misunderstanding of the word *incensum* in the text of the Exsultet. In context it means "lighted" and refers to the candle, but it was mistaken for another word spelled the same way but with a different meaning, "incense." The *Lutheran Book of Worship* in its conservatism thus preserves what may well be an error, although one of long standing.[160]

[*The assisting minster
may fix five grains of
incense in the candle.*]

The deacon singing the Exsultet now at last makes reference to the paschal candle itself, recalling its anticipation in the pillar of fire which led the Israelites through their nights in the wilderness and which was in fact God's own presence with his people.

[160]Nocent, 3:109; C. E. Pocknee, "Paschal Candle" in the *Dictionary of Liturgy and Worship* (1972).

Therefore, heavenly
Father, in the joy
of this night receive
our evening sacrifice
of praise,
your Church's
solemn
offering.
Accept this Easter
candle,

[Therefore in this night
of grace, receive O
holy Father, this
evening sacrifice
of praise; which the
Church lays before
you in the solemn
offering of the candle.
We sing the glories of
this pillar of fire,]

Holy Father, accept
our evening sacrifice
the offering of this
candle in your honor

The hymn praises the mystery of candlelight, endlessly divisible, yet without loss. The flame from which light is taken burns as brightly as before.

[*Tapers are lighted from
the paschal candle to
light other candles and
lamps as the Easter
Proclamation continues.*

[a flame divided but
undimmed, a pillar
of fire that glows to
the honor of God.]

the brightness of which
is not diminished,
even when its light
is divided and borrowed.]

The wonders of this night bind all creation together in one interdependent and mutually instructive whole. The natural world shows the ethical foundation of the cosmos and can teach the church lessons in sacrificial living. Bees give freely of themselves to provide the wax for the candle, and in its turn the candle gives unstintingly of itself for the benefit of others, giving itself so that the church might have light. The bees and the candle both provide an example for the church to emulate, as all imitate the *kenosis* of Christ, who emptied himself for the life of the world.[161] Thus the marriage metaphor is most apt.

[For it is fed by the
melting wax which
the bees, your servants,
have made for the
substance of this
candle.]

O night truly blessed
in which heaven and
earth are joined —

---

[161] See Shakespeare's Sonnet 73:
In me thou see'st the glowing of such fire,
That on the ashes of his youth doth lie,
As the death-bed whereon it must expire,
Consumed with that which it was nourished by.

things human and
things divine.

The soaring lyricism of the praise asks an apotheosis of the paschal candle:

[Let it mingle with	We, therefore, pray to you, O Lord, that this candle, burning to the honor of your name,	May it shine continually to
the lights of heaven and continue bravely burning] to dispel the darkness of this night!	will continue to vanquish the darkness of this night and [be mingled with the lights of heaven.]	drive away all darkness.

Candle and rising sun and Christ the rising Sun of Justice and Righteousness are all brought together when the full light shines.

May the Morning Star which never sets find this flame still burning: Christ that Morning Star, who came back from the dead, and shed his peaceful light on all mankind,	[May he who is the morning star find it burning — that morning star which never sets, that morning star which, rising again from the grave,] faithfully sheds light on all the human race.	May Christ, the Morning Star who knows no setting, find it ever burning — he who gives his light to all creation, and
	[And we pray, O Lord, rule, govern, and preserve with your continual protection your whole Church, giving us peace in this time of our paschal rejoicing;] through the same Lord, Jesus Christ,	
your Son who lives and reigns for	your Son, who lives and reigns with you and the Holy Spirit, one God, now and	who lives and reigns for
ever and ever. *Amen.*	forever. *Amen.*	ever and ever. *Amen.*

The theme of light, finally, is intensely eschatological and points not only to the resurrection but to the parousia as well. "Let your loins be girded and your lamps burning, and be like men who are waiting for their master to come home..." (Luke 12:35–37). At its close, the great hymn looks to the *eschaton* to which Easter points, when God will be all in all.[162]

2. THE SERVICE OF READINGS. The Vigil proper now begins. The preparatory service of light, from the striking of the new fire through the proclamation of Easter in the Exsultet, serves as an entrance rite for the Liturgy of the Word which follows it. Anciently, the lessons were the final instruction of the catechumens, and the series of readings extended through the night until cockcrow.

For both practical and symbolic reasons the lessons are read near and in the light of the paschal candle.[163] As the Old Testament prepared for Christ, waiting in hope for the fulfillment of God's promises, so the Christian church, the new life already begun, waits in hope for the consummation and the final revelation.

The Roman and Episcopal rites provide a helpful introduction to the readings, describing briefly the context in which they are to be proclaimed and heard, which may not be obvious to the congregation. "In these or similar words" the priest says,

The Sacramentary	*Book of Common Prayer*
Dear friends in Christ, we have begun our solemn vigil. Let us now listen attentively to the word of God, recalling how he saved his people throughout history and, in the fullness of time, sent his own Son to be our Redeemer. Through this Easter celebration, may God bring to perfection the saving work he has begun in us. (p. 187)	Let us hear the record of God's saving deeds in history, how he saved his people in ages past; and let us pray that our God will bring each of us to the fullness of redemption. (p. 288)

The Episcopal form is an adaptation of the address in the Roman sacramentary.

The number of lessons read at the Vigil has varied greatly. Medieval books give no fewer than four lessons (as, for example, in the Gregorian sacramentary) and as many as twelve (as in the Gelasian sacramentary). The liturgy for Holy Saturday in the 1570 Roman missal provided twelve Old Testament "Prophecies." The 1969 missal has reduced the number to seven (the holy number), followed by the Epistle and Gospel of the Eucharist, making nine lessons in all.

The Roman rite allows for the reading of fewer lessons than the seven provided "for pastoral reasons,"

---

[162] Roger Greenacre, *The Sacrament of Easter* (London: Faith Press, 1965), 74. See Rev. 2:28; 22:16; 2 Pet. 1:19; cf. Numb. 24:27.
[163] Nocent, 3:113.

but it must always be borne in mind that the reading of the word of God is the fundamental element of the Easter Vigil. At least three readings from the Old Testament should be read, although for more serious reasons the number may be reduced to two. The reading from Exodus 14, however, is never to be omitted.[164]

The *Lutheran Book of Worship* is slightly less forceful in its preference for the use of a large body of Scripture in the Vigil:

Twelve readings are appointed. The number may be reduced to seven or four, but the first and fourth lessons should always be read (Min. Ed., p. 147).

The *Book of Common Prayer* provides nine lessons but directs:

At least two of the following Lessons should always be read, of which one is always the Lesson from Exodus (p. 288).

Roman Catholic Liturgy of the Word	Lutheran Service of Readings	Episcopal Liturgy of the Word
I. Gen. 1:1–2:2 *or* 1:1, 26–31a *Ps. 104:1–2a, 5–6 10 & 12 Refrain v. 30* or *Ps. 33:4–5, 6–7, 12–13, 20 & 22 Refrain v. 5b*	I. Gen. 1:1–2:2 *or* 1:1–3:4	I. Gen. 1:1–2:2 *Ps. 33:1–11* or *36:5–10*
	II. Gen. 7:1–5, 11–18; 8:6–18; 9:8–13	II. Gen. 7:1–5, 11–18; 8:6–18; 9:8–13 *Ps. 46*
II. Gen. 22:1–18 *or* 22:1–2, 9a, 10–13, 15–18 *Ps. 16:5 & 8, 9–10, 11 Refrain v. 1*	III. Gen. 22:1–18	III. Gen. 22:1–18 *Ps. 33:12–22* or *Ps. 16*
III. Exod. 14:15–15:1 *Exod. 15:1–2, 3–4, 5–6, 17–18 Refrain v. 1a*	IV. Exod. 14:10–15:1a *or* 13:17–15:1a *Song of Moses and Miriam (Exod. 15:1b–2, 6, 11, 13, 17–18)*	IV. Exod. 14:10–15:1 *Song of Moses (Exod. 15:1–6, 11–13, 17–18)*
		V. Isa. 4:2–6 *Ps. 122*
IV. Isa. 54:5–14 *Ps. 30:2, 4, 5–6 11–12a, 13b Refrain v. 2a*		
V. Isa. 55:1–11 *Isa. 12:2–3, 4b–6 Refrain v. 3*	V. Isa. 55:1–11	VI. Isa. 55:1–11 *Isa. 12:2–6*

---

[164] *The Sacramentary*, 187.

VI. Baruch 3:9–15,   VI. Baruch 3:9–37
    32–4:4
    Ps. 19:8, 9, 10, 11
    Refrain John 6:69b

VII. Ezek. 36:16–17a, 18–28   VII. Ezek. 36:24–28
    Ps. 42:3, 5bcd; 43:3, 4   *Ps. 42:1–7*
    Refrain 42:2   or *Isa. 12:2–6*

                VII. Ezek. 37:1–14   VIII. Ezek. 37:1–14
                                        Ps. 30
                                  or *Ps. 143*

                                  IX. Zeph. 3:12–20
                                  Ps. 98
                                  or *Ps. 126*

                VIII. Isa. 4:2–4
                      The Song of the Vineyard
                      (Isa. 5:1–2b, 7a)

                IX. Exod. 12:1–14
                   or 12:1–24

                X. Jonah 3:1–10

                XI. Deut. 31:19–30
                      A Song of Moses
                      Deut. 32:1–4, 7, 36, 43a

                XII. Dan. 3:1–23 (Song of
                    the Three Young Men
                    1–2, 23–27) 24–29
                    or Dan. 3:1–29
                    Benedicite, Omnia Opera
                    (Song of the Three Young Men
                    35–60, 62–65)

The *Lutheran Book of Worship*, following its affinity for the Easter Vigil in the old Roman missal, gives the twelve lessons from the 1570 Roman missal, which are from the eighth-century *Comes* of Murbach, behind which lies the ten-lesson series of the old Gelasian sacramentary.

    The choice and significance of the Old Testament readings at the Easter Vigil can only be understood in the light of their Jewish background and use.[165] Genesis 1 is read first because the creation of the world is also a Passover and Easter event.[166] The pre-Christian Book of Jubilees places the creation of the world during the Passover month of Nisan, and for Philo of Alexandria the month of Nisan, together with the spring equinox, constitutes an image of the beginning of all things, and the Passover is a commemoration of the origin of the world. The New Testament describes the church as a new creation (2 Cor. 5:17;

---

[165]Rupert Berger and Hans Hollerweger, eds., *Celebrating the Easter Vigil*, trans. Matthew J. O'Connell (New York: Pueblo Publishing Co., 1983), 11.

[166]*Celebrating the Easter Vigil*, 24. See also Susan Niditch, *Chaos to Cosmos: Studies in Biblical Patterns of Creation* (Chico, CA: Scholars Press, 1985) and Mircea Eliade, *Cosmos and History: The Myth of the Eternal Return*, trans. Willard R. Trask (New York: Harper & Row, 1959), pub. in 1954 by Pantheon Books as *The Myth of the Eternal Return*.

Gal. 5:17), and the annual awakening of nature to new life each spring is richly symbolic of this spiritual renewal.[167]

An allegorical and typological interpretation of each reading is suggested by the prayer which follows each lesson, interprets it, and relates it to the paschal transition from death to life.[168] Following the first reading, the account of creation, the collect (no. 51) is from the Leonine sacramentary (no. 1239); Gregorian (no. 1025); it is, in a slightly different translation, the Prayer of the Day (no. 8) in the *Lutheran Book of Worship* for the First Sunday after Christmas (for the Second Sunday after Christmas in the *Book of Common Prayer*). The English translation in the Lutheran and Episcopal books derives from the proposed English Prayer Book of 1928.

The second lesson appointed in the *Lutheran Book of Worship* is the story of the flood (Gen. 7:1–5, 11–18; 8:6–18; 9:8–13), a "type" of baptism (see 1 Pet. 4:18–22). This lesson is followed by a collect (no. 52) from the Gelasian sacramentary (no. 432) and the Gregorian (no. 1027) as in the Roman Missal of 1570. In the Gelasian sacramentary this prayer was used after the first lesson, Genesis 1; the Roman sacramentary of 1969 appoints it after its seventh reading (Ezek. 36:16–17a, 18–28); the *Book of Common Prayer* appoints it after its ninth lesson (Zeph. 3:12–20). The English translation in the Lutheran book is a revision of the translation by William Bright in *Ancient Collects* (p. 92), which had been used in the *Service Book and Hymnal* (p. 218) as the first of the Collects and Prayers "For the Church."

Service Book and Hymnal	*Lutheran Book of Worship*
O God of unchangeable power and eternal light, look favorably on thy whole Church, that wonderful and sacred mystery; and, by the tranquil operation of thy perpetual Providence, carry out the work of man's salvation; and let the whole world feel and see that things which were cast down are being raised up, that things which had grown old are being made new, and that all things are returning to perfection through him from whom they	O God, strength of the powerless and light in all darkness: Look in mercy upon your Church, that wonderful and sacred mystery, that it may be an ark of peace in the midst of chaos.

Let the whole world experience and see that what has fallen is being raised up, that what was old is being made new, and that all things are being restored to wholeness through him from whom they |

---

[167]*Celebrating the Easter Vigil*, 25.

[168]On such typological interpretation see Northrop Frye, *The Great Code* (New York: Harcourt Brace Jovanovich, 1982), 78–123; Paul Minear, *The Literary Uses of Typology: From the Late Middle Ages to the Present* (Princeton: University Press, 1977); Adrian Wilson and Joyce Lancaster Wilson, *A Medieval Mirror: Speculum Humanae Salvationis 1324–1500* (Berkeley: University of California Press, 1985).

took their origin, even thy Son,
Jesus Christ our Lord.

first took being, your Son,
Jesus Christ our Lord.

The third lesson tells of Abraham's willingness to sacrifice Isaac, his only son. The Book of Jubilees (18:18–19; 17:15; 18:3) understands the sacrifice of Isaac as the origin of the week-long feast of unleavened bread at Passover. The sacrifice of Isaac is the prototype of all sacrifice, and the temple where sacrifices were performed was thought to have been built on the same site as the sacrifice of Isaac. The theme of the firstborn is common to the sacrifice of Isaac, Passover, and the crucifixion. God rescued Isaac and Israel from death, and for the church this was the pattern that was fulfilled by the resurrection of God's beloved firstborn and only-begotten.[169]

The prayer (no. 53) after the third lesson is from the Gelasian sacramentary (no. 434) and the Gregorian (no. 1029):

Deus, fidelium pater summe, qui in toto orbem terrarum promissionis tuae filios diffusa adoptione multiplicas et per paschale sacramentum Abraham puerum tuum universarum, sicut iurasti, gencium efficis patrem: da populis tuis digne ad graciam tuae vocationis intrare: per.

Each rite has its own translation of the collect.

Roman Catholic	Lutheran	Episcopal
God and Father of all who believe in you, you promised Abraham that he would become the father of all nations, and through the death and resurrection of Christ you fulfill that promise: everywhere throughout the world you increase your chosen people. May we respond to your call by joyfully accepting your invitation to the new life of grace. We ask this through Christ our Lord.	God and Father of all the faithful, you promised Abraham that he would become the father of all nations, and through this paschal mystery you increase your chosen people throughout the world. Help us to respond to your call by joyfully accepting the new life of grace. We ask this through your Son, Jesus Christ our Lord.	God and Father of all believers, for the glory of your Name multiply, by the grace of this Paschal sacrament, the number of your children; that your Church may rejoice to see fulfilled your promise to our father Abraham; through Jesus Christ our Lord.

The fourth lesson, required in all the rites, reports the central event of the Exodus and the formative act for ancient Israel, the passage through the Red Sea. God intervened decisively to deliver his people from bondage, to wall them off by water from their old life as slaves in a

---

[169] *Celebrating the Easter Vigil*, 22.

foreign country, and to lead them through the years of preparation to their own land. So God continues to lead his people through the waters of baptism to deliver them from slavery to sin and guide them to their promised heavenly home.

Following the fourth lesson, the prayer (no. 54) from the Gelasian sacramentary (no. 435) and Gregorian supplement (no. 1031) is appointed:

Deus, cujus antiqua miracula etiam nostris saeculis curruscare sentimus, dum quod uni populo a persecutione Aegyptia liberando dexterae tuae potentia contulisti, id in salute gentium per aquam regenerationis operaris: praesta, ut in Abrahae filios et in Israeliticam dignitatem tocius mundi transeat plenitudo: per.

The Gregorian sacramentary has a different version of this prayer (no. 365) associated with the same reading. The Lutheran translation is a slight adaptation of the collect in the *Book of Common Prayer*, altered, it was thought, to enhance the flow.

Roman Catholic	Lutheran	Episcopal
Father, even today we see the wonders of the miracles you worked long ago. You once saved a single nation from slavery, and now you offer that salvation to all through baptism. May the peoples of the world become true sons of Abraham and prove worthy of the heritage of Israel. We ask this through Christ our Lord.	O God, whose wonderful deeds of old shine forth even to our own day: By the power of your mighty arm you once delivered your chosen people from slavery under Pharaoh, a sign for us of the salvation of all nations by the water of baptism. Grant that all the peoples of the earth may be numbered among the offspring of Abraham and may rejoice in the inheritance of Israel; through your son Jesus Christ our Lord.	O God, whose wonderful deeds of old shine forth even to our own day, you once delivered by the power of your mighty arm your chosen people from slavery under Pharaoh, to be a sign for us of the salvation of all nations by the water of baptism. Grant that all the peoples of the earth may be numbered among the offspring of Abraham, and rejoice in the inheritance of Israel; through Jesus Christ our Lord.

or
Lord God,
in the new covenant
you shed light on the
miracles you worked
in ancient times:
the Red Sea is a symbol

of our baptism,
and the nation you
freed from slavery
is a sign of your
Christian people.
May every nation
share the faith and
privilege of Israel
and come to new birth
in the Holy Spirit.
We ask this through
Christ our Lord.

The alternative prayer in *The Sacramentary* is a translation of the same Latin collect but is an attempt at making more explicit for modern congregations the significance of the Old Testament types.

The fifth lesson in the Roman sacramentary and in the *Lutheran Book of Worship* (the sixth lesson in the *Book of Common Prayer*) is about salvation freely offered to all (Isa. 55:1–11). The Lutheran collect (no. 55) is borrowed from the *Book of Common Prayer;* it is based on an earlier composition by H. Boone Porter. In the Roman sacramentary the prayer following this reading is a new composition deriving from the Gelasian (no. 438) and the Gregorian sacramentary (no. 1039):

Almighty, ever-living God,
only hope of the world,
by the preaching of the prophets
you proclaimed the mysteries we are celebrating tonight.
Help us to be your faithful people,
for it is by your inspiration alone
that we can grow in goodness.
We ask this through Christ our Lord.

A rubric follows, "Prayers may also be chosen from those given after the following readings, if the readings are omitted."[170]

Following the sixth lesson, from Baruch about the fountain of wisdom, a collect (no. 56) from the Gregorian sacramentary (no. 1035) is appointed as in the 1570 Roman Missal:

Deus, qui ecclesiam tuam semper gentium vocatione multiplicas, concede propitius, ut, quos aqua baptismatis abluis, continua protectione tuearis.

The Sacramentary and the *Lutheran Book of Worship* each provide independent translations:

Roman Catholic	Lutheran
Father you increase your Church by continuing to call all people to	O God, you increase your Church by continuing to call all peoples to

---

[170] *The Sacramentary*, 190.

salvation. Listen to our prayers and always watch over those you cleanse in baptism. We ask this through Christ our Lord.

salvation. Let the cleansing waters of Baptism flow, and by your love watch over those whom you have called; through your Son, Jesus Christ our Lord.

The seventh lesson, Ezekiel 37, the valley of the dry bones, was at an early date used as the reading from the prophets on the Sabbath of passover week in the liturgy of the synagogue.[171] The Hebrew slaves in Egypt, their hope gone, were delivered and made into a mighty nation, and when they came into their own land they brought the bones of Joseph with them for burial.

After the lesson from Ezekiel, the Gelasian sacramentary (no. 437) and the Gregorian sacramentary (no. 1037) appointed this collect:

Deus, qui nos ad caelebrandum paschale sacramentum utriusque testamenti paginis inbuisti, da nobis intelligere misericordias tuas, ut ex perceptione praesentium munerum firma sit expectatio futurorum: per.

The prayer in the *Lutheran Book of Worship* (no. 57) following this lesson draws its address from the collect in the *Book of Common Prayer* which follows this reading and its petition from the Latin collect, which is translated in *The Sacramentary* as an alternative prayer following the seventh reading (Ezek. 36:16–17a, 18–28).

Roman Catholic	Lutheran	Episcopal
Father, you teach us in both the Old and the New Testament to celebrate this passover mystery. Help us to understand your great love for us. May the goodness you now show us confirm our hope in your future mercy. We ask this through Christ our Lord.	O God, by the Passover of the Son you have brought us out of sin into righteousness and out of death into life. Give us such an understanding of your mercy that, in receiving the gifts of Word and Sacrament now, we may learn to hope for all your gifts to come; Jesus Christ our Lord.	Almighty God, by the Passover of your Son you have brought us out of sin into righteousness and out of death into life: Grant to those who are sealed by your Holy Spirit the will and the power to proclaim you to all the world; through Jesus Christ our Lord. through your Son,

The Episcopal collect is based on an earlier composition by H. Boone Porter.

Following the eighth lesson, Isaiah's vision of God's presence in a renewed Israel (Isa. 4:2–6), the Gelasian sacramentary appoints this prayer (no. 438; Gregorian no. 1039):

---

[171] *Celebrating the Easter Vigil*, 24.

Deus, qui in omnibus ecclesiae tuae filiis sanctorum prophaetarum voce manifestasti in omni loco dominationis tuae satorem te bonorum seminum et electorum palmitum esse cultore: tribe populis tuis qui et vinearum apud te nomine censentur et segitum, ut spinarum et tribulorum squalore resecato digni efficiantur fruge foecundi: per.

The English translation was made for the *Lutheran Book of Worship* (no. 58).

Following the ninth lesson, about the passover lamb (Exod. 12:1–14 or 12:1–24), the Gelasian sacramentary (no. 433) and the Gregorian (no. 1041) appointed this prayer:

Omnipotens sempiterne Deus, qui in omnium operum tuorum dispensatione mirabilis es, intelligant redempti tui non fuisse excellentius quod initio factus est mundus, quam quod in finem saeculorum Pascha nostrum immolatus est Christus: per eundem dominum.

It was translated for the *Lutheran Book of Worship* (no. 59).

Following the tenth lesson, about Jonah's preaching in Nineveh (Jon. 3:1–10), a prayer from the Gelasian sacramentary (no. 439; Gregorian no. 1043) appointed:

Deus, qui diuersitatem omnium genitum in confessione tui nominis unum esse fecisti, da nobis et uelle et posse quae praecipis, ut populo ad aeternitatem uocato una sit fides mentium et pietas actionum: per.

The English translation was made for the *Lutheran Book of Worship* (no. 60).

Following the eleventh lesson, Moses' warning to the people (Deut. 31:19–30), the Gelasian sacramentary appointed this prayer (no. 440; Gregorian no. 1045):

Deus, celsitudo humilium et fortitudo rectorum, qui per sanctum Moysen puerum tuum ita erudire populos tuos sacri carminis tui decantatione uoluisti, ut illa legis iternacio fieret etiam nostra directio: excita in omnem justificatarum gencium plenitudinem potentiam tuam, et da laeticiam mitigando terrorem, ut omnium peccatis tua remissione deletis, quod denuntiatum est in ultionem transeat in salutem: per.

This prayer was translated for the *Lutheran Book of Worship* (no. 61).

3. THE SERVICE OF HOLY BAPTISM. In the Roman rite, the Liturgy of the Word continues with the Gloria in Excelsis, the Collect, the Epistle, Alleluia, Gospel, and homily. Then the third part of the Vigil, the Liturgy of Baptism, begins. This is an alternative practice permitted by the rubrics in the *Book of Common Prayer* (p. 292).

In the Lutheran rite, following the Prayer Book and the rite in the medieval missals, the service of readings is understood to be preparatory to the celebration of Holy Baptism, and that sacrament, or the renewal of baptismal vows if there are no candidates for baptism, follows directly.

The Lutheran rite, following the medieval missals, directs that the paschal candle be taken to the font for the Service of Baptism. The

Roman sacramentary directs that if there is to be a procession of some length to the baptistery, the Easter candle is carried first, followed by the candidates and their godparents, and the priest with the ministers.

In the Lutheran rite, the procession to the font is made during the singing of the canticle *Benedicite, Omnia Opera;* in the Roman sacramentary it may be during the singing of the abbreviated form of the Litany of the Saints. The Lutheran rite thus emphasizes the redemption of the cosmos and the role of nature in the praise of God while the Roman rite emphasizes the community of holy people into which the baptized are received.

Anciently, the Easter Vigil was the time for baptism, and the center of the rite still is the celebration of Holy Baptism or, if there are no candidates for baptism, the renewal of baptismal promises.

Continuing a custom that developed in the Middle Ages giving dramatic impact to the action at the font and tying the baptism, death, and resurrection of Christ to the baptismal dying and rising of the candidates, both the Roman and Lutheran rites permit the presiding minister to lower the paschal candle into the water one or three times at the conclusion of the Thanksgiving.[172] In the Roman rite the action clearly complements the words:

The priest may lower the Easter candle into the water either once or three times as he continues:
> We ask you, Father, with your Son
> to send the Holy Spirit upon the waters of this font.

He holds the candle in the water:
> May all who are buried with Christ
> in the death of baptism
> rise also with him to newness of life.
> We ask this through Christ our Lord.

Then the candle is taken out of the water as the people sing the acclamation:
> Springs of water, bless the Lord.
> Give him glory and praise for ever.

Since the candle represents Christ — ritually it *is* Christ — the action of lowering it into the font signifies Christ going into the Jordan to be baptized. And as the ancient church often declared, Jesus going into the Jordan baptized and sanctified the waters of the earth.

The sexual symbolism of the phallic candle entering the font which is called the womb of the Church from which new Christians will come forth is apparent to those who have been taught to see such things,[173] but it is not referred to in the text of the liturgy.

In the Lutheran rite, the renewal of the baptismal promises is made at the time of the profession of the faith by the candidates or, if there

---

[172] Min. Ed., p. 25; *The Sacramentary*, 202.
[173] See Alan Watts, *Myth and Ritual in Christianity* (Boston: Beacon Press, 1968), 179–180, n. 2. But see Alex Stock in *Blessing and Power*, ed. Mary Collins and David Power (Edinburgh: T. & T. Clark, 1985), 44–45.

are no candidates for baptism, by a separate renunciation of evil and profession of faith in the triune God. In the Roman and Episcopal rites, the renewal of baptismal promises is set out in a separate portion of the rite with an introductory address and a prayerful conclusion.

Roman Catholic	Episcopal

Roman Catholic

Dear friends,
through the paschal mystery
we have been buried with
Christ in baptism,
so that we may rise with him
to a new life.
Now that we have completed
our lenten observance,
let us renew the promises
we made in baptism
when we rejected Satan
and all his works,
and promised to serve God faithfully
in his holy Catholic Church.

And so:
Do you reject Satan?
I do.
And all his works?
I do.
And all his empty promises?
I do.

or

Do you reject sin, so as to
live in the freedom of God's
children?
I do.
Do you reject the glamor of evil,
and refuse to be mastered
by sin?
I do.
Do you reject Satan, the father
of sin and prince of darkness?
I do.

Do you believe in God, the
Father Almighty, creator of
heaven and earth?
I do.
Do you believe in Jesus Christ,
his only Son, our Lord, who was

Episcopal

Through the Paschal mystery,
dear friends,
we are buried with
Christ by Baptism into his death,
and raised with him
to newness of life.
I call upon you, therefore, now that
our lenten observance is ended
to renew the solemn promises
and vows of Holy Baptism,
by which we once renounced Satan
and all his works,
and promised to serve God faithfully
in his holy Catholic Church.

Do you reaffirm your renunciation
of evil and renew your commitment
to Jesus Christ?
I do.

Do you believe in God the Father?
*I believe in God, the Father
almighty, creator of heaven and
earth.*
Do you believe in Jesus Christ,
the Son of God?

born of the Virgin Mary, was
crucified, died, and was buried,
rose from the dead, and is now
seated at the right hand of
the Father?
I do.

*I believe in Jesus Christ, his
only Son, our Lord. He was
conceived by the power of the Holy
Spirit and born of the Virgin Mary.
He suffered under Pontius Pilate,
was crucified, died and was buried.
He descended to the dead. On the
third day he rose again. He ascended
into heaven, and is seated at the
right hand of the Father. He will
come again to judge the living
and the dead.*
Do you believe in God the Holy Spirit?
*I believe in the Holy Spirit,
the holy catholic Church,
the communion of saints,
the forgiveness of sins,
the resurrection of the body,
and the life everlasting.*

Do you believe in
the Holy Spirit,
the holy Catholic Church,
the communion of saints,
the forgiveness of sins,
the resurrection of the body,
and life everlasting?
I do.

Will you continue in the apostles'
teaching and fellowship, in the
breaking of bread, and in the
prayers?
I will, with God's help.
Will you persevere in resisting
evil, and, whenever you fall into
sin, repent and turn to the Lord?
I will, with God's help.
Will you proclaim by word and
example the Good News of God
in Christ?
I will, with God's help.
Will you seek and serve Christ in
all persons, loving your neighbor
as yourself?
I will, with God's help.
Will you strive for justice and peace
among all people, and respect the
dignity of every human being?
I will, with God's help.

God, the all-powerful Father
of our Lord Jesus Christ,
has given us a new birth
by water and the Holy Spirit
and forgiven
all our sins,
May he also keep us faithful

May Almighty God, the Father
of our Lord Jesus Christ,
who has given us a new birth
by water and the Holy Spirit,
and bestowed upon us
the forgiveness of sins,
keep us in eternal life by his grace,

to our Lord Jesus Christ   in Christ Jesus our Lord.
for ever and ever.
Amen.   *Amen.*

The introduction and conclusion of the Episcopal rite are taken from the Roman missal.

The Roman and Lutheran rites then suggest sprinkling the congregation with baptismal water.[174]

4. THE SERVICE OF HOLY COMMUNION. The Service of Holy Communion at the Easter Vigil begins with the joyful singing of the Hymn of Praise, properly not sung since the beginning of Lent. The Lutheran and Roman liturgies prescribe the Gloria in Excelsis,[175] during which the altar candles are lighted and the church bells rung to sound the joy of the resurrection.[176] The Prayer Book gives a choice of one of three canticles: the Gloria in Excelsis, the Te Deum, or "Christ our Passover," a creation of the 1549 Prayer Book for Morning Prayer on Easter Day.

The Roman sacramentary appoints a Prayer of the Day for the Vigil from the Gelasian (no. 454) and the Gregorian (no. 377) sacramentaries and the Bobbio missal (no. 258). The *Church Book* (1868) appointed that prayer for Easter Eve, and the *Common Service Book* appointed it for Saturday in Holy Week, although it clearly is appropriate only for a service at night. The translation in the *Church Book* was continued in the *Common Service Book:*

O God, Who didst enlighten this most holy night with the glory of the Lord's Resurrection; Preserve in all Thy people the spirit of adoption which Thou hast given, so that renewed in body and soul they may perform unto Thee a pure service; through the same, our Lord Jesus Christ, who liveth and reigneth with Thee and the Holy Ghost, ever one God, world without end.

The collect anticipates Easter dawn, recalls the custom of baptizing catechumens on this day, and may allude to the practice of lighting lamps in churches and homes on Easter Eve as the "new fire" shows the glory of the resurrection.[177]

The Prayer Book includes this collect for the first time, replacing one from the 1662 book, as an alternative to the prayer "O God, who for our redemption" described below.

The *Lutheran Book of Worship* provides no Prayer of the Day specifically for the Vigil (although the historic prayer was available in the *Common Service Book*), but the first prayer for Easter Day, "O God, you gave your only Son" (no. 62), may appropriately make the transition from Lent to Easter, from the old life under the power of death to the new life of daily repentance and joyful living.

---

[174]Min. Ed., p. 152: *The Sacramentary*, 205.

[175]Min. Ed., p. 152; *The Sacramentary*, 192.

[176]Marion Hatchett (p. 249) quotes the Sarum rubric in this regard: "All the bells shall be rung together in a clash."

[177]Reed, 462.

Roman Catholic	Episcopal
Lord God,	O God,
you have brightened this night	who made this most holy night to shine
with the radiance	with the glory
of the risen Christ.	of the Lord's resurrection:
Quicken	Stir up
the spirit of sonship	in your Church that Spirit of adoption
in your Church;	which is given to us in Baptism, that we,
renew us in mind and body	being renewed both in body and mind,
to give you whole-hearted service.	may worship you in sincerity and truth;
Grant this	
through our Lord Jesus Christ,	through Jesus Christ our Lord,
your Son,	
who lives and reigns with you	who lives and reigns with you
and the Holy Spirit,	in the unity of the Holy Spirit,
one God, for ever and ever.	one God, now and for ever.

The Latin original is:

Deus, qui hanc sacratissimam noctem gloriosae dominicae resurrectionis illustras, conserua, in noua familiae tuae progeniem adoptionis spiritum quem dedisti, ut corpore et mente renouati, puram tibi exhibeant servitutem: per dominum.

The *Lutheran Book of Worship* appoints no propers for the Vigil Eucharist, so one is free to choose from the eucharistic propers appointed for Easter Day. The Roman and Episcopal rites both make specific appointments of an Epistle, Psalm, and Gospel.

Roman Catholic	Episcopal
Romans 6:3–11	Romans 6:3–11
Ps. 118:1–2, 16ab–17, 22–23	Alleluia repeated and/or
refrain: Alleluia, alleluia,	Ps. 114 or another psalm
alleluia	or hymn
(A) Matthew 28:1–10	(ABC) Matthew 28:1–10
(B) Mark 16:1–8	
(C) Luke 24:1–12	

Marion Hatchett notes that Matthew 28:1–10 "is the Gospel that has been used in the Easter Vigil since the time of the earliest Roman lectionaries."[178]

The Roman and Episcopal rites both direct that a sermon be preached at the Vigil;[179] the *Lutheran Book of Worship* (Min. Ed., p. 153) permits its omission "because of the instructional character of the Service of Readings." The Lutheran book says nothing explicitly about the

---

[178] Hatchett, 250.

[179] *The Sacramentary*, 192; *Book of Common Prayer*, 292, 295. "It is expected that a sermon or homily will follow the Gospel if it has not followed one of the readings of the Vigil" (Hatchett, 250).

use of the Nicene Creed at the Vigil Eucharist, but the Notes on the Liturgy (Min. Ed., p. 28 #21) direct that

The use of two creeds in the same service is not desirable. The Creed is omitted at this point if Holy Baptism or another rite with a creed is celebrated within the service.

To avoid such duplication, the Nicene Creed is not used in the Roman or Episcopal rites.

The proper preface for Easter in all three rites dates from the Gelasian (no. 458) and the Gregorian (nos. 379, 385, 394, 417) sacramentaries and the Gallican Bobbio missal (no. 261). See also the *Missale Gallicanum vetus* (no. 182 and 233) and the *Missale Gothicum* (no. 286).

vere dignum iustum est, aequum et salutare te quidem, domine, omni tempore, sed in hac potentissimam noctem gloriosus praedicare, cum pascha nostrum immolatus est Christus. Ipse enim verus est agnus qui abstulit peccata mundi; qui mortem nostram moriendo distruxit et vitam resurgendo reparavit. Proptera profusis paschalibus gaudiis totus in orbe terrarum mundus exultat.

The English translation of the 1549 *Book of Common Prayer* was borrowed by Lutheran service books in English, beginning with the *Church Book* (1868).

Roman Catholic	Lutheran	Episcopal
We praise you with greater joy than ever on this Easter night (day), when Christ became our paschal sacrifice.	But chiefly are we bound to praise you for the glorious resurrection of our	But chiefly are we bound to praise you for the glorious resurrection of your Son Jesus Christ our
He is the true Lamb	Lord; for he is the true Passover Lamb who gave himself to	Lord; for he is the true Paschal Lamb, who was sacrificed
who took away	take away our sin,	for us, and has taken away the sin of the
the sins of the world. By dying he destroyed our death; by rising he restored our life. And so,	who by his death has destroyed death, and by his rising has brought us to eternal life. And so, with Mary Magdalene and Peter and all the witnesses of the resurrection, with earth and sea and all their creatures, and	world. By his death he has destroyed death, and by his rising to life again he has won for us everlasting life.
with all the choirs of angels	with angels and archangels, cherubim	

in heaven	and seraphim,
we proclaim your glory	we praise your name
and join their	and join their
unending hymn	unending hymn.
of praise.	

The *Lutheran Book of Worship*, expanding the conclusion of the long-traditional preface, joins the congregation to "the apostle to the apostles" (Mary Magdalene, who first saw the risen Lord) and Peter, first of the twelve, and all the other witnesses, together with all creation, echoing the *Benedicite Omnia Opera*, and all the company of heaven, echoing the Exsultet.

The Roman sacramentary provides five prefaces for the Fifty Days of Easter.

The *Lutheran Book of Worship* (Min. Ed., p. 153) permits the substitution of Psalm 136, a psalm in praise of the events of the Exodus, for the usual post-communion canticles.

The *Lutheran Book of Worship* recommends prayer 242 as the post-communion. It is the prayer after communion appointed in the Roman sacramentary for the Easter Vigil.

Roman Catholic	**Lutheran**
Lord, you have nourished us with your Easter sacraments. Fill us with your Spirit and make us one in peace and love. We ask this through Christ our Lord.	Pour out upon us the spirit of your love, O Lord, and unite the wills of those whom you have fed with one heavenly food; through Jesus Christ our Lord.

The original is from the Leonine sacramentary (no. 1049), the Gelasian sacramentary (no. 1330), and the Gregorian (nos. 164, 382, 388, 397, 618):

Spiritum nobis, Domine, tuae caritatis infunde; ut quos uno caelesti pane satiasti una facias pietate concordes.

The Lutheran translation derives from the *Service Book and Hymnal*, which introduced the collect to Lutheran use.

Pour forth upon us, O Lord, the spirit of thy love that by thy mercy thou mayest make of one will those whom thou hast fed with one heavenly food.

The Roman sacramentary enriches the dismissal by adding a double alleluia to the dismissal by the deacon and to the congregation's response. The Prayer Book permits the same. The singing of Alleluia, returned with joyful energy in the verse before the Gospel in the Vigil Eucharist, is characteristic of the liturgy for these days of rejoicing, made the more joyful because of the discontinuance of Alleluia during Lent.

EASTER: THE FIFTY DAYS

Easter, the oldest Christian feast, was understood anciently to be one continuous festival, the "Pentecost," the *quinquagesima*, the Great Fifty Days of rejoicing, corresponding to the Jewish "feast of Pentecost, which is the sacred festival of the seven weeks" (Tobit 2:1; see Lev. 23:15–21; Deut. 16:9–11).[180] It is a fifty-day-long Sunday. There was no fasting during these days, no kneeling, and Alleluia was its characteristic and repeated song.[181] The separation of the Pentecost, or Fifty Days, into the festivals of Easter, Ascension, and the Day of Pentecost took place in the fourth century.

Easter Day

The first Prayer of the Day in the *Lutheran Book of Worship* (no. 62) and in the *Book of Common Prayer* is from the Gregorian sacramentary (no. 324), in which it was appointed for Wednesday in Holy Week. In the Sarum rite it was among the devotions associated with the Easter procession, and the 1549 Prayer Book provided for its use prior to Matins on Easter Day. The collect then disappeared from the Prayer Book until the revision of 1892, which appointed it for a second celebration on Easter. It was then borrowed by the *Service Book and Hymnal* (1958) "For an Early Service" on Easter Day. The translation in the *Lutheran Book of Worship* is a revision of the translation in the Prayer Book.

The second Prayer of the Day in the Roman, Lutheran (no. 63), and Episcopal books is from the Gregorian sacramentary (no. 383), appointed for Easter in previous Lutheran books and the medieval missals. In the subtle and understated way of the historic collects, the prayer joins the risen Lord and the risen life, a prominent New Testament theme. (See Col. 3:1–3, the Second Lesson for Easter Day.) The reference in the introductory clause to opening the gates of life (see the Responsorial Psalm 118:19–20, "Open for me the gates of righteousness...") refers probably to the opening of Jesus' side, an idea taken from St. Augustine:

"One of the soldiers laid open his side, and forthwith came thereout blood and water." A suggestive word was made use of by the evangelist, in not saying pierced, or wounded his side, or anything else, but "opened"; that thereby, in a sense, the gate of life might be thrown open, from whence have flowed forth the sacraments of the Church, without which there is no entrance to the life which is true life.[182]

---

[180] See Tertullian, *On Prayer* 23.1; *On Idolatry* 14.7; *On Baptism* 19.2; Eusebius, *Life of Constantine* 4.64; Theodor H. Gaster, *Festivals of the Jewish Year* (New York: Morrow, 1953), 51ff.; the references in Geoffrey W. H. Lampe, ed., *A Patristic Greek Lexicon* (London: Oxford University Press, 1961), 1060ff.

[181] Tertullian, *The Chaplet* or *de corona* 3.4; *Egeria's Travels* 41; Canon 20 of the Council of Nicaea.

[182] Augustine, *On the Gospel of St. John*. Tractate 120.2. On "gates" see Ps. 107:16; Isa. 26:2; 45:1–2; 62:10; Jer. 17:25; 22:4; Rev. 21:25.

The First Lesson on the Sundays of Easter is always from the Acts of the Apostles. These accounts of the life, growth, and witness of the early church are understood as reports of the meaning of the resurrection, the life and work of the church being an extension of the life and work of the dying and rising Savior.

Singers in the Middle Ages vocalized a *jubilus* on the final syllable of Alleluia at the Gradual before the Gospel. These notes were then broken up into melodic phrases to enable singers to catch their breath. By the ninth century, words were added to the phrases, and these became a separate form called proses or *sequences* (additional words *following* the regular text). A great number of such sequences were written during the Middle Ages, enriching not only worship but hymnody and poetry as well. The *Lutheran Book of Worship*, like the Roman sacramentary, appoints one of the great classical sequences for use at Easter, *Victimae Paschali laudes* ("Christians, to the Paschal Victim," hymn 137). The hymn is ascribed in one manuscript (Einsiedeln, end of the eleventh century) to Wipo (ca. 1000–1050), who was a priest, a native of Burgundy, and chaplain to the emperors Conrad II and Heinrich III. *Victimae Paschali* is an example of the transition from the rhythmical but irregular rhymed sequences of authors like Notker to the regular rhyming sequences of Adam of St. Victor and later authors. It also played a noteworthy role in the transition from ritual to representational drama. Its dramatic portrayal of the experience of the resurrection encouraged the development of liturgical dramatization and then of more distinct forms.[183] From the *Victimae Paschali* the pre-Reformation German vernacular hymn "Christ ist erstanden" (hymn 136) is derived. Luther admired the hymn and incorporated its vivid picture of the conflict between Death and Life in the third stanza of his "Christ lag in Todesbanden" (hymn 134). Jane Eliza Leeson made a popular translation, "Christ the Lord Is Ris'n Today; Alleluia" (hymn 128).

Alone of the liturgical books of the three rites the *Lutheran Book of Worship* provides a prayer for Easter evening (no. 64). It derives from the collect for Easter in the Gelasian sacramentary (no. 464) and for Wednesday within the octave of Easter in the Gregorian sacramentary (no. 408), its use in the present Roman sacramentary. In *Contemporary Worship 6* the prayer was appointed for "Easter Evening or Easter Monday." Two additional Easter collects from the Gregorian sacramentary (nos. 371 and 389) were provided in the *Church Book*, the *Common Service Book*, and the *Service Book and Hymnal*. Their intended use was not specified.

"It takes a certain amount of time," notes Adolf Adam, "for moments of deep festivity to run their course."[184] The feast of Easter,

---

[183] See O. B. Hardison, Jr., *Christian Rite and Christian Drama in the Middle Ages* (Baltimore: Johns Hopkins University Press, 1965), especially essay 5, "The Early History of the *Quem quaeritis.*" See also John Julian, *A Dictionary of Hymnology*, 2nd ed. rev. (1907), "Victimae Paschali."

[184] Adam, 84.

therefore, does not end when Easter Day is over. The Fifty Days of Easter are regarded as a "week of weeks," a great octave of eight Sundays from Easter through Pentecost, and this great octave is mirrored in the smaller octave of the week following Easter Day, corresponding to the week-long celebration of the Passover (Exod. 12:15). Easter week as a time marked by special liturgical celebration dates from perhaps the second half of the third century,[185] thus balancing the emphasis on the days of Holy Week with an equal liturgical emphasis on the Easter octave. St. Augustine said that the week was the unanimous practice of the church, as ancient as Lent.[186] Indeed, until the eighth century it was the only octave customary in the church.

Easter week is a reflection of the mystery and glory of the resurrection as is evident in the name in Orthodox use, Bright Week — that is, the week of radiance. It was also a week in which particular attention was paid to the baptized. As the centuries passed, obligatory attendance at the services of Easter week was reduced to four days, then in 1094 to three (Sunday, Monday, and Tuesday) and so it remained in much of Europe even after the Reformation.[187] In North America the *Church Book*, the *Common Service Book*, and the *Service Book and Hymnal* made liturgical provision for Easter Monday; *The Lutheran Hymnal* provided for Easter Tuesday as well.[188] The 1928 Prayer Book introduced propers (Collect, Epistle, and Gospel) for the Monday and Tuesday of Easter Week; the 1979 Prayer Book, like the Roman sacramentary, provides full propers for each of the days of the Easter octave. The *Lutheran Book of Worship* is deficient in this regard. Surely Bright Week deserves an emphasis equal to that placed upon Holy Week, for these two weeks proclaim the two faces of one mystery: the death and resurrection of Christ.

The Second Sunday of Easter

This Sunday, which concludes the Easter octave, was known anciently as White Sunday (*dominica in albis*, the Lord's Day in white [robes]) because those who had been baptized at Easter wore their white robes all week as a sign of their new life. As early as the ninth century it was customary in Germany to have Confirmation on this Sunday, and the custom continued in some Lutheran churches after the Reformation. It is a time to be preferred to the other days Lutherans have often chosen

---

[185]See the homilies of Asterius the Sophist on the Pslams; Adam, 85, 116–17.

[186]Augustine, *Letters* 55, 32. Egeria reports of the Jerusalem church, "The eight days of Easter they celebrate till a late hour, like us, and up to the eighth day of Easter they follow the same order as people do everywhere else" (39.1).

[187]Egeria (39.2) observes that the Jerusalem church kept Easter Sunday, Monday, and Tuesday in the same way in the same place, the Great Church; on Easter Wednesday the site was the Mount of Olives, Thursday the site of the resurrection, Friday on Sion, Saturday "before the Cross."

[188]Curiously, the collects, two for Monday and three for Tuesday, seem to be different versions of but two prayers, one for Monday and one for Tuesday.

for Confirmation — Palm Sunday and Pentecost — and helps to rescue this Sunday from the oblivion to which it is often consigned.

The Prayer of the Day in the *Lutheran Book of Worship* (no. 65) is a translation of the collect in the older missals that Lutherans had become accustomed to since its introduction in the *Church Book*. The original is from the Gregorian sacramentary (no. 435) for the Second Sunday of Easter (*die domne post albas*). In earlier missals the collect expressed an appropriate idea, saying in the past tense, "we have celebrated the festival of the Lord's resurrection," for it marked the close of the Easter octave, and the Sundays following were counted "after Easter." Now that the ancient Pentecost, the fifty days of Easter, has been recovered, the note of conclusion which the prayer strikes is less appropriate. The Roman sacramentary therefore provides a prayer from the *Missale Gothicum* (no. 309) instead; it makes reference to Hebrews 9:12. The spare and flat translation in the *Lutheran Book of Worship* is a reduction of the earlier already terse translation of the *Church Book* and the *Common Service Book* and implies that Easter is now past, when in fact it has only begun.

The collect in the *Book of Common Prayer* is from the Gregorian sacramentary (no. 423) and is also appointed in the Prayer Book for Easter Thursday and for after the seventh lesson in the Easter Vigil.

From this Sunday until Pentecost the Second Lesson is from 1 Peter (Year A), 1 John (Year B), or Revelation (Year C) because "these texts seem most appropriate to the spirit of the Easter season, a spirit of joyful faith and confident hope."[189] On this Sunday of St. Thomas the Gospel from the ancient lectionaries reporting Thomas' encounter with the risen Christ eight days after Easter serves all three years of the lectionary cycle. It is the culmination of the Fourth Gospel and a central proclamation of Easter, for Easter is incomplete until it elicits an appropriate response from all who learn of it and celebrate it.

The Third Sunday of Easter

The Third Sunday of Easter continues the contemplation of the meaning of the resurrection by presenting accounts of appearances of the Lord. The mystery of the risen Christ is so radically different from all human expectations that the church takes weeks liturgically to ponder it. The Sundays move from mystery to mystery as the wonder of the new life deepens.

The *Lutheran Book of Worship* (no. 66) retains the collect from the Gelasian sacramentary (no. 541) and the supplement to the Gregorian sacramentary (no. 1114) which was appointed for this Sunday, the "Sunday after the octave of the pascha." The English translation dates from the *Church Book* (1868), in which the prayer was unique in the abruptness of its address, "God, who, by the humiliation of Thy Son . . ."); it

---

[189]Introduction to the *Roman Lectionary*, II.iv.1.

has been revised in the *Lutheran Book of Worship.* The Roman sacramentary has moved this prayer to the fourteenth Sunday of the year and has provided a new collect for this Sunday drawn from the Gelasian (no. 515) and the Leonine (no. 1148) sacramentaries.

The collect in the *Book of Common Prayer* was composed by John W. Suter, Jr., for Monday in Easter Week in the 1928 Prayer Book. In the 1979 book it is appointed for Wednesday in Easter Week in addition to this Sunday.

The Fourth Sunday of Easter

Good Shepherd Sunday distills the essence of Easter in a memorable and beloved image. The Lamb who was slain is one with the Shepherd who lays down his life for the sheep. The Good Shepherd shows the faithful care and self-sacrificing love for his own which characterizes the risen Lord. Moreover, as the Fourth Gospel presents the picture, when Jesus calls himself the Good Shepherd he is making a divine claim, appropriating an image that in the Old Testament was applied to God himself. In many of the ancient baptistries the figure of the Good Shepherd was a popular image, reinforcing its connection with Easter.

The Sunday of the Good Shepherd had in previous service books been kept on the previous Sunday, but in the present calendar it has been moved to this Sunday so as not to interrupt the sequence of the second and third Sundays of Easter which present accounts of appearances of the risen Christ.

The first Prayer of the Day in the *Lutheran Book of Worship* (no. 67) is a new composition, written for *Contemporary Worship 6* (1973). The opening address is from Hebrews 13:20. The image in the petition of the prayer, describing all the people of God as shepherds, is not a biblical image (in the Old Testament God is the Shepherd, in the New Testament the title is appropriated by Christ). In such passages as Ezekiel 34, the shepherds of God's people are those who have responsibility for guiding them. This prayer democratizes that image and gives to all the faithful the responsibility of oversight and care.

The second prayer in the *Lutheran Book of Worship* (no. 68) is from the Leonine sacramentary (no. 75) where it was among the masses of April. The Gelasian sacramentary (no. 546) appointed it for the second Sunday after the close of the Pascha (that is, the Third Sunday of Easter) as did the supplement to the Gregorian sacramentary (no. 1117). Previous Lutheran books, like the Roman missal, appointed it for this Sunday, then called Jubilate, the Third Sunday after Easter. The collect originally had reference to those recently joined to the family of the church through baptism at Easter. It is a wonderfully vigorous prayer. The Latin *respuere* (translated "resolutely reject") means to spit out (cf. Rev. 3:16). The opening address in the Latin says simply that God shows the light of his truth to the erring so that they may return "into the Way," referring probably to that most ancient designation of Christianity (Acts 9:2; 22:4).[190] The Roman sacramentary now appoints this prayer for the fifteenth Sunday of the year, and provides for this Sunday a prayer from the Gelasian sacramentary (no. 524). The Lutheran translation derives from the 1549 Prayer Book.

The *Book of Common Prayer* has substituted for this prayer a collect written by Massey H. Shepherd, Jr.

The Fifth Sunday of Easter

While all the days of Easter are to be understood as one feast, their unity and coherence is not static. Rather, week by week the mystery deepens. Beginning with the Fifth Sunday of Easter the attention moves toward the Ascension and the deeper communion between the Lord and the faithful which the end of the resurrection appearances was understood to have brought about.

The Prayer of the Day in the *Lutheran Book of Worship* (no. 69) is a translation of a collect in the Gelasian sacramentary (no. 551) and the supplement to the Gregorian sacramentary (no. 1120) assigned to this Sunday, "the third Sunday after the close of the Pascha." The English translation derives from the 1549 Prayer Book. The Roman sacramentary has moved this prayer to the twenty-first Sunday of the year and as the opening prayer for this Sunday provides a prayer from the Gelasian sacramentary (no. 522).

The collect in the *Book of Common Prayer* is a composition of the 1549 book formerly assigned to the Feast of St. Philip and St. James (May 1), and reassigned to this Sunday in the 1979 book because it had particular reference to the Gospel for Year A and suits the other years as well.[191]

The Gospels for the Fifth, Sixth, and Seventh Sundays of Easter are from the farewell discourses of Jesus at the Last Supper and from his high priestly prayer.

The Sixth Sunday of Easter

The Sixth Sunday of Easter looks to the Ascension and beyond it to the gift of the Paraclete, who will strengthen the faithful for their life of obedience, love, and service. The focus of the new life moves from Christ in his appearances to its manifestation in the lives of believers.

The Prayer of the Day (no. 70) in the Lutheran book is a translation of the collect in the Gelasian sacramentary (no. 556) and the supplement to the Gregorian sacramentary (no. 1123) assigned to "the fourth Sunday after the close of the Pascha." The English translation derives from the 1549 Prayer Book.

The collect in the *Book of Common Prayer* is from the Gelasian sacramentary (no. 1178) which in earlier Prayer Books had been appointed

---

[190]Reed, 511. Massey H. Shepherd, Jr. understands the Latin differently and translates, "O God, who showest thy light of truth that those wandering (*errantes*) in the way might return...." *Oxford American Prayer Book Commentary*, 172–173.

[191]Hatchett, 182.

for the sixth Sunday after Trinity. In the *Lutheran Book of Worship* this prayer is appointed for the Sixth Sunday after Pentecost.

The opening prayer in the Roman sacramentary is a new composition based on collects from the Leonine sacramentary (no. 229 and 1282) and the Gelasian sacramentary (no. 504).

In the year 470 Bishop Mammertus of Vienne in France ordered fasting, processions, and the praying of litanies on the Monday, Tuesday, and Wednesday before Ascension Day. The occasion seems to have been earthquakes and poor harvests. The practice spread and took on the aspect of prayer for a fruitful harvest, although the original penitential character remained in these "Rogation Days" (days of asking). Some sixteenth-century church orders retained the rogation days; more commonly they were replaced by penitential days set by proclamation as the need arose. In the *Church Book*, the *Common Service Book*, and the *Service Book and Hymnal* propers were provided for a Day of Humiliation and Prayer. A widespread European Lutheran custom set this observance on the Wednesday before the last Sunday after Trinity, the last Sunday of the church year. The *Lutheran Book of Worship* calls this occasion a Day of Penitence.

The Roman calendar now joins the rogation days to the ember days as times to pray for human needs, especially for the productivity of the earth and for human labor.[192] The time and the manner of the observance of these days are left to the episcopal conferences.

The *Book of Common Prayer* has broadened the use of the propers for the rogation days. Three sets of propers are provided "for use on the traditional days or at other times."[193] The Lutheran book has likewise provided propers for what it calls the Stewardship of Creation (Min. Ed., pp. 187–88), which are appropriate for use on the rogation days as well as at other times.

The Ascension of Our Lord

By the fourth century the Ascension was being celebrated on the fortieth day after Easter. St. Augustine declared that the feast was celebrated "all over the world."[194] The Lutheran church has generally retained the observance of Ascension Day on Thursday, the fortieth day after Easter, but in Prussia the festival was celebrated on the following Sunday,[195] and on the present Roman calendar, in places where Ascension Day is not a day of obligation, it is transferred to the following Sunday. The *Book of Common Prayer* and the *Lutheran Book of Worship* retain the observance on Thursday.

The Ascension is in part an enthronement festival. The coronation of Christ the King is celebrated, but so in him is the enthronement

---

[192]*General Norms for the Liturgical Year and the Calendar* (March 21, 1969), no. 45.
[193]*Book of Common Prayer*, 258.
[194]Augustine, *Sermon* 179.1. *PL* 39:2084.
[195]Horn, 147.

of humanity itself. John Chrysostom declared, "Our very nature...is enthroned today high above all cherubim."[196]

The Prayer of the Day in the *Lutheran Book of Worship* (no. 71), the opening prayer in the Roman sacramentary, and the second collect in the *Book of Common Prayer* all derive from sermon 73 by Leo the Great and a collect in the Gregorian sacramentary (no. 497). The last phrase echoes the eucharistic preface, "Lift up your hearts. *We lift them to the Lord.*" The English translation in the Lutheran and Episcopal books derives from the 1549 *Book of Common Prayer.* In past Lutheran practice, the *Church Book*, the *Common Service Book*, and the *Service Book and Hymnal* provided a second collect, an adaptation by the 1549 Prayer Book for the Sunday after Ascension Day of "the beautiful Antiphon addressed to God the Son at the Magnificat in Second Vespers, which the Venerable Bede is said to have repeated on his deathbed."[197] The theme is retained in hymn 158, "Alleluia! Sing to Jesus."

In the *Book of Common Prayer* the first collect for Ascension Day is from the Leonine sacramentary (no. 169) and was used as a post-communion prayer in the 1912 Scottish Prayer Book.

Until the reform of the calendar which began with the Roman sacramentary of 1969 and emphasized the unity of the Fifty Days, the paschal candle, which had been burning at gospel side of the altar to show the presence of the risen Lord with his church, was extinguished after the reading of the Ascension Gospel as an indication that the appearances of the risen Lord had come to an end. The present Roman book directs that the candle is to be kept burning through the Day of Pentecost as an indication of the unitive celebration of the resurrection-ascension-sending of the Spirit. The *Lutheran Book of Worship* takes a compromise course, leaning toward ending the use of the candle after the Ascension Gospel but allowing its use throughout the season.[198]

---

[196] John Chrysostom, *Sermon on the Ascension* 2. Nicholas Cabasilas (*De vita in Christo* VI.1) wrote:

Not only did he suffer the most terrible torments and receive agonizing wounds, but when he had returned to life and stolen his body away from corruption, he kept his wounds and wore their scars on his flesh; and with them he showed himself to the angels, so that his wounds were like an adornment, and he was pleased to show the marks of his suffering. All this happened when his body was glorified, without weight or dimension or any corporeal accident; and yet he never desired to put his wounds away or renounce his scars, believing he should preserve them by reason of his love for humanity, regained by him by virtue of these wounds, because these deathly hurts allowed him to conquer the object of his love. How otherwise can we explain the presence on his glorified body of wounds which nature or the art of medicine have sometimes been able to remove from mortal and corruptible bodies? One might almost say he wanted to suffer again and again for our sakes; but since this became impossible when his body was removed from all incorruptibility, and also to spare his executioners, he decided to keep on his body the proofs of his sacrifice and always to preserve the scars of those wounds, received on the Tree of crucifixion. So, in glory, he will be recognized after the event as the one who was crucified, whose side was pierced on behalf of slaves, and he will wear those scars eternally as a royal ornament.

[197] Reed, 514.

[198] The rubric is on p. 157 of the Ministers Edition.

The second proper preface in the Roman sacramentary and the preface in the Lutheran and Episcopal books are translations of the Preface for the Ascension in the Gregorian sacramentary (no. 499). The Lutheran translation was prepared originally for the *Common Service Book* (1917). The first Ascension preface in the Roman sacramentary is a new composition based in part on prefaces in the Leonine sacramentary (nos. 177, 176, 183)[199] and making the same basic point as the second preface. Noteworthy in the preface as well as in the Prayer of the Day is the belief that the Ascension celebrates not only the glorification of Christ but also in him the exaltation of the human race.

The Seventh Sunday of Easter

Although Ascension marks an important stage in the unfolding of the richness of the paschal mystery, it remains a part of Easter. Therefore the Sunday following Ascension Day is called the Seventh Sunday of Easter.

The Gelasian collect appointed in previous Lutheran and Roman books for this Sunday had no seasonal reference, and so the Roman and Lutheran liturgies now follow the Anglican tradition since 1549 and replace this collect. The first Prayer of the Day in the *Lutheran Book of Worship* (no. 72) is taken from the Roman sacramentary and is from the Gelasian sacramentary (no. 580). It alludes to the Gospel for Year A for Ascension Day (Matt. 28:16–20) and the Alleluia Verse (Matt. 28:19–20). The alternative Prayer of the Day (no. 73) in the Lutheran book is the Prayer of the Day for the occasion of Christian Unity (no. 147, Min. Ed., pp. 184–85) with the opening address slightly altered. This prayer, written for *Contemporary Worship 6* (p. 155), makes allusion to Jesus' high priestly prayer, especially portions read as the Gospel in Years B and C.

The present Prayer Book continues the use of the 1549 adaptation of the antiphon to the Magnificat which previous Lutheran books had appointed as an alternative collect for Ascension Day.

Pentecost

Pentecost, the Fiftieth Day of Easter, "is to be understood as the crowning close of the Easter season,"[200] not an independent festival of the Holy Spirit. It was anciently a time for the baptism of those who could not be baptized at the Easter Vigil; thus the Fifty Days began and ended with a baptismal vigil. The name Whitsunday (White Sunday) refers to the white garments worn by the newly baptized. The understanding of Pentecost as the close of the Fifty Days gradually broke down, and by the time of the Gelasian sacramentary there is provision for an octave of Pentecost.[201] In the Gregorian sacramentary there are services for Monday and Tuesday after Pentecost as the celebration spilled over into the

---

[199] Nocent, 3:235.
[200] Adam, 89.
[201] See also *Apostolic Constitutions* 5.20.

succeeding days, as happened with Christmas and Easter. So the *Church Book*, the *Common Service Book*, and the *Service Book and Hymnal* provide propers for the Monday after Pentecost; *The Lutheran Hymnal* gave propers for Monday and Tuesday "of Whitsun Week" (reflecting the name of the week in the *Common Service Book*).

THE VIGIL OF PENTECOST. The Roman, Lutheran, and Episcopal rites have all restored the vigil of Pentecost. The Roman and Lutheran books provide specific propers; the Prayer Book makes provision by way of a rubric (p. 227).

The Prayer of the Day (no. 74) for the Vigil of Pentecost in the *Lutheran Book of Worship* is a combination of the first opening prayer in the Roman sacramentary (from the Gelasian sacramentary, no. 637) and the petition of the alternative opening prayer of the Roman sacramentary (from the collect for the Vigil in the Gregorian sacramentary, no. 520). These prayers make clear the relationship between Easter and Pentecost. The "promise of Easter" is made in the Gospel for Easter evening and for the Ascension (Luke 24:49); the phrase also recalls the promises in the Gospels for the Sixth Sunday of Easter in Year A (John 14:16–17), and Year C (John 14:26). The petition for unity recalls the Gospels for the Seventh Sunday of Easter in all three years, Jesus' high priestly prayer, and looks forward to the Second Lesson on the Day of Pentecost. The reference to God's people "gathered in prayer, open to the Spirit's flame" shows the present church in a conscious imitation of the first-century Christian community gathering expectantly, according to the command of Christ, as on the first Pentecost (Acts 1:14; 2:1).

The *Book of Common Prayer* does not appoint a collect specifically for the Vigil of Pentecost but provides instead two collects for Pentecost. The first of these is similar to the Roman and Lutheran prayers and is based on the second of the collects for the mass of Pentecost in the Gelasian sacramentary (no. 638).[202]

The opening of the Gospel for the Vigil is to be heard as a key to understanding the unity of the Easter season: "on the last day of the feast, the great day...."

The proper preface for Pentecost in the *Lutheran Book of Worship* is a translation of the Preface of the Holy Spirit in the Gelasian sacramentary (no. 627), the Gallican *Missale Gothicum* (no. 357), and the Gregorian sacramentary (nos. 552 and 528). The translation was prepared for the *Church Book* (1868). Unfortunately the final phrase of the Gregorian preface has been omitted in the Lutheran translations. It continued, "and the heavenly hosts and angelic powers sing together a hymn to your glory, saying without ceasing, Holy, holy, holy...."

---

[202] Hatchett, 184. Hatchett translates the Gelasian collect,
  God, who on this festal day sanctified your universal church for every race and nation: Pour out through the whole world the gifts of your Holy Spirit, that what was begun among them at the beginning of the preaching of the Gospel with divine magnanimity may now also be poured out through the hearts of believers.

The preface in the *Book of Common Prayer* derives from Cranmer's new composition for the 1549 Prayer Book. The Roman sacramentary has replaced the ancient preface with a composition drawn from the Gelasian sacramentary (nos. 634 and 641), which brings out the relationship between Easter and Pentecost clearly.

THE DAY OF PENTECOST. Both Prayers of the Day for Pentecost (nos. 75 and 76) in the *Lutheran Book of Worship* are new compositions, written for *Contemporary Worship 6*. The scriptural allusion in the second prayer is to the confusion of tongues at Babel and the unity of language on Pentecost, the First and Second Lessons in Year C.

The opening prayer in the Roman sacramentary is from the Gelasian sacramentary (no. 638). The second collect in the *Book of Common Prayer* has its origins in the Gregorian sacramentary where it is appointed for the morning mass on Pentecost at St. Peter's Basilica (no. 526). This splendid prayer was the collect for Pentecost in all the earlier Prayer Books and in the Lutheran service books as well. It is preserved in the *Lutheran Book of Worship* among the Prayers, Intercessions, and Thanksgivings (no. 202, Min. Ed., pp. 110–11).

Instead of the psalm between the lessons the *Lutheran Book of Worship* permits the use of the hymn *Veni, Creator Spiritus* (hymns 472 and 473), a Latin hymn associated with Pentecost since its composition in the ninth century.

The Alleluia Verse before the Gospel is noteworthy, not being taken from Scripture but from an eleventh-century antiphon, *Veni, sancte spiritus, reple tuorum corda fidelium*. Luther based his hymn *Komm, heiliger Geist, Herre Gott* ("Come, Holy Ghost, God and Lord," hymn 163) on a German stanza which had developed from the Latin antiphon.

As at Easter and like the Roman sacramentary, the *Lutheran Book of Worship* appoints a sequence hymn for use following the Alleluia Verse. The sequence associated with Pentecost is *Veni, sancte spiritus*, the Golden Sequence, a masterpiece of Latin hymnody, composed about 1200 and ascribed variously to Hermannus Contractus, Robert II of France, Stephen Langton, Innocent III, and others. The hymn was included in the *Common Service Book* in Edward Caswall's translation, "Holy Spirit, Lord of Light" (no. 144).[203] It is unfortunately not included in the *Lutheran Book of Worship*, and so the sequence hymn listed in the propers is the *Veni, creator spiritus* ("Come, Holy Ghost, Our Souls Inspire," hymn 472, 473).

The traditional color for Pentecost is red, usually explained as suggesting the color of the fire of the Holy Spirit. Adolf Adam observes that the continued use of red may be regarded as a holdover from the time when Pentecost was treated as an isolated festival. "But it would surely be more meaningful for the entire great octave of Easter to show the

---

[203] See the spirited translation by John Austin in his *Devotions in the Ancient Way of Offices* (1668) and the study by Philip H. Pfatteicher, *The Life and Writings of John Austin*, dissertation, University of Pennsylvania, 1966.

same color as the principal feast itself"[204] and use white throughout, including the Day of Pentecost.

After the Day of Pentecost, the celebration of Easter being completed, the paschal candle is removed from its place in the chancel. The *Lutheran Book of Worship* directs that it be "moved to the baptismal font where it is lighted as a reminder of the resurrection character of Holy Baptism (Min. Ed., p. 157). The Roman sacramentary gives similar instruction.[205]

THE TIME AFTER PENTECOST

Since Pentecost, the fiftieth day, is the conclusion of Easter, "ordinary time" or the "green season," which had begun the Monday following the Baptism of the Lord and which was interrupted by Lent and Easter, resumes the Monday after Pentecost.[206] It is a mistake to understand the time after Pentecost as the "season of Pentecost," for the day marks the end and culmination, not a beginning.

The Roman calendar numbers the ordinary Sundays after the Baptism of Christ and after Pentecost consecutively, and so "ordinary time" includes thirty-three or thirty-four weeks. Any weeks not needed are omitted immediately following Pentecost. In Lutheran and Episcopal practice, the Sundays after the Epiphany form their own cycle, and when Easter is early, the latter weeks after the Epiphany are omitted that year. The time after Pentecost forms another cycle, from twenty-three to twenty-eight weeks long depending on the date of Easter, and the treatment of this time by Lutherans and by Episcopalians differs. The *Lutheran Book of Worship*, like earlier Lutheran books, deletes from the end of the series any propers that may not be needed that year. The result is that the eschatological thrust of the last Sundays after Pentecost is often weakened or absent. The *Book of Common Prayer* therefore has devised a scheme that deletes any supernumerary weeks from the

---

[204]Adam, 91.

[205]The candle "should be kept in the baptistery with due honor. During the celebration of baptism, the candles of the newly-baptized are lighted from it." *The Sacramentary*, p. 273.

[206]The Notes on the Liturgy (Min. Ed., p. 14), however direct that, following the customary Lutheran practice,

Propers appointed for Principal Festivals, Sundays, and Days of Special Devotion are used at Holy Communion during the weekdays following unless provision is otherwise made for a Lesser Festival.

In the daily prayer offices the use of the Psalms appointed for General Week I begins on the Monday following the Day of Pentecost.

The traditional summer Ember Days were the Wednesday, Friday, and Saturday following Pentecost — an indication that the ancient understanding was that the regular round of fasting, which had been suspended during the great Fifty Days, was resumed. (In both Roman and Episcopal practice these Ember Days are freed from their old connection with the turning of the four seasons and may be observed at times and in ways appropriate to local custom and practice (Adam, 189; Hatchett, 184).

beginning of the time after Pentecost rather than the end. Each week of the time after Pentecost is numbered (from one to twenty-nine) and assigned an approximate date. Proper 1, for example, is for the "Week of the Sunday closest to May 11." Moreover, the lectionary, but not the collects, for proper 1, 2, and 3 duplicates the lectionary for the Sixth, Seventh, and Eighth Sundays after the Epiphany. The result is that the Episcopal propers correspond closely to those of the Roman Catholic Church during the time after Pentecost. The Lutheran calendar is often out of step by several weeks.

The Holy Trinity. The First Sunday after Pentecost

In the eastern church the Sunday after Pentecost is a festival of All Saints. In the Gelasian and later Gregorian sacramentaries, the Sunday is the Octave of Pentecost. The Festival of the Holy Trinity was begun by Bishop Stephen of Liege (903–920) and spread rapidly in northern Europe; in 1334 Pope John XXII ordered the observance of the festival throughout the western church. The propers of the feast have their origins in a sacramentary of votive masses gathered by Alcuin for the private devotion of priests. The votive mass of the Holy Trinity was the basis for the prayers of the festival as it emerged in the tenth century.[207] The festival is perhaps best understood not as the feast of a doctrine[208] but as the celebration of the richness of the being of God (see the splendid hymn by Frederick W. Faber, "Most ancient of all mysteries," no. 138 in the *Service Book and Hymnal*) and the occasion of a thankful review of the now completed mystery of salvation, which is the work of the Father through the Son in the Holy Spirit.[209]

The first Prayer of the Day (no. 77) in the *Lutheran Book of Worship* and the opening prayer in the Roman sacramentary are new compositions, the Lutheran prayer composed for *Contemporary Worship 6*. The second prayer in the Lutheran book (no. 78), like the collect in the *Book of Common Prayer*, is a translation of the collect in later medieval books like the Leofric missal. The Lutheran version follows the later medieval prayers which address the Holy Trinity; the Prayer Book version, following earlier practice, addresses the prayer to the Father through the Son.

The proper preface in the *Lutheran Book of Worship* follows very closely the English translation in the Roman sacramentary. It appeared about the middle of the eighth century in the old Gelasian sacramentary. The proper preface used in the Prayer Book and in previous Lutheran

---

[207] A curiosity of the *Common Service Book*, continued in the *Service Book and Hymnal*, was the provision for the use of white garments on Trinity Sunday "and its Octave" ("through its Octave" according to the *Service Book and Hymnal*). Since the Feast of the Holy Trinity seems never to have had an octave, what the Lutheran churches were noting with the use of white on the Sunday following Trinity Sunday was rather the octave of Corpus Christi, the celebration of the sacrament of the Body and Blood of Christ, observed in the Roman Catholic Church on the Thursday following Trinity Sunday.

[208] See, for example, Horn, 157.

[209] Adam, 168.

service books is thought to be of Mozarabic origin[210] and is found in the Gelasian sacramentary (no. 680) and the Gregorian sacramentary (no. 1621) for the Sunday in the octave of Pentecost.

The Second Sunday after Pentecost
(Roman 9th Sunday of the Year; Episcopal Proper 4)

The Roman Catholic and Episcopal collect for this Sunday is from the Gelasian sacramentary (no. 1186) where it is the first prayer of the third of sixteen masses. It is included in the Gregorian sacramentary (no. 1150) as the prayer for the eighth Sunday after (the) Pentecost (octave). In earlier Lutheran service books it was the collect for the Seventh Sunday after Trinity; in the Roman missal of 1570 it was the collect for the Seventh Sunday after Pentecost; in previous Prayer Books, following the Sarum missal, it was the collect for the Eighth Sunday after Trinity. Luther Reed praised "the fine collect,"[211] but in the *Lutheran Book of Worship* it has been replaced with a new composition (no. 79) from *Contemporary Worship 6*.

In the proposed lectionary of the Consultation on Common Texts, the first lessons for the first Sundays after Pentecost in Year A are from the patriarchal narratives. The first lessons for Year B are from the Davidic tradition; for Year C they are from the prophetic tradition.

For the Sundays after Pentecost (and for optional use on the Sundays after the Epiphany) the *Book of Common Prayer* has provided three proper prefaces of the Lord's Day, written by H. Boone Porter and stressing Sunday as the day of creation, of the resurrection, and of the giving of the Holy Spirit.[212] The *Lutheran Book of Worship* has borrowed the second of these and appointed it for use on the Sundays after Pentecost. (It is inappropriate for use on weekdays, and a separate form is provided for use on days other than Sunday — the introductory and concluding phrases of the preface without the insertion of a proper preface.) The preface stresses the centrality of Sunday as the weekly celebration of the resurrection and recalls the language of the (alternative) Prayer of the Day for Easter Day (no. 63).

The Roman sacramentary provides eight proper prefaces for use on the Sundays in ordinary time; each centers on an aspect of the work of salvation. In addition six prefaces for weekdays are provided.

The Third Sunday after Pentecost
(Roman 10th Sunday of the Year; Episcopal Proper 5)

The Prayer of the Day (no. 80) in the *Lutheran Book of Worship* is translated from the Gelasian sacramentary in which the prayer (no. 566) is

---

[210]Hatchett, 402.

[211]Reed, 527. The opening phrase in the 1662 Prayer Book paraphrase, used in previous Lutheran books, "O God, whose never-failing providence ordereth all things both in heaven and earth," is more literally rendered "whose providence is not deceived in the management of its own" (Reed, 527) or "your providence never fails in ordering (*or* bringing about *or* managing) that which is proper to itself" (Hatchett, 187).

[212]Hatchett, 398.

the first collect for the sixth of the Sundays after the paschal octave, the first Sunday after the octave of Pentecost. In the Gregorian sacramentary (no. 1129) it is the collect for the first Sunday after (the octave of) Pentecost, that is, the Second Sunday after Pentecost. In previous Lutheran books, many medieval missals, and previous prayer books the prayer was assigned to the First Sunday after Trinity, the Second Sunday after Pentecost; in the Roman missal of 1570 the collect was used on Trinity Sunday after the Collect of the Day as a commemoration of the first Sunday after Pentecost. The prayer is also found in the *Missale Francorum* (no. 141) and in the Bobbio missal (no. 507). Luther Reed notes that the phrase "the weakness of our mortal nature" recalls Pope Gelasius's defense of the faith against Pelagianism.[213] The English translation originates in the 1549 Prayer Book; the *Lutheran Book of Worship* has followed Reed's suggestion that the translation would be more literal if "hope" were substituted for "trust" in the opening phrase.[214] The *Book of Common Prayer* now appoints this prayer for the Sixth Sunday after the Epiphany.

The prayer appointed for this Sunday in the Prayer Book and the Roman sacramentary is from the Gelasian sacramentary (no. 556) and the supplement to the Gregorian sacramentary (no. 1123) where it is appointed for the fourth Sunday after the Easter octave. In previous Roman, Lutheran, and Anglican books this prayer was appointed for the Fifth Sunday after Easter; the *Lutheran Book of Worship* retains its use there, now the Sixth Sunday of Easter (no. 70).

The Fourth Sunday after Pentecost
(Roman 11th Sunday of the Year; Episcopal Proper 6)

The Prayer of the Day (no. 81) in the *Lutheran Book of Worship* is a new composition, written for *Contemporary Worship 6*. The biblical allusion is to 1 Pet. 2:9 in which the vocation of Israel (Exod. 19:6; Isa. 61:6) is extended to the church (see also Rev. 1:6; 5:10).

The collect in the Prayer Book is a new composition by Massey H. Shepherd, Jr. The content is similar to that of the Lutheran prayer but is at once broader and more specific in its description of the Christian vocation.

The opening prayer in the Roman sacramentary derives from the Gelasian collect (no. 566; Gregorian no. 1129) previously appointed for the Second Sunday after Pentecost (the First Sunday after Trinity in previous Lutheran books).

The Fifth Sunday after Pentecost
(Roman 12th Sunday of the Year; Episcopal Proper 7)

The collect in the Roman Catholic and Episcopal books is a translation of a Gelasian collect for the Sunday after the Ascension (no. 586),

---

[213]Reed, 521.
[214]Ibid.

which was included in the supplement to the Gregorian sacramentary (no. 1132) as the collect for the second Sunday after (the) Pentecost (octave). The missals of Bamberg, Nuremberg, Constance, and Sarum appointed it for the Second Sunday after Trinity, and previous Lutheran and Episcopal books did likewise. The forthright Gelasian original departs from the usual collect form and, without an opening address giving the antecedent reason, begins directly with the petition.

The *Lutheran Book of Worship* has chosen to replace this collect with a new composition (no. 82) inspired by the Gospel for Year B.

The Sixth Sunday after Pentecost
(Roman 13th Sunday of the Year; Episcopal Proper 8)

The Prayer of the Day (no. 83) in the *Lutheran Book of Worship* is from the Gelasian sacramentary (no. 1178) where it is appointed for the first of sixteen masses for ordinary Sundays, and the Gregorian sacramentary (no. 1144) as the collect for the sixth Sunday after (the octave of) Pentecost. The collect was assigned to this Sunday in previous Lutheran books; the Roman missal of 1570 assigned it to the Fifth Sunday after Pentecost; the *Book of Common Prayer* to the Sixth Sunday after Trinity. The invocation is based on 1 Cor. 2:9. The Latin *invisibilia* suggests that which cannot be seen; the 1549 Prayer Book translation rendered it "the things which have not entered into man's heart"; later revision incorporated the phrase from Philippians 4:7, "which passes all understanding." Luther Reed suggested that the opening phrase, "those who love you," brings to mind Jesus' question to Peter, "Do you love me?" (The day of SS. Peter and Paul is near this Sunday). Reed moreover praises the prayer as "one of the finest in the Church's use, a prayer of rare spiritual beauty, perfect form, and fine diction."[215]

The Roman sacramentary has moved this prayer to the twentieth Sunday in ordinary time and has replaced it here with a prayer from the Bergamo sacramentary (no. 725). The *Book of Common Prayer* assigns to this day, the Sunday nearest to June 29, the festival of St. Peter and St. Paul, the collect formerly assigned to the feast of St. Simon and St. Jude (October 28), written for the 1549 Prayer Book.

The Seventh Sunday after Pentecost
(Roman 14th Sunday of the Year; Episcopal Proper 9)

The Prayer of the Day (no. 84) in the *Lutheran Book of Worship* is a new composition, inspired by the Gospel for Year C. The opening prayer for this Sunday in the Roman sacramentary is the collect formerly assigned to the Second Sunday after Easter, which in the Lutheran book is still appointed for what is now counted as the Third Sunday of Easter. The collect in the *Book of Common Prayer* is from the Leonine sacramentary, where it is associated with a September mass (no. 971). The translation

---

[215]Reed, 525.

is a revision of the translation included in *Parish Prayers*, edited by Frank Colquhoun (London: Hodder and Stoughton, 1967), no. 1555.[216]

The Eighth Sunday after Pentecost
(Roman 15th Sunday of the Year; Episcopal Proper 10)

Both prayers (nos. 85 and 86) in the *Lutheran Book of Worship* are new compositions. The first draws upon the images in the Gospel for Years A and B; the second upon the parable of the Good Samaritan, the Gospel for Year C.

The collect for Proper 10 in the *Book of Common Prayer* is the Gregorian collect (no. 86), which had been appointed for the First Sunday after the Epiphany in previous Episcopal, Lutheran, and Roman books. In the *Lutheran Book of Worship* it is now appointed for the Sixth Sunday after the Epiphany (no. 16). The opening prayer in the Roman sacramentary is the collect that had been appointed for the Third Sunday after Easter in previous Roman, Episcopal, and Lutheran books; it was moved to make room for a prayer more directly appropriate for Easter. The Lutheran book retains it for what is now counted the Fourth Sunday of Easter (no. 68).

The Ninth Sunday after Pentecost
(Roman 16th Sunday of the Year; Episcopal Proper 11)

The first Prayer of the Day (no. 87) in the *Lutheran Book of Worship* is from the earliest of the sacramentaries, the Leonine, in which it is appointed for one of the September masses (no. 1015). In the Gelasian sacramentary it is the fourth of the Sunday masses (no. 1190); the supplement to the Gregorian (no. 1153) appoints it for the ninth Sunday after (the) Pentecost (octave).[217] Lutheran books have appointed it for the Ninth Sunday after Pentecost; the 1570 Roman missal assigned it to the Eighth Sunday after Pentecost; previous Prayer Books to the Ninth Sunday after Trinity. The 1979 Prayer Book appoints it for Proper 14, and for this Sunday appoints a collect composed for the 1549 Prayer Book for use after the offertory when there was no communion.

The second Prayer of the Day (no. 88) in the *Lutheran Book of Worship* is a new composition related to the Gospel for Year C.

The Roman sacramentary appoints a collect from the Bergamo sacramentary (no. 719).

The Tenth Sunday after Pentecost
(Roman 17th Sunday of the Year; Episcopal Proper 12)

The Prayer of the Day (no. 89) in the *Lutheran Book of Worship* is an adaptation of the collect assigned to this Sunday in previous Lutheran

---

[216] Hatchett, 188.

[217] The Latin collect "is an early Leonine original of the fifth century which exhibits a fine balance of phraseology which is almost impossible to preserve in translation" (Reed, 528):
> Largire nobis, domine, quaesumus, spiritum cogitandi quae bona sunt promptius et agendi, ut qui sine te esse non possimus secundum te vivere valeamus: per

books. The original, an exhortation to the right kind of prayer, is from the Gelasian sacramentary (no. 1195) for the fifth of sixteen Sunday masses and is closely related to a similar prayer in the earlier Leonine sacramentary.[218] The collect is also included in the Gregorian sacramentary (no. 272) for Wednesday of the fourth week in Lent and the Gregorian supplement (no. 1156) for the tenth Sunday after (the octave of) Pentecost. It has been appointed for the Ninth Sunday after Pentecost in the 1570 Roman missal and for the Tenth Sunday after Trinity in the *Book of Common Prayer.*

The collect for Proper 12 in the Prayer Book and for the seventeenth Sunday in Ordinary Time in the Roman sacramentary is from the Gregorian sacramentary (no. 1158), appointed for the fourth Sunday after (the) Pentecost (octave). Previous Lutheran books used it on the Third Sunday after Trinity; the Sarum missal and previous Prayer Books assigned it to the Fourth Sunday after Trinity; the 1570 Roman missal used it on the Third Sunday after Pentecost. Luther Reed praised "this fine collect,"[219] but it has not been preserved in the *Lutheran Book of Worship.*

The Eleventh Sunday after Pentecost
(Roman 18th Sunday of the Year; Episcopal Proper 13)

The two Prayers of the Day in the *Lutheran Book of Worship* are both new compositions. The first prayer (no. 90) draws its imagery from the Gospel for Year B but is also appropriate for Year A. Its language recalls the third post-communion prayer in the *Service Book and Hymnal,* retained in the *Lutheran Book of Worship* and in *Occasional Services* (1982) as prayer 209. The second Prayer of the Day (no. 91) is appropriate for Year C and is similar in thought to the Prayer for the Right Use of God's Gifts (no. 38) in the *Book of Common Prayer* (p. 827), a prayer originally written for the 1928 Prayer Book.

The collect in the *Book of Common Prayer* is from the Gelasian sacramentary (no. 1218) from the eleventh of sixteen Sunday masses. It is appointed in the Gregorian supplement (no. 1174) for the sixteenth Sunday after (the) Pentecost (octave). In previous Lutheran use it was assigned to the Sixteenth Sunday after Pentecost (the Fifteenth after Trinity); in previous Prayer Books it was assigned to the Sixteenth Sunday after Trinity. The opening prayer in the Roman sacramentary derives also from this Gelasian collect and a collect in the Leonine sacramentary (no. 887).

The Twelfth Sunday after Pentecost
(Roman 19th Sunday of the Year; Episcopal Proper 14)

The Prayer of the Day (no. 92) in the *Lutheran Book of Worship* has its origin in a collect in the Leonine sacramentary (no. 917) where it

---

[218]Reed, 529.

[219]Ibid., 523. Hatchett, 189, discusses the translation.

is included among prayers for the autumn ember days. In a greatly revised form it is found in the Gallican *Missale Francorum* as the final collect in the prayers of the people at Sunday mass (no. 140) and in the Gelasian sacramentary (no. 1201) as the collect for the seventh of sixteen Sunday masses. In the Gregorian supplement it is assigned to the twelfth Sunday after (the) Pentecost (octave), no. 1162. Previous Lutheran books used this "remarkably fine collect"[220] on this Sunday, the 1570 Roman missal on the Eleventh Sunday after Pentecost, and previous Prayer Books on the Twelfth Sunday after Trinity. The 1979 Prayer Book assigns it to Proper 22; the Roman sacramentary to the Twenty-seventh Sunday of the Year.

The English translation for the 1549 Prayer Book was, except for the addition to the invocation of the phrase "who art always more ready to hear than we to pray," close to the Latin of the Gelasian, concluding "and giving unto us that our prayer dare not presume to ask." The revisers of 1662 altered the translation to the present fuller and smoother form.

The collect for this Sunday in the Roman sacramentary and in the *Book of Common Prayer* is the Leonine prayer (no. 1015) still assigned to the Ninth Sunday after Pentecost in the *Lutheran Book of Worship*.

The Thirteenth Sunday after Pentecost
(Roman 20th Sunday of the Year; Episcopal Proper 15)

The Prayer of the Day (no. 93) in the *Lutheran Book of Worship* is the collect (no. 110) appointed for St. Thomas's Day (December 21), with "that perfect faith" altered to "the perfect faith." The prayer is the *Service Book and Hymnal* revision of the collect written for the 1549 Prayer Book for St. Thomas's Day.

The opening prayer in the Roman sacramentary is the prayer from the Gelasian sacramentary retained in the Lutheran book on the Sixth Sunday after Pentecost. The collect for Proper 15 in the *Book of Common Prayer* was written for the 1549 Prayer Book and appointed for the second Sunday after Easter. The collect has been familiar to Lutherans since the *Service Book and Hymnal* introduced it as a post-communion prayer, a practice continued in the *Lutheran Book of Worship* (no. 243).

The Fourteenth Sunday after Pentecost
(Roman 21st Sunday of the Year; Episcopal Proper 16)

The Prayer of the Day (no. 94) in the Lutheran book is a new composition, inspired by the Gospel for Year C.

The collect for Proper 16 in the Prayer Book is a prayer written for the 1928 *Book of Common Prayer* for Tuesday in Whitsun Week; its preamble derives from a collect in the Gregorian sacramentary (no. 542) for Friday after Pentecost. The opening prayer in the Roman sacramentary is the prayer formerly assigned to the Fourth Sunday after Easter

---

[220]Reed, 531.

and retained in the Lutheran book on what is now counted the Fifth Sunday of Easter.

The Fifteenth Sunday after Pentecost
(Roman 22nd Sunday of the Year; Episcopal Proper 17)

The Prayer of the Day (no. 95) in the *Lutheran Book of Worship* is a new composition, inspired by the Gospel for Years A and C.

The prayer in the Roman sacramentary and in the *Book of Common Prayer* is from the Gelasian sacramentary for the second of sixteen Sunday masses (no. 1182). The supplement to the Gregorian sacramentary appointed it (no. 1147) for the seventh Sunday after (the) Pentecost (octave). Previous Lutheran books assigned it to the Sixth Sunday after Trinity; earlier Prayer Books to the Seventh Sunday after Trinity; the 1570 Roman missal to the Sixth Sunday after Pentecost. Luther Reed observes, "This Collect is a meaningful and forceful prayer from the Gelasian sacramentary which the English Reformers materially enriched by their free translation of 1549,"[221] but the prayer is not used in the *Lutheran Book of Worship*.

The Sixteenth Sunday after Pentecost
(Roman 23rd Sunday of the Year; Episcopal Proper 18)

The Prayer of the Day (no. 96) in the Lutheran book is a new composition, having affinities to the thought of many of the collects for the time after Pentecost in previous Lutheran books.

The collect in the *Book of Common Prayer* is from the Leonine sacramentary (no. 540); the translation is from William Bright's *Ancient Collects* (p. 74). The opening prayer for this Sunday in the Roman sacramentary is the same as the collect it appoints for the Fifth Sunday of Easter (Gelasian no. 522).

The Seventeenth Sunday after Pentecost
(Roman 24th Sunday of the Year; Episcopal Proper 19)

The Prayer of the Day (no. 97) in the *Lutheran Book of Worship* is from the Gelasian sacramentary (no. 1198), in which it is the initial prayer of the sixth of sixteen Sunday masses. The collect is included in the Gallican *Missale Gothicum* as the first prayer of the first of six Sunday masses (no. 477). The supplement to the Gregorian sacramentary appoints it (no. 1159) for the eleventh Sunday after (the) Pentecost (octave). The Roman missal of 1570 assigned it to the Tenth Sunday after Pentecost; previous Lutheran books to the Tenth Sunday after Trinity; previous Prayer Books to the Eleventh Sunday after Trinity. The 1979 Prayer Book appoints it for Proper 21; the Roman sacramentary for the Twenty-sixth Sunday of the Year. God's "mercy and pity," more literally God's sparing and showing compassion rather than his creating and

---

[221] Reed, 527. See the comments on the translation in Hatchett, 191.

sustaining the universe, are the principal manifestations of the divine almighty power.

The opening prayer in the Roman sacramentary for this Sunday is from the Leonine sacramentary (no. 1045). The collect for Proper 19 in the *Book of Common Prayer* was assigned in previous Lutheran books to the Eighteenth Sunday after Trinity, in previous Prayer Books to the Nineteenth Sunday after Trinity, in the 1570 Roman missal to the Eighteenth Sunday after Pentecost, and in the 1969 Roman sacramentary to the Eleventh Sunday of the year. It is from the Gelasian sacramentary (no. 1230), the first collect of the fourteenth of sixteen Sunday masses. The Gregorian sacramentary appointed it for the nineteenth Sunday after (the) Pentecost (octave).

The Eighteenth Sunday after Pentecost
(Roman 25th Sunday of the Year; Episcopal Proper 20)

The Prayer of the Day (no. 98) in the *Lutheran Book of Worship* is a new composition, inspired by the Gospel for Year A.

The collect for Proper 20 in the *Book of Common Prayer* is from the Leonine sacramentary (no. 173) where it appears as a prayer for Ascension Day. The translation is by William Bright. The opening prayer in the Roman sacramentary is a new composition combining collect no. 493 from the Leonine sacramentary and no. 1374 from the Mozarabic missal.

The Nineteenth Sunday after Pentecost
(Roman 26th Sunday of the Year; Episcopal Proper 21)

The Prayer of the Day (no. 99) in the *Lutheran Book of Worship* is derived from a prayer in the Gelasian sacramentary (no. 1213). The Latin original is an unusual form, voicing its petition in the first word before the usual invocation: *Custodi, domine, quaesumus, aecclesiam tuam protectione perpetua....*

The collect appointed for this Sunday in the Roman sacramentary and in the *Book of Common Prayer* is the Gelasian collect the Lutheran book assigns to the Seventeenth Sunday after Pentecost.

The Twentieth Sunday after Pentecost
(Roman 27th Sunday of the Year; Episcopal Proper 22)

The Prayer of the Day (no. 100) in the *Lutheran Book of Worship* is a new composition in a modern and almost brash style, written for *Contemporary Worship 6*. The immediate inspiration is the beginning of the Gospel for Year B. The prayer is also notable in being one of the few prayers in the liturgy that are addressed to the second person of the Holy Trinity in his human nature. Traditionally, liturgical prayer has been addressed to the Father through the Son in the Holy Spirit. The prayer is unusual in its lack of a termination, which adds to the abrupt, even unsatisfying effect of the composition.

The Prayer Book, like the Roman sacramentary, assigns to this Sunday the Leonine collect used by the *Lutheran Book of Worship* on the Twelfth Sunday after Pentecost.

The Twenty-first Sunday after Pentecost
(Roman 28th Sunday of the Year; Episcopal Proper 23)

The Prayer of the Day (no. 101) in the *Lutheran Book of Worship* is a revision of the collect for a Day of General or Special Thanksgiving, which was introduced in the *Church Book* (1868). The first sentence alludes to Lamentations 3:23.

The collect in the Roman sacramentary and in the *Book of Common Prayer* is familiar to Lutherans from its use in previous Lutheran books on the Sixteenth Sunday after Trinity. The collect is found in the Gregorian sacramentary among a group of prayers for morning and evening (no. 996) and in the supplement to the Gregorian sacramentary (no. 1177) as the collect for the seventeenth Sunday after (the) Pentecost (octave). In the Roman missal of 1570 it was appointed for the Sixteenth Sunday after Pentecost.

The Twenty-second Sunday after Pentecost
(Roman 29th Sunday of the Year; Episcopal Proper 24)

The Prayer of the Day (no. 102) in the *Lutheran Book of Worship* is borrowed word for word from the collect for Proper 24 in the *Book of Common Prayer*. It is the first of the solemn collects for Good Friday in the Gelasian sacramentary (no. 401), the *Missale Gallicanum vetus* (no. 95), the Gregorian sacramentary (no. 339), and the Sarum missal. The translation is based on that of William Bright in *Ancient Collects* (p. 98). The same prayer, but in the translation of *The Sacramentary*, is used as the first collect of the Bidding Prayer in the Good Friday liturgy in the *Lutheran Book of Worship* (Min. Ed., p. 139, no. 42).

The opening prayer in the Roman sacramentary is the collect from the Gelasian sacramentary (no. 561) that had been appointed for the Sunday after the Ascension in the 1570 missal and in previous Lutheran books.

The Twenty-third Sunday after Pentecost
(Roman 30th Sunday of the Year; Episcopal Proper 25)

The prayer for this Sunday in the Roman, Lutheran (no. 103), and Episcopal rites is the same. It is from the Leonine sacramentary (no. 598) where it is found among a series of prayers for use at Vespers. The Gelasian sacramentary appoints it for the eighth of the sixteen Sunday masses (no. 1209); the Gregorian supplement assigns it as the collect (no. 1168) for the fourteenth Sunday after (the) Pentecost (octave). In previous Lutheran books it was assigned to the Thirteenth Sunday after Trinity; in previous Prayer Books to the Fourteenth Sunday after Trinity; in the 1570 missal to the Thirteenth Sunday after Pentecost. A literal translation of the original Latin would have "that we may deserve to obtain," but by the omission of "deserve to" Cranmer eliminated any idea of merit from the prayer.[222]

The Twenty-fourth Sunday after Pentecost
(Roman 31st Sunday of the Year; Episcopal Proper 26)

The Prayer of the Day (no. 104) in the Lutheran book is a new composition, relating particularly to the three lessons for Year A.

The collect in the Roman sacramentary and in the *Book of Common Prayer* is from the Leonine sacramentary (no. 574) where it is among the masses for July. In the Gelasian sacramentary it is the second of the collects for the eighth of the sixteen masses (no. 1206); in the Gregorian supplement (no. 1165) it is appointed for the thirteenth Sunday after (the) Pentecost (octave). Previous Lutheran books assigned it to the Twelfth Sunday after Trinity; previous Prayer Books to the Thirteenth Sunday after Trinity; the 1570 Roman missal to the Twelfth Sunday after Pentecost.

The Twenty-fifth Sunday after Pentecost
(Roman 32nd Sunday of the Year; Episcopal Proper 27)

The Prayer of the Day (no. 105) in the *Lutheran Book of Worship* is found among a series of "daily prayers" in the Gregorian sacramentary (no. 894).[223] The collect was assigned to this Sunday in previous Lutheran books, to the Twenty-fifth Sunday after Trinity in the *Book of Common Prayer*, and to the Twenty-fourth Sunday after Pentecost in the 1570 Roman missal. The present translation is an adaptation of the free rendering in the 1549 *Book of Common Prayer* which had been in Lutheran use since the *Church Book* (1868). The opening words, "Stir up" (*excita*), anticipate the characteristic cry of the Advent prayers.

The opening prayer in the Roman sacramentary is a version of the Gelasian prayer which previous Lutheran books appointed for the Nineteenth Sunday after Trinity. The collect for Proper 27 in the *Book of Common Prayer* was composed, it is thought, by John Cosin for the 1662 revision of the Prayer Book for the Sixth Sunday after the Epiphany. This prayer, like the opening of the prayer in Lutheran use, reflects the lessons which begin to focus on the second coming, the glorious advent of Christ at the end of time.

The Twenty-sixth Sunday after Pentecost
(Roman 33rd Sunday of the Year; Episcopal Proper 28)

The Prayer of the Day (no. 106) in the *Lutheran Book of Worship* is a contribution of the Church of Sweden. The prayer first appeared in the *Evangeliebok* of the Church of Sweden (1639). The English translation

---

[222]Hatchett, 194; Reed, 534.
[223]Thus Reed, 544, and Shepherd, 225. Horn, 174, and Paul Zeller Strodach, *The Church Year* (Philadelphia: Board of Publication of the United Lutheran Church in America, 1924), 259, ascribe it to the Gelasian sacramentary.

dates from the *Church Book* (1868). In previous Lutheran books the collect was assigned to the Twenty-sixth Sunday after Trinity.

The opening prayer in the Roman sacramentary is from the Leonine sacramentary (no. 486). The *Book of Common Prayer* appoints for this Sunday the collect written for the Second Sunday in Advent in the 1549 *Book of Common Prayer*, based on Romans 15:4.

The Twenty-seventh Sunday after Pentecost

The *Lutheran Book of Worship*, numbering the Sundays after Pentecost with no overlapping of propers for the Sundays after the Epiphany, requires in years when Easter is very early an additional set of propers that does not have a parallel with the system of numbering the Sundays used in the Roman sacramentary or in the *Book of Common Prayer*. The Prayer of the Day (no. 107) is a new composition, inspired by Psalm 90.

Christ the King. The Last Sunday after Pentecost

The festival of Christ the King is of recent Roman Catholic origin. Pope Pius XI in 1925, the sixteenth centenary of the Council of Nicaea, set the new feast day on the last Sunday in October "chiefly in view of the coming feast of All Saints"[224] (and, it is thought, to combat the popularity of Reformation Sunday among Lutherans and others). The new feast achieved remarkable popularity.[225] Lutherans too picked up the title and frequently used it to name new congregations; as doctrine it was unimpeachable. The Roman calendar of 1969 moved the feast to the last Sunday of the liturgical year, the "final Lord's Day" with its eschatological emphasis. "The Solemnity of Our Lord Jesus Christ, the King of the Universe," as the title runs in Latin, is thus understood as a celebration of Christ the King as the goal of the liturgical year and of our earthly pilgrimage.[226] The framers of the *Lutheran Book of Worship* found in the feast of Christ the King a welcome emphasis on the eschatological vision of the last Sundays after Pentecost, much to be preferred to the custom that obtained in many places in Lutheranism of keeping the last Sunday of the church year as a *Todtenfest* in commemoration of those who had died during the previous year. The *Book of Common Prayer*, while not using the title, keeps the theme in the propers for the Sunday closest to November 23, Proper 29.

The opening Collect of the Day in all three rites derives from the collect for the feast of the Kingship of Our Lord Jesus Christ, introduced in the Roman Church in 1925. The Prayer Book provides a free translation by Howard Galley; the *Lutheran Book of Worship* (no. 108) has revised it slightly. The phrase "king of all creation" is taken not

---

[224] Adam, 177. *Quas primas* in *Acta apostolicae sedis* (1925), 593–610.

[225] See Josef A. Jungmann's reservations about "these interminable expansions of the liturgical picture of Christ" quoted in Adam, 178.

[226] Adam, 178.

only from the proper preface and alternative opening prayer of the Roman sacramentary,[227] it also recalls the phrase from the beloved hymn, "Beautiful Savior." The preposition in the Lutheran version, "restore all things *to* your beloved Son," seems to be a mistaken transcription from the Episcopal version, "restore all things *in* your well-beloved Son; no theological scruple was implied.

Thus, with the celebration of Christ the King, the church year completes its annual round and, turning in its seamless way, gives particular point to the alternative Gospels appointed in the *Lutheran Book of Worship* for the First Sunday in Advent, which tell of the triumphal entry of Christ into the holy city: "Behold, your king comes to you."

LESSER FESTIVALS

St. Andrew, Apostle. November 30

Andrew's feast day is November 30 in both the East (from the fourth century) and the West (from at least the sixth century). The commemoration of Andrew in Rome began after Pope Simplicius (468–483) dedicated a church to him.

The Prayer of the Day in the *Lutheran Book of Worship* (no. 109) is a modest revision of the collect which had been in previous Prayer Books since 1552[228] and in the *Service Book and Hymnal*. The 1979 Prayer Book more thoroughly revised the collect and included an emphasis on the missionary impulse inherent in Andrew's call.[229] Those who prepared the *Lutheran Book of Worship* chose however to adapt the collect familiar to Lutherans from the *Service Book and Hymnal* rather than borrow the Episcopal revision. The reference to Andrew's following Jesus "without delay" joins to this feast day the urgency of the message of Advent, which begins the Sunday nearest to St. Andrew's Day.[230]

The opening prayer in the Roman sacramentary is from the Gelasian sacramentary (no. 1080) and the Gregorian (no. 770).

The proper preface for apostles' days in the *Lutheran Book of Worship* is a slightly modified form of the preface for apostles and ordinations given in the *Book of Common Prayer*. It is from the trial Liturgy of the Lord's Supper (1967), which was a revision of the preface proposed in Prayer Book Studies IV (1953), which was based on the preface for ordinations in the Scottish Prayer Book revisions of 1912 and 1929. The biblical sources include John 10:11–18; 21:15–19; Hebrew 13:20;

---

[227]Father, all-powerful, God of love, you have raised our Lord Jesus Christ from death to life, resplendent in glory as King of creation. Open our hearts, free all the world to rejoice in his peace, to glory in his justice, to live in his love. Bring all mankind together in Jesus Christ your Son, whose kingdom is with you and the Holy Spirit, one God, for ever and ever.

[228]The only collect new to that revision (Hatchett, 196).

[229]Hatchett, 196.

[230]See Shepherd, 226–27.

and Matthew 28:18–20. The Lutheran form of this preface affirms the continuity of the twelve apostles with the twelve tribes (patriarchs) and with those who embody and proclaim God's message (Prophets). Thus, the apostles are understood to have a dual function.

St. Thomas, Apostle. December 21

The commemoration of Thomas was established in the Eastern church by the sixth century on October 6. The Gregorian sacramentary lists December 21 as Thomas's feast day, and the Lutheran and Episcopal books preserve that tradition. The Roman calendar, because of the importance of the Advent liturgies of December 17–24, moved the feast to July 3.

The Lutheran (no. 110) and Episcopal prayers for this day are both revisions of the collect written for the 1549 Prayer Book and introduced to Lutheran use by the *Service Book and Hymnal* (1958). The Lutheran book also uses the prayer on the Thirteenth Sunday after Pentecost (as no. 93). The opening prayer in the Roman sacramentary is from the Gelasian sacramentary (no. 1088). Appropriately, that collect says nothing about doubt; the sole emphasis is on Thomas's faith.

The Confession of St. Peter. January 18

In sixth-century Gaul there was a commemoration on January 18 of the giving of the primacy to Peter.[231] The feast was accepted by Rome about 600. The festival of the Confession of St. Peter was introduced into the 1979 *Book of Common Prayer*, marking the beginning of the Week of Prayer for Christian Unity; the *Lutheran Book of Worship* borrowed the festival from the Prayer Book. The week of prayer was first observed in January 1908. In 1935 Abbe Paul Courturier invited all Christians to join in a common observance of the week of prayer for the unity of the church; it was endorsed by the Commission on Faith and Order of the World Council of Churches.[232]

The Prayer of the Day (no. 115) in the *Lutheran Book of Worship* is an adaptation of the collect in the *Book of Common Prayer* drafted by Massey H. Shepherd, Jr., on the basis of the Gospel for the festival and the opening prayer in the Roman sacramentary. It is noteworthy that all three prayers make the foundation of the church not the person of Peter but his confession of faith.

The Conversion of St. Paul. January 25

A mid-fifth century martyrology from Italy speaks of a Roman commemoration of Paul on January 25; the festival of his conversion, unknown in the East, was accepted in Rome in the tenth century.

The Prayer of the Day (no. 116) in the *Lutheran Book of Worship* is

---

[231] Adam, 241.
[232] See Glenn C. Stone, "The Week of Prayer for Christian Unity," *Una Sancta* 19 (Presentation of Our Lord, 1962):18–22.

from the Gregorian sacramentary (no. 604) with the first phrase taken from an earlier Gelasian collect (no. 927) for the martyrdom of St. Paul. The English translation was introduced in the *Service Book and Hymnal* and revised in the *Lutheran Book of Worship*. Notable in the revision is the change, suggested by the Roman sacramentary and *The Lutheran Hymnal* (1941), from "may by his example be led to thee," following the Latin, to "may be witnesses to the truth of your Son." The goal is not personal salvation only but the evangelization of the world through personal proclamation and witness after the example of Paul the great preacher and missionary.

The collect in the Prayer Book is a revision of the translation prepared for the 1549 Prayer Book.

The Presentation of Our Lord. February 2

Egeria reports a celebration of the Presentation in fourth-century Jerusalem. Late in the seventh century, Pope Sergius (687–701) introduced a candlelight procession, and both the Roman sacramentary and the Episcopal *Book of Occasional Services* provide a form for the blessing and procession on Candlemas.

The Roman sacramentary, the Prayer Book, and previous Lutheran books all use the same collect, from the Gregorian sacramentary (no. 124). The *Lutheran Book of Worship* has replaced the traditional collect with a new composition (no. 117) after the manner of a berakah rather than a collect and making a problematic petition. It may be argued that inspiration by the Spirit is not a requirement for seeing Jesus with our own eyes (unless it is in the Johannine sense of seeing as the equivalent of believing).

The Lutheran book uses the preface of Christmas for the Presentation (it is the closing of the Christmas cycle); the Prayer Book uses the preface of the Epiphany with its emphasis on Christ the light; the Roman sacramentary has provided a new preface for the feast.

St. Matthias, Apostle. February 24

Matthias's feast day seems to have been introduced ca. 1000, although the Gelasian sacramentary includes his name in the canon of the mass. The 1969 Roman calendar has moved his feast out of Lent to May 14; the Eastern church commemorates Matthias on August 9.

The Prayer of the Day in the *Lutheran Book of Worship* (no. 118) is taken from the *Book of Common Prayer* for which it was composed in 1549. The opening prayer in the Roman sacramentary is a translation of the collect used in the 1570 Roman missal.

The Annunciation of Our Lord. March 25

As early as the third century, March 25, then the spring equinox, was regarded as the beginning of creation, the date of the incarnation, and the date of the crucifixion, symbolically tying the creation and the new creation together.[233] The date thus became new year's day through-out Europe from the sixth century and remained so in England (and America) until 1752.

The collect of the Day (no. 119) in the *Lutheran Book of Worship* and in the *Book of Common Prayer* is a translation of a collect in the Gregorian sacramentary (no. 143), used as a post-communion prayer for the Annunciation. The prayer joins in a noteworthy way the themes of annunciation and incarnation with the cross and resurrection, con-necting Christmas, three months earlier, with the Triduum, some days ahead. The Roman sacramentary uses another prayer from the Gre-gorian sacramentary (no. 140) and provides a proper preface for the day.

St. Mark, Evangelist. April 25

Mark's feast day is earlier than the eighth century in the East. Because he was buried elsewhere, his feast day was not introduced in Rome until the tenth or eleventh century.

The prayers in all three rites seem rooted in the same Gregorian collect. The 1549 Prayer Book adapted the collect, and it was further revised in 1662 and in that form made its way, with the specific reference to St. Mark broadened to "Evangelists and Apostles," into the *Church Book* (1868) as the second of three common collects for Evangelists', Apostles', and Martyrs' days. The *Common Service Book*, eliminating the reference to apostles, made it the common collect for Evangelists' days and in this form it was appointed for St. Mark's Day in the *Ser-vice Book and Hymnal*, thus returning it to the day from which it was borrowed. The revision in the *Lutheran Book of Worship* (no. 120) in-corporates the idea of not only believing but living the new life, a theme of the Roman collect.

St. Philip and St. James, Apostles. May 1

Philip and James, celebrated separately by the Eastern churches and the Mozarabic and Gallican liturgies, have been commemorated together in the West since their relics were brought to the Church of the Twelve Apostles, which had been built in the fourth century and completely rebuilt and consecrated by John III (561–574) on May 1, 570.[234] The Roman calendar of 1969 commemorates Philip and James on May 3 to make room for the commemoration of St. Joseph the Worker on May Day.

The Prayer of the Day in the *Lutheran Book of Worship* (no. 121) is a revision of the collect for this day in the *Service Book and Hymnal*, which in turn was borrowed from the 1549 Prayer Book and revised in 1662. Curiously, although characteristically (cf. St. Mark's prayer),

---

[233]Geoffrey Chaucer in the Nun's Priest's Tale of his *Canterbury Tales* speaks of
    ... the month in which the world bigan,
    That highte March, when God first maked man.... (ll. 367–68)
[234]Reed and Horn give the date as 561.

the *Service Book and Hymnal* deleted the reference to Philip and James who were being commemorated on this day, perhaps to avoid even the remotest suggestion that their aid was being invoked. The *Lutheran Book of Worship* continues the omission.

The 1969 Prayer Book provides a new collect, the old one having been moved to the Fifth Sunday of Easter. The model for the new composition is the second collect of the common of a bishop in the South African Prayer Book of 1954. The Roman sacramentary uses the collect (no. 860) from the Gelasian sacramentary.

The Visitation. May 31

Bonaventure introduced the feast of the Visitation to his Franciscan order in 1263, observing it on July 2, the day after the octave of the birth of John the Baptist (June 24). The feast received papal approval from Urban VI in 1389; the Council of Basel (1441) authorized the festival, and it entered the general Roman calendar under Pius V. The feast is not observed by the Eastern church.

The Prayer of the Day (no. 122) in the *Lutheran Book of Worship* is a revision of the collect which had been in Lutheran use in English translation since the *Church Book* (1868). It was translated from the earliest German church order, the vernacular mass of Theobald Schwartz (Nigri) in Strasbourg (1524). It is a remarkable prayer, which together with the Gospel for the day (The Magnificat), proclaims with clarity a central message of the festival: the revolutionary character of God's activity, putting down the mighty from their seats and exalting the lowly and the despised. This is the festival of the poor and the neglected of the world.

The collect in the Prayer Book is a revision of a prayer by William Bright.[235] The Roman sacramentary has provided a new prayer for this day.

St. Barnabas, Apostle. June 11

The commemoration of Barnabas began in the fifth century in the East and in the West from the ninth century. The feast was accepted at Rome in the eleventh century.

The collect for this festival in the *Book of Common Prayer*, borrowed by the *Lutheran Book of Worship* (no. 123), is a new composition by Massey H. Shepherd, Jr., "with specific reference to events in the life of the apostle."[236] Among the scriptural allusions in the prayer are Acts 4:32–37; 9:19–30; and 13:1–3.

The opening prayer in the Roman sacramentary is from the Parisian missal of 1736.

---

[235] William Bright, *Ancient Collects*, appendix, p. 236, under the title "On the example of the Blessed Virgin."
[236] Hatchett, 201.

317

The Nativity of St. John the Baptist. June 24

John's birthday is of very early observance. The Eastern date is January 7, the day after the Epiphany. In the West the feast dates from the fifth century.

The Prayer of the Day (no. 124) in the *Lutheran Book of Worship* is a flat, uninspired, and repetitious reduction of the collect for this day in the *Common Service Book* and the *Service Book and Hymnal*. It was in turn a translation of a German original found in the Lüneburg Order (1564) which derived from a collect in the Gelasian sacramentary (no. 901; Gregorian, no. 574). The Gelasian collect is used in the Roman sacramentary. The collect in the *Book of Common Prayer* was composed for the 1549 Prayer Book.

St. Peter and St. Paul. June 29

Peter and Paul, believed to have been executed in Rome in ca. 64, have been commemorated together on June 29 since the third century. Together, these two apostles represent the entire Christian mission to Jews and Gentiles, and moreover they represent the two biblical ways of faith, like Moses and Abraham.[237]

The Prayer of the Day (no. 125) in the *Lutheran Book of Worship* is borrowed from the *Book of Common Prayer*. It is a revision by Massey H. Shepherd, Jr., of the collect in the Leonine sacramentary (no. 280), which is also the basis for the opening prayer in the Roman sacramentary. The collect is also found in the Gelasian sacramentary (no. 921) and the Gregorian sacramentary (no. 594); there is a variant in the Gallican Bobbio missal (no. 329).

St. Mary Magdalene. July 22

Mary of Magdala has been commemorated in both East and West on July 22 since the tenth century.

The Prayer of the Day in the *Lutheran Book of Worship* (no. 126) is a revision of the collect in the *Book of Common Prayer*, which is based on the English proposed book of 1928. The Lutheran version loses the reference to knowing Christ in the power of his unending life, which is of course a reference to Mary's recognition of the risen Jesus in the garden. Jesus' calling of Mary Magdalene is his coming to her and sending her as a witness (John 20:17–18).

This festival was not in the *Common Service Book* or in the *Service Book and Hymnal*. It was on the calendar in *The Lutheran Hymnal* (1941); the collect was borrowed from the Prayer Book, then appointed for the Second Sunday after Easter and now appointed for Proper 15, the collect used in the *Service Book and Hymnal* as a post-communion prayer. The opening prayer in the Roman sacramentary is based on the

---

[237] See Franz Leenhardt, *Two Biblical Faiths: Protestant and Catholic* (Philadelphia: Westminster Press, 1964).

Parisian and Ambrosian missals and emphasizes Mary's role as a herald of the resurrection.

St. James the Elder. July 25

James's feast day has been celebrated in Rome since the ninth century. The supplement to the Gregorian sacramentary (no. 1640) gives the date of the observance as July 25.

The Lutheran Prayer of the Day (no. 127) is a revision of the collect in the *Book of Common Prayer*, revised to answer the objections of some that true authority in the church derives from more than the spirit of self-denying service. Charles M. Guilbert drafted the Episcopal prayer, which stresses two events in the life of St. James narrated in the Epistle (Acts 11:27–12:3) and the Gospel (Matt. 20:20–28). The Lutheran Gospel (Mark 10:33–45) is a departure from the Roman and Episcopal lectionaries. The opening prayer in the Roman sacramentary derives from the collect for the day in previous missals, adapted and revised.

The Transfiguration of Our Lord. August 6

The Notes on the Liturgy (Min. Ed., p. 14) permit the continuation of the ecumenical tradition, introduced into American Lutheran practice by the *Service Book and Hymnal* (1958), of observing the Transfiguration on August 6, the date on which it is observed in the Church of Sweden. Making use of the permission given in this rubric means that the Transfiguration will be celebrated twice during the year — on the last Sunday after the Epiphany and on August 6.[238] This double observance is not a peculiarity of the Lutheran liturgy. The Roman calendar, in addition to keeping August 6, also used the Transfiguration theme on the Second Sunday in Lent; the Prayer Book, in addition to August 6, uses the transfiguration theme on the last Sunday after the Epiphany.

Mary, the Mother of Our Lord. August 15

Several Lutheran church orders after the Reformation — Brandenburg-Nuremberg (1533), Nassau (1536), Mark Brandenburg (1540), Schwäbisch Hall (1543) — retained this feast day of St. Mary. Luther in his pamphlet "Concerning the Order of Public Worship" (1523) advised that the festivals of Mary's Nativity, Purification, Annunciation, and Assumption be observed in Evangelical churches as signs of continuity and order.

The Prayer of the Day in the *Lutheran Book of Worship* (no. 128) is borrowed from the Prayer Book and revised so that it makes no reference to Mary's death (or "departure" as the Schwäbisch Hall Order called it), only to her motherhood. The Episcopal collect is a revision of the prayer in the South African Prayer Book. The opening prayer in the Roman sacramentary derives from the Gelasian sacramentary (no. 994).

---

[238]Such is the intention of "also" in the rubrics.

St. Bartholomew, Apostle. August 24

Bartholomew's commemoration began in the East and has been on August 24 in the West since the eighth-century supplement to the Gregorian sacramentary (no. 1656).

The Prayer of the Day in the *Lutheran Book of Worship* (no. 129) is borrowed from the *Book of Common Prayer;* the translation is basically that of the 1549 Prayer Book. The prayer derives from a collect in the Leonine sacramentary (no. 1273), the Gregorian sacramentary (no. 74), and the Gallican *Missale Gothicum* (no. 322); in each of the three books it is appointed for the festival of St. John the Evangelist.

The opening prayer in the Roman sacramentary is a new composition.

Holy Cross Day. September 14

Helena's discovery of what was supposed to be the true cross on September 14, 320, and the dedication of three churches in Jerusalem in 355 led to an annual commemoration of the discovery and veneration of the cross on which Christ died. The commemoration spread to Constantinople in the fifth century and by the seventh century to Rome.

The Prayer of the Day (no. 130) in the *Lutheran Book of Worship* is adapted from the collect in the *Book of Common Prayer*. It is a new collect, drafted for the present book by Massey H. Shepherd, Jr. The opening prayer in the Roman sacramentary derives from the collect in the Gelasian sacramentary (no. 1023).

St. Matthew, Apostle and Evangelist. September 21

Matthew's feast day seems to be of Eastern origin; it had spread to the West by the time of the Gregorian supplement (no. 1671).

Each of the three prayers for the day is a new composition; all make a similar request. The Prayer of the Day in the Lutheran book (no. 131) is based primarily on the opening prayer in the Roman sacramentary from the Parisian missal. The Episcopal collect is a new prayer by Massey H. Shepherd, Jr.

St. Michael and All Angels. September 29

Michael the archangel, popular with the Jews as the protector of God's people (Dan. 10:13, 21; 12:1), has been honored since early times, and countless churches and chapels have been dedicated to him, especially since the fifth century.

All three rites use the same collect for this day, from the Gregorian sacramentary (no. 726). The *Lutheran Book of Worship* (no. 132), like its predecessors beginning with the *Church Book*, borrowed the translation of the *Book of Common Prayer*, made originally for the 1549 book and slightly revised in 1662 and 1979.

St. Luke, Evangelist. October 18

Luke's commemoration in Rome dates from the ninth century, as is evidenced by the supplement to the Gregorian sacramentary (no. 1681). His feast day in East and West is October 18.

The Prayer of the Day (no. 133) in the *Lutheran Book of Worship* is a revision of the collect in the *Book of Common Prayer*, which is itself a revision of the 1928 revision of the original collect written for the 1549 Prayer Book. The Roman sacramentary provides a new prayer for St. Luke's Day.

St. Simon and St. Jude, Apostles. October 28

Although in the Apostolic lists in the New Testament the two apostles Simon and Judas (not Iscariot) are paired, the Eastern church commemorates them separately, Simon on May 10 and Jude on June 19, as well as both together on July 1. Their feast came from Gaul to Rome at a relatively late date; the calendar of Charlemagne does not mention it; the supplement to the Gregorian sacramentary (no. 1684) provides propers.

The Prayer of the Day in the *Lutheran Book of Worship* (no. 134) is borrowed from the *Book of Common Prayer*. The collect previously associated with this day in the Prayer Book (and therefore in Lutheran books as well) has been moved to Proper 8 "for wider use and exposure."[239] It has unfortunately been moved out of the Lutheran book altogether. The new prayer in the Episcopal and Lutheran books was drafted by Massey H. Shepherd, Jr., and makes use of the characteristic of zeal associated with Simon in Luke 6:15 and Acts 1:13.

The opening prayer in the Roman sacramentary derives from various codices of the Gregorian sacramentary (no. 279*) and was the collect for this feast in previous missals.

Reformation Day. October 31

The annual celebration of the Reformation came slowly into the Lutheran churches. Only six of the several hundred sixteenth-century church orders provide for the celebration: Brunswick (1528), Hamburg (1529), Lübeck (1531), Elector Joachim (1563), and Pomerania (1568). The first three are all by Bugenhagen. The date varied, and the observances soon died out. The Thirty Years' War stirred a spirit of anti-catholicism, and in 1667 John George II, Elector of Saxony, ordered a Reformation festival to be celebrated on October 31. The observance spread and was often transferred to the nearest Sunday, before or after the date.

With the 450th anniversary of the Augsburg Confession (1980) interest has been fostered by the Graymoor Ecumenical Institute and the American Lutheran Publicity Bureau in the celebration of October 31 or the Sunday following as a festival of Reformation/Reconciliation in

---

[239]Hatchett, 206.

affirmation of the tragic necessity of the Lutheran Reformation but also of the goal of healing the breach of the sixteenth century.[240]

The Prayer of the Day (no. 135) is a revision of the English translation, in use since the *Church Book* (1868), of the German collect found in the Saxon (Duke Henry) Church Order (1539–1540). The first and second lessons are new appointments; Psalm 46, the basis for Luther's most famous hymn *Ein'feste Burg ist unser Gott*, is an almost inescapable selection, appointed in most previous books. The Gospel, John 8:31–36, was appointed in the *Common Service Book* and in the *Service Book and Hymnal*.

All Saints' Day. November 1

By the fourth century a commemoration of all the martyrs was celebrated in the East; the date varied. The observance was introduced in Rome under Boniface IV (608–615) with the dedication of the Pantheon on May 13, 609 (or 610) to the Virgin Mary and all the martyrs. In the middle of the eighth century in England and Ireland, November 1 was observed as All Saints' Day. Gregory IV in 835 requested the Holy Roman Emperor Louis the Pious to establish this as a feast throughout his realm.

The Prayer of the Day in the *Lutheran Book of Worship* (no. 136) is a revision of the collect written for the 1549 *Book of Common Prayer* and revised in 1662. It was introduced to Lutheran use in the *Common Service Book*.[241] The opening prayer in the Roman sacramentary derives from various codices of the Gregorian sacramentary (no. 290*) and was used in previous missals.

The proper preface for All Saints in the *Lutheran Book of Worship* is a composite of the preface which was in the *Service Book and Hymnal*, borrowed directly from the *Book of Common Order* of the Church of Scotland (p. 327), and the preface from the Prayer Book which entered the American book in 1928 from the Scottish Prayer Book of 1912. The scriptural allusions are Hebrew 12:1; Ephesians 1:13–18; Colossians 1:17. The Roman preface is a new composition, which broadens the concept of saints beyond those who have been canonized.

The *Service Book and Hymnal* (1958) in effect gave All Saints' Day an octave by prescribing red as the proper color "on All Saints' Day and the Sunday following."[242] The custom of celebrating the feast of All Saints for eight days was established by Pope Sixtus IV in 1430 for

---

[240]Luther chose to post his Ninety-five Theses on the door of the castle church in Wittenberg on the eve of All Saints' Day, and that association should not be overlooked. The *Book of Occasional Services* of the Episcopal Church provides a Service for All Hallows Eve (pp. 106–07), which is the service of light with appropriate lessons and prayers.

[241]Of the liturgical appointments for All Saints' Day, Luther Reed (p. 571) wrote, "The propers, in point of harmony, depth of sentiment, and poetic beauty, are unsurpassed by any series in the church's calendar."

[242]*Service Book and Hymnal*, p. 277. The primary purpose was to encourage the observance of the Festival of All Saints, if not on the day itself (November 1), then at least on the following Sunday. The rubric made little sense when November 1 fell on a Sunday.

the whole Western church. The octave was abolished in the Roman calendar of 1969.

COMMEMORATIONS

The Common of Saints

The Prayer of the Day (no. 137) in the *Lutheran Book of Worship* is a revision of the first of three collects for the common of a saint appointed in the *Book of Common Prayer*. The Episcopal collect is a revision of the second collect provided for a saint's day in the 1928 book. The scriptural allusion is Hebrew 12:1–2, then the Epistle and now the second lesson in the first set of lessons appointed by the Prayer Book for the commemoration of a saint. The scriptural allusion has been reduced somewhat in the Lutheran version of the prayer.

The Prayer Book provides three set of psalms and lessons for the common of a saint; the Lutheran book has selected from these to make its one set.

The Common of Martyrs

The Prayer of the Day in the *Lutheran Book of Worship* (no. 138) was composed for *Contemporary Worship 6* (1973) in preparation for the *Lutheran Book of Worship*. The final clause of the petition is a reminder of the derivation of the word "martyr" from the Greek "witness." The two alternative prayers in the Roman Catholic Common of Several Martyrs and the second prayer in the Common of One Martyr make the same play on words.

The Lutheran Alleluia Verse and its alternative are taken from the Roman lectionary; the Gospel, Mark 8:34–38, is from the Prayer Book Propers of a Martyr III.

The Common of Missionaries

Lutheran liturgical interest in missionaries derives in large measure from the nineteenth-century liturgical revival which coincided with the great age of missionary expansion. Many Lutheran groups in North America were themselves begun and supported by that drive to spread, plant, and nurture the Gospel.

The Prayer of the Day in the Lutheran book (no. 139) is a revision of the first collect from the Common of a Missionary in the *Book of Common Prayer*, which is itself a revision of a prayer in the *Book of Common Worship* of the Church of South India (p. 65), the Indian Prayer Book supplement, and the English Prayer Book of 1928. The scriptural allusions are Ephesians 3:8 and Colossians 2:19. The Roman sacramentary as part of the Common of Pastors provides a prayer for the commemoration of a missionary. The first sentence of the Lutheran prayer is a new composition, drawn in part from the thought of the Roman prayer, and reminds the assembly that the work of making the good news known is finally not the work of the missionary but of the Holy Spirit, who gives his gifts to his people and so "calls, gathers, enlightens, and sanctifies the whole Christian church on earth," as Luther says in his explanation of the third article of the Creed in the Small Catechism.

The Roman sacramentary provides propers for a mass For the Spread of the Gospel, from which the Lutheran book borrows the appointment of the Second Lesson (Rom. 10:11–17) and the Gospel (Luke 24:44–53). The *Book of Common Prayer* appoints the preface for Pentecost for the commemoration of a missionary; the Lutheran book makes no suggestion concerning a preface.

The color white, which is appointed in the Lutheran book, suggests Christ, who is the content of a faithful missionary's message, and recalls the Epiphany season with its emphasis on the manifestation of Christ to the nations. In view of the role of the Holy Spirit in the spread of the church, red would also be an appropriate choice.

The Common of Renewers of the Church

This category and the propers appointed for it are the contribution of the *Lutheran Book of Worship* to the ecumenical church. The category reminds the Christian community of a basic Reformation principle: the church is never beyond the need for change and is never reformed once and for all. The Prayer of the Day (no. 140) is a new composition, prepared for *Contemporary Worship 6* (1973).

The Common of Renewers of Society

The category Renewers of Society, the first Prayer of the Day (no. 141), and the selection of the lessons, responsorial psalm, Verse, and Offertory are the contributions of *Contemporary Worship 6* and the *Lutheran Book of Worship*. The address of the first Prayer of the Day is based on Matthew 20:28. The alternative Prayer of the Day (no. 142) is a revision of the prayer in the Proper for Social Justice in the *Book of Common Prayer*, which first appeared in the 1928 Prayer Book. The Prayer was composed, some say, by James Martineau; others say it was written by Edward Lambe Parsons.[243]

The Common of Pastors and Bishops

In churches with an episcopal polity the bishop is the chief pastor of the diocese; the presbyters are assistants who extend the bishop's pastoral ministry. The Roman Catholic and Episcopal churches provide propers for a common of Pastors. The *Lutheran Book of Worship* adds for clarification "and Bishops," reminding the church that the ministry of bishops is primarily not administrative but pastoral.

The *Lutheran Book of Worship* has borrowed from the Common of a Pastor in the *Book of Common Prayer* the first of the two collects,

---

[243]See Hatchett, 215.

one psalm, and the lessons. The Collect (no. 143) is derived from the prayer for the commemoration of pastors that was written for the *Book of Common Worship* of the Church of South India (p. 66). The petition contains an allusion to Ephesians 4:11–13. The second Prayer of the Day in the *Lutheran Book of Worship* (no. 144) is a new composition. The first prayer stresses the pastoral care by the shepherds of the church; the second, the leadership which makes ministry possible.

The Common of Theologians

Four Western doctors (from the Latin "teachers") of the church were recognized by Boniface VIII in 1298: Gregory the Great, Ambrose, Augustine, and Jerome. Three Eastern doctors — John Chrysostom, Basil the Great, and Gregory Nazianzus — were recognized by Pius V in 1568; Athanasius was added later. There are now more than thirty of these teachers on the Roman calendar.

The *Book of Common Prayer* and the *Lutheran Book of Worship* provide for the commemoration of Theologians. (The Prayer Book adds "Teachers" to the title.) The *Lutheran Book of Worship* has borrowed from the Prayer Book the first of the two Collects (no. 145), the psalm, and the lessons. The Episcopal collect, which was adapted by the Lutheran book, is a revision of the collect "Of a Doctor of the Church, Poet, or Scholar" in the 1959 Canadian Prayer Book, which was derived from the collect for St. Barnabas's Day in the 1549 Prayer Book. The first sentence of the prayer is based on 1 Corinthians 12:4–11.

The Roman sacramentary provides one prayer for the Common of Doctors of the Church for use if there is no proper prayer. Moreover, in the Common of Holy Men and Women there is a collect for a teacher.

The Common of Artists and Scientists

It is appropriate for the church which is proud to count among its most brilliant ornaments Johann Sebastian Bach, which has rejoiced in the richness of church music, and which has often encouraged rigorous thought and bold intellectual exploration, to provide for the remembrance of the contribution of practitioners of the arts and the sciences. The propers for Artists and Scientists were prepared for the *Lutheran Book of Worship*, a contribution to the ecumenical church. The Prayer of the Day (no. 146) was drafted by Philip H. Pfatteicher and draws in part on the thought of the fourth stanza of Henry Hallam Tweedy's hymn "Eternal God, whose power upholds/Both flower and flaming star" (no. 322 in the *Service Book and Hymnal*). The 1959 Canadian *Book of Common Prayer* provided a common "Of a Doctor of the Church, Poet, or Scholar."

OCCASIONS

In addition to the Lesser Festivals and the common propers for the various Commemorations, the *Lutheran Book of Worship* also provides propers for certain Occasions, a title borrowed from the *Book of Common Prayer.*

Unity

All three rites — Roman, Lutheran, and Episcopal — have provided propers for a Eucharist with its particular emphasis on unity. It is significant that the propers for the Unity of the Church are first among those provided for Occasions, indicating that the most important concern of the church at this time in its history is unity "so that the world may believe" (John 17:21).

The Prayer of the Day in the *Lutheran Book of Worship* (no. 147) was prepared for *Contemporary Worship 6* (1973) and derives from the collect in the *Book of Common Prayer* for the Unity of the Church, which is based on a prayer by William Temple.[244] In the Lutheran book this prayer, which is based on John 17:21–23, is also appointed as the alternative Prayer of the Day (no. 73) for the Seventh Sunday of Easter, the Gospel for which in all three years is drawn from Jesus' high priestly prayer in John 17.

The Roman sacramentary provides three sets of propers for Christian Unity, each with a choice of two opening prayers, and a proper preface for Christian Unity. The Prayer Book appoints the preface of Baptism or the preface of Trinity Sunday.

Dedication and Anniversary

The two Prayers of the Day in the *Lutheran Book of Worship* are new compositions, prepared for *Contemporary Worship 6*. The first prayer (no. 148) makes the ancient affirmation that what makes a church holy is not a particular rite of consecration but the use of the building. The opening of the prayer echoes Solomon's prayer at the dedication of the temple (1 Kings 8:27, from the first lesson for the occasion; 2 Chron. 6:18); the conclusion echoes Solomon's petition. The first sentence of the second prayer (no. 149) is grounded in Jesus' promise in Matthew 28:20; the last sentence of the petition recalls the collect for All Saints' Day.

The prayer in the Roman sacramentary is a translation of a collect in the Gregorian sacramentary (no. 1262) and the Bobbio missal (no. 390). The collect in the *Book of Common Prayer* is a new composition, derived from J. D. Wilkinson.[245] The Psalm and the First and Second Lessons in the Lutheran propers are borrowed from the Roman and Episcopal

---

[244] In *Parish Prayers*, ed. Frank Colquhoun (London: Hodder & Stoughton, 1967), no. 494. Hatchett, 212.

[245] In *The Calendar and Lessons for the Church Year* (London: SPCK, 1969), 89. Hatchett, 211.

rites. The Roman sacramentary provides two proper prefaces for the dedication of a church, one for use in the dedicated church and the other for use outside the church; the *Book of Common Prayer* has provided a new preface for the dedication and the anniversary of the dedication of a church.[246]

Harvest

The celebration of the harvest festival is a Lutheran custom of long standing. In European practice it is usually observed near St. Michael's Day (September 29), an association which adds an eschatological dimension to the celebration of harvest, for according to tradition St. Michael will gather the dead at the last day. In the United States, Thanksgiving Day began as a day of thanksgiving after the harvest in 1621, but when it was established as a national day of thanksgiving in 1863 its purpose was broadened beyond gratitude for the harvest. Therefore Lutheran congregations which observe a festival of harvest usually do so in addition to the national day of thanksgiving. The *Book of Common Prayer* does not provide for a festival of harvest, but the propers for Thanksgiving Day incorporate the harvest theme. The Roman sacramentary provides propers for a mass for productive land in addition to propers for a mass after harvest. Recognizing the overlapping of harvest and thanksgiving, the Roman Lectionary for Mass notes that "Readings from the Mass in thanksgiving may also be used."

The Prayer of the Day for Harvest in the *Lutheran Book of Worship* (no. 150) first appeared in the *Church Book* (1868); the present collect is a revision. The ethical turn of the original collect ("bless and protect the living seed of Thy Word sown in our hearts, that in the plenteous fruits of righteousness we may always present unto Thee an acceptable thankoffering") has been replaced in the revision with a request for environmental concerns ("Teach us to use your gifts carefully"), reflecting the increased awareness of the fragility of the earth. The first sentence recalls the versicle Luther suggests in the Small Catechism for grace before meals[247] (Ps. 145:16; see 104:28–29); the second sentence draws upon Psalm 65:9ff. The harvest festival is a very old celebration, as old as religion,[248] and an echo of ancient traditions, still full of significance to many, is heard toward the end of the prayer in the gender of the pronoun referring to the land ("her").

The First Lesson is borrowed from the *Church Book* and *The Lutheran Hymnal;* the Second Lesson from the *Common Service Book;* the Psalm from the *Church Book*, the *Common Service Book*, *The Lutheran Hymnal*, the *Service Book and Hymnal*, and the Roman lectionary. The Gospel, verse, and offertory are selections peculiar to the *Lutheran Book of Worship.*

---

[246] For further discussion of the rites of the dedication of churches see Philip H. Pfatteicher, *Commentary on the Occasional Services*, 250–91.

[247] *Book of Concord*, 353.

[248] See for example, Eliade, *Patterns in Comparative Religion*, 331ff.

For reasons not immediately apparent the *Common Service Book* and the *Service Book and Hymnal* appointed red as the proper liturgical color for the festival of harvest and for the Day of General or Special Thanksgiving. The Roman Catholic and Episcopal practice was to use white for thanksgiving. In the *Lutheran Book of Worship* the color for Harvest is the color proper to the season (therefore usually green); for a Day of Thanksgiving it is white.

Day of Penitence

The Lutheran church after the Reformation returned to the practice which had obtained before the establishment of the rogation days and provided appointments for what was often called a Day of Humiliation and Prayer, without naming any specific date for the observance. Later in many areas, especially after the deprivations of the Thirty Years' War, a fixed date was established for annual observance, sometimes on or near the rogation days. In places where the influence of the Reformed Church was strong (Cassel, Hesse, Württemberg, for example), quarterly or even monthly penitential days were appointed. After 1893, most Lutheran areas in central and northern Germany observed the Wednesday before the last Sunday after Trinity as a day of penitence.[249]

The propers, except the Gospel for the day (Luke 15:11–32) which had been appointed in the *Common Service Book*, are all new. The first Prayer of the Day (no. 151) replaces the one in previous books, translated from the Nuremberg church order (1691), which was long, repetitious, and more general than the new and more terse prayer that was prepared for *Contemporary Worship 6*. The second prayer (no. 152) was written by Charles A. Ferguson for the *Lutheran Book of Worship* to incorporate into a Christian liturgy the themes of the recent Jewish observance, Yom Hashoah, a remembrance of the Holocaust, established in 1952 on the anniversary of the uprising in the Warsaw Ghetto (February 1943). The observance now takes place in April. People of the Lutheran tradition were both executioners and victims in that unspeakable horror of the death camps, and so it is perhaps particularly fitting for a Lutheran book to take note of such an observance. The Roman sacramentary provides propers for a mass In Time of War and Civil Disturbances, which overlaps some of the themes of the Day of Penitence.

The *Common Service Book* and the *Service Book and Hymnal* prescribed the use of black only twice during the year: for a Day of Humiliation and Prayer and for Good Friday. The *Lutheran Book of Worship* prefers to associate black only with Ash Wednesday, the most somber day of desolation in the year, to leave Good Friday as anciently without liturgical color (the altar having been stripped bare on Maundy Thursday), and to soften the color of the Day of Penitence to purple, in line with the general brightening of the mood and spirit of worship in recent years.

---

[249]Reed, 574.

National Holiday

The provision of propers for the observance of a national holiday is new to the Lutheran tradition. Lutheran liturgists have consistently maintained that the liturgy of the church is international and universal, spanning the centuries and political systems and nationality; therefore no notice was taken liturgically of national holidays. In actual parish practice, however, the situation was quite different.

The *Lutheran Book of Worship* was prepared for Lutherans principally in two countries, the United States and Canada. Therefore any appointments for national holidays had to be handled in a general fashion. The Canadian *Book of Common Prayer* of 1922 provided for the observance of Dominion Day and other Occasions of National Thanksgiving. Independence Day (July 4) entered the American Prayer Book in 1928;[250] the 1979 Prayer Book provides propers for Independence Day and For the Nation. The Roman sacramentary provides propers for masses for several civil needs: For the Nation (State) or City; For Those Who Serve in Public Office; For the Assembly of National Leaders; For the King or Head of State; For the Progress of Peoples; For Peace and Justice; and In Time of War and Civil Disturbances. The American bishops have authorized propers for Independence Day for use in the United States.[251]

The Prayer of the Day in the *Lutheran Book of Worship* for a National Holiday (no. 153) is a new composition, written for *Contemporary Worship 6*. The Psalm and the First Lesson are new selections; the Second Lessons and the Gospel are those appointed in the *Book of Common Prayer* in the propers for the Nation. The extra-liturgical character of this observance is underscored in the Lutheran book by the lack of provision of a proper liturgical color for a National Holiday; the proper color is that of the liturgical season.

Peace

Although, like Unity, Peace may be said to be a theme of every Eucharist, the intention of these propers is to provide for a service the theme of which is civil peace between the peoples and nations of the earth. The modern church is learning to understand the social implications of the Gospel of peace, which overflows into all areas of life. In the Old Testament peace was a sign of the messianic kingdom; for Christians, too, peace is not simply a religious category but is ultimately indivisible, for as Eric Milner-White put it in a splendid prayer, "O God, it is your will to hold heaven and earth in a single peace."[252]

---

[250]See the review of the struggle from 1785 to 1789 in the Episcopal Church to introduce a service of thanksgiving for religious and civil liberty into the American Prayer Book given in Shepherd, 263–64.

[251]*The Sacramentary*, 663–64, 536–39.

[252]Prayer no. 166, Min. Ed., p. 105. Eric Milner-White, ed., *Memorials upon Several Occasions* (London: A. R. Mowbray, 1933), no. 7b. The original text began, "O God, who

The Prayer of the Day in the *Lutheran Book of Worship* (no. 154) is a revision of the collect in the *Book of Common Prayer* for a Eucharist for Peace. The collect is based on a prayer by Francis Paget, bishop of Oxford (1902–1911). It was included in the 1928 Proposed English Prayer Book and in the Prayer Books of South Africa, India, and Canada.[253]

The comparable propers in the Roman sacramentary are those for Peace and Justice.

Day of Thanksgiving

Nearly all Lutheran sixteenth-century church orders provide propers for a day of humiliation and prayer; very few provide for a day of thanksgiving. The propers for this occasion are most often used on the national Thanksgiving Day, but their use at other times when expressions of thanksgiving and gratitude are appropriate should not be overlooked.

The Prayer of the Day (no. 155) is the same as that appointed for the Twenty-first Sunday after Pentecost (no. 101). It is a revision for *Contemporary Worship 6* of the collect for the Day of General or Special Thanksgiving which first appeared in the *Church Book* of 1868 (The national Thanksgiving Day being but five years old). The same collect, in German, appears in Loehe's *Agenda* of 1844. Absent from the otherwise admirable prayer is the recognition of the needs of others, which is expressed in the Episcopal collect for Thanksgiving and in the opening prayer of the propers for Thanksgiving Day authorized for use in the Roman Catholic dioceses of the United States. The Roman sacramentary appoints a proper preface; the *Book of Common Prayer* appoints the preface of Trinity Sunday.

Stewardship of Creation

The traditional times for processions, litanies, and prayer for good harvests and for various civil needs were the three days before Ascension Day and, in the city of Rome, St. Mark's Day (April 25). Since both of these occasions fell within the Easter season, their penitential overtones were always at variance with the spirit of the fifty days of rejoicing. The Roman calendar of 1969 abolished the litanies on St. Mark's Day and combined the rogation days with the ember days, leaving the date and manner of their observance to the episcopal conferences of each nation. The *Book of Common Prayer* has preserved the rogation days but has expanded their purpose beyond agricultural needs and permits the propers to be used at other times besides the traditional days before Ascension Day.

The *Lutheran Book of Worship* has borrowed all three collects from the Episcopal series and has selected a Psalm, First and Second Lesson, and Gospel, and has set them all under one heading, Stewardship of

---

wouldst fold heaven and earth in a single peace..." as in the *Service Book and Hymnal*, no. 57 (p. 226).
[253]Hatchett, 214.

Creation. The first prayer (no. 156), for fruitful seasons, derives from the collect for the rogation days which was in the 1928 Prayer Book.[254] The second collect, for commerce and industry (it is the third collect in the Lutheran order, no. 158; see p. 396, no. 178), is based on the prayer for Industry in the Canadian Prayer Book. The third collect (the second in the Lutheran series, no. 157), for the stewardship of creation, is a revision of the prayer in the 1928 Prayer Book for Faithfulness in the Use of this World's Goods. That prayer seems to derive from a prayer "For the Rich" in the Book of Offices proposed to the General Convention of the Episcopal Church in 1889 (p. 89). Note: In early editions of the *Lutheran Book of Worship*, the First Lesson was given as Job 39:1–11, 16–18. This was a misprint; the correct reference is Job 38:1–11, 16–18.

The Episcopal *Book of Occasional Services* (pp. 101–03) provides additional lessons and prayers for the Rogation Procession.

New Year's Eve

For centuries the church struggled to keep the excesses of the celebration of the secular new year out of its solemnities. It was a losing battle. In Germany after the Reformation the New Year was given certain liturgical recognition. The *Church Book* (1868) provided a collect for the New Year and called the following Sunday "Sunday after New Year." The *Common Service Book* and the *Service Book and Hymnal* preserved the New Year collect. The American Book of Common Prayer has never provided anything for the new secular year.[255] There was a collect for the New Year in the English proposed book of 1928. Previous Roman Catholic missals provided nothing for the New Year, but the 1969 Roman sacramentary provides propers for a mass at the beginning of the New Year. In the *Lutheran Book of Worship*, to emphasize the extra-liturgical character of New Year's Eve services, the propers are not included with those for the church year and the holy days but rather with the Occasions. The rubric following the propers further guards against misunderstanding and misuse of these propers and assures the primacy of the church year.

The Prayer of the Day in the *Lutheran Book of Worship* (no. 159) is a new composition, prepared for *Contemporary Worship 6*. The Gospel (Luke 13:6–9) is from the lectionary of Thomasius for New Year's Eve.

Holy Baptism

The Prayer of the Day in the *Lutheran Book of Worship* (no. 160) is borrowed from the 1979 *Book of Common Prayer*, where it concludes the

---

[254]It seems to have been influenced by a prayer "For the Fruits of the Earth" written by Bishop John Cosin and first printed in his *Collection of Private Devotions* (1627); the revision uses phrases from a prayer by E. W. Benson in *Parish Prayers*, ed. Frank Colquhoun, no. 348. Hatchett, 214.

[255]The Episcopal *Book of Occasional Services*, 40–44, provides a Service for New Year's Eve, a vigil modeled on the Easter Vigil.

prayers for the candidates. Although a good bit of material from these prayers was borrowed for the *Lutheran Book of Worship*, in their Lutheran form the prayers conclude with the standard formula, "Into your hands, O Lord, we commend all for whom we pray...," thus freeing the Episcopal prayer for use elsewhere. The broad selection of psalms and lessons is drawn in part from the Roman lectionary and from the *Book of Common Prayer*. Only once in the propers is a text for the Prayers of the people provided: those for Holy Baptism. The Roman rite also provides model intercessions for Baptism (*The Rites*, pp. 264–67). The proper preface for Holy Baptism is taken from the *Book of Common Prayer* (p. 381); the preface was prepared for the 1979 Prayer Book. The three effects of baptism enumerated in the preface are all equally important. The post-communion prayer, like the Prayer of the Day, is simple and direct, almost to the point of abruptness. It was composed for *Contemporary Worship 7* and is a reminder that participation in the Supper is inherent in the baptismal adoption into the community of the faithful. The two sacraments are intimately related.

Additional discussion of the propers for Holy Baptism is provided above, pp. 33–34, 38, 61. The propers for Marriage, the Burial of the Dead, and Corporate Confession and Forgiveness are discussed in connection with the examination of each of those rites.

Table I
The Commons Provided by Four Liturgical Books

Roman Sacramentary	Book of Common Worship: Church of South India	Book of Common Prayer	Lutheran Book of Worship
Blessed Virgin Mary			
	Apostles		
Holy Men & Women		a Saint	Saints
Martyrs	Martyrs	a Martyr	Martyrs
Virgins	Faithful women		
		a Monastic	
	Preachers of the Gospel	a Missionary	Missionaries
	Prophets and Reformers		Renewers of the Church
			Renewers of Society
Pastors	Pastors	a Pastor	Pastors and Bishops
Doctors of the Church	Doctors of the Church	a Theologian and Teacher	Theologians
	Teachers		
	Healers of the Sick		
			Artists and Scientists
	Pioneers and Builders		
	Servants of the Church		

Note: Confessors is no longer a category for any of these traditions.

Table II
The Ancient Series of Collects,
Preserved in the Common Service, as Used in Revised Liturgies

An x indicates that the book includes the collect on its traditional date;
if it has been moved to a different date, the new date is given.

Common Service (Church Book, CSB, SBH)	Roman Missal 1570	Book of Common Prayer 1928	Roman Missal 1969	LBW 1978	Book of Common Prayer 1979
Advent 1	X		Fri. after Advent 1	X	
Advent 2	X		Thurs.	X	
Advent 3	X			X	
Advent 4	X	X	Thurs. after Advent 1	X	
Christmas early	X (midnight)		X	X	X
Christmas later	X (day)			X	
St. Stephen	X	X	X	X	X
St. John (Innocents)	X	X	X	X	X
Christmas 1	X		3d Sun. of year		
Circumcision		X			
The Epiphany	X	X	X	X	X
Epiphany 1	X	X		Epiphany 6	Proper 10
Epiphany 2	X	X	X	Epiphany 8	Epiphany 4
Epiphany 3	X	X			
Epiphany 4	X	X		X	
Epiphany 5	X	X	X	Epiphany 7	
Transfiguration	X (Aug. 6)			X (alt.)	
Septuagesima	X	X			
Sexagesima	X	X			
Quinquagesima	X	X			Epiphany 7
Ash Wednesday		X		X	X
Lent 1					
Lent 2	X	X			Lent 3
Lent 3	X	X			
Lent 4	X	X		X	
Lent 5	X	X			
Lent 6	X	X	X	X	X
Holy Monday	X		X		
Holy Tuesday	X		X		
Holy Wednesday	X		X		
Maundy Thursday				X (alt.)	
Good Friday	Super populum Wed. in Holy Week	X		X	X
Easter Eve	X		X		X
Easter Day	X	X	X	X	X
Easter 1	X		Sat. after Easter 7	X	

Table II (continued)

Common Service (*Church Book, CSB, SBH*)	Roman Missal 1570	*Book of Common Prayer 1928*	Roman Missal 1969	*LBW 1978*	*Book of Common Prayer 1979*
Easter 2	X		14th Sun. of Year	X	
Easter 3	X	X	15th Sun. of Year	X (alt.)	
Easter 4	X	X	21st Sun. of Year	X	Lent 5
Easter 5	X	X	10th Sun. of Year	X	Proper 5
Ascension Day	X	X	X	X	
Sunday after Ascension	X		29th Sun. of Year		
Pentecost	X	X			X
Mon. after Pent.	X				
Trinity Sunday	X	X	X	X (alt.)	
Trinity 1		X	11th Sun. of Year	Pentecost 3	Epiphany 6
Trinity 2	Pentecost 2	X	12th Sun. of Year		Proper 7
Trinity 3	Pentecost 3	Trinity 4	17th Sun. of Year		Proper 12
Trinity 4	Pentecost 4	Trinity 5	8th Sun. of Year		Proper 3
Trinity 5	Pentecost 5	Trinity 6	20th Sun. of Year	Pentecost 6	Easter 6
Trinity 6	Pentecost 6	Trinity 7	22d Sun. of Year		Proper 17
Trinity 7	Pentecost 7	Trinity 8	9th Sun. of Year		Proper 4
Trinity 8	Pentecost 8	Trinity 9	Thurs. after Lent 1	Pentecost 9	Proper 14
Trinity 9	Pentecost 9	Trinity 10		Pentecost 10	
Trinity 10	Pentecost 10	Trinity 11	26th Sun. of Year	Pentecost 17	Proper 21
Trinity 11	Pentecost 11	Trinity 12	27th Sun. of Year	Pentecost 12	Proper 22
Trinity 12	Pentecost 12	Trinity 13	31st Sun. of Year		Proper 26
Trinity 13	Pentecost 13	Trinity 14	30th Sun. of Year	Pentecost 23	Proper 25
Trinity 14	Pentecost 14	Trinity 15			
Trinity 15	Pentecost 15	Trinity 16	Mon. after Lent 3		Proper 13
Trinity 16	Pentecost 16	Trinity 17	28th Sun. of Year		Proper 23
Trinity 17	Pentecost 17	Trinity 18			
Trinity 18	Pentecost 18	Trinity 19	Sat. after Lent 4		Proper 19
Trinity 19	Pentecost 19	Trinity 20	32d Sun. of Year		

Table II (continued)

Common Service (*Church Book*, *CSB*, *SBH*)	Roman Missal 1570	*Book of Common Prayer* 1928	Roman Missal 1969	*LBW* 1978	*Book of Common Prayer* 1979
Trinity 20	Pentecost 20	Trinity 21		Burial	
Trinity 21	Pentecost 21	Trinity 22			
Trinity 22	Pentecost 22	Trinity 23			
Trinity 23	Pentecost 23	Trinity 24	Fri. after Lent 5		
Trinity 24	Pentecost 24 and last Sun.	Sun. next before Advent	Weekdays after 34th Sun. of Year	Pentecost 25	
Trinity 25					
Trinity 26				Pentecost 26	
Trinity 27 = 23					
St. Andrew		X			
St. Thomas		X		Pentecost 13	
Conv. St. Paul	X				
Presentation	X		X		
St. Matthias		X			
Annunciation		X	Advent 4		
St. Mark		X			
SS. Philip & James		X			Easter 5
Visitation					
Nativity John B.					
SS. Peter & Paul		X			
St. James		X			
St. Bartholomew		X			
St. Matthew		X			
St. Michael	X	X			
St. Luke		X			
SS. Simon & Jude		X			Proper 8
Reformation					
All Saints		X			
Harvest					
Humiliation					
Thanksgiving				Pentecost 21	

BIBLIOGRAPHY

Advent

Burlin, Robert. *The Old English Advent.* New Haven: Yale University Press, 1967.

Cowley, Patrick. *Advent: Its Liturgical Significance.* London and New York: Faith Press, 1960.

Liturgy 4:3 (Summer 1984). An issue devoted to Advent, Christmas, and Epiphany.

Merton, Thomas. "The Advent Mystery," *Worship* 38 (December 1983):17–25.

Christmas and Epiphany

Coffin, Tristam P. *The Book of Christmas Folklore.* New York: Continuum, 1973.

Cullmann, Oscar. *Weinachten der alter Kirche.* Basel, 1947. English translation in *The Early Church*, edited by A. J. B. Higgins. Philadelphia: Westminster Press, 1956. Pp. 17–36.

Duchesne, Louis. *Origines du culte Chrétien.* 1899. English translation, *Christian Worship: Its Origin and Evolution.* 5th ed. London: SPCK, 1949.

Gunstone, John T. A. *Christmas and Epiphany.* London: Faith Press, 1967.

Samuelson, Sue. *Christmas: An Annotated Bibliography of Analytical Scholarship.* New York: Garland, 1982.

Studwell, William E. *Christmas Carols: A Reference Guide.* New York: Garland, 1985.

Usener, Hermann Karl. *Das Weinachtsfest.* 2nd ed. by Hans Lietzmann. Bonn: F. Cohen, 1911.

Weiser, Francis X. *The Christmas Book.* New York: Harcourt Brace, 1952.

Lent and Holy Week

Bennett, J. A. W. *Poetry of the Passion: Studies in Twelve Centuries of English Verse.* Oxford: Clarendon Press, 1982.

Bugnini-Braga. *Ordo Hebdomadae Sanctae Instauratus.* Rome, 1956.

Crichton, J. D. *The Liturgy of Holy Week.* Rev. ed. Dublin: Veritas Publications; Leominster, Herefordshire: Fowler Wright Books, 1983.

Davies, J. Gordon. *Holy Week: A Short History.* Ecumenical Studies in Worship No. 11. Richmond, VA: John Knox Press, 1963.

Freedman, Ruth G. *The Passover Seder.* Philadelphia: University of Pennsylvania Press, 1980.

Greenacre, Roger. *The Sacrament of Easter: An Introduction to the Liturgy of Holy Week.* Studies in Christian Worship No. 4. London: Faith Press, 1965.

Loehr, Aemiliana. *The Great Week.* Translated by D. T. H. Bridgehouse. Westminster, MD: Newman Press, 1958.

Mackowski, Richard M. *Jerusalem: City of Jesus.* Grand Rapids, MI: Eerdmans, 1980. Note especially pp. 149–59, a discussion of the Church of the Holy Sepulchre.

McManus, Frederick R. *The Rites of Holy Week.* Patterson, NJ: St. Anthony Guild Press, 1956.

Miller, J. J. "The History and Spirit of Holy Week," *American Ecclesiastical Review* (April 1957).

Music for the Vigil of Easter. Minneapolis: Augsburg Publishing House and Philadelphia: Board of Publications, Lutheran Church of America, 1979.

Peters, F. E. *Jerusalem: The Holy City in the Eyes of Chroniclers, Visitors, Pilgrims, and Prophets from the Days of Abraham to the Beginnings of Modern Times.* Princeton: University Press, 1985.

Talley, Thomas J. "The Origins and Shape of Lent," *Liturgy* 4 (Winter 1983): 9–13.

Tierney, Mark. *Holy Week: A Commentary.* Dublin: Browne and Nolan, 1958.

Easter

Beckwith, Roger T. "The Origin of the Festivals of Easter and Whitsun," *Studia Liturgica* 13 (1979):1–20.

Berger, Rupert, and Hans Hollerweger, eds. *Celebrating the Easter Vigil.* Translated by Matthew J. O'Connell. New York: Pueblo Publishing Co., 1983.

Gunstone, John T. A. *The Feast of Pentecost.* London: Faith Press, 1967.

Huck, Gabe, and Mary Ann Simcoe. *A Triduum Sourcebook.* Chicago: Liturgy Training Publications, 1983.

Liturgy 3:1 (Winter 1982). An issue devoted to "Easter's Fifty Days."

Nardone, Richard. "The Roman Calendar in Ecumenical Perspective," *Worship* 50 (May 1976):238–46.

Nocent, Adrian. "Liturgical Catechesis of the Christian Year," *Worship* 51 (November 1977):496–505.

Regan, Patrick. "The Fifty Days and the Fiftieth Day," *Worship* 55 (May 1981): 194–218.

———. "The Three Days and the Forty Days," *Worship* 54 (January 1980):2–18.

Talley, Thomas J. "History and Eschatology in the Primitive Pascha," *Worship* 47 (April 1973):212–21.

Weiser, Francis X. *The Easter Book.* New York: Harcourt Brace, 1954.

Saints

Atkinson, Clarissa. *Mystic and Pilgrim: The Book and the World of Margery Kempe.* Ithaca, NY: Cornell University Press, 1986.

Berger, Pamela. *The Goddess Obscured: Transformation of the Grain Protectress from Goddess to Saint.* Boston: Beacon Press, 1985.

Brown, Peter. *The Cult of the Saints: Its Rise and Function in Latin Christianity.* London: SCM, 1981; Chicago: University Press, 1982.

Butler's Lives of the Saints. Ed., rev., and supplemented by Herbert Thurston and Donald Attwater. 4 vols. New York: Kenedy, 1956.

Cohen, Henig, and Tristam Coffin, eds. *The Folklore of American Holidays.* Detroit: Gale Research Co., 1986.

Cox, Pamela. *Biography in Late Antiquity: A Quest for the Holy Man.* Berkeley: University of California Press, 1984.

Cunningham, Lawrence. *The Meaning of Saints.* San Francisco: Harper & Row, 1980.

———. *The Mother of God.* San Francisco: Harper & Row, 1982.

Delaney, John. *Dictionary of Saints.* Garden City, NY: Doubleday, 1980.

———. *Saints Are Now: Eight Portraits of Modern Sanctity.* Garden City, NY: Doubleday, 1983.

Farmer, David Hugh, ed. *The Oxford Dictionary of Saints.* 2nd ed. New York: Oxford University Press, 1987.

Ferguson, Charles A. "Saints' Names in American Lutheran Church Dedications," *Names* 14 (1966):76–82.

Foxe, John. *Acts and Monuments* .... Ed. Stephen Reed Cattley. New York: AMS, 1965 [1837–41]. Ed. and abridged by G. A. Williamson as Foxe's *Book of Martyrs.* Boston: Little, Brown, 1966.

Gordon, Ernest. *A Book of Protestant Saints.* Chicago: Moody Press, 1946.

Gunn, Janet Varner. *Autobiography: Toward a Poetics of Experience.* Philadelphia: University of Pennsylvania Press, 1982.

Grabar, Andre. *Christian Iconography: A Study of Its Origins.* Princeton: University Press, 1968.

Jegen, Carol Frances, ed. *Mary According to Women.* Kansas City: Leaven Press, 1985.

Liturgy 5:2 (Fall 1985). An issue devoted to "With all the Saints."

Martindale, C. C. *What Are Saints? Fifteen Chapters in Sanctity.* London: Sheed and Ward, 1932.

Nicholl, Donald. *Holiness.* New York: Seabury Press, 1981.

O'Connell, Michael. *Theotokos: A Theological Encyclopedia of the Blessed Virgin Mary.* Wilmington, DE: Michael Glazier, 1982.

Pelikan, Jaroslav, David Flusser, Justin Lang. *Mary: Images of the Mother of Jesus in Jewish-Christian Perspective.* Philadelphia: Fortress Press, 1986.

Perham, Michael. *The Communion of Saints.* London: SPCK, 1982.

Pfatteicher, Philip H. *Festivals and Commemorations: Handbook to the Calendar in the Lutheran Book of Worship.* Minneapolis: Augsburg Publishing House, 1980.

Post, Willard E. *Saints, Signs, and Symbols.* New York: Morehouse-Barlow, 1974.

Purcell, William. *Martyrs of Our Time.* St. Louis: CBP Press, 1985.

Sherry, Patrick. *Spirit, Saints, and Immortality.* Albany, NY: State University of New York Press, 1984.

Ward, Benedicta. *Miracles and the Medieval Mind: Theory, Record, and Event 1000–1215.* Philadelphia: University of Pennsylvania Press, 1982.

Weinstein, Donald, and Rudolph M. Bell. *Saints and Society: The Two Worlds of Western Christendom 1000–1700.* Chicago: University Press, 1982.

Wescott, Glenway. *A Calendar of Saints for Unbelievers.* Hauppauge, NY: Leete's Island Books, 1976 [1932].

Weiser, Francis X. *The Holyday Book.* New York: Harcourt Brace, 1956.

Wilson, Stephen, ed. *Saints and Their Cults: Studies in Religious Sociology, Folklore, and History.* Cambridge and New York: Cambridge University Press, 1983.

Wright, Elliott. *Holy Company: Christian Heroes and Heroines.* New York: Macmillan, 1981.

Occasions — Unity

Asmussen, Hans, et al. *The Unfinished Reformation.* Translated by Robert J. Olsen. Notre Dame, IN: Fides, 1961.

Brown, Robert McAfee. *The Ecumenical Revolution.* Garden City, NY: Doubleday, 1967.

Facing Unity: Models, Forms, and Phases of Catholic-Lutheran Church Fellowship. By the Roman Catholic/Lutheran Joint Commission. Geneva, Switzerland: Lutheran World Federation, 1985.

Fries, Heinrich, and Karl Rahner. *Unity of Christians: An Actual Possibility.* Translated by Ruth C. L. Gritsch and Eric Gritsch. Philadelphia: Fortress and New York/Ramsey, NJ: Paulist Press, 1985.

Goodall, Norman. *The Ecumenical Movement: What It Is and What It Does.* 2nd ed. London and New York: Oxford University Press, 1964.

Rusch, William G. *Ecumenism: A Movement Toward Church Unity.* Philadelphia: Fortress Press, 1985.

Occasions — Dedication and Anniversary

Crichton, J. D. *The Dedication of a Church.* Dublin: Veritas Publications, 1980.

Muncey, Raymond W. *A History of the Consecration of Churches and Churchyards.* Cambridge: W. Heffer & Sons, 1930.

Occasions — Stewardship of Creation

Brooks, Paul. *Speaking for Nature: How Literary Naturalists from Henry Thoreau to Rachel Carson Have Shaped America.* Boston: Houghton Mifflin Co., 1980.

Eisley, Loren. *The Immense Journey.* New York: Vintage Books, 1959.

Marx, Leo. *The Machine in the Garden: Technology and the Pastoral Ideal in America.* New York: Oxford University Press, 1964.

Merchant, Carolyn. *The Death of Nature: Women, Ecology, and the Scientific Revolution.* New York: Harper & Row, 1980.

Montefiore, Hugh, ed. *Man and Nature.* London: Collins, 1975.

Roberts, Laurence D., ed. *Approaches to Nature in the Middle Ages: Medieval and Renaissance Texts and Studies*, vol. 16. Binghamton: State University of New York Center for Medieval and Early Renaissance Studies, 1982.

Santmire, H. Paul. *Brother Earth.* New York: Thomas Nelson, 1970.

―――. "The Liberation of Nature: Lynn White's Challenge Anew," *Christian Century* 102 (May 22, 1985):530–33.

―――. *The Travail of Nature: The Ambiguous Ecological Promise of Christian Theology.* Philadelphia: Fortress Press, 1985.

Williams, Raymond. *The Country and the City.* New York: Oxford University Press, 1973.

Liturgical Color

Braun, Joseph. *Die liturgischen Paramente in Gegenwart und Vergangenheit.* Freiburg im Breisgau: Herder, 1924.

Hope, W. H. St. J., and E. G. C. F. Atchley. *English Liturgical Colours.* New York: Macmillan, 1918. Incorporating *The Transactions of the St. Paul's Ecclesiological Society.* Vols. I and II.

Jacobs, Henry E., and John A. W. Haas. *The Lutheran Cyclopedia.* New York: Scribners, 1899, 364–65.

Legg, John W. *Notes on the History of the Liturgical Colours.* London: J. S. Leslie, 1882.

Pocknee, C. E. *Liturgical Vesture.* London: Mowbray, 1960.

Staley, Vernon. *Ceremonial of the English Church.* 4th ed., rev. London: Mowbray, 1927.

6

DAILY PRAYER

Ministers Edition, pp. 46–78, 92–104, 14–17

Parallel Rites

Roman Catholic	*Liturgy of the Hours*, 4 vols. (New York: Catholic Book Publishing Co., 1975–1976)
Episcopal	The Daily Office (Morning Prayer, Evening Prayer, Compline, An Order of Service for Noonday, An Order of Service for the Evening, Daily Devotions for Individuals and Families), *Book of Common Prayer*, pp. 35–146, 934–1001.
Lutheran	An Order of Evening Service, *Church Book* (1868), pp. 24–38. Matins, Vespers, *Common Service Book* (text ed.), pp. 25–36, 191–206, 486–88, 497–514; *Service Book and Hymnal*, pp. 129–52, 275–76, 280–83. *Contemporary Worship 9: Daily Prayer of the Church*, 1976.
Orthodox	Great Vespers, Matins, the First Hour, the Third Hour, the Sixth Hour, the Ninth Hour, the Typical Psalms, *Service Book*, pp. 1–63.
Presbyterian	Morning Prayer (for Daily Use), Evening Prayer (for Daily Use), *Worshipbook* (1972), pp. 56–61.
Church of South India	Order for Morning and Evening Worship, *Book of Common Worship*, pp. 73–101.

Purpose

The mystery of God in Christ is the center of the liturgy of the church. By celebrating the Liturgy of the Hours at certain times of the day which recall creation and re-creation, the church, gathered together in the Holy Spirit, hears the life-giving Word of God and in response to it voices the praise of creation, joins with the songs of heaven, shares in Christ's perpetual intercession for the world. This cycle of praise and prayer transforms our experience of time, deepening our understanding of how day and night can proclaim and celebrate the paschal mystery. Thus, the

340

daily liturgy of the hours supplements and contrasts with the centrality of the Sunday Eucharist in the life of the church, edifying the one holy people of God until all is fulfilled in the kingdom of heaven.[1]

Characteristics

Daily prayer is designed for use by all the people of God, not just clergy; it belongs to the whole church, even as all Christians have the obligation of frequent, indeed unceasing prayer. It is, moreover, corporate prayer, not private prayer; even when prayed by one alone it is prayed in union with all the church on earth and in heaven and with all creation. Third, while it is primarily praise directed to the eschatological dimension, mirroring the heavenly liturgy, daily prayer seeks a balance between three traditional uses: to sing psalms, to hear Scripture, to intercede for the world.

Background

The church year invests the annual cycle with sacred significance, making it a commemoration of the incarnation, life, passion, death, resurrection, ascension, reign, and return of Christ. Behind that annual commemoration lies a still deeper, more obvious, and more archetypal cycle — the daily round of night and day, especially the last hour of the day at dusk when the lamps are lighted and at the first hour of the day when the rising sun dispels the last shadow of night.[2] For those with eyes to see and ears to hear, the regular succession of darkness and light is a powerful proclamation of praise to the Creator, who brought light into darkness, life out of death. Nature itself participates in this praise, waking to new life with the coming of spring and the coming of the dawn.[3]

"Sing unto the Lord a new song," the Psalter enjoins us again and again. It is the Christ-hymn, new every morning, that the family fellowship strikes up at the beginning of the day, the hymn that is sung by the whole Church of God on earth and in heaven, and in which we are summoned to join. God has prepared for Himself one great song of praise throughout eternity, and those who enter the community of God join in this song.... In the morning of every day the Church on earth lifts up this song and in the evening it closes the day with this

---

[1] This statement of the purpose and function of the liturgy of the hours was drafted in large measure by Philip H. Pfatteicher and adopted by the study group on the Liturgy of the Hours of the North American Academy of Liturgy meeting in Los Angeles, January 7, 1981. It was subsequently presented with German and French translations to the 1981 meeting of Societas Liturgica and published by Thaddaeus Schnitker, "La prière publique de l'église," *Questions liturgiques* 63 (1982):41–44.

[2] *The Liturgy of the Hours*, The General Instruction on the Liturgy of the Hours with a Commentary, by A.M. Roguet, trans. Peter Coughlin and Peter Perdue (London: Geoffrey Chapman, 1971), 17.

[3] The Yaqui Indians regard song as a *lingua franca* of the intelligent universe through which experience with other living things is made accessible to the human community. See Larry Evers and Filipe Molina, *Yaqui Deer Songs: A Native American Poetry* (Tucson: University of Arizona Press, 1986).

hymn. It is the triune God and His works that are extolled. This song has a different ring on earth from what it has in heaven. On earth it is the song of those who believe, in heaven the song of those who see.[4]

Most ancient societies have marked the new year, the turning of the seasons, sunset and sunrise with prayer. Judaism marked the morning and the evening with sacrifices in the temple at Jerusalem and with a series of psalms and prayer in mid-morning and mid-afternoon. Private prayers were offered three times a day — evening, morning, and noon (Ps. 55:17)[5] — or even seven times a day (Ps. 119:164). Nine, noon, and three o'clock were also the principal divisions of the Roman day.

Christianity inherited and continued such daily public and private prayer. The *Didache* (8.3) says that the Lord's Prayer should be said three times a day, probably at the three traditional times for prayer. By the second century at least, the morning service consisted of psalms, canticles, and prayers, and sometimes in some places scripture reading. The evening service, rooted in the domestic necessity of lighting the lamps, was introduced by a service of light consisting of psalms, prayers, and occasionally readings.[6]

The obligation to pray was not, however, discharged with prayer at certain times of the day. The devout Christian was expected to take seriously St. Paul's injunction to "pray without ceasing" (1 Thess. 5:17), which is quoted by many writers from Ignatius of Antioch onward.[7] Clement of Alexandria (ca. 150 – ca. 215) portrays the Christian as constantly engaged in praising God at every moment of life, in every task and occupation.[8] Certain times of day were nonetheless set aside for prayer: at meals,[9] morning, noon, evening, and during the night. The *Apostolic Tradition* of Hippolytus (d. 235) reports the pleasant conceit that at midnight all nature pauses briefly for prayer and praise.

For the elders who gave us the tradition taught us that at that hour all creation is still for a moment, to praise the Lord; stars, trees, waters stop for an instant, and all the host of angels (which) ministers to him praises God with the souls of

---

[4]Dietrich Bonhoeffer, *Life Together*, trans. John W. Doberstein (New York: Harper and Bros., 1954), 57–58.

[5]See Paul F. Bradshaw, *Daily Prayer in the Early Church* (New York: Oxford University Press, 1982), 8–10, and Robert Taft, *The Liturgy of the Hours in East and West* (Collegeville: Liturgical Press, 1986), 3–11.

[6]1 Clement 40:1–4 and especially 24:1–3:
Let us consider, beloved, how the Lord continually manifests to us the resurrection to come, whose first fruits he made Christ by raising him from the dead. We see, beloved, that the resurrection was accomplished according to the time. Day and night make visible to us a resurrection. Night goes to sleep, the day rises; the day departs, the night follows.

[7]Bradshaw, 47.

[8]Clement of Alexandria, *Stromata* 7.7; see also Origen, *On Prayer* 12.2

[9]Clement of Alexandria, *Pedagogue* 2.9–10; also Tertullian, *On Prayer* 25.

the righteous in this hour. That is why believers should take good care to pray at this hour.[10]

Such prayer at midnight probably goes back to the beginning of Christianity and may be rooted in ancient Jewish tradition. It reflects the strong eschatological emphasis of that time: one was to sleep so as to be easily awakened to greet the parousia.[11] The *Apostolic Tradition* urges prayer at cockcrow (although this is probably a later addition to the text),[12] upon rising, at each of the three divisions of the day (nine, noon, and three o'clock), at bedtime, and at midnight.[13] This is apparently chiefly private prayer but an accepted cycle nonetheless.[14]

By the middle of the third century, Cyprian, bishop of Carthage, recommended that all Christians observe daybreak as the celebration of the resurrection, the third hour as the commemoration of the descent of the Holy Spirit or of the condemnation of the Savior, the sixth hour as the time of the crucifixion, the ninth hour as the time of Christ's death, and the evening as a time to recognize that Christ must bring his light into our darkness.[15] Tertullian connects the third hour with the descent of the Spirit, the sixth hour with Peter's prayer on the housetop (Acts 10:9), the ninth hour with Peter and John healing the paralytic (Acts 3:1).[16] The three daytime hours were at least in some places understood to be supplementary to the principal times of prayer at morning and evening and came to be called "the little hours" or "the hours of the Passion" (Christ's condemnation, crucifixion, death).

After the recognition of Christianity under Constantine, the new and splendid church buildings invited frequent use. Lauds at sunrise and Vespers at sunset, *ingressu lucis et noctis*, at the coming of light and of night, in Tertullian's phrase, were prayed in the cathedrals and churches as the daily public prayer of Christianity. Chrysostom's writings show that the morning and evening offices at Antioch were primarily psalmody and intercession. Psalm 63[17] was said in the morning; Psalm 141 in the evening; the intercessions were for the church and for the whole world. This was the public "cathedral office."[18]

At the same time, the office was taking a different direction within the monastic movement. Those who had given their lives to prayer had the time[19] and the desire to enrich the hours with prayers, hymns, and antiphons. But most of all they desired to pray the whole Psalter and to

---

[10]*Apostolic Tradition* 41.

[11]Clement of Alexandria, *Pedagogue* 2.9; Bradshaw, 37–39, 57; Taft, 15.

[12]See Bradshaw, 55.

[13]*Apostolic Tradition* 35–36, 41.

[14]On the difficulties of interpreting this, see Bradshaw, 53; Taft, 21–25.

[15]Cyprian, *On Prayer* 34.

[16]Tertullian, *On Prayer* 24–25.

[17]Eusebius of Caesarea, *Commentary on Psalm 142* 8.

[18]Bradshaw, 18, 74; Taft, 32.

[19]Alexander Schmemann, *Introduction to Liturgical Theology* (London: Faith Press, 1966), 107.

read or hear the Scriptures regularly. The psalms therefore came to be prayed "in course" over a period of one to fourteen days. In addition to Lauds and Vespers and the three Little Hours, Matins (devotions at midnight or at cockcrow) and Compline (devotion at bedtime) were added. Later, Prime was introduced to complete the hours of prayer seven times a day, as the psalmist had said (119:164), when Matins and Lauds were combined into one office as was done in some places. What was being developed in this process was not simply an elaboration of prayer but a new concept of prayer. The monks were not creating corporate worship but forms of private prayer to be practiced in common.[20]

John Cassian (ca. 360–ca. 435), traveling from Gaul to Eastern monasteries in the last decade of the fourth century, describes in detail the divine office he found in Egypt. Lauds and Vespers were said as a public prayer with twelve psalms at each and two lessons, one from the Old Testament and one from the New Testament, although on Saturday and Sunday and throughout Easter both lessons were from the New Testament. The psalms, following a common custom, were chanted by a single voice while the rest of the company listened. Silence and meditation and a prayer followed each psalm.[21]

Prime was created in Bethlehem, Cassian reports,[22] to prevent the more slothful in the community from sleeping through the expected meditation between Lauds at dawn and the third hour of Terce. Prime was introduced to announce the beginning of work.

At the little hours the general custom was to recite three psalms at each hour, but in some monasteries three psalms were sung at the third hour, six at the sixth, and nine at the ninth hour. St. Columban required twelve psalms at night during the summer but more as the nights grew longer; on Saturday and Sunday at least eighteen psalms were sung, usually thirty-six, and sixty-five during Saturday and Sunday vigils.

The *Rule* of St. Benedict is more restrained. The psalter was prayed weekly; shorter psalms were chosen for the daytime offices to leave time for work. The *Rule* of St. Benedict, "the creator of the breviary of the West," is the first record of Compline, although it may be much older.

The two forms of the divine office, cathedral and monastic, were not completely separate,[23] and for several centuries they continued side by side or combined in places where monks worshiped in parish churches or where the parish clergy were bound to monastic rules. Egeria described the office in fourth-century Jerusalem, in which the monks assembled at the appointed times to pray the office; the clergy and laity joined

---

[20]W. Jardine Grisbrooke in *The Study of Liturgy*, ed. Cheslyn Jones, Geoffrey Wainwright, Edward Yarnold (New York: Oxford University Press, 1978), 360; Taft, 57ff.

[21]John Cassian, *Institutes of the Cenobites* 2, 3.

[22]Ibid., 3.6; but see *The Study of Liturgy*, 361 no. 5.

[23]See Grisbrooke, *The Study of Liturgy*, 362–63.

them at the principal services.[24] In other places, the monastic office was attached to the congregational morning and evening services and to make the resulting services of a more reasonable length, the lessons and instruction (considered by Gregory of Tours to be an essential element of the office) were eliminated except for Matins.

As the Middle Ages progressed, the office became more and more the property of monks and clergy. When Charlemagne imposed the Roman service books throughout his kingdom, the Roman divine office was required of all clergy attached to cathedrals and parish churches. Since the end of the ninth century the Roman office has been used throughout the Latin church, except in Milan and Toledo, which enjoy special privilege and have their own rites (Ambrosian and Mozarabic). There was, however, no uniformity, and there was a great variety of offices said in various regions and even in the same city.[25] Ceremonies and devotions multiplied (with the decline in manual work, according to Edmund Bishop). Benedict of Aniane at his monastery at Inde directed his monks before Matins to visit all the altars and say the Lord's Prayer and Creed at each and, having returned to their places in choir, recite the fifteen gradual psalms (Psalms 120–134). By the tenth century the recitation of these fifteen psalms before praying the office had become a universal monastic practice. The creed, Ave Maria, and confession of sins were added to some forms of the office. Beginning in the tenth century, supplementary offices abounded: the Office of the Blessed Virgin, of the Holy Cross, of the Holy Trinity, of the Holy Spirit.

The office having become the property of monks and clergy, pious laypeople desired to imitate their devotion, so in the fourteenth century the laypeoples' prayer book appeared, called the Book of Hours, or the Primer. An invariable office, adapted from the hours of the Virgin, it was a book of instruction, summarizing what every Christian should know, as well as a book of devotion. The primer enjoyed enormous popularity.

The name "breviary" apparently derives from books which gave only the initial words of liturgical texts as cue lines, the rest having been committed to memory by repeated use.[26]

It became the custom of the Roman curia to shorten the office to suit the convenience of the cardinals. The office was further shortened so that the reading of Scripture was almost entirely suppressed. The papal captivity at Avignon further curtailed the ceremonies of the office. The multiplication of feasts of saints and of octaves of feasts made the recitation of the ferial (daily) office infrequent and the weekly recitation of the Psalter impossible. Humanists attempted to purify what they saw as the inelegances of the office. By the time of the

---

[24]Egeria's Travels 24. *Egeria's Travels to the Holy Land*, trans. John Wilkinson, rev. ed. (Jerusalem: Ariel Publishing House and Warminster, England: Aris and Phillips, 1981), 123–25.

[25]J. D. Crichton in *The Study of Liturgy*. 370.

[26]*The Study of Liturgy*, 379; Pierre Salmon, *The Breviary through the Centuries*, trans. Sister David Mary (Collegeville: Liturgical Press, 1962), 60.

Reformation the venerable divine office was in a state of considerable disrepair.

The need for reform was urgent. Cardinal Quiñones made a revision of the breviary to insure that the Psalter be recited once a week and the principal parts of the Bible be read once a year, the office be of approximately the same length each day, and that the Sunday office not be inordinately long. His *Breviarium Sanctae Crucis* (1535, 2d ed. 1536) gained immediate popularity. John Henry Newman wrote of Quiñones's purpose,

His object was to adapt the Devotions of the Church for private reading, rather than chanting in choir, and so to encourage something higher than that almost theatrical style of worship, which, when reverence is away, will prevail alternately with a slovenly and hurried performance.... [27]

The book was suppressed in 1568 to make way for the official *Breviarium Romanum*, but its influence remains. Cranmer made use of it in his revisions of the office for the *Book of Common Prayer*.

The churches of the Reformation also revised the office for their use, for beneath the daunting complexity and the clutter of saints' feasts and legends, the Lutheran and Anglican reformers could still see the gem of value. It had been customary in some places in the late Middle Ages to group Matins, Lauds, and Prime together to facilitate their use and to say Vespers and Compline together. Both in England and on the continent the reformers recognized morning and evening prayer as the two principal hours of prayer and gathered elements of Matins, Lauds, and Prime to form what was called Matins or Morning Prayer and of Vespers and Compline to form what was called Vespers or Evening Prayer.

The first revised offices to come from the Reformation were Lutheran. In his "Concerning the Order of Public Worship"[28] (1523), Martin Luther outlines an hour-long service at four or five in the morning (the Old Testament lesson appointed for Matins, sermon, praise and prayer consisting of psalms, responsories, and antiphons) and a service in the evening at five or six o'clock (New Testament reading, sermon, praise, song, and prayer); a mid-day service is commended but no form is suggested. In addition to these services for "priests and pupils," Luther says that the whole congregation should assemble on Sundays for mass and Vespers; normally the sermon at mass was on the Gospel for the day, the sermon at Vespers on the Epistle.

In his *Formula Missae*, published in December of 1523, Luther commends Matins "with its three lessons,"[29] the minor hours, Vespers, and Compline. These offices were primarily for schools. Luther assumes

[27] *Tracts for the Times* no. 25, p. 13.

[28] Martin Luther, "Concerning the Order for Public Worship," *Luther's Works* 53:11–14. See also J. Neil Alexander, "Luther's Reform of the Daily Office," *Worship* 57 (1983): 348–60.

[29] Martin Luther, "An Order of Mass and Communion for the Church at Wittenberg," *Luther's Works* 53:37–39. On "the three lessons" of Matins, Paul Z. Strodach in the Philadelphia Edition of *The Works of Martin Luther* (Philadelphia: Muhlenberg Press,

that "the whole Psalter" and "the entire Scripture" will be used (the lesson in the morning from one testament, the lesson in the evening from the other). He assumes (incorrectly) that this was the original purpose of the office — reading and preaching the Bible — and that later, "when evil times came," these were replaced by "psalms, hymns, and other things... in boring repetition."

The offices Luther outlines in his *Deutsche Messe* (1526)[30] were more clearly for schools. Sunday was to begin with Matins at five or six in the morning (psalms, sermon on the Epistle, antiphon, Te Deum or Benedictus, Lord's Prayer, collects, and *Benedicamus domino*). Mass was celebrated later in the morning with a sermon on the Gospel for the day. Vespers was sung in the late afternoon with two lessons, one from the Old Testament on which the sermon was based and the other from the epistles. The congregation was thus to hear three sermons on Sunday. On weekdays Luther emphasizes instructional lessons: Monday and Tuesday there was to be a German "lesson" (i.e., sermon) on the Catechism; on Wednesday a sermon on Matthew's gospel (because of its ethical emphasis); on Thursday and Friday sermons on the rest of the New Testament; on Saturday a sermon on John's gospel. In these daily services, after the psalms, there was a reading from the Latin New Testament and the same chapter was read again in German; there was an antiphon, a sermon, a German hymn or at Vespers the Magnificat, the Lord's Prayer said silently, a collect, and the *Benedicamus domino*. The chief purpose of these offices was instruction, primarily for the young, to train them in the Bible. It was thus a departure from the traditional purpose of the church's daily prayer (for which Luther made a small provision in the morning and evening prayers he outlined in the Small Catechism), but it may be understood as a recovery of an ancient practice reported in the *Apostolic Tradition* of Morning Prayer and "instruction" and Egeria's description of the presence of the faithful with baptismal candidates at the bishop's daily morning catechesis in Jerusalem.[31]

Many church orders follow Luther's pattern, some make no provision for daily services, some combine services. Bugenhagen's forms for north Germany (e.g., Brunswick, 1528) are similar to Luther's forms. He retains the preces before the collect. In his order for Denmark (1537) he combines Vespers and Compline, since Compline is in many ways a duplication of Vespers. Brandenburg-Nuremberg (1533) mixes Morning Prayer with the liturgy of the word in ante-communion: psalms, Epistle, hymn, Gospel, Te Deum, and three collects. Such a joining of Morning Prayer to the beginning of the Holy Communion also became a not uncommon Anglican practice.

1932) 6:116 n. 146 suggests that the reference is to the ferial office when but one nocturn is said.

[30]Luther, "The German Mass and Order of Service," *Luther's Works* 53:68–69.

[31]*Apostolic Tradition* 35, 39, 41; *Egeria's Travels* 46.1ff.

In Strasbourg the Reformed Church preserved a vernacular daily Morning and Evening Prayer with a *lectio continua* of the Bible (New Testament in the morning, Old Testament in the evening), followed by a sermon.[32]

In the Lutheran tradition, Matins and Vespers remained in use chiefly in schools and were in time lost to congregations until they were recovered in the nineteenth-century liturgical revival.[33] Theodor Kliefoth (1810–1895) in northern Germany devised forms of Matins and Evening Prayer. Loehe's liturgy included a Breviary for use of the Pastor, consisting of Morning Prayer, "on going to church," "in sacristy," confession of sins, "thanksgiving after the completion of worship," and prayers for the young, especially catechumens.

Dieffenbach and Müller's *Evangelisches Brevier* (1857) was also a book for the clergy. It provided Matins, not in its traditional form but as a form of ante-communion consisting of Introit, Kyrie, Gloria Patri, collect, lesson, preces, Creed, Sanctus, Our Father, and Aaronic benediction. There was an office for going to church consisting of versicles, collect, and psalm with Gloria Patri. Lauds consisted of versicles, hymn, and psalm. There was a short office for use after church. A form for meditation consisting of verses, collect, psalm, and Magnificat was provided. Compline included Introit, hymn, collect, lesson, and prayer.

Matins and Vespers in their historic Western form revised for congregational use as in the *Book of Common Prayer* (Matins joined with Lauds and elements of Prime; Vespers combined with Compline) were provided for American Lutherans in the *Kirchenbuch* (1877) and in English in the Common Service (1888). In addition to congregational use, chiefly as Sunday Vespers, the historic office provided the basis for the forms provided for church school worship. Accompanying the *Church Book* was *The Sunday School Book* for the Use of Evangelical Lutheran Congregations by the authority of the General Council of the Evangelical Lutheran Church in America (Philadelphia: Lutheran Book Store, 1891). It was revised and enlarged in 1896 and issued by the United Lutheran Publication House in Philadelphia. Accompanying the *Common Service Book* was the *Parish School Hymnal* authorized by the United Lutheran Church in America, 1926). Students in Lutheran church schools thus gained at least a passing acquaintance with some elements of the historic office. The use of the office as private prayer was practically unknown.

The twentieth-century revival of Protestant religious communities in Europe, largely ecumenical, has increased an awareness of the divine office: the Evangelical Sisters of Mary at Darmstadt, the sisters of the

---

[32]Hughes Oliphant Old, "Daily Prayer in the Reformed Church of Strasbourg, 1525–1530," *Worship* 52 (1978):121–38.

[33]A notable exception was Leipzig. See Günther Stiller, *Johann Sebastian Bach and Liturgical Life in Leipzig*, trans. Herbert J. A. Bouman et al. (St. Louis: Concordia Publishing House, 1984).

Castell Circle in the Schwanberg Castle near Kitzingen; the French communities at Granchamp, Pomeyrol, and especially Taizé in Burgundy. Other forms have been produced for more general use by the Brotherhood of St. Michael's *Stundengebet* (3rd ed. 1953) and the *Allgemeine evangelische Gebetbuch* (1955).

In 1931 another *Evangelisches Brevier*, edited by Oskar Mehl, appeared. It followed closely the Roman breviary. Matins, for example, consisted of versicles, Venite with proper invitatories, psalms with antiphons, a hymn followed by a versicle, a lesson, a variable canticle, preces, and Aaronic benediction. Offices were provided for morning, noon, evening, and night prayer. In the mid-twentieth century the Church of Sweden published a breviary for its priests, modeled closely on the Roman form.

In America in 1948 a Committee on Faith and Life of the United Lutheran Church in America urged:

> In order to strengthen the pastor's devotional life, it is earnestly recommended that a pastor's office book be provided. This office book may contain a collection of Psalter selections, New Testament lections (both quoted and referenced), prayers concerned with the pastor's needs (Luther's Sacristy Prayer), appropriate hymn texts, significant religious poetry, questions to measure and encourage faithfulness and loyalty to the ministerial office, etc.[34]

Work was begun on the project; a few sample sections were published following the Roman office for Advent, but nothing further came of the project.

In 1959, John W. Doberstein published *Minister's Prayer Book*, an anthology of prayers and meditations relating to the work of the ministry. It attained considerable popularity, and, because no other similar books were available, it was reprinted in 1986 by Fortress Press with revisions by Philip H. Pfatteicher.

Herbert Lindemann edited *The Daily Office* (St. Louis: Concordia Publishing House, 1965), which was a book for laity and clergy alike, following the historic pattern of the breviary. It was a book primarily for reading and meditation.

In England at the Reformation, Thomas Cranmer revised the divine office on the basis of the work of Quiñones and the German church orders. The Psalter was to be read through monthly; most of the Old Testament and the Apocrypha were read yearly; the New Testament (except for Revelation) thrice yearly. The framework of the late medieval rites remained largely intact, but antiphons, responsories, and office hymns were removed to simplify the office, and the clergy in charge of congregations were to say daily Morning and Evening Prayer publicly in their churches in English "to the end that the congregation may be thereby edified." Alone of all Western Christian churches, Anglicanism preserved daily Morning and Evening Prayer as a living part of parish worship.[35]

---

[34]United Lutheran Church in America *Minutes* 1948, p. 304.
[35]Taft, 323; Louis Bouyer, *Liturgical Piety* (Notre Dame: University Press, 1955), 47.

In the Roman Breviary after 1570 minor revisions were made. During the seventeenth and eighteenth centuries in France most of the dioceses attempted a reform of the breviary. In 1736 the Archbishop of Paris, Charles de Vintmille, had a reformed breviary published which continued in use until modern times. It gave Sunday greater prominence, shortened the ferial (daily) office, provided that the ferial office was never suppressed during Lent, reclassified festivals, allowed only approved histories as lessons, and grouped the daily psalms around particular themes.

Vatican Council I (1869–1870) ordered the reform of the breviary, but not until 1911 was the reform inaugurated (in *Divina afflatu* of Pius X, November 1911), It consisted chiefly of rearranging the Psalter, asserting the primacy of the weekdays of Lent, and shortening the office.

The Second Vatican Council (1962–1965) ordered a far more thoroughgoing reform, which emphasized the two chief hours of Morning and Evening Prayer as the hinges on which the office turns and encouraged all the people of God to join in their family prayer. Matins, now called the Office of Readings, has been adapted so that it may be prayed at any hour; Prime is suppressed; any one of the Little Hours may be selected according to the time of day when it is said; the psalms are spread over the course of a month; the hymns are not limited to the traditional office hymns.[36]

On the basis of contemporary research in the origin, development, and purpose of the office, the Episcopal and Lutheran churches revised their forms of Morning and Evening Prayer. The subcommittee of the Inter-Lutheran Commission on Worship which drafted Matins, Vespers, Compline, the suffrages, and the Litany consisted of Mark P. Bangert, Marianka Fousek, Brian L. Helge, Philip H. Pfatteicher, who chaired the committee, and Edward D. Roe. Their work was published as *Contemporary Worship 9: Daily Prayer of the Church* (1976).

In the Eastern Orthodox churches the structure of the offices is elaborate and quite different from the Western form which is common to the Roman Catholic, Lutheran, and Episcopal churches.[37]

The Byzantine Office

Orthros (Morning Prayers)	Vespers
1. Royal Office Pss. 20, 21 Trisagion Our Father Troparion Litany	1. Initial prayers

---

[36] *Constitution on the Sacred Liturgy*, IV: The Divine Office, in *The Documents of Vatican II*, ed. Walter M. Abbott (New York: The America Press, 1966), 163–67; *General Instruction on the Liturgy of the Hours.*

[37] See Taft, 219–91.

2. Hexapsalm
Pss. 3, 38, 63, 88, 103, 143
meanwhile: 12 prayers of
sunrise

3. Great Litany of Peace

4. Verses from Isa. 26
or Ps. 118

5. Troparion

6. Reading of the Psalter

7. On Sundays and Feast Days
Gradual (Ps. 129:1, 5–6)

8. On Sundays: Gospel
Gospel
Hymn of the Resurrection

9. Ps. 51

10. On Sundays and in Lent
solemn prayer

11. The Canon (Canticles from
OT and NT

12. Pss. 148–150

13. Troparia

14. Weekdays and in Lent
Lord have mercy (40 times)
Prayer of St. Ephraim
Our Father

15. Ps. 34 and Final Prayers

16. Dismissal

---

2. Introductory Psalm
Ps. 104

3. Great Litany of Peace

4. Reading of the Psalter

5. Lucernarium
Pss. 141, 142, 130, 117

Entrance Procession

6. Phos hilaron

7. Prokimeon (psalm verses)
Readings

8. Prayer

9. On Sundays and major feasts
procession

10. Psalm verses

11. Nunc Dimittis

12. Trisagion

Our Father

13. Gloria in Excelsis
(lesser doxology in Lent
and on weekdays)

14. Litany

15. Texts from Pss. 90, 91

16. Trisagion
Our Father

17. In Lent, on weekdays, and
minor feasts
Troparion and litany

18. Final Prayers

19. Dismissal

351

THE SERVICES IN DETAIL

EVENING PRAYER: VESPERS. The Orthodox churches, with their close ties to Old Testament traditions, reckon the day according to the Jewish and biblical pattern, from sundown to sundown.[38] Vespers is the key to understanding the entire office, for it is the beginning as well as the ending of the daily cycle. In such a pattern night serves as a preparation for the following day and every night becomes a vigil, awaiting the celebration of the resurrection with the rising sun and awaiting as well the dawn of the great and final day.

In common with general ecumenical practice (the Roman Catholic Church, the Episcopal Church, the Presbyterian Church, and others) the service known to previous generations of Lutherans and Roman Catholics by its traditional Latin name, Vespers, is now in the *Lutheran Book of Worship* called Evening Prayer. Vespers is retained as a subtitle to preserve that ancient name, familiar in many contexts still, a name which ought not to be forgotten or allowed to fall into disuse. Evensong, the lovely name in common use in England and Scandinavia, has not been in general Lutheran use in North America.

The Service of Light. Light is one of the most powerful and evocative symbols in the history of religion.[39] A devotional understanding of the lighting of the lamps as evening comes on long antedates Christianity. Indeed, the power of that moment lasted until the introduction of electricity which rendered unnecessary the lighting of the gas street lamps in cities in the nineteenth century. Widespread in the ancient world, the lighting of the lamps was a part of the public worship of the ancient Hebrews (Exod. 30:7–8) and was part of the liturgy done in families, the lighting of the Sabbath lights, which continues down to our own time. It became a daily Christian practice too,[40] derived perhaps from the lighting of the lamp in Jerusalem.[41] In the *Apostolic Tradition* Hippolytus describes a service of light in connection with an evening *agape*.[42] The lucernarium, the office of light (in Greek *lichnikon*, from *lychnia*, lamps) which introduced the evening prayers at the dinner table was eventually brought into the church building and remains at the center of Eastern Orthodox Vespers and is found in the Mozarabic and Ambrosian rites.[43]

---

[38] *Service Book of the Holy Orthodox–Catholic Apostolic Church*, trans. Isabel Florence Hapgood, rev. ed., 5th ed. (Englewood, NJ: Antiochian Orthodox Christian Archdiocese, 1975), 582.

[39] Mircea Eliade, *Patterns in Comparative Religion* (Cleveland and New York: World, 1963), chap. 3 and 4; Lev. 24:3–4; Exod. 25:31–40; Rev. 1:12–13. See especially the splendid passage in T. S. Eliot's "Choruses from 'The Rock,'" X, "O Light Invisible we praise Thee!" and John Milton's *Paradise Lost* III.1ff., "Hail, holy light."

[40] See perhaps Acts 20:7–8.

[41] Gregory Dix, *The Shape of the Liturgy*, 2nd ed. (Westminster: Dacre Press, 1945), 87; Gabriele Winkler, "Über die Kathedralvesper in den verschiedenen Riten des Ostens und Westens," *Archiv für Liturgiewissenschaft* 16 (1974):60–61.

[42] *Apostolic Tradition* 25.

[43] See *Egeria's Travels*, 123–24; Taft, 223, 235–36, 277–78, 285–87; also Lancelot Andrewes, *Preces Privatae* (New York: Meriden, 1961), pp. 104, 107, evening prayers.

As every Sunday is an echo of Easter, so each evening the service of light is a simplified service of light of the Easter Vigil, including a procession in which three verses are sung, followed by a hymn, the dialogue between an assisting minister and the congregation, and a proclamation of thanksgiving.

In Evening Prayer, the first pair of verses said during the procession with the candle is based on John 1:14; the second pair is Luke 24:29 in the translation of the New English Bible; the third pair is based on 2 Corinthians 4:6 and the Exsultet ("Be glad also O mother Church, clothed with the brightness of such a light," Min. Ed., pp. 144, 146).

In the Propers for Daily Prayer (Min. Ed., pp. 92–95) proper versicles for Advent, Christmas/Epiphany, Lent, and Easter are provided. The biblical translation is primarily the Revised Standard Version. The Advent verses are drawn from Revelation 22:17, 2 Timothy 4:8; and Romans 8:22. The response to each verse is the ancient cry of longing, *maranatha*, Revelation 22:20. The verses expand from the Spirit-filled church to all who await Christ's appearing, including those outside the church, to the whole of the creation.

The Christmas/Epiphany verses are drawn from Isaiah 9:2a and John 1:5; Isaiah 9:2b and John 1:14b; Isaiah 9:6 and John 1:4. (This last response is one place in the *Lutheran Book of Worship* where exclusive language remains. "Man" is of course used in the generic sense and was intended to be somewhat less exclusive than the Revised Standard Version's "men." Many doubtless will want to correct it to "mortals" or "the world.")

The Lenten versicles are drawn from 2 Corinthians 6:2a and b; Psalm 85:4 and 4:6b; Malachi 4:2 (see Matt. 14:33) and Psalm 113:7.

The Easter versicles are drawn from Romans 6:9a; Isaiah 60:3; Romans 6:9b. The response to each is the three-fold Alleluia, the Easter song and the eternal theme of the church.

The invariable hymn to Christ the light of the Father's glory (*phos hilaron* in Greek) — see the Ambrosian hymn, "O Splendor of the Father's Light" (no. 271) — which follows the introductory versicles, is one of the oldest in the church's treasury, already ancient in the time of Basil the Great of Caesarea (d. 379), so old that he did not even know who wrote it.[44] The hymn seems to date from the late second to the early third century; its author is unknown.[45]

Pagans greeted the light *Chaire phos agathon* (Hail, good light) or *Chaire phos philon* (Hail, friendly light!), and Clement of Alexandria records that Christians greet the true God with "Hail, Light."[46] By their

---

[44]Basil the Great, *Treatise on the Holy Spirit* 29; Taft, 38, 286; F. Dölger, "Lumen Christi: Der christliche Abendhymnus *Phos hilaron*," *Antike und Christentum* 5 (1936):1–43; A. Tripolitis, "*Phos hilaron:* Ancient Hymn and Modern Enigma," *Vigiliae Christianae* 24 (1970):189–96.

[45]The Orthodox Great Vespers credits Sophronius, Patriarch of Jerusalem, with its composition. *Service Book*, 8.

[46]Clement of Alexandria, *Protrepticus* 11, 114.1.

hymn of greeting, Christians express their conviction that "the light of the world is not the sun of creation by day nor the evening lamp by night, but the eternal Son of God, the 'true light that enlightens everyone,' in the words of St. John's Gospel (1:9),"[47] enlightening, that is saving, the world. Moreover, the practice of orientation, turning to the East to pray facing the rising sun, symbolizing Christ the light of the world and sun of justice, first testified to by Clement of Alexandria,[48] is a declaration of the same conviction.

The translation as well as the melody to which *Phos hilaron* is set in the *Lutheran Book of Worship* is by Roger Petrich, made for the book;[49] hymn 279, "O Gladsome Light," is a metrical paraphrase of the hymn. The hymn is addressed to Christ, the brightness of the Father's glory (Hebrews 1:3). He is the glad, joy-giving, joyful, happy, blessed Light from Light as the Fourth Gospel and the Nicene Creed declare. As the sun sets and the lamps are lighted, the congregation praises the Holy Trinity,[50] and concludes the song with a further ascription of praise to the Son of God, the giver of life (John 3:14–16; 10:10), whose splendor all the universe proclaims and glorifies. The cycles of night and day, the lighted candles and lamps, light and darkness, the church on earth in union with the choirs of heaven all combine to give him praise.

The thanksgiving concludes the service of light. A solemn prefatial blessing,[51] the Christian child of the Jewish *berakah* formula, it consists of the preface verses except for "Lift up your hearts. *We lift them to the Lord*," according to the custom giving by Hippolytus in the *Apostolic Tradition* (25) that these verses are limited to the eucharistic dialogue. The blessing itself is from *Morning Praise and Evensong*.[52] This proclamation of praise and thanksgiving is in the Jewish manner and recalls the constant guidance of God's people in the wilderness (Exod. 13:21, etc.). The pillar of cloud has reference in part to the incense which may be used to honor the candle and the fire recalls the candle itself which led the procession at the beginning of the service of light and is the central symbol and focus of attention during the service of light. More generally, cloud and fire became traditional expressions of God's continuing presence, care, and guidance. "Enlighten our darkness by

---

[47] Taft, 286.

[48] Clement of Alexandria, *Stromata* 7.7; see also Origen, *On Prayer* 32; Tertullian, *Apology* 16; *To the Nations* 1.13.

[49] Other translations are in the *Taizé Office Book* (London: Faith Press, 1966), 22; the *Book of Common Prayer*, 112 (made by Charles M. Guilbert); Lucien Deiss, *The Springtime of the Liturgy* (Collegeville: Liturgical Press, 1979), 251–52. See M. Eleanor Irwin, "PHOS HILARON: The Metamorphoses of a Christian Hymn," *The Hymn: A Journal of Congregational Song* 40 (April 1989):7–12.

[50] "No Byzantine service begins without a blessing or glorification of the Holy Trinity, the ultimate aim of all worship" (Taft, 284).

[51] From the same word from which the liturgical "preface" derives, *praefatio*, a solemn proclamation of praise.

[52] *Morning Praise and Evensong*, ed. William G. Storey, Frank C. Quinn, David F. Wright (Notre Dame: Fides Press, 1973), 73–74.

the light of your Christ" (that is, of your Anointed) is an allusion to the Gelasian collect used in Compline (no. 261), "Be our light in the darkness, O Lord."[53] Moreover, God's word, the psalmist said, was a lamp to our steps and a light to our path (Ps. 119:105), another expression of God's guiding care of his people on their journey through this world.

Two other thanksgivings for light are provided on page 95 of the Ministers Edition. The first, Thanksgiving for Light I, is from the *Apostolic Constitutions* (ca. 380)[54] as translated in *Morning Praise and Evensong*.[55] Thanksgiving for Light II is from the *Apostolic Tradition* (ca. 215)[56] as translated in *Morning Praise and Evensong*[57] with one change: the *Lutheran Book of Worship* text has "to you *in* the Holy Spirit" in the doxology, following the text of Thanksgiving for Light I; *Morning Praise and Evensong* has "to you *and* the Holy Spirit."[58]

A literal offering of incense, recalling Exodus 30:7–8, was added to the ritual lighting of the lamps beginning perhaps in Syria in the fourth century.[59] This use of incense encouraged the penitential character of the evening office since in the Old Testament incense was understood to represent purification and the expiation of sin (Numb. 16:46–47), derived from its practical use as a fumigant.

Psalmody. Psalm 141 is the traditional evening psalm[60] in Christian (although not Jewish) use.[61] In the *Lutheran Book of Worship*, verses 1–4a and 8 are used as the invariable psalm of repentance. The translation is that of the Psalter of the *Book of Common Prayer* and the *Lutheran Book of Worship*, slightly revised for the musical setting. John Cassian commented on the significance of this vesper psalm:

This evening sacrifice ... may be more fully understood as that true evening sacrifice which was given in the evening by our Lord and Savior when he instituted the most holy mysteries of the Church at supper with his apostles; or which on the following day he offered for all time to his Father by the raising up of hands for the salvation of the whole world.[62]

---

[53]Min. Ed., 75; *Book of Common Prayer*, 133. The earlier translation in the *Service Book and Hymnal* (p. 230) and the 1928 *Book of Common Prayer* began "Lighten our darkness, we beseech thee, O Lord." See 2 Samuel 22:29.

[54]*Didascalia et constitutiones apostolorum*, ed. F. X. Funk (Paderborn: F. Schoeningh, 1905), 8.37.

[55]*Morning Praise and Evensong*, 2.

[56]*La Tradition Apostolique de Saint Hippolyte*, ed. Bernard Botte (Münster, Westfalen: Aschendorffsche Verlagsbuchhandlung, 1963), 64.

[57]*Morning Praise and Evensong*, 26.

[58]See Deiss, 147: "with the Holy Spirit." The Latin is *cum sancto spiritu.*

[59]The earliest evidence for the use of incense at Vespers may be Ambrose, *De Virginibus* 3, and the Spanish poet Prudentius (348–405), *Hymnus ad incensum lucernae*. Taft, 143, 157.

[60]See John Chrysostom, *Exposition of Psalm 140:1* [141:1]; see *Apostolic Constitutions* 2, which also notes the use of Psalm 143.

[61]The earliest reference to Psalm 141 in Evening is Origen, *On Prayer* 32. See also Taft, 33ff.

[62]John Cassian, *Institutes* 3.3

The psalm prayer (no. 254) which follows Psalm 141 is from *Morning Praise and Evensong;*[63] the Roman Catholic Liturgy of the Hours which does not have an invariable psalm of repentance uses a different prayer with this psalm; the *Lutheran Book of Worship* (Min. Ed., p. 435) uses that prayer (no. 419) as the psalm prayer to Psalm 141 in the Psalter.

Additional psalms and a New Testament canticle may be sung. The table of Psalms for Daily Prayer (Min. Ed., p. 96) gives two additional psalms for evening and for morning for each of the seasons and times of the year. The psalm appointments have been selected from the collection of psalms appointed in the eucharistic lectionary in order to keep the pew edition of the *Lutheran Book of Worship* of manageable size. Following Jewish and ancient Christian practice, particularly of the cathedral office, no attempt is made to make use of the entire Psalter.

The appointment of proper antiphons for seasons has been declining in Lutheran service books even as the use of antiphons has been increasing. The *Common Service Book* and the *Service Book and Hymnal* gave four antiphons for Advent, Christmas, Epiphany, Lent, and Easter; three for Ascension Day, Pentecost, and Trinity Sunday (the *Common Service Book* gave only one for Trinity Sunday); and one for Reformation Day. The *Common Service Book* also provided a list of sixteen antiphons "for other times" (text ed., p. 202). The *Lutheran Book of Worship* provides two antiphons for each season for use with the additional psalms and canticles.

For Advent the first psalm antiphon, "In that day...," is from the Roman Liturgy of the Hours Morning Prayer for the First Sunday in Advent;[64] the second, "the uneven ground...," is from Sunday Evening Prayer for the Fourth Sunday in Advent.[65] For Christmas/Epiphany the first psalm antiphon, "A prince from the day of your birth," is from second evening prayer for Christmas in the Roman Liturgy of the Hours;[66] the second, "Come, you peoples," is from Morning Prayer for the Baptism of our Lord in the Roman rite.[67] For Lent the first antiphon, "Return to the Lord," is from Joel 2:13, which is also the Verse for Ash Wednesday and the Verse appointed for Lent when the proper verses are not sung. The second, "The Lord delivers us," is from Colossians 1:13 and is used at second Evening Prayer on the Fifth Sunday of Easter in the Roman rite.[68] For Holy Week the first antiphon, "Christ has humbled himself," is from Philippians 2:8; the second, "He was wounded for our transgressions," is from Isaiah 55:5. For Easter the first antiphon, "The glory of the Lord," is from Revelation 21:23; the second, "God feeds us with finest wheat," is from Psalm 81:16.

---

[63] *Morning Praise and Evensong*, Tuesday Evening, p. 59.

[64] *Liturgy of the Hours* (New York: Catholic Book Publishing Co., 1975), 1:144.

[65] Ibid., 1:315.

[66] Ibid., 1:415.

[67] Ibid., 1:637.

[68] *Liturgy of the Hours* 2 (1976):821.

In early monastic practice the psalms were sung either *directly*, that is in their entirety, by a single voice or by the whole community in unison; or *alternately*, with the congregation divided into two choirs and alternating the verses. If the psalm text included an "alleluia" response, the psalm might be sung *responsorially* with a single voice singing the psalm and the community responding "alleluia" to each verse. Later monastic usage followed the practice of the cathedral office and used the responsorial method with any psalm, selecting a verse of the psalm to serve as its refrain. *Antiphonal* practice appears from the fourth century. The Gloria Patri, never found in responsorial psalmody, is added to conclude the unit; refrains not drawn from Scripture sometimes replace scriptural antiphons; and the congregation, divided into two choirs, responds to the verse alternately with antiphons. In more recent Latin and Lutheran use, the antiphon is used simply at the beginning and the end of the psalm.[69]

Although the Gospel canticles Magnificat, Benedictus, and Nunc Dimittis have long been part of the office, the use of hymns and hymn-like passages from the Epistles and Revelation as part of the psalmody of Evening Prayer is in large measure an innovation introduced by the Roman Liturgy of the Hours (1970) based on modern biblical scholarship, which has noted the presence of such hymns in the New Testament documents.[70] The use of the Beatitudes as a canticle was known to Ambrose, and the practice continues in the Eastern Church.[71] Following such ancient manuscripts as the fifth-century Codex Alexandrinus, the *Common Service Book* included twelve canticles immediately after its collection of psalms; among these were the Beatitudes and a new canticle created for the book from passages in Rev. 5, 15, and 19, called the *Dignus est Agnus*.[72] In the present Roman Liturgy of the Hours there are seven New Testament canticles appointed for Evening Prayer, one for each day of the week:

Saturday	Philippians 2:6–11
Sunday	from Revelation 19:1–7
Monday	Ephesians 1:3–10
Tuesday	Revelation 4:11; 5:9, 10, 12
Wednesday	Colossians 1:12–20
Thursday	Revelation 11:17–18; 12:10b–12a
Friday	Revelation 15:3–4

At second Evening Prayer on Sundays in Lent, instead of the Alleluia canticle from Revelation, 1 Peter 2:21–24 is used; at first Evening Prayer on the Epiphany and at second Evening Prayer on the Transfiguration (August 6) the canticle is from 1 Timothy 3:16. The *Lutheran Book of*

---

[69] Taft, 139.

[70] See, for example, Jack T. Sanders, *The New Testament Christological Hymns* (Cambridge: University Press, 1971).

[71] Taft, 142, 241.

[72] *Common Service Book*, text ed., pp. 362–63.

Worship gives two of these canticles, Philippians 2:6–11 (Canticle 20) in a translation by Philip Pfatteicher and Revelation 15:3–4 (Canticle 21) in the translation made for the *Book of Common Prayer* by Charles M. Guilbert. In addition, following the Liturgy of St. John Chrysostom[73] and the *Common Service Book*,[74] the Beatitudes (Matthew 5:3–10) are provided as a third canticle from the New Testament (Canticle 17). The translation is that of the New English Bible with the word "sons" changed in the *Lutheran Book of Worship* to "children."

To maintain chronological sense, the Hebrew psalms are sung or said first and the New Testament canticle is sung last. "The constant rule of tradition is retained in the arrangement of the psalmody and the readings: first the Old Testament, then the Apostle, and finally the proclamation of the Gospel."[75] So the order of the biblical songs is Hebrew psalms, New Testament canticle from "the Apostle," and finally the Gospel Canticle.

The Council of Vaison (529) directed the use of the Gloria Patri (in the form "Glory to the Father and to the Son and to the Holy Spirit now and forever," the usual Eastern form) at the end of the psalms — that is, once, after all the psalms had been sung — to defend against Arianism. In Gaul, each psalm was concluded with the Gloria Patri,[76] and this became a distinguishing feature of the use of psalmody in the West; in the East, Gloria Patri concluded a unit of psalms.[77] On November 1, 589, canon 2 of a synod at Narbonne in southern Gaul ordered the Gloria Patri to be added to the end of each psalm or section of longer psalms.

The *Lutheran Book of Worship*, like the Roman Catholic Liturgy of the Hours, has recovered the more ancient practice of the psalm prayers, which give a Christian interpretation to the psalms, and has rejected the use of the Gloria Patri after the psalms as unnecessary and redundant.

The Office Hymn. The first Christian hymns derived from the Jewish liturgy and had their origin in the catechetical schools of Alexandria under Clement (d. ca. 215). A hymn by Clement, translated as "Shepherd of Tender Youth," was included in the *Service Book and Hymnal* (no. 179). Other early hymn writers included Methodius (d. ca. 311), Gregory Nazianzus (d. 389), and Synesius, bishop of Cyrene (d. 430).

It was probably through the monastic offices that hymns became a regular part of Christian worship.[78] Egeria notes that hymns were sung at every office she attended in Jerusalem.[79] The writing of Latin hymns began in the fourth century with Hilary (d. 366), who had been banished

---

[73]*Service Book*, 83–84.

[74]*Common Service Book*, text ed., p. 362 no. 11.

[75]*General Instruction on the Liturgy of the Hours* III.V.139; Roguet, 47.

[76]John Cassian, *Institutes* 2.8 (ca. 417–425); see also the *Rule of the Master* 33.42.5 and the *Rule* of St. Benedict 11.3.

[77]Taft, 97, 150.

[78]They are found for the first time in the rules of Arles. Taft, 103–04.

[79]*Egeria's Travels* 24.1–2.

by the emperor Constantius to Asia Minor in 356 and was profoundly impressed by the singing of Greek hymns in the churches of that region. When he returned to the West, he brought some hymns with him. The singing of hymns was given great impetus by Ambrose, bishop of Milan, "the father of Latin hymnody and the real inaugurator of modern hymnody in every tongue."[80] Besieged with his supporters in his new basilica in Milan in 385 by the imperial troops of the empress Justina, Ambrose preached and arranged a course of devotions in which he taught the people to sing his hymns.[81] He used the simplest of lyric meters, a stanza of four eight-syllabled iambic lines, which survives as the familiar long meter of modern hymnals. St. Augustine reports in his *Confessions* the impact of Ambrose's hymns on him.[82] Others imitated the popular form and a body of Ambrosian hymns arose. Benedict of Nursia made hymn-singing a regular part of his influential *Rule* in his monasteries. Aurelian, bishop of Arles, did the same. A Council at Tours in 567 recommended the use of hymns by other authors in addition to Ambrose.

Opposition to song which was not derived from Scripture was strong, however, and for five centuries Rome stood firm for the exclusive use of "the Bible only" as church song.[83] By the seventh century, Ambrosian hymns were found in the office in Spain and Gaul, but not until the twelfth century were non-biblical hymns admitted to the Roman office.

The preparation of local breviaries especially in France in the late seventeenth and eighteenth centuries gave a fresh impulse to the use of hymns in the daily office. The brothers de Santeuil contributed to the Cluniac breviary and Charles Coffin (1676–1749), whose hymns "The Advent of Our God" (no. 22) and "On Jordan's Banks the Baptist's Cry" (no. 36) are included in the *Lutheran Book of Worship*, contributed to the Paris breviary.

Office hymns have been treated like psalmody for they function as an extension of the psalms, and thus have traditionally concluded with a doxology, usually addressed to the same person of the Trinity as the hymn itself.

For the Roman Church the Liturgy of the Hours (1970) has opened the hymnic treasures of the church and allowed for greater variety. In the Latin form of the office, for the sake of variety there are two series of hymns for each hour for the time "throughout the year" to be used in alternate weeks. In the vernacular office the conference of bishops of a nation may introduce new compositions "provided they suit the spirit of the hour, season, or feast; one should constantly beware of permit-

---

[80]Louis Fitzgerald Benson, *The Hymnody of the Christian Church* (Richmond: John Knox Press, 1956 [1927]), 65.

[81]Augustine, *Confessions* IX.7.

[82]Augustine, *Confessions* IX.6.

[83]Benson, 73.

ting those popular songs which are of no artistic value and completely unworthy of the liturgy."[84]

The *Lutheran Book of Worship* provides a table listing the Office Hymns included in its hymnal (Min. Ed., pp. 499–500). Most of them are associated with particular seasons or times in the more important breviaries:

A Patre unigenitus (83)	Epiphany Matins and Lauds
A solis ortus cardine (64)	Christmas
Ad regias Agni dapes (210)	Easter 2
Caelestis (Coelestis) forman gloriae (90)	Transfiguration
Christe cunctorum dominator alme (375)	Dedication of a Church
Christe qui lux es et die (173)	Lent Compline
Christe Redemptor omnium (49)	Christmas
Claro paschali gaudio (154)	Common of Apostles
Conditor alme siderum (323)	Advent 1
En clara vox redarguit (37)	Advent
Hostis Herodes impie (85)	the Epiphany
Hymnum canamus gloriae (157)	Ascension
Instantis adventum Dei (22)	Advent
Jam lucis orto sidere (268)	Prime
Jesu, dulcedo cordium (356)	Transfiguration
Jesu, dulcis memoria (316)	Holy Name of Jesus
Jesu, nostra redemptio/ Amor et desirderium (300)	Ascension
Jesu, Rex admirabilis (537)	Holy Name of Jesus
Jordanis oras praevia (36)	Advent
Nocte surgentes vigilemus omnes (267)	Sunday Matins
O lux beata Trinitas (275)	2nd Sunday after the Octave of the Epiphany
O Pater sancte, mitis atque pie (169)	Trinity Sunday
O sola magnarum urbium (81)	The Epiphany
Pange lingua gloriosi corporis (120)	Corpus Christi
Pange lingua gloriosi proelium (155, 118)	5th Sunday in Lent, Palm Sunday, Good Friday
Splendor paternae gloriae (271)	Monday Lauds; the Epiphany
Stabat Mater dolorosa (110)	Seven Sorrows of the Virgin Mary
Te lucis ante terminum (277)	Compline
Veni, Creator Spiritus (472, 473, 284)	Pentecost
Veni Redemptor omnium gentium (28)	Christmas Day
Vexilla regis prodeunt (124, 125)	5th Sunday in Lent, Palm Sunday, Good Friday

Others, although not in the important medieval breviaries, were included in some office books:

---

[84] *General Instruction on the Liturgy of the Hours* III.X.178; Roguet, 54.

O filii et filiae (139)   Easter
Quem pastores laudavere (68)   Christmas Matins and Vespers
Rex Christe, factor omnium (101)   Passiontide (the last two weeks of Lent).

"O amor quam extaticus" is the fifth line of *Apparuit benignitas*, a late medieval hymn on the incarnation, translated in a cento version by Benjamin Webb for *The Hymnal Noted* (1854). It was not an office hymn.

The Lessons. The cathedral offices were services of praise and intercession, and there were no scripture lessons in the normal cathedral office except in Egypt and Cappadocia.[85]

By the ninth century at least, a lectionary had been developed which provided for the reading of the whole Bible at Matins in the course of a year. Genesis through Judges was read from Septuagesima to Palm Sunday; Jeremiah in Lent; Isaiah and Lamentations in Holy Week; Epistles, Acts, and Revelation during Easter; Old Testament historical books, the Wisdom literature, and the Apocrypha during the time after Pentecost; Isaiah, Jeremiah, and Daniel from Advent to the Epiphany; Ezekiel, the minor prophets, and Job in the time after Epiphany. The gospels and the Pauline epistles were read through at mass during the year. The sequence was almost completely obscured by the vast multiplication of saints' day and octaves during the later Middle Ages.

The 1549 *Book of Common Prayer* followed the civil year in its daily lectionary, and it was not until the twentieth-century revisions that the church year was used as the basis for the daily readings in the Prayer Book.

For Lutheran use, the *Common Service Book* (1919) provided three lessons (Old Testament, Epistle, and Gospel) for each Sunday and certain festivals and days of the church year, according to four series, including the lectionaries of Gottfried Thomasius, the church of Hannover, and the Eisenach Conference. In a separate table, one lesson for morning and one lesson for evening were appointed for each weekday of the year;[86] *The Lutheran Hymnal* also included this weekday lectionary. The *Service Book and Hymnal* provided two lessons for Matins and two lessons for Vespers for each Sunday and Holy Day (pp. 280–81), derived principally from table A of the *Common Service Book* (text ed., pp. 497–98). A daily lectionary was included in the text edition of the *Service Book and Hymnal* (1967), which gave only one lesson, usually from the New Testament, for each weekday of the year.

The Inter-Lutheran Commission on Worship, recognizing the deficiencies of the lectionaries available in Lutheran books and aware of the long and constant tradition of the daily reading of Scripture in the services of the Anglican churches, chose to borrow the daily office lectionary from the *Book of Common Prayer*. In this lectionary, the New Testament is read through twice in the two-year cycle and the Old Testament once, and the books are so arranged that they are read at suitable

---

[85]Taft, 32–33.
[86]*Common Service Book*, text ed., pp. 497–506, 507–12.

and traditional times in the church year. The Prayer Book lectionary has been revised slightly for use in the Lutheran book, and there has been some reordering of lessons, especially those from the Old Testament. For example, in the week of Pentecost 17 in year 2, Job 32 is read before chapter 29 to make a smoother narrative by reading Elihu's speeches before the replies of Job and of God. On Sundays the Old Testament continues to be read in course; the Second Lesson and the Gospel are often chosen to fit with the theme of the Old Testament lesson. There is a modest number of readings from the Apocrypha to reacquaint Lutherans with those books which Luther included in his translation of the Bible as profitable to be read, but in each case an alternative lesson from the Hebrew Old Testament is also provided. There was no biblical, theological, or confessional issue involved; it was rather a matter of pastoral concern for those within and outside the church who were unfamiliar with the Lutheran attitude toward the apocryphal books.

In the Roman Liturgy of the Hours there is a one-year cycle of readings, and there is a second lectionary provided for optional use which follows a two-year cycle. The Liturgy of the Hours does not use gospel readings at the office because the whole of the four gospels is read each year at mass in the daily and Sunday eucharistic lectionary.

The Episcopal and Lutheran daily lectionary follows a two-year cycle. Year 1 is used beginning on the First Sunday in Advent preceding odd-numbered years; Year 2 is used beginning on the First Sunday in Advent preceding even-numbered years. The church year begins with Advent, and the pattern is that Year 1 is for odd-numbered years and Year 2 is for even-numbered years.

Three readings are provided for each day. Without laying down a rule, the Notes on the Liturgy lean toward the suggestion that the first two lessons (from the Old Testament and from an epistle) be read in the morning and the Gospel be read in the evening if two services are prayed each day. The *Book of Common Prayer* (p. 934) recommends that the Gospel be read in the evening in Year 1 and in the morning in Year 2. Both books agree that there should be a balance between the Old Testament and the New: when more than one reading is used, the first should be from the Old Testament and when two lessons are desired for both morning and evening, the Old Testament lesson from the alternate year may be used.[87] The in-course sequence is emphasized in both books. When a festival or commemoration interrupts the sequence or readings they may be reordered to secure continuity or to avoid repetition.

The three readings for each day (Old Testament, Epistles or Acts, and Gospel) can also serve as readings for weekday Eucharists if it is not desirable to repeat the readings from the previous Sunday. (December 26 is the one exception, but this, being St. Stephen's Day, has its own proper eucharistic lessons.)

---

[87] Min. Ed., p. 18; *Book of Common Prayer*, 934.

The printed format of the daily lectionary in the *Lutheran Book of Worship* is not helpful, for it is difficult to tell whether one is looking at the appointments for Year 1 or for Year 2. The format in the *Book of Common Prayer* is much less confusing with Year 1 and Year 2 on facing pages and is much to be preferred.

The *Lutheran Book of Worship* gives no direction concerning the announcement of the lessons in Morning and Evening Prayer. The announcement, if given at all, should be kept as brief as possible: "A reading from First Kings." Chapter and verse citations are altogether unnecessary. Nothing need be said at the conclusion of the lesson; the reader ceasing and returning to a seat is sign and notice enough that the reading has been concluded.

The silence after each lesson is a constituent part of this portion of the service and must not be neglected. The office is not a traditional time for preaching, and the silence is an opportunity for the congregation to reflect upon the meaning of the words which have just been proclaimed. The silence is another way of preaching, another form of the proclamation of the Word of God.

The verse said after the readings and the silence is from Hebrews 12:1–2a. The translation is adapted from the Revised Standard Version.

The Gospel Canticle. The Gospel Canticle is not only drawn from a gospel narrative, it is a proclamation of the Gospel of revolutionary liberation, freedom, light, and peace and therefore should be "accorded the same solemnity and dignity as is usual for the hearing of the Gospel."[88] It is an invariable and constituent element in the service, never to be omitted. The congregation stands to sing it, to proclaim and to hear this song of the gospel.

Probably since St. Benedict's *Rule* (540), the use of the Magnificat has been virtually universal in Evening Prayer in the Western churches.[89] The translation in the *Lutheran Book of Worship* is by the International Consultation on English Texts.[90] The theme of this Song of Mary, who is understood to represent the church, is similar to that of Evening Prayer. The assembly gives thanks for what has been bestowed during the day and for the mighty deeds God has done throughout the world, remembering his ancient covenant and keeping his promise of mercy.[91] The interest of the writer of Luke in reconciling the coming of God with the humble and obscure circumstances in which the advent occurred comes to a focus in Mary. The Magnificat is the praise of and by the Virgin Mary as the preeminent example of those who fear God and who rejoice in God's merciful and revolutionary strength.

---

[88] *General Instruction on the Liturgy of the Hours* III.V.138; Roguet, 47.

[89] Earlier, and in the Eastern Church still, it is an element in Morning Prayer. Taft, 112, 128–29, 222, 241, 281.

[90] See *Prayers We Have in Common*, 2nd rev. ed. (Philadelphia: Fortress Press, 1975), 25–26 for details on the translation.

[91] See the *General Instruction on the Liturgy of the Hours* II.II.39; Roguet, 30; and Robert C. Tannehill, "The Magnificat as Poem," *Journal of Biblical Literature* 93 (1974):263–375.

The Lutheran church orders in Germany praised the Magnificat, retaining it sometimes in Latin, sometimes in a German translation. The German Magnificat was remarkably popular, and people "loved to sing this song of Mary."[92] The most frequently used tone was *tonus peregrinus* of the Gregorian series.[93] The Wittenberg order of 1533 suggested a practice common for a time in which each verse of the German or Latin text was followed by a German hymn stanza which elaborated the thought. One of Luther's finest writings in his 1521 exposition of the Magnificat, "this sacred hymn of the most blessed Mother of God."[94]

The *Lutheran Book of Worship* provides proper antiphons to the Gospel Canticle. For Advent the antiphon is from Luke 1:30–31 and is used in the Roman Liturgy of the Hours at second Evening Prayer of the First Sunday in Advent. For the last part of Advent the seven "O antiphons" are appointed. They are of unknown authorship but were already in use by the eighth century. They were highly regarded in the Middle Ages; chanting them was assigned to dignitaries of the monastery or cathedral chapter; the largest bell was rung during the singing of the O Antiphon and the Magnificat. The structure of each resembles that of a collect. Each begins with an invocation of the Messiah under an Old Testament title ("O Wisdom," for example); an amplification giving an attribute of the Messiah and developing the invocation follows ("proceeding from the mouth of the Most High, pervading and permeating all creation, mightily ordering all things"); finally there is an appeal, beginning always with "Come" (*veni*) and making reference to the initial invocation ("come and teach us the way of prudence").[95] The texts are almost entirely a mosaic of scriptural verses; only "come and save us" from O Emmanuel and "come quickly to deliver us" from O Root of Jesse do not seem to be a direct scriptural quotation. The sources are these:

O Wisdom (*O Sapientia*)	Ecclesiasticus 24:3; Wisdom 8:1; Isaiah 40:3–5
O Adonai (*O Adonai*)	Exodus 6:2, 3, 12; 3:2: 6:6
O Root of Jesse (*O Radix Jesse*)	Isaiah 11:10; Romans 15:12 Isaiah 5:15; Habakkuk 2:3; Hebrews 10:37
O Key of David (*O Clavis David*)	Isaiah 22:22; Revelation 3:7 Isaiah 42:7; Psalm 107:14; Luke 1:79
O Dayspring (*O Oriens*)	Zechariah 6:12; Hebrews 1:3; Malachi 4:2; Luke 1:78–79; Isaiah 9:2
O King of the nations (*O Rex Gentium*)	Haggai 2:8; Isaiah 28:16;

---

[92] Luther D. Reed, *The Lutheran Liturgy*, rev. ed. (Philadelphia: Fortress Press, 1960), 439.
[93] *Luther's Works* 53:176–79.
[94] *Luther's Works* 21:297–358.
[95] Michel Huglo, "O Antiphons," *New Catholic Encyclopedia.*

	Ephesians 2:14; Genesis 2:7
O Emmanuel (*O Emmanuel*)	Isaiah 7:14; 8:8; 32:22; Genesis 49:10

The titles *Sapientia, Radix Jesse, Rex Gentium,* and *Emmanuel* were applied to Christ by Pope Damasus (366–384) in his *Carmen de cognomentis Salvatoris; Clavis David* was applied to Christ by Ambrose.[96] Although there is some variation in order and number, the seven antiphons in the present order seem to be original. One indication is that in reverse order the first letter of each title of Christ (Sapientia, Adonai, Radix, Clavis, Oriens, Rex, Emmanuel) spell ERO CRAS (I shall be there tomorrow), an answer by Christ to the pleas of his people. In the Middle Ages such word-play was extremely popular.

The first Gospel Canticle antiphon for Christmas is from the second Evening Prayer of Christmas Day in the Roman Liturgy of the Hours;[97] the second is from the first Evening Prayer of the Epiphany.[98] The Gospel Canticle antiphon for Lent is from Amos 5:24. The antiphon for Holy Week is from Galatians 6:14 in an ancient liturgical form which added "in him is salvation, life, and resurrection" and which was used on Tuesday and Thursday of Holy Week as the Introit antiphon in the Roman Missal and the Common Service. It is the entrance antiphon for Tuesday and Thursday in the present Roman sacramentary.

The Gospel Canticle antiphon for Easter is from Psalm 118:24, a verse long associated with Easter. It is even more to the point in the translation in the Episcopal and Lutheran Psalter, "On this day the Lord has acted."

Hymn 180, "My Soul Now Magnifies the Lord," is a metrical paraphrase of the Magnificat.

The Litany. Intercessions were a principal part of the ancient office.[99] John Chrysostom indicates the scope of these prayers by making reference to 1 Timothy 1:1–4.[100] The intercessions were for the church and the world. The form was a series of biddings with *Kyrie eleison* as the response.[101] Evening Prayer as it came to be observed in the West eventually ended with a brief litany or simply the three-fold Kyrie[102] or preces and the Lord's Prayer. The litany in the text of Evening Prayer in the *Lutheran Book of Worship* is a re-working of the deacon's litany (*synapte*) in the Liturgy of St. John Chrysostom. The text of this litany in the Orthodox liturgy is given above (pp. 118–120) in connection with the Kyrie of the Holy Communion. Instead of this Eastern litany, the West-

---

[96] Ambrose, *De institutione virginis* 9.62
[97] *Liturgy of the Hours* 1:418.
[98] Ibid., 1:547.
[99] *Apostolic Constitutions* 8.34; *Egeria's Travels* 24:5–6.
[100] John Chrysostom, Sermon on 1 Timothy, chapter 6; sermon on Matthew 3; see also Tertullian, *Apology* 39.
[101] *Apostolic Constitutions* 8:34, 6–10.
[102] Second Council of Vaison (529), canon 3; see Taft, 148.

ern Litany, Responsive Prayer 2, or other prayers may be used (Min. Ed., p. 17 #11).

In the *Apostolic Constitutions* (8.10) after the bids to pray, the deacon tells the people to bow their heads while the bishop says a prayer over them. Following this general pattern and following the long Western tradition of concluding a litany with prayers, the *Lutheran Book of Worship* concludes the evening litany with the collect for peace (no. 255). It was the opening collect in a mass for peace in the Gelasian (no. 1472) and the Gregorian (no. 1343) sacramentaries; in the Sarum processional it was included among the prayers after the rogation litany, and in the Sarum breviary was used at Vespers. The *Book of Common Prayer* has therefore consistently given it as one of the fixed collects for Evening Prayer. It is found in many Lutherans church orders of the sixteenth century and was used by the nineteenth-century Lutheran liturgists as the concluding prayer at Vespers.

The collect is rich in historic associations. It reflects the troubled times in the latter half of the fifth century when it was composed, "when sieges and barbaric invasions made men's hearts fail for fear, when Rome but narrowly escaped the Huns and did not escape the Vandals; when the Western Empire itself passed away before Odoacer, and Odoacer was overthrown by Theodoric."[103] The prayer is for the profound peace of which Christ speaks and which he alone can give (John 14:27), which defends against all enemies — internal and external, spiritual and physical — and which is obtained by living in harmony with the will of God. The first clause of the collect rehearses the development of the Christian life: from initial desire through purposeful resolves and sound judgments, to just and righteous deeds.[104] The prayer therefore asks not for freedom from trouble but freedom from fear. God's gift of peace issues in a determined obedience to his commands as our response to his prevenient gift, and our being defended (and at last delivered) from fear of all enemies issues in a life of peace and contentment, which reflects God's initial gift.

Apparently in imitation of monastic practice, canon 10 of the Council of Gerona (517) directed that the Lord's Prayer should be added to the end of Morning and Evening Prayer each day. (Priests said the final collect, but in the absence of a priest the Lord's Prayer was used instead.) The innovation was only slowly accepted. Canon 10 of the Fourth Council of Toledo (633) criticized those who continued to use the Lord's Prayer only on Sunday.

In the practice which Tertullian describes, the Our Father is prayed first and then the community offers its intercessions. This was the pattern of prayer at the office in previous Roman and Lutheran books and is still the pattern in the *Book of Common Prayer*. The Roman Liturgy of

---

[103] William Bright, quoted in Reed, p. 447.

[104] Massey H. Shepherd, Jr., *Oxford American Prayer Book Commentary* (New York: Oxford University Press, 1950), 31.

the Hours and the *Lutheran Book of Worship*, however, have adopted a different model, which for Lutherans is the model of ante-communion, culminating in the Lord's Prayer. The Our Father thus is the conclusion of the office, gathering all the needs and desires of the congregation into the words, rooted in Old Testament prayer, which Christ taught to his church. Tertullian called the Lord's Prayer "the prescribed and regular prayer" (*legitima et ordinaria oratio*) but observed that to it was added "a superstructure of petitions for additional desires."[105] Such a practice merged again in Luther's German Mass when he directs that after the sermon be offered a paraphrase of the Lord's Prayer which involved an admonition to those who desired to partake of the Holy Communion.[106]

The Lord's Prayer is introduced by a verse which joins Luke 23:42 and 11:1 with a phrase from the Great Entrance in the Liturgy of St. John Chrysostom, "May the Lord God remember in his kingdom all you Orthodox Christians, now and always, and for ever and ever."

In the *Apostolic Constitutions*, after the prayer which concludes the intercessions, the deacon dismisses the people. In the Roman Breviary from ca. 1000, derived probably from Gallican use, the *Benedicamus domino* ("Let us bless the Lord") was the conclusion of each hour. The Lutheran church orders retained it, and when the service was led by a layperson, this verse concluded the office. The verse draws upon the conclusion of each of the first four books of the Psalter (41:13; 72:18; 89:52; 106:48); the response can be related to 1 Corinthians 15:57. The Benedicamus is the traditional conclusion to the office and not a verse introducing the benediction as the salutation introduces the prayer of the day. Because Lutherans have come to expect a benediction at the conclusion of every service, the misunderstanding of the function of the Benedicamus has arisen. When the preaching office is added to Matins or Vespers, the office of Matins or Vespers concludes with the Benedicamus and the benediction concludes the preaching office.

THE PREACHING OFFICE. When it is desired to have a sermon in connection with Morning or Evening Prayer, a brief preaching office is attached to the conclusion of Morning or Evening Prayer, following the Benedicamus. It consists of offering, hymn, sermon, prayer, and blessing.

The first of the prayers after the sermon, "Almighty God, grant to your Church your Holy Spirit" (no. 250), is a translation which first appeared in the *Church Book* (1868);[107] it was number 38 of the Collects and Prayers in the *Common Service Book*,[108] and number 2 of the

---

[105] Tertullian, *On Prayer* 10.
[106] *Luther's Works* 53:78–80.
[107] *Church Book*, p. 91, no. 10.
[108] *Common Service Book*, text ed., p. 216.

Collects and Prayers in the *Service Book and Hymnal*.[109] It was used in *The Lutheran Hymnal* in the Order of Morning Service Without Communion.[110] The prayer was used in the Brandenburg-Nuremberg church order (1533), but it is even older. It was used in Andreas Althamer's *Katechismus*, the first Lutheran Catechism (1528). The original prayer was considerably longer.

The second of the prayers, "Lord God, you have called your servants" (no. 251), is from Eric Milner-White and George Wallace Briggs's *Daily Prayer*.[111] It was number 96 of the Collects and Prayers in the *Service Book and Hymnal* (p. 231).

The third of the prayers, "Lord, we thank you that you have taught us" (no. 252), is the closing prayer from the *Lutheran Hymnary* of the Norwegian Evangelical Lutheran Church.

Canon 2 of the Council of Barcelona (540) ordered that a blessing should conclude the morning and evening office. The blessing given in the *Lutheran Book of Worship* is a version of a blessing in common use in the Roman Catholic Church for papal benedictions.

PRAYER AT THE CLOSE OF THE DAY: COMPLINE. Compline seems to have originated in the fourth century as the prayers of the monks as they went to bed. It duplicates Vespers in several ways, which in the cathedral office reviewed and concluded the day. Benedict of Nursia in the sixth century in his *Rule* described the content of this office:

At Compline they shall recite three psalms only [4, 91, 134], without antiphon and plainly. Afterwards the proper hymn: lesson: versicle: *Kyrie eleison*, and the blessing to end.[112]

Later in the Middle Ages as Vespers was moved earlier in the day, Compline was often said in the church and there attracted additions: Our Father and Ave Maria,[113] antiphons to the psalms, Nunc Dimittis, Apostles' Creed, confession and absolution, concluding prayers.

In the twentieth century there has been a renewal of interest in Compline in Anglican and Lutheran churches. People came to know it as the going to bed prayer at retreats and conferences and came to love its simple and profound beauty. The Irish Prayer Book (1926), the proposed English Prayer Book (1928), the Scottish Prayer Book (1929), the

---

[109] *Service Book and Hymnal*, p. 218.

[110] *The Lutheran Hymnal* (1941), p. 14.

[111] Eric Milner-White and George Wallace Briggs, *Daily Prayer* (London: Oxford, 1941), p. 14. The phrase "ventures of which we cannot see the ending" may be derived in part from Samuel Johnson's *Rasselas*, chapter 15:

"I am almost afraid," said the princess, "to begin a journey of which I cannot perceive an end, and to venture into this immense plain where I may be approached on every side by men whom I never saw." The prince felt nearly the same emotions, though he thought it more manly to conceal them.

[112] *Rule* of St. Benedict 17 in *Western Asceticism* (Philadelphia: Westminster Press, 1958), 308.

[113] In modern Roman use, a Marian antiphon, which may be the *Ave Maria, Alma Redemptoris Mater* ("Loving mother of the Redeemer"), or *Salve Regina* ("Hail, holy queen"), is said in English or Latin at the end of Compline.

Canadian Prayer Book (1959), the Indian Prayer Book (1963), and the American Prayer Book (1979) included Compline among the daily offices. Except for the *Worship Supplement* (1969), the *Lutheran Book of Worship* is the first Lutheran book in North America to include this office. The musical setting is by Carlos R. Messerli.

The structure of Compline in the Roman Catholic, Lutheran, and Episcopal forms is similar:

Roman Catholic Liturgy of the Hours (Night Prayer)	Lutheran Book of Worship	Book of Common Prayer (An Order for Compline)
Ps. 70:1 and Gloria Patri	The Lord almighty...	The Lord almighty...
	Ps. 92:1–2	Ps. 124:8
(Penitential rite)		Confession
		Ps. 70:1 and Gloria Patri
Hymn	Night Hymn	
	Confession	
Psalm	Psalm(s)	Psalm(s)
Reading	Brief Lesson	Brief Lesson
Responsory	Responsory	Responsory
Nunc Dimittis with antiphon	Office Hymn	
Prayer	Preces	Kyrie
	Prayer	Our Father
	Our Father	Prayer
	Nunc Dimittis with antiphon	Nunc Dimittis with antiphon
		Benedicamus
The Lord almighty...	Blessing	Blessing
Marian antiphon		

In the Lutheran and Episcopal forms, Compline begins with a blessing, a post-Reformation addition to the office. The *Lutheran Book of Worship* has altered the form in the Prayer Book, "The Lord almighty grant us a quiet night and a perfect end," to prevent unseemly amusement; the Lutheran form concludes "and peace at the last." The phrase is echoed in prayer 260 at the end of the office.

The verses which follow the opening blessing in the Lutheran form are from Psalm 92:1–2 (cf. 7:17; 9:2). The translation was made for the *Lutheran Book of Worship*. The verses introduce the first hymn.

Confession is in one of two forms. The first is a prayer of confession by the congregation with a declaration of grace by the leader. The forms were written for the present Lutheran book. The second form is from the Confiteor at the beginning of Mass in the 1570 missal and from Compline in the Roman Breviary (1570) in which the leader confesses before the congregation, which then asks God's forgiveness upon the leader and then confesses their sins with a response by the leader. The confession in the *Book of Common Prayer* follows the first form, a confession by officiant and people and a request for forgiveness by the officiant. The Roman Liturgy of the Hours permits but does not require confession:

A brief examination of conscience may be made. In the communal celebration of the office, a penitential rite using the formulas of the Mass may be inserted here.

Benedict required three invariable psalms at Compline — 4, 91, 134; they have been traditional in the West since then. The *Book of Common Prayer* adds Psalm 31:1–5 from Compline in the Sarum breviary and permits other suitable psalms. The Roman Liturgy of the Hours uses Psalms 4 and 134 at Saturday Compline, 91 at Sunday Compline, 86 on Monday, 143:1–11 on Tuesday, 31:1–6 and 130 on Wednesday, 16 on Thursday, and 88 on Friday; the Sunday form of Compline, however, may be used throughout the week.

The Roman Liturgy of the Hours provides a brief lesson for each day of the week; the Lutheran and Episcopal rites provide a list from which the lesson may be chosen. The Prayer Book says "one of the following, or some other suitable passage of Scripture, is read." The Lutheran book says "As a Brief Lesson one or more of the following is read." It is, however, difficult to imagine circumstances in which more than one brief lesson would be desirable.

	Roman Catholic **Liturgy of the Hours**	*Lutheran Book* *of Worship*	*Book of* *Common Prayer*
Saturday	Deut. 6:4–7		
Sunday	Rev. 22:4–5		
Monday	1 Thess. 5:9–10		
Tuesday	1 Pet. 5:8–9a	1 Pet. 5:6–9a	1 Pet. 5:8–9a
Wednesday	Eph. 4:26–27		
Thursday	1 Thess. 5:23		
Friday	Jer. 14:9a	Jer. 14:9	Jer. 14:9, 22
		Matt. 11:28–30	Matt. 11:28–30
			Heb. 13:20–21
		John 14:27	
		Rom. 8:38–39	

Jeremiah was the usual reading in medieval Compline; 1 Peter 5 was often used at the beginning of the office.

Since the curtailment of the reading of Scripture in the office except at Matins, the brief lesson, sometimes called a "chapter," has been characteristic of Lauds, Vespers, and the Little Hours as well as Compline. The churches of the Reformation naturally have not found this brevity attractive and have sought to provide for fuller readings at the major hours of the day, morning and evening. In keeping with the simplicity of Compline, however, it seems desirable to provide simply a verse or two of Scripture for meditation as one concludes the day and prepares for bed.

The Responsory. The Responsory in the Lutheran and Roman rites is the same, from Psalm 31:5; the Lutheran form is cast consistently in the singular, the Roman has "You have redeemed us, Lord God of truth." The Episcopal response takes the form of versicles and responses to be said responsively; the first pair of verses is Psalm 31:5, the second, used later in the Lutheran office before the prayer, is from Psalm 17:8.

The Office Hymn. The hymn in widespread use in the West at Compline is *Te lucis ante terminum* ("To You before the Close of Day," no. 277), found in the earliest Ambrosian manuscripts although it is not attributed to Ambrose. This hymn is given as the first of several choices in the Roman Liturgy of the Hours. The other hymn used in medieval forms of Compline, especially in Lent, is *Christe qui lux es et dies* ("O Christ You Are the Light and Day," no. 273). It is first cited in the Rule of St. Caesarius, ca. 502.

In the Roman form of Compline the hymn is sung before the psalmody; in Benedict's *Rule* and the older Roman rite it came after the psalmody. In the Sarum breviary and early English Primers, the hymn was sung after the lesson, and this is its location in the Lutheran rite.

Prayers. A traditional verse at Compline was Psalm 17:8. In the Roman Breviary of 1570 it was used as verse and response following the Responsory. The *Lutheran Book of Worship* has used two verses from that psalm (17:1, 15) in addition to the traditional verse to form the brief preces which introduce the prayer.

The first prayer, "Be present, merciful God" (no. 259), is a revision of a translation in Compline in the *Book of Common Prayer* of a collect from the Leonine sacramentary (no. 593) and the Gregorian sacramentary (no. 941). The translation in William Bright's *Ancient Collects* is:

Be present, O Lord, to our prayers, and protect us by day and night; that in all successive changes of times we may ever be strengthened by Thine unchangeableness; through Jesus Christ our Lord.[114]

The second prayer, "O Lord, support us all the day long of this troubled life" (no. 260), was found or composed in or before 1876 by George W. Douglas from a passage in Sermon XX of a volume of sermons by John Henry Newman, *Sermons on Subjects of the Day*.[115] It

---

[114]Bright, 10.
[115]Hatchett, 568; Shepherd, 594–95. See *The Living Church* June 8, 1935.

was included in the *Book of Common Prayer* in 1928 and is no. 63 (p. 833) in the 1979 Prayer Book.

The third prayer, "Be our light in the darkness" (no. 261), is a translation of a Gelasian collect for Vespers (no. 1589), *Illumina, quaesumus domine, tenebras nostras*, which was no. 186 in the *Service Book and Hymnal* (p. 230). It was also included in the Bobbio missal (no. 565), the Gregorian sacramentary (no. 936), and at Compline in the Sarum missal. A version of the prayer is given in Tuesday Compline in the Roman Liturgy of the Hours. The translation in the *Lutheran Book of Worship* is borrowed from the *Book of Common Prayer* (p. 133). The biblical allusion, clearer in the older translation "lighten our darkness," is to 2 Samuel 22:29.

The fourth prayer, "Visit our dwellings, O Lord" (no. 262), is the collect of the Roman breviary for Compline and is used in the Liturgy of the Hours as the collect for solemnities that do not occur on Saturday or Sunday. The translation in the *Lutheran Book of Worship* is borrowed from the *Book of Common Prayer* (p. 133) with the phrase "this place" changed to "our dwellings."

The fifth prayer, "Eternal God, the hours of both day and night are yours" (no. 263), is based on a form of intercession in the version of Compline which appeared in the Episcopal *Authorized Services* (1973),[116] which was part of the process of revision of the American Prayer Book.

The sixth prayer, "Gracious Lord, we give you thanks for the day" (no. 264), was written by Edward D. Roe for the *Lutheran Book of Worship*.

The Gospel Canticle. After the Benedictus, which looks forward to the birth of John the forerunner, and after the Magnificat, which looks to the birth of the Messiah, a third Lukan song breathes the confidence of completion: "Your word has been fulfilled." The long-awaited promised salvation of the world has been embodied in the infant whom Simeon holds in his arms, and the trustful serenity of Simeon's' song makes it remarkably appropriate for the close of the day. Christians noticed this quite early, and the Nunc Dimittis was part of an evening prayer given in the fourth-century *Apostolic Constitutions* (7.48). The canticle with its excellent invariable antiphon, a late medieval contribution, was introduced into Compline during the Middle Ages.

---

[116]*Authorized Services* (New York: Church Hymnal Corporation, 1973), p. 195:
Eternal God, to you, our heavenly Father, the darkness and the light are both alike, and the night is as clear as the day. We therefore pray you to be with those who watch and work throughout the night on behalf of others:
Here the leader or members of the congregation may mention specific persons and occupations
Grant them courage in danger, diligence in emergencies, and the presence of your Holy Spirit in the long and lonely hours. When we awake may we be thankful for their labors and take thought in turn for their needs; through Jesus Christ our ever-reigning Lord.

In the medieval order of Compline the Nunc Dimittis came after the brief lesson and before the concluding prayer. The *Lutheran Book of Worship*, borrowing the order of the *Book of Common Prayer*, has moved the canticle to the conclusion of the office so that it serves as the departure song of the congregation. As is the case with the other Gospel Canticles, the translation is that of the International Consultation on English Texts.[117]

Not to be overlooked in Compline are the reminders that as the day comes to its close, so one day will each life. The dying of the day is a sign of the death of the individual and the eventual death of the universe. The Nunc Dimittis, it should be noted, is part of the Commendation of the Dying[118] as well as part of Prayer at the Close of the Day.

The blessing is from the *Book of Common Prayer* and derives from medieval blessings in the Roman rite.

MORNING PRAYERS: MATINS. Following general ecumenical practice, the service known to previous generations of Lutherans as Matins is in the *Lutheran Book of Worship* called Morning Prayer, as it is in the Liturgy of the Hours, the *Book of Common Prayer*, the *Worshipbook* of the Presbyterian Church, and others. This office has gone by various names through the centuries — Matins in some places, Lauds in others. In the Latin Liturgy of the Hours it is called Ad laudes matutinas. In French, Office du matin: laudes. The service called Matins in previous Lutheran books has been a blending of elements from Matins, Lauds, and Prime. Matins is preserved in the *Lutheran Book of Worship* as a subtitle.

Morning Prayer (more accurately, Morning Praise) is the celebration of dawn in its rich associations. For Christians dawn signifies the resurrection of Christ, who is the rising Sun (Mal. 4:2), the true light (John 1:9), the dawn from on high (Luke 1:78, from the Benedictus).[119] "We should pray in the morning," said St. Cyprian, "to celebrate the resurrection of the Lord with morning prayer."[120] Dawn is a triumphant hour, driving out the last vestiges of light. Its rising brightness looks to the unfolding future of the day and of the life of the world.[121]

The earliest available accounts of the office indicate that in the Western church Morning Prayer began with Psalm 51[122] or at least the versicle from Psalm 51:16, "O Lord, open my lips *and my mouth shall declare your praise.*" In modern Jewish use, the Eighteen Benedictions

---

[117] *Prayers We Have in Common*, 27.

[118] *Occasional Services* (Minneapolis: Augsburg Publishing House and Philadelphia: Board of Publication, Lutheran Church in America, 1982), 106.

[119] Clement of Alexandria, *Stromata* 7.7, 43.6–7; Taft, 14–15 n. 2.

[120] Cyprian, *On the Lord's Prayer* 35.

[121] *General Instruction on the Liturgy of the Hours*, Roguet, 103; see also Bradshaw, 38–39. Dietrich Bonhoeffer in *Life Together* (p. 40) observes, "The Old Testament day begins in the evening and ends with the going down of the sun. It is the time of expectation. The day of the New Testament church begins with the break of day and ends with the dawning light of the next morning. It is the time of fulfillment, the resurrection of the Lord."

[122] Cassian, *Institutes* 3.6.

are preceded with this verse; it may be a pre-Christian element in the office. In the Roman Liturgy of the Hours it is now an invitatory which is said at the beginning of each day's prayer whether the Office of Readings (formerly Matins) or Morning Prayer (formerly Lauds); it is followed by Psalm 95 (or 100 or 67 or 24) with its antiphon and the Gloria Patri. For the beginning of other offices Psalm 70:1 is prescribed: "God, come to my assistance. *Lord, make haste to help me.*"

Lutheran and Episcopal use follows the medieval form of Matins in the Roman Breviary and begins Morning Prayer with Psalm 51:16 as a verse and response and the Gloria Patri sung in unison as in earlier Western practice. The translation of the Gloria Patri is by the International Consultation on English Texts.[123]

The "lesser doxology" (the Gloria in Excelsis is the greater doxology) probably began as an adaptation of Jewish blessings of God and such early Christian expressions of praise as Romans 16:27, Ephesians 3:21, Philippians 4:20, 2 Peter 3:18, Jude 25, and Revelation 5:13. The form was influenced by the baptismal formula in Matthew 18:19. The Gloria Patri has been used at the end of whole psalms from the beginnings of antiphonal psalmody in Antioch. The original wording apparently was "Glory to the Father through the Son in the Holy Spirit now and forever." In opposition to the Arians who used the form to support their contention that there was a time when the Son was not, the Western churches in the sixth century changed the form to make the three persons of the Trinity clearly equal, "Glory to the Father and to the Son and to the Holy Spirit" and added "as it was in the beginning, is now, and will be forever," to assert the eternity of the Son. In the Middle Ages, particularly in Germany, as throughout the East, the sign of the cross was made at the beginning of the Gloria Patri in recognition of its significance as a profession of faith.[124]

In the medieval office Alleluia was added to the Gloria Patri at the beginning of Matins except during pre-Lent and Lent. The *Lutheran Book of Worship* uses a double alleluia to make a more satisfying musical phrase.

John Chrysostom[125] and the *Apostolic Constitutions*[126] indicate that Psalm 63 was the traditional morning psalm. In the sixth century, Benedict of Nursia in his *Rule* directed that Psalm 95 be sung with an antiphon as the first psalm at Nocturns each day. The antiphons (sometimes called invitatories) to Psalm 95 relieve the tedium of daily use of this psalm, emphasize the season of the church year, and provide for congregational participation when it is used as a refrain during the psalm. Following Lutheran custom, the last four verses of Psalm 95 are omitted in the *Lutheran Book of Worship*.

---

[123] See *Prayers We Have in Common*, 19.
[124] Reed, 412. See Eric Werner, *The Sacred Bridge* (New York: Columbia University Press, 1959), chap. 9, "The Doxology in Synagogue and Church."
[125] John Chrysostom, *Commentary on Psalm 140*.1. See Bradshaw, 74.
[126] *Apostolic Constitutions* 2.59; cf. 8.34–39.

The invitatory antiphon for general use was composed for the *Lutheran Book of Worship* and reflects the sunrise and the renewal of life at the beginning of the daylight and recalls the Johannine equation of light and life.

The proper invitatory antiphon for Advent (Min. Ed., p. 92) is drawn from the antiphon for the first part of Advent (through December 16) in the Liturgy of the Hours, "Come, let us worship the Lord, the King who is to come." The proper invitatory antiphon for Christmas/Epiphany (Min. Ed., p. 93) is from John 1:14; the antiphon for Lent (Min. Ed., p. 94) is from Psalm 145:18. The antiphon for Easter (Min. Ed., p. 94) is from Luke 24:24 and was appointed in the *Common Service Book* and the *Service Book and Hymnal*. It is similar to the invitatory antiphon in the Liturgy of the Hours, "The Lord is risen, alleluia."

Psalms. The psalms of Morning Prayer were chosen in harmony with a long tradition. The first psalm appointed in the table of Psalms for Daily Prayer is a psalm appropriate to the morning; the last is one of the laudate Psalms (145–150). These psalms, especially 148–150, were anciently used to end Lauds and perhaps gave the name to this office. The ancient Roman offices, according to John Cassian, had fixed psalms at Lauds — 51, 63, 67, 148–150 — and one daily variable psalm (100, 5, 43, 65, 90, 143, 92). Paul Bradshaw suggests, however, that Psalms 148–150 were originally part of the night prayer of the monastic tradition and only later became part of Morning Prayer.[127]

An Old Testament canticle may be sung between the two daily psalms. In the Liturgy of the Hours, because of the abundance of song in the Old Testament besides the psalms, each weekday of the four-week cycle has its own proper canticle. In the *Lutheran Book of Worship*, Canticle 14, "Listen! You Nations of the World," is from Jeremiah 31:10–14 in a version by John Arthur. These verses from Jeremiah are used in the Liturgy of the Hours as the canticle for Morning Prayer on Thursday of Week I.

Canticle 15, "Seek the Lord" *Quaerite Dominum*, a Song of Isaiah), is from Isaiah 55:6–11 in a version prepared by Philip Pfatteicher on the basis of the Revised Standard Version, the New English Bible and Canticle 10 in the *Book of Common Prayer* (pp. 86–87).

Canticle 16 "I Will Sing the Story of Your Love," is drawn from Psalm 89:1 (antiphon-refrain), Jeremiah 33:10–11, and Psalm 100:5. The texts were arranged by Philip Pfatteicher, primarily on the basis of the New English Bible.

Canticle 18, "All You Works of the Lord" (*Benedicite, omnia opera*), is from the Apocryphal addition to Daniel, the Song of the Three Young Men verses 35–65.[128] The translation is a conservative revision of the translation which previous Lutheran books had borrowed from the *Book*

---

[127]Cassian, *Institutes* 3.6. Bradshaw, 82–83, 109–10, but see Taft, 79–81, 97–100, and especially 193–201.

[128]A standard canticle at Sunday Matins in East and West. Taft, 127, 129, 146, 159, 162.

of Common Prayer, with the refrain "praise him and magnify him for-ever" repeated after every third verse. The structure of the hymn is to be noted (as the headings in the *Book of Common Prayer* make clear): the first two lines are a general invocation of all creation to bless the Lord; the next section ("You angels of the Lord, bless the Lord") specif-ically invokes particular aspects of the cosmic order; the next section ("Let the earth bless the Lord"), the earth and its creatures; the next section ("You people of God, bless the Lord"), the people of God; the last two lines are a concluding Trinitarian doxology. Two different treat-ments of the hymn are given in the Prayer Book: the version in the Tudor language is in Morning Prayer I (pp. 47–49) and a modern ver-sion is in Morning Prayer II (pp. 88–90). In the Liturgy of the Hours this canticle is appointed for Morning Prayer on Sunday in Week I and Week III. It is used in the Lutheran version of the Easter Vigil after the twelfth lesson.

Canticle 19 is the Song of Moses and Miriam from Exodus 15:1–2, 6, 11, 13, 17–18. The translation is a composite of the Revised Stan-dard Version and the *Book of Common Prayer* (p. 85). The phrase "my father's God" is unfortunate; the Prayer Book has a superior rendering ("the God of my people") at that point. This canticle is appropriate for Easter and is used in the Easter Vigil after the fourth lesson (Min. Ed., p. 148). In the Liturgy of the Hours this canticle is used at Morning Prayer on Saturday of Week I.

Other Old Testament canticles are given in the Easter Vigil: *Vinea facta est:* The Song of the Vineyard (Isaiah 5:1–2b, 7; (Min. Ed., p. 149) and *Attende, caelum:* A Song of Moses (Deuteronomy 32:1–4, 7, 36a, 43a; Min. Ed., p. 150). The translation is basically from the New English Bible, revised with phrases from the Revised Standard Ver-sion. The *Apostolic Constitutions* (ca. 380) give the *Gloria in Excelsis* ("Glory to God in the highest") as a "morning hymn."[129]

The Athanasian Creed was used until 1955 in the Roman Catholic Church at Prime on most Sundays of the year; after 1955 until the publication of the Liturgy of the Hours which suppressed Prime it was used on Trinity Sunday. This practice is still observed in some places in the Lutheran church. On Trinity Sunday, therefore, when it is desired the Athanasian Creed may be sung or said as the canticle between the psalms.

The Office Hymn. The office hymn follows as a continuation of the praise of God in psalms and hymns (see Eph. 5:18–19 and Col. 3:16).[130]

Detailed comments on the use of the office hymn are included above under Evening Prayer, pp. 358–361.

The Lessons. The lessons are read according to the lectionary for the daily office. When Morning Prayer is used instead of ante-communion as the principal service of a congregation on Sunday, it is appropriate to

---

[129]*Apostolic Constitutions* 7.
[130]See Bradshaw, 43–45.

use the three readings from the eucharistic lectionary instead of those from the daily lectionary.[131]

Detailed comments on the daily lectionary and the readings are included above under Evening Prayer, pp. 361–363.

Responsory. A responsory may follow the lessons. It is an ancient chant form, already prescribed by Benedict's *Rule* (ca. 540) and originally sung after each lesson at Matins. It assumed a pattern in which Scripture was used to comment on itself; sometimes brief liturgical compositions were included. Amalarius of Metz in the ninth century first describes the characteristic form which developed in the Gallican church and which was later adopted in Rome. The responsorial form of chant was used formerly in the Gradual and the Offertory of the Eucharist.

The first part of the responsory, the responsory proper, is a series of verses and responses. The second part, called the "verse," is so constructed that its conclusion could be used as a response to each part of the responsory proper. Then the first (and older) part of the Gloria Patri (without "as it was in the beginning, is now, and will be forever") is said, after which the concluding part of the verse is repeated. In Lent the Gloria Patri was omitted from the Responsory.

Many of the historic responsories were superb liturgical texts. The responsory for the First Sunday in Advent (*Aspiciens a longe*), for example, is

> Watching from afar, I see the power of God advancing,
> and a cloud covering the whole earth.
> Go out to meet him and say,
>> Tell us if you are the one who is to come
>> to reign over your people Israel.
> All peoples of the earth, all children of mortals,
>> rich and poor alike, go out to meet him and say,
> Shepherd of Israel, hear us,
> you who lead Joseph's race like a flock,
>> Tell us if you are the one.
> Open wide the gates, you princes,
> let the King of glory enter,
>> who is to reign over the people of Israel.
> Watching from afar, I see the power of God advancing,
> and a cloud covering the whole earth.
> Go out to meet him and say,
>> Tell us if you are the one who is to come
>> to reign over the people of Israel.

The German reformers attempted to preserve at least some of the responsories with their music and provided for the use of a responsory after the lessons in Vespers as well as in Matins. With the general neglect of Matins and Vespers as a form of congregational worship during the periods of Pietism and Rationalism, the Lutheran churches in Europe

---

[131] This is in fact required by the *Book of Common Prayer*, 888.

lost the responsory and antiphons. The Common Service restored them to North American Lutheran use.

The Liturgy of the Hours has a short responsory after the lesson in Lauds and Vespers; formerly such a *responsum breve* was used following the brief lesson ("chapter") in Prime, the Little Hours, and Compline.

The Gospel Canticle. The Benedictus is the Gospel Canticle at Morning Prayer according to a long tradition in the Western church. It may have been the Gospel Canticle in Lauds according to Benedict's *Rule* and it is part of Morning Prayer (*Orthros*) in the Eastern Church. Like the whole of Morning Prayer, Benedictus is oriented toward the future, to the dawn of salvation and the dawn of the last day of fulfillment. The first eight verses parallel the Magnificat and are drawn from the Old Testament; the last four speak of John the Baptist as the one who will prepare the way for the Messiah, "the dayspring from on high" (Mal. 4:2).

The Benedictus in its liturgical use is a proclamatory celebration of the God-given freedom to live the new life as the new day dawns and unfolds its promise and hope. The translation is by the International Consultation on English Texts.[132]

Proper antiphons are given with the propers for Daily Prayer (Min. Ed., pp. 92–95).

Further comments on the Gospel Canticle and the antiphons are given above under Evening Prayer, pp. 363–365.

The Prayers. The Lutheran reformers made no change in the traditional conclusion of Matins and Vespers as they knew them from the local breviaries in Germany and elsewhere. The offices concluded with the Kyrie, Lord's Prayer, and collects. In the *Lutheran Book of Worship*, following the Liturgy of the Hours, the Kyrie is no longer used and the Lord's Prayer is the concluding prayer of the office.

The Prayer of the Day follows the Benedictus as a kind of psalm prayer to the Gospel Canticle. Other prayers may follow.

The collect for grace (no. 249) is used to conclude the series. It is derived from the Gelasian sacramentary (no. 1576) and the Gregorian sacramentary (no. 1491) and the Gallican Bobbio missal (no. 569) and was the concluding prayer in the daily office of Prime. It was probably made from two prayers of St. Basil, based chiefly on the psalms for that hour.[133] The *Common Service Book* and the *Service Book and Hymnal* used the *Book of Common Prayer* translation; the *Lutheran Book of Worship* has slightly altered the revision in the present Prayer Book (p. 100).

The Lord's Prayer is the culmination and conclusion of the prayers.

---

[132]See *Prayers We Have in Common*, 20–21, for details of the translation; see also Raymond E. Brown, "The Annunciation to Zechariah, the Birth of John the Baptist, and the Benedictus," *Worship* 62 (1988):482–96.

[133]Philip Freeman, *The Principles of Divine Service*, 2nd ed. (London: Parker, 1866), 1:222. Cited in Reed, 425.

For comments on the Benedicamus and the preaching office, see above under Evening Prayer, p. 367.

The Paschal Blessing. The Paschal Blessing, a little office of the resurrection, has its origin in the practice developed by the church in Jerusalem described by Egeria. There it was a weekly commemoration of the resurrection in the very place where the event happened.[134] Egeria reports that on Sundays the bishop reads the gospel of the Lord's resurrection at first cockcrow. The gospel is read in the tomb which Christ used, the bishop sitting where the angel sat and announced the same news to the women. The commemoration is made at cockcrow, at the end of the night, rather than at the first light of dawn. Thus the commemoration of the resurrection has been drawn from the night service into the morning service.

The *Apostolic Constitutions* (8.38) have a thanksgiving for morning, which parallels the thanksgiving for light in the evening:

O God, the God of spirits and of all flesh, beyond compare, standing in need of nothing, you have given the sun to rule over the day and the moon and stars to rule over the night. Look down upon us with gracious eyes and receive our morning thanksgivings and have mercy on us; for we have not stretched out our hands to some strange god [Ps. 44:20]; for there is not among us any new god, but you, the eternal God, without end, who gave us our being through Christ and give us our well-being through him. Vouchsafe us also, through him, eternal life, with whom glory and honor and worship be to you and the Holy Spirit for ever.[135]

Recalling this ancient practice and bringing together the themes of dawn and resurrection and baptism, light and life, the *Lutheran Book of Worship* provides for a commemoration of the resurrection for use at the font on Sundays, the day of the Lord's rising.

The Sunday resurrection vigil in the ancient cathedral office culminated in the proclamation of the Paschal Gospel. The Paschal Blessing in the Lutheran book follows the precedent. A verse from Galatians 3:37 with the Easter song, Alleluia, as the response introduces the singing of the Easter Gospel.

The church's great song of thanksgiving, Te Deum, follows as a response. This Latin Hymn in rhythmical prose has been variously attributed. A popular tradition beginning in perhaps the eighth century imagined that it had been composed spontaneously by Ambrose and Augustine at Augustine's baptism. In some ancient Irish manuscripts it is attributed to Bishop Nicet, who, according to Dom G. Morin's suggestion in 1894, has been identified with Niceta(s) of Remesiana (modern

---

[134] *Egeria's Travels* 27.2 John Wilkinson comments, "Here is a service which was celebrated on the day of the resurrection, and in the very place which was its testimony. Where the bishop reads the Gospel the angel once sat and announced the same news to the women" (p. 65).

[135] *Apostolic Constitutions* 8.38.

Nish in Yugoslavia), who died after A.D. 414.[136] It can be said with some certainty only that the hymn was composed at the beginning of the fifth century in Latin. (The Greek text is a ninth-century translation of the Latin.) The earliest manuscript is the seventh-century Bangor (Ireland) antiphonary. The use of the Te Deum in the morning office is referred to in the *Rule* of St. Caesarius (ca. 500) and in the *Rule* of St. Benedict (530). In the Roman breviary, Te Deum was used after the last lesson at Matins; now in the Liturgy of the Hours it occurs in the Office of Readings.

Luther loved this noble hymn, and in his book *The Three Symbols or Creeds of the Christian Faith* (1538) he praised the Te Deum together with the Apostles' and Athanasian creeds.[137] His German translation became as popular in the Lutheran church as the Latin version had been before.

The Te Deum may be understood as a Western relative of the Gloria in Excelsis, the structure of which it parallels. The translation is by the International Consultation on English Texts and is closer to the original Latin than the older English version in previous Episcopal and Lutheran books, which derived from the King's Primer (1545), "We praise thee, O God." The older opening vocative "O God" is inaccurate; the Latin is literally "You (*te*) as God (*deum*) we praise (*laudamus*)." An effort was made by the consultation to preserve in English the opening poetic triplets in a clearly parallel structure: "You are God...," "You are the Lord...," "You are the eternal Father...."

The hymn begins with this three-fold acclamation of God who is Lord and Father of all creation. The heavenly hosts of angels sing God's praise in the words of the Sanctus (Isa. 6:3); the translation is deliberately identical with that of the Sanctus. From their places in heaven three classes of New Testament royalty join the song — apostles, prophets, and martyrs. In this context the prophets are those of the early church (see Rev. 18:20; Eph. 2:20, 3:5, 4:11) rather than the Old Testament prophets. On earth the church militant echoes the heavenly praise and acclaims the triune God, who is the Father of unbounded (*immensae*) majesty, the Son, worthy of all worship (*venerandum*), and the Holy Spirit, advocate and guide (*Paracletum*).

The second part of the hymn, alluding to Psalm 24, glorifies Christ, eternal Son and King, who became incarnate to overcome death (literally to draw or extract the stinger of death or to neutralize the effects of the sting; see 1 Cor. 15:56) and open the kingdom of heaven to all believers (see the Prayer of the Day for Easter, no. 63), who now reigns in glory, and who will come to judge the world. Because of the motives for the incarnation the promised arrival of the Judge does not evoke terror but rather the confident plea, with which the

---

[136]Andrew E. Burn, *Niceta of Remesiana: His Life and Works* (Cambridge: University Press, 1905). Also his *The Hymn Te Deum and Its Author* (London: Faith Press, 1926).
[137]See *Luther's Works* 34:202; 53:171–75.

hymn concludes, for Christ who bought us with the price of his blood (that is, his life; see 1 Cor. 6:20; 7:23) to come to help (*subveni*) his people now and bring (*munerari*, reward, or *numerari*, number) them at last to enjoy that eternal glory which the Son shares with the Father. The conclusion of the circle will then be complete as the hymn returns to the vision of everlasting splendor with which it began.

In several manuscripts certain verses were added to the text of the hymn: Psalms 28:10; 145:2; 123:3; 56:1, 3; 31:1. The *Lutheran Book of Worship* does not include them, but they may occasionally be read or sung responsively as preces to introduce the prayer. (See *Manual on the Liturgy*, p. 295).

The concluding prayer of the Paschal Blessing (no. 253), a kind of psalm prayer to the canticle, is a version of the first Prayer of the Day for Easter (no. 62, Min. Ed., p. 153) which was written for the *Lutheran Book of Worship*.

The Psalter
(Ministers Edition, pp. 340–422, 18, 20)

Jews and Christians through the centuries have found in the psalms not only the compelling voice of ancient poets but expressions which give voice to their own joys and fears, distress and faith. Joan Webber has demonstrated that John Donne in his sermons regularly identifies his voice with that of the psalmist, so that "almost all his sermons on the Psalms have an urgent immediacy that distinguishes their tone from that of others."[138]

The psalter has served for millennia as a principal hymnbook for Jews and Christians alike, "an inexhaustible mine of devotion."[139] Luther, reflecting both his monastic training and his biblical scholarship, praised the psalms.

The Psalter ought to be a precious and beloved book, if for no other reason than this: it promises Christ's death and resurrection so clearly — and pictures his kingdom and the condition and nature of all Christendom — that it might well be called a little Bible. It is really a fine enchiridion or handbook. In fact, I have a notion that the Holy Spirit wanted to take the trouble himself to compile a short Bible and book of examples of all Christendom or all saints, so that anyone who could not read the whole Bible would here have anyway almost an entire summary of it, comprised in one little book.

Beyond all that, the Psalter has this noble virtue and quality. Other books make much ado about the works of the saints, but say very little about their words. The Psalter is a gem in this respect.... It presents to us not the simple ordinary speech of the saints, but the best of their language, that which they used when they talked with God himself in great earnestness and on the most

---

[138] Joan Webber, *Contrary Music: The Prose Style of John Donne* (Madison: University of Wisconsin Press, 1963), 167.
[139] Reed, 393.

important matters.... There you look into the hearts of all the saints, as into fair and pleasant gardens, yes, as into heaven itself....

In a word, if you would see the holy Christian Church painted in living color and shape, comprehended in one little picture, then take up the Psalter.[140]

In Jewish use in the temple and synagogue and in Christian use in cathedrals and churches daily prayer made selective use of the psalms, choosing those which were appropriate to the occasion. The monastic practice, however, was to pray 150 psalms in course, daily for some Eastern monks, weekly for the monks of Rome, fortnightly for monks in Gaul. As the medieval period progressed, the Roman system came to prevail in the West. Certain psalms were prayed at certain offices; the rest of the psalter was distributed throughout the week. The multiplication of saints' days and other feasts complicated and obscured the scheme.

Musical treatment of the psalms was noteworthy. There were nine psalms tones or melodies, eight regular and one irregular (*tonus peregrinus*), called the Gregorian tones. They manifested great variety, and each psalm had its antiphon sung to its proper melody. Properly to render the entire psalter therefore required trained singers. "The chanting of the Latin Psalter to these fine melodies for a millennium and more is one of the most impressive features of the liturgical and musical literature of the church."[141]

The Lutheran reformers attempted to retain the chanting of the psalms to their historic melodies. Many of the church orders printed the psalm tones, and cantionales gave them in complete form. The church orders often continued or adapted the practice which had been traditional in the West since the time of Benedict. Psalms 1–109 were assigned to Matins; Psalms 110–150 to Vespers. The entire Psalter was used, but no effort was made to match days and times with appropriate psalms. The development of vernacular hymnody, the dissolution of monastic communities, the discontinuance of corporate clerical communities, changes in worship caused in part by married clergy and families, eventually led to the decline and near loss of the chanted psalter to the Lutheran church.

The *Church Book*, the *Common Service Book*, and the *Service Book and Hymnal* gave a collection of selected psalms in the Authorized Version of the Bible.[142] The *Common Service Book* gave a table of proper psalms for festivals and seasons (text ed., pp. 513–14). This was expanded in the *Service Book and Hymnal* (pp. 282–83) so proper psalms were appointed for Matins and Vespers for every Sunday and festival

---

[140]Martin Luther, "Preface to the Psalter" 1545 (1528), *Luther's Works* 35:254–57.

[141]Reed, 394.

[142]Luther Reed and Harry Archer in their *Psalter and Canticles Pointed for Chanting to the Gregorian Psalm Tones* (Philadelphia: General Council Publication Board, 1901) were the first to give a plainsong setting to the entire Psalter in the Authorized Version. See also Herbert Lindemann, ed., *The Psalter of the Authorized Version of the Scriptures* (Minneapolis: Augsburg Publishing House, 1940).

of the church year and other occasions. No effort was made to cover the entire Psalter. (*The Lutheran Hymnal* distributed the 150 psalms over thirty-one days.) The psalms were identified by number and by the Latin *incipit;* the seven penitential psalms were noted and Psalm 22 was described as "a Psalm of the Passion." The translation of the Authorized Version was printed in an uninviting, tight, double-column format which was not easy to read and nearly impossible to sing. The *Common Service Book* provided 101 psalms, including twenty-two sections of Psalm 119; the *Service Book and Hymnal* added fourteen, deleted one (curiously, Psalm 141), making room for the additional psalms by reducing Psalm 119 to three sections. Some psalms (for example, 18 and 89) were abbreviated without indication; Psalm 137 was expurgated; in at least three places "prevent" was replaced with "came upon" (Psalm 18 twice) or "meetest" (Psalm 2), demonstrating a certain uneasiness with the language of the Authorized Version.

The *Lutheran Book of Worship* provides the complete Psalter in the Ministers Edition; the pew edition contains only those 122 psalms appointed for use in the Eucharist or other offices. There is a complete psalm table in weekly cycles for the season of the church year. No attempt has been made to include all 150 psalms in the table. The "General" section of the table, since it is used most through the year, is spread over a cycle of four weeks to prevent undue repetition. Week 1 is used beginning with the Monday following the First Sunday after the Epiphany, the Baptism of Our Lord; and beginning with the Monday after the Day of Pentecost. Weeks 2, 3, and 4 follow successively, and the cycle is repeated until Lent or Advent begins.

The format of the Psalter in the *Lutheran Book of Worship* is less crowded and more inviting than in the predecessor books, and the psalms look like poetry on the page. A still more inviting format is found in the present *Book of Common Prayer.*

Following ancient practice and the Roman Liturgy of the Hours, a psalm prayer is provided (in the Ministers Edition) for each psalm.[143] (See Appendix 2, pp. 517–518, for sources of these psalter collects.)

In the 1549 *Book of Common Prayer* the 150 psalms were spread in numerical order over the course of a month. The American revisions of the Prayer Book beginning in 1789 began to introduce selections from the psalms with increasing attention to the church year; these attempts were an alternative to the traditional monthly arrangement. In the 1979 book there is a seven-week pattern for the entire psalter (except for Christmastime, Holy Week, and Easter), but the traditional thirty-day division remains as an alternative.

The Psalter of the 1549 Prayer Book was from the Great Bible of 1539, Coverdale's revision of his 1535 translation. As the centuries

---

[143]The use of a prayer after each psalm is ancient and widespread. Basil (*Letter* 207.3) speaks of "psalmody interrupted by prayers"; Egeria (24.1, 8, 9) mentions "a prayer between each of the hymns"; Cassian, *Institutes* 2.5, 7; Caesarius of Arles, *Sermon* 76.1, 3; Canon 30 of the Council of Agde (506); the Fourth Council of Toledo (633).

passed, changes were made to correct, clarify, or modernize what were considered to be obsolete words. In the 1979 Prayer Book the Psalter is the result of a thorough and systematic examination of the Hebrew original, but keeping Coverdale's masterful rhythm.[144]

The translation was prepared by a committee headed by Robert C. Dentan of the General Theological Seminary in New York; other scholars in Hebrew, Greek, and Latin worked with him for some ten years as did also specialists in liturgical chant and English literature, among whom, until his death in 1973, was W. H. Auden. The result of their work is a continuation of the revision, begun in America in 1790 and continued in 1793, 1827, 1845, 1871, 1892, and especially in 1928, of the Psalter in the *Book of Common Prayer*. A most helpful introduction by Charles M. Guilbert to this revised Psalter is included in *The Psalter: A New Version for Public Worship and Private Devotion* (New York: Seabury Press, 1978).

In the new version the psalms are printed in lines of poetry corresponding to Hebrew versification, which is based on a parallelism of ideas, a symmetry of form and sense rather than sound. The line length of the psalms is clearer on the broad pages of the Prayer Book than in the double columns of the *Lutheran Book of Worship*.

Because of the Anglican long experience with daily use of the psalter and to secure an ecumenical bond, the Inter-Lutheran Commission on Worship chose to use the Psalter of the *Book of Common Prayer* rather than a less thoroughly tested version. Only one change was made: Psalm 8 in the Prayer Book version begins, "O Lord our Governor"; the Lutheran book follows the more familiar rendering of previous Lutheran books, "O Lord our Lord."

The psalter in its Episcopal and Lutheran forms uses small capital letters to represent the tetragrammaton YHWH, the personal name of the deity: LORD; it uses "Lord" as a translation of *Adonai*. In Psalm 68:4 and 83:18 the verse construction requires that the divine Name be spelled out, and it appears as Yahweh. The Prayer Book form capitalizes Name when it refers to God, for it is a reference to God himself; the

---

[144]Ian A. Gordon, *The Movement of English Prose* (Bloomington and London: Indiana University Press, 1966), 99–100, praises the achievement of Coverdale, "a preacher":

> Coverdale's sense of what could be effectively read aloud (rather than what could be meaningfully read in private, which was what Geneva derived from Tyndale) is best seen in his own sections of the Old Testament, notably in the Prophets and the Psalter:
>
> Haue mercy vpon me (O God) after thy goodness, and accordinge vnto thy greate mercies, do away myne offences.
>
> Wash me well fro my wickedness, and clense me fro my synne. For I knowledge my fautes, and my synne is euer before me.
>
> [Psalm 50 (51 in A.V.)]
>
> This is quite different from the 'chronicle' prose of Tyndale. The Hebrew parallelism shapes the syntax but is adapted to English structure. It is pre-eminently a prose that can be intoned, and Coverdale's Psalter is still that of the Prayer Book. Coverdale's instinct for native English is as fine as Tyndale's — but he draws on different sources.

Lutheran form in the Psalter, as elsewhere in the Lutheran book, keeps the letters of "name" all lower case.

Imprecatory or cursing verses and psalms present a problem. In the Roman Liturgy of the Hours these offending psalms (58, 83, 109) and verses have been removed from the liturgical psalter.[145] The *Book of Common Prayer* and the *Lutheran Book of Worship* retain the biblical psalter intact.

It should be noted that many psalms in this version have one verse more than in other translations because of the effort to represent more accurately the parallelisms of the Hebrew original. Thus the Notes on the Liturgy in the Lutheran book (Min. Ed., p. 20) caution, "Psalm references and verse divisions reflect the versification of the psalms in this book. If a psalm is read from the Bible or another source, it is important to check the versification against the psalter in this book [the *Lutheran Book of Worship*]." The description of the traditional methods of reciting the psalms, given in the Notes on the Liturgy (Min. Ed., p. 20), is to be noted.[146] An asterisk divides each verse into two parts for chanting; the asterisk marks the conclusion of the first half of the chant. When the psalms are read, the Prayer Book rubrics note that "a distinct pause should be made at the asterisk" (p. 583). The mark was introduced into the 1662 Prayer Book to facilitate unison reading or chanting. Others have noted a parallel with Old English poetry in which each line was divided with a distinct caesura.

Table I
Canticles Included in Three Books

Common Service Book	Service Book and Hymnal	Lutheran Book of Worship
1. Magnificat	1. Magnificat	Evening Prayer; No. 6
2. Nunc Dimittis	2. Nunc Dimittis	Compline; Holy Communion
3. Te Deum	3. Te Deum	Paschal Blessing; No. 3
4. Benedictus	4. Benedictus	Morning Prayer; No. 2
5. Benedicite	5. Benedicite	Easter Vigil; No. 18
6. Confitebor tibi (Isa. 12)	6. Confitebor tibi (Isa. 12)	
7. Exultavit cor meum (1 Sam. 2)	7. Exultavit cor meum (1 Sam. 2)	
8. Cantemus Domino	8. Cantemus domino	Easter Vigil; No. 19
9. Domine, audivi (Hab. 3)	9. Domine, audivi (Hab. 3)	
10. Audite coeli	10. Audite coeli	Easter Vigil (*Attende, caelum*)
11. Beatitudes		17. How blest are those
12. Dignus est Agnus		

---

[145] See Roguet, 116–17.
[146] The information was borrowed from the *Book of Common Prayer*, p. 582.

	11. Song of Hezekiah	
	12. Song of David	
Agnus Dei	Agnus Dei	1. Jesus, Lamb of God
Venite	Venite	4. Come, let us sing to the Lord
		5. Let my prayer rise before you
		7. Climb to the top
		8. The people who walked
		9. I called to my God
		10. Sing praise to
		11. Now, listen, you servants of God
		12. God, who has called you
		13. Keep in mind
		14. Listen! You nations
		15. Seek the Lord
		16. I will sing the story
		20. Christ Jesus,
		21. O Ruler of the Universe
		Vinea facta est (Easter Vigil)

BIBLIOGRAPHY

Daily Prayer

Bäumer, Suitbert. *Geschichte des Breviers.* Freiburg im Breisgau, 1895.

Battifol, Pierre. *Historie du Breviare romain.* Paris, 1898. English translation, *History of the Roman Breviary.* London and New York: Longmans, Green and Co., 1912.

Baudot, Jules. *Le Breviare romain.* Paris, 1907. English translation, *The Roman Breviary: Its Sources and History.* St. Louis: B. Herder, 1909.

Baumstark, Anton. *Comparative Liturgy.* London: Mowbrays, 1958.

Benson, Louis Fitzgerald. *The English Hymn: Its Development and Use in Worship.* Philadelphia: Presbyterian Board of Publication, 1915.

————. *The Hymnody of the Christian Church.* New York: George H. Doran Co., 1927.

Bishop, William Chatterley. *The Mozarabic and Ambrosian Rites: Four Essays in Comparative Liturgiology.* Edited by C. L. Feltoe. London: Mowbray, 1924.

Botte, Bernard, ed. *La Tradition Apostolique de Saint Hippolyte.* Münster, Westfalen: Aschendorffsche Verlagsbuchandlung, 1963 [Paris, 1946].

Bradshaw, Paul F. *Daily Prayer in the Early Church: A Study of the Origin and Early Development of the Divine Office.* New York: Oxford University Press, 1982.

——. "Prayer Morning, Evening, and Midnight — An Apostolic Custom?" *Studia Liturgica* 13:1 (1979):57–62.

Britt, Matthew. *The Hymns of the Breviary and Missal*. New York: Benziger, 1922.

Brooks, Robert J. "Have the Time of Your Life with the Liturgy of the Hours," *Liturgy* 26 (November–December 1979):13–17.

Brou, Louis, ed. *The Psalter Collects from V–VIIth Century Sources*. Henry Bradshaw Society vol. 83. London: Henry Bradshaw Society, 1949.

Chadwick, Owen. "The Origins of Prime," *Journal of Theological Studies* 49 (1948):178–82.

Connelly, Joseph. *Hymns of the Roman Liturgy*. Westminster, MD: Newman, 1957.

Crichton, J. D. *Christian Celebration: The Prayer of the Church*. London: Chapman, 1976.

Cullmann, Oscar. *Early Christian Worship*. Napierville, IL: Allenson, 1953.

Cuming, Geoffrey J. *Hippolytus: A Text for Students*. Bramcote, Notts.: Grove Books, 1976.

——. "The New Testament Foundation of Common Prayer," *Studia Liturgica* 10 (1974):88–105.

de Sainte Marie, H. "The Psalter Collects," *Ephemerides liturgicae* 65 (1951): 105–10.

Delling, Gerhard. *Worship in the New Testament*. Translated by Perry Scott. Philadelphia: Westminster Press, 1962.

Dix, Gregory. *The Apostolic Tradition of St. Hippolytus*, 1937. 2d ed. with preface and corrections by Henry Chadwick. London: SPCK, 1968.

Dugmore, C. W. "Canonical Hours," *Dictionary of Liturgy and Worship*, ed. J. G. Davies. New York: Macmillan, 1972. Revised as the *New Westminster Dictionary of Liturgy and Worship*. Philadelphia: Westminster Press, 1986.

——. *The Influence of the Synagogue upon the Divine Office*. Alcuin Club Collections 45. Westminster: Faith Press, 1964 [1944].

Fischer, Balthasar. "The Common Prayer of Congregation and Family in the Ancient Church," *Studia Liturgica* 10 (1974):106–24.

Gelineau, Josef. *Voices and Instruments in Christian Worship*. Translated by Clifford Howell. Collegeville: Liturgical Press, 1964.

Grisbrooke, W. Jardine. "A Contemporary Liturgical Problem: The Divine Office and Public Worship," *Studia Liturgica* 8:3 (1971–1972):129–68; 9:1–3 (1973):1–18, 81–106.

Hughes, H. V. *Latin Hymnody: An Enquiry into the Underlying Principles of the Hymnarium*. Church Music Monographs no. 5. London: Faith Press, 1922.

Jasmer, P. "A Comparison of the Monastic and Cathedral Vespers up to the Time of St. Benedict," *American Benedictine Review* 34 (1983):337–60.

Jasper, Ronald C. C., ed. *The Daily Office*. London: SPCK, 1968.

Jeremias, Joachim. *The Prayers of Jesus*. Napierville, IL: A. R. Allenson, 1974.

Jones, Cheslyn, Geoffrey Wainwright, and Edward Yarnold, eds. *The Study of Liturgy*, Chapter 5, "The Divine Office." New York: Oxford University Press, 1978.

Julian, John, ed. *Dictionary of Hymnology*. 2 vols. New York: Dover, 1957 [1907].

Jungmann, Josef A. *Pastoral Liturgy*. New York: Herder and Herder, 1962.

Liturgy 18:5 (May 1973). An issue devoted to the Liturgy of the Hours.

McCarthy, M. C. *The Rule for Nuns of St. Caesarius of Arles: A Translation with a Critical Introduction.* Catholic University Studies in Medieval History. New Series, vol. 16. Washington, DC: Catholic University Press, 1960.

Martimort, A., ed. *The Church at Prayer: Introduction to the Liturgy.* Vol. 4 *Liturgy and Time.* Collegeville: Liturgical Press, 1986.

Mateos, Juan. "The Morning and Evening Office," *Worship* 42 (1968):31–47.

———. "Office de minuit et office du matin chez S. Athanase," *Orientalia Christiana Periodica* 28 (1962):173–80.

———. "L'office monastique à la fin du IVe siècle: Antioche, Palestine, Cappadoce," *Oriens Christianus* 47 (1963):53–88.

———. "The Origins of the Divine Office," *Worship* 41 (1967):477–85.

———. "Quelques anciens documents sur l'office du soir," *Orientalia Christiana Periodica* 35 (1969):347–474.

———. "La Synaxe monastique des vêpres byzantines," *Orientalia Christiana Periodica* 36 (1970):248–50.

———. "La vigil cathederale chez Egérie," *Orientalia Christiana Periodica* 27 (1961):281–312.

Mearns, J. *The Canticles of the Christian Church Eastern and Western in Early and Medieval Times.* Cambridge: University Press, 1914.

Messenger, Ruth Ellis. *Latin Hymns of the Middle Ages.* Papers of Hymn Society of America XIV. New York: Hymn Society of America, 1948.

———. *The Medieval Latin Hymn.* Washington, DC: Capital Press, 1953.

Moule, C. F. D. *Worship in the New Testament.* London: Lutterworth Press, 1962.

Pascher, Joseph. *Das Stundengebet der römischen Kirche.* Munich: K. Zink, 1954.

Pfatteicher, Philip H. "Daily Prayer," chapter 7 of *Manual on the Liturgy.* Minneapolis: Augsburg Publishing House, 1979. Pp. 263–304.

———. *The Life and Writings of John Austin.* Ph.D. dissertation University of Pennsylvania, 1966.

Raby, F. J. E. *A History of Christian–Latin Poetry from the Beginnings to the Close of the Middle Ages.* Oxford: Clarendon Press, 1927.

Ratcliff, E. C. "The Choir Offices," *Liturgy and Worship.* Edited by W. K. Lowther Clarke and Charles Harris. London: SPCK, 1932. Pp. 257–95.

Response in Worship, Music and the Arts 17:3 (1977). An issue devoted to daily prayer.

Roguet, A.-M. *The Liturgy of the Hours: The General Instruction on the Liturgy of the Hours with a Commentary by A.-M. Roguet.* Translated by Peter Coughlin and Peter Perude. London: Chapman, 1971.

Salmon, Pierre. *The Breviary through the Centuries.* Collegeville: Liturgical Press, 1962.

———. *L'office divin au moyen âge.* Paris: Éditions du Cerf, 1967.

Schmemann, Alexander. *Introduction to Liturgical Theology.* London: Faith Press, 1966.

Schnitker, Thaddäus A. "The Liturgy of the Hours and the History of Salvation," *Studia Liturgica* 15.3/4 (1982–1983):145–57.

Storey, William G. "The Liturgy of the Hours: Principles and Practice," *Worship* 46 (April 1972):194–203.

Studia Liturgica 10 (1975) is devoted to the theme of Common Prayer.

Taft, Robert. *The Liturgy of the Hours in the Christian East: Origins, Meaning, Place in the Life of the Church*. Cochin, Kerala (India): KCM Press, 1984.

———. *The Liturgy of the Hours in East and West: The Origins of the Divine Office and its Meaning for Today*. Collegeville: Liturgical Press, 1985.

———. *"Quaestiones disputatae* in the History of the Liturgy of the Hours: The Origins of Nocturns, Matins, Prime," *Worship* 58 (1984):130–58.

The Taizé Office. London: Faith Press, 1966.

Van Dijk, S. J. P., and Joan Hazelden Walker. *The Origins of the Modern Roman Liturgy: The Liturgy of the Papal Court and the Franciscan Order in the Thirteenth Century*. London: Darton, Longman & Todd, 1960.

Verbraken, Patricius. *Oraisons sur les 150 psaumes: Lex Orandi 42*. Paris: Éditions du Cerf, 1967.

Walker, Joan Hazelden. "Terce, Sext, and None, an Apostolic Custom" *Studia Patristica* 5 (1962):206–12.

Wallwork, N. "The Psalter and the Divine Office," *Studia Liturgica* 21.1 (1977): 46–64.

Walpole, A. S. *Early Latin Hymns*. Cambridge: University Press, 1922.

Werner, Eric. *The Sacred Bridge: Liturgical Parallels in Synagogue and Early Church*. New York: Schocken, 1970 [1959].

Winkler, Gabrielle. "New Study of the Early Development of the Office," *Worship* 56 (January 1982):27–35.

The Work of God: A Study in the Divine Office of the Church by a Religious of C.S.M.V. London: Faith Press, 1964.

The Psalter

Anderson, Bernhard W. *Out of the Depths: The Psalms Speak for Us Today*. Rev. and expanded ed. Philadelphia: Westminster Press, 1983.

Barth, Christopher F. *Introduction to the Psalms*. Translated by R. A. Wilson. New York: Scribners, 1966.

Bonhoeffer, Dietrich. *Life Together*. Translated by John W. Doberstein. New York: Harper and Bros., 1954. Pp. 44–50.

Brueggemann, Walter. *Praying the Psalms*. Winona, MN: St. Mary's Press, 1982.

Clarke, W. K. Lowther, and C. Harris, eds. *Liturgy and Worship*. London: SPCK, 1964 [1932]. Pp. 51–99, 287–92, 685–89.

Dahood, Mitchell. *Psalms*. 3 vols. Garden City: Doubleday, 1965–1972.

Drijvers, Pius. *The Psalms: Their Structure and Meaning*. New York: Herder and Herder, 1965.

Gelineau, Joseph, and D. Rimbaud. *Le psautier de la Bible de Jerusalem*. Paris: Éditions du Cerf, 1961.

Gunkel, Hermann. *The Psalms: A Form-Critical Introduction*. Translated by Thomas M. Horner. Philadelphia: Fortress, 1967.

Keel, Othmar. *The Symbolism of the Biblical World: Ancient Near Eastern Iconography and the Book of Psalms*. New York: Seabury Press, 1978.

Lamb, John Alexander. *The Psalms in Christian Worship*. London: Faith Press, 1962.

Lewis, C. S. *Reflections on the Psalms*. New York: Harcourt, Brace & Co., 1958.

Merton, Thomas. *Bread in the Wilderness*. Philadelphia: Fortress Press, 1987.

Mowinkel, Sigmund. *The Psalms of Israel's Worship*. Translated by D. R. Ap-Thomas. New York and Nashville: Abingdon, 1962.

Osterley, W. O. E. *The Psalms: Translated with Text-Critical and Exegetical Notes.* London: SPCK, 1939.

Paterson, John. *The Praises of Israel: Studies Literary and Religious in the Psalms.* New York: Scribners, 1950.

Patrick, Millar. *Four Centuries of Scottish Psalmody.* London, Glasgow, and New York: Oxford University Press, 1949.

The Psalms: A New Translation from the Hebrew Arranged for Singing to the Psalmody of Joseph Gelineau. London: Collins, 1963. Philadelphia: Westminster Press, 1964 [New York, Paramus, and Toronto: Paulist Press, 1968].

The Psalter: A New Version for Public Worship and Private Devotion. Introduced by Charles Mortimer Guilbert. New York: Seabury Press, 1978.

Ringgren, Helmer. *The Faith of the Psalmists.* Philadelphia: Fortress, 1963.

Robinson, Theodore W. *The Poetry of the Old Testament.* New York: Scribners, 1947.

Scott, R. B. Y. *The Psalms as Christian Praise.* New York: Association Press, 1958.

Shepherd, Massey H., Jr. *A Liturgical Psalter for the Christian Year.* Minneapolis: Augsburg Publishing House and Collegeville: Liturgical Press, 1976.

———. *The Psalms in Christian Worship: A Practical Guide.* Minneapolis: Augsburg Publishing House and Collegeville: Liturgical Press, 1976.

Terrien, Samuel. *The Psalms and Their Meaning for Today.* Indianapolis and New York: Bobbs-Merrill, 1952.

Van Doren, Mark, and Maurice Samuel. *The Book of Praise: Dialogues on the Psalms.* Edited by Edith Samuel. New York: John Day, 1974.

Weiser, Artur. *The Psalms: A Commentary.* Philadelphia: Westminster Press, 1962.

Westerman, Claus. *The Praise of God in the Psalms.* Translated by Keith R. Crim. Richmond: John Knox Press, 1965.

7

PETITIONS, INTERCESSIONS, AND THANKSGIVINGS
RESPONSIVE PRAYER 1
RESPONSIVE PRAYER 2
THE LITANY
THE ATHANASIAN CREED

Ministers Edition, pp. 105–17, 79–91, 118–20, 25, 17–18

The five sections of the *Lutheran Book of Worship* included in this chapter are all supplementary to the offices of daily prayer.

PETITIONS, INTERCESSIONS, AND THANKSGIVINGS
(Ministers Edition, pp. 105–17)

Parallel Collections

Episcopal   Prayers and Thanksgivings, *Book of Common Prayer*, pp. 810–41.

Lutheran   General and Special Collects, *Church Book* (1868), pp. 89–112 (77 provided).
Collects and Prayers, *Common Service Book* (1919), text ed. pp. 207–35 (101 provided).
Collects and Prayers, *Service Book and Hymnal* (1958), pp. 218–35 (123 provided, plus 15 for private devotion).

Presbyterian   Other Prayers for Christian Worship, *The Worshipbook* (1972), pp. 179–202.

Purpose

The *Lutheran Book of Worship* is primarily a book for use in connection with congregational worship. The collection of prayers, therefore, is chiefly for use with Morning and Evening Prayer, Responsive Prayer 1 and 2, the Litany, the Service of the Word, or the Holy Communion when there is no Communion. They may also suggest ideas for those who write the intercessions for the prayers in the Eucharist. These prayers may also serve as private prayers for families and individuals.

Characteristics

The collection of prayers in the *Lutheran Book of Worship* focuses not only on individual needs and the needs of the church but on the whole fabric of social and political life in which the church finds itself. Awareness of the church's social responsibility and a commitment to prayer and action on behalf of the world are clear characteristics of these prayers.

Background

The prayers in the *Church Book* were almost exclusively concerned with the needs of the church, including the spiritual needs of its members. Broadening of these concerns has been developing through the twentieth century, through the *Common Service Book* and the *Service Book and Hymnal* to the *Lutheran Book of Worship*. The last two books are notable for their breadth of concern. (See Table, pp. 414–423.)

Sources of the Petitions, Intercessions, and Thanksgivings

PEACE AMONG THE NATIONS (no. 165)
Source: *Book of Common Prayer* (p. 816)
No. 5: For Peace among the Nations

> Almighty God our heavenly Father, guide the nations of the world into the way of justice and truth, and establish among them that peace which is the fruit of righteousness, that they may become the kingdom of our Lord and Savior Jesus Christ.

The prayer was written by Edward Lambe Parsons, recalling James 3:18 and Revelation 11:15.[1] It was included in the 1928 Prayer Book (p. 44).

PEACE (no. 166)
Source: *Service Book and Hymnal* (p. 226)
No. 57: For Peace

---

[1] Massey H. Shepherd, Jr., *Oxford American Prayer Book Commentary* (New York: Oxford University Press, 1950), 44–45; Marion Hatchett, *Commentary on the American Prayer Book* (New York: Seabury Press, 1981), 557. The 1979 *Book of Common Prayer* can be said to be the source of prayers in the 1978 *Lutheran Book of Worship* because Eugene L. Brand and Philip H. Pfatteicher, who made the selection of prayers, had before them the 1976 *Proposed Book of Common Prayer*, as well as its predecessor, the *Draft Proposed Book of Common Prayer*, which originally included most of the prayers. Upon the approval of the Episcopal Church's General Convention in 1979, the *Proposed Book of Common Prayer* became the *Book of Common Prayer*. The texts of the two books are identical.

O God, who wouldst fold both heaven and earth in a single peace: Let the design of thy great love lighten upon the waste of our wraths and sorrows; and give peace to thy Church, peace among the nations, peace in our dwellings, and peace in our hearts; through thy Son, our Saviour, Jesus Christ.

The prayer was taken from Eric Milner-White, *Memorials upon Several Occasions* (London: A. R. Mowbray, 1933), no. 7b.

SOCIAL JUSTICE (no. 167)
Source: *Book of Common Prayer* (p. 823)
No. 27: For Social Justice

Grant, O God, that your holy and life-giving Spirit may so move every human heart [and especially the hearts of the people of this land], that barriers which divide us may crumble, suspicions disappear, and hatreds cease; that our divisions being healed, we may live in justice and peace; through Jesus Christ our Lord.

The author is unknown. The prayer is new to the 1979 *Prayer Book*.[2]

THE VARIETY OF RACES AND CULTURES (no. 168)
Source: *Book of Common Prayer* (p. 840)
Thanksgiving no. 7: For the Diversity of Races and Cultures

O God, who created all peoples in your image, we thank you for the wonderful diversity of races and cultures in this world. Enrich our lives by ever-widening circles of fellowship, and show us your presence in those who differ most from us, until our knowledge of your love is made perfect in our love for all your children; through Jesus Christ our Lord.

The prayer was drafted for the 1979 Prayer Book by Caroline Rose.[3]

OUR COUNTRY (no. 169)
Source: *Book of Common Prayer* (p. 820)
No. 18: For our Country

Almighty God who hast given us this good land for our heritage: We humbly beseech thee that we may always prove ourselves a people mindful of thy favor and glad to do thy will. Bless our land with honorable industry, sound learning, and pure manners. Save us from violence, discord, and confusion; from pride and arrogance, and from every evil way. Defend our liberties, and fashion into one united people the multitudes brought hither out of many kindreds and tongues. Endue with the spirit of wisdom those to whom in thy Name we entrust the authority of government, that there may be justice and peace at home, and that, through obedience to thy law, we may show forth thy praise among the nations of the earth. In the time of prosperity, fill our hearts with thankfulness, and in the day of trouble, suffer not our trust in thee to fail; all which we ask through Jesus Christ our Lord.

The Prayer, sometimes called "George Washington's prayer for his country," was written in 1882 by George Lyman Locke and this emended form was first included in the 1928 *Prayer Book*.[4]

[2]Hatchett, 561
[3]Ibid., 570.
[4]Shepherd, 35–36, 36–37; Hatchett, 560.

PETITIONS, INTERCESSIONS, AND THANKSGIVINGS

STATE/PROVINCIAL AND LOCAL GOVERNMENTS (no. 170)
Source: *Book of Common Prayer* (p. 822)
No. 23: For Local Government

> Almighty God our heavenly Father, send down upon those who hold office in this State (Commonwealth, City, County, Town, _____) the spirit of wisdom, charity, and justice; that with steadfast purpose they may faithfully serve in their offices to promote the well-being of all people; through Jesus Christ our Lord.

This is a revision for the 1979 American Prayer Book of a prayer in the 1959 Canadian Prayer Book.[5]

RESPONSIBLE CITIZENSHIP (no. 171)
Source: Derived from *Book of Common Prayer* (pp. 821–22)
No. 22: For Sound Government

> O Lord our Governor, bless the leaders of our land, that we may be a people at peace among ourselves and a blessing to other nations of the earth.
> *Lord, keep this nation under your care.*
> To the President and members of the Cabinet, to Governors of States, Mayors of Cities, and to all in administrative authority, grant wisdom and grace in the exercise of their duties.
> *Give grace to your servants, O Lord.*
> To Senators and Representatives, and those who make our laws in States, Cities, and Towns, give courage, wisdom, and foresight to provide for the needs of all our people, and to fulfill our obligations in the community of nations.
> *Give grace to your servants, O Lord.*
> To the Judges and officers of our Courts give understanding and integrity, that human rights may be safeguarded and justice served.
> *Give grace to your servants, O Lord.*
> And finally, teach our people to rely on your strength and to accept their responsibilities to their fellow citizens, that they may elect trustworthy leaders and make wise decisions for the well-being of our society; that we may serve you faithfully in our generation and honor your holy Name.
> *For yours is the kingdom, O Lord, and you are exalted as head above all.*

The prayer was composed by Caroline Rose for the 1979 *Prayer Book*.[6]

THOSE IN CIVIL AUTHORITY (no. 172)
Source: *Book of Common Prayer* (p. 820)
No. 19: For the President of the United States and all in Civil Authority

> O Lord our Governor, whose glory is in all the world: We commend this nation to *thy* merciful care, that being guided by *thy* Providence, we may dwell secure in *thy* peace. Grant to the President of the United States, the Governor of this State (*or* Commonwealth), and to all in authority, wisdom and strength to know and to do *thy* will. Fill them with the love of truth and righteousness, and make them ever mindful of their calling to serve this

---

[5] Hatchett, 561.
[6] Ibid.

people in *thy* fear; through Jesus Christ our Lord, who *liveth* and *reigneth* with *thee* and the Holy Spirit, one God, world without end.

This prayer was written for the 1928 *Book of Common Prayer*, revised from the prayer for the sovereign in the *English Prayer Book*.[7]

COURTS OF JUSTICE (no. 173)
Source: *Book of Common Prayer* (p. 821)
No. 21: For Courts of Justice

Almighty God, *who sittest* in the throne judging right: We humbly beseech *thee* to bless the courts of justice and the magistrates in all this land; and give *unto* them the spirit of wisdom and understanding, that they may discern the truth, and impartially administer the law in the fear of *thee* alone; through him who shall come to be our Judge, *thy* Son our Savior Jesus Christ.

This prayer was written for the 1928 Prayer Book. The opening address comes from Psalm 9:4; the petition echoes Isaish 11:2; the final clause recalls the Te Deum.[8]

CITIES (no. 174)
Source: *Book of Common Prayer* (p. 825)
No. 33: For Cities

Heavenly Father, in your Word you have given us a vision of that holy City to which the nations of the world bring their glory: Behold and visit, we pray, the cities of the earth. Renew the ties of mutual regard which form our civic life. Send us honest and able leaders. Enable us to eliminate poverty, prejudice, and oppression, that peace may prevail with righteousness, and justice with order, and that men and women from different cultures and with differing talents may find with one another the fulfillment of their humanity; through Jesus Christ our Lord.

J. Robert Zimmerman drafted the prayer for the 1979 Prayer Book.

TOWNS AND RURAL AREAS (no. 175)
Source: Derived from *Book of Common Prayer* (p. 825)
No. 34: For Towns And Rural Areas

Lord Christ, when you came among us, you proclaimed the kingdom of God in villages, towns, and lonely places: Grant that your presence and power may be known throughout this land. Have mercy upon all of us who live and work in rural areas [especially _____]; and grant that all the people of our nation may give thanks to you for food and drink and all other bodily necessities of life, respect those who labor to produce them, and honor the land and the water from which these good things come. All this we ask in your holy Name.

This prayer was drafted for the 1979 Prayer Book by H. Boone Porter.[9]

THE NEIGHBORHOOD (no. 176)
A new prayer, composed for the *Lutheran Book of Worship*. The reference is to Jeremiah 29:7.

---

[7]Shepherd, 18; Hatchett, 560.
[8]Shepherd, 35–36.
[9]Hatchett, 563.

THE HUMAN FAMILY (no. 177)
Source: *Book of Common Prayer* (p. 815)
No. 3: For the Human Family

> O God, you made us in your own image and redeemed us through Jesus your Son: Look with compassion on the whole human family; take away the arrogance and hatred which infect our hearts; break down the walls that separate us; unite us in bonds of love; and work through our struggle and confusion to accomplish your purposes on earth; that, in your good time, all nations and races may serve you in harmony around your heavenly throne; through Jesus Christ our Lord.

This prayer was written for the 1979 Prayer Book by Charles P. Price.[10]

COMMERCE AND INDUSTRY (no. 178)
Source: *Book of Common Prayer* (p. 259)
Collects for Various Occasions, no. 19. II: For Commerce and Industry

> Almighty God, whose Son Jesus Christ in his earthly life shared our toil and hallowed our labor: Be present with your people where they work; make those who carry on the industries and commerce of this land responsive to your will; and give to us all a pride in what we do, and a just return for our labor; through Jesus Christ our Lord, who lives and reigns with you, in the unity of the Holy Spirit, one God, now and for ever.

This prayer is modeled after a prayer "For Industry" in the Canadian Prayer Book."[11] See above p. 331, prayer no. 158.

THE UNEMPLOYED (no. 179)
Source: *Book of Common Prayer* (p. 824)
No. 30: For the Unemployed

> Heavenly Father, we remember before you those who suffer want and anxiety from lack of work. Guide the people of this land so to use our public and private wealth that all may find suitable and fulfilling employment, and receive just payment for their labor; through Jesus Christ our Lord.

This prayer is a revision of the prayer of the Industrial Christian Fellowship:

> O Lord and Heavenly Father, we commend to Thy care and protection the men and women of this land who are suffering distress and anxiety through lack of work. Strengthen and support them, we beseech Thee; and so prosper the counsels of those who govern and direct our industries, that Thy people may be set free from want and fear to work in peace and security, for the relief of their necessities and the well-being of this realm; through Jesus Christ our Lord.[12]

OUR ENEMIES (no. 180)
Source: *Book of Common Prayer* (p. 816)
No. 6: For Our Enemies

---

[10]Ibid., 557.

[11]Ibid., 214.

[12]Published in *The Prayer Manual*, ed. F. B. Macnutt (London: A. R. Mowbray, 1951), no. 117. Quoted in Hatchett, 562.

O God, the Father of all, whose Son commanded us to love our enemies: Lead them and us from prejudice to truth; deliver them and us from hatred, cruelty, and revenge; and in your good time enable us all to stand reconciled before you; through Jesus Christ our Lord.

This is a revision of a prayer by an anonymous writer in *The Living Church* (September 8, 1968).[13]

THE POOR AND THE NEGLECTED (no. 181)
Source: *Book of Common Prayer* (p. 826)
No. 35: For the Poor and the Neglected

> Almighty and most merciful God, we remember before you all poor and neglected persons whom it would be easy for us to forget: the homeless and the destitute, the old and the sick, and all who have none to care for them. Help us to heal those who are broken in body or spirit, and to turn their sorrow into joy. Grant this, Father, for the love of your Son, who for our sake became poor, Jesus Christ our Lord.

This is a revision of a prayer "For all Poor, Homeless, and Neglected Folk," first published among the proposals for the 1892 revision of the Prayer Book in *The Book Annexed* (1883) and added to the 1928 Prayer Book (p. 599). Franklin D. Roosevelt made it famous as "The Forgotten Man's Prayer."[14]

THE OPPRESSED (no. 182)
Source: *Book of Common Prayer* (p. 826)
No. 36: For the Oppressed

> Look with pity, O heavenly Father, upon the people in this land who live with injustice, terror, disease, and death as their constant companions. Have mercy upon us. Help us to eliminate our cruelty to these our neighbors. Strengthen those who spend their lives establishing equal protection of the law and equal opportunities for all. And grant that every one of us may enjoy a fair portion of the riches of this land; through Jesus Christ our Lord.

The prayer was written by Caroline Rose.[15]

THE PROPER USE OF WEALTH (no. 183)
Source: *Book of Common Prayer* (p. 827)
No. 38: For the Right Use of God's Gifts

> Almighty God, whose loving hand *hath* given us all that we possess: Grant us grace that we may honor *thee* with our substance, and, remembering the account which we must one day give, may be faithful stewards of *thy* bounty, through Jesus Christ our Lord.

This collect, which was introduced in the 1928 Prayer Book, is a revision of a prayer "For the Rich" from a book of offices proposed to the General Convention of the Episcopal Church in 1889.[16] See Luke 16:1ff.

---

[13]Hatchett, 557.
[14]Shepherd, 599; Hatchett, 563.
[15]Hatchett, 564.
[16]Shepherd, 599; Hatchett 564.

SCHOOLS (no. 184)
Source: *Book of Common Prayer* (p. 824)
No. 31: For Schools and Colleges

> O Eternal God, bless all schools, colleges, and universities [and especially
> _____], that they may be lively centers for sound learning, new discovery,
> and the pursuit of wisdom; and grant that those who teach and those who
> learn may find you to be the source of all truth; through Jesus Christ our
> Lord.

The original prayer, by an unknown author, was published in the Scottish Prayer
Book of 1912. It was revised for inclusion in the 1928 Prayer Book (p. 42.).[17]

AGRICULTURE (no. 185)
Source: *Book of Common Prayer* (p. 824)
No. 29: For Agriculture

> Almighty God, we thank you for making the earth fruitful, so that it might
> produce what is needed for life: Bless those who work in the fields; give us
> seasonable weather; and grant that we may all share the fruits of the earth,
> rejoicing in your goodness; through Jesus Christ our Lord.

This prayer was composed by the English revisers of 1689 for Rogation Sunday
(now the Sixth Sunday of Easter). It was included in the American Prayer Book
of 1892.[18]

PRISONS AND CORRECTIONAL INSTITUTIONS (no. 186)
Source: *Book of Common Prayer* (p. 826)
No. 37: For Prisons and Correctional Institutions

> Lord Jesus, for our sake you were condemned as a criminal: Visit our jails
> and prisons with your pity and judgment. Remember all prisoners, and bring
> the guilty to repentance and amendment of life according to your will, and
> give them hope for their future. When any are held unjustly, bring them
> release; forgive us, and teach us to improve our justice. Remember those
> who work in these institutions; keep them humane and compassionate; and
> save them from becoming brutal or callous. And since what we do for those
> in prison, O Lord, we do for you, constrain us to improve their lot. All this
> we ask for your mercy's sake.

This is a new prayer by Charles P. Price.[19]

THOSE WHO SUFFER FOR THE SAKE OF CONSCIENCE (no. 187)
Source: *Book of Common Prayer* (p. 823)
No. 26: For those who suffer for the sake of Conscience

> O God our Father, whose Son forgave his enemies while he was suffering
> shame and death: Strengthen those who suffer for the sake of conscience;
> when they are accused, save them from speaking in hate; when they are
> rejected, save them from bitterness, when they are imprisoned, save them
> from despair; and to us your servants, give grace to respect their witness and
> to discern the truth, that our society may be cleansed and strengthened. This
> we ask for the sake of Jesus Christ, our merciful and righteous Judge.

---

[17]Shepherd 42; Hatchett, 562–63.
[18]Shepherd, 39–40; Hatchett, 562. In the 1928 Prayer Book the prayer is on page 39.
[19]Hatchett, 564.

This is a new prayer by Charles P. Price.[20]

USE OF LEISURE (no. 188)
Source: *Book of Common Prayer* (p. 825)
No. 32: For the Good Use of Leisure

O God, in the course of this busy life, give us times of refreshment and peace, and grant that we may so use our leisure to rebuild our bodies and renew our minds, that our spirits may be opened to the goodness of your creation; through Jesus Christ our Lord.

This is a new prayer by James G. Birney.[21]

THE CHURCH (no. 189)
Source: William Laud, *A Summarie of Devotions* (Oxford, 1667), p. 192

Gracious Father, I humbly beseech thee, for thy holy Catholick Church, fill it with all truth; in all truth with all peace. Where it is corrupt, purge it: where it is in error, direct it: where it is superstitious, rectifie it: where any thing is amiss, reform it: where it is right, strengthen and confirm it: where it is in want, furnish it: where it is divided and rent ansunder, make up the breaches of it, O thou holy one of Israel.

The prayer, in a slightly revised form, was included in the 1928 Prayer Book and in the *Service Book and Hymnal* (1958), pp. 218–19, no. 4. The version in the *Lutheran Book of Worship* closely resembles that in *Book of Common Prayer* (p. 816), no. 7: For the Church.[22]

SPREAD OF THE GOSPEL (no. 190)
Source: *Book of Common Worship* (Presbyterian Church, U.S.A. [1906]), p. 133

Increase, O God, the faith and the zeal of all Thy people, that they may more earnestly desire, and more diligently seek, the salvation of their fellow-men, through the message of Thy love in Jesus Christ our Lord. Send forth a mighty call unto Thy servants to preach Thy Word, and multiply the number of those who labour in the Gospel; granting unto them a heart of love, sincerity of speech, and the power of the Holy Ghost, that they may be able to persuade men to forsake sin and turn unto Thee. And so bless and favor the work of Thine evangelists that multitudes may be brought from the kingdom of evil into the kingdom of Thy dear Son, our Saviour Jesus Christ.

This prayer, slightly abbreviated, appeared as no. 10: For the Spread of the Gospel (Evangelistic Work) in the *Service Book and Hymnal* (p. 219). It has been more radically revised for the *Lutheran Book of Worship*.

MISSIONS (no. 191)
Source: *Book of Common Prayer* (Scotland, 1912), p. 51.

Almighty God, our heavenly Father, who in thy goodness hast caused the light of the Gospel to shine in our land; Extend thy mercy, we beseech thee, to the nations of the world that still walk in darkness. Enlighten the Moslems with the knowledge of thy truth; and grant that the Gospel of salvation may

---

[20]Ibid., 561.
[21]Ibid., 563.
[22]Shepherd, 36–37; Hatchett, 557.

be made known in all lands, that the heart of the peoples may be turned unto thee, through Jesus Christ our Lord.

This prayer, slightly revised, was included in the *Service Book and Hymnal* as no. 32 of the Collects and Prayers (For Islam, p. 223).

THE MISSION OF THE CHURCH (no. 192)
Source: *Book of Common Prayer* (p. 816)
No. 8: For the Mission of the Church

Everliving God, whose will it is that all should come to you through your Son Jesus Christ: Inspire our witness to him, that all may know the power of his forgiveness and the hope of his resurrection; who lives and reigns with you and the Holy Spirit, one God, now and for ever.

This is a new prayer, written by Caroline Rose.[23]

THE SAINTS (no. 193)
Source: *Book of Common Prayer* (p. 838)
Thanksgiving no. 4: For the Saints and Faithful Departed.

We give thanks to you, O Lord our God, for all your servants and witnesses of time past: for Abraham, the father of believers, and Sarah his wife; for Moses, the lawgiver, and Aaron, the priest; for Miriam and Joshua, Deborah and Gideon, and Samuel with Hannah his mother; for Isaiah and all the prophets; for Mary, the mother of our Lord; for Peter and Paul and all the apostles; for Mary and Martha, and Mary Magdalene; for Stephen, the first martyr, and all the martyrs and saints in every age and in every land. In your mercy, O Lord our God, give us as you gave to them, the hope of salvation and the promise of eternal life; through Jesus Christ our Lord, the first-born of many from the dead.

This prayer is an expansion of a section of the prayers in the Order of Worship of the Consultation on Church Union, 1968 (p. 26).[24] It is a revision of the commemoration of saints in the Eucharist of the Taizé community.

MINISTERS OF THE WORD (no. 194)
Source: *Book of Common Prayer* (1549)
St. Peter's Day (June 29)

Almightie God, whiche by thy sonne Jesus Christe haste geuen to thy Apostle saincte Peter many excellente giftes, and commaundedste him earnestly to feede thy flocke: make wee beseche thee, all bishops and pastors diligently to preache thy holy worde, and the people obediently to folowe thesame, that they maye receiue the croune of euerlasting glory, through Jesus Christ our Lord.

This collect, without the reference to St. Peter, was appointed in the *Service Book and Hymnal* for the Festival of St. Peter and St. Paul (June 29), p. 110. The biblical allusion is John 21:15ff.

[23] Hatchett, 557.
[24] *An Order of Worship for the Proclamation of the Word of God and the Celebration of the Lord's Supper* (Cincinnati: Forward Movement, 1968), 26; Hatchett, 570.

THE ELECTION OF A PRESIDENT OR PASTOR (no. 195)
Source: *Book of Common Prayer* (p. 818)
No. 13: For the Election of a Bishop or other Minister

Almighty God, giver of every good gift: Look graciously on your Church, and so guide the minds of those who shall choose a bishop for this Diocese (*or*, rector for this parish), that we may receive a faithful pastor, who will care for your people and equip us for our ministries; through Jesus Christ our Lord.

This prayer is based on a collect in the proposed revision of the English Prayer Book (1928).[25] The Lutheran revision does not use the title "bishop" because when the book was published (1978) the title was not yet in official use in the Lutheran bodies in North America; it had been accepted before the publication of *Occasional Services* (1982).

DEACONESSES AND DEACONS (no. 196)
Source: *Service Book and Hymnal* (p. 228)
No. 69: For Deaconesses

O God, the Father of Jesus Christ our Lord, who in olden time didst call holy women to the service of thy Church: Let thy blessing rest upon all who are set apart for the work of serving love; grant them knowledge of thy Gospel, sincerity of purpose, true diligence in service, and beauty of life in Christ; that many souls may rise up to bless them, and that thy holy Name may be glorified; through the same thy Son, Jesus Christ our Lord.

The prayer is based on a prayer in the Order for the Consecration of Deaconesses in the *Ritual of the Methodist Episcopal Church*, 1916 (p. 129), naming Phoebe and Dorcas, which was in turn based on a prayer mentioning Old Testament women in the 1908 *Ritual*. These prayers were expanded to nearly the Lutheran form in the Methodist Book of Worship, 1944 (p. 452).

CHURCH MUSICIANS AND ARTISTS (no. 197)
Source: *Book of Common Prayer* (p. 819)
No. 17: For Church Musicians and Artists

O God, whom saints and angels delight to worship in heaven: Be ever present with your servants who seek through art and music to perfect the praises offered by your people on earth; and grant to them even now glimpses of your beauty, and make them worthy at length to behold it unveiled for evermore; through Jesus Christ our Lord.

This is the prayer of the Royal School of Church Music, revised to include other artists in addition to musicians.[26]

TEACHERS (no. 198)
This is a new prayer, written for the *Lutheran Book of Worship.*

RENEWAL (no. 199)
Source: *Book of Common Prayer* (p. 254)
Collects for Various Occasions, no. 10: At Baptism

---

[25] Hatchett, 559.
[26] Ibid., 560.

Almighty God, by our baptism into the death and resurrection of your Son Jesus Christ, you turn us from the old life of sin: Grant that we, being reborn to new life in him, may live in righteousness and holiness all our days; through Jesus Christ our Lord, who lives and reigns with you and the Holy Spirit, one God, now and for ever.

This new collect was drafted for the 1979 *Book of Common Prayer.*[27]

RENEWAL (no. 200)
Source: *Book of Common Prayer* (p. 254)
Collects for Various Occasions, no. 11: At Confirmation

Grant, Almighty God, that we, who have been redeemed from the old life of sin by our baptism into the death and resurrection of your Son Jesus Christ, may be renewed in your Holy Spirit, and live in righteousness and true holiness; through Jesus Christ our Lord, who lives and reigns with you and the Holy Spirit, one God, now and for ever.

This new collect was drafted for the 1979 *Book of Common Prayer.*[28]

GRACE TO RECEIVE THE WORD (no. 201)
Source: *Book of Common Prayer* (1549)
Second Sunday in Advent

Blessed lord, which hast caused al holy scriptures to bee written for our learnyng: Graunt vs that we maye in such wise heare them, read, marke, learne, and inwardly digeste them: that by pacience and coumfort of thy holy woorde, we may embrace and euer hold fast the blessed hope of euerlasting life, which thou hast giuen vs in our sauiour Jesus Christe.

The prayer entered Lutheran use in the Church Book (1868), no. 49, and was given special prominence in *The Lutheran Hymnal* as the Collect for the Word, which concluded the Order of Morning Service without Communion (p. 14). Thomas Cranmer constructed the collect on the basis of such scriptural ideas as John 5:39, Acts 17:11, 1 Corinthians 10:11; 2 Timothy 3:16–17.[29]

ENLIGHTENMENT OF THE HOLY SPIRIT (no. 202)
Source: Gregorian Sacramentary
No. 526: The morning mass at St. Peter's Basilica

Deus qui hodierna die corda fidelium sancti spiritus inlustratione docuisti. da nobis in eodem spiritu recta sapere. et de eius semper consolatione gaudere. Per dominum.

This was the collect for Pentecost in previous Lutheran and Anglican books, based on widespread medieval use.[30] (It is found in the Bamberg, Constance, Nuremberg, and Sarum missals).

SELF-DEDICATION (no. 203)
Source: *Book of Common Prayer* (pp. 832–33)
No. 61: A Prayer of Self-Dedication

---

[27] Ibid., 211.
[28] Ibid.
[29] Shepherd, 92.
[30] Ibid., 180; Hatchett, 184.

Almighty and eternal God, so draw our hearts to *thee*, so guide our minds, so fill our imaginations, so control our wills, that we may be wholly *thine*, utterly dedicated *unto thee;* then use us, we pray *thee*, as *thou wilt*, and always to *thy* glory and the welfare of *thy* people; through our Lord and Savior Jesus Christ.

This prayer, written by William Temple, the Archbishop of Canterbury (1942–1944), was taken from *the Prayer Manual*, no. 255[31] for the 1979 Prayer Book.

TRUSTFULNESS (no. 204)
Source: *Book of Common Prayer* (pp. 216–17)
Collect for the Eighth Sunday after the Epiphany

Most loving Father, whose will it is for us to give thanks for all things, to fear nothing but the loss of you, and to cast all our care on you who care for us: Preserve us from faithless fears and worldly anxieties, that no clouds of this mortal life may hide from us the light of that love which is immortal, and which you have manifested to us in your Son, Jesus Christ our Lord; who lives and reigns with you, in the unity of the Holy Spirit, one God, now and for ever.

This collect was written by William Bright and was included in the appendix to his *Ancient Collects* (pp. 234–35). It was included in the 1928 Prayer Book among the additional family prayers (p. 596). The opening of the prayer alludes to 1 Timothy 2:1, Philippians 3:8, and 1 Peter 5:7. In their commentaries both Marion Hatchett and Massey Shepherd note that in the view of Scripture, the antithesis of faith is not doubt but fear, for faith is essentially trust in God's love, grace, and care.[32]

BEFORE WORSHIP (no. 205)
Source: *Book of Common Prayer* (p. 833)
No. 64: Before Worship

O Almighty God, *who pourest* out on all who desire it the spirit of grace and supplication: Deliver us, when we draw near to *thee*, from coldness of heart and wanderings of mind, that with steadfast thoughts and kindled affections we may worship *thee* in spirit and truth; through Jesus Christ our Lord.

This prayer, written by William Bright, was included in the appendix to his *Ancient Collects* (p. 233). The address combines Zechariah 12:10 and John 4:23. The 1928 Prayer Book omitted the opening clause, which was based on James 1:17, "from whom every good prayer cometh."[33]

BEFORE WORSHIP (no. 206)
Source: *Collects and Prayers for Use in Church* (p. 41)
No. 71: Upon Entering Church

Bless me, O God, with a reverent sense of thy Presence, that I may be still and adore thee: through Jesus Christ our Lord.

---

[31] Hatchett, 568.
[32] Shepherd, 596; Hatchett, 172–73.
[33] Shepherd, 594; Hatchett, 569.

This prayer was included in the Collects and Prayers section of the *Service Book and Hymnal* as no. 1 under Private Devotion (p. 234).[34]

BEFORE HOLY COMMUNION (no. 207)
Source: *Book of Common Prayer* (p. 834)
No. 66: Before Receiving Communion

> Be present, be present, O Jesus, our great High Priest, as you were present with your disciples, and be known to us in the breaking of bread; who live and reign with the Father and the Holy Spirit, now and for ever.

The prayer is from the Mozarabic liturgy[35] and is included in the *Book of Common Worship* of the Church of South India (p. 14). It was introduced to Lutheran use in *Contemporary Worship 2: The Holy Communion* (1970) (p. 19), and the continued use of a version of this prayer at the breaking of the bread is permitted by the Notes of the Liturgy (Min. Ed., p. 29 #34).

BEFORE HOLY COMMUNION (no. 208)
Source: *Book of Common Prayer* (p. 337)

> We do not presume to come to this thy Table, O merciful Lord, trusting in our own righteousness, but in thy manifold and great mercies. We are not worthy so much as to gather up the crumbs under thy Table. But thou art the same Lord whose property is always to have mercy. Grant us therefore, gracious Lord, so to eat the flesh of thy dear Son Jesus Christ, and to drink his blood, that we may evermore dwell in him, and he in us.

This is the prayer of humble access in Holy Eucharist I. It first appears in the Order of the Communion, 1548, and was incorporated into the 1549 Prayer Book and has been a characteristic feature of the Anglican rite ever since.[36] The prayer was given in the *Service Book and Hymnal* as no. 7 of the prayers for private devotion. The prayer includes phrases and ideas from the Liturgy of St. Basil, Mark 7:28, a Gregorian collect (nos. 851 and 1327), John 6:56, and Thomas Aquinas's *Summa Theologica* (III.74.1).

AFTER HOLY COMMUNION (no. 209)
Source: *The Kingdom, the Power and the Glory*
(*The Grey Book*, Part III), 3d ed. (London, 1925), p. 69

> Almighty God, who hast given to thy people the true Bread who cometh down from heaven, even thy Son Jesus Christ; grant that our souls may be so fed by him who giveth health unto the world, that we may abide in him and he in us, and thy Church be filled with the power of his deathless life; through the same Jesus Christ our Lord.

---

[34] The Prayer was taken from *Collects and Prayers for Use in Church*. Authorized by the United Lutheran Church in America. Prepared by the Common Service Book Committee (Philadelphia: Board of Publication of the United Lutheran Church in America, 1935), p. 41. The Index of Sources of *Collects and Prayers* (p. 252) credits *Oremus: Collects, Devotions, Litanies from Ancient and Modern Sources*, ed. Paul Zeller Strodach (Philadelphia: United Lutheran Publication House, 1925), 122:
> Bless me, O God, with the vision of Thy being and beauty, that in the strength of it, we may work without haste and without rest; through....
The prayer is said (p. 208) to be taken from *Prayers for Students*.

[35] Hatchett, 569.

[36] Shepherd, 82; Hatchett, 381–82.

A revision of this prayer, on which the *Lutheran Book of Worship* version is based, was given in the *Service Book and Hymnal* both as one of the post-communion prayers (pp. 14, 39, 69) and as one of the prayers for private devotion, no. 10 (p. 235).

AFTER WORSHIP (no. 210)
Source: *Book of Common Prayer* (p. 834)
No. 68: After Worship

Grant, we beseech *thee*, Almighty God, that the words which we have heard this day with our outward ears, may, through *thy* grace, be so grafted inwardly in our hearts, that they may bring forth in us the fruit of good living, to the honor and praise of *thy* Name; through Jesus Christ our Lord.

This prayer was composed for the 1549 Prayer Book as one of the six collects provided for use after the offertory when there was no communion.[37]

ANSWER TO PRAYER (no. 211)
Source: *Book of Common Prayer* (1549)

Almightie God, the fountayn of all wisdome, which knowest our necessities beefore we aske, and our ignoraunce in asking: we beseche thee to haue compassion vpon our infirmities, and those thynges whiche for our vnwoorthines we dare not, and for our blindness we can not aske, vouchsafe to geue vs for the woorthines of thy soone Jesu Christ our Lorde.

This prayer was written for the 1549 Prayer Book as one of the six collects provided for use after the offertory when there was no communion. In the 1552 and succeeding revisions these prayers were permitted after Morning or Evening Prayer or Communion or the Litany. The scriptural allusions include Ecclesiasticus 1:5, Matthew 8:8, and Romans 8:26.[38] Other revisions of the prayer are given in the 1979 Prayer Book as the Collect for Proper 11 (p. 11) and as one of the collects at the Prayers (no. 4, pp. 394–95).

ANSWER TO PRAYER (no. 212)
Source: Liturgy of St. John Chrysostom
The Prayer of the third antiphon

Ὁ τὰς κοινὰς ταύτας καὶ συμφώνους ἡμῖν χαρισάμενος προσευχάς, ὁ καὶ δύο καὶ τρισὶ συμφωνοῦσιν ἐπὶ τῷ ὀνόματί σου τὰς αἰτήσεις παρέχειν ἐπαγγειλάμενος αὐτὸς καὶ νῦν τῶν δούλων σου τὰ αἰτήματα πρὸς τὸ συμφέρον πλήρωσον χορηγῶν ἡμῖν ἐν τῷ παρόντι αἰῶνι τὴν ἐπίγνωσιν τῆς σῆς ἀληθείας καὶ ἐν τῷ μέλλοντι ζωὴν αἰώνιον χαριζόμενος.

This prayer appears in late medieval manuscripts in the liturgies of St. John Chrysostom and St. Basil but not in the earliest manuscripts. The English translation dates from a prayer printed at the conclusion of Cranmer's English Litany (1544).[39] The *Lutheran Book of Worship* uses the translation in the 1979 *Book of Common Prayer* (pp. 102 and 126). The biblical reference is Matthew 18:19–20. The prayer in the older Prayer Book version was included in the *Service Book and Hymnal* as no. 121 of the Collects and Prayers (p. 234). In its English

---

[37] Shepherd 49–50; Hatchett, 569.
[38] Shepherd, 49–50; 1928 *Book of Common Prayer*, pp. 49–50; Hatchett, 189.
[39] Shepherd, 20; Hatchett, 130–31.

form the prayer lacks a doxology; in the Eastern liturgies the priest says this prayer while the deacon's litany is sung and the doxology concludes both: "for you are a good God and love the human race, and to you we ascribe glory, to the Father, and to the Son, and to the Holy Spirit, now and ever and unto ages of ages." (See Hapgood, *Service Book*, p. 83.)

A PRAYER ATTRIBUTED TO ST. FRANCIS (no. 213)
Source: *Book of Common Prayer* (p. 833)
No. 62: A Prayer attributed to St. Francis

The author of this prayer is not known; it cannot be traced back earlier than the twentieth century.[40] The Lutheran and the Episcopal forms are identical except that the Lutheran book prints the prayer in sense lines.

GENERAL THANKSGIVING (no. 214)
Source: *Book of Common Prayer* (p. 101)
The General Thanksgiving

Bishop Edward Reynolds of Norwich (1661–1676) composed this prayer for the 1662 Prayer Book. Its scriptural allusions include Colossians 1:27, Psalms 51:15, and Luke 1:75.[41] The revision of this prayer in the Lutheran and Episcopal books is identical except that the Prayer Book sets it in sense lines. See Augustine on Psalm 32, sermon 1.7: "Let us sing a new song not with our lips but with our lives."

HARVEST OF LANDS AND WATERS (no. 215)
Source: *Book of Common Prayer* (p. 828)
No. 42: For the Harvest of Lands and Waters

> O gracious Father, *who openest thine* hand and *fillest* all things living with plenteousness: Bless the lands and waters, and multiply the harvests of the world; let *thy* Spirit go forth, that it may renew the face of the earth; show *thy* loving-kindness, that our land may give her increase; and save us from selfish use of what *thou givest*, that men and women everywhere may give *thee* thanks; through Christ our Lord.

This prayer is a revision of a prayer new to the 1892 Prayer Book and taken from a collection authorized by Cortlandt Whitehead, bishop of Pittsburgh

---

[40]Hatchett, 569. The prayer has been adapted by the Missionaries of Charity as the "Daily Prayer of the Co-workers of Mother Teresa":

> Make us worthy, Lord, to serve our fellow men throughout the world who live and die in poverty and hunger. Give them, through our hands, this day their daily bread, and by our understanding love, give peace and joy.
> Lord, make me a channel of Thy peace that, where there is hatred, I may bring love; that where there is wrong, I may bring the spirit of forgiveness; that where there is discord, I may bring harmony; that where there is error, I may bring truth; that where there is doubt, I may bring faith; that where there is despair, I may bring hope; that where there are shadows I may bring light; that where there is sadness, I may bring joy.
> Lord, grant that I may seek rather to comfort than to be comforted, to understand than to be understood, to love than to be loved; for it is by forgetting self that one finds; it is by forgiving that one is forgiven; it is by dying that one awakens to eternal life. Amen.

[41]Shepherd, 19; Hatchett, 130.

(1882–1922).[42] The scriptural allusions are to Psalm 145:17 and 104:31, the first familiar to Lutherans from the table grace Luther suggested in the Small Catechism.

CONSERVATION OF NATURAL RESOURCES (no. 216)
Source: *Book of Common Prayer* (p. 827)
No. 41: For the Conservation of Natural Resources

Almighty God, in giving us dominion over things on earth, you made us fellow workers in your creation. Give us wisdom and reverence so to use the resources of nature, that no one may suffer from our abuse of them, and that generations yet to come may continue to praise you for your bounty; through Jesus Christ our Lord.

This is a new prayer, drafted by Charles W. F. Smith.[43]

THANKS FOR THE HARVEST (no. 217)
Source: *Book of Common Prayer* (p. 840)
Thanksgiving no. 9: For the Harvest

Most gracious God, by whose knowledge the depths are broken up and the clouds drop down the dew: We yield thee hearty thanks and praise for the return of seedtime and harvest, for the increase of the ground and the gathering in of its fruits, and for all the other blessings of thy merciful providence bestowed upon this nation and people. And, we beseech thee, give us a just sense of these great mercies, such as may appear in our lives by a humble, holy, and obedient walking before thee all our days; through Jesus Christ our Lord, to whom, with thee and the Holy Ghost be all glory and honor, world without end.

This is a slightly revised form of a prayer which dates from the proposed Prayer Book of 1786 which appointed it for use at Morning Prayer on Thanksgiving Day.[44] It is based on Psalm 145 and quotes Proverbs 3:20 and Genesis 8:22.

IN TIME OF SCARCE RAINFALL (no. 218)
Source: *Book of Common Prayer* (p. 828)
No. 43: For Rain

O God, heavenly Father, who by *thy* Son Jesus Christ *hast* promised to all those who seek *thy* kingdom and its righteousness all things necessary to sustain their life: Send us, we entreat *thee*, in this time of need, such moderate rain and showers, that we may receive the fruits of the earth to our comfort and to *thy* honor; through Jesus Christ our Lord.

This is a slightly revised version of a prayer in the 1549 Prayer Book.[45]

DANGERS OF ABUNDANCE (no. 219)
Source: Eric Milner-White, *Daily Prayer* (London: Oxford, 1941), p. 75.

O God, who in thy love hast bestowed upon us gifts such as our fathers never knew nor dreamed of: Mercifully grant that we be not so occupied

---

[42]Shepherd, 39–40; Hatchett, 565.
[43]Shepherd, 39–40; Hatchett, 565.
[44]Shepherd, 50; Hatchett, 571.
[45]Shepherd, 39–40; Hatchett, 565.

with material things that we forget the things which are spiritual; lest, having gained the whole world, we lose our own soul; for thy mercy's sake.

This prayer was included in the *Service Book and Hymnal* as no. 74 among the Collects and Prayers (p. 228). The scriptural allusions are Philippians 3:19 and Mark 8:36.

GUIDANCE (no. 220)
Source: Gregorian sacramentary (no. 198)

Actiones nostras quaesumus domine et aspirando praeueni. et adiuuando prosequere. ut cuncta nostra operatio. et a te semper incipiat. et per te coepta finiatur. per dominum.

In the Gregorian sacramentary this is one of the prayer said after a lesson in the liturgy of the word during the vigil at the climax of the Lenten Ember days. The English translation dates from the 1549 Prayer Book. In the 1979 Prayer Book it is no. 57 of the prayers (p. 832.)[46] In the *Service Book and Hymnal* it was no. 113: For Divine Assistance (p. 233).

GENERAL INTERCESSION (no. 221)
Source: *Service Book and Hymnal* (p. 230)
No. 85: Evening

Watch thou, dear Lord, with those who wake, or watch, or weep tonight, and give thine angels charge over those who sleep. Tend thy sick ones, O Lord. Rest thy weary ones. Bless thy dying ones. Soothe thy suffering ones. Pity thine afflicted ones. Shield thy joyous ones. And grant all, for thy love's sake, in Jesus Christ our Lord.

The prayer, from Selina Fox's *A Chain of Prayer Across the Ages*, is said to be derived from the writings of St. Augustine.[47] It is given in the 1979 Prayer Book as one of the collects for mission in Evening Prayer (pp. 71 and 124) and in Compline (p. 134).

PROTECTION THROUGH LIFE (no. 222)
Source: *Book of Common Prayer* (p. 832)
No. 60: For Protection

Assist us mercifully, O Lord, in these our supplications and prayers, and dispose the way of *thy* servants towards the attainment of everlasting salvation; that, among all the changes and chances of this mortal life, they may ever be defended by *thy* gracious and ready help; through Jesus Christ our Lord.

This prayer comes from the Gelasian sacramentary (no. 1313); it is also in the Gregorian supplement (no. 1317) and the Bobbio missal (no. 400). In each of these it was used in a votive mass for travelers.[48] The English translation dates from the 1549 Prayer Book.

---

[46]Shepherd, 49–50; Hatchett, 567–68.

[47]Selina F. Fox, *A Chain of Prayer across the Ages*, 5th ed. (New York: E. P. Dutton, 1928), 189, attributed it to St. Augustine. Luther Reed, in his list of sources of the collects and prayers in the *Service Book and Hymnal* (*The Lutheran Liturgy*, p. 608), identifies the source of the prayer as simply "St. Augustine (?)"; Marion Hatchett (pp. 143, 147) says "from the writings of Saint Augustine of Hippo."

[48]Shepherd, 49–50; Hatchett, 568.

THOSE IN AFFLICTION (no. 223)
Source: Gelasian sacramentary
No. 411: For Good Friday

> Omnipotens sempiterne Deus, maestorum consolatio, laborantium forti-
> tudo, perueniant ad te praeces de quacumque tribulatione clamantium, ut
> omnes sibi in necessitatibus suis misericordiam tuam gaudeant adfuisse. Per
> Dominum.

The English translation originates with Eric Milner-White, *The Occasional
Prayers of the 1928 Book Reconsidered* (London, 1930), p. 25. The last sentence
of the translation is from the Liturgy of St. Mark. The prayer was included in
the *Service Book and Hymnal* as no. 35 among the Collects and Prayers (p. 223).

THOSE IN MENTAL DISTRESS (no. 224)
Source: *Book of Common Prayer*, 1928 (p. 598)
For Those in Mental Darkness

> O heavenly Father, we beseech thee to have mercy upon all thy children
> who are living in mental darkness. Restore them to strength of mind and
> cheerfulness of spirit, and give them health and peace; through Jesus Christ
> our Lord.

The prayer, new to the 1928 Prayer Book, is thought to be by Charles Lewis
Slattery.[49] It is not included in the 1979 Prayer Book.

THOSE IN TROUBLE OR BEREAVEMENT (no. 225)
Source: *Book of Common Prayer* (p. 831)
No. 55: For a Person in Trouble or Bereavement

> O merciful Father, who hast taught us in thy holy Word that thou dost not
> willingly afflict or grieve the children of men: Look with pity upon the sorrows
> of thy servant for whom our prayers are offered. Remember *him*, O Lord,
> in mercy, nourish *his* soul with patience, comfort *him* with a sense of thy
> goodness, lift up thy countenance upon *him*, and give *him* peace; through
> Jesus Christ our Lord.

This is one of the occasional prayers introduced in the 1789 revision of the
Prayer Book. The opening alludes to Lamentations 3:33, the conclusion to
Numbers 6:26.[50]

RECOVERY FROM SICKNESS (no. 226)
Source: *Book of Common Prayer* (p. 458)
For Recovery from Sickness

> O God, the strength of the weak and comfort of sufferers: Mercifully accept
> our prayers, and grant to your servant *N.* the help of your power, that *his*
> sickness may be turned into health, and our sorrow into joy; through Jesus
> Christ our Lord.

This prayer was written for the 1928 Prayer Book apparently by Howard Bald-
win St. George.[51]

---

[49]Shepherd, 598.
[50]Ibid., 44–45; Hatchett, 567.
[51]Shepherd, 309–11; Hatchett, 468.

THOSE SUFFERING FROM ADDICTION (no. 227)
Source: *Book of Common Prayer* (p. 831)
No. 56: For the Victims of Addiction

> O blessed Lord, you ministered to all who came to you: Look with compassion upon all who through addiction have lost their health and freedom. Restore to them the assurance of your unfailing mercy; remove from them the fears that beset them; strengthen them in the work of their recovery; and to those who care for them, give patient understanding and persevering love.

This prayer, drafted by Charles W. F. Smith, is new to the 1979 Prayer Book.[52]

RESTORATION OF HEALTH (no. 228)
Source: *Book of Common Prayer* (p. 841)
Thanksgiving no. 11: For the Restoration of Health

> Almighty God and heavenly Father, we give *thee* humble thanks because *thou hast* been graciously pleased to deliver from *his* sickness *thy* servant *N.*, in whose behalf we bless and praise *thy* Name. Grant, O gracious Father, that *he*, through *thy* help, may live in this world according to *thy* will, and also be partaker of everlasting glory in the life to come; through Jesus Christ our Lord.

This is a revision of the thanksgiving "For a Child's Recovery from Sickness" which entered the Prayer Book in 1892 and which was a variant of the thanksgiving in the Thanksgiving of Women after Childbirth in the 1789 Prayer Book.[53]

THE AGED (no. 229)
Source: *Book of Common Prayer* (p. 830)
No. 49: For the Aged

> Look with mercy, O God our Father, on all whose increasing years bring them weakness, distress, or isolation. Provide for them homes of dignity and peace; give them understanding helpers, and the willingness to accept help; and, as their strength diminishes, increase their faith and their assurance of your love. This we ask in the name of Jesus Christ our Lord.

This is a new prayer composed by Ivy Watkins Smith and Charles W. F. Smith.[54]

FAMILIES (no. 230)
Source: *Book of Common Prayer* (pp. 828–29)
No. 45: For Families

> Almighty God, our heavenly Father, who settest the solitary in families: We commend to thy continual care the homes in which thy people dwell. Put far from them, we beseech thee, every root of bitterness, the desire of vainglory, and the pride of life. Fill them with faith, virtue, knowledge, temperance, patience, godliness. Knit together in constant affection those who, in holy wedlock, have been made one flesh. Turn the hearts of the parents to the children, and the hearts of the children to the parents; and so enkindle fervent charity among us all, that we may evermore be kindly affectioned to one another; through Jesus Christ our Lord.

---

[52] Hatchett, 567.
[53] Shepherd, 53; Hatchett, 571.
[54] Hatchett, 566.

This prayer, written by Frederick Dan Huntington, entered the Prayer Book in 1928. Among the biblical allusions are Psalm 68:6, Hebrews 12:15, Galatians 5:26, 2 Peter 1:5–6, Genesis 2:24, and Malachi 4:6.[55]

BIRTH OF A CHILD (no. 231)
Source: *Book of Common Prayer* (p. 841)
Thanksgiving no. 10: For the Gift of a Child

Heavenly Father, you sent your own Son into this world. We thank you for the life of this child, *N.*, entrusted to our care. Help us to remember that we are all your children, and so to love and nurture *him*, that *he* may attain to that full stature intended for *him* in your eternal kingdom; for the sake of your dear Son, Jesus Christ our Lord.

This is a new prayer, written by Caroline Rose.[56]

THE CARE OF CHILDREN (no. 232)
Source: *Book of Common Prayer* (p. 829)
No. 46: For the Care of Children

Almighty God, heavenly Father, you have blessed us with the joy and care of children: Give us calm strength and patient wisdom as we bring them up, that we may teach them to love whatever is just and true and good, following the example of our Savior Jesus Christ.

On the basis of a much longer prayer by William Austin Smith, John W. Suter, Jr., drafted this prayer, which first entered the Prayer Book in 1928. The biblical allusion is to Philippians 4:8.[57]

YOUNG PERSONS (no. 233)
Source: *Book of Common Prayer* (p. 829)
No. 47: For Young Persons

God our Father, you see your children growing up in an unsteady and confusing world: Show them that your ways give more life than the ways of the world, and that following you is better than chasing after selfish goals. Help them to take failure, not as a measure of their worth, but as a chance for a new start. Given them strength to hold their faith in you, and to keep alive their joy in your creation; through Jesus Christ our Lord.

This is a new prayer, drafted by Ann Brooke Bushong.[58]

THOSE WHO LIVE ALONE (no. 234)
Source: *Book of Common Prayer* (p. 829)
No. 48: For Those Who Live Alone

Almighty God, whose Son had nowhere to lay his head: Grant that those who live alone may not be lonely in their solitude, but that, following in his steps, they may find fulfillment in loving you and their neighbors; through Jesus Christ our Lord.

[55]Shepherd 598; Hatchett, 565.
[56]Hatchett, 571.
[57]Shepherd, 596; Hatchett, 565.
[58]Hatchett, 565.

This is a new prayer, drafted by Paul E. Langpaap.[59]

REMEMBRANCE OF THE FAITHFUL DEPARTED (no. 235)
Source: *Book of Common Order*, Church of Scotland, 1940 (p. 59)

> With reverence and affection we remember before Thee, O everlasting God, all our friends and kindred who have passed within the veil. Keep us in union with them here, through faith and love towards Thee, that hereafter we may enter into Thy blessed presence, and be numbered with those who serve Thee and behold Thy face, in glory everlasting; through Jesus Christ our Lord, unto whom with Thee and the Holy Spirit, be glory and praise, now and for evermore.

This prayer was introduced to Lutheran use in the *Service Book and Hymnal* as no. 43 of the Collects and Prayers (p. 224).

PRAYER OF THE CHURCH (Min. Ed., pp. 116–17)
Source: *Service Book and Hymnal* (pp. 6–8)

> Almighty God, the Father of our Lord Jesus Christ: We give thee praise and hearty thanks for all thy goodness and tender mercies. We bless thee for the love which hath created and doth sustain us from day to day. We praise thee for the gift of thy Son, our Saviour, through whom thou hast made known thy will and grace. We thank thee for the Holy Ghost, the Comforter; for thy holy Church, for the means of Grace, for the lives of all faithful and godly men, and for the hope of the life to come. Help us to treasure in our hearts all that our Lord hath done for us; and enable us to show our thankfulness by lives that are given wholly to thy service;
> *We beseech thee to hear us, good Lord.*
> Save and defend thy Church Universal, purchased with the precious Blood of Christ. Give its pastors and ministers according to thy Spirit, and strengthen it through the Word and the holy Sacraments. Make it perfect in love and in all good works, and establish it in the faith delivered to the saints. Sanctify and unite thy people in all the world, that one holy Church may bear witness to thee, the God and Father of all;
> *We beseech thee to hear us, good Lord.*
> Upon all in any holy office in thy Church bestow thy wisdom and heavenly grace, and enable them to fulfill their duties in thy fear and in purity of heart. Let thy gracious benediction rest upon our clergy and people, and upon all who are set over us in the Lord; that faith may abound, and thy kingdom increase;
> *We beseech thee to hear us, good Lord.*
> Send forth thy light and thy truth into all the earth, O Lord. Raise up, we pray thee, faithful servants of Christ to labor in the Gospel at home and in distant lands;
> *We beseech thee to hear us, good Lord.*
> According to thy merciful goodness, O God, extend thy saving health and strength to the younger Churches. Grant that they may rejoice in a rich harvest of souls for thy kingdom. Support them in times of trial and weakness, and make them steadfast, abounding in the work of the Lord;

---

[59] Ibid., 566.

We beseech thee to hear us, good Lord.

Preserve our Nation in righteousness and honor, and continue thy blessings to us as a people, that we may lead a quiet and peaceable life, in all godliness and honesty. Grant health and favor to all who bear office in our land (especially to the President and the Congress, the Governor and Legislature of this State *or,* in *Canadian Churches:* especially to Her Gracious Majesty the Queen, the Prime Minister and the Parliament, and all Provincial Authorities), and help them to acknowledge and obey thy holy will;

We beseech thee to hear us, good Lord.

Give to all men the mind of Christ, and dispose our days in thy peace, O God. Take from us all hatred and prejudice, and whatever may hinder unity of spirit and concord. Prosper the labors of those who take counsel for the nations of the world, that mutual understanding and common endeavor may be increased among all peoples;

We beseech thee to hear us, good Lord.

Bless, we pray thee, the schools of the Church, universities and centers of research, all institutions of learning, and those who exercise the care of souls therein. Withhold not, we pray thee, thy Word and Wisdom, but bestow it in such measure that men may serve thee in Church and State, and our common life be brought under the rule of thy truth and righteousness;

We beseech thee to hear us, good Lord.

We pray thee especially, heavenly Father, to sanctify our homes with thy light and joy. Keep our children in the covenant of their baptism, and enable their parents to rear them in a life of faith and godliness. By the spirit of affection and service unite the members of all Christian families, that they may show forth thy praise in our land and in all the world;

We beseech thee to hear us, good Lord.

God of mercies, we pray thee to comfort with the grace of thy Holy Spirit all who are in sorrow or need, sickness or adversity. Remember those who suffer persecution for the faith. Have mercy upon those to whom death draws near. Bring consolation to those in sorrow or mourning. And to all grant a measure of thy love, taking them into thy tender care;

We beseech thee to hear us, good Lord.

Let thy blessing rest upon the seed-time and harvest, the commerce and industry, the leisure and rest, and the arts and culture of our people. Take under thy special protection those whose toil is difficult or dangerous, and be with all who lay their hands to any useful task. Give them just rewards for their labor, and the knowledge that their work is good in thy sight, who art the Maker and Sustainer of all things;

We beseech thee to hear us, good Lord.

We remember with thanksgiving those who have loved and served thee in thy Church on earth, who now rest from their labors (especially those most dear to us, whom we name in our hearts before thee). Keep us in fellowship with all thy saints, and bring us at length to the joy of thy heavenly kingdom;

We beseech thee to hear us, good Lord.

(Here special Supplications, Intercessions, and Thanksgivings may be made.)

All these things, and whatever else thou seest that we need, grant us, O Father, for his sake who died and rose again, and now liveth and reigneth with thee in the unity of the Holy Ghost, one God, world without end. *Amen.*

The Prayer of the Church was written for the *Service Book and Hymnal* (1958) to replace the rather windy and, to many, tediously long and uninterrupted monologue of the General Prayer of the Common Service.

Table II
Comparative Index of Topics
in Prayer Collections in Four Lutheran Service Books

Church Book		*Common Service Book*		*Service Book and Hymnal*		*Lutheran Book of Worship*
				Abundance, dangers of #74		Abundance, Dangers of #219
						Addiction, Those Suffering from #227
Affliction, for those in #33	=	Affliction, for those in #62		Affliction, for those in #35		Affliction, Those in #223
#35	=	#63				
#37	=	#64	=	#36		
Affliction, in Time of #34	=	(Burial of the Dead)		Affliction, in Time of Priv. dev. #14		
Affliction, Steadfastness in #34	=	Affliction, Steadfastness in #31	=	Affliction, Steadfastness in #111		
						The Aged #229
						Agriculture #185
				All People, for #62		
						Alone, Those who Live #234
				Anniversary of a Church Building #11, 12		
Answer to Prayer #75	=	Answer to Prayer #82	=	Answer to Prayer #121	=	Answer to Prayer #212
#76	=	#83	=	#122	=	#211
#77	=	#84	=	#123		
				Armed Forces of the Nation, for the #50		
		Army, for the #90				

		Bereaved, for the		Bereaved, for the	Bereavement, Those in Trouble or #225
		#96	=	#53	
					Birth of a Child #231
				Brotherhood #60	
		Catechumens #48	=	Catechumens #16	
		Chaplains #93	=	Chaplains #52	
Charity #69	=	Charity #16	=	Charity #100	
				Children #40, 41	Children, Care of #232
Children of the Church #14	=	Children of the Church #46	=	Children of the Church #17	
		Children of the Parish #47			
				Christian Service #68	
the Church		the Church		the Church #1 #2 #3 #4	the Church #189
#10	=	#38			
#11	=				
#13	=	#40 #39			
				#5	
				the Church and the Community #67	
				the Church and the World #61	
		the Church in Time of War or Distress #87 #88 #89	=	the Church in Time of War or Distress #14	
Protection of the Church #18	=	Protection of the Church #41	=	Protection of the Church #15	
				The Church Militant #6	

Table II (continued)

Church Book	Common Service Book	Service Book and Hymnal	Lutheran Book of Worship
			Church Musicians and Artists #197
			Cities #174
			Citizenship, Responsible #171
Civil Authority, for Those in #25 =	Civil, Authority, for Those in #74		Civil Authority, Those in #172
		Coming of the Kingdom #28	
			Commerce and Industry #178
		Compassion #70	
		Conference of Christian People #18	
			Conscience, Those Who Suffer for the Sake of #187
		Consecration #105	
			Conservation of Natural Resources #216
	Constancy #12		
	Contentment #30 =	Contentment #110	
		the Consummation #33	
	our Country/ Nation	our Country/ Nation	our Country #169
	#72 = #73 = #85 =	#47 #46 #45	
			Courts of Justice #173
		Deaconesses #69	Deaconesses and Deacons #196

Death, for a Blessed #72	= 	Death, for a Blessed #35	
		Departed, Thanksgiving for the Faithful #43 =	Departed, Remembrance of the Faithful #235
Drought, in Time of #40	= 	Drought, in Time of #70	see Rainfall #218
			Election of a President or Pastor #195
Enemies, for our #26 #27	 =	Enemies, for our #68	Enemies, our #180
		Enemies of the Nation #99	
Erred, for Those who have #19 #20	 = =	Erred, for Those who Have #42 #43	
Evening #47	= 	Evening #61 =	Evening #86 #83 #84 #85 Priv. dev. #15
			Evildoers, against #55
Faith #58	= 	Faith #11 =	Faith #103 #102
Faith, Hope, and Love #1	= 	Faith, Hope, and Love #13 =	Faith, Hope, and Love #97

Families
#230

Friends
#38

Fruits of
the Earth
#77, 78

General
Intercession
#221

	Gospel, the Maintenance of the #100 =	Gospel, the Maintenance of the #27

417

Table II (continued)

Church Book	Common Service Book	Service Book and Hymnal	Lutheran Book of Worship
		Gospel, Spread of the #10	Gospel, Spread of the #190
			Governments State/provincial and Local #170
Grace to do God's Will #55	= Grace to do God's Will #17	= Grace to do God's Will #101	
Grace to know and Follow Christ #62 #63	= Grace to Know and Follow Christ #28 = #27	= Grace to Follow Christ #107 (= SS. Philip & James)	
Grace to Receive the Word #49	= Grace to Receive the Word #10	= Grace to Receive the Word #93	= Grace to Receive the Word #201
Grace to Use our Gifts #48	= Grace to Use our Gifts #18	= Grace to Use our Gifts #106	
Guidance, Divine #59 #60 #9	= Guidance, Divine #19 = #20 = #21	= Assistance, Divine #113 #94, 95, 96	= Guidance #220
Guidance into Truth #50	= Guidance into Truth #9	= Guidance into Truth #92	
			Harvest of Lands and Waters #215
			Harvest, Thanks for the #217
			Health, Restoration of #228
Heathen #24	= Heathen #56	Heathen #30	
Heaven, Blessedness of #73	= Heaven, Blessedness of #36	= Heaven, Blessedness of #118	
Holiness #67	= Holiness #34		
		Holy Communion, after Priv.. dev. #8, 9, 10, 11	Holy Communion, after #209

			Holy Communion, before Priv.. dev. #5, 6, 7	Holy Communion, before #207, 208
Holy Spirit		Holy Spirit	Holy Spirit	Holy Spirit, Enlightenment of the #202
#3	=	#1		
#4	=	#2	= #91	
#5				
#6				
#7	=	#3		
#64	=	#4		
#65	=	#5	= #90	
			Home and Kindred #39	
				Human Family #177
Humility #70	=	Humility #32		
Faith #58	=	Faith #11	(= St. Thomas)	
Imprisoned #31	=	Imprisoned #67		
			Industrial Peace #72	
			Islam, for #32	
Jews, for the #23	=	Jews, for the #57	Jews, for the #31	
			Kingdom, for the #64	
			Knowledge of God #116	
			Labors of Men #73	
				Leisure, Use of #189
Love to God #56	=	Love to God #15	= Love to God #98	
#68	=	#14	#99	
			Marriage, for the Sanctity of #42	
			Meekness, for #109	
				Mental Distress, Those in #224

419

Table II (continued)

Church Book		Common Service Book		Service Book and Hymnal		Lutheran Book of Worship
Ministry, for the		Ministry, for the		Ministry, for the		Ministers of the Word
#15	=	#51	=	#19		
#16	=	#49				
#17	=	#50		(= SS. Peter & Paul) #20	=	#194
				Ministry, for the Increase of the #21		
		Ministry of Mercy #94				
						Mission of the Church #192
		Missionaries, Commissioning of #55				
				Missionary Work #25, 29		
Missions #12	=	Missions #52 #53, 54	=	Missions #23 #24, 26		Missions #191
		Morning #59 #60	= =	Morning #80 #81 #82		
		Morning, Sunday #58		Lord's Day, Right Use of the #79		
Mothers #38	=	Mothers #66				
National Distress #28 #29 #30	= = =	National Distress #75 #76 #77				
		Navy, for the #91				
						Neighborhood #176
				New World, for the #66		
						The Oppressed #182
Pardon #53	=	Pardon #25				

421

Table II (continued)

Church Book	Common Service Book	Service Book and Hymnal	Lutheran Book of Worship
		Relations of Men to One another #71	
Renewal	Renewal	Renewal, Spiritual	Renewal
#8 =	#6 =	#88	#199, 200
#51 =	#7 =	#89	
Repentance #52 =	Repentance #24 =	Repentance Priv. dev. #13	
		Saints #44	The Saints #193
			Schools #184
		Seafarers #51	
			Self-dedication #203
Sick, for the	Sick, for the	Sick, for the	Sickness, Recovery from
#36 =	#65 =	#37	#226
#37 =	#64 =	#36	
	Sick, Wounded, and Captives #95		
Sickness, in Time of Great #39 =	Sickness, in Time of Great #69		
Sin, Deliverance from #54/ =	Sin, Deliverance from #26		
			Social Justice #167
Spiritual Illumination #61 =	Spiritual Illumination #8		
Spiritual	Spiritual	Spiritual Synods of the Church #13	
			Teachers #198
Temptation, for Aid in #57 =	Temptation, for Aid in #22 #23 =	Temptation, for Aid in Priv. dev. #12	
Thanksgiving, General	Thanksgiving, General		Thanksgiving, General
#42 =	#81		#214
#45			

Thanksgiving, National #43 #44	= =	Thanksgiving, National #78 #79	=	Thanksgiving, National #56	

Theological
Seminaries
#22

Towns and
Rural Areas
#175

Trustfulness
#204

Unemployed #76   Unemployed #179

Unity in the Faith #21 #22 = =   Unity in the Faith #45 #44   Unity, Church #7, 8

Variety of
Races and
Cultures
#168

Victory, for #97 = Victory, for #54

Vocation
#117

War, for Those in Our Country's Service in Time of #92 = War, for Those in Our Country's Service in Time of #49

Wealth, Right Use of #75   Wealth, Proper Use of #183

Weather, in Time of Unseasonable #41 = Weather, in Time of Unseasonable #71

Worship, after
#210

Worship, before Priv. dev. #1 #2, 3, 4, = Worship, before #206 #205

Young Persons
#233

Zeal
#104

RESPONSIVE PRAYER 1 AND 2
(Ministers Edition, pp. 79–81, 82–85, 17)

Parallel Texts

Episcopal   The Suffrages in Morning and Evening Prayer, *Book of Common Prayer*, pp. 97–98, 121–22

Lutheran   The Suffrages, *Church Book* (1868), pp. 118–20
The Suffrages, the Morning Suffrages, the Evening Suffrages *Common Service Book* (1919), text ed., pp. 242–49
The Suffrages, the Morning Suffrages, the Evening Suffrages, *The Lutheran Hymnal* (1941), pp. 113–16
The General Suffrages, the Morning Suffrages, the Evening Suffrages, *Service Book and Hymnal* (1958), pp. 153–56.
Responsive Prayer 1 and 2, *Contemporary Worship 9: Daily Prayer of the Church* (1976), pp. 58–64.

Purpose

Responsive Prayer 1 may be used as the prayers at Morning Prayer; Responsive Prayer 2 may be used as the prayers at Evening Prayer, replacing the litany. Responsive Prayer 1 or 2 may be used separately as a simple office either in place of Morning or Evening Prayer or to supplement these offices when a fuller cycle of daily prayer is desired.

Characteristics

Responsive Prayer 1 is less tied to the beginning of the day than Morning Prayer is; Responsive Prayer 2 is not associated with sunset as is Evening Prayer but is adaptable for noon, afternoon, or evening. When used alone as separate services, these offices are more appropriate to times later in the morning than Morning Prayer is and earlier or later in the afternoon and evening than Evening Prayer is. Responsive Prayer 2 is also for use before travel, an echo of the medieval office of Itinerarium.

Development of the Suffrages

The title "Suffrages" is from the Latin *suffragium*, a prayer of intercession; the suffrages are sometimes called *preces*, a Latin word meaning prayers, requests.

Wilhelm Loehe, aware of the limited opportunity for intercession in the historic form of Matins and Vespers as they had been preserved in the Lutheran church orders, included in his Agenda of 1844, which he prepared for Lutheran congregations in North America, the suffrages he found in the Roman breviary in connection with morning and evening prayers. He included the Suffrages, which were used at Lauds and Vespers in the Roman office, the Morning Suffrages, which were used at Prime, and the Evening Suffrages, which were used at Compline. The *Church Book* (1868) provided an English translation of the Suffrages with the rubric, "The Suffrages may be used at Morning or Evening Service in the same manner as the Litany" (p. 118). The Common Service

(1888) added an English translation of the Morning and the Evening Suffrages, and these three forms were continued in the *Common Service Book* (1917), *The Lutheran Hymnal* (1941), and the *Service Book and Hymnal* (1958). Beginning with the *Common Service Book* provision was made for the Morning and Evening Suffrages to be used alone as a separate office.

In 1955 Pope Pius XII and the Sacred Congregation of Rites issued a simplification of the rubrics of the Roman breviary and missal. This simplification was enacted by Pope John XXIII, who ordered that the previous rubrics were inoperative after January 1, 1961. The preces which the *Service Book and Hymnal* called the "General" Suffrages (in previous Lutheran books they were simply the Suffrages), which were used at Lauds and Vespers, were limited to Wednesdays and Fridays of Advent, Lent, and Passiontide; the Ember Wednesday and Friday in September; and Lauds of Ember Saturdays, except within the octave of Pentecost. Thus they were made a penitential addition to the office. The preces which the Lutheran books called the Morning Suffrages and which had been taken from Prime were eliminated; the preces which the Lutheran books called the Evening Suffrages, which had been taken from Compline, were likewise removed from that office. With the publication of the Liturgy of the Hours, the preces are eliminated entirely, and instead Morning and Evening Prayer use brief litanies of intercession, and different prayers are used on each day of the year.

THE SUFFRAGES IN DETAIL

Responsive Prayer 1 is a revision of what Lutheran books had called the Morning Suffrages, which had come from medieval forms of Prime, now suppressed in the Roman Liturgy of the Hours. The earlier Roman and Lutheran forms had begun with the three- or six-fold Kyrie. In the *Lutheran Book of Worship* a version of the Trisagion of the Eastern churches is used: "Holy, God, holy and mighty, holy and immortal, *have mercy and hear us.*" The Eastern text concludes simply "have mercy on us," and *Occasional Services* (1982) uses this text (p. 108). The Trisagion in its Latin translation was used in the middle of the weekday preces in the Roman office of Prime and so suggested itself to the Lutheran revisers. The Lord's Prayer follows in both the Roman and Lutheran orders. (An interesting feature of the former General Suffrages and of the Morning and Evening Suffrages as they were used in *The Lutheran Hymnal* was that the Lord's Prayer did not include the doxology "for thine is the kingdom and the power and the glory, forever and ever," reminding users that the doxology was a later addition to the prayer.)

In both Roman and Lutheran forms, the Apostles' Creed is said next. Although the use of this creed in the office cannot be traced back earlier than the eighth century,[60] Ambrose urged that "we ought also specially to

---

[60] Ibid., 121.

repeat the creed as a seal upon our hearts daily before light."[61] Augustine also teaches catechumens to adopt the practice of reciting the Creed daily "before you go to sleep, before you go forth."[62] The Creed has been a characteristic feature of Morning and Evening Prayer in the *Book of Common Prayer* since 1549, following the medieval forms of the office.

The versicles (the suffrages proper) in Responsive Prayer 1 and the rest of the order are selected from the Roman rite as this table shows:

Roman Breviary	*Common Service*	*Lutheran Book of Worship*
Sundays and Weekdays		
Psalm 88:13	Psalm 88:13	Psalm 88:13
71:8	71:8	51:12
51:9	51:9	71:8
51:10	51:10	
51:11	51:11	
51:12	51:12	
Weekdays		
140:1		
59:1		
59:2		
145:2		145:2
65:5		65:5
70:1		
Holy God, Holy Mighty,		
Holy Immortal		
103:1		103:1
103:2		
103:3		
103:4		
103:5		103:5
Sundays and Weekdays		
124:8		
Confiteor		
Misereatur		
Indulgentiam		
Vouchsafe, O Lord	Vouchsafe, O Lord	
Have mercy...	Have mercy...	
Let thy mercy...	Let thy mercy...	
102:1	102:1	102:1
The Lord be with you	The Lord be with you	The Lord be with you
Let us pray	Let us pray	Let us pray
Collect for Grace	Luther's Morning Prayer	Luther's Morning Prayer
Benedicamus	Benedicamus	Benedicamus
	The grace...	Blessing

---

[61] *De virginibus* 3.20; see also *Exhortatio virginitatis* 58.
[62] *De symbolo ad catechumenos* 1.

426

Luther's Morning Prayer is taken from the Small Catechism;[63] the translation (no. 265) was made for the *Lutheran Book of Worship*. Luther Reed suggests with some justification that this prayer by Luther is an expansion of the collect for grace (no. 249, given in the *Lutheran Book of Worship* at the conclusion of Morning Prayer), which was the prayer used at the office of Prime.

In all his Collects and prayers, Luther kept within the great Christian tradition. There was no striving for originality. On the other hand, there is every evidence of church consciousness, respect for historical continuity, and liturgical restraint. With these principles in view, Luther treated the ancient forms freely, infusing into them a warmth peculiarly his own, yet ever retaining the hard core of these expressions of centuries of Christian experience.[64]

In Responsive Prayer 2 the preces are the first set of suffrages from Morning Prayer II in the *Book of Common Prayer* (pp. 97–98). These are based on those of the 1549 Prayer Book, and several of them had been part of the Sarum office of Prime. The biblical sources are:

Show us your mercy, O Lord,	
and grant us your salvation.	Psalm 85:7
Clothe your ministers with righteousness	
Let your people sing with joy.	132:9
Give peace, O Lord, in all the world;	see 122:7
for only in you can we live in safety.	see 4:8
Lord, keep this nation under your care,	
and guide us in the way of justice and truth.	
Let your way be known upon earth;	
your saving health among all nations.	67:2
Let not the needy, O Lord, be forgotten,	
nor the hope of the poor be taken away.	9:18
Create in us clean hearts, O God,	51:11a
and sustain us with your Holy Spirit.	51:13b

The fourth set of verses derives from a phrase in the prayer for Peace among the Nations given in the *Book of Common Prayer:*

Almighty God, our heavenly Father, guide the nations of the world into the way of justice and truth. . . .[65]

The prayer for noon (no. 266) is from Herbert Lindemann's *The Daily Office.*[66]

The prayer for afternoon (no. 267) is A Collect for Guidance from Morning Prayer II in the *Book of Common Prayer* (p. 100). It was given

---

[63] On Luther's prayers see the devotional reflection by Arthur Carl Piepkorn, "This Little Prayer in Addition," *Response* 5:2 (St. Michael and All Angels, 1963):70–73. See also Piepkorn's reflections on the forms in the Small Catechism for grace at meals, "Benedicite and Gratias," *Response* 5:3 (Epiphany 1964):139–40.

[64] Reed, 641.

[65] *Book of Common Prayer*, 816.

[66] *The Daily Office* (St. Louis: Concordia Publishing House, 1965), 684.

in Selina Fitzherbert Fox's *A Chain of Prayer across the Ages* as "from an ancient collect."[67] From there it entered the Canadian Prayer Book of 1922.

The prayer for evening (no. 268) is from Luther's Small Catechism. A problematic phrase in this prayer as in Luther's Morning Prayer is the phrase "Let your holy angels have charge of us." Luther's prayers are cast in the singular and the German has "let your holy angel." This could be a reference to one's guardian angel, and thus when the prayer is put in the plural the noun angel should logically be made plural also. Luther may, however, have had in mind the Hebrew reference to God as an angel as in Isaiah 63:9 ("the angel of his presence saved them"), Genesis 48:16, Exodus 23:20, 33:2; in that case the translation of the Common Service is preferable, "let your angel have charge concerning us," and the meaning would be "may you yourself take charge of us."

As the popularity of pilgrimages increased in the Middle Ages, a brief office for travelers as they set out was created to pray for their safe passage and return. This office, called Itinerarium (or Itinerary), in its structure parallels the Suffrages. Its incorporation of the Benedictus suggests that it was attached to Lauds after the Gospel Canticle as travelers would set out after their morning prayers at sunrise. The Benedictus with its reference to the dawn would also be an appropriate canticle for those traveling east to the Holy Land. In the *Roman Ritual* the office opens with the Benedictus with the antiphon

May the almighty and merciful Lord lead us in the way of peace and prosperity. May the Angel Raphael be our companion on the journey and bring us back to our homes in peace, health, and happiness.

The Our Father and a series of versicles follow, then four collects, and the concluding verse

> Let us go forth in peace.
> *In the name of the Lord. Amen.*

The prayer Before Travel (no. 269) in Responsive Prayer 2 is derived from the traditional prayers, conflating and abbreviating them into one, and using three great biblical journeys as a pattern for our own passage through this world toward the eschatological destination of all such travel.

---

[67]Fox, 2.

THE LITANY
(Ministers Edition, pp. 86-91, 17-18)

Parallel Texts

Roman Catholic	The Litany of the Saints, *The Sacramentary*, pp. 194–95; *The Rites*, pp. 95–96.
Episcopal	The Great Litany, *Book of Common Prayer*, pp. 148–55.
Lutheran	The Litany, *Church Book* (1868), pp. 113–18 The Litany, *Common Service Book* (1919), text ed., pp. 236–41 The Litany, *Service Book and Hymnal* (1958), pp. 156–61 The Litany, *Contemporary Worship 9: Daily Prayer of the Church* (1976), pp. 65–67.

Purpose

The Litany may be used as the Prayer in Morning Prayer or as the Prayer in Evening Prayer replacing the litany given in the text of that service. It may be used as the prayer in the Service of the Word. It may serve as the entrance hymn in the Eucharist. The Litany may be used as a separate penitential service.

Characteristics

The Litany is a repeated, insistent, responsive prayer recalling Jesus' parable of the importunate friend (Luke 11:5–10). It is primarily penitential, but it reaches to include the whole range of human need in its embrace, "mighty in its grasp of the grounds for divine compassion."[68] The litany form of prayer is popular in many traditions, in liturgical and non-liturgical churches,[69] in liturgies and in para-liturgical forms.[70] Its popularity derives in part from the hypnotic effect of the repetition, which in ritual use is often associated with the accumulation of power,[71] gathering and uttering again and again the forceful energies of language which have their roots in the divine breath and spirit. In Christian use, more specifically, Robert Taft had shown that litanies represent a development from the bidding form of prayer in which the repeated response

---

[68] Reed, 623.

[69] See, for example, the Byzantine liturgies; the Presbyterian *Worshipbook* (1972), pp. 105–31. See also *The Wideness of God's Mercy: Litanies to Enlarge our Prayer*, complied and adapted by Jeffrey W. Rowthorn, 2 vols. (Minneapolis: Winston-Seabury Press, 1985).

[70] See, for example, the Litany of the Holy Name of Jesus, the Litany of the Blessed Virgin Mary (Loreto), the Litany of the Sacred Heart of Jesus in *A Manual of Prayer for the Use of the Catholic Laity* (Baltimore: John Murphy, 1930). See also the Litany of Our Lord Present in the Holy Eucharist, the Litany of Repentance, the Litany for Advent, the Litany of the Word Incarnate Our Lord Jesus Christ in *The Treasury of Devotion*, ed. T. T. Carter (New York: Thomas Nelson, 1938).

[71] See Margot Astrov, ed., *American Indian Prose and Poetry* (New York: Capricorn, 1962), 12. Originally published as *The Winged Serpent*, 1946.

replaces the silent prayer after the bid to pray and the minister's collect is postponed until the conclusion of the intercessions.[72]

Development of the Litany

The litanaic form of prayer was in use long before Christian times (see Psalm 118 and 136 with their repeated refrains).

In the Christian East, the first evidence of a litany is from the second half of the fourth century at Antioch.[73] By the end of the century a litany of intercession was used in Jerusalem,[74] and it spread throughout the East.

The litany form of intercession was used in Rome in the time of Pope Gelasius I (492–496) at the beginning of the mass. Gregory the Great (590–604) reduced this litany on non-festival days to the simple responses *Kyrie eleison.*

Responsorial prayer was used not only in church but outside the buildings in procession. Basil in Cappadocia and John Chrysostom in Antioch report processions sometimes in competition with Arian-sponsored processions. Such processions replaced pagan processions asking for safety for the crops. Bishop Mamertus of Vienne ca. 467 inaugurated processional litanies on the Monday, Tuesday, and Wednesday before Ascension Day to avert an earthquake and other calamities which had devastated the region and which had left him alone kneeling before the altar when the people had fled in panic. Such processions on these Rogation Days spread throughout Gaul and to England in 741 (the council of Cloveshoe) and to Rome in the time of Leo III (795–816).

A Greek-speaking pope from Syria, Sergius I (687–701) introduced in Rome another type of litany originally for private use, which included an invocation of saints and special devotion to the Holy Cross and to Christ as the Lamb of God, and consisting of only one intercession with the response, "We ask you to hear us."[75] Anciently, only classes of saints were invoked; individual names were added later.[76]

Eventually these two types of litanies combined, and the resulting form was in general use throughout the West in the later Middle Ages. It consisted of

1. an introductory Kyrie and invocations of the Persons of the Holy Trinity with the response "Have mercy on us" (*miserere nobis*);

2. the invocations of the saints with the response "Pray for us" (*ora pro nobis*);

---

[72]Robert F. Taft, "The Structural Analysis of Liturgical Units: An Essay in Methodology," *Beyond East and West: Essays in Liturgical Understanding* (Washington, DC: Pastoral Press, 1984), 154–56. See also John F. Baldovin, "Kyrie Eleison and the Entrance Rite of the Roman Eucharist," *Worship* 60 (July 1986):336.

[73]*Apostolic Constitutions* 8.6.

[74]*Egeria's Travels* 24.5–6.

[75]Shepherd, 54; Hatchett, 155.

[76]Reed, 626.

3. the deprecations (from *deprecari*, to avert by prayer) or supplications for deliverance with the response "Deliver us, Lord" (*libera nos domine*);

4. the obsecrations (from *obsecrare*, to ask on religious grounds) or appeals for deliverance by virtue of events in Christ's life, with the response "Deliver us, Lord" (*libera nos domine*);

5. the intercessions with the response "We ask you to hear us" (*te rogamus audi nos*);

6. invocations of the Lamb of God, the Kyrie, and the Our Father;

7. versicles and collect(s) concluded the prayer.

The Litany was used on April 25 and the Rogation Days and, usually in a shorter form, at the Easter Vigil before the blessing of the font, at ordinations, and at the dedication of churches. The Litany was sung in procession on Sundays and festivals before the high mass; during Lent it was said daily after the mid-morning office of Terce. Wednesday and Friday came to be associated with the Litany; the Litany was sung in procession after the little hour of None (noon) before Mass on Wednesday and Friday and in times of necessity and emergency it was used in procession on Wednesday and Friday. In Lutheran and Anglican use Wednesday and Friday continued to be regarded as litany days.

Luther had a deep love for the Litany. The threat of the Turks' advance to the gates of Vienna in 1528 led him to suggest in a pamphlet "The War against the Turks" (October 1528) the use of the Litany after the sermon or at Matins and Vespers "especially by the young." On February 13, 1529 he wrote to Nicholas Hausmann that the Litany was sung in Latin and German; he published music for the two litanies later that year.

The two litanies as Luther revised them are nearly the same; both closely follow the Roman Litany of the Saints. Luther, however, omitted the invocations of the saints as well as the intercessions for the pope and the departed, made the intercessions more specific and extended than in the Roman form, and simplified the music, especially for the responses. The music for the Latin Litany Corrected is derived from the traditional music of the Litany of the Saints; the music of the German Litany is original with Luther.[77] It proved to be popular and was almost universally associated with the Litany in Lutheran use through the publication of the *Common Service Book* (1917). The *Service Book and Hymnal* provided a less heavy and more attractive melody adapted from traditional Latin forms. The *Lutheran Book of Worship* has provided a melody composed by Gerhard M. Cartford.

Luther's Litanies were intended to be sung antiphonally by two choirs; the response was made to each petition, maintaining the momentum of the prayer.

---

[77] See *Luther's Works* 53:147–70.

His German Litany spread from Wittenberg and Magdeburg to Leipzig, Erfurt, Lübeck, Rostock, Austria, and Scandinavia. There was far less deviation from Luther's text of the Litany than there was from his Latin and German masses. The penitential character of the Litany was emphasized especially in southern Germany. Receiving it more as a musical composition than a congregational prayer, the church orders appointed it for Wednesday and Friday (sometimes Saturday) Vespers in place of the Magnificat; on Sundays in towns and villages it was used before the service, or after the Epistle, or after the sermon when there were no communicants.

In 1544 Thomas Cranmer published his English Litany based on the Sarum litany, Luther's revision,[78] and the litany in the Liturgy of St. John Chrysostom. This work was the beginning of his liturgical reform, the beginning of the *Book of Common Prayer*. Notable is the change in the rhythm of the Litany which Cranmer effected by grouping several suffrages under one response.

The "Church Litany" and "The Litany of the Life, Passion, and Death of Jesus Christ" are in regular use among the Moravians. Litany hymns have been popular with the Moravians and with the Oxford Movement in England. Private litanies have abounded in books of devotion.

In the Roman Catholic Church the popularity of the litany form grew so great that in the seventeenth century there were at least eighty different litanies in use. Clement VIII in 1601 forbade the use of all but two, the Litany of the Saints and the Litany of Loreto. In the nineteenth and twentieth centuries the number has expanded again. The Litany of the Saints was revised in 1969 and appears in three forms: the long form for solemn intercessions at any time; a shorter form for use at ordinations, dedications of churches, and the Easter Vigil; and a short form for use at the commendation of the dying.

In the *Lutheran Book of Worship*, although revised to include present-day concerns, the Litany parallels more closely than did the form in the *Service Book and Hymnal* Luther's forms, which themselves were conservative renderings of the Litany of the Saints. The Litany also follows earlier Lutheran forms in English and, following Cranmer's style, groups petitions together followed by a single response. Luther, like the Litany of the Saints which he adapted, requires a response after each petition.

LITANY IN DETAIL

Lucas Lossius, the church musician and friend of Melanchthon, called the Litany an exposition of the Lord's Prayer (*explicatio orationis dominicae*),[79] and the parallel is evident, for both move from adoration

---

[78] See Henry E. Jacobs, *The Lutheran Movement in England*, rev. ed. (Philadelphia: Frederick, 1894), 230ff. See also E. C. Ratcliff, "The Choir Offices: The Litany," in *Liturgy and Worship*, ed. W. K. Lowther Clarke (London: SPCK, 1932), 282–87.

[79] Reed, 623.

through petitions for various needs of the community to a concluding doxology.[80] The parallel with the classic collect form is also apparent.

The introductory portion, like the address of the collect, names the one to whom the prayer is offered. In the *Lutheran Book of Worship* the Kyrie is in a form closer to the original Greek, *Kyrie eleison.* The verse "O Christ, hear us," serves as a reminder that the Litany is a prayer primarily addressed to God the Son. The invocations of the persons of the Holy Trinity remain as in earlier forms, naming the fullness of God which Christians have come to know.

The transition to the body of the prayer is simplified so that the response to the repeated "Be gracious to us" is also repeated, making a somewhat repetitious pair of verses. The original has as the response "Spare us, good Lord" and "Help us, good Lord."

The deprecations have been gathered into three groups: deliverance from the work of Satin (sin, evil, error, cunning, unprepared death); deliverance from the violence of political quarrels and injustice; deliverance from the violence of nature. The final line asks deliverance from everlasting death — the worst ill that can befall us, who may be required to endure all the rest of the evils against which we pray.

In the first group of petitions, the death we pray to be delivered from is no longer described, as it was in earlier forms of the Litany, as "sudden" (many now in fact hope and pray for a swift death in view of the modern ability to prolong the process of dying) but more accurately as "unprepared and evil." The Latin litany had *ad subitanea et improvisa morte*, from a sudden and unprepared death, "unprepared" explaining why a "sudden" death would be thought of as evil.[81]

In the second group of petitions, the prayer is no longer against rebellion, for that may be the last recourse of an oppressed people, but is against treason and against corrupt and unjust government which may drive the people to understandable and justifiable rebellion. The third group adds prayers against drought and earthquake.

The obsecrations, like the antecedent reason in the classic collect, lay the foundation for a confident appeal for divine aid. Liturgical theology understands every act of Christ's life to have "its appropriate saving energy."[82] Again, there are three groups of petitions: those dealing with the mystery (not in the sense of a marvel but in the theological sense

---

[80]See the devotional reflections by Arthur Carl Piepkorn, "Let Us Pray for the Church," *Response* 6:2 (St. Michael and All Angels, 1964):69–72; "Let Us Pray for the State," *Response* 6:3 (Epiphany, 1965):121–25; "Good Lord, Deliver us!...Help Us, Good Lord!" *Response* 7:1 (Pentecost, 1965):22–28; "Let Us Pray for Our Fellow-Pilgrims," *Response* 7:3 (Epiphany, 1966):134–37. See also Charles Gore, *Reflections on the Litany* (London: Mowbray, 1932).

[81]See Elie Wiesel, *The Gates of the Forest*, trans. Frances Frenaye (New York: Schocken, 1982), 24: Gregor's father says, "Don't let death take you by surprise"; and p. 134: "He was sure that his father died without warning, that death had not left him time to face it and fight it."

[82]William Bright in John Henry Blunt, *The Annotated Book of Common Prayer* (London: Rivingtons, 1866), 51.

of a sacramental sign) of Christ's coming into the world; those dealing with his life of struggle, suffering, and death; and those dealing with the mystery of his new life, the three-fold Easter mystery of resurrection-ascension-sending of the Spirit. The obsecrations in the Litany in the *Lutheran Book of Worship* parallel those in previous forms of the Litany.

The supplications or prayers for ourselves are brief, revealing "the broad and unselfish spirit of the Litany itself."[83] The petitions are those of previous Lutheran versions of the Litany; only the petition for deliverance in the day of judgment and the last line "we sinners, ask you to hear us" were in the pre-Reformation forms.

The intercessions are largely Luther's own creation. The first section prays for the welfare, peace, and unity of the church. The vigorous phrase "to beat down Satin under our feet" is from Romans 16:20 and alludes also to the eucharistic prayer of Hippolytus (Min. Ed., pp. 226, 262, 298: Prayer IV). The second section prays for the work of the church. The third section prays for civil justice and peace and recalls 2 Timothy 2:2. The fourth section prays for specific classes of people, and adds to those listed in previous versions of the Litany families and friends of the sick, families in discord, the unemployed and needy, all who are in prison (not only those innocently imprisoned), and widowers (as well as widows). The fifth section includes those things mentioned in earlier versions, but it asks not that our enemies' hearts be turned (as if they were the ones in the wrong) but that we be reconciled with them (for both they and we may be at fault). It asks not simply that we receive the fruits of the earth but that we wisely use them with the treasures of the sea and air, reflecting modern environmental awareness.

The conclusion of the Litany, comparable to the concluding doxology of the collects, reverses the order of the introduction. The Son of God is named again as the one to whom the prayer has been addressed (the verse is similar to the "Be gracious to us" of the beginning), and a three-fold invocation of the Lamb of God, comparable to the invocation of the Holy Trinity at the beginning, is sung. "O Christ, hear us" follows, and the Litany concludes as it began, with the Kyrie. Thus the rounded form of the Litany of the Saints and of Luther's revisions, which was truncated as repetitious[84] in the *Service Book and Hymnal*, has been restored.

In its earlier Lutheran and in its Anglican forms the Litany concludes with the Lord's Prayer and a collect. Luther's Latin Litany had five collects, each introduced by a versicle; his German Litany had six versicles and four collects. The versicles and collects were drawn from the old litany forms.[85] The *Church Book* (followed by the *Common Ser-*

---

[83] Reed, 632.

[84] Reed, 633.

[85] See Paul Zeller Strodach in the Philadelphia Edition of the *Works of Martin Luther*, vol. 6 (Philadelphia: Muhlenberg Press, 1932):319ff.; Paul Althaus, *Sur Einführung in die Quellengeschichte der kirchlichen Kollekten in den lutherischen Agenden des 16. Jahrhunderts* (Leipzig: Edelmann, 1919), 12.

vice Book and the *Service Book and Hymnal*) retained these verses and collects, although in a different order, and added the collect for peace from Vespers.[86]

The use of a prayer to conclude the litany is appropriate and is to be connected with the use of the Prayer of the Day as a prayer to conclude the Kyrie litany in the Eucharist (when the Hymn of Praise is omitted), and the use of the Collect for peace to conclude the litany in Evening Prayer.

The following table compares the texts of the Roman, Lutheran, and Anglican litanies. The pre-Reformation texts have been assembled in one column based on the work of Paul G. Drews, *Beiträge zu Luthers liturgischen Reformen* (Tübingen: Mohr, 1910), pp. 24–32, supplemented by Paul Zeller Strodach in the Philadelphia Edition of *The Works of Martin Luther*, vol. VI, pp. 249–60. Luther's principal source was the breviary of the Augustinian Eremites; material from Luther's other contemporary sources is indicated as follows: that from the Magdeburg Breviary as supplied by Drews is marked (M.B.), that from the Augsburg Breviary, a conventual use, as supplied by Strodach is marked (A.B.). The table is originally the work of Luther Reed,[87] revised to suit the *Lutheran Book of Worship* and the 1979 *Book of Common Prayer*.

Table I
Texts of the Roman, Lutheran, and Anglican Litanies

Pre-Reformation *Breviary Augustinian Eremites*	Luther's *Latina Litania Correcta*	Luther's *Deutsche Litanei*	*Lutheran Book of Worship*	*American Book of Common Prayer*
Kyrieleison	Kyrie *Eleison*	Kyrie *Eleison*	Lord, have mercy. *Lord, have mercy*	
Christe eleyson	Christe *Eleison*	Christe *Eleison*	Christ, have mercy. *Christ, have mercy*	
Kyrie Eleison (A.B.)	Kyrie *Eleison*	Kyrie *Eleison*	Lord, have mercy. *Lord, have mercy*	
Christe audi nos *Christe exaudi nos*	Christe *Exaudi nos*	Christe *Erhöre uns*	O Christ, hear us. *In mercy hear us.*	
Pater de coelis deus *miserere nobis*	Pater de coelis deus *Miserere nobis*	Her Got vater ym himmel *Erbarm dich vber vns*	God, the Father in heaven, *have mercy on us.*	O God, the Father, Creator of heaven and earth, *Have mercy upon us*

[86] The first collect in the *Church Book* (the third in Luther's litanies) is from the Leonine sacramentary; the second (the second in Luther's Latin Litany, the fourth in his German Litany) is from the Gelasian sacramentary; the third (the first in Luther's litanies) is from the Bamberg and Sarum Missals; the fourth (the fourth in Luther's Latin Litany, the third in his German Litany) is the collect for the Fourth Sunday after the Epiphany in the Roman Missal of Luther's time and the church orders also and is from the Gregorian sacramentary; the fifth is the fifth in Luther's Latin Litany.

[87] Reed, 734–50.

Table I (continued)

Pre-Reformation Breviary Augustinian Eremites	Luther's Latina Litania Correcta	Luther's Deutsche Litanei	Lutheran Book of Worship	American Book of Common Prayer
Fili redemptor mundi deus *miserere nobis*	Fili redemptor mundi deus *Miserere nobis*	Her Got son der welt heiland *Erbarm dich vber vns*	God, the Son, Redeemer of the world, *have mercy on us.*	O God the Son, Redeemer of the world, *Have mercy upon us.*
Spiritus sancte deus *miserere nobis*	Spiritus sancte deus *Miserere nobis*	Herr Gott heiliger geist *Erbarm dich vber vns*	God, the Holy Spirit, *have mercy on us.*	O God the Holy Ghost, Sanctifier of the faithful. *Have mercy upon us.*
Sancta trinitas unus Deus *miserere nobis* (A.B.) (Nomina Sanctorum et Sanctarum)			Holy Trinity, one God, *have mercy on us.*	O holy, blessed, and glorious Trinity, one God, *Have mercy upon us.*
Propitius esto: *parce nobis domine* Propitius esto *Exaudi nos domine* A peccatis nostris: *libera nos domine* (M.B.) (*Repeated after each prex.*)	Propitius esto: *parce nobis domine* Propitius esto: *Libera nos domine* (*Repeated after each prex.*)	Sey uns gnedig *Verschon vnser lieber herre Got* Sey vns gnedig: *hilff vns lieber Herre Gott*	Be gracious to us. *Spare us, good Lord.* Be gracious to us. *Spare us, good Lord.*	Remember not, Lord Christ, our offenses, nor the offenses of our forefathers; neither reward us according to our sins. Spare us, good Lord, spare thy people, whom thou hast redeemed with thy most precious blood, and by thy mercy preserve us for ever. *Spare us, good Lord.*
Ab omni malo	Ab omni peccato:	Für allen sünden *Behüt vns lieber Herre Gott* (*After each prex.*)	From all sin, from all error, from all evil; from the cunning assaults of the devil;	From all evil and wickedness; from sin; from the crafts and assaults of the devil; and from everlasting damnation, *Good Lord, deliver us.*
Ab omni peccato	Ab omni errore	Für allem yrsal		
Ab ira tua (*See below*)	Ab omni malo Ab insidiis diaboli	Für allem vbel Für des teuffels trug vnd list		
Ab subitanea et improvisa morte Ab insidiis diaboli	Ab subitanea et improvisa morte (*See above*)	Für bösem schnellen tod (*See above*)	from an unprepared and evil death: *Good Lord, deliver us.*	(*See below*)
				From all blindness of heart; from pride, vainglory, and hypocrisy; from envy, hatred, and malice; and from all want of charity, *Good Lord, deliver us.*
(*See below*)				From all inordinate and sinful affec- tions; and from all the deceits of the world, the flesh, and the devil, *Good Lord, deliver us.*

	(*See below*)	(*See below*)	(*See below*)	From all false doctrine, heresy, and schism; from hardness of heart, and contempt of thy Word and commandment, *Good Lord, deliver us.*
	(*See below*)	(*See below*)	From war, bloodshed, and violence; from corrupt and unjust government; from sedition and treason: *Good Lord, deliver us.*	(*See below*)
	A peste et fame	Für pestilentz vnd tewer zeit	From epidemic, drought, and famine; from fire and flood, earth quake, lightning and storm; and from everlasting death: *Good Lord, deliver us.*	From lightning and tempest; from earthquake, fire and flood; from plague, pestilence, and famine. *Good Lord, deliver us.*
	A bello et caede	Für krieg vnd blut	(*See above*)	From all oppression, conspiracy, and rebellion; from violence, battle, and murder; and from dying suddenly and unprepared, *Good Lord, deliver us.*
	(*See above*)	(*See above*)		
Ab ira et odio et omni mala voluntate A spiritu fornicatoris				(*See above*)
	A seditione et simultate	Für auffrhur vnd zwitracht	(*See above*)	(*See above*)
A fulgure et tempestate	A fulgure et tempestatibus	Für hagel vnd vngewitter	(*See above*)	(*See above*)
A morte perpetua	A morte perpetua	Für dem ewigen Tod	(*See above*)	(*See above*)
Ab omni malo (M.B.)	(*See above*)	(*See above*)	(*See above*)	(*See above*)
Per mysterium sanctae incarnationis tuae	Per mysterium sanctae incarnationis tuae		By the mystery of your incarnation;	By the mystery of thy holy Incarnation;
Per adventum tuum				
Per nativitatem tuam	Per sanctam nativitatem tuam	Durch dein heilig geburt	by your holy birth: *Help us, good Lord.*	by the holy Nativity
				and submission to the Law;
Per baptismum et sanctum jejunium tuum	Per baptismum, jejunium et tentationes tuas		By your baptism, fasting, and temptation;	by thy Baptism, Fasting, and Temptation, *Good Lord, deliver us.*
	Per agoniam et sudorem tuum sanguineum	Durch dein todkampff vnd blutigen schweiss	by your agony and bloody sweat;	By thine Agony and Bloody Sweat;
Per crucem et passionem tuam	Per crucem et passionem tuam	Durch dein Creutze	by your cross and suffering;	by thy Cross and Passion;
Per mortem et sepulturam tuam	Per mortem et sepulturam tuam	vnd tod	by your death and burial: *Help us, good Lord.*	by thy precious Death and Burial;

Table I (continued)

Pre-Reformation Breviary Augustinian Eremites	Luther's Latina Litania Correcta	Luther's Deutsche Litanei	Lutheran Book of Worship	American Book of Common Prayer
Per sanctam resurrectionem tuam	Per resurrectionem	Durch dein heiliges aufferstehn	By your resurrection	by thy glorious Resurrection
Per admirabilem ascensionem tuam	et ascensionem tuam	und hymelfart	and ascension;	and Ascension;
Per adventum spiritus sancti paracliti	Per adventum spiritus sancti paracliti		by the gift of the Holy Spirit; *Help us, good Lord.*	and by the Coming of the Holy Ghost *Good Lord, deliver us.*
	In omni tempore tribulationis nostrae		In all time of our tribulation;	In all time of our tribulation;
	In omni tempore facilitatis nostrae		in all time of our prosperity;	in all time of our prosperity;
	In hora mortis	In vnser letzten stund	in the hour of death;	in the hour of death,
In die judicii	In die judicii	Am jüngsten gericht	and in the day of judgment: *Save us, good Lord.*	and in the day of judgment, *Good Lord, deliver us.*
Peccatores *te rogamus audi nos*	Peccatores *te rogamus audi nos*	Wir armen sünder bitten *Du wollest vns hören lieber herre Gott*	Though unworthy, we implore you *to hear us, Lord our God.*	We sinners do beseech thee to hear us, O Lord God;
(Te rogamus, etc. *follows each prex*)	(Te rogamus, etc. *follows each prex*)			
Ut nobis parcas				
Ut nobis indulgeas				
Ut ad veram poenitentiam nos perducere digneris				
Ut dominum apostolicum et omnes ecclesiasticos ordines in sancta religione conservare digneris....				
Ut inimicos sanctae ecclesiae humiliare digneris				
Ut ecclesiam tuam sanctam regere et conservare digneris	Ut ecclesiam tuam sanctam catholicam regere et gubernare digneris	Vnd deine heilige Christliche Kirche regieren und füren	To rule and govern your holy catholic Church;	and that it may please thee to rule and govern thy holy Church Universal in the right way, *We beseech thee to hear us, good Lord.*
	Ut cunctos Episcopos, Pastores et ministros ecclesiae in sancto verbo et sancta vita servare digneris	Alle bischoff, pfarrherr, vnd kirchendiener ynn heilsamen wort vnd heiligen leben behalten	to guide all servants to your Church in the love of your Word and in holiness of life;	That it may please thee to illumine all bishops, priests, and deacons, with true knowledge and understanding of thy Word; and that both by their preaching and living, they may set

				it forth, and show it accordingly, *We beseech thee to hear us, good Lord.*
(See below)	*(See below)*	*(See below)*	*(See below)*	That it may please thee to bless and keep all thy people, *We beseech thee to hear us, good Lord.*
Ut sectas et omnia scandala tollere digneris	Allen rotten und ergernissen wehren	to put an end to all schisms and causes of offense to those who would believe;	*(See above)*	
Ut errantes et seductos reducere in viam veritatis digneris	All yrrigen vnd verfürten wider bringen	and to bring into the way of truth all who have gone astray: *We implore you to hear us, good Lord.*	*(See below)*	
Ut Satanam sub pedibus nostris conterere digneris	Den Satan vnter unser füsze treten	To beat down Satan under our feet;	*(See below)*	
Ut operarios fideles in messem tuam mittere digneris	Trew arbeiter ynn deine erndte senden	to send faithful workers into your harvest;	That it may please thee to send forth laborers into thy harvest, and to draw all mankind into thy kingdom, *We beseech thee to hear us, good Lord.*	
Ut incrementum verbi et fructum spiritus cunctis audientibus donare digneris	Deinen geist vnd krafft zum wort geben	to accompany your Word with your Spirit and power;	That it may please thee to give to all people increase of grace to hear and receive thy Word, and to bring forth the fruits of the Spirit, *We beseech thee to hear us, good Lord.*	
Ut lapsos erigere et stantes confortare digneris		to raise up those who fall and to strengthen those who stand;	*(See below)*	
Ut pusillanimes et tentatos consolari et adiuvare digneris	Allen betrübten vnd blöden helffen vnd trösten	and to comfort and help the fainthearted and the distressed: *We implore you to hear us, good Lord.*	*(See below)*	
(See above)	*(See above)*	*(See above)*		That it may please thee to bring into the way of truth all such as have erred, and are deceived, *We beseech thee to hear us, good Lord.* That it may please thee to give us a heart to love and fear thee, and diligently to live after thy commandments, *We beseech thee to hear us, good Lord.*
(See below)	*(See below)*	*(See below)*	*(See below)*	That it may please thee so to rule the hearts of thy servants, the President of the United States

Table I (continued)

Pre-Reformation Breviary Augustinian Eremites	Luther's Latina Litania Correcta	Luther's Deutsche Litanei	Lutheran Book of Worship	American Book of Common Prayer
				(*or* of this nation), and all others in authority, that they may do justice, and love mercy, and walk in the ways of truth, *We beseech thee to hear us, good Lord.*
	(*See above*)	(*See above*)	(*See above*)	That it may please thee to make wars to cease in all the world;
Ut regibus et principibus christianis pacem et veram concordiam largiri (donare) digneris	Ut regibus et principibus cunctis pacem et concordiam donare digneris	Allen königen vnd fürsten frid vnd eintracht geben	To give to all nations justice and peace;	to give to all nations unity, peace, and concord;
				and to bestow freedom upon all peoples, *We beseech thee to hear us, good Lord.*
			to preserve our country from discord and strife;	
	Ut Caesari nostro perpetuam victoriam contra hostes suos donare digneris	Unsern Kaiser stet sieg widder seine feinde gönnen		
Ut antistitem nostrum cum omnibus sibi commissis in sancta (vera) religione conservare digneris (M.B.)	Ut principem nostrum cum suis praesidibus dirigere et tueri digneris	Unsern Landherrn mit allen seinen gewaltigen leiten und schützen	to direct and guard those who have civil authority;	(*See above*)
Ut cuncto populo christiano pacem et unitatem largiri digneris				
Ut nos metipsos in tuo sancto servitio confortare et conservare digneris				
Ut cunctum populum christianum percioso sanguine tuo redemptum conservare digneris (M.B.)				
Ut mentes nostras ad coelestia desideria erigas				
Ut omnibus benefactoribus nostris sempiterna bona retribuas				
Ut animas nostras fratrum propinquorum et benefactorum				

nostrorum ab aeterna damnatione eripias				
	Ut magistratum et plebem nostram benedicere et custodire digneris	Vnsern Rat vnd gemeine segnen und behüten	and to bless and guide all our people: *We implore you to hear us, good Lord.*	(*See above*)
	Ut afflictos et periclitantes respicere et salvare digneris (*See below*)	Allen, so yn not vnd far sind, mit hülff erscheinen (*See below*)	To behold and help all who are in danger, need, or tribulation; (*See below*)	(*See below*)
				That it may please thee to show thy pity upon all prisoners and captives, the homeless and the hungry, and all who are desolate and oppressed, *We beseech thee to hear us, good Lord.*
(*See below*)	(*See below*)	(*See below*)	(*See below*)	That it may please thee to give and preserve to our use the bountiful fruits of the earth, so that in due time all may enjoy them, *We beseech thee to hear, us good Lord.*
				That it may please thee to inspire us, in our several callings, to do the work which thou givest us to do with singleness of heart as thy servants, and for the common good, *We beseech thee to hear us, good Lord.*
			to protect and guide all who travel;	That it may please thee to preserve all who are in danger by reason to their labor or of their travel, *We beseech thee to hear us, good Lord.*
	Ut praegnantibus et lactentibus felicem partum et incrementum largiri digneris	Allen schwangern vnd seugern, fröliche frücht vnd gedeyen geben	to preserve and provide for all women in childbirth;	That it may please thee to preserve, and provide for, all women in childbirth;
	Ut infantes	Alle kinder	to watch over children and to guide the young;	young children
	et aegrotos fovere et custodire digneris	vnd kranken pflegen vnd warten	to heal the sick and to strengthen their families and friends; (*See below*)	(*See below*)
			to bring reconciliation to families in discord;	and orphans, the widowed, and all whose homes are broken or torn by strife, *We beseech thee to hear us, good Lord.*

Table I (continued)

Pre-Reformation Breviary Augustinian Eremites	Luther's Latina Litania Correcta	Luther's Deutsche Litanei	Lutheran Book of Worship	American Book of Common Prayer
			to provide for the unemployed and for all in need;	(See below)
	Ut captivos liberare digneris	Alle gefangene los vnd ledig lassen	to be merciful to all who are imprisoned;	(See above)
	Ut pupillos et viduas protegere et providere digneris	Alle witwen vnd waisen verteydigen vnd versorgen	to support, comfort, and guide all orphans, widowers, and widows;	(See above)
	(See above)		(See above)	That it may please thee to visit the lonely; to strengthen all who suffer in mind, body, and spirit; and to comfort with thy presence those who are failing and infirm, *We beseech thee to hear us, good Lord.*
	(See above)		(See above)	That it may please thee to support, help, and comfort all who are in danger, necessity, and tribulation, *We beseech thee to hear us, good Lord.*
	Ut cunctis hominibus miserere digneris	Aller menschen dich erbarmen	and to have mercy on all your people: *We implore you to hear us, good Lord.*	That it may please thee to have mercy upon all mankind, *We beseech thee hear us, good Lord.*
				That it may please thee to give us true repentance; to forgive us all our sins, negligences, and ignorances; and to endue us with the grace of the Holy Spirit to amend our lives according to thy holy Word, *We beseech thee to hear us, good Lord.*
	Ut hostibus, persecutoribus, et calumniatoribus nostris ignoscere et eos convertere digneris	Unsern feinden, verfolgern vnd lestern vergeben vnd sie bekeren	To forgive our enemies, persecutors, and slanderers, and to reconcile us to them;	That it may please thee to forgive our enemies, persecutors, and slanderers, and to turn their hearts, *We beseech thee to hear us, good Lord.*
Ut fructus terrae dare et conservare digneris	Ut fruges terrae dare et conservare digneris	Die frücht auff dem lande geben und bewaren	to help us use wisely the fruits and treasures of the earth, the sea, and the air;	(See above)

(*See above*)	(*See above*)	(*See above*)	That it may please thee to strengthen such as do stand; to comfort and help the weak-hearted; to raise up those who fall; and finally to beat down Satan under our feet, *We beseech thee to hear us, good Lord.*	
Ut omnibus fidelibus defunctis requiem aeternam donare digneris			That it may please thee to grant to all the faithful departed eternal life and peace, *We beseech thee to hear us, good Lord.*	
			That it may please thee to grant that, in the fellowship of [_____ and] all the saints, we may attain to thy heavenly kingdom, *We beseech thee to hear us, good Lord.*	
Ut nos exaudire digneris	Ut nos exaudire digneris	·Vnd vns gnediglich erhören	and graciously to hear our prayers: *We implore you to hear us, good Lord.*	
Fili dei *Te rogamus audi nos*	Fili dei *Te rogamus audi nos*	O Jhesu Christ Gottes son *Erhöre vns lieber herre gott*	Lord Jesus Christ, Son of God, *We implore you to hear us.*	Son of God, we beseech thee to hear us. *Son of God, we beseech thee to hear us.*
Agnus dei qui tollis peccata mundi *parce nobis domine* (or) *miserere nobis* (M.B.)	Agne dei qui tollis peccata mundi *miserere nobis*	O du Gottes lam das der welt sünde tregt *Erbarm dich vber vns*	Lamb of God, you take away the sin of the world; *have mercy on us.*	O Lamb of God that takest away the sins of the world, *Have mercy upon us.*
Agnus dei qui tollis peccata mundi *parce nobis domine* (or) *miserere nobis* (M.B.)	Agne dei qui tollis peccata mundi *miserere nobis*	O du Gottes lam das der welt sünde tregt *Erbarm dich vber vns*	Lamb of God, you take away the sin of the world; *have mercy on us.*	O Lamb of God that takest away the sins of the world, *Have mercy upon us.*
Agnus dei qui tollis peccata mundi *miserere nobis (or) dona nobis pacem* (M.B.)	Agne dei qui tollis peccata mundi *da nobis pacem*	O du Gottes lam das der welt sünde tregt *Verley vns steten frid*	Lamb of God, you take away the sin of the world; *give us peace. Amen.*	O Lamb of God that takest away the sins of the world, *Grant us thy peace.*
Christe audi nos *Christe exaudi nos*	Christe *exaudi nos*	Christe *Erhöre vns*	O Christ, hear us. *In mercy hear us,*	O Christ, hear us. *O Christ, hear us.*
Kyrieleyson	Kyrie *eleison*	Kyrie *eleison*	Lord, have mercy. *Lord, have mercy.*	Lord, have mercy upon us. or Kyrie eleison
Christeleison	Christe *eleison*	Christe *eleison*	Christ, have mercy. *Christ, have mercy*	*Christ, have mercy upon us,* or *Christe eleison*
Kyrieleison	(*Both choirs together:*) Kyrie eleison. Amen.	(*Both choirs together:*) Kyrie eleison, Amen.	Lord, have mercy. *Lord, have mercy.*	Lord, have mercy upon us. or Kyrie eleison
Pater noster	Pater noster			[Our Father]

THE ATHANASIAN CREED
(Ministers Edition, pp. 118–20)

Parallel Texts

Episcopal   Historical Documents of the Church: Quicunque Vult commonly called the Creed of Saint Athanasius, *Book of Common Prayer*, pp. 864–65

Lutheran   *The Lutheran Hymnal* (1941), p. 53
Church Book (1891), p. 266

Purpose

The Athanasian Creed is, with the Nicene and Apostles' creeds, one of the three ecumenical creeds of Western Christianity. In Lutheran practice its liturgical use has been associated with Trinity Sunday on which it is used as part of the psalmody at Matins.[88]

Characteristics

The Athanasian Creed is a profession of the Christian faith in forty rhythmical sentences, dealing with the Holy Trinity and the Incarnation. If differs from the Nicene and the Apostles' creeds in its inclusion of anathemas of those who hold a contrary view. This creed, called the Quicunque Vult from its opening words in Latin, is not recognized as a standard of faith in the East, in part because of its inclusion of a *filioque* clause ("the Spirit . . . is proceeding from the Father and the Son"), although with that clause removed it has been used in the Russian Church since the seventeenth century.

Development of the Symbol

The Quicunque Vult, composed in Latin, originated probably in southern Gaul in the region of Lerins, probably after 435.[89] The first certain witness to its existence is a sermon by Caesarius of Arles (ca. 470–542), although the first manuscripts in which it occurs are from the seventh and eighth centuries.

Originally private and non-liturgical, the creed found its way into the Western liturgy, no doubt in part because of the creed's insistence on the worship of, rather than simply the belief in, the Holy Trinity. By the ninth century it was used in Germany on Sundays after the sermon. Elsewhere it was used at Prime on Sundays, sometimes treated as a psalm with an antiphon and Gloria Patri. Scholastics of the thirteenth

---

[88] *The Lutheran Hymnal* (1941) General Rubrics allowed that "On Trinity Sunday, at Matins, the Athanasian Creed may be used instead of the Psalmody" (p. 4); the text of the creed was given on page 53. This usage was encouraged by Arthur Carl Piepkorn, editor of the Lutheran Liturgy edition of the liturgical calendar published annually by the Ashby Company of Erie, Pennsylvania. The present editor, Hans Boehringer, suggests the use of the Athanasian Creed in place of the Nicene Creed at the Holy Communion on Trinity Sunday and at Morning Prayer after the final psalm.

[89] See J. N. D. Kelly, *The Athanasian Creed* (New York: Harper & Row, 1964), 112.

century put it on a plane with the Nicene and Apostles' creeds, and this tradition was preserved in the Lutheran *Book of Concord* in which it is one of the three catholic or ecumenical creeds. (Earlier Luther had written a pamphlet on *The Three Symbols or Creeds of the Christian Faith*, 1538, by which he meant the Apostles' Creed, the Athanasian Creed, and the Te Deum laudamus; he added the Nicene Creed as a kind of afterthought at the end.)[90]

In the Roman Breviary the Athanasian Creed was used at Prime on most Sundays until Pius X (1903–1914) limited its use to the Sundays after the Epiphany and after Pentecost. After the revision of the rubrics ordered in 1955, it was used only on Trinity Sunday. With the revision of the Divine Office in 1970 in which Prime was suppressed, the liturgical use of the Athanasian Creed in the Roman rite ceased.

In the 1549 *Book of Common Prayer* the Athanasian Creed was printed with the Gloria Patri for use after the Benedictus (apparently as a second canticle) on Christmas, the Epiphany, Easter Day, Ascension, Pentecost, and Trinity Sunday. The 1552 revision extended its use to seven other holy days so that it would be used approximately monthly.[91] The 1662 Prayer Book directed that it replace the Apostles' Creed on these thirteen days.

In North America, the Athanasian Creed was included in *The Lutheran Hymnal* (1941), reflecting German use.

The translation of the Quicunque Vult in the *Lutheran Book of Worship* is by Ralph Quere.

---

[90] *Luther's Works* 34:197–229.

[91] The other days were St. Matthias, St. John the Baptist, St. James, St. Bartholomew, St. Matthew, SS. Simon and Jude, St. Andrew. See E. C. Ratcliff, "The Choir Offices: The Athanasian Creed," in *Liturgy and Worship*, ed. W. K. Lowther Clarke (London: SPCK, 1932), 280–82.

8

THE SERVICE OF THE WORD

Ministers Edition, pp. 313–17, 32–33

Parallel Rites

Lutheran

The Lutheran Hymnary (1913).
The Concordia I Hymnal (1932).
The Concordia II Hymnal (1933).
A Service of Prayer and Preaching I, II, III, *Worship Supplement* authorized by the Commission on Worship of the Lutheran Church–Missouri Synod and the Synod of Evangelical Lutheran Churches, 1969.
Contemporary Worship 5: Services of the Word (for Advent, Christmas and Epiphany, Lent, Easter, General I, General II), 1972.

Church of
South India

Third Order of Service, *Book of Common Worship* (1963), pp. 93–99. The first order is ante-communion; the second is Morning and Evening Prayer.

Presbyterian

The Order of Public Worship (five orders for morning and five orders for evening), the *Book of Common Order* of the Church of Scotland (1940), pp. 11–74.

World
Council
of Churches

Venite Adoremus II. Geneva: World Student Christian Federation, n.d. [1968?], pp. 1–57.

There is no parallel service in the Roman Catholic liturgy, the *Book of Common Prayer*, or the Presbyterian *Worshipbook* (1972). For those Sundays when the Lord's Supper is not celebrated the *Worshipbook* provides ante-communion.

Purpose

The Service of the Word emphasizes the reading and exposition of Scripture and is intended for use at those times when the celebration of the Holy Communion is inappropriate or not desirable. Ante-communion, the usual Lutheran alternative to the Holy Communion, truncates the fullness of the eucharistic liturgy; Morning Prayer, the usual Anglican alternative to the Holy Communion, is not in its historic form designed to include preaching (and the gathering of an offering).

Characteristics

The Service of the Word has similarities to the synagogue service and to the liturgy of the word as it developed in Christianity as part of the Eucharist and in another form as the daily office, but it is a new creation drafted without reference to any precedents. Its similarities to ancient forms of a liturgy of the word are due not to conscious imitation but to the natural logic of such a service and what is to be included in it and in what order.

By its use of the Apostles' Creed, the Service of the Word has a certain baptismal emphasis which distinguishes it from the Holy Communion. Moreover, like Morning Prayer and unlike the Holy Communion, the Service of the Word does not require an ordained minister for the leadership of the services.

The celebration of the Eucharist requires a diversity of liturgical ministers: presiding minister, assisting ministers, cantor, readers, choir, congregation. The preaching service, however, requires only a preacher and a congregation, assisted perhaps, but not necessarily, by a choir. There are no choir elements in the Service of the Word as there are in the Holy Communion (proper verse, proper offertory). The function of the choir in the Service of the Word is entirely auxiliary; in the Holy Communion it is virtually required.

The Service of the Word centers around the pulpit and lectern; the altar need not be used at all. In the Holy Communion, on the other hand, the locus is the nave and the pulpit and the altar, for the Holy Communion employs dramatic, symbolic, and necessary movement. The Service of the Word requires none.

The Service of the Word makes only limited use of the church year. Apart from the opening dialogue and the Prayer of the Day, it has no proper. In the Holy Communion, however, the polarity between ordinary and proper is constitutive of the celebration.[1]

The Service of the Word, like all preaching services, gravitates toward speaking, unlike the Holy Communion which is in the usual practice a sung service. In the Service of the Word the only elements which are sung are the two hymns, the two canticles, and the "psalm, hymn, or anthem" between the lessons.

Background

Hebrew religion as a religion of revelation leaned heavily on the reading of the sacred books which recorded God's mighty acts of self-disclosure

---

[1] This whole series of contrasts between preaching services and the Holy Communion is drawn from Eberhard Weisman, "Der Predigtgottesdienst und die verwandten Formen," *Leiturgia* III (Kassel: Johannes Stauda, 1956):3–4.

and of deliverance of his people. The daily devotion of every pious Jew included the *Shema*, "The Prayer" (*Tefillah*), and the orderly and continuous meditation of the Word of God. Little is known in detail about the synagogue liturgy of Jesus' time, but the few descriptions that are available (from later centuries) indicate that the Sabbath service opened with psalm verses and the weekday service with a salutation, an exhortation to prayer, and praise of God the creator of all things. Second, there was a prominent feature of Jewish worship then and now, the *Shema*, a profession of faith from Deuteronomy 6:4–9; 11:13–21; and Numbers 15:37–41. The nucleus of the synagogue service was the reading of the Scripture,[2] preceded and followed by several prayers of praise (*berakah*). There were two readings, the first from the Law (Torah) according to a *lectio continua* pattern, the second from the Prophets, usually chosen at will.[3] A sermon was included (see Acts 4:16–20; 12:15ff.), sometimes after the Prophetic reading but usually after the first reading. There was a prayer, principally the *Tefillah*, often called the Eighteen Benedictions.[4] Songs probably were a part of the service, but their place in the liturgy is not known.[5]

By the time of Justin Martyr (d. ca. 165), the outline of the liturgy of the Lord's Day is clear:

The memoirs of the apostles or the writings of the prophets are read as long as time allows.

When the lector has finished, the president addresses us and exhorts us to imitate the splendid things we have heard.

Then we all stand and pray.[6]

The eucharistic breaking of bread follows. As the centuries passed, however, preaching began to move out of the eucharistic setting so that every mass did not invariably include a sermon. Parish priests, trained primarily to say mass, seldom preached, and in the Middle Ages preaching was done primarily by monks, many of whom, like Bernard of Clairvaux, became remarkably popular itinerant preachers who would deliver a series of sermons in a parish church in the manner of the preaching mission of recent times.[7]

In sixth-century Gaul, vernacular preaching services, freer in form than the Eucharist and centered in the pulpit, which in medieval churches stood in the nave where hearers could gather around, became

---

[2] Eric Werner, *The Sacred Bridge* (New York: Schocken, 1959), 8–9; but see Paul Bradshaw, *Daily Prayer in the Early Church* (New York: Oxford University Press, 1982), 12–15, 20, 86.

[3] Bradshaw, 19; Werner, 9; see Luke 4:16–30.

[4] Bradshaw, 16–19.

[5] See Bradshaw, 21–22.

[6] *Apology* 1.67 given in Lucien Deiss, *The Springtime of the Liturgy*, trans. Matthew J. O'Connell (Collegeville: Liturgical Press, 1979), 93.

[7] Eugene L. Brand, "The Liturgical Life of the Church," in *A Handbook of Church Music*, ed. Carl Halter and Carl Schalk (St. Louis: Concordia Publishing House, 1978), 38.

a feature of church life.[8] Part of the liturgical reform under Charlemagne was a renewed emphasis on preaching. He directed that sermons be preached regularly at mass, and these sermons, in part fulfilling an educational purpose, accumulated a series of elements of pedagogical and devotional intent. Thus in the ninth century a para-liturgical pulpit office called Prone (*pronaus*)[9] developed which consisted of varying elements in varying order but often included a collect, the Apostles' Creed, sometimes the Decalogue, the Lord's Prayer, intercessions, announcements and notices, and instruction. One such order is this from Biberach: (1) bells are rung, (2) Ave Maria, (3) reading the Holy Gospel, (4) sermon on the Gospel, (5) announcements, (6) confession, (7) giving holy water, (8) hymn, if a feast day. A highly evolved form of the Prone is this order from Basel, the work of John Ulrich Surgant (*Manuale Curatorum*, 1502): (1) "In the name of the Father..." in Latin, (2) sermon text in Latin, (3) German votum with a congregational *Amen*, (4) sermon text in German, (5) invocation of the Holy Spirit, (6) sermon, (7) parish notices, (8) intercessions, (9) Our Father and Ave Maria, (10) Apostles' Creed, (11) Decalogue, (12) confessions, (13) closing votum. The Prone came to be understood as standing apart from the mass. Sometimes it was done before the Eucharist; sometimes it was an entirely separate service. The importance of such preaching services by the fifteenth century is evident in the establishment in larger churches and foundations the *Prädikaturen*, the office of preacher.[10]

In the Reformed tradition, worship patterns, apart from the quarterly celebration of the Lord's Supper, usually are clearly derived from the office of the Prone.[11]

After the Reformation in Lutheran territories, if there were no communicants the Holy Communion would be terminated before the Preface. As the desire to commune declined in the ages of rationalism and pietism, this abbreviation of the Eucharist became a regular pattern. In North America because of this long-established custom and because of the insufficient supply of clergy to serve each congregation weekly, the ante-communion became the regular Sunday service to which the Holy Communion was occasionally added.

Although the Holy Communion is being recovered as the regular Sunday service in many congregations, joining the Lord's Supper and the Lord's Day, some congregations still desire a non-eucharistic service

---

[8]Henry G. J. Beck, *The Pastoral Care of Souls in South-East France during the Sixth Century* (Analecta Gergoriana 51, Rome, 1950), 259–83.

[9]Weisman, 23–24. The name derives from *praeconium* (announcement) and the French *prône*, a grille which separated the chancel and the place from which announcements were given.

[10]Brand, 39.

[11]J. Neil Alexander, "Luther's Reform of the Daily Office," *Worship* 57 (July 1983):357; F. E. Brightman and K. D. Mackenzie, "The History of the Book of Common Prayer down to 1662," *Liturgy and Worship*, ed. W. K. Lowther Clarke (London: SPCK, 1981 [1932]), 142–43; "Prône," *New Catholic Encyclopedia*.

centered on reading and expounding the Scriptures. It is not particularly desirable to truncate the Holy Communion into ante-communion, for it destroys the sense of the unity and integrity of the whole service and implies that the Holy Communion is something to be added occasionally to the "normal service." Morning Prayer is not designed to be a preaching service. The Inter-Lutheran Commission on Worship, therefore, provided the Service of the Word as an alternative for those occasions when the Holy Communion was not desired. The wisdom of the decision is debatable.[12]

THE SERVICE IN DETAIL

Although it was not intentionally so constructed, the Service of the Word has certain affinities with the ancient synagogue service as it can be reconstructed. There are three principal sections.

THE PRAISE OF GOD. The first section of the Service of the Word centers on the Creed. Like the synagogue liturgy, the Service of the Word begins with praise of God the creator. There is a hymn followed by the verses of the dialogue.

The first dialogue is from a New Testament blessing of God and his Anointed.

Holy is the Lord, the Almighty.
He was, he is, and he is to come. see Rev. 4:8
He is worthy of glory and honor and power.
He created all things. By his will they came to be. see Rev. 4:11
Worthy is Christ, the Lamb who was slain;
worthy to take the scroll and break its seals. see Rev. 5:9
By his blood he purchased for God
people of every race and tongue, of every folk and nation. see Rev. 5:9
Christ made of them a kingdom
and priests to serve our God.
And they shall reign on earth forever. see Rev. 5:10
Amen. Come, Lord Jesus. Rev. 22:20

The alternative dialogue is cast in the style of the Jewish *Berakah*, which praises God by thanking him for his greatness and power. In its opening verses this dialogue recalls the *Birkat yotser*,[13] a "doorway of praise" which in Jewish practice leads to the profession of the *Shema*.

Blessed are you, O Lord our God,
king of the universe, see Ps. 72:18–19; Dan. 4:37
for in your wisdom you have formed us. Ps. 104:24; Prov. 3:19
You feed the hungry and clothe the naked. Ps. 146:7; Isa. 58:7; Ezek. 18:7, 16
We bless you and praise your name forever. Ps. 145:1
You set free those who are bound. Isa. 61:1
We bless you and praise your name forever. Ps. 145:1

---

[12]See for example, Brian L. Helge, "Services of the Word: Good, Bad, Unnecessary," *Lutheran Forum* 7 (August 1973):14–15; Alexander, 357.
[13]Deiss, 15–16.

You raise up those whose courage falters.	Isa. 61:1; 40:29, 31
We bless you and praise your name forever.	Ps. 145:1
You provide for our every need.	Ps. 34:9–10
Accept our grateful praises.	
You have called us from all peoples.	Ps. 22:27
We rejoice and bless your name forever.	
You bless your people with peace.	Ps. 29:11
We bless you and praise your loving grace.	
Blessed are you, O Lord our God,	
king of the universe,	see Ps. 72:18–19; Dan. 4:37
for in your wisdom you have formed us.	Ps. 104:24; Prov. 3:19

Special dialogues for Advent and Lent are provided, for the Service of the Word may during these seasons be useful as a midweek service at a time when Evening Prayer may no longer be appropriate, a time too late for Evening Prayer (a service for sunset) and too early for Compline (a service before going to bed).

The dialogue for Advent has these sources:

Blessed is he who comes as king,	
who comes in the name of the Lord.	Luke 19:38
Glory to God in the highest,	
and peace to his people on earth.	Luke 2:14; 19:38
I will hear what the Lord God has to say —	
a voice that speaks for peace.	Ps. 85:8
Peace for all people and for his friends	
and those who turn to him in their hearts.	Ps. 85:8
His help is near for those who fear him,	
and his glory will live in our land.	Ps. 85:9
Blessed is he who comes as king,	
who comes in the name of the Lord.	Luke 19:38
Glory to God in the highest,	
and peace to his people on earth.	Luke 2:14; 19:38

The dialogue for Lent has these sources:

Grace and peace from God our Father and the Lord Jesus Christ.	2 Cor. 1:2
Praise be God, the Father of our Lord Jesus Christ,	
the Father of all mercies, and the God of all consolation.	2 Cor. 1:3
Seek the Lord while he may be found.	
Call upon him while he is near.	Isa. 55:6
Let the wicked abandon their ways,	
and the unrighteous their thoughts.	Isa. 55:7
Let them turn to the Lord for mercy,	
to our God, who is generous in forgiving.	Isa. 55:7
All you who are thirsty, come to the water.	
You who have no money, come, receive bread, and eat.	
Come without paying and without cost, drink wine and milk.	Isa. 55:1
Praised be God, the Father of our Lord Jesus Christ,	
the Father of all mercies, and the God of all consolation.	2 Cor. 1:3

The baptismal creed occupies a place in the Service of the Word which corresponds to the place of the *Shema* in the synagogue service. By confessing the faith of the church, the congregation praises God whose mighty deeds the creed summarizes and triumphantly confesses the catholic faith against all adversaries as an encouragement of those who have been baptized into it, even as the *Shema* is a proclamation of praise, a ringing defense of monotheism, and a reminder to Israel to be faithful to its historic faith. The introduction to the Creed, a new composition, summarizes these ideas.

The Old Testament canticle, which helps to maintain the continuity with Israel, concludes this section of the service.

PROCLAMATION OF THE SCRIPTURES. The second part of the Service of the Word centers on the reading and exposition of Scripture. The lessons and the silence and the sermon are introduced by the Prayer of the Day, which prepares the congregation for the proclamation of the Word of God.

It may be observed that the Bible is a wonderfully rich book, and the church responds to it in various ways. The congregation sometimes sits and sometimes stands when a reading is from the Gospel because the lesson serves different functions in different services. The Service of the Word is a preaching service in which the emphasis is on hearing the Word. In this service the church building is not unlike a classroom, and the congregation sits to be instructed by the lessons and the sermon. The order of the readings is flexible: Old Testament and New Testament, but not necessarily in that order. The last lesson is the sermon text (Min. Ed., p. 33 #17). In Morning and Evening Prayer, the emphasis is on praise and prayer, and in that context the Word of God is heard and meditated upon devotionally. The congregation sits for these readings also.[14] In the Eucharist there is a further elaboration of the readings, and the three lessons are understood in a richly symbolic way. They are read in an ascending order: the First Covenant of promise, the Apostle (usually St. Paul), and then the Lord himself. The third lesson is seen as the culmination of the readings as Christ is the fulfillment of the Scripture, and this third lesson is surrounded with ceremonies: congregation standing, acclamations before and after the reading, sometimes with a Gospel procession, perhaps with candles and incense. These ceremonies are to be understood in the context of the whole eucharistic action: Christ comes to his people in Scripture and sacrament, and they stand (or kneel) to receive him. In the Holy Communion, the third lesson is more than just another reading. It is the Holy Gospel, which is heard as the voice of the living Lord in the midst of his people, who is soon to break bread with them and enter then in a yet more personal and intimate way in the Supper. (So the reading of the Holy Gospel is traditionally reserved to those who have been or-

---

[14]It may be noted that there is a practice among some Roman Catholics of standing for any reading from the gospels in whatever context it is read.

dained.) In the Eucharist, Christ's active presence is celebrated; he acts and his people respond by hearing and by doing. In the Service of the World, the action is primarily mental and spiritual, and considerably less physical.

The hymn, which corresponds to the Hymn of the Day in the Holy Communion, concludes this section of the service, even as in the synagogue service the reading of scripture was preceded and followed by several *berakot*.

PRAYERS AND INTERCESSIONS. The third section of the service, corresponding to the *Kaddish* (Aramaic for "sanctification"), the great doxology which concluded the service in the synagogue and the first two petitions of which inspired the first two petitions of the Lord's Prayer,[15] is the prayer of intercession. As is the case with the other central items of the other two sections of the Service of the Word, the prayer is preceded and followed by an offering of praise and thanksgiving.

Before the prayer an offering may be received. Although this action has a primarily practical purpose — the collection of donations to keep the congregation functioning — it may also be understood as an offering of thanksgiving and praise to God the creator who has given us all that we possess. It is a gathering of a sacrifice of praise.

The prayer given in the text of the Service of the Word is a classic text of the Lutheran church in North America. Its precise origin is unknown; the author seems to have been Joseph A. Seiss,[16] who may have drawn on various German sources in composing or translating the prayer.[17] It first appeared in the *Church Book* (1868) of the General Council[18] and was preserved in the *Common Service Book*[19] and the *Service Book and Hymnal*.[20] In *The Lutheran Hymnal* (1941) which added the next to last paragraph concerning the offerings, it was the General Prayer in The Order of Morning Service without Communion (p. 13).

Other forms of prayer may be used: Responsive Prayer 1 or 2, the Litany, the Prayer of the Church (Min. Ed., pp. 116–17), a series of collects, or the form of intercession from the Holy Communion.

The New Testament canticle, which may be understood as comparable to the third-century addition to the synagogue service, *Alenu*, an

---

[15] Deiss, 17.

[16] Dr. Seiss, pastor of the Church of the Holy Communion in Philadelphia 1875–1904, with a keen interest in the Second Coming of Christ, anglicized the pronunciation of his name so that it was pronounced "cease."

[17] Luther D. Reed, *The Lutheran Liturgy*, rev. ed. (Philadelphia: Fortress Press, 1960), 662.

[18] *Church Book*, no. IV, pp. 122–24. The earliest Lutheran General Prayer in English was translated from the Reformation of Cologne (1543), perhaps by Cranmer, in *A Simple and Religious Consultation* (1548). The German prayer was translated by Joseph A. Seiss for the 1891 *Church Book* (pp. 153–54); a briefer version was included in the *Common Service Book* (pp. 256–57). The prayer was not included in the *Service Book and Hymnal*. See Reed, *The Lutheran Liturgy* (1947), pp. 577–79, and the revised edition (1960), p. 662.

[19] *Common Service Book*, no. I, pp. 253–54.

[20] *Service Book and Hymnal*, no. III, p. 239.

affirmation of monotheism couched in hymnic language and similar to the Te Deum, is the concluding burst of praise.[21]

The benediction is the priestly blessing of the Old Testament, the Aaronic benediction much beloved in Lutheran use.[22] This blessing, "which the Lord himself appointed,"[23] was thought by Luther to have been the blessing Jesus gave to his apostles at the Ascension.[24] The Hebrew is difficult to render in contemporary English, and the Inter-Lutheran Commission on Worship, finding no suitable translation, composed its own out of existing translations, casting it in the third person in the text of the service for leaders who may be laypeople, commenting in the Notes on the Liturgy (Min. Ed., p. 33 #17) that "when the leader is a pastor, the Benediction should be used in declarative form:"

The Lord bless you and keep you.	Revised Standard Version, New American Bible, New American Standard, *The Torah*[25]
The Lord make his face shine on you and be gracious to you.	New American Standard
The Lord look upon you with favor	New American Bible ("The Lord look upon you kindly") and *The Torah* ("The Lord bestow his favor upon you")
and give you peace.	Revised Standard Version. New American Bible, New American Standard, New English Bible

[21] Werner, 7.

[22] See H. H. Rowley, *Worship in Ancient Israel: Its Forms and Meaning* (Philadelphia: Fortress Press, 1967), 237.

[23] Martin Luther, "An Order of Mass and Communion for the Church at Wittenberg" (1523), *Luther's Works* 53:30.

[24] Ibid., 30; or, Luther thought, Jesus might have used a blessing like Psalm 67:6–7.

[25] *The Torah: The Five Books of Moses* (Philadelphia: Jewish Publication Society of America, 1962), 256.

9

Marriage

Ministers Edition, pp. 328–330, 189–190, 36–37

Parallel Rites

Roman Catholic
: Rite of Marriage (during mass, outside of mass, between a Catholic and an unbaptized person), *The Rites*, pp. 529–70.

Episcopal
: The Celebration and Blessing of a Marriage, *Book of Common Prayer*, pp. 422–38.

Lutheran
: The Order of Marriage, *The Book of Worship* (General Synod 1867), pp. 87–90.

  Order for the Solemnization of Holy Matrimony, *The Liturgy of the Evangelical Lutheran Church* (General Synod 1881), pp. 73–84.

  The Solemnization of Marriage, *Church Book* (1891), pp. 374–77.

  The Marriage Service, *Forms for Ministerial Acts* (General Synod 1900), pp. 97–102.

  Order for the Solemnization of Marriage, *A Liturgy for the Use of Evangelical Lutheran Pastors* (Joint Synod of Ohio 1912), pp. 144–47.

  Order for Marriage, *Common Service Book* (1919), text ed., pp. 449–53.

  Marriage: First Form, Second Form, *Liturgy and Agenda* (Missouri Synod, 1921), pp. 340–48.

  The Order of a Marriage (The Congregation Participating; The Congregation Not Participating: A Short Form), *The Lutheran Agenda* (Synodical Conference, 194–), pp. 35–52.

  Order for Marriage, *Service Book and Hymnal* (1958), pp. 270–73.

  Contemporary Worship 3: The Marriage Service (1972).

Orthodox
: The Rite of Holy Matrimony, *Service Book*, pp. 291–305.

Presbyterian
: The Marriage Service, *Worshipbook* (1972), pp. 65–68.

Methodist
: A Service of Christian Marriage (1979)

Church of   The Marriage Service, *Book of Common Worship* (1963), pp.
South India   139–47.

Purpose

The marriage service provides a context of praise, Scripture, and prayer
(and the Lord's Supper) within which a man and a woman make with
each other a lifelong covenant of commitment and fidelity according to
the ordinance and institution of God (Mark 10:2–12).

Characteristics

The marriage rite is a service of worship filled with joy and gladness and
gratitude for the goodness of creation, in which the people are not mere
spectators but an active congregation participating in the celebration
and representing to the couple the presence and support of the church.

Marriage is not a peculiarly Christian or even biblical institution; it
is part of the universal order of creation, God's gift to the world. In the
evangelical view there is no such thing as "Christian marriage"; there
is marriage between Christians.

The primary metaphors of the marriage service have to do with
covenantal fidelity, made specific in the love of God for Israel and Christ
for the church, which steadfast and self-giving love the couple is called
to reflect in their relationship with each other. A second set of images
in the marriage service has to do with a banquet, combining a marriage
feast and the eschatological messianic banquet, and coming to a focus in
the eucharistic banquet at which Christ the Bridegroom is the host and
which prepares the church for the final appearance of the Bridegroom
(Matt. 22:30; Mark 12:25; Luke 20:34–36). The metaphors of the marriage rite join the gladness of the celebration of marriage with the joy in
the fulfillment of creation when Christ will be joined in permanent and
triumphant and intimate communion with his bride, the church.

In the tradition of the Western church, marriage is understood not as
a union made by the minister or the minister's words but by the couple
themselves.[1] The man and the woman who establish a covenant of

---

[1] See Dietrich Bonhoeffer, *Ethics*, ed. Eberhard Bethge, trans. Neville Horton Smith
(New York: Macmillan, 1955), 130:

> Marriages are not concluded either by the Church or by the state, and it is not
> solely from these institutions that they derive their title. Marriage is concluded
> rather by the two partners. The fact that a marriage is performed publicly in the
> presence of the state and in the presence of the Church signifies no more than the
> civil and ecclesiastical public recognition of marriage and its inherent rites. That
> is the Lutheran doctrine.

See A. N. Niebergall "Marriage: 9. Lutheran," in *The New Westminster Dictionary of Liturgy and Worship*, ed. J. G. Davies (Philadelphia: Westminster Press, 1986). See also
Massey H. Shepherd, Jr., *The Oxford American Prayer Book Commentary* (New York:
Oxford University Press, 1950), 300: "The two parties to the contract marry each other
and are the ministers of the nuptial bond." See also Philip T. Weller, *The Roman
Ritual*, complete ed. (Milwaukee: Bruce Publishing Co., 1964), 272: "The mutual consent . . . constitutes the essence of the sacrament."

fidelity with each other by their vows are thus the principal ministers of the rite. The presiding minister is the principal witness to what they do.

The covenant of fidelity which is the essence of marriage in the evangelical view is intended to be lifelong, until death parts the couple. Only such lifelong, unconditional promises give the time necessary for the couple to develop the depth of character, truthfulness, forgiveness, and trust which are to characterize married Christians. Without the lifelong commitment, one may expect only superficial encounters, short-term relationships which last only as long as happiness continues.

Background

To understand the rites of marriage, attention to the context in which they are performed is even more essential than is the case with other liturgical rites, for marriage rites are intimately related to society, custom, and culture.

There is no description of the ancient Christian marriage rites, but they were built on prevailing pre-Christian customs primarily of the Romans. Marriage within Christianity is a continuation of an institution common to all humanity enriched with Jewish and Christian experiences of God's faithfulness and steadfast love for his people. For many centuries into the common era, marriage remained a civil contract and ceremony, indeed a family function.

In the early church, although a clear distinction was drawn between the betrothal (engagement) and the marriage, the former was considered no less binding than the latter. The betrothal, according to Ignatius,[2] took place only with the bishop's approval and involved the giving of money as a pledge that the promised marriage would take place, and the giving to the wife a ring,[3] used for the sealing of household goods, as an indication that the woman would have charge of the home. The ring was also a promise of the dowry. The woman was veiled,[4] a regular part of the dress of betrothed and married women. The couple's hands were joined,[5] and a kiss was exchanged.[6] The wedding, according to Tertullian,[7] involved the celebration of the Eucharist and a blessing. This was the distinctively Christian ceremony connected with marriage.

In later forms in the East, the man was given a crown, a sign of victory, according to John Chrysostom (d. 407), indicating that the man came to the marriage bed unconquered by pleasure.[8] The crowning remains the high point of the Orthodox marriage rite as the priest places crowns on the heads of the man and the woman, showing them to be king

---

[2] Ignatius, *Letter to Polycarp* 5. See "Marriage" in *The New Westminster Dictionary of Liturgy and Worship.*

[3] Isidore of Seville, *On Ecclesiastical Offices* 2.20.8.

[4] Ambrose, *Letter to Virgil* 7.

[5] Gregory of Nazianzus, *Letter* 193.

[6] Tertullian, *Apology* 6; *On the Veiling of Virgins* 11.

[7] Tertullian, *To His Wife* 2.6

[8] John Chrysostom, *Sermon on 1 Timothy* 9.

and queen of a little image of the kingdom of God, and, recalling the martyrs' crowns, reminding them that they are to be living witnesses to Christ.

Only when the social order broke down during the seventh and eighth centuries did the church preside at the giving of matrimonial consent, and it did so in order to protect the freedom of those who entered marriage and to prevent forced marriages. Such declaration of free consent has been the central element of church marriages ever since. The marriage liturgy in the early sacramentaries (Leonine, Gelasian, Gregorian) is not obligatory. The rite of marriage was done at the doors of the church (*in facie ecclesiae*), first reported in Normandy in the early twelfth century. (Chaucer's Wife of Bath twice speaks of the five husbands she "had at church doore."[9]) The minister inquired concerning the consent of each, the bride was given to the man (a Teutonic contribution to the ceremony), the dowry was reported, the ring was blessed and given to the bride, the groom gave some gold and silver, and the priest blessed the couple. If a mass followed, the couple entered the church. The nuptial blessing was said during which the veil was laid on the head of the bride and the shoulders of the groom.

It was also in the twelfth century that the doctrine of the seven sacraments emerged,[10] the number seven having long suggested perfection and plenitude. Marriage was included in this number on the basis of Augustine's broad definition of a sacrament as a sign of a sacred thing or event. Several factors led to the inclusion of marriage: weakness in civil government and the accompanying increase of church influence in civil affairs, a concern to protect the public nature of marriage and the rights of women, resistance to the Catharist and Albigensian heresies, which considered marriage as evil, and the description of marriage as a *sacramentum* in the Vulgate translation of Ephesians 5:32.

The Roman Ritual of 1614 is derived from the medieval rite but allows for the continuation of the many local customs.[11] In the East, the rite used by the Orthodox Church assumed its present form only in the seventeenth century.

At the time of the Reformation, marriage law and rites were still in process of development. The Roman, Germanic, canon, and imperial law understood the mutual consent of the couple to be the foundation of their marriage: *consensus facit nuptias*. The church consistently opposed secret marriages.

During the sixteenth century, marriage in church became increasingly important in Catholic and Protestant understanding. After the Reformation, Lutheran areas often adapted the use of their local Roman Catholic diocese.

---

[9] Geoffrey Chaucer, *Canterbury Tales*, Wife of Bath's Prologue l. 462; Wife of Bath's Tale, l. 6

[10] See Christopher Kiesling, "How Many Sacraments?" *Worship* 44 (May 1970):268–76.

[11] Gerard S. Sloyan, "The New Rite for Celebrating Marriage," *Worship* 44 (May 1970):259.

The oldest evangelical marriage rite comes from 1524, probably drafted by Johannes Bugenhagen at Wittenberg. There is an address based on Genesis 1–3, the couple is asked, "N., will you take N. to be your wedded wife/husband according to God's ordinance?" Rings are exchanged, and the pastor gives them in wedlock in the name of the Holy Trinity. Matthew 19:6 and other New Testament readings were added in some places as the form spread, especially in southern Germany. The pronouncement of the couple to be husband and wife and the use of Matthew 19:6 were commonly used in various parts of Germany before the Reformation.

Another form developed in Strasbourg, following the diocesan liturgy of 1513. It was printed in 1525 and regarded the blessing of marriage as a confirmation of what the couple had done by the exchange of vows.

Luther's Traubüchlein (1529) had great influence. He provided the order only with some reluctance, saying, "Since marriage and the married estate are worldly matters, it behooves us pastors or ministers of the church not to attempt to order or govern anything connected with it, but to permit every city and land to continue its own use and custom in this connection."[12] He provided his form for blessing the couple "before the church or in the church" when those asked to preside at the marriage did not know anything better. Moreover, since it had been customary "to surround the consecration of monks and nuns with such great ceremonial display ... how much more should we honor this divine estate [of marriage] and gloriously bless and embellish it and pray for it.... It should be accounted a hundred times more spiritual than the monastic state...." Also, Luther said, the blessing of a marriage would help teach young people "to take this estate seriously."[13]

Luther's Order of Marriage for Common Pastors (1529) followed the Wittenberg order but also incorporated Roman Catholic forms and early church traditions. There were three parts to the rite: the banns (public announcement), the betrothal (*copulatio*) at the church door, and the blessing before the altar in the church. The banns were primarily to request prayers for the couple and secondarily to discover impediments. At the entrance of the church the questions of consent are asked, rings are exchanged, the couple join hands with Matthew 19:6, and the pastor joins them in marriage. The blessing or confirmation in the church before the altar, presumably on the day after the betrothal, after the marriage has been consummated by the couple, involves scripture lessons and prayer. The first lesson, Genesis 2:18, 21–24, serves as a kind of words of institution for marriage.[14] Three lessons addressed to the couple tell of God's commandment (Eph. 5:25–29, 22–24), the cross (Gen. 3:16–19), and comfort (Gen. 1:27–28, 31). Proverbs 18:22 concludes the

[12]Martin Luther, "The Order of Marriage for Common Pastors" (1529), *Luther's Works* 53:111.

[13]Ibid., 112.

[14]Alfred Niebergall, "Marriage: 9. Lutheran," in *The New Westminster Dictionary of Liturgy and Worship*, ed. J. G. Davies (Philadelphia: Westminster Press, 1986).

readings. The benediction is a prayer, prayed with hands outstretched over the bride and groom.

To Luther's provisional order various church orders added other biblical readings such as Matthew 19:3–9 and John 2:1–11.

The Brandenburg-Nuremberg order (1533) allows a declaration by the couple to replace the question regarding their consent in marriage: "I N. take you N. as my wedded spouse and pledge you my troth." Augsburg (1527) and Hesse (1539) permit the omission of the question. In northern Germany the pastor "pronounces" or "makes" the couple husband and wife; in Strasbourg and Brandenburg-Nuremberg the orders have, "The obligation of marriage, which you have commended to each other before God, and his congregation, I confirm at the behest of the Christian congregation in the name of the Father and of the Son and of the Holy Spirit." By the end of the sixteenth century there was a clear tendency to understand the church ceremony as the constitutive act which made the marriage; earlier the betrothal had this function.

By the seventeenth century the questions had become more imperative, and the couple promised love, fidelity, and support for each other "until death parts us." In the eighteenth century under the influence of legal opinions, church marriage had become a legal act which the church performed on behalf of the state. In the nineteenth century in Europe an obligatory civil ceremony was introduced.

In the Roman Catholic Church the Constitution on the Sacred Liturgy of the Second Vatican Council directed the revision and enrichment of the marriage rite. Variety is encouraged; the "nuptial blessing" which had been a prayer for the bride was to be expanded to be a prayer for both spouses. Marriage was normally to be celebrated within mass after the Gospel and sermon.[15]

The marriage rite of the Inter-Lutheran Commission on Worship was drafted by Earl J. Lund, Edward C. May, Philip H. Pfatteicher, who chaired the committee, Olive Wise Spannaus, and John F. Steinbruck. It was published in 1972 as *Contemporary Worship 3* and was slightly revised for inclusion in the *Lutheran Book of Worship*.

THE SERVICE IN DETAIL

The Marriage service is printed for use by itself (Min. Ed., pp. 328–30), but it may when desired be used within a celebration of Holy Communion. In that case, it follows the sermon and Hymn of the Day and begins with the address.

The marriage service, like the Holy Communion, begins (after the entrance)[16] with the Apostolic Greeting from 2 Corinthians 3:14.

---

[15] *Constitution on the Liturgy* III.77–78.

[16] The affected hesitation step (the "Alexandra step") which has been popular in some places began with the wedding of Princess Alexandra of England, who had a limp. To make her less conspicuous, the entire wedding party walked in imitation of her halting steps.

When marriage is celebrated within the Holy Communion, the Hymn of Praise is canticle 16, "I will sing the story of your love, O Lord." The canticle is drawn from Psalm 89:1 (antiphon-refrain), Jeremiah 33:10–11, and Psalm 100:5. The texts were arranged by Philip Pfatteicher, primarily on the basis of the New English Bible.

The Prayer of the Day (no. 162) gathers New Testament references to the joy of marriage and sets them in the context of the fulfillment at the end of time, which in the New Testament is frequently seen under the image of a wedding banquet.

The Rites of the Catholic Church	*Lutheran Book of Worship*	*Book of Common Prayer*
Father, you have made the bond of marriage a holy mystery, a symbol of Christ's love for his Church. Hear our prayers for N. and N. With faith in you and in each other they pledge their love today. May their lives always bear witness to the reality of that love. We ask this through our Lord....		

or

Father, hear our prayers for N. and N., who today are united in marriage before your altar. Give them your blessing and strengthen their love for each other. We ask this through our Lord....

or

Almighty God, hear our prayers for N. and N., who have come here today to be united in the sacrament of marriage. Increase their faith in you and in each other, and through them bless your Church (with

Christian children).
We ask this through
our Lord....

or

Father, when you created mankind you willed that man and wife should be one. Bind N. and N. in the loving union of marriage; and make their love fruitful so that they may be living witnesses to your divine love in the world.	Eternal God, our creator and redeemer, as you gladdened the wedding at Cana in Galilee by the presence of your Son, so bring your joy to this wedding by his presence now. Look in favor upon __name__ and __name__, and grant that they, rejoicing in all your gifts, may at length celebrate the marriage feast which has no end	O gracious and everliving God, you have created us male and female in your image: Look mercifully upon this man and this woman who come to you seeking your blessing, and assist them with your grace, that with true fidelity and steadfast love they may honor and keep the promises and vows they make;
We ask this through our Lord Jesus Christ, your son, who lives and reigns with you and the Holy Spirit, one God, for ever and ever.	with Christ our Lord, who lives and reigns with you and the Holy Spirit, one God, now and forever.	through Jesus Christ our Savior, who lives and reigns with you in the unity of the Holy Spirit, one God, for ever and ever.
(pp. 561–62)	(p. 189)	(p. 425)

The prayer in the *Lutheran Book of Worship* derives from a collect by George Koski, written while he was a student at the Lutheran Theological Seminary at Philadelphia. The first prayer in the Roman rite is a new composition; the second is a revision of the prayer at the blessing of the ring in the former rite; the third is a new composition; the fourth is a revision of the first prayer at the nuptial blessing in the former rite.[17] The collect in the *Book of Common Prayer*, drafted by Charles M. Guilbert, preserves the main themes of the first prayer of the marriage rite in the 1549 Prayer Book, which was based upon the Sarum form for the blessing of the ring.[18]

There are many points of agreement between the three rites with regard to the appointments for the liturgy of the word at a marriage.[19]

---

[17] Lord, be favorable to our prayers and graciously protect your ordinance, whereby you have provided for the propagation of humanity; that what is now joined together by your authority may be preserved by your help; through our Lord....

[18] Marion Hatchett, *Commentary on the American Prayer Book* (New York: Seabury Press, 1981), 434; Shepherd, 302–03.

[19] See Reginald H. Fuller, "Lectionary for Weddings," *Worship* 55 (May 1981):244–59 for expository and exegetical comments on the readings.

Roman Catholic	Lutheran	Episcopal
Gen. 1:26–28, 31a	Gen. 1:26–31	Gen. 1:26–28
2:18–24	2:18–24	2:4–9, 15–24
24:48–51, 58–67		
Song of Sol. 2:8–10, 14,	Song of Sol. 2:10–13	Song of Sol. 2:10–13
16a		
8:6–7a	8:7	
	Isa. 63:7–9	
Jer. 31:31–32a, 33–34a		
Tobit 7:9c–10, 11c–17		
8:5–10		Tobit 8:5b–8
Ecclus. 26:1–4, 16–21		
Ps. 33	Ps. 33	
34		
103		Ps. 67
112		
	127	127
128	128	128
	136	
145		
149		
	150	
Rom. 8:31b–35, 37–39		
12:1–2, 9–18	Rom. 12:1–2	
1 Cor. 6:13c–15a, 17–20		
12:31–13:8a	1 Cor. 12:31–13:13	1 Cor. 13:1–13
		Eph. 3:14–19
Eph. 5:2a, 21–33	Eph. 5:21–33	5:1–2, 21–33
Col. 3:12–17		
1 Pet. 3:1–9		
1 John 3:18–24		
4:7–12		1 John 4:7–16
Rev. 19:1, 5–9a		
Verse		
1 John 4:8, 11		
4:12	1 John 4:12	
4:16		
4:7b		
	Ps. 85:7 (Advent 1)	
	Lam. 3:22 (Epiph. 8)	
	John 3:16 (Lent 4)	
	14:23 (Pent. 11)	
Matt. 5:1–12		Matt. 5:1–10
5:13–16		5:13–16
7:21, 24–29		7:21, 24–29
19:3–6	Matt. 19:4–6	
22:35–40		

Mark 10:6–9		Mark 10:6–9, 13–16
John 2:1–11	John 2:1–10	
15:9–12	15:9–12	John 15:9–12
15:12–16		
17:20–26		

The three paragraphs of the address follow the three-part outline of Luther's arrangement of biblical texts in his Traubüchlein (1529): commandment, cross, and consolation. The *Common Service Book* had formed an address from an arrangement of biblical passages — Genesis 2:18; Matthew 19:4–6; Ephesians 5:25, 22 — prefaced with an introduction,

Dearly beloved, forasmuch as marriage is a holy estate, ordained of God, and to be held in honor by all, it becometh those who enter therein to weigh, with reverent minds, what the Word of God teacheth concerning it;

and concluded with a clear statement about the reality of the effects of sin in human relationships and of God's grace,

and although, by reason of sin, many a cross hath been laid thereon, nevertheless our gracious Father in heaven doth not forsake His children in an estate so holy and acceptable to Him, but is ever present with His abundant blessing.

Lutheran rites have consistently preserved this pattern, declaring by Scripture and liturgical text God's institution of marriage, the cross of adversity which falls upon those who are joined in marriage, and God's abundant grace and support.[20]

The first paragraph of the address in the rite in the *Lutheran Book of Worship*, reflecting Genesis 1:26–31, affirms the goodness of sexuality and the relationship of marriage to human community. John Macquarrie has written,

Sex is the most obvious indicator of the fundamentally communal character of human existence, no single existent being complete in himself or herself. Marriage is the institutional form which protects and stabilizes the sexual relation. But this means that in the "natural" order, marriage is the simplest and most fundamental form of human community.[21]

Human community is rooted in God's intention of joy for his creation. It should be noted that what "is brought to perfection in the life to come" is not the couple's marriage but the joy of which their marriage is an expression and sign.[22] Joy is understood here to be the intention of God and a sure sign of his presence.

---

[20] See, for example, the 1867 *Book of Worship* of the General Synod; the 1868 *Church Book* of the General Council; the Liturgy of the Joint Synod of Ohio (1912); the *Liturgy and Agenda* of the Lutheran Church–Missouri Synod (1921).

[21] John Macquarrie, *Principles of Christian Theology*, 2d ed. (New York: Scribners, 1977), 513.

[22] See Ps. 16:11; John 3:29; 15:11; 16:24; 17:13; 1 John 1:4; 2 John 12; Jude 24.

The second paragraph acknowledges sin and its impact upon human relationships. Previous rites spoke of the "cross" which is laid upon marriage, but in the *Lutheran Book of Worship* the address makes clear that suffering and hardship are not God's doing; they are the consequences of our doing, our sin defined as our "age-old rebellion." This rebellion perverts God's goodness and gifts, and makes of them less than God intended.

The third paragraph declares that marriage is not only acceptable to God; God himself in fact established it and continues to bless it and support it. The "joy" of the first paragraph is repeated and restored (John 15:11–17; Rev. 21:1–4).

Earlier rites preserved both the betrothal questions (the declaration of consent) and the more recent addition of the marriage vows. Both the *Common Service Book* and the *Service Book and Hymnal* betray some ambiguity about the form. Both books have the declaration of consent, which in medieval rites accomplished the marriage:[23]

N., wilt thou have this Woman/Man to thy wedded wife/husband, to live together after God's ordinance in the holy estate of Matrimony? Wilt thou love her/him, comfort her/him, honor and keep her/him in sickness and in health, and, forsaking all others, keep thee only unto her/him, so long as ye both shall live? *I will.*

The *Common Service Book* then directed the couple to say to each other the simple formula couched in archaic language,

I, *N.*, take thee, *N.*, to my wedded Wife/Husband, and plight thee my troth, till death us do part.

The ring or rings may then be given, and the minster pronounces them "Man and Wife." But an alternative "simpler form" is provided (p. 453), which requires simply the couple's declaration of consent, after which the minister pronounces them man and wife. In this form, following European precedent, the vows are not said, and there is no provision for the giving of the ring(s).

The *Service Book and Hymnal*, after the declaration of consent, provided a full form of the marriage vows taken from the *Book of Common Prayer* (the 1928 Book, pp. 301–02):

I, N., take thee, N., to my wedded wife/husband, to have and to hold from this day forward, for better for worse, for richer for poorer, in sickness and in health, to love and to cherish, till death us do part, according to God's holy ordinance; and thereto I plight thee my troth.

An alternative "shorter form" is provided — the simple form of the vow from the *Common Service Book.*

The difference between the declaration of consent and the marriage vows had become unclear, and they seemed to be variants of the same

---

[23]See Weller, 272.

action, the later vows repeating the earlier ones.[24] In the *Lutheran Book of Worship* therefore the betrothal question is incorporated into the introduction to the marriage vows:

_____ and _____ , if it is your intention to share with each other your joys and sorrows and all that the years will bring, with your promises bind yourselves to each other as husband and wife.

The couple affirm their intention to join each other in marriage by exchanging the vows. The introductory statement preserves the long-standing insistence of the church that the vows be exchanged freely without constraint and also makes clear that marriage is the covenant of fidelity which the man and the woman make with each other by their vows.

The giving of the bride, an optional element in the *Common Service Book* and in the *Service Book and Hymnal* (it did not appear in the rite in the *Church Book*), was brought into the Lutheran rite from the *Book of Common Prayer*, which took the action from the Sarum and York rites.[25] It is omitted from the *Lutheran Book of Worship* rite (see note, Min. Ed., p. 36).

The joining of the hands is a pre-Christian practice, observed by the Jews (Tobit 7:13), Greeks, and Romans, and is "the essential ceremonial action" of the vows.[26]

The vow given in the text promises (1) unreserved sharing, (2) fidelity, (3) until death parts the couple. A deep and powerful sign of their becoming "one flesh," their "joining," is the consummation of the marriage in sexual union.

Other forms of the vows are given in the Notes on the Liturgy (Min. Ed., p. 36 #3). All the vows were written for the *Lutheran Book of Worship;* the first alternative was adapted from a form written by William and Diane Edwards, who were married in Salem Lutheran Church in Glendale, California, in March 1971. In the *Book of Common Prayer* there is no provision for variation from the vow provided in the text of the marriage rite; in the Roman rite the only variation permitted is whether the couple declare their consent by a statement or by responding to the priest's question. In the United States an alternative form is permitted, based on the widely-imitated form from the *Book of Common Prayer,*

I, N., take you, N., for my lawful wife/husband, to have and to hold, from this day forward, for better, for worse, for richer, for poorer, in sickness and in health, until death do us part.

The marriage rite in the *Lutheran Book of Worship* reflects the usual North American practice and assumes that two rings will be used. Lutheran rites have not made provision for the blessing of the ring(s); the

---

[24]Shepherd, 301–02.
[25]Hatchett, 434; see Shepherd, 301–02.
[26]Shepherd, 301–02.

1549 Prayer Book likewise removed the blessing of the ring from the rite. The 1928 Prayer Book added a blessing, "Bless, O Lord this ring, that he who gives it and she who wears it may abide in thy peace and continue in thy favour, unto their life's end; through Jesus Christ our Lord." The "Additional Orders and Offices" added to the 1962 Lutheran *Occasional Services* provided a form for the blessing of a wedding ring (along with a prayer for blessing palms and one for blessing fishing boats) similar to the Episcopal form, with apologetic rubric,

In the use of the following forms of blessing, it must be clear that all of God's creation is good, and that these forms are intended to set apart certain things for specific use, and that the principal blessing is upon those that use them for the specific purpose (p. 215).

The 1979 Prayer Book provides an optional blessing of the ring(s) and the Roman rite provides a blessing and two alternative forms.

The form provided in the Lutheran book for the giving of the rings emphasizes the intention of the giver, as does the form in the Prayer Book:

Lutheran Book of Worship	*Book of Common Prayer*
I give you this ring as a sign of my love and faithfulness.	N., I give you this ring as a symbol of my vow, and with all that I am, and all that I have, I honor you, in the Name of the Father, and of the Son, and of the Holy Spirit (*or* in the Name of God). (p. 427)

Previous Lutheran forms, like the present Roman form, emphasized the understanding of the recipient:

Service Book and Hymnal	*The Rites of the Catholic Church*
Receive this ring as a token of wedded love and troth.	N., take this ring as a sign of my love and fidelity. In the name of the Father, and of the Son, and of the Holy Spirit. (p. 542)

"Token" has taken on connotations of less significance, and so the *Lutheran Book of Worship* uses "sign"; the previous form defined the love which is so signified as "wedded love." ("Troth" meant truth, fidelity.)

It was a medieval custom to slip the ring on the thumb, the second, and the third fingers at the words Father, Son, and Holy Spirit respectively and finally on the fourth finger at the Amen.[27] Placing the ring upon the fourth finger of the woman's hand is a survival of an ancient

---

[27] Ibid.

Roman custom before the introduction of Christianity; it was thought that a special nerve or vein connected this finger with the heart.

Recognizing that the couple have made themselves husband and wife by the exchange of their vows, the minister as the principal witness to their action, speaking for all in proclamation and thanksgiving, announces (no longer "pronounces," for the only other formal use of this verb is to pronounce someone dead) them thus bound to one another. As a further proclamation of praise and thanksgiving, the congregation gives thanks to the Holy Trinity, and the minister adds the warning of Matthew 19:6, a verse associated with marriage rites since before the Reformation.

The blessing of the couple is adapted from the form in the *Common Service Book* and the *Service Book and Hymnal*, which was taken from the Sarum rite and the 1549 *Book of Common Prayer*.[28] It echoes Genesis 2 with the title "the Lord God" and the allusion to Adam and Eve. The revised form emphasizes not only continuance but growth in holy love throughout the lifetime of the couple.

The parents (and the wedding party) may add their blessing with the text from Psalm 61:7 (adapted from the New English Bible); the Notes on the Liturgy (Min. Ed., p. 37 #7) provide a verse of the companions in the Song of Songs 1:4 (New English Bible), which was judged by some to be a bit strong for some parents to say to their children, and so it was relegated to the Notes.

The three prayers (nos. 276, 277, 278) are all newly composed. When the Holy Communion is celebrated, these prayers serve as the prayers of intercession of the Eucharist, and the service continues with the Peace and the Offering.

No proper Offertory is provided for the occasion of a marriage. If one is desired, the one appropriate for the day according to the liturgical calendar may serve.

The proper preface for marriage is new to Lutheran use and was composed by Philip Pfatteicher. The beginning,

For your love is firm as the ancient earth, your faithfulness fixed as the heavens,

is from Psalm 89:2 in the translation of the New English Bible. The preface continues by acknowledging marriage as an order of creation which proclaims the steadfast love of God even to those who know nothing of the biblical faith. A similar idea is expressed in the Roman Catholic eucharistic prayer for marriage (III):

---

[28]"Almighty God, who at the beginning did create our first parents, Adam and Eve, and did sanctify and join them together in marriage: Pour upon you the riches of his grace, sanctify and bless you, that ye may please him both in body and soul, and live together in holy love unto your lives' end." Given in Richard Tatlock, *An English Benedictional* (London: Faith Press, 1964), 22 #17. Compare the Nuptial Blessings in the *English Ritual* (Collegeville: Liturgical Press, 1964), 370–72; Weller, 277–78; the *Book of Common Prayer,* 430–31.

You created man in love to share your divine life.
We see his high destiny in the love of husband and wife,
which bears the imprint of your own divine love.
Love is man's origin,
love is his constant calling,
love is his fulfillment in heaven.
The love of man and woman
is made holy in the sacrament of marriage
and becomes the mirror of your everlasting love.

The *Book of Common Prayer* provides a simple preface, explicitly Christian in its metaphors:

Because in the love of wife and husband, you have given us an image of the heavenly Jerusalem, adorned as a bride for her bridegroom, your Son Jesus Christ our Lord; who loves her and gave himself for her, that he might make the whole creation new (p. 381).

This self-giving love is also the theme of the newly-composed post-communion prayer in the *Lutheran Book of Worship*. The prayer (no. 163) bears some similarity also to the second of the alternative prayers after communion in the Roman rite.

The Rites of the Catholic Church	*Lutheran Book of Worship*	*Book of Common Prayer*
Lord, we who have shared the food of your table pray for our friends N. and N., whom you have joined together in marriage. Keep them close to you always. May their love for each other proclaim to all the world their faith in you. We ask this through Christ our Lord. (pp. 568–69)	Lord Jesus Christ, as you freely give yourself to your bride the Church, grant that the mystery of the union of man and woman in marriage may reveal to the world the self-giving love which you have for your Church; and to you with the Father and the Holy Spirit be glory and honor now and forever. (p. 190)	O God, the giver of all that is true and lovely and gracious: We give you thanks for binding us together in these holy mysteries of the Body and Blood of your Son Jesus Christ Grant that by your Holy Spirit, *N.* and *N.*, now joined in Holy Matrimony, may become one in heart and soul, live in fidelity and peace, and obtain those eternal joys prepared for all who love you; for the sake of Jesus Christ our Lord. (p. 432)

The Lutheran prayer is unusual in that it is addressed to the second person of the Holy Trinity. The scriptural allusions are Revelation 19:7 and Ephesians 5:25. The self-giving love of the couple is for the sake not of each other only but of the world. It is their witness and testimony to the love which has found them and which their example is to call the world to imitate.

The blessing is derived from the excellent alternative blessing first provided in the *Service Book and Hymnal.*

Service Book and Hymnal	*Lutheran Book of Worship*
God Almighty send you his light and truth to keep you all the days of your life. The hand of God protect you; his holy Angels accompany you. God the Father, God the Son, and God the Holy Ghost, cause his grace to be mighty upon you. (p. 273)	Almighty God, Father, + Son, and Holy Spirit, keep you in his light and truth and love now and forever.

The three gifts of God spoken of in the *Lutheran Book of Worship* form — light, truth, and love — can be loosely related to the three persons of the Holy Trinity. The Father is the source of light (Gen. 1:3; Ps. 27:1; Is. 60:19; John 1:7–9; 2 Cor. 4:6; James 1:17); the Son is the truth of God (2 Cor. 11:10; Eph. 4:21; 1 Tim. 2:7); the Holy Spirit is the source of love (Rom. 15:30; Col. 1:8). It is unfortunate that the full form of the blessing in the *Service Book and Hymnal* with its invocation of El Shaddai and rich Old Testament allusions (Ps. 43:3) was not preserved. It was a noteworthy contribution.

No proper color is indicated in the propers for marriage (Min. Ed., p. 190) but the rubric regarding liturgical colors (Min. Ed., p. 21) notes, "The color for a season of the church year is not affected by the celebration of Holy Baptism or marriage...." Thus the tradition established in the *Common Service Book* is retained: "The Celebration of the Holy Communion, the Solemnization of Holy Matrimony, and the Order for the Burial of the Dead, shall not affect the Proper Color for the Day or Season in use when these Services may be held."[29] Paul Zeller Strodach, speaking of the use of the proper color of the day or season for marriage and for burial of the dead, explains, "the color of the day or season *remains unchanged* in these circumstances, carrying its testimony to the believers through all conditions under which they are called to live."[30]

In the Roman rite the proper color for a marriage is white; the *Book of Common Prayer* does not prescribe liturgical color, but the use of white is the common practice in Episcopal churches.

The *Church Book* preserved the traditional closed time (*tempora clausa*): "The Seasons of Advent and Lent, from of old, have been regarded as unsuitable times for marriages."[31] The *Common Service Book*

---

[29] *Common Service Book*, text ed., p. 489.

[30] Peter Zeller Strodach, *A Manual on Worship*, rev. ed. (Philadelphia: Muhlenberg Press, 1946), 134.

[31] *Church Book* (1868), 374.

and the *Service Book and Hymnal* made no mention of the ancient practice. The *Lutheran Book of Worship* restricts the closed time to Holy Week: "Marriage should not be celebrated during Holy Week because of the solemn character of the time" (Min. Ed., p. 36). The present Roman rite says simply, "When a marriage is celebrated during Advent or Lent or other days of penance, the parish priest should advise the couple to take into consideration the special nature of these times."[32]

Table I
Comparison of Rites

The Rites of the Catholic Church	Lutheran Book of Worship	Book of Common Prayer
		Entrance
	The grace	
		Address
		Declaration of consent
	Hymn of Praise	
Opening Prayer	Prayer of the Day	Collect
Readings	Readings	Readings
Sermon	(Sermon)	(Sermon)
	(Hymn of the Day)	
Address	Address	
Questions		
Declaration of Consent	Vows	Vows
Blessing and		(Blessing and)
Exchange of rings	Exchange of rings	Exchange of rings
	Announcement	Pronouncement
	Matt. 19:6	Matt. 19:6
	Blessing of couple	
		Our Father
General intercessions	Prayers	Prayers
		Blessing of the marriage
	(The Peace)	The Peace
Offertory	(Offertory)	Offertory
Great Thanksgiving	(Great Thanksgiving)	Great Thanksgiving
Our Father	Our Father	
Nuptial Blessing		
Communion	(Communion)	Communion
Benediction	Benediction	Benediction

---

[32]*The Rites of the Catholic Church* (New York: Pueblo Publishing Co., 1976), 536.

Table II
Development of Rite

Luther 1529	Church Book	Common Service Book Service Book and Hymnal	Lutheran Book of Worship
At the entrance of the church Declaration of Consent Exchange of Rings Matt. 19:6 Pronouncement		Invocation	The grace... (Lessons)
	Address Gen. 1:18, 14	Address Gen. 1:18 Matt. 19:4–6	Address a) commandment
	Eph. 5:25–29 Gen. 3:16–17 Gen. 1:27–28, 31	Eph. 5:25, 22	b) cross c) comfort
		(*SBH:* Eph. 5:25, 28b–29, 22–23; 1 Pet. 3:4b, 7)	
	Banns	Banns Declaration of Intent	
Before the Altar Gen. 1:18, 21–24 Eph. 5:25–29, 22–24 Gen. 3:16–19 Gen. 1:27–28, 31 Prov. 18:22		*At the altar*	
	Giving of ring Vows Matt. 19:6	Vows Giving of ring	Vows Giving of ring(s)
	Pronouncement	Pronouncement Matt. 19:6	Announcement Matt. 19:6
Blessing	Blessing from Luther	Blessing	Blessing(s)
		Prayer(s)	Prayers (Holy Communion)
	Our Father Aaronic benediction (Te Deum)	Our Father Aaronic benediction	Our Father Benediction

BIBLIOGRAPHY

Braddock, Joseph. *The Bridal Bed.* New York: John Day, 1961.

Brundage, James A. *Law, Sex and Christian Society in Medieval Europe.* Chicago: University Press, 1988.

Cooke, Bernard, ed. *Christian Marriage.* Vol. 5 of Alternative Futures for Worship. Collegeville: Liturgical Press, 1986.

Dominian, Jack. *Marriage, Faith, and Love.* New York: Crossroad Publishing Co., 1982.

Everett, William Johnson. *Blessed Be the Bond: Christian Perspectives on Marriage and the Family.* Philadelphia: Fortress Press, 1985.

Fuchs, Eric. *Sexual Desire and Love: Origins and History of the Christian Ethic of Sexuality and Marriage.* New York: Seabury Press, 1983.

Goody, Jack. *The Development of the Family and Marriage in Europe.* Cambridge: University Press, 1983.

Gruenenfelder, John. "The Unity of the Marital Act," *Worship* 42 (October 1968):495–501.

Hansen, Paul G., Oscar E. Feucht, Fred Kramer, Erwin Lueker. *Engagement and Marriage: A Sociological, Historical, and Theological Investigation of Engagement and Marriage.* St. Louis: Concordia Publishing House, 1959.

Heaney, Seamus P. *The Development of the Sacramentality of Marriage from Anselm of Laon to Thomas Aquinas.* Washington, D.C.: Catholic University Press, 1963.

James, Edwin O. *Marriage Customs Through the Ages.* New York: Collier, 1965. [1952].

Kasper, Walter. *Theology of Christian Marriage.* Translated by David Smith. New York: Seabury Press, 1980.

Lazareth, William H. *Luther on the Christian Home.* Philadelphia: Muhlenberg Press, 1960.

Leclercq, Jean. *Monks on Marriage: A Twelfth Century Christian View.* New York: Seabury Press, 1982.

Lowther Clarke, W. K. "Solemnization of Matrimony." In *Liturgy and Worship*, edited by W. K. Lowther Clarke and Charles Harris. London: SPCK , 1932.

Luhmann, Niklas. *Love as Passion: The Codification of Intimacy.* Oxford: Polity Press, 1986.

Luther, Martin. "The Estate of Marriage" (1522). *Luther's Works* 45:11–49.

———. "On Marriage Matters" (1530). *Luther's Works* 46:259–320.

———. "Sermon on the Estate of Marriage" (1519). *Luther's Works* 44:3–14.

Mackin, Theodore. *What is Marriage? Marriage in the Catholic Church.* New York: Paulist Press, 1982.

Pfatteicher, Philip H. *In Love and Faithfulness.* Philadelphia: Parish Life Press, 1982.

Ritzer, Korbinian. *Formen, Riten und religiöses Brauchtum der Eheschliessung in der christlichen Kirchen des ersten Jahrtausends.* Münster im Westf.: Aschendorff, 1962.

Rothman, Ellen K. *Hands and Hearts: A History of Courtship in America.* New York: Basic Books, 1984.

Schillebeeckx, Edward C. F. A. *Marriage: Human Reality and Saving Mystery.* Translated by N. D. Smith. New York: Sheed and Ward, 1965.

Stevenson, Kenneth. *Nuptial Blessing: A Study of Christian Marriage Rites.* Alcuin Club collections 64. New York: Oxford University Press, 1983.

———. *To Join Together.* Studies in the Reformed Rites of the Catholic Church vol. 5. New York: Pueblo Publishing Co., 1987.

Thurian, Max. *Marriage and Celibacy.* Translated by Norma Emerton. London: SCM Press, 1959.

10

Burial of the Dead

Ministers Edition, pp. 331–339, 190–191, 37–38

Parallel Rites

Roman Catholic	Rite of Funerals, *The Rites*, pp. 643–720.
Episcopal	The Burial of the Dead: Rite One; The Burial of the Dead: Rite Two, *Book of Common Prayer*, pp. 468–507.
Lutheran	Burial of the Dead, *The Book of Worship* (General Synod 1867), pp. 127–36. Order for the Burial of the Dead, *The Liturgy of the Evangelical Lutheran Church* (General Synod 1881), pp. 84–111. The Burial Service, *Forms for Ministerial Acts* (General Synod 1900), pp. 103–26. The Burial of the Dead, *A Liturgy for the Use of Evangelical Lutheran Pastors* (Joint Synod of Ohio 1912), pp. 147–50. The Burial of the Dead, *Church Book* (General Council 1891), pp. 406–21. Order for the Burial of the Dead, *Common Service Book* (1919), text ed., pp. 430–48. The Burial of the Dead, *Liturgy and Agenda* (Missouri Synod 1921), pp. 352–75. The Order for the Burial of the Dead; A Reading Service for the Burial of the Stillborn, *The Lutheran Agenda* (Synodical Conference 194–), pp. 67–103. Order for the Burial of the Dead, *Service Book and Hymnal* (1958), pp. 253–69. *Contemporary Worship 10: Burial of the Dead* (1976).
Orthodox	The Order for the Burial of the Dead (Laymen), The Order for the Burial of the Dead (Priests), The Order for the Burial of a Child, The Order for the Burial of Those Who Die at Holy Easter and During the Whole of the Bright Week, The Requiem Office for the Dead, *Service Book*, pp. 368–453.
Methodist	A Service of Death and Resurrection (1980)

Purpose

The Burial of the Dead is an expression of the faith and hope of the community of those who have been baptized into the death and resurrection of Christ in the face of the death of one of its members. This expression takes three aspects: (1) prayer for the one who has died, commending that person to the care of God;[1] (2) comfort of the bereaved with the assurance of the power and goodness of the living God; and (3) praise of God "to whom all things live," the destroyer of death and the source of life and salvation.

Characteristics

The structure of the Burial of the Dead as it appears in the *Lutheran Book of Worship* is a significant change from the structure in previous service books. In earlier Lutheran and Episcopal books the Burial of the Dead was derived from the Office of the Dead and was an office (like Morning and Evening Prayer) of Psalms (with antiphons), readings (with responsories), and prayers. In the present Lutheran and Episcopal books, however, as in the Roman rite, the structure of the Burial of the Dead is that of the Holy Communion, indicating a renewed appreciation of the centrality of the sacrament in Christian life and its appropriateness in a variety of circumstances.

The present order is less easily adapted and is indeed less appropriate to funerals of those who die "without the sign of faith" than was the older order for the Burial of the Dead. It is a service for members of the Christian community, and adaptation for others is possible but not without awkwardness.

The *Lutheran Book of Worship* order is the first North American Lutheran burial rite to take clear notice of the one who as died. Earlier rites reflected a fear even of prayers which mention the departed, which was an exaggerated form of the Reformers' rejection of the offering of masses for the dead, sometimes years after their death.[2] Prayers that mention the departed may not have been familiar to many Lutherans for several generations, but such prayers are in harmony with Lutheran theology. The *Apology* of the Augsburg Confession declares, "We know that the ancients speak of prayers for the dead which we do not prohibit."[3] At

---

[1] Luther did not reject prayer for the dead in connection with a commendation of them to God's care. See *Luthers Werke*, WA 10.3, p. 409, which admits such prayer "once or twice"; see also "The Babylonian Captivity of the Church," *Luther's Works* 35:35. His objection was to the transfer of merits to the dead and the use of the mass to effect such transfer.

[2] Eugene L. Brand in the ILCW *Worshipbrief* no. 6 (March 1977) made this point in response to those who objected that prayer which mentions the departed was "unLutheran."

[3] *Apology* XXIV.96. See also *Apology* XXIV.94–96.

the time of the funeral the dead are not forgotten as if the service were only for the living. Death cannot break the communion of saints, who are "knit together in one holy Church, the body of Christ our Lord"[4] by their baptism. Prayer that God would give to the deceased eternal life in the fellowship of all the saints is an expression of the faith and hope of the Christian community.

Prayers for the dead were offered in the time of intertestamental Judaism (2 Macc. 12:43–45), and the origins of such prayers among Christians is traceable from the second century. Tertullian speaks of "oblations" for the departed "on the anniversary of their [heavenly] birth."[5] In the catacombs of St. Calixtus outside the walls of Rome may still be seen a number of inscriptions echoing the last words of dying Christians, "In your prayers remember us who have gone before you."[6] The Hannover Church Order (1536) calls the practice of offering prayers for the departed "a fine, ancient custom," but because of the abuses and superstitions which became attached to the practice through the centuries, any hint of the practice was generally abandoned in the Lutheran churches.[7]

The full liturgical expression of the church's faith and pastoral concern at the time of death includes the Commendation of the Dying (*Occasional Services*, pp. 103–07),[8] Comforting the Bereaved (*Occasional Services*, pp. 108–12), and Burial of the Dead. All three rites are to be understood as comprising a unified service.

The Burial of the Dead is informed throughout by a paschal spirit. The Commendation of the Dying and Comforting the Bereaved emphasize penitence and the sense of loss and grief. The Burial of the Dead, while not neglecting such emotions, is thus freed to proclaim more clearly the themes of triumph and victory and Easter joy. Following ancient Christian practice, grief is acknowledged, for death clearly involves loss, but mourning is excluded,[9] because Christ by his resurrection has destroyed death and opened the gate of everlasting life.[10]

In Lutheran theology death is a stage in the fulfillment of Baptism. Luther wrote eloquently,

This significance of baptism — the dying or drowning of sin — is not fulfilled completely in this life. Indeed this does not happen until man passes through bodily death and completely decays to dust. As we can plainly see, the sacrament or sign of baptism is quickly over. But the spiritual baptism, the drowning of

---

[4] Prayer of the Day for All Saints' Day, November 1.

[5] Tertullian, *The Chaplet* or *de Corona* 3; see also *On Monogamy* 10.

[6] Noted by William D. Bosenhofer, "Prayers for the Dead — A Layman's Reflections," *The Bride of Christ* VI.4 (Ordinary Time 1982):32.

[7] See Paul Zeller Strodach, *A Manual on Worship*, rev. ed. (Philadelphia: Muhlenberg Press, 1946), 353.

[8] See Richard Rutherford, *The Death of a Christian: The Rite of Funerals* (New York: Pueblo, 1980), 42; Alfred C. Rush, "The Eucharist: The Sacrament of the Dying in Christian Antiquity," *The Jurist* 34 (1974):10–35.

[9] Rutherford, 15. Ambrose (*de excessu fratris* 1.5) said that tears washed away sins.

[10] The (second) Prayer of the Day for Easter Day; Col. 1:1–3.

sin, which it signifies, lasts as long as we live and is completed only in death. Then it is that a person is completely sunk in baptism, and that which baptism signifies comes to pass.

Therefore this whole life is nothing else than a spiritual baptism which does not cease till death, and he who is baptized is condemned to die. It is as if the priest, when he baptizes, were to say, "Lo, you are sinful flesh. Therefore I drown you in God's name and in his name condemn you to death, so that with you all your sins may die and be destroyed." Wherefore St. Paul in Romans 6 [:4], says, "We were buried with Christ by baptism into death." The sooner a person dies after baptism, the sooner is his baptism completed.... There is no help for the sinful nature unless it dies and is destroyed with all its sin. Therefore the life of a Christian, from baptism to the grave, is nothing else than the beginning of a blessed death. For at the Last Day God will make him altogether new.

Similarly the lifting up out of the baptismal water is quickly done, but the thing it signifies — the spiritual birth and the increase of grace and righteousness — even though it begins in baptism, lasts until death, indeed, until the Last Day. Only then will that be finished which the lifting up out of baptism signifies. Then shall we arise from death, from sins, and from all evil, pure in body and soul, and then shall we live eternally. Then shall we be truly lifted up out of baptism and be completely born, and we shall put on the true baptismal garment of immortal life in heaven.[11]

The Burial of the Dead is a baptismal and an Easter liturgy setting forth the paschal passage from death to life.

Background

Funeral ritual is part of the heritage of the human community. All societies and religions have a ritual to deal with what is for all the critical fact of death. In the first-century church, funeral rites reflected both Jewish funerary rites with their stark simplicity and "consciousness of the righteous justice and faithfulness of God who is to be praised in death as well as in life,"[12] and also the funeral customs of the Mediterranean world of the time[13] in which the last honor paid to the dead was deeply rooted.[14] There was (1) a gathering of relatives and close friends by the bedside of the dying person; (2) prayer in the house while the body was washed and anointed and clothed in white linen; (3) a procession (from which come

---

[11] Martin Luther, "The Holy and Blessed Sacrament of Baptism" (1519), *Luther's Works* 35:30–31. This passage was also quoted above (p. 56) in connection with baptism, for in Luther's view, baptism and death belong together.

[12] Geoffrey Rowell, *The Liturgy of Christian Burial* (London: SPCK, 1977), 3–8. See also Jack Reimer, ed., *Jewish Reflections on Death* (New York: Schocken, 1974). On death in Scripture see Richard J. Dillon, "The Unavoidable Discomforts of Preaching about Death," *Worship* 57 (November 1983):486–96. See also "Burials" in *The New Westminster Dictionary of Liturgy and Worship*, ed. J.G. Davies (Philadelphia: Westminster Press, 1986).

[13] See Jocelyn M.C. Toynbee, *Death and Burial in the Roman World* (Ithaca: Cornell University Press, 1971), 43–51. See also Donna C. Kurtz and John Boardman, *Greek Burial Customs* (Ithaca: Cornell University Press, 1971).

[14] Rutherford, 6. See Cyril Bailey, *Religion in Virgil* (Oxford: Clarendon Press, 1935), 287–91; Virgil, *The Aeneid* 6, 212–35; Homer, *The Iliad* 23, 109–256.

the funerary terms *exsequiae* and *prosequi*) to church or cemetery during daylight (in ancient Roman times funerals were conducted at night) with symbols not of mourning but of victory and triumph — white garments, psalms of hope, repeated alleluias, palms of victory, incense;[15] (4) the office, a short service of praise and thanksgiving with biblical readings and psalms; (5) the celebration of the Eucharist, corresponding to the funerary feast, *silicernium*, eaten at the grave of the deceased, to emphasize the unbroken communion between living and dead; and (6) burial, often in shelves cut in the rock walls of hypogea and catacombs, with feet to the east signifying the expectation of the rising of the Sun of Righteousness. The third, ninth, and fortieth days after the funeral were times for relatives and friends to assemble for hymns and prayers. The dominant themes were joy and hope.

During the first three centuries of the church's life, the earliest witnesses to Christian care of the dead are the cemeteries,[16] which were apparently public rather than secret burying places, the graves of Christians identified by symbolic decorations which set forth the motif of life: Baptism with which the life in Christ began, loaves and fish pointing to the Eucharist which nourished that life, the Good Shepherd who leads his people through death into the pastures of everlasting life. In the fourth century, after the Edict of Milan, and the legalization of Christianity, these symbols give way to deliverance motifs: the sacrifice of Isaac, Daniel among the lions, Jonah freed from the fish, the three young men in the fiery furnace, Job delivered from misery; Christ healing the man born blind, Christ raising Lazarus, Peter's denial at cockcrow (representing the dawn of new life after the forgiveness of sins).

Prayer for the faithful departed was taken for granted as an expression of the communion of saints, living and dead, the unity of the church militant and triumphant.[17] Those who died outside communion with the church were believed to be beyond the help of prayer.[18] The prayers, like the iconography on the tombs, used images of light, rest, and deliverance without attempts at precise definition; Augustine wrote, "Now he lives in the bosom of Abraham whatever is signified by that bosom, there my Nebridus lives, that sweet friend of mine."[19] (The hymn by Frederick Lucian Hosmer [1840–1929] included in the *Service Book and Hymnal* [no. 600] sang in a similar vein, "O Lord of life, where'er they be, / Safe in thine own eternity, / Our dead are living unto thee. / Alleluia." A striking example of an ancient prayer for the departed is found

---

[15]See E.G.C.F. Atchley, *A History of the Use of Incense in Divine Worship*, Alcuin Collection 13. London: Longmans, Green, and Co., 1909.

[16]See John Chrysostom's discussion of the name "cemetery" *In coemeterii appellationem* (*Eis to onoma tou koimeiteirou*), Migne *PG* 49, 393.

[17]See Augustine, *The City of God* 2.9; *The Care to Be Taken for the Dead* (*de cura pro mortuis gerenda*) 6–7, 22.

[18]Rutherford, 15.

[19]Augustine, *Confessions* 9.3.6.

in the *Euchologion* or Prayer Book of Serapion, Bishop of Thmuis in the first half of the fourth century:

O God, you have authority of life and death, God of the spirits and master of all flesh; you kill and make alive, you bring down to the gates of Hades and bring up; you create the spirit of mortals within them and take to yourself the souls of the saints and give rest; you alter and change and transform your creatures, as is right and expedient, being yourself alone incorruptible, unalterable and eternal.

We pray to you for the repose and rest of this your servant; give rest to his soul, his spirit, in green places, in chambers of rest with Abraham and Isaac and Jacob and all your saints; and raise up his body in the day when you have ordained, according to your promises which cannot lie, that you may render to it also the heritage of which it is worthy in your holy pastures. Remember not his transgressions and sins and cause his going forth to be peaceable and blessed. Heal the grief of his relatives who survive him with the spirit of consolation, and grant to us all a good end, through your only-begotten Son, Jesus Christ, through whom to you is the glory and the strength in the Holy Spirit, for ever and ever.[20]

The prayer is a remarkable conflation of Hebrew and Greek thought.

By the time of Gregory the Great (d. 604), the idea of expiation becomes important in explanations of prayer for the dead: the prayer of the church brought about the liberation of the departed from the purifying fire of expiation of sin;[21] before long this fire would become localized as "purgatory."[22] Trust in God's mercy was giving way to a fear of God's judgment. This preoccupation with the lot of the dead approaching judgment is expressed in the last seven stanzas of the hymn attributed to Columba the Elder of Iona (d. ca. 597), "In Praise of the Father (*Altus prosator*)," and in a twelfth-century responsory *Libera me, Domine:*

From everlasting death, deliver me, O Lord, in that awful day when the heavens and the earth shall be moved, when you will come to judge the world by fire. Dread and trembling have laid hold of me, and I fear exceedingly because of the judgment and the wrath to come. O that day, that day of wrath, of sore distress and of all wretchedness, that great and exceedingly bitter day, when you will come to judge the world by fire.

It is also expressed most powerfully in the famous sequence *Dies Irae* (twelfth–thirteenth century).

In the liturgical books of the twelfth and thirteenth centuries the funeral mass celebrated for the departed before burial had become a mass other than one of the scheduled celebrations of the day. Rather than keeping watch by the body until the regular morning mass, a special mass had become part of the burial rite. This requiem mass became in the 1570 Roman missal the normative funeral mass, taking little note

---

[20] See Lucien Deiss, *The Springtime of the Liturgy* (Collegeville: Liturgical Press, 1979), 207–08; *Liturgy and Worship*, ed. W. K. Lowther Clarke (London: SPCK, 1932), 619.

[21] Rutherford, 26.

[22] See Jacques Le Goff, *The Birth of Purgatory*, trans. Arthur Goldhammer (Chicago: University of Chicago Press, 1984).

of the church year or of the community of the congregation. An absolution service was added to the conclusion of the funeral mass, reflecting medieval dread and trembling in the face of death and serving as a *memento mori* to the living who prayed for the departed.

The blessing of the grave was added in the tenth century.

Toward the end of the Middle Ages, forms for the burial of children began to appear.[23] Later Lutheran and Anglican rites would preserve some elements of such rites for children.

By 1500 the funeral liturgy revealed great diversity and was standardized only in the Roman Ritual of 1614.

Luther produced manuals for baptism and marriage but none for burial. He simply published a few German and Latin hymns for that purpose. There is therefore a great and confusing number and variety of forms and order for burial in individual Lutheran churches and areas. In general, the focal point was the resurrection, and, as it was for the Jews, the burial was understood as an act of charity toward the departed. "For the dead are still our brothers and have not fallen from our community by death; we still remain members of a single body" (Schwäbisch-Hall 1526, Richter I.47). The funeral was understood as a reminder of one's own death, as it had been in the Middle Ages.[24] As with marriage, there was opposition to secrecy with regard to burial. There are some instances of prayer for the dead in the Lutheran church orders.[25]

At first the coffin was lowered into the grave to the singing of a hymn; later, affirmations were added: Genesis 3:19,[26] Revelation 14:13,[27] or as earth is cast on the coffin three times,

Of the dust you have been made, and to dust you must return. May the Lord Jesus Christ raise your body and soul that you may rise again with the righteous on the last day. Amen.[28]

A sermon was preached for people of some standing, usually as a memorial some time after the burial. Occasionally brief admonitions were given in connection with the readings, 1 Thessalonians 4:13–18 and John 11:21–27. Eventually a sermon became an essential part of the funeral. The Wittenberg order (1533) directed that common people be buried without bells, those of middle degree with the singing of school children, and honorable persons with a procession and the great bells.[29]

---

[23] Rutherford, 84.

[24] See Württemberg (1536) in Aemilius L. Richter, ed., *Die evangelischen Kirchenordnungen des sechzehnten Jahrhunderts*, vol. 1 (Weimar: Land-industriecomptoir, 1846), 273.

[25] Württemberg (1536) in Richter I, 273; Hessen (1566 and 1574) in Emil Sehling, ed., *Die evangelischen Kirchenordnungen des XVI Jahrhunderts*, vol. 8 (Tübingen: Mohr, 1955), 336, 450.

[26] Dessau (1532) in Sehling i.2, 541.

[27] Pfalz-Neuburg (1543) in Sehling 13, 90.

[28] Waldeck (1556) in Richter vol. 2 (Leipzig: Günther, 1871), 171.

[29] Sehling 1, 1, 195.

Such classification of funerals lasted down to the beginning of the twentieth century in Germany and involved the entire form of the funeral.

The sermons of the sixteenth century were predominantly biblical and christological. In the seventeenth century a review of the person's life was added, and the eulogy eventually became a main theme.

Wilhelm Loehe and other leaders of the nineteenth-century liturgical revival prepared complete funeral liturgies for the first time in the Lutheran church, based on portions of sixteenth-century church orders and the English Prayer Books. A typical form followed the medieval office of the dead: Psalm 130 or another psalm, one or two lessons, a sermon, prayer. At the graveside as the coffin was lowered into the grave the form of committal from the *Book of Common Prayer* was sometimes used, occasionally with the additional words,

From the earth you are taken; to the earth you shall return. Jesus Christ our Redeemer will raise you on the last day.[30]

A lesson and prayers are provided also. The committal in the burial rite of the Liturgy of the Joint Synod of Ohio (1912) is remarkable in its starkness. The traditional antiphon "In the midst of life" is said, the body is lowered into the grave, and the formula of committal is said; that is all.

Philippe Aries has traced the history of Western attitudes toward death.[31] He observes that until the twelfth or thirteenth century "tame" death was integrated into the life of the community. Death was understood to be central to life, even as the burial ground was located in the ecclesiastical center of the town. During the thirteenth to the fifteenth centuries a new individualism led to a developing concern for one's own death, the judgment, and personal reckoning. A fascination with death and decay abounds (cf. the *transi* tombs), which was in part a rebellion against death as a defeat. By the seventeenth century people began to worry obsessively about their own mortality, and anxiety about death and a concern for the salvation of the souls of the deceased became common. The nineteenth century saw a fascination with a romanticized view of death, which gradually became a forbidden topic, so that in the twentieth century one finds obscene and hence invisible death.

In the latter half of the twentieth century considerable attention was given in medical and psychological literature to the subjects of death and dying, opening up the discussion of what had been a forbidden topic.[32]

---

[30]Prussia (1895).

[31]Philippe Aries, *Western Attitudes Toward Death: From the Middle Ages to the Present* (Baltimore: Johns Hopkins University Press, 1974).

[32]Among the many books were Jessica Mitford, *The American Way of Death* (New York: Simon and Schuster, 1963); Joseph Head and S. L. Cranston, eds., *Reincarnation: The Phoenix Fire Mystery. An East-West Dialogue on Death and Rebirth from the Worlds of Religion, Science, Psychology, Philosophy, Art, and Literature, and from Great Thinkers of the Present* (New York: Julian Press, 1977); John H. Hick, *Death and Eternal Life* (New York: Harper & Row, 1976); Quincy Howe, Jr., *Reincarnation for the Christian* (Philadelphia: Westminster Press, 1974); Elisabeth Kübler-Ross, *On Death and Dying* (New York:

Fear and embarrassment in the face of death had been developing for a century. G. K. Chesterton in his remarkable and delightful book *Orthodoxy* (1908) observed, "Some religious societies discouraged men more or less from thinking about sex. The new scientific society definitely discourages men from thinking about death; it is a fact, but it is considered a morbid fact."[33] In an essay in 1955 Geoffrey Gorer, the British anthropologist, used the phrase "The Pornography of Death." His point was that, like sex, death had become unmentionable in polite society.[34]

The opening of the once-veiled subject of death had an impact on liturgy. In 1969 the Roman Catholic Church as part of the liturgical reform ordered by the Second Vatican Council published *Ordo Exsequiarum* (The Rite of Funerals), embodying a broad understanding of the obsequies surrounding dying, death, burial, and final leave-taking, and emphasizing the paschal mystery and the consequent faith and hope.[35] A revised English translation with supplementary material was issued in October 1985.

The Episcopal and Lutheran churches in their liturgical reform made considerable use of the Roman Catholic liturgy, especially in their adoption of the eucharistic form as the normative order, turning away from their earlier structure of an office of psalms, readings, and prayers, in recognition of the historical evidence that "the Church's oldest memories of Christians caring for the dead included the celebration of the Lord's Supper."[36]

The Burial of the Dead was drafted by Hans C. Boehringer and published as *Contemporary Worship 10*. Philip V. Anderson, Thetis Cromie, Robert Fuller, and Johan A. Thorson served as consultants.

THE SERVICE IN DETAIL

The title of this service, Burial of the Dead, continues a Lutheran tradition which was introduced in the 1867 *Book of Worship* of the General

---

Macmillan, 1970) and *Questions and Answers on Death and Dying* (New York: Macmillan, 1974); Raymond A. Moody, *Life after Life: The Investigation of a Phenomenon — Survival of Bodily Death* (Harrisburg, PA: Stackpole Books, 1976), and *Reflections on Life After Life* (Harrisburg, PA: Stackpole Books, 1977); E. Garth Moore, *Try the Spirits: Christianity and Psychical Research* (New York: Oxford University Press, 1977); Karlis Osis and Erlendur Haraldsson, *At the Hour of Death* (New York: Avon Books, 1977); John L. Randall, *Parapsychology and the Nature of Life* (New York: Harper & Row, 1975); Ian Stevenson, *Telepathic Impressions: A Review and Report of Thirty-Five New Cases* (Charlottesville: University of Virginia Press, 1970), and *Twenty Cases Suggestive of Reincarnation*, 2nd rev. ed. (Charlottesville: University of Virginia Press, 1974).

[33] Gilbert K. Chesterton, *Orthodoxy* (New York: John Lane Co.), 36.

[34] See Russell Baker, *Growing Up* (New York: Congdon and Weed, 1982), chap. 4, on how rural Virginia in the 1930s had not yet developed the modern disgust with death.

[35] See Robert Sparkes and Richard Rutherford, "The Order of Christian Funerals: A Study in Bereavement and Lament," *Worship* 60 (November 1986):499–510; Robert J. Hoeffner, "A Pastoral Evaluation of the Rite of Funerals," *Worship* 55 (November 1981):482–99; Robert W. Hovda, "The Amen Corner," *Worship* 59 (March 1985):148–54 and 59 (May 1985):251–60 on the North American cultural setting for funerals and "Reclaiming the Church for the Death of a Christian."

[36] Rutherford, 56–57.

Synod and continued in the 1891 *Church Book*, the *Common Service Book* (1917), and the *Service Book and Hymnal* (1958). The title had been borrowed from the *Book of Common Prayer*. It is to be understood broadly, including use after cremation and for memorial services.

There is no indication of a proper liturgical color for Burial of the Dead with the propers for that occasion (Min. Ed., pp. 190–91); the color is to be understood as the color of the season or holy day. The Notes on the Liturgy (Min. Ed., p. 21) direct, "The color for a season of the church year is not affected by the celebration of Holy Baptism or marriage; the color is not changed for funerals...." Paul Zeller Strodach observed concerning this Lutheran practice or retaining the seasonal color for the personal occasions of marriage and burial, "The color of the day or season *remains unchanged* in these circumstances, carrying its testimony to the believers through all conditions under which they are called to live."[37] The Roman Sacramentary directs the use of white for the mass of the resurrection, emphasizing its paschal nature. The *Book of Common Prayer* gives no directions concerning liturgical color, although white is becoming popular in Episcopal churches.

The Burial of the Dead begins at the entrance of the church as the ministers meet the bereaved and the coffin of the deceased. (The *Lutheran Book of Worship* has consistently resisted the common euphemism "casket," which can mean any small box or container for valuables, and uses the straightforward and unambiguous word "coffin.") The presiding minister says the blessing from 2 Corinthians 1:3–4 which praises God and tells of consolation and its purpose. The Roman Catholic rite provides this verse or a version of the Apostolic Greeting.[38] The Burial Service of the Church of South India introduced the use of this verse at the beginning of the service.

If a pall is used, the verses from Romans 6:3–5 may be said to accompany and explain the action, relating the pall to the garment given at baptism. The Roman rite suggests

On the day of his (her) baptism, N. put on Christ. In the day of Christ's coming, may he (she) be clothed with glory.

In both rites the pall may be spread in silence.

The pall which covers the coffin is a kind of "body mask,"[39] symbolically showing the deceased clothed in the righteousness of Christ, wearing the robe of resurrection put on at baptism which makes the whole life from baptism to its completion in death a transitional state. The medieval formula for giving the white robe (*Westerhemd*) immediately following baptism, used in Luther's 1523 *Order of Baptism*, was

---

[37]Strodach, 134.

[38]*The Rites of the Catholic Church* (New York: Pueblo Publishing Co., 1976), 673; see p. 662.

[39]Anthropologists often note the use of masks in connection with rites of passage as a sign of the transitional state. See A. David Napier, *Masks, Transformation and Paradox* (Berkeley: University of California Press, 1986).

Receive the white, holy, and spotless robe which thou shalt bring before the judgment seat of Christ so as to receive eternal life.[40]

Thus clothed in the funeral pall, the body is brought into the church even as the person, clothed in the robe of Christ's righteousness, will be brought before the Judge, who is Love himself.

The procession is a dramatic and symbolic enactment of the passage through this world to that which is to come. In that brief walk our life is done; we see "the shortness and uncertainty of human life."[41] The procession is a reminder and an expression of mortality: we move daily toward death, but then through death to life. The pilgrimage procession is an evocative symbol, as ancient as Abraham, used by the writer to the Hebrews (11:8ff.) and by John Bunyan in his most popular allegory, *The Pilgrim's Progress from This World to That Which Is to Come*. The Burial of the Dead itself may be understood as a stational procession moving from the church door to the pulpit to the altar to the cemetery. Each stop along the way marks an important development of the fullness of the proclamation of this liturgy.

The psalms appointed for the procession into the church (Min. Ed., p. 190) are in part from the Roman rite at the home of the deceased (Ps. 23, 130).[42] Psalm 23, together with Psalm 93, was a favorite psalm to accompany the washing of the body in the ancient rites; Psalm 23 with its double theme of God as shepherd and host, pointing to baptism and the eucharist, was especially favored.

The verses are in part from the *Book of Common Prayer* (John 11:25–26, a frequent appointment in the burial forms in the church orders; Rom. 14:7–9; Rev. 14:13, used in several church orders at the committal). The 1549 *Book of Common Prayer* provided three anthems to be said or sung in procession from the churchyard gate to the church or the grave. The first was John 11:25–26, an antiphon at Lauds in the Sarum rite; the second was Job 19:25–27, a responsory after the first lesson at Matins in the Sarum office; this is included in the present Prayer Book but in the *Lutheran Book of Worship* it is not used here but at the procession to the grave. The 1979 Prayer Book uses Romans 14:7–8 and Revelation 14:13 as the third anthem; the verse from Revelation had been used in the Sarum rite and earlier Prayer Books after the committal.

The third option in the *Lutheran Book of Worship*, hymn 350, "Even as We Live Each Day," is a hymnic version of an anthem said (unreliably) to have been composed by Notker Balbulus (the Stammerer), a monk of St. Gall in Switzerland (d. 910), while watching the construction of a bridge over a gorge of the Goldach and realizing the danger which threatened the workers. The anthem, *Media vita in morte sumus*, was popular in Germany; several German versions were in existence

---

[40] *Luther's Works* 53:101.
[41] Min. Ed., 333, prayer no. 282.
[42] *The Rites*, 669.

in the fifteenth century. Luther's metrical translation of it (1524) made the hymn a statement of faith rather than a desperate cry and added two stanzas of Luther's composition.[43] The anthem or Luther's hymn was used in the burial rites of the German church orders and in the burial rites in North America. *The Book of Worship* of the General Synod (1867) and the *Liturgy of the Joint Synod of Ohio* (1912) borrowed the form from the *Book of Common Prayer* (the Joint Synod of Ohio adapting it to the Authorized Version), which prefixed Job 14:1–2 to the medieval antiphon that was sung after the Nunc Dimittis in the Sarum Compline office from the third to the fifth Sunday in Lent.

Man, that is born of a woman, hath but a short time to live, and is full of misery. He cometh up, and is cut down, like a flower; he fleeth as it were a shadow, and never continueth in one stay.

In the midst of life we are in death; of whom may we seek for succor, but of thee, O Lord, who for our sins art justly displeased?

Yet, O Lord God most holy, O Lord most mighty, O holy and most merciful Saviour, deliver us not into the bitter pains of eternal death.

Thou knowest, Lord, the secrets of our hearts; shut not thy merciful ears to our prayer; but spare us, Lord most holy, O God most mighty, O holy and merciful Saviour, thou most worthy Judge eternal, suffer us not, at our last hour, for any pains of death, to fall from thee.[44]

An abbreviated form was given as an alternative verse with which the service at the grave began in the *Common Service Book* (text ed., p. 447) and the *Service Book and Hymnal* (p. 268). The anthem is reminiscent of the Trisagion of the Eastern Liturgy, and the version in the present Prayer Book (p. 492) emphasizes that relationship.

The liturgy of the word follows. The first prayer, "O God of grace and glory" (no. 279), is slightly revised from the *Book of Common Prayer* Rite II, the third prayer at the burial of an adult (p. 493), which was drafted by Virginia Harbour on the basis of a prayer from Huub Oosterhuis' *Your Word Is Near.*[45]

Lutheran Book of Worship	*Book of Common Prayer*
O God of grace and glory, we remember before you today our *brother/sister*, ___name___ . We thank you for giving *him/her* to us to know and to love as a companion in our pilgrimage on earth. In your boundless	O God of grace and glory, we remember before you this day our brother (sister) *N.* We thank you for giving *him* to us, *his* family and friends, to know and to love as a companion on our earthly pilgrimage. In your boundless

[43] *Luther's Works* 53:274–76.

[44] *Book of Common Prayer* (1928), 332.

[45] Marion J. Hatchett, *Commentary on the American Prayer Book* (New York: Seabury Press, 1981), 486; see Huub Oosterhuis, *Your Word Is Near* (New York and Paramus: Newman Press, 1968), 77–87.

compassion, console us who mourn. Give us your aid, so we may see in death the gate to eternal life, that we may continue our course on earth in confidence until, by your call, we are reunited with those who have gone before us; through your Son, Jesus Christ our Lord. (Min. Ed., p. 332)	compassion, console us who mourn. Give us faith to see in death the gate of eternal life, so that in quiet confidence we may continue our course on earth, until, by your call, we are reunited with those who have gone before us; through Jesus Christ our Lord. (p. 493)

The opening address quotes Harry Emerson Fosdick's familiar hymn (no. 415).

The second prayer, "Almighty God, source of all mercy" (no. 280), is slightly revised from the *Book of Common Prayer* in which it is the last of the "Additional Prayers" (pp. 489, 505). It has been attributed to Bishop Charles Lewis Slattery of Massachusetts (d. 1930); the phrase "never-failing care and love" appears in another prayer by Bishop Slattery, "For those we love" (no. 54, p. 831, in the 1979 Prayer Book.) This prayer first appeared in the English proposed book of 1928 and was in the 1928 American Prayer Book (p. 342).[46]

Lutheran Book of Worship	*Book of Common Prayer*
Almighty God, source of all mercy and giver of comfort: Deal graciously, we pray, with those who mourn, that, casting all their sorrow on you, they may know the consolation of your love; through your Son, Jesus Christ our Lord.	Almighty God, Father of mercies and giver of comfort: Deal graciously, we pray, with all who mourn; that, casting all their care on you, they may know the consolation of your love; through Jesus Christ our Lord. (p. 505)

The prayer contains an allusion to Matthew 5:4.

The third prayer, "Almighty God, those who die in the Lord" (no. 281), is a revision of one of the "Additional Prayers" in the *Book of Common Prayer* (Rite I, p. 488; Rite II, p. 503). It first appeared in the 1549 Prayer Book, incorporating lines from various medieval burial offices.[47] It was revised in 1552 and 1662 and in the American Prayer Book of 1789, and was incorporated in the *Common Service Book* (text ed., p. 445) and the *Service Book and Hymnal* (p. 265).

Lutheran Book of Worship	*Book of Common Prayer*
Almighty God, those who	Almighty God, with whom still live the spirits of those who

---

[46] Massey H. Shepherd, Jr., *The Oxford American Prayer Book Commentary* (New York: Oxford University Press, 1950), 340–42; Hatchett, 498.

[47] Hatchett, 495–96.

die in the Lord still live with you in joy and blessedness. We give you heartfelt thanks for the grace you have bestowed upon your servants who have finished their course in faith and now rest from their labors. May we, with all who have died in the true faith, have perfect fulfillment and joy in your eternal and everlasting glory, through your Son, Jesus Christ our Lord.	die in the Lord, and with whom the souls of the faithful are in joy and felicity: We give you heartfelt thanks for the good examples of all your servants, who, having finished their course in faith, now find rest and refreshment. May we, with all who have died in the true faith of your holy Name, have perfect fulfillment and bliss in your eternal and everlasting glory, through Jesus Christ our Lord. (p. 503)

The 1549 original is given in Hatchett (pp. 495–96).

The fourth prayer, "O God, your days are without end" (no. 282), was adapted by the 1789 American Prayer Book from Jeremy Taylor (1613–1667), *The Rule and Exercises of Holy Dying* (5.7) and given as the sixth of the "Additional Prayers" in Rite I in the 1979 Prayer Book (p. 489).[48]

Lutheran Book of Worship	*Book of Common Prayer*
O God, your days are without end and your mercies cannot be counted. Make us aware of the shortness and uncertainty of human life, and let your Holy Spirit lead us in holiness and righteousness all the days of our life, so that, when we shall have served you in our generation, we may be gathered to our ancestors, having the testimony of a good conscience, in the communion of your Church, in the confidence of a certain faith, in the comfort of a holy hope, in favor with you, our God, and in peace with with all humanity; through Jesus Christ our Lord.	O God, whose days are without end, and whose mercies cannot be numbered: Make us, we beseech thee, deeply sensible of the shortness and uncertainty of life; and let thy Holy Spirit lead us in holiness and righteousness all our days; that, when we shall have served thee in our generation, we may be gathered unto our fathers, having the testimony of a good conscience; in the communion of the Catholic Church; in the confidence of a certain faith; in the comfort of a reasonable, religious, and holy hope; in favor with thee our God; and in perfect charity with the world. All which we ask through Jesus Christ our Lord.

---

[48]Shepherd, 316; Hatchett, 497.

The prayer was familiar to Lutherans from its use in the *Service Book and Hymnal* (p. 266). It is also found in the *Book of Common Order* of the Church of Scotland (p. 179).

The prayer at the burial of a child (no. 283) is from the *Book of Common Prayer* (p. 494), a revised version of a prayer first printed in the 1928 American Prayer Book (p. 342) and derived from a prayer by John Dowden which had appeared in the 1912 Scottish Prayer Book. [49]

Lutheran Book of Worship	*Book of Common Prayer*
O God our Father, your beloved Son took children into his arms and blessed them. Give us grace, we pray, that we may entrust __name__ to your never-failing care and love, and bring us all to your heavenly kingdom; through your Son, Jesus Christ our Lord.	O God, whose beloved Son took children into his arms and blessed them: Give us grace to entrust *N.*, to your never-failing care and love, and bring us all to your heavenly kingdom; through Jesus Christ our Lord, who lives and reigns with you and the Holy Spirit, one God, now and for ever. (p. 494)

There is considerable similarity in the appointed psalms[50] and readings. The lesson from Wisdom can be traced back to the *Apostolic Constitutions* (ca. 380).

Roman Catholic Lectionary	*Lutheran Book of Worship*	*Book of Common Prayer*
Job 19:1, 23–27a	Job 19:23–27a	Job 19:23–27a
Isaiah 25:6a, 7–9	Isaiah 25:6–9	Isaiah 25:6–9
	Isaiah 61:1–3	Isaiah 61:1–3
Lamentations 3:17–26	Lamentations 3:22–26, 31–33	Lamentations 3:22–26 31–33
Daniel 12:1–3		
Wisdom 3:1–9		Wisdom 3:1–5, 9
Wisdom 4:7–15		
2 Maccabees 12:43–46		
Psalm 23		
Psalm 25:6–7, 17–18, 20–21		
Psalm 27:1, 4, 7, 8b–9a, 13–14		
Psalm 42:2, 3, 5; 43:3–5	Psalm 42:1–7	Psalm 42:1– 7
	Psalm 46:1–7	Psalm 46
Psalm 63:2–9		

---

[49]The text is given in Hatchett, 486.

[50]On the use of Psalm 25 see Rutherford, 48; on the use of Psalm 42 see Rutherford, 49–50.

		Psalm 90:1–12
Psalm 103:8, 10 13–18		
Psalm 115:5–6; 116:10–11, 15–16	Psalm 121	Psalm 121
Psalm 122:1–9		
Psalm 130		Psalm 130
		Psalm 139:1–11
Psalm 143:1–2, 5–8, 10	Psalm 143	
Acts 10:34–43		
Romans 5:5–11	Romans 5:1–11	
Romans 5:17–21	Romans 5:17–21	
Romans 6:3–9		
Romans 8:14–23		Romans 8:14–19 34–35, 37–39
Romans 8:31–35, 37–39	Romans 8:31–35, 37–39	
Romans 14:7–9, 10b–12		
1 Cor. 15:20–24a, 25–28	1 Cor. 15:12–26	1 Cor. 15:20–26, 35–38, 42–44, 53–58
1 Cor. 15:51–57		
2 Cor. 5:1, 6–10		2 Cor. 4:16–5:9
Philippians 3:20–21		
1 Thess. 4:13–18		
2 Timothy 2:8–13		
1 Peter 1:3–9		
1 John 3:1–2	1 John 3:1–2	1 John 3:1–2
1 John 3:14–16		
Revelation 14:13		
	Revelation 7:9–17	Revelation 7:9–17
Revelation 20:11–21:1		
Revelation 21:1–5a, 6b–7	Revelation 21:2–7	Revelation 21:2–7

Verses: Matt. 11:25
Matt. 25:34
John 3:16
John 6:39
John 6:40
John 11:25a, 26
Phil. 3:20
2 Tim. 2:11–12a
Rev. 1:5–6
Rev. 14:13

Matthew 5:1–12a	
Matthew 11:25–30	Matthew 11:25–30
Matthew 25:1–13	Matthew 25:1–13
Matthew 25:31–46	
Mark 15:33–39; 16:1–6	
Luke 7:11–17	

Luke 12:35–40	Luke 12:35–40	
Luke 23:33, 39–43		
Luke 23:44–49; 24:1–6a		
Luke 24:13–35		
	John 5:24–29	John 5:24–29
John 6:37–40	John 6:37–40	John 6:37–40
John 6:51–58		
		John 10:11–16
John 11:17–27	John 11:21–27	John 11:21–27
John 11:32–45		
John 12:23–38		
John 14:1–6	John 14:1–6	John 14:1–6
John 17:24–26		

The Lutheran rite requires a sermon; the Roman rite encourages one; the Episcopal rite permits one.

The preacher needs to come to terms with death and speak forthrightly of its terror, its fearsomeness, its broken power. The responsible preacher will not only confront death directly but will also proclaim the hope which the death and resurrection of Christ bestow, without becoming overly cheerful, which can be a danger in modern funeral services. Death and life contend for mastery, and everyone experiences both and the conflict between them. A sermon needs to take into account both guilt over what we have not done for the deceased and what we can no longer do as well as the proclamation of the forgiveness of sins.[51] The purpose of the funeral sermon is to participate in God's work of healing.

The Apostles' Creed in used in the Lutheran and Episcopal rites, introduced with a statement to make its baptismal and paschal connections clear:

Lutheran Book of Worship	*Book of Common Prayer*
God has made us his people through our Baptism into Christ. Living together in trust and hope, we confess our faith.	In the assurance of eternal life given at Baptism, let us proclaim our faith and say....

The prayers of intercession emphasize the "whole Church in heaven and on earth," the communion of saints which is unbroken by death. The prayers acknowledge the sorrow of the moment, but set the present anguish of the mourners in the context of eschatological hope and joyful expectation.

The prayers are taken from the prayers in Rite I of the burial office in the *Book of Common Prayer* (pp. 480–81). They were drafted

---

[51] Reginald H. Fuller, "Lectionary for Funerals," *Worship* 56 (January 1982):36–63; Robert A. Krieg, "The Funeral Homily: A Theological View," *Worship* 58 (May 1984):222–39. See also Søren Kierkegaard, "The Decisiveness of Death: At the Side of a Grave" in *Thoughts on Crucial Situations in Human Life*, trans. David Swenson (Minneapolis: Augsburg Publishing House, 1941), 75–115.

by Robert H. Greenfield from familiar prayers in various editions of the Prayer Book,[52] familiar also to Lutherans from their use in Lutheran books. Rite I continues the use of Tudor language; the *Lutheran Book of Worship* closely follows the Prayer Book but has modernized the language.

The address in the first paragraph is from the prayer from All Saints' Day; the petition is from the first of the Prayers for the Departed.

Lutheran Book of Worship	*Book of Common Prayer*
Almighty God, you have knit your chosen people together in one communion in the mystical body of your Son, Jesus Christ our Lord.	Almighty God, you have knit together your elect in one communion and fellowship in the mystical body of your Son Christ our Lord: Give us grace to follow your blessed saints in all virtuous and godly living, that we may come to those ineffable joys that you have prepared for those who truly love you. (p. 245)
Give to your whole Church in heaven and on earth your light and your peace.	Eternal Lord God, you hold all souls in life: Give to your whole Church in paradise and on earth your light and your peace; and grant that we, following the good examples of those who have served you here and are now at rest, may at last enter with them into your unending joy. (p. 253)

The second paragraph of the prayer, "Grant that all who have been baptized," is based on the collect for Easter Even in the Prayer Books from 1662 through 1928. The phrase "may die to sin and rise to newness of life" is from Cranmer's translation of the form for the blessing of the font: "O merciful God, grant that like as Christ died and rose again, so *this Child* (*this* thy *Servant*) may die to sin and rise to newness of life. *Amen.*"[53]

Grant that all who have been baptized into Christ's death and resurrection	Grant, O Lord, that as we are baptized into the death of thy blessed Son, our Saviour Jesus Christ, so by continual mortifying our corrupt affections we may be
may die to sin and rise to newness of life and that through the grave and gate of death	buried with him; and that through the grave, and gate of death,

---

[52] Hatchett, 488.

[53] *Book of Common Prayer* (1928), 278. Shepherd, 278–79.

we may pass with him to our joyful resurrection.	we may pass to our joyful resurrection. (1928 Prayer Book, p. 161)

The first part of the third paragraph, the petition, "Grant that we who are still in our pilgrimage," is based on 2 Corinthians 5:7 and on a prayer in the 1892 and 1928 Prayer Books (1892, p. 301; 1928, p. 336), taken from an Office for the Burial of Children given in Littledale and Vaux, *The Priest's Prayer Book* and derived from the Roman ritual. The second part of the paragraph, the result clause, is from the prayer by Jeremy Taylor given in the *Lutheran Book of Worship* as one of the five opening prayers of the burial rite (no. 282) and used previously in the Prayer Book as "a Prayer which may be said by the Minister in behalf of all present at the Visitation" [of the sick].[54] It recalls a phrase from the Benedictus of Morning Prayer.

	Most merciful Father, who hast been pleased to take unto thyself the soul of this thy servant [*or* this child];
Grant to us who are still in our pilgrimage, and who walk as yet by faith, that	Grant to us who are still in our pilgrimage, and who walk as yet by faith, that having served thee with constancy on earth, we may be joined hereafter with thy blessed saints in glory everlasting.
	O God, whose days are without end, and whose mercies cannot be numbered; Make us, we beseech thee, deeply sensible of the shortness and uncertainty of human life;
your Holy Spirit may lead us in holiness and righteousness all our days.	and let thy Holy Spirit lead us in holiness and righteousness, all our days: that, when we shall have served thee in our generation, we may be gathered unto our fathers, having the testimony of a good conscience; in the communion of the Catholic Church; in the confidence of a certain faith; in the comfort of a reasonable, religious, and holy hope; in favour with thee our God, and in perfect charity with the world. (1928 Prayer Book, pp. 316–17; 1979 Prayer Book, p. 489)

---

[54] *Book of Common Prayer* (1928), 316–17. Shepherd, 316.

492

The fourth paragraph, "Grant to your faithful people," is from the collect for the Twentieth Sunday after Trinity in previous Lutheran books (the Twenty-first Sunday after Trinity in the *Book of Common Prayer*). The prayer is from the Gelasian sacramentary (no. 1238); the translation is from the 1549 Prayer Book.

Grant to your faithful people pardon and peace, that we may be cleansed from all our sins and serve you with a quiet mind.	Grant, we beseech thee, merciful Lord, to thy faithful people pardon and peace, that they may be cleansed from all their sins, and serve thee with a quiet mind. (*Service Book and Hymnal*, p. 103)

The fifth paragraph, "Grant to all who mourn," is based on a prayer in the 1928 Prayer Book (p. 342) for use at the burial of a child.[55] This prayer is the basis for the second of the Prayers of the Day in the *Lutheran Book of Worship* for the Burial of the Dead, "Almighty God, source of all mercy" (no. 280).

	Almighty God, Father of mercies and giver of all comfort; Deal graciously, we pray thee, with
Give to all who mourn a sure confidence in your loving care, that, casting all their sorrow on you, they may know the consolation of your love.	those who mourn, that, casting every care on thee, they may know the consolation of thy love. (1928 Prayer Book, p. 342; see 1979 Prayer Book, p. 505)

The sixth paragraph, "Give courage and faith," is based on a collect in the 1926 Irish Prayer Book and included as the next to last of the additional prayers in Rite II of the burial office in the American Prayer Book.[56] "The comfort of a holy and certain hope" echoes prayer no. 282.

Give courage and faith to those who are bereaved, that they may have strength to meet the days ahead in the comfort of a holy and certain hope, and in the joyful expectation of	Grant, O Lord, to all who are bereaved the spirit of faith and courage, that they may have strength to meet the days to come with steadfastness and patience; not sorrowing as those without hope, but in thankful remembrance of your great goodness, and in the joyful expectation of

[55] Shepherd, 340–42; Hatchett, 498.
[56] Hatchett, 489.

eternal life with those they
love.

eternal life with whose they
love.
(*Book of Common Prayer*, p. 505)

The seventh paragraph, "Help us, we pray," is based on a prayer in the 1954 revision of the South African Prayer Book. [57]

O heavenly Father, who in thy
Son Jesus Christ, hast given us
a true faith, and a sure hope:

Help us, we pray,
in the midst of things we
cannot understand,
to believe and trust in the
communion of saints, the
forgiveness of sins, and
the resurrection to life
everlasting.

Help us, we pray thee, to live

as those who believe in the
Communion of Saints, the
forgiveness of sins, and
the resurrection to life
everlasting, and strengthen this
faith and hope in us all the days
of our life.
(Hatchett, p. 489)

The eighth paragraph, "Grant us grace to entrust __name__ to your never-failing love," is from three prayers included in the burial rite in the *Book of Common Prayer:* at the Burial of a Child (see above, p. 488), the Commendation (see below, p. 498f.), additional prayers in Rite I.

O God, whose beloved Son took
children into his arms and blessed

Grant us grace to entrust
__name__ to your never-failing
love which sustained *him/her*
in this life.

them: Give us grace to entrust
N., to your never-failing
care and love,

and bring us all to your heavenly
kingdom.
(*Book of Common Prayer*, p. 494;
see also no. 54, p. 831)

Into your hands, O merciful
Savior, we commend your servant *N.*
Acknowledge, we humbly beseech you,
a sheep of your own fold, a lamb
of your own flock, a sinner of

Receive *him/her*
into the arms of your mercy,

your own redeeming. Receive *him*
into the arms of your mercy,
into the blessed rest of everlasting

---

[57] Ibid.

494

peace, and into the glorious
company of the saints in light.
(*Book of Common Prayer*, p. 499)

and remember *him/her* according to the favor which you bear for your people.	Remember thy servant, O Lord, according to the favor which thou bearest unto thy people; and grant that, increasing in knowledge and love of thee, *he* may go from strength to strength in the life of perfect service in thy heavenly kingdom. (*Book of Common Prayer*, p. 488)

The prayer "Remember thy servant," by an unknown author, was introduced in the 1928 *Book of Common Prayer*.

In the *Lutheran Book of Worship* the first concluding prayer, "God of all grace" (no. 284), is from the 1940 *Book of Common Order* of the Church of Scotland[58] and became familiar to Lutherans from its use as the concluding prayer in the *Service Book and Hymnal* burial order (p. 267).

Lutheran Book of Worship	*Book of Common Order*
God of all grace, you sent your Son, our Savior Jesus Christ, to bring life and immortality to light. We give you thanks because by his death Jesus destroyed the power of death and by his resurrection has opened the kingdom of heaven to all believers. Make us certain that because he lives we shall live also, and that neither death nor life, nor things present nor things to come shall be able to separate us from your love which is in Christ Jesus our Lord, who lives and reigns with you and the Holy Spirit, one God, now and forever.	God of all grace, who didst send Thy Son our Saviour Jesus Christ to being life and immortality to light; most humbly and heartily we give Thee thanks, that by His death He destroyed the power of death, and by His glorious resurrection opened the kingdom of heaven to all believers. Grant us assuredly to know that because He lives we shall live also, and that neither death nor life, nor things present nor things to come, shall be able to separate us from Thy love, which is in Christ Jesus our Lord.

The prayer derives from Romans 8:35–39. The opening address is from 2 Timothy 1:10; "opened the kingdom of heaven to all believers" is from the Te Deum.

---

[58] *The Book of Common Order* of the Church of Scotland (London: Oxford University Press, 1940), 175.

The alternative concluding prayer, "God, the generations rise and pass away before you" (no. 285), is from the burial order of the *Service Book and Hymnal* (p. 266). The opening clause of the original prayer, "O God, before whose face the generations rise and pass away," is from the *Book of Common Order* of the Church of Scotland (p. 176).[59] The graceful language of the original is markedly superior. In one case the modernized language is particularly unfortunate: the original had "Give us at length our portion"; the revision has "Give us in time" although it is of course not in time but in eternity that the inheritance will be enjoyed.

Lutheran Book of Worship	*Service Book and Hymnal*
God, the generations rise and pass away before you. You are the strength of those who labor; you are the rest of the blessed dead. We rejoice in the company of your saints. We remember all who have lived in faith, all who have peacefully died, and especially those most dear to us who rest in you. . . . Give us in time our portion with those who have trusted in you and striven to do your holy will. To your name, with the Church on earth and the Church in heaven, we ascribe all honor and glory, now and forever.	O God, before whose face the generations rise and pass away, the strength of those who labor, and the repose of the blessed dead: We rejoice in the communion of thy saints; we remember all who have faithfully lived; all who have peacefully died; and especially those most dear to us who rest in thee. Give us at length our portion with those who have trusted in thee and striven in all things to do thy holy will; and unto thy Name, with the Church on earth and the Church in heaven, we ascribe all honor and glory, world without end.

The Holy Communion is appropriate at the death of a Christian because of the paschal character of the Eucharist, which celebrates and makes new Christ's passion, death, and resurrection. It binds those who share it in intimate communion with God and his church, with angels and all the saints, living and departed. In the Holy Communion, the church militant and the church triumphant are one. It is therefore appropriate at a funeral to share the meal which gives strength and hope and a promise of eternal life.

In the context of the funeral liturgy the peace can fulfill most effectively its intended purpose, showing dramatically and tangibly the presence and support of the surrounding community. It can moreover remind the congregation of the cloud of witnesses which surrounds the church (Heb. 12:1) and the angelic guard which keeps watch over God's people.

---

[59] Ibid., 176.

"Let the vineyards be fruitful" is the more appropriate offertory for a funeral. It speaks of the gathering of the harvest, which in devotion is often related to the gathering of those who die (see hymn 407, especially the third and fourth stanzas, and hymn 412, the third stanza) and the gathering of the hopes and dreams of all. Some of the dreams are now broken, but the offertory looks toward the messianic feast of victory of which the Supper is a foretaste.

The *Lutheran Book of Worship* appoints a proper preface for the Burial of the Dead (Min. Ed., pp. 190–91). It is loosely based on the preface for Christian Death I in the Roman Sacramentary and the preface in the *Book of Common Prayer*, which are both translations of the oldest extant proper preface for the commemoration of the departed, which is in the Mozarabic *Missale Mixtum*.[60]

Roman Sacramentary	Lutheran Book of Worship	Book of Common Prayer
through Jesus Christ our Lord. In him, who rose from the dead, our hope of resurrection dawned. The sadness of death gives way to the bright promise of immortality. Lord, for your faithful people life is changed, not ended. When the body of our earthly dwelling lies in death we gain an everlasting dwelling place in Heaven. (p. 527)	through Christ our Lord, who brought to light the living hope of a blessed resurrection, that, in our grief, we may rejoice in full assurance of our change into the likeness of his glory.	Through Jesus Christ our Lord; who rose victorious from the dead, and comforts us with the blessed hope of everlasting life. For to your faithful people, O Lord, life is changed, not ended; and when our mortal body lies in death, there is prepared for us a dwelling place eternal in the heavens. (p. 382)

The scriptural allusions include 2 Timothy 2:10; 1 Peter 1:3; Hebrews 6:11; 10:22; and Philippians 3:20–21. Music for the proper preface appropriate to each of the three musical settings of the Holy Communion in the *Lutheran Book of Worship* is available in *Of Resurrection and Life*.[61]

The Holy Communion concludes with the Nunc Dimittis ("Lord, now you let your servant go in peace"), a beloved canticle long associated in Lutheran orders with burial, and the proper post-communion prayer (no. 164), which is revised from the post-communion prayer in the *Book of Common Prayer*.

---

[60] J. P. Migne, *PL* 85.1089.

[61] Philip H. Pfatteicher and S. Anita Stauffer, *Of Resurrection and Life*, Pastors Guide (Philadelphia: Parish Life Press, 1987), 55–57.

Lutheran Book of Worship	*Book of Common Prayer*
Almighty God, we thank you that in your great love you have	Almighty God, we thank you that in your great love you have fed us with the spiritual food and drink of the Body and Blood of your Son Jesus Christ, and have
given us a foretaste of your heavenly banquet. Grant that this Sacrament may be to us a comfort in affliction and a pledge of our inheritance in that kingdom where there is no death, neither sorrow nor crying, but the fullness of joy with all your saints; through your Son, Jesus Christ our Lord.	given us a foretaste of your heavenly banquet. Grant that this Sacrament may be to us a comfort in affliction, and a pledge of our inheritance in that kingdom where there is no death, neither sorrow nor crying, but the fullness of joy with all your saints; through Jesus Christ our Savior. (p. 498)

The prayer was drafted by Massey H. Shepherd, Jr.,[62] and concludes the celebration of the Holy Communion on a note of triumph.

Since many of those who attend the funeral service in the church do not go to the cemetery for the burial, the Episcopal and Lutheran books have added at the end of the Eucharist a Commendation of the departed to God's care, corresponding to the Final Commendation and Farewell which follows the mass in the Roman rite.

The Prayer Book provides verses from the Eastern Orthodox rite as an optional anthem, which echoes the post-communion collect, for use as the ministers take their places at the coffin.

> *Give rest, O Christ, to your servant(s) with your saints,*
> *where sorrow and pain are no more,*
> *neither sighing, but life everlasting.*

You only are immortal, the creator and maker of mankind; and we are mortal, formed of the earth, and to earth shall we return. For so did you ordain when you created me, saying, "You are dust, and to dust you shall return." All of us go down to the dust; yet even at the grave we make our song: Alleluia, alleluia, alleluia.

> *Give rest, O Christ, to your servant(s) with your saints,*
> *where sorrow and pain are no more,*
> *neither sighing, but life everlasting.* (p. 499)

The Commendation in the *Lutheran Book of Worship* (no. 286) is identical with that in the *Book of Common Prayer* from which it was taken. It is a slightly abbreviated form of "A Commendatory Prayer

---

[62]Hatchett, 490.

when the Soul is Departed" in the litany for the dying which was introduced in the 1928 Prayer Book from John Cosin's *Collection of Private Devotions* (1627).[63]

The commendation asks the Good Shepherd to receive the deceased. It recalls Jesus' last prayer from the cross, "Father, into your hands, I commend my spirit" (Luke 23:46); it also recalls the antiphon to the Nunc Dimittis in Compline, "Into your hands, I commend my spirit." The prayer is a concluding statement of trust to console the living with the knowledge of God's care for all his children now and forever. With joy the church once again relies on what God has done in Holy Baptism and commends the servant of God to Christ as "your own . . . your own . . . your own." The words and action of Baptism are recalled, "Child of God, you have been sealed by the Holy Spirit and marked with the cross of Christ forever." Now by death Baptism has reached its consummation. The child of God is indeed God's own.[64]

The dismissal is the required conclusion of the commendation in the *Lutheran Book of Worship*; in the *Book of Common Prayer* the commendation may be concluded with a blessing or a dismissal or both.

Lutheran Book of Worship	*Book of Common Prayer*
Let us go forth in peace.	Let us go forth in the name of Christ.
In the name of Christ. Amen.	*Thanks be to God.* (p. 500)

The Lutheran form is a standard form of the verse often used at the beginning of liturgical processions. Its emphasis on peace has special importance in the context of a funeral.

As the body is taken from the church, a psalm, hymn, or anthem may be sung. The Benedictus is a traditional canticle[65] ("The dawn from on high shall break upon us, to shine on those who dwell in darkness and the shadow of death"); it was appointed in the *Service Book and Hymnal* (p. 269). The traditional antiphon since medieval times has been "I am the resurrection and the life; he who believes in me, though he die, yet shall he live, and whoever lives and believes in me shall never die" (John 11:25–26).[66]

---

[63]Shepherd, 319; Hatchett, 491.

[64]In the Roman rite the commendation begins with an introduction by the priest. After silent prayer, the body is sprinkled with holy water and incensed as a responsory is sung. The prayer of commendation follows:

Father, into your hands we commend our brother (sister). We are confident that with all who have died in Christ he (she) will be raised to life on the last day and live with Christ for ever. (We thank you for all the blessings you gave him [her] in this life to show your fatherly care for all of us and the fellowship which is ours with the saints in Jesus Christ.) Lord, hear our prayer: welcome our brother (sister) to paradise and help us to comfort each other with the assurance of our faith (until we meet in Christ to be with you and with our brother [sister] for ever.) (We ask this) through Christ our Lord. (*The Rites*, 678.)

[65]Perhaps a relic of the fourteenth-century practice of singing Lauds of the Dead after the requiem mass.

[66]See Rutherford, 68, 81–82, 96–97.

The *Book of Common Prayer* provides five brief anthems, which may be sung or said (p. 500). The last of these, *In Paradisum*, probably of Gallican origin, is found in manuscripts from the beginning of written funeral rites (at least as early as the tenth century) and was used in medieval rites to accompany the procession to the church or to the grave.[67]

> Into paradise may the angels lead you.
> At your coming may the martyrs receive you,
> and bring you into the holy city Jerusalem.

The Roman rite also suggests the use of this chant as a recessional song after the commendation.[68] In the *Lutheran Book of Worship*, hymn 325 (stanza 3) expresses similar thoughts.

Psalm 114, "When Israel came out of Egypt," has long been associated with processions with the deceased;[69] it was understood to express the release of the Christian from this world into the freedom of the next, crossing over into the promised land. "Thank God almighty, I'm free at last!" was the expression of this idea in the American spiritual and is the inscription on Martin Luther King, Jr.'s tombstone.

During the procession to the cemetery or within the cemetery to the place of interment, verses may be sung. The first set of verses provided in the *Lutheran Book of Worship*, from Psalm 118, is also appointed in the Roman rite and was common in ancient rites proclaiming the Easter faith in the face of death.[70] The second verse, Job 19:25–26, is used in the *Book of Common Prayer* at the procession into the church. The third and fourth verses, Romans 14:7–8 and John 11:25–26a, are used in the *Book of Common Prayer* and in the *Lutheran Book of Worship* at the procession into the church. The Prayer Book permits these or "In the midst of life" to be used again, but appoints another anthem, from the 1928 Prayer Book, made of John 6:37, Romans 8:11, and Psalm 16:9, 11. Lutheran rites of the past, following medieval precedents, commonly used "In the midst of life" at the beginning of the service at the grave.

The prayer "Almighty God, by the death and burial of Jesus" (no. 287), which is a consecration of the grave, is drawn from the Roman rite.

Roman Catholic Rite of Funerals	*Lutheran Book of Worship*
Lord Jesus Christ, by the three days you lay in the tomb you	Almighty God, by the death and burial of Jesus, your anointed,

---

[67] Hatchett, 491.

[68] *The Rites*, 679; an alternative is provided:
> May the choirs of angels welcome you.
> Where Lazarus is poor no longer,
> may you have eternal rest.

Or John 11:25–26 may be sung. See also Rutherford, 48.

[69] Rutherford, 42–43.

[70] Ibid., 49.

made holy the graves of all
who believe in you; and even
though their bodies lie in the
earth, they trust that they,
like you, will rise again.
Give our brother (sister)
peaceful rest in this grave,
until the day when you, the
resurrection and the life,
will raise him (her) up
in glory. Then may he (she)
see the light of your
presence, Lord Jesus, in
the kingdom where you
live for ever and ever.
(*The Rites*, p. 680)

you have destroyed death and
sanctified the graves of all
your saints.

Keep our *brother/sister*,
whose *body* we now lay to rest,
in the company of all your saints
and, at the last,
raise *him/her* up to share with
all your faithful people the
endless joy and peace won through
the glorious resurrection of
Christ our Lord, who lives and
reigns with you and the Holy
Spirit, one God, now and forever.

The sanctification of the graves of the saints has been accomplished by Christ's destruction of death and his planting hope even in the place of decay.

Scripture readings at the graveside have been a common Lutheran custom, and the present rite provides for its continuation. The first reading, John 12:23–36, is also appointed in the Roman rite (with John 12:35–36 as an alternative.) The lesson continues the harvest theme heard in the offertory and draws upon ancient mythological understandings that derive from the insights of planting societies which knew the mystery that a seed must be buried in order for it to come to life.

The other two lessons, 1 Corinthians 15:51–57 and Philippians 3:20–21, are appointed in the Roman rite for use at the service in the church. The lesson from 1 Corinthians, with its reminders of Handel's *Messiah*, draws upon a different mythological picture than the lesson from John. It is the last trumpet, the opening of all graves, the great transformation, and the triumphant taunting of death.

The third lesson, from Philippians, speaks more simply of the change which Christ will effect on the Last Day.

The coffin is lowered into the grave or placed in its resting place, and the committal is said by the minister. The first form of committal is identical with that in the *Book of Common Prayer*. The first half is basically from the 1552 Prayer Book, which was taken in part from the beginning of the second funeral sermon in Archbishop Hermann's Consultation. [71] Alternatives to earth burial are provided: burial at sea ("the deep"), cremation ("the elements"), burial in a crypt or mausoleum ("its resting place"). The second half of the formula of committal is the familiar Aaronic benediction.

[71] Hatchett, 492.

The alternative form of committal is identical with that in the Roman rite[72] with the additional provisions for committal to the deep, to the elements, to its resting place.

The committal is the turning point for the mourners. They must let go of the deceased. As they turn from the grave to return to their lives, there is a dramatic portrayal that those who survive must go on living now without the one who has died. An ancient custom enacts the acceptance of death: each person throws some dirt on the coffin in its grave, helping in the burial, admitting an acceptance of the fact of death.

The Our Father is introduced with the phrase from Morning and Evening Prayer, especially appropriate at the burial: "Lord, remember us in your kingdom." The source is Luke 23:42, the Liturgy of St. John Chrysostom, and Luke 11:1. The verse declares our eschatological hope and asks for a deepened experience of prayer because of this death.

As the introduction to the Our Father recalls the daily cycle of prayer, the regular round of night and day, so the prayer (no. 288) which follows the Lord's Prayer makes the parallel between sleeping and waking, dying and rising. This concluding prayer is from Littledale and Vaux's *The Priest's Prayer Book*, "For a Happy Death."[73] It entered the 1892 American *Book of Common Prayer* (p. 301) as the second of three "additional prayers" in the Burial of the Dead and from there came into the *Common Service Book*[74] and the *Service Book and Hymnal*.[75] It recalls 1 Corinthians 15:55–57, the second of the optional lessons at the grave.

The verse, "Rest eternal grant *him/her*, O Lord" is based on 2 Esdras 2:34–35 and is found in the supplement to the Gregorian sacramentary (no. 1406) where it is used with the psalms of the burial office. (The first word of this verse in Latin, *requiem*, with which the Introit of the medieval mass for the dead began, became the identifying name of the mass for the departed.) With this versicle the Roman rite concludes.[76]

In medieval rites a brief prayer was attached to this versicle at the commendation of the dying and as the dismissal after the committal of the body to the grave:

May *his* soul, and the souls of all the faithful departed, through the mercy of God, rest in peace.

This prayer follows the versicle in the *Book of Common Prayer* (p. 502).

The benediction, from Hebrews 13:20–21, concludes the rite. It has been in Lutheran use at the close of the service at the grave at least since the *Forms for Ministerial Acts* (1900) of the General Synod. More common was the use of "The grace of our Lord Jesus Christ, and the

---

[72] *The Rites*, p. 681.
[73] *Book of Common Prayer* (1928), 336; Shepherd, 336; Hatchett, 489. Richard F. Littledale and J. Edward Vaux, *The Priest's Prayer Book*, 7th ed. (London: Masters & Co., 1890 [1864]).
[74] *Common Service Book* (text ed.), p. 448.
[75] *Service Book and Hymnal*, p. 269.
[76] *The Rites*, 683.

Love of God, and the Communion of the Holy Ghost be with you all." The benediction from Hebrews entered Episcopal use in the 1928 Prayer Book (p. 335).[77]

The dismissal, "Let us go in peace" is assigned to the presiding minister so that a statement by the funeral director will not intrude. The last word of the burial liturgy should linger and echo in the minds of the mourners.

Thus the burial liturgy as well as the entire liturgy comes to a conclusion with an affirmation of that peace which the world cannot give, that deep and enduring peace which passes all understanding. It is the peace promised by the Sabbath, wrought by the cross, enjoyed in a proleptic manner by the faithful even now, and which will crown the work of the Creator at the last when the kingdom will be delivered by the Son to the Father, and God will be all in all.

---

[77] *Book of Common Prayer* (1928), 335; Shepherd, 335.

Appendix I
Comparison of Rites

The Rites of the Catholic Church	Lutheran Book of Worship	Book of Common Prayer
1. At home of the deceased		
2. In the church		
2 Cor. 1:3–4 or Greeting	2 Cor. 1:3–4	
Placing pall	Placing pall (Rom. 6:35)	
		Verses
Prayer	Prayer	Prayer
Lessons(s)	Lessons(s)	Lessons(s)
Verse	(Verse)	
Gospel	Gospel	Gospel
Homily	Sermon	(Homily)
	Hymn	
	Apostles' Creed	Apostles' Creed
Intercessions	Prayers	Prayers
Holy Communion	(Holy Communion)	(Holy Communion)
Commendation	Commendation	Commendation
3. At the cemetery		
(Blessing of grave)		
Committal		
		(Consecration of grave)
(Reading)		
(Psalm)	Verses	Verses
Prayer	Prayer	
	(Lesson)	
	Committal	Committal
Our Father	Our Father	Our Father
	Prayer	
Eternal rest....	Rest eternal....	Rest eternal....
	Blessing	Dismissal

BIBLIOGRAPHY

Aries, Philippe. *Death in America.* Edited by David E. Stannard. Philadelphia: University of Pennsylvania Press, 1975.

————. *The Hour of Our Death.* Translated by Helen Weaver. New York: Knopf, 1981.

————. *Images of Man and Death.* Translated by Janet Lloyd. Cambridge, MA: Harvard University Press, 1985.

————. *Western Attitudes Toward Death from the Middle Ages to the Present Time.* Translated by Patricia M. Ranum. Baltimore: John Hopkins University Press, 1974.

Bailey, Lloyd R. *Biblical Perspectives on Death.* Philadelphia: Fortress Press, 1979.

Becker, Ernest. *The Denial of Death.* New York: Free Press, 1973.

Benoit, Pierre, and Roland Murphy. *Immortality and Resurrection.* Concilium 60. New York: Seabury Press, 1970.

Boase, Thomas S. R. *Death in the Middle Ages: Mortality, Judgment, and Remembrance.* New York: McGraw-Hill, 1972.

Burns, Norman T. *Christian Mortalism from Tyndale to Milton.* Cambridge, MA: Harvard University Press, 1972.

Cameron, J. M. "On Death and Human Existence," *Worship* 50 (May 1976):246–60.

Clark, James M. *The Dance of Death in the Middle Ages and Renaissance.* Glasgow University Publications 86. Glasgow: Jackson, 1950.

Coffin, Margaret. *Death in Early America: The History and Folklore of Customs and Superstitions of Early Medicine, Funerals, Burials and Mourning.* Nashville: Nelson, 1976.

Cohen, Kathleen. *Metamorphosis of a Death Symbol: The Transi Tomb in the Late Middle Ages and the Renaissance.* California Studies in the History of Art XV. Berkeley, Los Angeles, and London: University of California Press, 1973.

Cope, Gilbert, ed. *Dying, Death, and Disposal.* London: SPCK, 1970.

Cullmann, Oscar. *Immortality of the Soul or Resurrection of the Dead? The Witness of the New Testament.* London: Epworth, 1958.

Curl, James S. *A Celebration of Death: An Introduction to Some of the Buildings, Monuments, and Settings of Funerary Architecture in the Western European Tradition.* New York: Scribners, 1980.

————. *The Victorian Celebration of Death.* Detroit: Partridge Press, 1972.

Davidson, Glen W. *Living with Dying.* Minneapolis: Augsburg Publishing House, 1975.

————. *Understanding Mourning: A Guide for Those Who Grieve.* Minneapolis: Augsburg Publishing House, 1984.

"Death and Funerals." *Liturgy* 15:9 (November 1970).

Duncan-Jones, A. S. "The Burial of the Dead," *Liturgy and Worship.* Edited by W. K. Lowther Clarke and Charles Harris. London: SPCK, 1932.

Dunne, John S. *The City of the Gods: A Study in Myth and Mortality.* New York: Macmillan, 1965.

————. *A Search for God in Time and Memory.* New York: Macmillan, 1969.

————. *Time and Myth.* New York: Doubleday, 1973.

Enright, D. J., ed. *The Oxford Book of Death*. New York: Oxford University Press, 1983.

Etlin, Richard A. *The Architecture of Death: The Transformation of the Cemetery in Eighteenth Century Paris*. Cambridge, MA: M.I.T. Press, 1985.

Gatch, Milton McC. *Death: Meaning and Mortality in Christian Thought and Contemporary Culture*. New York: Seabury Press, 1969.

Gorer, Geoffrey. *Death, Grief, and Mourning*. New York: Doubleday, 1965.

Grollman, Earl, ed. *Concerning Death: A Practical Guide for the Living*. Boston: Beacon Press, 1974.

Habenstein, Robert W., and William M. Lamers. *Funeral Customs the World Over*. Milwaukee: Bulfin, 1960.

Harrah, Barbara K., and David F. Harrah. *Funeral Service: A Bibliography of Literature of Its Past, Present, and Future. The Various Means of Memorialization*. Metuchen, NJ: Scarecrow Press, 1976.

Hendin, David. *Death as a Fact of Life*. New York: Norton, 1973.

Holck, Frederick H., ed. *Death and Eastern Thought*. New York: Abingdon, 1974.

Hoon, Paul W. "Theology, Death, and the Funeral Liturgy," *Union Seminary Quarterly Review* 31:3 (Spring 1976).

Hovda, Robert W. *American Funeral Customs and the Value of Faith*. Collegeville: Liturgical Press, 1985.

Hughes, Robert G. *A Trumpet in Darkness: Preaching to Mourners*. Philadelphia: Fortress Press, 1986.

Huntington, Richard, and Peter Metcalf. *Celebrations of Death: The Anthropology of Mortuary Ritual*. New York: Cambridge University Press, 1979.

Irion, Paul. *Cremation*. Philadelphia: Fortress Press, 1968.

——. *The Funeral and the Mourners*. Nashville: Abingdon, 1954.

——. *The Funeral: Vestige or Value?* Nashville: Abingdon, 1966.

Kübler-Ross, Elisabeth. *On Death and Dying*. New York: Macmillan, 1970.

Lewis, C. S. [N. W. Clark, Pseud.] *A Grief Observed*. Greenwich, CT: Seabury Press, 1963 [1961].

Mack, Arien, ed. *Death in American Experience*. New York: Schocken, 1973.

McManners, John. *Death and the Enlightenment: Changing Attitudes toward Death among Christians and Unbelievers in Eighteenth Century France*. New York: Oxford University Press, 1981.

Motter, Alton, ed. *Preaching about Death*. Philadelphia: Fortress Press, 1975.

Neale, Robert E. *The Art of Dying*. New York: Harper & Row, 1973.

Nouwen, Henri. *A Letter of Consolation*. New York: Harper & Row, 1982.

Oates, Wayne E. *Pastoral Care and Counselling in Grief and Separation*. Philadelphia: Fortress Press, 1976.

O'Connor, Sister Mary C. *The Art of Dying Well: The Development of the Ars Moriendi*. New York: Columbia University Press, 1942.

Parabola: Myth and the Quest for Meaning 2:1 (Winter 1977). An issue devoted to death.

Pelikan, Jaroslav. *The Shape of Death: Life, Death, and Immortality In the Early Fathers*. New York: Abingdon, 1961.

Pfatteicher, Philip H., and S. Anita Stauffer. *Of Resurrection and Life*. Philadelphia: Parish Life Press, 1987.

Ragon, Michael. *The Space of Death: A Study of Funerary Architecture, Decora-*

tion, and Urbanism. Translated by Alan Sheridan. Charlottesville: University of Virginia Press, 1983.

Rahner, Karl. *On the Theology of Death.* Translated by Charles H. Henkey. New York: Seabury Press, 1973 [1961].

Rowell, Geoffrey. *The Liturgy of Christian Burial: An Introductory Survey of the Historical Development of Christian Burial Rites.* Alcuin Club no. 59. London: SPCK, 1977.

Rush, Alfred C. *Death and Burial in Christian Antiquity.* The Catholic University Studies in Christian Antiquity 1. Washington, DC: Catholic University of America Press, 1941.

Rutherford, Richard. *The Death of a Christian: The Rite of Funerals.* Studies in the Reformed Rites of the Catholic Church, vol. 7. New York: Pueblo Publishing Co., 1980.

Sacks, Peter M. *The English Elegy: Studies in the Genre from Spenser to Yeats.* Baltimore: John Hopkins University Press, 1985.

Schwarz, Hans. *Beyond the Gates of Death: A Biblical Examination of Evidence for Life after Death.* Minneapolis: Augsburg Publishing House, 1981.

Schibles, Warren. *Death: An Interdisciplinary Analysis.* Whitewater, WI: Language Press, 1974.

Stannard, David E., ed. *Death in America.* Philadelphia: University of Pennsylvania Press, 1974.

Stein, Arnold. *The House of Death: Messages from the English Renaissance.* Baltimore: John Hopkins University Press, 1986.

Stephenson, John S. *Death, Grief, and Mourning: Individual and Social Relations.* New York: Free Press, 1986.

Thielecke, Helmut. *Death and Life.* Philadelphia: Fortress Press, 1970.

————. *Living with Death.* Translated by Geoffrey Bromiley. Grand Rapids: Eerdmans, 1983.

Toynbee, Jocelyn M. C. *Death and Burial in the Roman World.* Ithaca: Cornell University Press, 1971.

Wagner, Johannes, ed. *Reforming the Rites of Death.* Concilium 32. New York: Paulist Press, 1968.

Weir, Robert F., ed. *Death in Literature.* New York: Columbia University Press, 1980.

Westerhoff, John, and William Willimon. *Liturgy and Learning through the Life Cycle.* New York: Seabury Press, 1980. Chapter 15: "Ministration at the Time of Death and the Burial of the Dead."

Willimon, William. *Worship as Pastoral Care.* Nashville: Abingdon, 1979. Chapter 5: "Liturgy and Life's Crises: The Funeral."

11

EPILOGUE

The nineteenth century has been described as "the century of greatest change in the history of Western civilization,"[1] and these revolutionary changes naturally had an impact on liturgy. The Oxford Movement in England and Loehe's work in Germany are two European examples. In the nineteenth century North American Lutherans began a process of liturgical change and development, moving to the use of English in worship, recovering and establishing the sixteenth-century Lutheran traditions in liturgy.

In 1868 a remarkable liturgical achievement of the Lutherans in North America, the *Church Book*, was published. One hundred years later, in 1968, the Inter-Lutheran Commission on Worship began work on what was to become the *Lutheran Book of Worship*, published in 1978. This commentary on that book was completed during the centennial of the Common Service.[2]

Much of what was said of the Common Service in its Preface of 1888[3] may also by extension be said of the 1978 *Lutheran Book of Worship*. Both were the results of the joint action of the three principal Lutheran bodies of the time: in 1878, the General Synod South, the General Synod, and the General Council; in 1968, the Lutheran Church–Missouri Synod, the American Lutheran Church, and the Lutheran Church in America. Both publications took a decade to prepare: the invitation to cooperate in the production of a Common Service came in 1878; the Inter-Lutheran Commission on Worship began its work in 1968. Both efforts sought to recover more venerable and more authentic traditions: in 1888, "the old Lutheran service"; in 1978, a larger ecumenical heritage. Both therefore claim not to be new and original work but faithful representations of the structures and outlines of the service of the Western Church enriched with embellishments and certain new features. Both claim to share in the communion of saints common to the Roman Catholic, Lutheran, and Anglican churches, and both bear

---

[1] *The Norton Anthology of World Masterpieces*, ed., Maynard Mack et al., 5th ed., vol. 2 (New York: W. W. Norton & Co., 1985), 815.

[2] For the history of the Common Service see Luther D. Reed, *The Lutheran Liturgy* (Philadelphia: Muhlenberg Press, 1947), 181–216; rev. ed. (Philadelphia: Fortress Press, 1960), 182–204.

[3] Preface to the Common Service, 1888, given in the *Common Service Book*, text ed., pp. 529–33.

a notable similarity to the contemporary Roman Catholic and Anglican rites. Both claim to be "the Common Service of the Christian Church of all ages." Both acknowledge the inevitable tension between freedom and tradition, part of which was the struggle to put the old service into a new language, the contemporary language of the people. Both flowed from a "strong desire for this bond of union . . . longing for unity in the Service of worship between all believers."[4] Both achieved a remarkable unanimity of approval.

Liturgical revision in the nineteenth and twentieth centuries not only preceded the unification of church bodies but encouraged and facilitated the process. The Common Service of 1888 and the *Common Service Book* of 1917 led to the formation of the United Lutheran Church in America. The *Service Book and Hymnal* of 1958 led to the creation of the Lutheran Church in America and the American Lutheran Church. The *Lutheran Book of Worship* of 1978 led to the formation of the Evangelical Lutheran Church in Canada and the Evangelical Lutheran Church in America. Churches cooperating in revising their liturgical heritage came to trust each other as they worked in concert toward a common goal. Their work implied the conviction that a revitalized historic service furnishes a solid basis for such agreement. "Orthodoxy," understood as both "right belief" and "right worship," issues in and evidences unity.[5] Thus in 1978 as in 1888, one may proclaim that "the continuous succession of pure service was unbroken."[6]

Nonetheless, there is still important work ahead, for no liturgy is a permanently finished product, completed for all time. A liturgy does not mark the conclusion of a development but only a pause along the way of pilgrimage. There is unfinished business in the development of the liturgy, and Lutherans must frankly admit that they have not achieved agreement among themselves on certain features of their liturgical heritage. A number of issues remain for Lutherans and for the whole church:

1. The necessity of a preparatory confession as a fixed order attached to the beginning of the Holy Communion remains a matter of controversy for Lutherans.

2. The validity and admissibility of a eucharistic prayer or more specifically the inclusion of the *verba testamenti* within a prayer of thanksgiving is a peculiar Lutheran problem that has lingered since the Reformation. To some, the separation of the Verba from the prayer is the hallmark of an authentic Lutheran liturgy and is its desirable, even necessary distinctive feature. To others, it is an aberration which compounds the medieval isolation of a moment and a means of consecration. Some indeed will not tolerate any prayer, except the Lord's Prayer, in connection with the proclamation of the Verba.

---

[4]Ibid., pp. 532–33.
[5]See Jeffrey W. Rowthorn, "Prayer in the Spirit of the Liturgy," *Liturgy* 5:1 (Summer 1985): 21–27.
[6]Preface, p. 530.

3. The language of public prayer is a principal ecumenical question, requiring careful and sustained attention. The language needs to be at once inclusive, allusive, and elevated. Should all gender-specific nouns (Lord, King, Father) and pronouns (he, his, him) be excluded when referring to God? Should neutral words (Sovereign, Parent) be used instead? Should feminine nouns and pronouns be introduced? How allusive can twentieth-century liturgical language be? Is, for example, the traditional text of the Exsultet utterly beyond the grasp of modern congregations? How can the language of prayer be accessible and still resound movingly and convincingly with elevated dignity and compelling power? As in the past decades anthropology has usefully informed the study of liturgy, so it may perhaps be that literary study will be a principal influence in the next decades. For naming, especially the naming of God, is a searching, not "a fixing of images and names that stills the poetic sense."[7] Names and metaphorical language should open up and release the energies of language so that surprise, revelation, and discovery are facilitated.

4. Inclusive language in the translation of Scripture is another important concern touching on the essence of Christianity. To what extent is it acceptable to alter the original Hebrew and Greek texts in translation in the interest of avoiding exclusive language? To what extent does the incarnation — God's choice of a particular time and a particular place to be born among his people — determine the language we use about God and about our experience of God's revelation to us?

5. The indigenization and cultural adaptation of liturgy is of increasing importance and urgency. No longer can one assume a bland and homogeneous group. A pluralistic society and a shrinking globe require an understanding of separate ethnic identities within the whole church, each with its own images, customs, and values. How are profound and significant human experiences and rituals to be incorporated into the proclamation of the Gospel of Jesus Christ in Scripture and in sacrament so that the various peoples of the world can in their own voices and in their own natural ways share in the historic worship of the catholic church?

6. The revival, development, and use of the catechumenate is a promising area of liturgical recovery and adaptation, especially in places where adult baptism is becoming the normal practice. How is this to be made again a vital part of the life of the Christian church?

7. Ecumenical celebrations of baptism must be fostered and encouraged so that no longer will individual congregations or denominations celebrate the sacrament of Christian initiation in isolation without the participation of other members and representatives of the household of faith. A common ecumenical baptismal rite would assist in encouraging the understanding that in baptism one is made a member of the Chris-

---

[7]David N. Power, "Liturgical Praxis: A New Consciousness at the Eye of Worship," *Worship* 61 (1987):298.

tian church, not simply a member of a denomination or congregation of the church.

8. The administration of the Holy Communion to all the baptized of whatever age, even infants, is a matter for ecumenical discussion. Are there any necessary qualifications to understanding the Holy Communion as the birthright of the baptized?

9. The value and meaning of confirmation, now that the wholeness of the baptismal rite has been set forth clearly and richly in the reformed baptismal rites, is even less clear than it has been in the past. Should confirmation survive as a separate rite?

10. The course of the Prayers of the Day in the *Lutheran Book of Worship* needs to be reviewed in the light of the reordering of the collects in the Roman sacramentary and in the *Book of Common Prayer* in order to restore as much unanimity and unity as possible in the use of these prayers.

11. Lectionary reform remains unfinished. The proposed lectionary of the Consultation on Common Texts with the deletion of extra appointments at the beginning rather than at the end of the time after Pentecost has great promise as a widely-accepted ecumenical course of readings. The publication of a lectionary in inclusive language with the psalms and their antiphons in place between the first and second lessons, the verse printed before the Gospel, and the forms of announcing the lessons printed in the text to guide the reader is desirable.

12. The legitimacy of the Apocrypha for use in the church's lectionary needs careful examination. Such study would help deepen the understanding of the meaning of the canon.

13. A course of post-communion prayers, at least a seasonal series, could enrich the liturgy of Holy Communion.

14. A series of solemn blessings or prayers over the people as in the Roman and Episcopal rites could be a useful addition to the service.

15. The liturgies for Ash Wednesday, the Sunday of the Passion, Maundy Thursday, Good Friday, and the Easter Vigil should be integrated with the other appointments for those days and harmonized with them when necessary to eliminate the contradictions and confusion that currently exists with regard to the use of these appointments. Common ecumenical forms for these liturgies should be drafted.

16. Daily Prayer needs to be encouraged so that all the people of God whether alone or in families or in assemblies can join the praises of all creation as "earth rolls onward into light."[8] The publication of an office book for all the people of God remains a matter of urgency.

17. Hymn texts, which in the various hymnals have recently gone their own way in the course of revision and alteration, should be examined with a view to providing common translations or adaptations so that the churches can again sing the same hymns with the same words if not always to the same tunes.

---

[8] John Ellerton, "The Day You Gave Us, Lord, Has Ended," hymn 274, stanza 2.

18. The burial rite perhaps should make provision for an office of the dead, similar to the *Common Service Book* and *Service Book and Hymnal* orders, for use as a service for those who have little or no church relationship and for whom the eucharistic form in the *Lutheran Book of Worship* is inappropriate.

To move the discussion of the controversial issues forward beyond mere repetition of centuries-old positions, these issues deserve to be treated as one treats all ecumenical theological issues: avoid the assumption that the other side is wrong or heretical, seek to understand why the other side takes the position it does, and, if possible, seek a common position that safeguards the legitimate concerns of each side guided by Scripture and informed by the long traditions of (Jewish and) Christian experience.

The Lutheran church in North America has a clear obligation to world-wide Lutheranism in confessional matters, for the Lutheran church is a confessional movement. The obligation to the Lutheran churches elsewhere in the world in liturgical matters is less strict. It is appropriate and proper for North American Lutherans to seek first of all the convergence of the various Christian communions on a continent that is rich with diversity and ecumenical promise.

It is therefore to be hoped that the *Lutheran Book of Worship* will be the last North American Lutheran liturgical book. When the time comes for the next revision of the liturgy, it should no longer be done exclusively by Lutherans. The next book should be the work of several denominations in cooperation, working out together the liturgical implications of the *Baptism, Eucharist and Ministry* document of the World Council of Churches, and acting upon the developing eucharistic sharing between the denominations. The next book must be the work of an ecumenical commission as an evidence of their common faith and worship and commitment.

The noble vision that inspired the liturgists of 1888, encouraging the recognition of the Augsburg Confession as the central confession and the Common Service as the central service of the Protestant churches is today even grander, still more faithful to the biblical injunctions to unity, going beyond the Protestant appeal and extending to include the Church of Rome as well. The primary goal of the Lutheran church is not to be a central beacon to the Protestant churches but to heal the breach of the sixteenth century. Even as the Augsburg confession has been proposed in the twentieth century as it was in the sixteenth as a catholic document presenting an authentic exposition of the faith of the catholic church of the West, so the service found in the *Lutheran Book of Worship* is a form of the principal liturgy of the Western church — Catholic and Protestant, Roman and non-Roman. The years ahead should find the church moving still farther, still more joyfully and confidently into the larger heritage of the catholic church.

The prayerful hope of the reformers of 1888 remains alive and compelling:

We would gladly behold the day when the One, Holy Christian Church shall use one Order of Service, and unite in one Confession of Faith.[9]

As the twentieth century draws to a close and the third millennium dawns, that hope, even in an age of pluralism and diversity, continues to press the church to grow into ever greater, ever more compelling expressions of its unity.

---

[9] Preface, p. 533.

Appendix 1

Membership on the Inter-Lutheran Commission on Worship

During its existence (1966–1978), the Inter-Lutheran Commission on Worship and its four working committees consisted of the following members:

Inter-Lutheran Commission on Worship

Henry C. Abram (LCMS) 1976–78; Louis Accola (ALC) 1975–78; John W. Arthur (LCA) 1966–78; Ruth Becker (LCA) 1972–73; Eugene L. Brand (ALC) 1966–71, (LCA) 1972–75; Edgar S. Brown, Jr. (LCA) 1966–70; Paul G. Bunjes (LCMS) 1966–72; Walter E. Buszin (LCMS) 1966–68; L. Crosby Deaton (LCA) 1966–72; E. Theodore DeLaney (LCMS) 1969–76; Gilbert E. Doan, Jr. (LCA) 1970–78; Mandus A. Egge (ALC) 1966–78; Paul Ensrud (ALC) 1966–68; Carl Fischer (ALC) 1968–74; Paul Foelber (LCMS) 1969–78; Edward A. Hansen (ALC) 1966–78; Tiovo K. I. Harjunpaa (LCA) 1970–78; Richard P. Hermstad (ALC) 1975–78; Edward T. Horn, III (LCA) 1966–72; Frederick F. Jackisch (LCA) 1966–78; Herbert Kahler (LCMS) 1966–75; Hans F. Knauer (ALC) 1966–68; A. R. Kretzmann (LCMS) 1966–69; Ulrich S. Leupold (LCA) 1966–70; Theodore S. Liefeld (ALC) 1966–78; L. R. Likness (ELCC) 1966–78; Herbert F. Lindemann (LCMS) 1966–69; Shirley McCreedy (LCA) 1974–78; Daniel Moe (LCA) 1966–78; Harold W. Moench (ALC) 1968–74; Constance Parvey (LCA) 1972–78; Paul K. Peterson (LCMS) 1972–78; Fred L. Precht (LCMS) 1966–76; Alf Romstad (ALC) 1966–67; Warren G. Rubel (LCMS) 1968–74; Leland B. Sateren (ALC) 1966–78; Rodney Schrank (LCMS) 1974–78; Ralph C. Schultz (LCMS) 1969–72; Martin L. Seltz (LCMS) 1966–67; Krister Stendahl (LCA) 1966–70; Clifford J. Swanson (ALC) 1971–78; Jaroslav J. Vajda (LCMS) 1966–78; Ralph R. Van Loon (LCA) 1970–71, 1975–78; Willis Wright (LCMS) 1972–78. Eugene L. Brand served as Project Director 1975–78 and Robert A. Rimbo as Project Assistant 1976–78.

Church Staff

John Becker (LCA) 1974–78; Eugene L. Brand (LCA) 1972–74; Edgar S. Brown, Jr. (LCA) 1966–70; E. Theodore DeLaney (LCMS) 1969–78; Mandus A. Egge (ALC) 1966–76; Jerry A. Evenrud (ALC) 1976–78; Janet Moede (ALC) 1966–73; Mons A. Teig (ALC) 1974–78; R. Harold Terry (LCA) 1973–74; Ralph R. Van Loon (LCA) 1972–78. Albert E. Anderson, Leonard Flachman, and Karen Walhof represented Augsburg Publishing House; Ralph L. Reinke represented

Concordia Publishing House; Frank G. Rhody represented the Board of Publication of the Lutheran Church in America.

Liturgical Text Committee

John W. Arthur (LCA) 1967–78; Hans C. Boehringer (LCMS) 1967–78; Eugene L. Brand (ALC) 1967–71; Charles A. Ferguson (LCA) 1968–78; Edward T. Horn III (LCA) 1967–68; A. R. Kretzmann (LCMS) 1967–69; L. R. Likness (ELCC) 1973–78; Herbert F. Lindemann (LCMS) 1967–78; Paul K. Peterson (LCMS) 1973–78; Philip H. Pfatteicher (LCA) 1968–78; Fred L. Precht (LCMS) 1969–72; Ralph W. Quere (ALC) 1971–78; Krister Stendahl (LCA) 1967–68; Clifford J. Swanson (ALC) 1967–73; Johan A. Thorson (ALC) 1967–78; Ralph R. Van Loon (LCA) 1972–78.

Liturgical Music Committee

Robert A. Bornemann (LCA) 1967–71; Paul G. Bunjes (LCMS) 1967–72; Gerhard M. Cartford (ALC) 1967–78; L. Crosby Deaton (LCA) 1967–68; Donna Zierdt Elkin (LCA) 1973–78; Paul Ensrud (ALC) 1967–68; Carl Fischer (ALC) 1968–78; Richard P. Hermstad (ALC) 1975–78; Richard W. Hillert (LCMS) 1967–78; Donald Hinkle (LCA) 1971–78; Ulrich S. Leupold (LCA) 1967–70; Carlos R. Messerli (LCMS) 1967–78; Daniel T. Moe (LCA) 1967–78; Reuben G. Pirner (ALC) 1967–75; Fred L. Precht (LCMS) 1973–78; Stanley Yoder (LCA) 1970–72.

Hymn Texts Committee

Bessie Coleman (ALC) 1970–73; L. Crosby Deaton (LCA) 1968–70; E. Theodore DeLaney (LCMS) 1967–78; Gilbert E. Doan, Jr. (LCA) 1967–78; Gracia Grindal (ALC) 1973–78; Edward A. Hansen (ALC) 1967–78; Edward T. Horn, III (LCA) 1967–68; Joel W. Lundeen (LCA) 1967–78; John Milton (ALC) 1967–68; Hilton C. Oswald (LCMS) 1967–78; Martin L. Seltz (LCMS) 1967; Gerald Thorson (ALC) 1968–78; George Utech (ALC) 1967–70; Jaroslav Vajda (LCMS) 1967–78; Marilyn Waniek (LCA) 1970–72; Stanley Yoder (LCA) 1973–78.

Hymn Music Committee

Charles R. Anders (LCA) 1967–78; Jan Bender (LCMS) 1967–70; Walter E. Buszin (LCMS) 1967–68; Paul Christiansen (ALC) 1967–69; Jerry A. Evenrud (ALC) 1975–78; Paul Foelber (LCMS) 1970–78; Larry Houff (LCA) 1974–78; Frederick F. Jackisch (LCA) 1967–78; Edward Klammer (LCMS) 1967–78; Ludwig Lenel (LCA) 1967–74; Ronald Nelson (ALC) 1974–78; Ruth Olson (ALC) 1969–74; Leland B. Sateren (ALC) 1967–78; Carl Schalk (LCMS) 1968–78; Dale Warland (ALC) 1967–74.

Appendix 2

Sources of the Psalm Prayers

The psalm prayers or psalter collects in the Ministers Edition of the *Lutheran Book of Worship* are drawn primarily from the Roman series prepared for the Liturgy of the Hours (LH). In the Roman series the prayers are often related to the antiphon, which underscores a central theme of the psalm. Nearly all the prayers taken from the Roman series have been slightly altered by Philip H. Pfatteicher; more substantial alterations are indicated "alt." A second source is a series of psalm prayers drafted by Frank C. Senn and his students in liturgy at Christ Seminary–Seminex in 1975–1976. A few of the prayers come from other sources.

Psalm

1	LH draft
2	LH
3	Jack Bailey, alt.
4	LH draft for Compline
5	LH
6	LH
7	J. Bailey
8	Philip H. Pfatteicher
9	LH alt.
10	LH alt.
11	Bailey and LH alt.
12	LH alt.
13	LH
14	LH alt.
15	LH draft alternate alt.
16	LH alt.
17	LH draft alt.
18	LH
19	John W. Suter, Jr., in the 1928 *Book of Common Prayer*, p. 596, "For Joy in God's Creation"
20	LH
21	LH
22	LH alt.
23	LH
24	LH draft alternate
25	LH draft alternate alt.
26	LH
27	LH alt.
28	LH draft alternate alt.
29	LH draft alternate
30	LH

31	LH draft alternate
32	LH
33	LH draft alternate
34	LH alt.
35	LH alt.
36	LH draft alternate alt.
37	LH alt.
38	LH alt.
39	LH
40	LH alt.
41	LH alt.
42	LH draft alternate
43	LH
44	LH alt. (Week II, Thursday, Office of Readings)
45	LH
46	LH draft alternate
47	LH draft alternate alt.
48	LH
49	LH draft alternate
50	LH (Week IV, Saturday Morning Prayer)
51	*Morning Praise and Evensong,* ed. William G. Storey, Frank C. Quinn, David F. Wright (Notre Dame, IN: Fides Publishers, 1973), p. 97.
52	LH alt.
53	LH alt.
54	LH draft alternate alt.
55	LH
56	LH
57	LH

Psalm

58	LH	105	LH
59	LH	106	LH alt.
60	LH	107	LH
61	LH	108	LH
62	LH alt.	109	LH
63	LH	110	LH alt. (Week II, Sunday Evening
64	LH		Prayer II)
65	Mark Felde	111	LH draft alternate alt.
66	LH alt.	112	LH alt.
67	LH draft alternate	113	LH alt.
68	LH	114	LH
69	LH	115	LH alt.
70	Embolism to the Lord's Prayer	116	LH alt. (Ps. 116:1–9)
	in the Roman Mass	117	LH draft alternate alt.
71	LH	118	LH
72	LH draft alternate alt.	119	LH to section XVII (Pe),
73	LH draft alternate alt.		Ps. 119:129–136
74	LH alt.	120	LH
75	LH	121	LH
76	LH	122	LH
77	LH	123	Bill Schreiber
78	LH to Ps. 78:1–39	124	LH
79	P. Pfatteicher, based on prayers	125	LH alt.
	by Felde and in LH	126	LH draft alternate
80	LH	127	LH alt.
81	LH draft alternate	128	LH draft alternate alt.
82	LH draft alt.	129	LH
83	LH	130	LH draft alternate
84	LH draft alternate	131	LH
85	LH draft alternate	132	LH draft alt.
86	LH	133	LH draft alternate alt.
87	LH alt.	134	LH draft
88	LH alt.	135	P. Pfatteicher
89	LH alt. to Ps. 89:2–38	136	LH draft alternate alt.
90	P. Pfatteicher	137	LH draft alternate alt.
91	LH	138	LH alt.
92	LH	139	LH draft alternate
93	LH draft alternate	140	LH alt.
94	LH	141	LH
95	LH draft	142	LH draft alt.
96	LH draft alternate	143	LH alt.
97	LH	144	LH
98	Frank C. Senn	145	P. Pfatteicher, based on
99	F. Senn		a prayer by Edward Tilley
100	George Loewer	146	LH
101	LH	147	LH to Ps. 147:1–11
102	LH draft alternate	148	LH draft
103	LH	149	LH
104	LH draft alternate	150	P. Pfatteicher

INDEX

ISBN 0-8006-0392-3